NOT A GOOD DAY TO DIE

THE UNTOLD STORY OF OPERATION ANACONDA

NOT A GOOD DAY TO DIE

SEAN NAYLOR

BERKLEY CALIBER BOOKS, NEW YORK

THE BERKLEY PUBLISHING GROUP
Published by the Penguin Group
Penguin Group (USA) Inc.
375 Hudson Street, New York, New York 10014, USA
Penguin Group (Canada), 90 Eglinton Avenue East, Suite 700, Toronto, Ontario M4P 2Y3, Canada
(a division of Pearson Penguin Canada Inc.)
Penguin Books Ltd., 80 Strand, London WC2R 0RL, England
Penguin Group Ireland, 25 St. Stephen's Green, Dublin 2, Ireland (a division of Penguin Books Ltd.)
Penguin Group (Australia), 250 Camberwell Road, Camberwell, Victoria 3124, Australia
(a division of Pearson Australia Group Pty. Ltd.)
Penguin Books India Pvt. Ltd., 11 Community Centre, Panchsheel Park, New Delhi—110 017, India
Penguin Group (NZ), 67 Apollo Drive, Rosedale, North Shore 0632, New Zealand
(a division of Pearson New Zealand Ltd.)
Penguin Books (South Africa) (Pty.) Ltd., 24 Sturdee Avenue, Rosebank, Johannesburg 2196,
South Africa

Penguin Books Ltd., Registered Offices: 80 Strand, London WC2R 0RL, England

Cover design and art by Steve Ferlauto
Text design by Tiffany Estreicher

PRINTING HISTORY
Berkley Caliber hardcover / March 2005
Berkley Caliber trade paperback / March 2006
Berkley Caliber trade paperback ISBN: 978-0-425-20787-1

The Library of Congress has catalogued the Berkley Caliber hardcover as follows:

Naylor, Sean
Not a good day to die / Sean Naylor.—1st ed.
p. cm.
ISBN 978-0-425-19609-0
1. Operation Anaconda, 2002. I. Title.

DS371.4123.O64N39 2005
958.104'7—dc22
2004057465

PRINTED IN THE UNITED STATES OF AMERICA

20 19 18 17 16 15 14 13

For my brother, Mark

ACKNOWLEDGMENTS

THIS book could not have been written without the help of scores of people, the vast majority of whom are U.S. servicemen and servicewomen.

Thanks are due to all the people I interviewed—in Afghanistan, the United States, and elsewhere—most of whom are listed at the end of this book. Their willingness to patiently recount events to me is one I truly appreciated. Their stories form the core of this book. Even those not quoted by name in the text helped frame issues and events for me, or provided invaluable photos, documents and maps. I owe a particularly large debt of gratitude to the troops who came forward to be interviewed against the wishes of their chains of command, in order to help me get the full truth.

Others deserving of special recognition are Captain Kevin Butler, the commander of A Company, 2-187 Infantry, and his first sergeant, Jonathan Blossom, who were gracious hosts when I and *Army Times* photographer Warren Zinn embedded with their company for Operation Anaconda. Lieutenant Colonel "Chip" Preysler of 2-187 and his command sergeant major, Mark Nielsen, were also very supportive of my project when it would have been easy for them not to be. The same can be said of their brigade commander, "Rak 6," Colonel Frank Wiercinski.

Many military public affairs officers went above and beyond the call of duty to ensure that I had access to the right people and information. The names on this honor roll include: Commander Kevin Aandahl of Special Operations Command, Central Command; Lieutenant Colonel Hans Bush, U.S. Army Special Operations Command; Carol Darby, U.S. Army Special Operations Command; Colonel Garrie Dornan, Office of the Chief of Public Affairs, U.S. Army; Major Karen Finn, Air Force Special Operations Command; Major General Larry Gottardi, Chief of Public Affairs, U.S. Army; Major Rob Gowan, U.S. Army Special Operations Command; Major Bryan Hilferty, 10th Mountain Division; Major Stephanie Holcombe, U.S. Air Force Public Affairs; Lieutenant

Colonel Tim Nye, U.S. Special Operations Command; Captain Jeff Poole, Coalition Forces Land Component Command; Walter Sokalski, U.S. Army Special Operations Command.

Kathryn Meeks of U.S. Special Operations Command's Freedom of Information Act office was always courteous and patient in dealing with my frustration at her command's slowness in processing my requests. Brigadier General John Brown, Richard Stewart and the rest of the staff at the Army Center for Military History were also extremely helpful. Army Vice Chief of Staff General John M. "Jack" Keane and officers at U.S. Central Command helped open doors that might otherwise have remained firmly closed to me. Retired Colonel Mike Kershner read through most of the first section of the book and provided invaluable suggestions on how to improve it. He and retired Lieutenant Colonel Kalev Sepp also broadened and deepened my understanding of special operations.

I am profoundly grateful to my editors at Army Times Publishing Company—especially Elaine Howard, Tobias Naegele, Robert Hodierne and Alex Neill—for allowing me so much time away from the office to complete this project. In addition, Robert Hodierne, senior managing editor at the company, helped cut my manuscript down to size. Chris Broz, also of the Army Times Publishing Company, brought enthusiasm and expertise to the essential task of drafting the maps to help readers navigate the geography of the Shahikot Valley and its environs. *Army Times* photographer Warren Zinn was my partner in crime during Anaconda whose boundless energy and sense of humor made the long separation from home so much easier to bear.

I could never have accomplished this project without my agent, Scott Miller, whose sage counsel has been my guide since I returned from Afghanistan. Natalee Rosenstein, my editor at Berkley Books, has, like Scott, shown enormous patience and understanding from the moment she acquired the rights to my book.

Finally, I would like to thank Kristina Maze—who provided unflagging love and support throughout the two-and-a-half years it took me to research and write the book—and my family and friends, who saw so little of me while I immersed myself in the events that transpired on snowy mountainsides half a world away.

Sean Naylor
Washington, D.C.
October, 2004.

CONTENTS

Reporting *Not a Good Day to Die* xi
Cast of Characters xiii
Glossary xvi
Prologue 1

IPB 8
REACTION TO CONTACT 184
TAKUR GHAR 300
WINDING DOWN 369

Notes 379
Interviewees 404
Bibliography 411
Index 415

REPORTING *NOT A GOOD DAY TO DIE*

THIS was not an easy book to report.

Researching and explaining a complex and controversial operation fought by a dozen task forces was always going to be a challenge, despite the advantage I enjoyed having been present at the rehearsals for and some of the combat during Operation Anaconda. But even I, after thirteen years of covering the military, had not expected to find so many obstacles placed in my path by a handful of individuals with reputations to protect.

A deal struck between U.S. Central Command and U.S. Special Operations Command banned personnel from either command from discussing Anaconda with the press. The commands established the ban to prevent disclosure of the truth behind the Takur Ghar episode. But the gag order caught all special operations forces, including those who had nothing to do with Takur Ghar, in its net, slowing my ability to report on the Special Forces' side of the Anaconda story. Meanwhile, both commands stalled for many months before answering my Freedom of Information Act requests (in CENTCOM's case even claiming to have "lost" mine). When they finally responded, the results were so heavily redacted as to be almost unusuable. Despite the efforts of the generals involved, however, information nevertheless found its way to me from a variety of sources ideally placed to provide a comprehensive view of Anaconda. But the climate of fear the ban created forced me to use ambiguous phrases like "special ops sources" when attributing some of these facts. While this may seem frustratingly vague, the reader should be under no doubt that these sources knew what they were talking about.

The ban was only lifted in early 2004, after Generals Franks, Holland, and Dailey had left CENTCOM, SOCOM, and Joint Special Operations Command respectively. This allowed me to interview—usually under very controlled conditions—members of the 160th Special Operations Aviation Regiment, the Rangers and other special operations units, with the proviso in some cases that their full names not be used in print. These interviews helped me confirm information gleaned from other sources and flesh out passages describing events about which I had only scant details. Other vital information came from documents, some of which were sent to me anonymously. When it became clear that I knew more than they wished, U.S. Special Operations Command officials launched an internal investigation. The investigation's ostensible purpose was to probe the alleged release of classified material, but its real goal was to punish those who might have helped me compile the facts, and to send a message to others tempted to break ranks and tell the truth.

In contrast to CENTCOM and SOCOM, the conventional Army was for the most part refreshingly straightforward and easy to deal with. Its soldiers and leaders made themselves readily available for interviews. Without their cooperation, I would still be researching and writing.

Sean Naylor
October 2004
Washington, D.C.

CAST OF CHARACTERS

LIEUTENANT Colonel Pete Blaber—The Delta Force officer who commanded AFO and believed in "Patton's three principles of war—audacity, audacity, and audacity."

Technical Sergeant John Chapman—The Air Force NCO who accompanied Mako 30 into combat on Takur Ghar.

Major General Dell Dailey—The head of Joint Special Operations Command. A special operations aviation officer, he was opposed to AFO's involvement in Anaconda.

Major General Warren Edwards—The Army officer who was deputy commanding general for operations at Coalition Forces Land Component Command.

General Tommy Franks—The commander of U.S. Central Command.

Command Sergeant Major Frank Grippe—The tall, jut-jawed infantryman who was the top NCO in 1-87 Infantry.

Lieutenant Colonel Chris Haas—The highly-respected commander of 1st Battalion, 5th Special Forces Group, who formed a close-knit team in Gardez with Blaber and Spider.

Major General Franklin "Buster" Hagenbeck—The 10th Mountain Division commander in charge of all U.S. forces in Anaconda except for the JSOC/TF 11 elements.

Chief Warrant Officer 4 Jim Hardy—The experienced pilot who was the maintenance guru for the Apache helicopters that flew into the Shahikot Valley.

Brigadier General Gary Harrell—The former commander of Delta Force who Franks had placed at the head of Task Force Bowie, the intelligence "fusion cell" at Gardez.

Lieutenant Commander Vic Hyder—The SEAL officer sent by Trebon and Kernan to oversee the insertion of TF Blue elements into the Shahikot. Hyder's recent history of poor judgment made him a dubious choice for the mission.

Major Jimmy—The Delta Force officer who was Blaber's second-in-command in AFO and also functioned as Blaber's liaison officer in the Mountain operations center.

Captain Joseph Kernan—The SEAL Team 6 and Task Force Blue commander. He had a reputation as one of the best swimmers in the Navy.

Lieutenant Colonel Paul LaCamera—The commander of 1-87 Infantry. His Ranger background gave him a bond with many of the other officers in Task Force Rakkasan.

Lieutenant Colonel Jim Larsen—The Task Force Rakkasan executive officer who represented Wiercinski in the early planning sessions at Bagram and Kabul.

Zia Lodin—The leader of the Afghan forces who fought on the Americans' side in Anaconda.

Lieutenant General Paul Mikolashek—The Army officer who headed Coalition Forces Land Component Command.

Colonel John Mulholland—The 5th Special Forces Group commander who headed Task Force Dagger. His A-teams had helped the Northern Alliance to topple the Taliban.

Command Sergeant Major Mark Nielsen—The combat-focused senior NCO in 2-187 Infantry, who was viewed as a voice of common sense by the battalion's soldiers.

Staff Sergeant Randel Perez—A 1-87 Infantry squad leader who had made the almost unheard-of switch to infantry from the supply corps because he wanted more of a challenge.

Lieutenant Colonel Charles "Chip" Preysler—The 2-187 Infantry commander who was the first field grade officer into the Shahikot.

Petty Officer First Class Neil Roberts—A SEAL NCO who was part of Task Force Blue's Mako 30 reconnaissance team.

Staff Sergeant Andrzej Ropel—A 1-87 Infantry squad leader; a Polish immigrant fighting for a country of which he was not yet a citizen.

Lieutenant Colonel Mark Rosengard—The TF Dagger operations officer who combined a flamboyant bravado with a tremendous work ethic and an ability to inspire subordinates.

Captain Nathan Self—The commander of 1st Platoon, A Company, 1st Ranger Battalion—the TF 11 quick reaction force sent to the top of Takur Ghar mountain.

"Slab"—The SEAL senior chief petty officer who led Mako 30. Blaber had a high regard for Slab, whom he knew from their days in the Balkans together.

"Speedy"—The Delta Force master sergeant called Kevin W. who headed AFO's India Team. His background as a triathlete and backwoods hunter gave him an edge in the Shahikot.

"Spider"—Also known as "the Wolf," this CIA operative headed the agency's operations in Gardez. Well known to Blaber, he proved an invaluable asset.

Captain Glenn Thomas—The leader of ODA 594, aka Texas 14; the first U.S. officer to venture into the Shahikot.

Brigadier General Gregory Trebon—The Air Force special operations officer who was Dailey's deputy in JSOC, and who Dailey placed in command of TF 11.

Colonel Frank Wiercinski—The seasoned commander of Task Force Rakkasan.

Major Paul Wille—The lead planner for Task Force Mountain forced to design a plan based on the compromises reached between several different task forces.

GLOSSARY

AC-130—The gunship used by U.S. Air Force Special Operations Command and based on the C-130 Hercules transport aircraft. The H-model of the AC-130 is called the Spectre. The newer U-model is called the Spooky.

AFO—Advance Force Operations, the "black" special operations outfit tasked with conducting high-risk reconnaissance missions in enemy-held territory.

AK-47—The Soviet-designed assault rifle ubiquitous in most guerrilla campaigns. More modern versions include the AKM and AKS. AK-style weapons are often referred to as "Kalashnikovs" after Mikhail Kalashnikov, who designed the original AK-47.

AMF—Afghan military forces or Afghan militia forces, the terms applied to the Afghan fighters who allied themselves with the United States in the fight against Al Qaida and the Taliban.

AOB—Advanced operating base, where a Special Forces company makes its headquarters in the field.

CAOC—Combined Air Operations Center; collocated with Moseley's CFACC headquarters at Prince Sultan Air Base in Saudi Arabia, the CAOC was where air support for the war in Afghanistan was coordinated.

CENTCOM—U.S. Central Command, the four-star headquarters commanded by General Tommy Franks that had charge of U.S. military operations in Afghanistan, Central Asia and the Middle East (minus Israel).

CFACC—Coalition Forces Air Component Command, the three-star headquarters commanded by Air Force Lieutenant General T. Michael "Buzz" Moseley that ran U.S. and coalition air missions in the CENTCOM area of responsibility, including Afghanistan.

CFLCC—Coalition Forces Land Component Command, the three-star headquarters commanded by Army Lieutenant General Paul Mikolashek that was located in Kuwait and controlled all U.S. and allied conventional and "white" special operations forces in the CENTCOM area of responsibility, including Afghanistan.

CinC—Commander-in-chief, the phrase used to refer to the four-star flag officers who head up each of the Pentagon's regional commands. Tommy Franks was a CinC. (Defense Secretary Donald Rumsfeld banned the use of the phrase "commander-in-chief" in this context, however, and ordered the military to instead use the words "combatant commander.")

ETAC—Enlisted tactical air controller, the airman who accompanies a ground unit into battle and is responsible for calling in close air support for that unit.

FARP—Forward arming and refueling point; a spot where helicopters can refuel and rearm in relative safety without having to fly all the way back to the air base from which they launched. During Anaconda FARP was code-named Texaco.

GPS—Global Positioning System; the satellite system that provided U.S. forces with accurate data on their exact location.

HUMINT—Human intelligence, gained through old-fashioned spying such as paying people for information, as distinct from intelligence gained via overhead imaging systems or high-tech eavesdropping.

IMU—The Islamic Movement of Uzbekistan, the radical Islamist guerrilla movement dedicated to overthrowing the Uzbekistan government. Considered the Central Asian franchise of Al Qaida, the IMU provided hundreds of the fighters in the Shahikot valley.

IPB—Intelligence preparation of the battlefield, the process of building as accurate a picture as possible of the enemy force before battle is joined.

ISR—Intelligence, surveillance and reconnaissance.

JSOC—Joint Special Operations Command, the two-star headquarters at Pope Air Force Base, North Carolina, in charge of the classified U.S. special operations forces such as 1st Special Forces Operational Detachment—Delta (i.e., Delta Force). Major General Dell Dailey commanded JSOC during the war in Afghanistan.

Kalashnikov—The name given to any of the AK series of weapons (such as the AK-47) designed by Mikhail Kalashnikov.

LZ—Landing zone (for a helicopter). Strictly, this is called a PZ (pickup zone) when it refers to a spot at which troops are waiting for a helicopter to collect them.

MBITR—Multiband Intra/Inter Team Radio, a handheld radio used by the U.S. military for communication over short distances.

MC-130—The Combat Talon, the special operations version of the venerable C-130 Hercules, equipped with in-flight refueling equipment, terrain-following and terrain-avoidance radar, as well as inertial and Global Positioning System satellite-guided navigation systems.

Mi-17—The Soviet-designed "Hip" transport helicopter used by both sides in the Afghan civil war between the Northern Alliance and the Taliban, as well as by the Central Intelligence Agency.

NCO—Noncommissioned officer, an enlisted soldier of the rank of corporal or above (in the Army); all sergeants are, by definition, NCOs.

NSA—National Security Agency; headquartered at Fort Meade, Maryland, the NSA is the largest of the U.S. intelligence agencies. Its job is to intercept foreign communications while protecting U.S. communications.

ODA—Operational Detachment Alpha, the 12-man (ideally) A-team around which the U.S. Army's Special Forces units are organized.

P-3—The U.S. Navy's Orion turboprop aircraft, originally designed for tracking submarines, the Orion has spawned several high-tech offshoots, such as the EP-3, which can intercept communications and film action on the ground from high altitude.

Rakkasans—The name given to the 187th Infantry Regiment by the Japanese after World War II. The regiment was a paratroop unit and *Rakkasan* loosely translates as "falling umbrella." Three battalions of the regiment made up the 3rd Brigade of the 101st Airborne Division (Air Assault) at the time of Anaconda.

RP—Release point, the predetermined location during a helicopter mission at which pilots know that by flying in a certain direction at a certain speed for a given amount of time they will arrive at their LZ.

RPG-7—The standard rocket-propelled grenade weapon designed by the Soviet Union and used by guerrilla forces the world over. It consists of a reusable launcher and a grenade with a high-explosive warhead.

RTO—Radio-telephone operator; the soldier whose job it is to man the radio.

SCIF—Secure, compartmented intelligence facility; the part of a military base at which the most sensitive intelligence issues are discussed.

SEALs—The Navy's Sea-Air-Land commandos.

SF—Special Forces, the Army's unconventional warfare troops, not to be confused with special operations forces.

SIGINT—Signals intelligence, i.e. intelligence derived from intercepting radio, telephone, computer or other communications.

SOF—Special operations forces; in the U.S. military, this consists of all the forces under the command of U.S. Special Operations Command, including Army Special Forces, 160th Special Operations Aviation Regiment, Delta Force, Navy SEALs, and the Air Force's MC-130 and AC-130 units and special tactics squadrons.

Texas 14—The code name given to Operational Detachment Alpha 594, the Special Forces A-team led by Captain Glenn Thomas.

TF—Task force; the designation given to any military unit that has been specially configured for a particular mission.

TOC—Tactical operations center, the field headquarters for a military unit; in joint (i.e., multiservice) task forces, this is sometimes referred to as the joint operations center, or JOC.

UAV—Unmanned aerial vehicle, a drone that is remotely piloted.

VTC—Video-teleconference. A meeting at which participants may be on separate continents, but can see each other via a system of video cameras and monitors at each location.

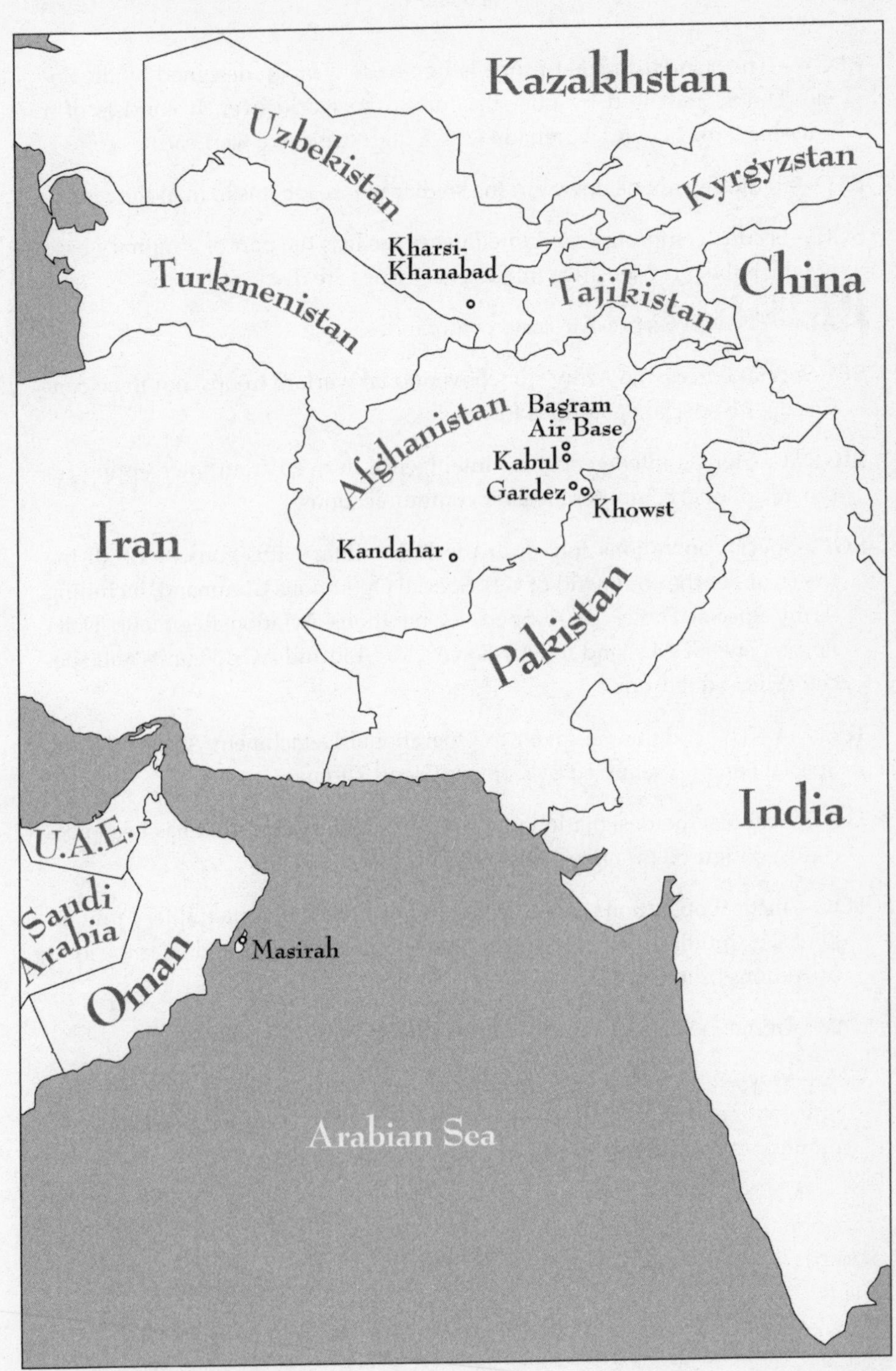
Kazakhstan
Uzbekistan
Kyrgyzstan
Kharsi-
Khanabad
Turkmenistan
Tajikistan
China
Afghanistan
Bagram
Air Base
Kabul
Gardez
Khowst
Iran
Kandahar
Pakistan
India
U.A.E.
Saudi
Arabia
Oman
Masirah
Arabian Sea

PROLOGUE

THE first gray fingers of dawn were gripping the mountaintops as the three helicopters hurtled between the snowcapped peaks. Packed like sardines inside each of the ungainly Chinooks were over forty combat-laden soldiers, and the aircraft's twin sets of rotor blades wilted visibly under the strain, making a deeper *whoompah! whoompah! whoompah!* sound than normal as they bludgeoned the thin mountain air into submission. Two minutes behind them another three Chinooks followed the same route, hurdling saddles and sweeping through passes.

On each helicopter, cramped soldiers sat facing inward on red nylon seats along the sides of the cabin. A third row sat between them on the floor facing the tail ramp. Wedged among a welter of rucksacks, rifles, mortars, and machine guns, and further constrained by their bulky webbing, helmets, and body armor, few soldiers could do more than turn their heads a few inches from side to side. The din of the engines made conversation impossible, and many soldiers sheltered under blankets the aircrew had handed out as shields against the icy blasts blowing in through the open side doors and tail ramps.

The harsh, jagged terrain of eastern Afghanistan sped past a couple of hundred feet below, an alien landscape dotted with mud-brick villages little changed since Alexander's hoplites marauded through the region 2,300 years previously. Those soldiers close enough to see out of one of the Chinooks' few windows peered down to spy villagers gazing up in awe and astonishment at the war machines thundering overhead. It was as if the sky belonged to a different century than the earth below. A few Pashtun tribesmen hazarded a wave at the aircraft. Others pointed and gaped, and one woman threw herself back into her home through a window, such was her haste to escape the scrutiny of the twenty-first century warriors above her.

Sergeant Carl Moore, the lead Chinook's left door gunner, glanced over his shoulder into the aircraft's interior and saw a sea of faces, most so young they wouldn't seem out of place crowding a high school corridor. The average age of the men in the back of the helicopter was twenty years old. But these teens and twenty-somethings weren't on their way to class, but to a trial by fire at 8,000 feet. Nestled in a mountain valley somewhere ahead, their commanders had told them, were hundreds of enemy fighters. It was going to be the job of the soldiers on the helicopters to capture or kill them before they could escape to Pakistan or foment rebellion against the American-installed government inside Afghanistan. When word of the mission had started to leak out a few days previously, the young Americans were excited. They had grown tired of the tedious duty of guarding air bases, which was all most had been doing since they arrived months before in central Asia. But now they were minutes away from combat. For all but a handful, it would be their first taste of "real-world" action, and intimations of their own mortality naturally intruded. Moore saw fear on several faces.

His counterpart manning the right door gun, Sergeant Eddie Wahl, also looked back inside the aircraft and saw a range of emotions on the young faces. One soldier stared blankly ahead. Another nervously checked and rechecked his weapon and ammo pouches, making sure everything he would need in a fight was instantly accessible.

Specialist Matthew Edwards, a clean-cut twenty-four-year-old armed with a light machine gun called the Squad Automatic Weapon, or SAW, kept his eye on his squad leader, Staff Sergeant Chris Harry. As a private in the 75th Ranger Regiment, Harry had parachuted into a fierce firefight at Rio Hato airfield during the 1989 invasion of Panama. That experience made him the only combat veteran among the infantry in the Chinook. Edwards, a lean, thoughtful soldier with a finance degree from Virginia Tech, tried to take his cue from Harry's demeanor. The squad leader didn't let him down. When Moore and Wahl test-fired their M60 machine guns halfway through the flight, several troops glanced up, alarmed. But Harry smiled broadly and looked around as if to say *Here we go, boys; don't be nervous, this is what we train for.* Edwards felt a surge of confidence. *We're ready for this,* he thought.

Private First Class Jason Wilson, a rascal-faced nineteen-year-old Oklahoman so short and skinny that his platoon sergeant referred to him as "an elf," allowed himself to be rocked to sleep by the vibrations. His SAW leaned between his knees, barrel pointing down so in case of an accidental discharge the bullet would shoot harmlessly through the floor, not into the rotor blades churning overhead. Several of Wilson's comrades also dozed fitfully, a common reaction of soldiers flying toward combat. These troops were "Screaming Eagles" of the 101st Airborne Division, and their predecessors in that storied unit had slumbered in much the same way in the transports that flew across the English Channel in the early hours of June 6, 1944, or, more recently, when Black Hawk helicopters ferried them into battle in the 1991 Gulf War.

Wilson and his buddies had been in grade school when the United States and its allies crushed the Republican Guard and the rest of the Iraqi military in that conflict. Since then, the "peace dividend" defense cuts of the 1990s had almost halved the Army that drove Saddam Hussein's legions from the field. As training funds dried up and peacekeeping missions proliferated, combat readiness suffered. The privates, specialists, and buck sergeants in the Chinooks swooping through the mountains belonged to what their elders disparagingly referred to as "the Nintendo generation." They came of age in the era of Internet chat rooms, gangsta rap, and grunge. Senior NCOs in the Army that Wilson joined complained that recruits at the turn of the twenty-first century showed up at basic training softer and less fit than their predecessors. As the United States lamented the passing of "The Greatest Generation" that secured victory in World War II, many Americans—and many enemies of America—questioned whether this latest generation of Americans had the stomach for a fight.

NOT all the passengers aboard that first Chinook bore the stamp of fresh-faced youth. Seated toward the front were Lieutenant Colonel "Chip" Preysler and Command Sergeant Major Mark Nielsen. Preysler, forty-one, the senior officer on the helicopter and the infantrymen's battalion commander, spent the flight glued to his radio, monitoring the brigade command net. Nielsen was his wiry sergeant major straight out of central casting—five feet eight inches and 169 pounds of weather-beaten rawhide toughened by fifteen years in the Ranger Regiment. Sergeant First Class Anthony Koch, thirty-four, the platoon sergeant of the infantrymen on the Chinook, thought the forty-eight-year-old Nielsen looked grizzled enough to have been in the War of 1812. But like Koch and Preysler, the sergeant major had yet to hear a shot fired in anger.

In the cockpit Chief Warrant Officer 3 Brett Blair, the pilot in command, removed his night-vision goggles as the light of dawn spread across the horizon. His adrenalin started pumping in earnest. When they had taken off, the weather brief had been "Clear, blue, and twenty-two," aviator talk for perfect flying weather. But now the Chinooks were squeezing through a 100-foot gap between a bank of fog beneath them and layer of cloud above. Hesitating, the three Chinooks circled as the clouds seemed to close in. *Hell, we're gonna screw the whole thing up because we can't get in,* Blair thought.

Then, scanning the thin strip of pale sky between the fog and the clouds, he glimpsed a white-capped mountain range in the distance. It was a moment of decision for the nineteen-year veteran. Blair got on the VHF radio to the other two birds in his serial. "Follow me, we're going through," he said. Pulling the thrust lever up with his left hand while using his right to push the cyclic lever, Blair put the Chinook into a rapid right turn. The other helicopters followed suit.

They flew on, dead east, and the skies began to clear. Blair's instincts had been sound. He picked up speed and lost altitude, taking the helicopter down to just thirty feet above the ground, hugging the terrain. About an hour after taking off from Bagram air base, he made a final sharp turn to the north as he closed on the valley. The helicopters behind him fell in trail. Now he was just a couple of kilometers from the release point, the predetermined location at which pilots are free to drop their maps because they know that by flying in a certain direction for a given amount of time at a certain speed, they will arrive at their landing zones. Over the intercom Blair told the crew in the back that they were ten minutes out from the LZ. In a sequence repeated on each of the Chinooks, Moore and Wahl turned to the infantrymen closest to them. "Ten minutes!" they shouted, holding all ten fingers up simultaneously in case the troops couldn't hear above the noise of the engines.

The word got passed quickly down the helicopter, each soldier tapping the grunt next to him on the shoulder and repeating the "Ten minutes!" shout while showing all ten fingers. The warning galvanized the troops. Those who had been huddled under blankets threw them off. No one was sleeping now. There was a distinct change in the atmosphere aboard the Chinook as the infantrymen's restlessness to escape the cramped confines of the aircraft mingled with their anxiety about what they would encounter on the ground. Soldiers fastened and refastened the straps on their Kevlar helmets and cinched their assault packs a little tighter so they wouldn't lose anything if they had to run. To Moore, the troops' faces reflected their realization that *Oh, shit, we're really doing this.*

As if to underline the proximity of danger, the lingering aroma of high-explosive bombs dropped on suspected Al Qaida positions near the LZs a few minutes previously now filled the helicopter. One young soldier looked confused by the acrid smell filling his nostrils. "That's just the Air Force doing its job!" Nielsen yelled at him.

As Blair coaxed and wrestled the helicopter between craggy outcrops, a voice crackled over the radio with alarming news. Special Forces troops near the valley had come under attack, and a "litter urgent" casualty required evacuation by helicopter ASAP. *Litter urgent.* The words resonated in the cockpits of all six Chinooks. It was an anodyne Army phrase that referred to a casualty so badly wounded that he had to be evacuated within the hour to stand a chance of survival. This wasn't good. The infantry weren't even on the ground yet, and already a friendly soldier's life was ebbing away somewhere ahead of and below them. It was the first sign anyone on the Chinooks had that events weren't going completely to plan.

The release point was in a draw just to the east of a ridgeline that jutted into the southern end of the valley. Despite the fog, the Chinooks hit the RP right on time. As they flew into the valley, the ground dropped away before them. The pilots began sweeping the terrain a couple of miles ahead with their eyes, searching for their LZs. By now Blair was flying along what aviators call "the nap of the earth," scudding just fifteen to twenty feet above the ground at the base of the valley's eastern ridgeline. A few hundred meters to the west lay the mud-colored villages in the center of the valley. To American ears, these villages had odd, exotic-sounding names—Serkhankhel, Babulkhel, Zerki Kale—but the troops knew them simply as Objective Remington.

Looking out of his open window across the terraced fields toward the villages, Moore swiveled his M60 machine gun back and forth. These were the most dangerous moments of the flight. His body tensed as he watched and waited for the sudden appearance of tracers arcing out of the village, or even worse, the small orange fireball of an incoming rocket-propelled grenade. Across the cabin the part-Cherokee, part-French-Canadian Wahl did likewise, searching for any sign of the enemy in the snow and rocks of the mountainside that stretched up for several thousand feet. Here and there cave mouths appeared as black gashes in the rock face. But there was no sign of life. Nothing, it seemed, was stirring. Maybe, just maybe, the air assault had achieved surprise after all.

IN fact, there were at least thirteen fighters hidden in the crags and crevices up ahead who knew the Chinooks were coming and were eagerly awaiting their arrival. But these men were all Americans, members of the U.S. military's most elite units. In the dead of night they had ridden on all-terrain vehicles and marched over frozen ridgelines through thigh-deep snow to emerge unseen in the heart of the enemy's last remaining stronghold in Afghanistan. They had already saved the operation from catastrophe once and would do so again in the days ahead. But few of the men sitting in the helicopters would ever realize the debt they owed to these secretive athlete-warriors who embodied their commander's credo of "audacity, audacity, and audacity."

WITH five, three, and two minutes to go, the air crew repeated the "*x* minutes out" warning, each alert ratcheting the tension up another notch inside the helicopter. As the minutes wound down, Captain Frank Baltazar, the troops' popular company commander, insisted on repeatedly high-fiving the soldier beside him, Specialist Dan Chapman. The twenty-one-year-old team leader understood this to be his commander's way of dealing with his nerves. Other soldiers made hasty, last-minute adjustments to their equipment.

At the three-minute mark the troops stopped checking their gear and focused their gaze on the rear of the helicopter, each mentally planning his route off the bird and going over in his mind what actions he was supposed to take immediately upon hitting the ground. A few got a kick out of the patch the Chinook's rear crew chief, Sergeant Mike Cifers, had Velcroed to the back of his helmet. "Fun Meter," it said, with a little arrow pointing all the way to the right. *Maximum fun. Yeah, right.*

At "Two minutes!" Koch barked a simple yet profound order: "Lock and load!" Simple, because it only required the troops to chamber a round in their M4 assault rifles, which they each did instantly with a series of metallic *kerr-chunks.* Profound, because the order is only given when combat may be imminent.

After careful analysis of maps and satellite photographs, the planners had given Blair an LZ next to a walled compound just north of a gully that ran west into the valley from the eastern ridgeline. But maps of the valley were notoriously unreliable, and satellite photos could be deceptive. A couple of days previously the CIA had flown a Russian-made Mi-17 helicopter over the area, filming the valley floor. Blair and the other pilots had watched the video, but it still hadn't been clear enough to tell him whether or not the spot picked out for his LZ was really suitable. To minimize the chance of a helicopter being shot down, the Chinook pilots were told that under no conditions were they to double back and fly south—they were never to fly over the same piece of terrain twice. Therefore the pilots had agreed with the infantry officers that they would put the troops down at "the first sure thing" close to their assigned LZs.

As Blair approached the compound, he saw a perfect spot about 100 meters south of the gully in a tiny terraced field.

"Thirty seconds!" Wahl yelled to the soldier next to him. The Chinook slowed to a hover. Blair put the helicopter into what pilots call its "landing attitude," with its nose pointing slightly upward to ensure the rear wheels touch down first. "Aircraft clear?" he asked over the intercom. It was the job of the three crewmen in the back to check for obstacles or hollows on the LZ that might disrupt the landing. "Clear to the left!" replied Moore. "Clear to the right!" yelled Wahl. "Clear to the rear!" shouted Cifers.

With the Chinook facing north toward the compound, Blair slowly lowered the big helicopter to the ground. In the cabin every infantryman was now wearing his "game face"—a look of focused determination—and had one arm through the harness of his rucksack, ready to move. As Cifers watched the dirt field rise up to meet him, he talked Blair through the last few seconds of the landing. "Aft wheels off ten feet!" he yelled over the intercom. "Five . . . four . . . three . . . two . . . one."

The moment that the Chinook's rear wheels hit the ground, the soldiers rose as one. Some wobbled under their huge packs before bracing themselves in an awkward runner's stance. They were relieved to be on the ground, where they could regain some measure of control over their fates. In the air they were nothing but a big target. Blair brought the front wheels down gently. The helicopter bounced along the ground for a few feet, then stopped. The troops were instantly on their feet, shouldering their rucks. Cifers had raised the ramp a few degrees as the helicopter descended, so it would not bang off the ground. Now he depressed the short lever beside the ramp to lower it again. Nielsen bellowed blunt orders from the front of the helicopter: "Go! Go! Go! Move! Move! Move!" Other NCOs took up the shout.

Sergeant Scotty Mendenhall was closest to the ramp as it began to fall. His location there was no accident. The beefy six-footer carried one of the platoon's two M240B machine guns—heavier, more lethal weapons than the SAWs. If the enemy was lying in wait for the Americans as they came off the helicopter, the firepower he laid down could provide the margin between life and death for him and his buddies. Impatient to get out, Mendenhall stepped onto the ramp while it was still descending. Holding the machine gun in one hand, he ran halfway down the ramp and jumped. It was just past 6:30 a.m. and the sun had not yet climbed over the mountains when his boots landed in the hard, gravelly dirt of the Shahikot Valley.

IPB

1.

IT was a raw, biting wind that swept down from the Hindu Kush in the first weeks of 2002, and the militiamen guarding the Ariana Hotel in downtown Kabul stamped their feet and blew on their hands to fight off the chill.

Behind them the hotel sat squat, yellow, and ugly. The Ariana was owned by the Afghan government, which in reality meant whichever guerrilla army happened to be in charge of Kabul at the time. It also meant the hotel had played several cameo roles in the decade of civil war that had wracked Afghanistan since the pro-Soviet government fell to the mujahideen in 1992. When the Taliban army of fundamentalist Muslim students routed the weak central government in 1996, their first order of business had been to drag Najibullah, the last pro-Soviet Afghan dictator, from the United Nations compound in which he and his brother had sheltered since their government fell in 1992. After torturing them, the Taliban death squad murdered the brothers and then hung their bodies from a makeshift scaffold in the traffic circle in front of the Ariana. Thereafter, the Taliban used the hotel as an R & R spot for troops rotating back from the front line in the war against the Northern Alliance forces of Ahmad Shah Massoud, and as a way station for Pakistani volunteers en route to the front. By way of payback, a Northern Alliance jet dropped a bomb on the hotel in 1997.

Now the tables had turned again. Al Qaida, the Islamist terrorist organization that had found a welcoming home in Afghanistan under the Taliban, had hijacked four planes in the United States and flown two of them into the World Trade Center and one into the Pentagon, killing thousands and stirring the world's only superpower to action. The Americans had come to Afghanistan, embraced the Northern Alliance, and driven the Taliban from power. And so it was that the guards lounging by the large concrete steps that led up to the

Ariana's main entrance were tough-looking Northern Alliance fighters, hard men down from the Panjshir Valley whose fingers never wandered far from the triggers of their Kalashnikov assault rifles. Some of these men had been fighting—against the Soviets, Najibullah's regime, other mujahideen militias, and the Taliban—for more than twenty years, and it showed on their dark, worn faces and dirty, calloused hands.

But the balance of power had not shifted completely in the Northern Alliance's favor. Not yet. The big dog on the block was the United States, and so while the Panjshiri guards shivered outside in their motley camouflage uniforms provided by the Central Intelligence Agency, inside the Ariana's bullet-scarred walls the Americans held court. The CIA had rented the entire hotel, retained the staff, and set up its Kabul station there. It made sense for the spooks to use the Ariana. It was centrally located, just a couple of blocks from the Presidential Palace, and the safe house being used by the Special Forces, but it was protected from the busy street by a ten-foot wall. The only other defenses the Americans had added were a string of concertina wire atop the wall and a sandbagged guard post on the flat roof, manned twenty-four hours a day by a couple of Northern Alliance fighters.

Easy living it wasn't. The plumbing was atrocious, even by Afghan standards, and the hotel was in a general state of disrepair. But it was warm, and the dining room still offered simple but delicious dishes of beans and rice and other staples of Afghan cuisine.

On this frigid mid-January afternoon a handful of men were gathered in one of the hotel's upstairs rooms for a meeting. The CIA personnel conducted most of their meetings in this room during those first turbulent months after the fall of Kabul, but on this occasion only one agency officer was present—a thin, bearded man with long sandy hair called John, who was the deputy chief of station. The rest of the men were soldiers, special operators from the units that had been at the forefront of the war in Afghanistan. Like John, they were dressed in civilian clothes and wore their hair longer than most American soldiers are allowed. All sported the beards that were ubiquitous among American special operators and intelligence operatives in Afghanistan. Most were armed with M4 carbines or 9mm Beretta pistols.

It was a dark-walled room made even darker by the curtains drawn to prevent any snipers from drawing a bead on those inside. Dust motes swam in a single shaft of intense sunlight that exploited a small gap between the curtains. A lamp resting on an end table cast shadows on a floor covered by an Afghan rug, and the men sat on a tatty, overstuffed sofa and similarly worn but comfortable chairs.

As the Americans sipped green tea from a service that a member of the hotel staff had set on a glass-topped coffee table, the mood was businesslike. The Taliban had been defeated, the Northern Alliance had swept into Kabul, and the whole country was—in theory—under the control of the Americans and the Afghan warlords with whom they had allied themselves. But the men in the room were not celebrating. The Taliban were gone and Al Qaida's guerrillas were on the run, but there was still much to do. Six weeks earlier the Americans thought they had Al Qaida's leaders holed up at Tora Bora in the White Mountains that straddle the border with Pakistan. Reluctant to put too many American troops on the ground, U.S. commanders had relied on their Afghan allies backed up by Special Forces to snare Osama bin Laden and his henchmen. But this time the Americans' faith in their militia allies was misplaced, and a failure to block escape routes into Pakistan from Tora Bora meant bin Laden and hundreds of Al Qaida's most hardened fighters had slipped the net.

So long as those guerrillas remained at large, the Americans knew they could not rest. And so as usual in these brainstorming sessions, which John convened daily in his excuse for a sitting room, the talk this afternoon was where to focus next.

As the meeting was breaking up, John looked across the table and spoke directly to one of the special operators—an Army officer dressed in a thick, long-sleeved shirt with an Afghan scarf around his neck. Clipped into the waistband of his cargo pants was a black leather holster in which nestled a semiautomatic Glock pistol with a twenty-round extended clip. Over six feet tall with dark hair and a goatee that framed an open and honest face, the officer was forty years old, yet still had the lean, hard physique of the track and field champion he had been in his youth. He exuded the self-confident air of a man used to not just living but succeeding on his wits. His name was Pete Blaber and he was a lieutenant colonel in 1st Special Forces Operational Detachment—Delta, better known to the public as "Delta Force."

The agency was getting a lot of reports that Al Qaida forces were regrouping in a mountainous region south of Gardez in eastern Afghanistan's rugged Paktia province, John said. "What's it called?" Blaber asked. The CIA officer told him. Blaber, who had been in Afghanistan for a month and thought he knew the lay of the land, had never heard of the place. "How do you spell it?" he said, eyes narrowing with curiosity as he grabbed a mechanical pencil to jot the name down in his day planner.

As Blaber scribbled, the CIA officer spoke each letter in turn: "S-H-A-H-I-K-H-O-T."

2.

THE spooks and operators at the Ariana weren't the only Americans in central Asia to have taken a sudden interest in the Shahikot Valley. Two weeks earlier, and 350 miles (about 563 kilometers) to the northwest, at a remote air base in Uzbekistan, two Army officers had been poring over maps of eastern Afghanistan. Major Paul Wille and Captain Francesca Ziemba were on the staff of the 10th Mountain Division, and they were working on an urgent tasking from the division commander, Major General Franklin "Buster" Hagenbeck.

A native Floridian and West Point graduate, Hagenbeck had taken command of the division in August, having previously seen combat in Grenada with the 82nd Airborne Division in 1983.

By late December 2001, Hagenbeck was a frustrated man. He'd left 10th Mountain's home post of Fort Drum in upstate New York a month earlier in the expectation that he would soon be commanding troops in combat in Afghanistan. Although it had been America's commandos who had carried the fight to the enemy so far, Hagenbeck was sure the conventional Army's battalions, brigades, and divisions would be essential in defeating the Taliban. He was by no means alone in believing that victory in Afghanistan would likely require conventional forces sooner rather than later. When the first CIA operatives and Special Forces soldiers had flown into Afghanistan in September to link up with the Northern Alliance, U.S. commanders were not planning for victory by Christmas. Their ambitions were far more modest: to use the Northern Alliance, emboldened by the precise lethality of America's air power and the tactical savvy of her special operators, to carve out a foothold in northern Afghanistan before the onset of the dreaded Afghan winter. The aim was to seize at least one airfield in the north into which conventional troops could be flown, if necessary, in time to launch a spring offensive.

When, against all expectations, one province after another fell quickly to the Northern Alliance, the Americans instead began planning to introduce conventional forces in a battle for Kabul, in case the Alliance's attack stalled at the gates of the Afghan capital. The plan was to airdrop a brigade of the 82nd Airborne Division to seize Kabul's airport, through which would flow the conventional units charged with taking control of the city. But the Taliban's hasty retreat from the capital on November 13 obviated the need for such an assault. (This was fortunate. With no permission to stage the airborne assault from bases in neighboring countries, it would have taken every tanker aircraft in the

Air Force's fleet to refuel the C-17 and C-141 transports flying the paratroopers from Pope Air Force Base, North Carolina, to the dark skies over Kabul. This would have left no tankers for the bombers that would be expected to conduct preassault strikes on Kabul's defenses.) Similar plans for a conventional assault on the southern city of Kandahar, the Taliban's spiritual home, also went by the wayside when the regime failed to make the last ditch defense of the city expected by U.S. commanders.

So instead of pitting their wits against the Taliban and Al Qaida, the end of 2001 found Hagenbeck and his staff sitting on the sidelines, itching to get into the action. Hagenbeck's mission was to be the forward headquarters in the Afghanistan theater for Lieutenant General Paul Mikolashek, who commanded all of America's conventional ground forces in a swathe of the globe that encompassed twenty-five countries stretching from Sudan to Kazakhstan. That was the territory for which U.S. Central Command (CENTCOM)—one of the Pentagon's five regional commands—was responsible, and Mikolashek's boss was CENTCOM commander General Tommy Franks. In peacetime Mikolashek's command was known as the Army component of Central Command, or ARCENT. But during the war in Afghanistan, as other ground forces—U.S. Marines, as well as U.S. and allied special ops units—were placed under Mikolashek, Franks gave it the tongue-twisting title of Coalition Forces Land Component Command, or CFLCC (pronounced "sea-flick").

ARCENT's headquarters at Fort McPherson in Atlanta, Georgia, was too far away from Afghanistan for Mikolashek's taste, so he moved it to the high-tech facilities at Camp Doha in Kuwait. But he wanted a headquarters element even closer, so the Army gave him the 10th Mountain division HQ, which is how Hagenbeck found himself at the windblown base at Kharsi-Khanabad, Uzbekistan. He and his headquarters arrived at K2, as it quickly became known, on December 1.

By the time Hagenbeck's troops had pitched their tents in K2, the Taliban had abandoned Kabul and retreated to their power base in the southern city of Kandahar, where their resistance evaporated by December 9. Meanwhile, bin Laden and hundreds of his fighters had fled to their Tora Bora stronghold. When Franks declined to commit conventional troops to stop those fighters from escaping into Pakistan, another opportunity to get into the fight seemed to have slipped through Hagenbeck's fingers. But he wasn't about to give up. Although an even-tempered officer of patrician countenance, the division commander was, by his own admission, "chomping at the bit to do something." He knew there were still enemy forces in Afghanistan. That much was clear from the daily video-teleconferences (VTCs) through which CENTCOM ran the war from its headquarters at MacDill Air Force Base in Tampa, Florida. These video-teleconferences, in which the senior figures from each headquarters sat in front of a TV camera–monitor combination that automatically broadcast the picture of whoever was talking to the other headquarters watching, were a feature of daily life for the colonels and generals planning and fighting the war. In these discussions CENTCOM officials referred to remaining concentrations of Al Qaida fighters in Afghanistan as "puddles of resistance."

Hagenbeck gathered his staff in late December and told them to collect all the intelligence they could about the situation in Afghanistan and to draw up rough plans—concepts of operations, in Army lingo—for missions in which the Mountain headquarters could be used to command and control conventional and special operations forces. Hagenbeck's aim was to demonstrate his headquarters' value to Mikolashek, in the hope of persuading the three-star general to give Mountain a combat operation to head up.

Wille and Ziemba got to work. A brawny, likable and plainspoken man, Wille was the division's chief of plans. His job was to coordinate the efforts of all the other planners in the division staff and subordinate units. Ziemba, a slender brunette who as a West Point cadet had somehow acquired the incongruous nickname "Ox," was the plans officer in the division's intelligence section. "Okay, where's some enemy activity?" Wille asked the intel officer. "Right here," she said, indicating a digital map display on her laptop, her finger pointing right at the Shahikot. "There's some enemy activity in this valley." The Shahikot area had been a mujahideen stronghold during the Soviet-Afghan war, she added. To Wille that seemed as good a place as any for which to plan an operation. He and Ziemba applied themselves to the task assiduously. Their "office" was the plans tent, the only unheated tent in the entire command post. In the chill of the Uzbek winter, they often typed with their gloves on. Operating on two hours of sleep a night, supplemented by copious amounts of coffee, the two officers scrutinized maps, analyzed intelligence reports, and put together a rough plan.

Their job was made all the harder by the fact that no one at the Mountain headquarters, including Hagenbeck himself, had access to the most current intelligence about events in Afghanistan. This was a function of the compartmentalized approach to intelligence gathering in the war, in which, for reasons of operational security and bureaucratic turf protection, intelligence gathered by one U.S. agency or command was often not shared with other senior U.S. officials or military commanders in the region. CENTCOM even held back intelligence from Mikolashek's headquarters. Nevertheless, by the end of December, Wille and Ziemba produced a well-developed concept paper that showed how the Mountain HQ could use conventional and unconventional forces to crush Al Qaida guerrillas in the Shahikot. Wille presented it to Hagenbeck, who liked what he saw. The concept was forwarded to Mikolashek and his CFLCC planners in the first week of January.

Hagenbeck heard nothing back from Mikolashek. His frustration gave way to resignation. On January 25 he boarded a plane and flew to Kuwait, there to brief Mikolashek on another plan his staff had drawn up: the one for their imminent return to Fort Drum.

3.

WITHIN forty-eight hours of his return to K2 after briefing Mikolashek on his plan to take his headquarters back to the States, Hagenbeck was finally read in on some of the compartmentalized intelligence hitherto denied him. The man sharing the intel was Colonel John Mulholland, a bear of a man who commanded 5th Special Forces Group. Mulholland had every right to be pleased with the course of his war so far. Under his command a task force of just 316 Special Forces soldiers had entered Afghanistan, organized, trained, and, in some cases, equipped the Northern Alliance and the anti-Taliban Pushtun militias, toppled the Taliban government in Kabul and routed its fielded forces. The entire campaign, from the first A-team flying into Afghanistan on October 19 to the collapse of the Taliban's home base in Kandahar on December 6, had lasted only forty-nine days. Notwithstanding the critical contributions made by the CIA, air power, and other special operations forces, the defeat of the Taliban was Special Forces' finest hour.

Special Forces have been part of the Army since 1952. For much of that time they have been treated like a bastard child. The "big Army" never really felt comfortable with the independence bred and trained into SF soldiers. Unlike the conventional Army, which often maneuvered in 600-soldier battalions, Special Forces' cutting edge was provided by twelve-man operational detachments alpha, more commonly known as ODAs or A-teams. By 2001 Special Forces focused on "unconventional warfare"—teaching insurgents how to wage war against enemies of the United States. Afghanistan seemed to validate their approach. But that didn't stop CENTCOM from ensnaring Special Forces in a confusing and often conflicting chain of command that was to affect with nearly disastrous results the rest of the war in Afghanistan.

The commander of all of CENTCOM's "white" (i.e., those whose existence is not classified) special operations forces was a former head of SEAL Team 6, the Navy's rough equivalent of the Army's Delta Force. That officer, Rear Admiral Albert Calland, split the special ops command in Afghanistan. In the north, where the Northern Alliance's presence offered great opportunities for unconventional warfare, he created Task Force Dagger, with Mulholland's 5th Group at its core. To special ops planners, the south offered more potential for a force designed to conduct special reconnaissance and direct action; in other words, a force that specialized first in finding the enemy, then killing him. The force Calland established to do that—Joint Special Operations Task Force (South)—was led by another SEAL, Commodore Robert Harward, and comprised largely special ops units from allied countries, rounded out by some SEALs and Special Forces. It was called Task Force K-Bar.

Many, especially those in the Army, worried about Navy operators being thrust into extended land operations. But in the north the plan worked better than anyone had dared hope.

WITH Mikolashek's support, Task Force Dagger put unconventional warfare (UW) doctrine to work on a massive scale in Afghanistan, allying with the warlords who would become American surrogates or, in the language of UW, "G-chiefs" (the *G* stands for *guerrilla*). According to Lieutenant Colonel Mark Rosengard, Dagger's operations officer, the key to understanding and implementing that doctrine was to reduce it to its bare essentials. For a UW operation to work, a potential G-chief must be able to answer "yes" to three simple questions, he said.

"The first one is 'Do we have a common goal today, recognizing tomorrow may be different?' The second question is 'Do you have a secure backyard?'" Rosengard said. Without a sanctuary in which Special Forces could meet with and organize indigenous troops, "we'll only run away from the enemy all the time and never get anywhere."

The third question is even more basic: "Are you willing to kill somebody?"

"With those three things, I can do business," Rosengard said. "It's no more complicated than that. Bragg [Fort Bragg, North Carolina, where Special Forces doctrine is written and taught] will make that a mile long and teach people a course for eight weeks."

In the Northern Alliance, Task Force Dagger found an organization whose leaders could answer with a resounding "yes" to each of the three questions. Despite the assassination of its charismatic leader, Ahmad Shah Massoud, only two days before the September 11 attacks, the alliance remained a force in being, with its own "secure backyard" in northeastern Afghanistan. Once the A-teams got their feet on the ground and put their heads together with their chosen G-chiefs, the combination of American know-how and air power with Northern Alliance muscle proved unstoppable when opposed by the Taliban's ragtag army.

The Taliban's collapse heralded an extraordinary success for Task Force Dagger, but it also posed new and difficult challenges. The Northern Alliance had proven worthy allies in the fight to topple the Taliban. But once that victory had been achieved, the alliance's leaders were more interested in consolidating power for themselves in Kabul, or in fighting among themselves, than they were in crushing the Al Qaida forces that, along with the remnants of the Taliban army, had fled to the mountains that lined the border with Pakistan. This was to be expected. The Northern Alliance was dominated and led by fighters from the two largest ethnic groups in northern Afghanistan, the Tajiks and the Uzbeks. The Taliban, on the other hand, was a movement that emerged from the Pushtun tribes concentrated along both sides of the border with Pakistan. The Pushtuns had traditionally controlled Afghanistan's central government, and what the Northern Alliance leaders were really interested in was ejecting their hated Pushtun rivals from power, and then enjoying the fruits of victory. They had little incentive to risk their lives chasing Al Qaida's highly motivated foreign fighters through the mountains.

At this point American interests diverged from those of the Northern Alliance. U.S. commanders had little interest in rounding up the Taliban's foot soldiers, most of whom had returned to their farms and villages or fled to Pakistan. But the Americans had every intention of killing or capturing the hundreds—perhaps thousands—of Al Qaida fighters now on the run in eastern Afghanistan, as well as Taliban leader Mullah Mohammed Omar and his immediate subordinates. Task Force Dagger was given permission to extend its unconventional warfare campaign into the Pushtun lands of southern and eastern Afghanistan. However, having allied themselves with the Northern Alliance, dominated by the Pushtuns' historical enemies, the Americans had—perhaps unavoidably—set themselves a difficult task when it came to winning Pushtuns over to their cause. To make matters worse for the Americans, Al Qaida had also been a stronger presence in the eastern provinces than elsewhere in the country, buying friends and influence with cash.

The TF Dagger leaders realized allies would not be as easy to find in eastern Afghanistan as they had been in the north. Working out of bases in Pakistan, Dagger teams cobbled together a few Pushtun tribal militias and tagged them the "Eastern Alliance," as a counterweight to the Northern Alliance. For a time this approach seemed to be working. It was Dagger, with help from the CIA and other special ops units, which brought Pushtun leader Hamid Karzai into Afghanistan from obscurity and exile in Pakistan, then fought with him until the Taliban were vanquished and he could assume power as the United States' handpicked head of state in Kabul. Other A-teams found Pushtun chiefs willing—for a price—to help them pursue Al Qaida in the mountains of northeast Afghanistan. But the Americans' luck ran out at a place called Tora Bora.

4.

NESTLED in the White Mountains on the north edge of a finger of Pakistan that jutted fifty miles into eastern Afghanistan, Tora Bora was one of several complexes along that part of the border that had served as bases for the mujahideen during their war against the Soviets and had since been taken over by the Taliban or Al Qaida. The bases were in the Pushtun heartland, just across the border from Pakistan. This meant they could be easily resupplied by Pakistan's Inter-Services Intelligence Directorate, which in the past had supplied both men and materiel to the mujahideen and the Taliban. Most of these bases shared the same features: natural and man-made caves, bunkers, antiaircraft defenses, logistics depots, and convenient escape routes back into Pakistan.

In late November intelligence reports indicated that a significant Al Qaida force was coalescing at Tora Bora. There were strong suggestions that bin Laden was also there, although firm intelligence on the movements of bin Laden and other Al Qaida leaders was hard to come by. Bin Laden had lived among the Pushtuns for all but six of the last nineteen years. Many families in the region had benefited from his generosity. Like bin Laden, the Pushtun tribesmen were fiercely Islamic, but the Pushtuns also lived by a strict honor code that set great store by the sheltering of guests from their enemies. Few were willing to cooperate with the Americans. Fewer still could be fully trusted. Even with a $5 million reward on his head, bin Laden was safer among the Pushtuns than he was almost anywhere else on earth.

Without good intelligence, the Americans faced a daunting challenge in assaulting Al Qaida's mountain fastness in Tora Bora. They went with the modus operandi that had worked for them up to now: unconventional warfare. Dagger's success around Kandahar with Karzai and his fellow Pushtun leader, Gul Agha Sherzai, had given the task force's leaders confidence that they could take the momentum they had gained with the Northern Alliance and transfer it to the Pushtun heartland. They found a few local militia leaders they thought they could work with in the Tora Bora area and, with CIA officers handing out wads of greenbacks, set about using them to hunt bin Laden down.

But the truth was it didn't matter much whether or not the Dagger leaders or the generals at CFLCC headquarters in Kuwait thought unconventional warfare alone would be enough to destroy the Al Qaida forces at Tora Bora. They had no other option. From the very start of the war, CENTCOM had been extraordinarily reluctant to introduce conventional forces into Afghanistan. This approach reflected what Franks was being told by Defense Secretary Donald Rumsfeld. "The message was strong from the national level down: 'We are not going to repeat the mistakes of the Soviets. We are not going to go in with large conventional forces,'" recalled Major General Warren Edwards, who was Mikolashek's deputy commanding general for operations at CFLCC. "This was so embedded in our decision-making process, in our psyche."

"We don't want to make the same mistakes as the Russians, we don't want to look like an invading force" became a mantra, an article of faith for U.S. officials from senior figures in the Bush administration to field grade officers in Afghanistan. This represented a very simplistic view of the Soviets' defeat in Afghanistan, which owed as much to their attempt to impose an alien, morally bankrupt political system on the Afghan population using scorched-earth tactics as it did to the raw number of troops they put into the country. It also ignored the possibility of a middle ground somewhere between the 120,000 troops that the Soviets had in Afghanistan at the height of their war in the 1980s and the few hundred special operators that the United States had in Afghanistan. Even had the United States put two light divisions—say the 101st Airborne and 10th Mountain divisions—into Afghanistan, the numbers would not have exceeded 30,000, only a quarter of what the Soviets deployed.

Inside the Pentagon the three figures at the head of the Army—Secretary of the Army Tom White, Chief of Staff General Eric "Ric" Shinseki, and Vice Chief of Staff General Jack Keane—argued for a larger role for their service. Afghanistan was a large, landlocked country, after all. It had no air force to speak of, and no navy. But when Shinseki, who represented the Army when the Joint Chiefs of Staff met to discuss strategy, pushed for a greater deployment of regular Army units to Afghanistan, he was repeatedly rebuffed by the defense secretary and the loyal coterie of political appointees who surrounded him in the Pentagon. "Ric was always for more conventional force than the guys down the hallway, and Rumsfeld in particular," White said. It didn't help the Army leaders' cause that Shinseki's relations with Rumsfeld had been strained since the early days of the defense secretary's tenure. Rumsfeld arrived at the Pentagon in January 2001 determined to restructure the military so that it could more efficiently and effectively meet the challenges of the twenty-first century. In an ironic twist he called this process "transformation," hijacking a term Shinseki had been using since October 1999 to describe his plans to modernize the Army. Rumsfeld spoke of transforming the entire military, but he had the Army foremost in his sights. The Army's senior generals, he believed, were too wedded to their Cold War-era heavy armored and mechanized divisions and lacked the imagination necessary to break with the ways of the past in order to create the more flexible formations and doctrine Rumsfeld believed were the keys to success on future battlefields. In the months prior to September 11, the media had been full of stories suggesting that Rumsfeld was looking to do away with two of the Army's ten active duty divisions and use the savings to fund the development of precision munitions, which he and his advisers viewed as the route to success in future conflicts. Although Rumsfeld's rhetoric about transformation in many ways echoed Shinseki's, the personality clash between the brash, arrogant defense secretary and the low-key chief of staff did much to create an atmosphere of mutual distrust between the office of the secretary of defense and the Army leadership. In this light, it is hardly surprising that Rumsfeld resisted the Army leaders' suggestions to deploy more conventional forces to Afghanistan. As the combination of Special Forces and airpower helped sweep the Taliban from power, it appeared the Afghanistan campaign was validating Rumsfeld's vision of twenty-first-century warfare.

The Pentagon's—and, by extension, CENTCOM's—obsession with minimizing the presence of U.S. conventional troops in Afghanistan translated into an arbitrary cap on the number of U.S. personnel that Franks would allow on Afghan soil at any one time.

THUS the attack on Al Qaida's positions at Tora Bora that began November 30 followed the same pattern as previous operations: an assault by Afghan fighters, advised by Dagger A-teams, Delta Force operators, and CIA operatives, and supported by a massive aerial bombardment. For the first time the formula failed. The CIA and Dagger had recruited a local Pushtun militia led by a warlord named Hazrat Ali for the assault. But Ali and his troops did not share the Northern Alliance's enmity for the Taliban's foreign allies and prosecuted their attacks halfheartedly. Even had they been more highly motivated, the challenges of assaulting such inaccessible, heavily defended positions would almost certainly have proved beyond the capabilities of the hastily organized force.

"That was the most formidable terrain that we fought in," said Rosengard, Dagger's operations officer. Valleys were no more than snow-filled defiles whose sheer rock walls soared skyward to become jagged peaks up to 15,000 feet high. "Given the availability of that cover and concealment [to the enemy], with the Afghans, and particularly with the Pushtun Afghans—the General Hazrat Ali guys—we did not have the fire and maneuver available to us to get in there and root guys out," Rosengard said. "We just didn't have the skill to overcome the combination of that enemy and that terrain."

The Dagger leaders assumed a portion of the Al Qaida force would fight to the death, but only to protect their comrades, including bin Laden and other senior leaders, as they tried to escape. This is exactly what happened. The Tora Bora base backed on to the porous Pakistan border, across which lay the Pushtun tribal areas of the Northwest Frontier Province, whose inhabitants were sympathetic to the Taliban and largely beyond the control of the central government in Islamabad. With no U.S. conventional forces to block their escape, hundreds of Al Qaida fighters slipped into Pakistan.

It seems incredible in retrospect, but this turn of events had not been foreseen at CENTCOM or CFLCC. "There was some knowledge that this might be the last great stand, that bin Laden might be there, the senior leadership might be there," said Edwards, Mikolashek's deputy. "But the mindset was, we're gonna push forward, we're gonna strike 'em with air, we're gonna kill 'em all up here in the valley. Not, they're gonna flee outta there." A few days into the fighting the Americans intercepted a radio communication out of Tora Bora from bin Laden himself. But even then, with the prospect of their highest-value target escaping with the core of his remaining force, U.S. commanders remained oblivious to the strategic disaster unfolding. "When Tora Bora started to bog down, I'm not sure anybody understood how many were escaping," Edwards said.

The American generals might not have realized how many foes were escaping, but after several days of inconclusive fighting around Tora Bora, they became frustrated with the operation's slow pace. "The whole issue between CENTCOM and CFLCC and Dagger during Tora Bora was keeping up the momentum," Edwards said. The Afghan allies would make an attempt at an attack, then go home and drink tea. "It wasn't moving fast enough for the CinC [commander-in-chief, i.e., Franks]."

American surveillance planes spotted scores of intense heat sources—interpreted as campfires—in the snowy heights. There were no settlements at that altitude. The perception at CFLCC was that these fires were keeping enemy fighters warm as they made their way to Pakistan. The generals in Kuwait recommended bombing the positions as soon as possible. But Franks and his staff did not see it like that. "They might be shepherds" was Central Command's attitude, according to two officers who sat in on video-teleconferences in which the matter was discussed. At CFLCC that theory didn't wash. The idea that scores of shepherds were tending their flocks in drifting snow at 10,000 feet in the middle of winter was implausible. But the higher headquarters prevailed and refused to target the hot spots because no one could prove that they were enemy campfires. Whoever set the fires—Al Qaida fighters or a midwinter gathering of shepherds—survived to make a safe passage over the border.

At least two Dagger A-teams were sent across the border to help Pakistani troops whom the Americans wanted to block Al Qaida's path. This was a vain hope. The Pakistani military was reluctant to stray into the Pushtun tribal areas that straddled the border, and the effort foundered. The Pakistanis intercepted about 300 Al Qaida troops, but roughly 1,000 escaped. Among those who got away, almost certainly, was Osama bin Laden. Franks would later say that he remained unconvinced that bin Laden was at Tora Bora. Deputy Defense Secretary Paul Wolfowitz told Congress in June 2002 that Franks had believed that conducting the Tora Bora operation with U.S. conventional forces would have required "a massive, highly visible buildup" of troops that would have tipped off the Al Qaida forces, allowing them to flee. But among American officials familiar with the battle, Franks was in the minority. The prevailing opinion was that, despite the scores of enemy fighters killed by American bombs, Tora Bora represented a failure, a defeat for the Americans, and CENTCOM was to blame for not using conventional forces.

For the first time the unconventional warfare approach had come up short. The point was lost on neither TF Dagger nor the higher-ups in CFLCC and CENTCOM. "Certainly [Tora Bora] has got to be quantified as a failure for not having drug out of there who everybody believed was there," Rosengard said. "[That failure] drove home to much greater clarity the fact that we did indeed lack the fire and maneuver to do all things for all people in Afghanistan." But to CFLCC's planners, Tora Bora also underlined the consequences of CENTCOM's bias against committing the conventional forces required to destroy the remaining Al Qaida elements in Afghanistan. "There was a constant—in our mind—disconnect between mission and assets allowed to be available to do the mission," Edwards said. That disconnect would reassert itself ten weeks later in the Shahikot.

5.

IN the cold, muddy tent city at K2, the Tora Bora failure prompted long conversations among the senior Dagger officers as the unconventional warfare maestros reconsidered their approach to what remained of the war in

Afghanistan. As the officers talked long into the dark Uzbek nights, one thick Boston accent rose loudly above the whine of C-17 engines and the roar of MC-130 Combat Talon turboprops from the nearby runways. The voice belonged to Lieutenant Colonel Mark Rosengard.

Until October, Rosengard had been deputy commander of 10th Special Forces Group, which is headquartered at Fort Carson, Colorado, but specializes in operations in Europe. Then he received a call from Special Forces Command at Fort Bragg telling him to pack his bags—he was headed to K2 to serve as Dagger's new operations officer. (A Special Forces group's operations officer was usually a major, but when transformed into a joint special operations task force, the group was entitled to a lieutenant colonel in that position.) Even if he'd been a bland operator who preferred to stay in the background, Rosengard's job as the officer in charge of coordinating Dagger's current missions while planning future operations would have made him one of the most important of the fifty-plus augmentees who arrived at K2 to beef up Mulholland's staff. But Rosengard wasn't that type, and the inspiring force of his personality rendered his impact on the task force, and the coming operation, all the greater.

Possessed of an exuberant self-confidence, the forty-four-year-old Rosengard had been seasoned by years spent operating in Bosnia, Kosovo, and northern Iraq. That experience, combined with his extraordinary energy and drive, meant he commanded instant respect among his subordinates in the "3 shop," as an Army unit's plans and operations directorate is known. Rosengard was "a fireball" who motivated his men to work eighteen-hour days, seven days a week, said Captain Tim Fletcher, who, as commander of 5th Group's Headquarters and Headquarters Company, observed Rosengard at close quarters for several months.

Rosengard's ability to work long hours with no apparent diminishment in his judgment or equilibrium astonished his subordinates. Fueled by a constant intake of caffeine and nicotine, Rosengard would literally work until he dropped. "He wouldn't sleep unless he basically just shut down," said Fletcher. After being evacuated—against his will—to a U.S. military hospital in Incirlik, Turkey, suffering from chest pains that turned out to be nothing more serious than acid reflux, Rosengard quit his pack-a-day-of-Marlboro-Lights habit on January 1, impressing colleagues with his ability to do so without becoming short-tempered. But that was his only lifestyle concession. He only relaxed when reading letters from his wife and two children. Then he would slip into a comalike sleep. On those occasions his staff would let him doze through small crises or moments of decision, because he needed the rest, even though they knew their failure to rouse him would bring a rocket when he finally awoke.

Rosengard was a man who found it easy to get along with others, and for whom subordinates would gladly work themselves into the ground. This was an invaluable trait for an officer who arrived as an unknown quantity in the pressurized atmosphere of Dagger's headquarters. "He's a phenomenal man that I'd work for again in a heartbeat," Fletcher said. Rosengard quickly formed a good working relationship with Major Perry Clark, 5th Group's operations officer who now worked for him. Clark knew the personalities in the headquarters and the operators on the teams. Rosengard brought experience.

But there was also a flamboyant side to Rosengard, a former college hockey goalie whose black mustache was as thick as his vowels were broad. He gave briefings at high volume, accentuating his remarks by using a red laser aiming device attached to his 9mm Beretta pistol. His over-the-top, all-action style unsettled some soldiers, who had to suppress laughter when confronted with this vociferous, pistol-waving officer. But Rosengard never used his outspokenness to demean. If he was angry with someone, he let them know privately. "If you ever got pulled aside, and talked to nice and quietly, you knew you were in a world of hurt, because that's when he was serious," Fletcher said.

American bombs were still falling on Tora Bora when Rosengard and his staff met December 8 to consider where next to focus Dagger's energies. There were probably still some Taliban elements in the desert provinces south and west of the city of Kandahar city, but U.S. commanders considered these an insignificant threat. "We knew where we had a problem, where the sanctuary was, where there were people that would support [the enemy] we were going to get," Rosengard said. That sanctuary was Paktia's mountainous border with Pakistan. "The place where we had the littlest influence that had the most significance was Paktia province. . . . We knew there was order of battle [there] that we had not yet encountered and had not accounted for in any way," he said. Dagger's planners concluded that "tactically, Paktia was the biggest deal left on the plate."

But as they were figuring out *where* they should next take the fight to their enemy, U.S. commanders were also rethinking their "all UW, all the time" approach. The war had changed course. They were now facing a different enemy than they had encountered—and conquered—using unconventional warfare. For the past two months Dagger's Special Forces operators and CIA operatives had used the Northern Alliance to roll back an enemy that consisted largely of the Taliban's peasant infantry. But by now the Taliban had been evicted from all major towns. Most Taliban fighters not killed or captured had returned to their farms and villages or crossed into Pakistan. Al Qaida, however, was another matter. Its fighters had no hometowns or villages in Afghanistan to which to return. The option of simply surrendering or switching sides, as many Taliban-affiliated militias had done when it was clear which way the war was headed, did not exist for Al Qaida. They were outsiders, foreigners from Uzbekistan and Chechnya, as well as Saudi Arabia and other Arab states. They could expect no quarter from the Northern Alliance and little from the Americans. Nor could they return to the homes they had left. Most were on the run from the authorities in their native countries, who preferred to export Islamic extremism rather than let it fester at home.

What's more, Al Qaida troops' religious fervor made them highly motivated soldiers. During the war with the Northern Alliance, the Taliban's 55th Brigade—composed entirely of Al Qaida fighters—was one of the Taliban order of battle's most effective formations. Al Qaida fighters were also, almost by definition, vehemently anti-American. With their most senior leaders still at large, they would not consider themselves defeated. Some had made it into Pakistan from Tora Bora or elsewhere. There they might find refuge in the tribal areas. A few leaders, perhaps, could hide in plain sight in the sprawling metropolises of Rawalpindi, Lahore, or Karachi. But most Al Qaida fighters would remain close to their bases along the border. Many had traveled thousands of miles to learn the skills of jihad in Al Qaida's Afghan training camps. Now the infidels had come to Afghanistan. The prospects for jihad could not be better. With no way home and the chance for victory or martyrdom before them, they could be expected to fight.

The disappointing performance of Hazrat Ali's forces at Tora Bora, where the Americans' nominal allies accepted bribes to allow Al Qaida safe passage, combined with the knowledge that they now faced a more skilled and determined enemy, forced Dagger's senior officers to reassess the wisdom of relying on local militias. Unconventional warfare was yielding diminishing returns. Perhaps it was time for a new approach.

BY mid-December a new place name was appearing in reports being sent back to K2 about Al Qaida activity in eastern Afghanistan: Shahikot. When used by the Special Forces' indigenous allies, it referred to an area south of Gardez, rather than to any particular valley. The focus on Paktia, where the Shahikot was, sent the Dagger folks searching for copies of two books Mulholland had arranged to have shipped to them before they left 5th Group's home post of Fort Campbell, Kentucky: *The Bear Went Over the Mountain* and *The Other Side of the Mountain.* Translated and edited by Lester Grau, a retired U.S. Army officer who worked at the Army's Foreign Military Studies Office at Fort Leavenworth, Kansas, *The Bear Went Over the Mountain* was a collection of tactical vignettes from the Soviet war in Afghanistan, written by Soviet officers. *The Other Side of the Mountain,* written by Grau with Ali Ahmad Jalali, a former mujahed, followed a similar format, only with a different set of vignettes seen this time from the perspective of mujahideen commanders. Both books featured detailed analyses of combat operations in eastern Afghanistan in general and Paktia in particular. When read together, they provided Dagger personnel valuable insight into how their enemies might operate in Paktia, and which tactics would work best against them.

While most Dagger staff boned up on eastern Afghanistan's recent military history and brainstormed on what to do next, one officer adopted a more scientific approach. Captain Brian Sweeney was attached to the Dagger staff from the Land Information Warfare Activity, an Army organization that specialized in tracking patterns of enemy activity in order to discern enemy networks and command and control nodes. Beginning in December, on his own initiative, Sweeney patiently correlated the information that Dagger and CIA teams were sending back from eastern Afghanistan with technical information on the location and movement of Al Qaida forces provided by spy planes and satellites. Sitting in Dagger's secure, compartmented intelligence facility, or SCIF—a long tent, surrounded by razor wire, guarded by 10th Mountain troops and permeated by the smell of burnt coffee—Sweeney worked to paint a picture of Al Qaida's network of safe houses, transportation nodes and escape routes out of Afghanistan, which he called "ratlines." He identified three separate ratlines.

Although working as an information operations specialist, Sweeney, described by a colleague as a tall, dark-haired, "James Bond-looking guy," was also a Special Forces officer. This was a key attribute. As an SF officer, Sweeney "brought a Special Forces background and mindset to the analysis process that the technicians had not previously thought about," Rosengard said. Dagger's intelligence cell was dominated by Air Force personnel who had been brought in to aid 5th Group's transformation to a joint special ops task force, but even the SF soldiers from 5th Group's intel shop failed to put the pieces together as well as Sweeney. "It was brilliant," Rosengard said.

As the Shahikot assumed a higher profile in Dagger's planning, the special ops staffers began feeding intelligence tidbits to their Mountain counterparts and K2 neighbors, allowing Wille and Ziemba to draw up their own plans for how to deal with the Al Qaida force said to be assembling south of Gardez. But despite the growing frequency of references to the region in intel reports, Dagger did not make the Shahikot its primary focus until mid-January. When it did, it was partly on the basis of information received from an A-team codenamed Texas 14.

6.

THE convoy of mud-splattered pickup trucks that wound its way through the muddy, crowded streets of Gardez on January 4, 2002, was manned by a motley crew of Americans and Afghans, and led by an American who looked like an Afghan.

The Americans were the SF soldiers of Texas 14, the call sign for ODA 594, an A-team from 5th Group's 3rd Battalion, along with a couple of CIA operatives. The Afghans included the beginnings of a private Pushtun army that Texas 14 and the agency were starting to assemble. And the American who looked like an Afghan was Texas 14's leader, Captain Glenn Thomas, an officer of Japanese descent whose black beard and longish black hair meant he could pass as a local for as long as he could go without speaking.

Thomas and his men were tired, but still hungry for action. While other A-teams had distinguished themselves in actions around Kandahar, Kabul, and Mazar-i-Sharif, Texas 14 had spent most of the last two months in Afghanistan but had yet to find itself at the center of a major operation.

In mid-December the team relocated to Logar province—south of Kabul, but north of Paktia—to work with a couple of small militia factions. Afghanistan's ethnic boundaries merge in Logar, and few of the forces with which Texas 14 was working were Pushtuns. But on January 2 a group of thirty Pushtun fighters from Logar arrived on the team's doorstep. Already vetted by the CIA, they were clearly of a higher caliber than the other Afghans Texas 14 was training. The A-team was particularly taken by the anti-Taliban firebrand who led this new group. The man's name was Zia Lodin, and, unbeknownst to him, Americans he had never met would soon assign him a key role in the biggest battle of their war in Afghanistan.

A scion of the Lodin tribe, whose patriarch had nominated him to lead the American-paid force, Zia was estimated to be in his thirties or early forties. At least six feet tall, he had dark brown hair, a short dark beard, and puffy cheeks. He did not have a fighter's background. But to the men of Texas 14 and their bosses at K2, Zia had enormous potential. They immediately entrusted his men with their personal protection. Within a few days of being introduced to Zia, Thomas decided the charismatic Zia met all three rules of UW. Zia's fierce animosity toward the Taliban and Al Qaida impressed Texas 14, as did his personal courage and other qualities the SF soldiers and CIA operatives associated with strong leadership. But the Dagger men were also drawn to Zia because he seemed to represent an enlightened sort of Afghan strongman, a rare commodity among their G-chiefs. "He was not interested in just doing what other people told him to do," recalled Rosengard, Dagger's operations officer. "He was a young man with his own vision, which didn't include hanging women because they looked at him strangely one day, and it certainly didn't include not sending his kids to school, and his vision probably didn't include a society that allowed exportation of terrorism. He was a pretty idealistic young man. He was a young man of moxy."

When Mulholland ordered Thomas to push south into Paktia toward Gardez, Texas 14 decided to form their collective of little militia factions (now emboldened by CIA cash) into one warrior band, which they would use as armed reconnaissance during the move to Gardez. By the time Texas 14's small convoy reached Gardez, their faith in Zia was solid. "Everything that he had said he would do, he did," Rosengard said. "He was willing to go with us and take us places, and everything he told us turned out to be true." With the help of the CIA's open bags of cash, Texas 14 had found their G-chief.

THE town into which Texas 14's little convoy was making its way had a feel of past grandeur gone to seed. A couple of the downtown streets were almost European-style boulevards, bisected by median strips and flanked by buildings whose paint had long since worn off. The town's veneer of affluence had peeled away, but its population was booming and its barely paved roads were choked with people. In 1979, when the Soviets invaded Afghanistan, Gardez had a population of fewer than 10,000. By 2002 it had swelled tenfold. The increase could be mostly attributed to an influx of people who had fled to Pakistan as refugees during the Soviet war and returned—many with new families—in the 1990s. Like many of those refugees, when Texas 14 rolled into Gardez, their first order of business was to find themselves a home. The technical term for what the SF soldiers and their CIA counterparts were seeking was a "safe house." But when the CIA found and rented the perfect place on the town's eastern outskirts, that phrase did not do it justice. Typical of the compounds inhabited by families of means in Afghanistan, it was more of a fortress than a house. Protected on all sides by tapered mud-brick walls about 100 meters long, twenty-five feet high, six feet thick at the bottom, and about four feet thick at the top, the square, Alamo-like compound had an enormous dirt courtyard entered via a steel gate that, when opened, was wide enough to accommodate the Americans' pickup trucks.

The Americans moved into the compound. Their Afghan allies camped outside. To eliminate the threat of a drive-by shooting from the main road that ran east to west in front of the compound, Texas 14's Afghans established check-points over a mile from the safe house in each direction. Normal traffic was blocked and had to take a long detour—a clear indication that, in terms of the local population, at least, the Americans were now operating in uncharted territory.

Once settled into their new home, the safe house residents set about doing their respective jobs. For the CIA, that meant putting out feelers to try to develop sources of human intelligence in Gardez, talking with locals in order to get harder information about the whereabouts of Al Qaida forces. The SF soldiers got down to the business of instructing their Afghan force, which included Hazaras and Tajiks from central and northern Afghanistan who were distinctly unwelcome in the Pushtun heartland, but who Texas 14 felt they needed to protect the safe house and provide added muscle during forays into the countryside. Training their polyglot Afghan force in basic infantry tactics was no small task for, oddly enough, given the mission the Americans would ask them to perform a few weeks later, one field in which Zia and his small band of peasant warriors—only half the size of a U.S. infantry company when he joined forces with Texas 14—had almost no experience was combat.

7.

THE bulky, powerful C-17 Globemaster III taxied slowly along the Bagram runway before coming to a standstill. As the giant turbofan engines wound down with a high-pitched whine, the crew lowered the back ramp, revealing the Afghan night sky inch by gray-black inch. It was the first week of January, and bitterly cold air flooded the transport's cabin. Rising from his nylon seat, Pete Blaber shouldered his ruck and braced himself against the midnight chill before striding down the back ramp and climbing into a waiting SUV. Sitting behind the wheel in civilian clothes was a paunchy reserve officer named Scott. In civilian life Scott was a cop, but here in Bagram he was the deputy commander of a top-secret intelligence outfit. It was only a two-minute drive to the broken-down building where Scott was taking Blaber to spend the night, but that was all the time the Delta officer needed to take in the bleak, moonlit landscape. Perhaps Scott's civilian background was not as incongruous as it might first appear, because this place looked like it needed a new sheriff.

Located thirty miles north of Kabul on a high, broad plain at the southern edge of the Hindu Kush, the base was built in the late 1950s as part of a Soviet aid package for Afghanistan's left-leaning government. The Soviets were not acting out of generosity. They knew they might find it useful to have a few good air bases in Afghanistan someday. Sure enough, the first wave of the Soviet force that invaded Afghanistan in December 1979 flew into Bagram. The base served as the hub of Soviet air operations during the 1980s and was frequently attacked by guerrillas. Peaks as high as 15,000 feet dominated the approaches to the airfield on three sides, and the huge Soviet transport planes would land and take off in tight corkscrew patterns to avoid flying over the mountains and becoming targets for mujahideen armed with shoulder-held antiaircraft missiles. After the Soviets left, the base was on the frontlines of the various Afghan civil wars. Like the Ariana hotel, it bore the scars.

The first American troops into Bagram belonged to ODA 555 (the "Triple Nickel"), who arrived with the Northern Alliance on October 21. The Special Forces soldiers found the base in terrible condition. Bullets had pockmarked the low-quality concrete every building was made of. Here and there a larger hole had been punched through a wall by a tank main gun round, or the corner of a roof ripped off by a rocket-propelled grenade. There was no electricity or running water. All that remained of the Afghan air force was a jumbled pile of broken and rusting MiGs beside the runway.

A few of the Americans at the base were conventional soldiers conducting support operations. But the vast majority looked a little different from the denizens of most American military camps. Few complete uniforms were in evidence. These troops wore jeans, T-shirts, and photojournalist vests, plus fleece jackets to shield themselves from the harsh Afghan winter. Their hair hung lank around their ears. All had thick, bushy beards. But appearances can be deceiving, and in this case were intended to be so. These scruffy men were among the most skilled warriors and covert operatives in the world. America had sent the best it had to Afghanistan in the wake of September 11. Now many of them had set up shop in Bagram's dilapidated hangars and barracks.

They belonged to a variety of organizations, some of which were well known to the American public. But others had names that rarely if ever appeared in print. By late January they had been assigned a series of exotic code names: Bowie, Dagger, and K-Bar. In fact, many troops at Bagram in January belonged to a top-secret unit that had already changed its name since deploying to Afghanistan. It started the war as Task Force Sword, but by January had been renamed Task Force 11.

Task Force 11 had only one goal: to kill or capture so-called "high-value targets" (HVTs), the phrase the U.S. military used to describe senior Al Qaida and Taliban leaders.

Task Force Sword had included 2,200 to 2,500 personnel, making it one of the biggest agglomerations of "black" special operators ever assembled. ("Black" special operations forces, such as Delta and SEAL Team 6, also known as "special mission units," are those whose existence the Pentagon refuses to formally acknowledge.) Inside Sword were several component task forces, but from October until early January its principal muscle had been provided by a 100-strong squadron of Delta Force operators and support troops, code-named Task Force Green. These were the men at the very core of Task Force Sword, the direct action force trained to kick in doors, overwhelm a numerically superior force, and kill or capture America's most dangerous enemies.

Established in 1977 at Fort Bragg as the United States' premier counterterrorist unit, Delta had grown from a few dozen soldiers to a force of almost 1,000. Only about 250 were "operators," super-fit commandos who executed direct action missions. They were divided into three squadrons—A, B, and C—of about seventy-five to eighty-five soldiers each. Within each squadron were three troops (not three soldiers, but three company-equivalent formations). Two were assault troops specializing in direct action. After completing Delta's six-month operator training course, newcomers were assigned to an assault troop. A few handpicked veterans would graduate to the squadron's reconnaissance and surveillance, or "recce," troop. Smaller than the other troops, the recce troop's missions included penetrating enemy lines unseen, watching enemy positions, and sniping. (The use of the British abbreviation *recce,* rather than the more American *recon,* reflected Delta's roots as an organization modeled along the lines of the British Special Air Service, or SAS, by its founder, Colonel Charlie Beckwith, who had served with the SAS as an exchange officer.) For reasons of operational security and practicality, Delta, now known also by its cover name of Combat Applications Group, was a very self-contained organization. The rest of the unit consisted of superbly trained and equipped mechanics, communications specialists, intelligence analysts, and other support troops, plus a headquarters staff. In addition, Delta had an aviation squadron based elsewhere on the East Coast, which also flew missions for the CIA.

The first Delta squadron to deploy as TF Green for the war in Afghanistan was B Squadron. It came home in December. A Squadron took its place, but only for a few weeks. By January 1 A Squadron had been replaced by another commando element. But these operators were from SEAL Team 6 and went by the name Task Force Blue.

Formed in 1980, SEAL Team 6 recruited its personnel from the rest of the Navy's SEAL teams. The unit's job was to conduct the same sort of antiterrorist direct action missions in which Delta specialized, but in a maritime environment. In other words, if terrorists threatened a cruise ship or an oil rig, Team 6 would likely get the call to take care of the situation. But the unit got off to a rocky start.

Richard Marcinko, the unit's charismatic and hard-drinking founder and first commanding officer, was a legendary SEAL. But his flamboyant—some would say cowboylike—personality proved divisive within the team and the wider SEAL community. He changed command in 1983, but the damage to the team's reputation did not pass so easily. Marcinko's abrasive personality and the freewheeling, devil-may-care attitude he imprinted on the new organization ensured that for the rest of the decade many Delta soldiers viewed their Navy counterparts with suspicion verging on scorn. In 1990, Marcinko was sentenced to twenty-one months in jail after being convicted of several charges in connection with a scheme to use his former Team 6 colleagues to bilk the U.S. Treasury of over $100,000. His conviction further tarnished the reputation of the organization he had built from the ground up.

It took a few years, but after Marcinko's departure, Team 6 slowly gained a measure of professionalism and respect. It also expanded, but, lacking Delta's extensive support structure, it never grew to more than about a third of the size of its Army counterpart. Like Delta, the team acquired a cover name—Naval Special Warfare Development Group, or DevGru—and matured so that by the early 1990s even some Army special operators felt its professionalism matched Delta's. But as Team 6 became more proficient, the scorn Delta felt toward it evolved into antagonism as the Navy operators began to encroach on Delta's turf, taking on land-based direct action missions that had been Delta's exclusive preserve. Some of the bitterness—which was mutual—could be attributed to the fierce rivalry that had always existed between the respective special operations communities of the Army and Navy, from which both units recruited most of their men. One Navy officer who worked closely with both Army and Navy special ops forces described their relationship as "at best analogous to a sibling rivalry, and at worst, to a marriage coming apart."

Joint Special Operations Command (JSOC), the higher headquarters for both units, instituted a joint training regimen in the early 1990s that required both organizations to train with each other every three months. After a few years of this routine, the leaders in each organization had grown up beside each other. A mutual respect ensued. By the mid-1990s the friction had become a healthy rivalry rather than outright animosity. Strong friendships developed between operators in each organization.

Nevertheless, JSOC commander Major General Dell Dailey's insertion of TF Blue into Afghanistan irked Army special operators, and Delta men in particular, who worried that their Navy counterparts' limited land warfare training did not adequately prepare them for the extraordinarily demanding missions presented by operations in Afghanistan. They noted, disapprovingly, that while Delta would never seek to conduct a direct action mission at sea, Team 6 had no inhibitions about taking on missions that required a deep understanding of land warfare. "A lot of the SEALs are just boat guys, and you can't shake and bake an infantry guy," an Army operator in Afghanistan said. In the eyes of the Delta operators, much of the blame lay with Joint Special Operations Command, which seemed determined to treat Delta and Team 6 as interchangeable, despite their vastly different areas of expertise. The decision to withdraw Delta's A Squadron early and put Team 6's squadrons into the TF 11 rotation before all three Delta squadrons had seen action seemed nonsensical to Army types. The operators in Delta's C squadron "were borderline suicidal that they weren't in the fight yet," according to an Army special ops source.

But Dailey, an Army special operations helicopter pilot who had also served in the Rangers, had little sympathy for the Delta operators. His decision to use the SEALs reflected his view that the "war on terror" had to be viewed in the same context as the Cold War: a long, drawn-out marathon, not a short sprint to victory. He expected the new war to last forty years and was determined to ensure JSOC could prosecute the fight with intensity over the long haul. Therefore he decided to give Delta a rest. Committing the unit to Afghanistan indefinitely, he believed, would burn Delta out within nine months. He knew Delta was superior to Team 6 in land operations, but he thought each unit easily surpassed the standard required for success.

Dailey applied the same thought process to the leadership of TF 11. In October Sword's joint operations center moved from JSOC headquarters at Pope Air Force Base in North Carolina to Masirah Island, off the coast of Oman in the Indian Ocean. Dailey went along as Sword's commander. But in a move that roughly coincided with the change from Sword to 11, he put his entire operation in Masirah and Afghanistan, including his position as the task force commander, on a ninety-day rotation cycle. So in January he and his principal staff returned to Pope. His replacement was his deputy, Air Force Brigadier General Gregory Trebon. Curiously, although Task Force 11's raison d'être was reconnaissance and direct action against high-value targets, Trebon had no background in those fields. A vastly experienced pilot who had logged over 7,000 flight hours in fifty-five different military and civilian airframes, Trebon was also a free-fall–qualified parachutist. He had spent most of his career in special operations and enjoyed a reputation for being a solid professional. But Trebon's special ops assignments had been spent in aircraft units or coordinating the special operations air component on larger Air Force or joint staffs. His specialty was piloting C-141 transports specially configured for landing on dirt airstrips or dropping Rangers on low-level parachute missions. An expert at integrating Air Force special ops into commando operations, he had had no opportunity to learn the tactics, techniques, and procedures involved in hunting down and killing enemies on the ground.

Some JSOC personnel thought Dailey should have placed Delta's commander, Colonel Jim Schwitters, or Captain Joe Kernan, the Team 6 commander, in charge of TF 11, depending on whether it was the turn of TF Green or TF Blue to take the lead in the task force. Dailey knew Trebon lacked boots-on-the-ground experience, but he believed he had an obligation to develop his deputy by giving Trebon responsibility. Dailey also knew that Tommy Franks preferred to work through generals whenever possible, and that Trebon was the protégé of Air Force General Charlie Holland, who as commander of U.S. Special Operations Command was Dailey's boss.

In contrast with Trebon, there was one general in Bagram who knew all about how to chase down and kill "bad guys," as the U.S. military liked to refer to its enemies. That was Brigadier General Gary Harrell. A barrel-chested man with a viselike handshake his aides felt compelled to warn visitors about, Harrell was a legendary special operator. He had spent all but eighteen months between December 1985 and July 2000 in a variety of jobs in Delta and JSOC, rising to command Delta between 1998 and 2000. Harrell was no stranger to manhunts. As Delta's C Squadron commander, he had tracked drug kingpin Pablo Escobar in Colombia and warlord Mohammed Farah Aidid in Somalia. Later, in the 1990s, he helped locate and capture war criminals in the Balkans.

Despite his background, Harrell was not in charge of any "door-kickers" in Afghanistan. Since July 2000 he had headed CENTCOM's Joint Security Directorate, which oversaw the protection of U.S. forces across CENTCOM's slice of the globe. But in November 2001 Franks ordered him to Afghanistan to command an intelligence "fusion cell" that would take all the intelligence being produced by U.S. assets in—or over—Afghanistan and fuse it together to be "stovepiped" back to Franks. The CENTCOM commander placed a lot of faith in Harrell, whom he referred to as his "quarterback," and sent him to Afghanistan to bring more focus to the intel collection process. The burly one-star showed up in Bagram on November 25. Staffed with personnel from the military, the CIA, and other agencies, his fusion cell's task was to sift through the reams of information the United States was gathering on the movements of high-value targets and decide what constituted "actionable" intelligence. The cell started off small, but after Harrell arrived it expanded to a force of fifty or sixty people. Like TF 11, Harrell's new organization, which he named Task Force Bowie, worked directly for Franks, with no requirement to report to Mikolashek. Unlike TF 11, however, Bowie was located in Bagram, which was fast becoming the dominant military headquarters in Afghanistan. Harrell was also in charge of Bagram's detention facility, a large multistory gray building where Taliban and Al Qaida prisoners were held and interrogated by U.S. intelligence personnel. In the opinion of special operators in Afghanistan, Harrell's location gave him a substantial advantage over anyone back in Masirah.

Those on the ground in Bagram realized Harrell was more than an intelligence conduit. He was Franks's personal representative at Bagram. "He [Franks] wanted his guy on the ground to make sure that things were going the right way," said an officer who worked close to Harrell. Harrell not only brought a general's star to bear, but also an intimidating weight of experience that few, if any, at Bagram, could match.

Nested inside Bowie, but reporting to TF 11, was a small organization that would soon have a major impact on the war. Called Advance Force Operations, or AFO, its mission was to conduct high-risk reconnaissance missions deep into enemy territory. AFO was not a standing organization back in the States, but rather a concept coordinated by a JSOC headquarters cell that could draw personnel from any special operations unit to meet a particular mission's requirements. Troops attached to AFO were equally at home conducting deep tactical reconnaissance on a conventional battlefield or infiltrating a foreign capital wearing suits and carrying false passports in order to rent vehicles and office space in preparation for a direct action mission. AFO could also conduct terminal guidance (spotting targets for aircraft to strike), sniper missions, and direct action, if necessary. "The intent is to tailor the force for the situation, so it's never quite the same, but it's always small, it's always cross-functional, and it's always the best of the best working in it," said an officer familiar with AFO.

Although AFO was small, relative to a typical Delta squadron, its mission—challenging even when compared to the Herculean tasks often required of Delta—was reflected in the seniority of its personnel. The AFO commander was usually a senior lieutenant colonel who had already commanded a Delta squadron, and almost all the NCOs were master sergeants or sergeants major—seasoned operators who could each draw on fifteen to twenty-five years of experience. "The ability to do that stuff required a degree of self-control and just being cool that almost went beyond what you would expect of anybody in the squadrons," said an officer who worked on the JSOC staff in the 1990s.

The man JSOC chose to run AFO in Afghanistan was Pete Blaber.

Prior to taking charge of AFO early January, Blaber had been Delta's operations officer, having already commanded B Squadron. As the operations officer, he had deployed to Masirah and then Afghanistan with TF Green before returning to the States in December. Now he was back to run what was arguably the most challenging mission in TF 11, the on-the-ground reconnaissance efforts in the search for the most senior enemy leaders. To cover Afghanistan's 647,500 square kilometers Blaber had a tiny force of about forty-five operators, intel analysts, and commo guys. The bulk of these troops were divided into six teams—half in southern Afghanistan, led by a major, and half in northeastern Afghanistan, also commanded by a major. The small headquarters element Blaber would head up was based at Bagram with TF Bowie.

But all was not well in Bagram. The several hundred special ops troops gathering in khaki tents and ramshackle buildings at the base were some of the planet's finest warriors, backed by a world-class intelligence capability. In briefings and planning sessions they exuded a calm, professional aura so polished it positively shone. But beneath the surface, tensions were pulling at the unity of the operation at Bagram. Some operators felt that the force gathering there was neither organized nor led in the most effective, logical manner; that it was not, in military-speak, "optimized for mission success." Many were concerned at Trebon's appointment as TF 11 commander and JSOC commander Dailey's decision to replace Delta's experienced land warriors with Team 6's "boat guys." To Army special ops types at Bagram, these steps smacked, at the very least, of a misplaced commitment to the U.S. military principle of "jointness"—the notion that combat effectiveness is always enhanced by the closest possible integration of the four military services. "The Green position was 'We should do this, give it to us. We don't need anybody replacing us, we'll just do this ourselves,'" recalled a JSOC officer.

Dailey was a divisive figure in the special operations community. A former head of the 160th Special Operations Aviation Regiment, his appointment as JSOC commander made him the latest in a string of Army and Air Force pilots to be given senior positions in U.S. Special Operations Command and JSOC. This trend upset many of JSOC's ground warriors, who viewed their direct action missions as JSOC's raison d'être and couldn't see why aviators were placed in charge of such operations. "Guys who come from aviation units know how to manage money, but they don't know how to tactically employ their ground elements," said a Delta NCO. Among these men, Dailey had a reputation for parochialism and risk aversion. An officer who worked for him said Dailey nurtured "a long-held gripe" against ground special ops units. Other operators agreed that Dailey's experiences in the 160th, whose pilots are often referred to as "taxi drivers" or "bus drivers" by the operators they ferry into combat, had left him with a big chip on his shoulder. In after-action reviews of training exercises and combat missions, 160th officers often were sharply criticized by their Delta, Ranger, and Special Forces peers if the helicopter portion of an operation was less than perfect. It was easy to see how such experiences might have left Dailey bearing a grudge that came to the fore when he took command of JSOC, they said. "Now the guy who was head of the fleet of taxi cabs is running the show," noted a special operations source in Bagram. Dailey also believed, according to an Army officer, that a general, simply by virtue of his rank, was automatically qualified to command and control ground operations, even if he had no real ground experience.

But other officers, particularly those who knew Dailey through service in the 160th, had a far more positive view of the general. "He always seemed to me to be a fair-minded, pretty smart tactical leader," said a field grade officer who had worked for Dailey in the 160th. "He was very popular as commander of the 160th—very charismatic." These officers were skeptical of the view that Dailey was biased against ground-pounders. As a junior officer he had served in the Rangers, they said, noting that near his Master Aviator Badge he still wore the Expert Infantryman Badge, an award given only to infantrymen who pass an exacting series of field tests.

In theory, Dailey was not in Trebon's chain of command, which ran straight to Franks, who had operational control of TF 11. But in reality, as the deputy JSOC commander, Trebon frequently answered to Dailey, who from his North Carolina headquarters continued to exert control over how his forces were used in Afghanistan.

Dailey's performance during video-teleconferences with TF 11's staff did little to alter his reputation as a micromanager—some JSOC staffers referred to him as "the 6,000-mile screwdriver"—and a black special ops elitist averse to having JSOC forces work with white special ops forces, let alone the conventional troops now deploying into Afghanistan. Given these circumstances, it was almost inevitable that tensions would arise between Trebon, the Air Force officer in charge of a manhunt, and Harrell, whose résumé seemed to make him more qualified to do Trebon's job than Trebon himself.

Edwards, the deputy CFLCC commander watching events unfold from Kuwait, could see Harrell pushing the envelope of the authority Franks had given him. The CENTCOM commander placed great trust in Harrell, Edwards noted, "but he gave Gary no operational responsibilities when he put him over there." Harrell strained against these restrictions. "Gary's a good officer," Edwards said. "And good, intelligent, aggressive officers tend to fill vacuums." In this case, the vacuum was the lack of strong, experienced leadership being applied by Trebon, and both Harrell and Dailey were trying to fill it. "There was clearly friction between what Gary Harrell was doing or thought he was doing, and what Dell Dailey was doing or thought he was doing," Edwards said. "Now, I say that very cautiously, because probably never in the United States' history was there as much cooperation as was shown there, but that didn't eliminate all of the tensions over who was actually going to control black SOF [special operations forces] in country, and exactly what Gary and his little Task Force Bowie was to do as an intelligence fusion operation, and who had operational control."

Some in TF 11 were also unhappy with Dailey's and Trebon's concept for how the task force was to operate, which was to keep the direct action force—first Green, and then Blue—based intact at Bagram, waiting for intelligence from Bowie to pinpoint a high-value target, at which point the door-kickers would launch on a raid to kill or capture the target. The hours required to fly from Bagram to the eastern provinces where bin Laden and the other senior enemy figures were probably hiding made some think it would have been better to divide the direct action force into smaller elements and push them out to safe houses in those provinces. "It became an unwieldy process," an operator said. "Most of the guys knew it wasn't the best way of operating. . . . You cannot fly in a helicopter in real time to a target from Bagram and have a high likelihood of killing or capturing someone. You have to be deployed forward."

But in Masirah, Trebon and his staff were juggling competing missions. CENTCOM had ordered them to have commandos on standby at Bagram twenty-four hours a day for what were called "time-sensitive targeting" missions. This assignment came after it took four days to get U.S. troops to a snowbound site in the mountains where the Americans had conducted an airstrike on a man they hoped might be one of the "big three"—bin Laden, his deputy, Ayman al-Zawahiri, and Mullah Omar. After that fiasco CENTCOM ordered TF 11 to handle such missions. "So they added that to our rucksack, which meant all the guys had to sit strip alert, basically," a TF 11 officer said. In addition, Dailey knew that if he pushed TF Blue out from Bagram to safe houses in the hinterland, he'd need to deploy more Rangers to guard them, and he was desperately trying to control the size of his force in Afghanistan. (Rangers provided a supporting direct action element, named Task Force Red, to act in concert with Green or Blue.) To some, TF Blue was complicit in this arrangement. Eager for action, but lacking a thorough grounding in reconnaissance, the SEALs were reluctant to go searching for high-value targets. "They weren't proactive," a special ops source said. "They wanted the HVT to come to them with a fucking ribbon on him."

Not surprisingly, the Rangers were perhaps the most frustrated troops at the base. Their commander, Lieutenant Colonel Tony Thomas, was one of the most seasoned special ops officers in Afghanistan. One of the few soldiers of any rank with two combat jumps to his credit, he had parachuted into Grenada as a Ranger platoon leader in 1983 and into Panama in 1989 as a Ranger company commander. He spent most of the 1990s in Delta, participating in major operations in the Balkans and rising to command B Squadron. Now he was back in another combat zone, but this time forced to work under officers with far less experience of such circumstances. "He was as good of a guy as we had," said a special operator with extensive Afghanistan experience.

TF Red had been sharply reduced at the end of the year. The original TF Red, consisting of the 3rd Ranger Battalion, was replaced by Thomas's task force, which included only a reinforced company (a rifle company plus mortars, snipers, and scouts), and a large battalion headquarters from Thomas's 1st Ranger Battalion. Like all Rangers, Thomas's troops specialized in direct action and prided themselves on their ability to conduct detailed mission planning. TF Red had a large staff trained in planning dangerous missions in a way that left as little as possible to chance. The size of Thomas's staff allowed him to put his operations center at Kandahar while keeping his operations officer and a rump staff at Bagram. TF Blue's SEALs, by contrast, were not renowned for their planning skills, and often asked the Rangers for help in planning missions in Afghanistan. Thomas and his men found it incredible that they were acting as glorified gate guards for a unit that didn't have the wherewithal to plan its own missions. The 1st Battalion commander stewed in frustration as he watched the SEALs "fooling around," a special ops source said. "He had to bite his tongue to keep from just fucking killing somebody."

"Red knew they should have been the lead unit working missions, but they were standing guard and task organized under the [SEALs]," commented another observer at Bagram. "What a waste."

This was the situation that confronted Blaber when he walked off the C-17 that first week in January. Blaber was by now an old hand at parachuting (sometimes literally) into a situation and having to take it all in at a glance. A former enlisted man and Ranger who gained his commission via the Army's Officer Candidate School, he had joined Delta in 1991 and was a combat veteran who had seen action all over the globe, including Panama, Somalia, and the Balkans. It didn't take him long to get the lay of the land in Bagram.

Blaber had long believed in "the power of combinations," putting together cross-functional teams from black and white SOF, conventional forces, and the CIA in order to maximize the potential of each. At this stage in the war the other key players on the ground in Afghanistan were Dagger and the CIA. It was they who were out in the hinterlands, conducting UW with Afghan militias and keeping an ear to the ground for useful information about the location of Al Qaida troops and HVTs. Blaber's first act after arriving was to ensure that his AFO teams were joined at the hip in what were called "pilot teams" with the Dagger and CIA personnel operating out of the safe houses in Gardez, Khowst, and other provincial towns. But for these teams to be truly effective, they needed greater on-site communications bandwidth and intelligence analysis capability. So Blaber flattened his organization, taking almost all his intel analysts and commo guys out of Bagram and pushing them down to empower the pilot teams in the safe houses. That joined the information users (the operators) with the information gatekeepers (the intel analysts), allowing data to flow from one to the other smoothly and efficiently, without being contaminated by layers of staff in between. Blaber decided that Bagram held no appeal for him. He joined his northern AFO command element in the CIA "station annex" in the Ariana, taking a commo guy and an intel analyst. In the Ariana he was plugged into the heart of the CIA's operation in Afghanistan and was just two blocks from Dagger's Kabul safe house. Both Dagger and the Agency had more to offer Blaber in the way of useful intelligence than had anyone at Bagram.

He left two analysts at Bagram, plus an air operations officer and a major called Jimmy, who was his deputy commander. Another former Ranger, Jimmy was in his late thirties, six feet tall, and weighed about 180 pounds. He had the lean, athletic physique typical of Delta operators. He wore his black hair long, slicked back, with a full black beard. Dark brown eyes and perfect white teeth only added to his movie-star good looks. A 10th Mountain officer said Jimmy resembled Al Pacino in the lead role of the movie *Serpico*. Indeed, in some quarters Jimmy had the reputation for being "a Hollywood-type Delta guy." But others who knew him well said that was unfair, and that those who made that criticism were just jealous of Jimmy's professionalism. "If you're going to go into a combat operation, he's one of the guys you want on your team," said an operator who served with Jimmy. Blaber and Jimmy went back a long way. They had first met when Jimmy was a Ranger lieutenant and Blaber was a major in Delta. They had worked closely together when Jimmy was the operations officer in Delta's A Squadron, and Blaber held the same job for the entire unit. This was the first time they had served together on a combat op, but Blaber had complete trust in Jimmy. He knew he would need a liaison officer and go-to guy in Bagram upon whom he could depend. He had no hesitation in making Jimmy that guy.

In the space of a few days Blaber had dramatically reshaped his organization to take full advantage of its capabilities, as well as those of Dagger and the CIA. Now the pieces were in place. The AFO troops were ready to take on whatever challenges lay in store. They would not have long to wait.

8.

FOR a week after moving to Kabul in the first few days of the year, Blaber met daily at the Ariana with John, the CIA's deputy station chief, and TF Dagger's Lieutenant Colonel Chris Haas, the highly respected commander of 5th Special Forces Group's 1st Battalion. Then, on January 16, John mentioned for the first time that intelligence indicated the presence of a significant enemy force in the Shahikot area.

The meeting marked a turning point in the war. Since mid-December, the station chief—a tall, quiet, intelligent, and very self-assured CIA officer named Rich—had been telling the military that U.S. forces needed to focus their search for Al Qaida on the Gardez-Khowst area. Rich was a man whose counsel the military leaders had learned to heed. A case officer in Algeria during the Islamist rebellion of the early 1990s, he had been appointed chief of the CIA's "bin Laden unit" in 1999. In that job he had visited the strip of Afghanistan held by Ahmad Shah Massoud. He probably knew more about the country than any other U.S. offical in Afghanistan in early 2002. When Edwards, the deputy CFLCC commander, visited that month, Rich told him he expected "the last battle" of the war to be fought in the Gardez-Khowst region. Now, a few weeks later, the CIA had sharpened its focus from "Gardez-Khowst" to "Shahikot." From the moment that John first uttered the word in the meeting at the Ariana, the CIA and AFO made building the intelligence picture of the Shahikot region their highest priority.

In Rich and John the CIA had two of the smartest Americans in Afghanistan. All the military folks who dealt with either of the Agency's top two in Kabul came away impressed. "In no conversation that I've ever had with [Rich] has he turned out to be wrong," Edwards said. "He had a much better feel for Afghanistan than most of the people I talked to. Most of the people thought they knew a lot more than they really did."

AFTER receiving intelligence tips that Al Qaida and Taliban forces were moving into the town of Zermat, eighteen kilometers southwest of Gardez, Texas 14 drove into Zermat on January 16 with about 300 Afghans. The Afghan forces included 170 troops under two commanders named Kabir and Ziabdullah who had accompanied Texas 14 from Logar, Zia's thirty men as the Americans' personal security detail, and 100 men provided by the Gardez shura, which was essentially a town council made up of the tribal elders. The Americans included Thomas's men and several CIA operatives. But when they reached Zermat, it was clear any enemy force had been forewarned and made itself scarce. Instead the U.S. troops were greeted by curious crowds. At the Islamic school, or *madrassa,* which they thought was an enemy base, they instead found the town elders waiting for them with a lunch laid out. If anything this experience made the Americans even more suspicious about Zermat and its environs. The next day they headed down the same road again, and Zia's men spotted a Russian-made Kamaz truck a couple of kilometers away heading east toward the Shahikot (which no one had told Texas 14 was an area of interest, despite the attention the valley was receiving at higher headquarters). Zia's men gave chase but couldn't catch the vehicle. However, en route they captured another Kamaz truck and a taxi. A search of the truck turned up a bag full of bomb-making documents, plus food and clothing that Zia's men said were definitely Arabian.

The incident drew Glenn Thomas's attention to the Shahikot. He took immediate action. The next day another convoy departed the safe house, bound for the Shahikot. Most of the force consisted of 100 Afghan militiamen, including thirty from Zia plus a large Gardez shura contingent. The U.S. element included Texas 14, several CIA men, a signals intelligence team, and a couple of Team 6 SEALs attached to the AFO element now resident in the Gardez safe house. The Americans' intent was to drive down the Zermat road, turn off toward the Shahikot, and split their force as they approached the huge hump-back mountain that marked the valley's western edge. One half of the force would set up a blocking position just south of the mountain while the rest of the force would enter the valley from the north.

As they moved toward the valley, the signals intelligence team picked up several transmissions in Arabic from Zermat describing the convoy and trying to figure out where it was going. Then the plan fell apart. The Gardez shura troops drove off and made a beeline for the valley, leaving the Americans in their dust. When Thomas's men caught up with them at the valley's southern entrance (not the northern one the shura troops were supposed to head toward), they told the Americans some of their vehicles had already entered the valley and one of their men had been captured. Then the "captured" man suddenly reappeared, still with his weapon. The U.S. troops grew suspicious. Thomas sent some Gardez shura fighters into the nearest village to find out what was going on. They were gone for hours. Before they returned, the Americans saw a woman in a burkha leave one of the villages and climb into the mountains. Then a small boy in tears passed them leading a camel loaded with household goods out of the valley. When asked why he was crying he replied that the men in his village had told him to leave because there was going to be a big fight. Zia's men, who the Americans trusted more than any other Afghans, were visibly nervous and repeatedly told Thomas that they should leave before the sun set. Meanwhile a white van could be seen driving back and forth between the villages in the middle of the valley and the mountainous ridgeline that formed the Shahikot's eastern wall.

The shura troops came back with two locals who said no Al Qaida fighters were in their village. They invited the Americans for tea. Thomas and the others were not convinced. All their senses told them they were in a perilous situation. With the sun setting they decided to head back to Gardez before dark. As they drove back to the Zermat road, they couldn't help but notice that the Gardez shura troops who had earlier claimed total ignorance of the Shahikot knew the route well enough to lead the convoy out in blacked-out conditions. Back at the safe house two of Zia's senior lieutenants told Thomas that while in the Shahikot they had seen "Chechens" setting up DShK (pronounced "dishka") 12.7mm heavy machine guns and other weapons on the high ground overlooking the route the Americans would have to take into Babulkhel. The "Chechens" shouted down to Zia's fighters to "do their Muslim duty" by leading the Americans into what was clearly a trap. Zia's men had no intention of betraying their American allies but were reluctant to tell Thomas of the episode while still in the valley. They thought that if the shura troops heard they might turn on the Americans.

Yet again Zia's fighters had proven their worth. It wasn't long before the Americans eased Kabir's men out of the picture and placed Zia in overall charge of the little Afghan army they were assembling in Gardez.

9.

BY January 20 reports from Gardez, combined with Sweeney's analysis, had persuaded Mulholland to make the Shahikot Dagger's top priority. While Sweeney sat in the SCIF tracing ratlines south and east of Gardez, other planners worked to piece together other parts of the puzzle in Dagger's Joint Operations Center (JOC).

Dagger's JOC, like TF 11's, consisted of a series of interconnected, white-walled, temperature-controlled nylon tents that hummed with nonstop staff activity interspersed with the scratchy insistence of radio chatter. The plethora of laptops made it resemble a high-tech stenographer's pool. Racks of communications gear lined the walls, and the tables were strewn with maps and notebooks, as well as the coffee machines ubiquitous to all military operations centers. In a tent corner sat a couple of boxes filled with snacks from MREs—Meals, Ready to Eat, the U.S. military's calorie-filled ration packs—that hungry staffers grazed on day and night.

Two of Rosengard's key planners were SF warrant officers who had served on teams that had just returned to K2 from north of Gardez. One warrant was analyzing the Shahikot area to determine where Al Qaida might have training or logistics bases and how enemy fighters might travel between them. The other leaned over a planning table in a different tent, using his knowledge of key personalities in that part of Paktia to draw up a "people network" not only of likely Taliban or Al Qaida leaders or supporters, but also those figures who might become U.S. allies.

By now Mulholland, the Dagger commander, had decided the intelligence justified a major operation aimed at the Shahikot. Planning proceeded, but was still very compartmentalized. Much of the nuts-and-bolts work was confined to the tent Rosengard's planning cell shared with CIA officers attached to Dagger. In addition to Mulholland, Air Force Colonel Frank Kisner (Mulholland's deputy who also commanded the AC-130 gunships and MC-130s at K2), Rosengard, Sweeney, and the two warrants, only a few staffers with a "need to know" were aware something big was in the works.

AS Dagger's planners and analysts pored over intel reports, maps, and satellite photos, they became increasingly familiar with the Shahikot, which had previously been to them just a vague area south of Gardez.

There were in fact two Shahikot valleys—an Upper Shahikot Valley and a Lower Shahikot Valley. The two valleys ran parallel on a line south southwest to north northeast, separated by a mountainous ridgeline over 9,000 feet high. The Upper Shahikot Valley, which lay to the east, was aptly named. It had a higher elevation, and the valley floor appeared on maps as a thin ribbon of land no more than a couple of hundred meters wide, hemmed in by craggy mountain peaks. No one appeared to live there. But the Lower Shahikot Valley—soon known as *the* Shahikot—was a different proposition. Depending on where you measured, the valley was about five miles (eight kilometers) long by two-and-a-half miles (four kilometers) wide. An arrowhead-shaped ridgeline jutted into the valley's southern end, creating southwestern and southeastern entrances. This ridgeline became known as "the Finger." The valley was bordered on the east by the ridgeline dividing it from the Upper Shahikot. At its southern end this ridgeline peaked at a mountain called Takur Ghar, which at 10,469 feet dominated the valley. An equally imposing terrain feature marked the valley's western edge: a humpback ridgeline almost 9,000 feet high, over four miles long and almost a mile wide. This ridge was called Tergul Ghar (Ghar means "mountain" in Pushto), but its distinctive shape caused American planners to dub it "The Whale," after a similar rocky mass at the Army's National Training Center in California's Mojave Desert.

Unlike its inhospitable eastern neighbor, the Lower Shahikot's floor was reasonably suited to human habitation. It was flat enough to support subsistence farming, and several creeks ran through it. As a result, there were four villages in the valley, each with no more than a couple of hundred inhabitants. The farthest south was Marzak, located between Takur Ghar and the Finger. The tiny hamlet of Zerki Kale was just to the north of the Finger's tip, about 1,000 meters southwest of Babulkhel. Serkhankhel, the largest village, sat squarely in the middle of the valley. The Shahikot's main entrance lay to the southwest, between the southern end of the Whale and the western side of the Finger. Beyond lay Zermat, about nine miles to the west northwest, and Gardez, eighteen miles to the north. But there were other exits from the Shahikot, for those who wished to seek them: heading south, past Marzak, a determined traveler could climb through saddles and passes, or head east through the steep-sided gorge along the southern base of Takur Ghar. There were also several high passes through the eastern ridge into the Upper Shahikot, as well as an obvious route to the northwest around the Whale's northern end. The most logical avenues of ingress and egress were those to the west around the Whale, but it was those that pointed south and east for which anyone headed to Pakistan in a hurry would likely opt.

After studying the intelligence, Rosengard's planning cell concluded that the Shahikot held three types of people: Afghan civilians who had no stomach for a fight and would try to escape west out of the valley as soon as the shooting started; enemy leaders (no one knew how senior, but everyone at K2 and Bagram was hoping a genuine HVT was hiding in the Shahikot) who would also try to slip away, either by hiding among noncombatants or by heading toward Pakistan; and last, hard-core fighters, who might have no option but to stick around and cover their leaders' escape before also trying to make their getaway. No firm estimate on the number of enemy fighters existed, but overhead imagery showed considerable traffic along a route running due east out of Serkhankhel through a pass in the eastern ridge. This trail—no more than a goat path—was assumed to be how the most senior enemy figures in the valley would choose to exit the Shahikot in case of attack. Rosengard decided the key to the operation lay in forcing the enemy to try to escape along that route. He called this "convincing the enemy to do what he already wants to do."

Despite the evidence from Tora Bora that relying on Afghan allies was a high-risk strategy in the Pushtun provinces, Rosengard initially explored the possibility of an operation in the Shahikot geared entirely around friendly Afghan fighters—in the blizzard of acronyms that characterized the war in Afghanistan, these were known as Afghan military forces, or AMF—with the usual complement of Special Forces advisers. To Rosengard and other Dagger leaders, there were two overriding reasons why the AMF still represented the force of choice. First, reports from Gardez suggested that any Al Qaida forces in the Shahikot were intermingled with up to 1,000 Afghan civilians. These included the village residents as well as people brought in from nearby towns to work as the guerrillas' "indentured servants." When attacking the Shahikot, Dagger officers thought, it would be essential to have troops who could quickly distinguish between local civilians on the one hand and the Arabs, Uzbeks, and other foreigners the Americans wanted to kill on the other. Rosengard et al. didn't trust any Americans—not even their own Special Forces—to be able to make that distinction. The alternative, in the Dagger officers' minds, was to risk a slaughter of civilians, with a negative strategic impact that would outweigh any benefits gained. Rosengard worried aloud about sending a U.S. conventional force into the Shahikot, seizing the objective, and then civilian survivors of the assault telling CNN: "These Americans came in and killed my sister and my brother and all these Afghans."

The second reason the Dagger leaders thought it vital to use AMF for the attack was a desire to give the Afghans a feeling of "ownership" over the victory the Americans presumed would ensue. This harkened back to the U.S. desire to not appear as an occupying or invading force. "In the end we want the Afghans to feel ownership of having liberated their country, and having participated as a partner in [eradicating] the sanctuary" that Al Qaida had created for themselves, Rosengard said. Asked whether, in a country so fragmented along ethnic lines, the average Afghan grasped that concept, Rosengard thought for a moment before replying that Zia, at least, understood it.

10.

AT his Kuwait headquarters Mikolashek's strategic thinking paralleled that of Mulholland and Rosengard. The general had been following intel reports since late December about Al Qaida regrouping in the Shahikot. Every day he would walk the 300 meters between the warehouse that was home to his headquarters and the CFLCC intelligence center, which was housed in a brick building inside another warehouse. There he would spend an hour or more picking the brains of analysts who were poring over raw intelligence from Afghanistan. A new human intelligence report would surface every couple of days indicating enemy activity in and around the valley. Marzak was the first village to crop up, followed a few days later by Serkhankhel. Mikolashek's interest was piqued. *This is bigger than a bread box,* he thought.

As evidence mounted that Al Qaida forces were coalescing in the Shahikot, the generals running the war in Afghanistan considered their next move. To Mikolashek, eastern Afghanistan was the last part of the country allied forces did not control. Estimates of enemy strength in the Shahikot area varied wildly. For a long time the intel folks' best guess was that fewer than 100 Al Qaida fighters were in and around the valley. That figure grew steadily, with estimates ranging from a couple of hundred to several thousand. Mikolashek and other U.S. leaders concluded that their next step in the war must be to bring a significant force to bear to crush the enemy in the Shahikot.

Based on intelligence he was receiving, Mikolashek assessed the enemy fighters gathering in the Shahikot to be members of the Islamic Movement of Uzbekistan (IMU). The IMU was a radical Islamist group that had spent the last decade fighting Uzbekistan's authoritarian government from bases in neighboring Tajikistan. By September 11, the IMU had become the central Asian franchise of Al Qaida. Its fighters had gathered in strength in Afghanistan to defend bin Laden in his fight against the Americans. The IMU fighters in the Shahikot had been driven out of the Kunduz area in northern Afghanistan, and then had escaped again from Tora Bora, Mikolashek figured. Reluctant to enter Pakistan because their different ethnicity would make them stick out there, the Uzbeks were probably biding their time in the Shahikot before either attempting a return to Tajikistan, or launching a fresh assault on U.S. forces and the provisional government in Kabul, Mikolashek thought. He was determined to prevent them taking either course of action.

HAVING decided to act against Al Qaida in the Shahikot, senior U.S. commanders then had to decide when and how to attack, and with what forces. Despite the Tora Bora debacle, Franks and Mikolashek opted to stick with the formula that had brought them success against the Taliban: unconventional warfare plus airpower. "We followed our guiding principles," Mikolashek said. "This [would] be an unconventional operation, and the main effort [would] be AMF forces." The fact that intelligence indicated that the enemy in the Shahikot were not the Taliban's farmers-cum-fighters, but hardened Al Qaida and IMU guerrillas, did nothing to change the generals' minds.

If it was to be an unconventional operation, Mikolashek had to choose one of the two joint special ops task forces under his control—Dagger (Mulholland's unconventional warfare task force) or K-Bar (Harward's direct action and special reconnaissance task force)—to pull the attack together. It was not a difficult decision. Mulholland's Special Forces teams had demonstrated time and again an ability to mold Afghan militias into effective combat units. The acknowledged masters of unconventional warfare in Afghanistan, they were already working on the challenge presented by the Shahikot. The disparate special ops units in K-Bar had not developed the same ties with Afghan forces that Dagger had. As special reconnaissance and direct action specialists, that was not their job. To Mikolashek, there was only one option: let Mulholland take this one and run with it.

Mulholland was already running with it, but he was also running into problems in the Pushtun heartland as he tried to replicate his successes with the Northern Alliance. Despite its name, the "Eastern Alliance" organized by Dagger teams in other Pushtun provinces was not a coherent organization, just a collection of unconnected militias, none of which hailed from the Gardez-Shahikot area. There was no "Eastern Alliance" available for the Shahikot mission. Dagger had been active in Paktia only since December, but even before it became clear the Shahikot would demand his attention, Mulholland had wanted a force in the province capable of conducting operations. There was no local anti-Taliban force in being, and recruiting and training one would take time. With higher commanders impatient for action, Mulholland decided to use the one force he had available: Texas 14's Afghan fighters under Zia Lodin.

In Gardez, Glenn Thomas and his A-team was working hard to transform Zia's troops into an effective combat force, but by early February it was clear they had a long way to go before they would be ready to take on Al Qaida. That wasn't good news for Mikolashek. He wanted to attack the Shahikot as soon as possible and waited anxiously for Texas 14 to complete their preparations with Zia. "Trying to find, recruit, train, equip, and supply these guys took a lot longer than we would have wanted it to," Mikolashek said. "If we would have had by early February a force in being, we probably would have gone in there [to the Shahikot] about that time." But there was a "force in being" available to Mikolashek. By mid-January the 101st Airborne Division's 3rd Brigade had deployed to Kandahar to replace the Marines. Although the brigade had only one of its three infantry battalions in Kandahar, it had another guarding the airfield in Jacobabad, Pakistan, while 10th Mountain's 1-87 Infantry was at K2. Thus U.S. commanders had three battalions of highly trained light infantry available to them in theater, had they wanted to use them instead of Zia's forces as the main effort in the attack. But CENTCOM's obsession with minimizing the role of U.S. conventional troops meant this option was never seriously considered.

However, CENTCOM, CFLCC, and Dagger had learned one important lesson from their embarrassment at Tora Bora: the need to block any escape route to Pakistan. The terrain around the Shahikot was more conducive than at Tora Bora to establishing blocking positions along the ratlines that ran toward Pakistan. The Americans were determined not to let their enemies escape again. "What we didn't want . . . was the effect of not having a backstop," Mikolashek said. "One of the things that we learned from Tora Bora was the need to have blocking positions."

But who would man such positions? The answer seems obvious in hindsight: U.S. infantry. But to the generals, that wasn't clear at the time. If the CIA and Mulholland's A-teams could have recruited enough militiamen, Mikolashek probably would have "defaulted" to the Afghans-plus-Special Forces formula yet again. But even though Dagger was recruiting a company-sized Pushtun force in the Gardez area to bolster Zia's tiny militia, there still weren't enough AMF to conduct the classic hammer-and-anvil operation the Dagger staff envisioned for the Shahikot. Meanwhile, officers up and down the chain of command continued to analyze the intelligence picture as it was pieced together like a jigsaw. With estimates of the enemy force mounting and no other troops to establish the desired blocking positions, Mulholland decided the operation in the Shahikot presented a good opportunity to use U.S. conventional forces in large-scale combat for the first time in Afghanistan. Mikolashek's staff had come to the same conclusion independently. CENTCOM finally came on board in late January. At one of the innumerable video-teleconferences through which Franks and Mikolashek ran the war, CENTCOM issued orders to focus intelligence, surveillance and reconnaissance assets on, and expedite operations in, the Khowst-Gardez area with a view to eliminating pockets of Al Qaida resistance. CENTCOM further directed that a combination of Afghan, SF, and conventional forces be used to conduct these operations. "That was the first time that CENTCOM acknowledged that we could use and should use conventional forces for offensive operations," Edwards said.

As January shivered into February in Afghanistan, generals and colonels at MacDill, Camp Doha and K2 began to pepper their discussions on how to approach the challenges in Paktia with a new, oddly Japanese-sounding word: Rakkasan.

11.

IT was a cold, crisp night in Kandahar and the phone on the desk in Frank Wiercinski's cramped office in the airport's dusty terminal building was ringing insistently. The brigade commander answered. On the line was a TF Dagger officer in Bagram. His message was brief and to the point. Wiercinski's presence was required at a meeting to be held in Bagram in a couple of days to discuss an upcoming operation. The tall, solidly built infantry colonel replaced the receiver and glanced vacantly around the sparsely decorated room. A stand by his desk held an American flag and the 187th Infantry regimental colors. On the wall hung a rug presented to him by a local Afghan commander and the 101st Airborne Division flag, which showed the head of a bald eagle, its orange beak open as if in mid-scream, against a black background. There were no maps. Wiercinski received too many visitors here who weren't cleared to view them. All the maps were on the walls of his tactical operations center just forty feet away. *An upcoming operation?* he thought. *Now, this is interesting.*

WIERCINSKI'S life had been a blur since he had answered another phone call in entirely different circumstances almost five months previously. He had been stepping out of the shower at home after doing physical training with his troops on the morning of September 11. When he picked up the phone, he heard the urgent voice of Bruce Meyers, a family friend. "Have you seen the TV yet?" Meyers asked. "No." "Turn it on." Wiercinski's TV screen flashed to life moments before the second plane hit the World Trade Center. "No way," the still-dripping colonel muttered under his breath as he watched the orange ball of flame burst from the skyscraper. As news filtered through of a plane hitting the Pentagon and of another that had crashed in mysterious circumstances in Pennsylvania, it quickly dawned on Wiercinski that someone had attacked his country. The United States was at war. Wiercinski hurriedly pulled his uniform on—he lived only six minutes from Fort Campbell's main gate, and always came home to shower after PT—before jumping in his red Mazda pickup truck and racing back on post.

As he pulled into the brigade commander's parking slot behind the 101st Airborne Division's 3rd Brigade headquarters, his staff was already buzzing with nervous energy. Returning salutes en route to his office, the colonel found himself looking into many familiar pairs of eyes. He had been in command for over a year, living, eating, and breathing the brigade's business. Brigade command was an extraordinarily stressful stint of an officer's career. Preparing several thousand men and women for the savagery of ground combat could not be otherwise. But Wiercinski had solid subordinates upon whom he could count for support. He didn't get to select his three battalion commanders—the Army assigned its most promising lieutenant colonels to those positions—but he had handpicked each of his majors, placing trustworthy officers upon whom he knew he could rely into the crucial brigade and battalion staff jobs. He had also inherited a first-class brigade command sergeant major in Iuniasolua Savusa, an imposing slab of Samoan muscle whose professionalism set a tremendous example for the brigade's enlisted soldiers.

There was an extra edge to the hustle and bustle in the brigade headquarters, even accounting for the extraordinary scenes being replayed on every television in the building. The brigade was preparing to go on "black cycle," meaning that for the next six to eight weeks, it would be the first of the division's three infantry brigades to deploy somewhere should the Pentagon order the 101st to war.

Wiercinski felt a surge of excitement. What a job he had. It was his dream posting. The Army had 320 infantry colonels and only twenty-five infantry brigades, so most colonels never even got to command a brigade. But Wiercinski wasn't commanding just any brigade. He had one of the most famous brigades in the Army: the 3rd Brigade of the 101st Airborne Division (Air Assault)—*the Rakkasans.*

THE 101st Airborne Division began life in 1942 as a glider and parachute unit. In the general order that gave birth to the 101st, Major General William C. Lee, the division's first commander, told his troops that although the 101st had no history, it had "a rendezvous with destiny." The phrase became the title of the division song, but also imbued the 101st with a sense of uniqueness. "Let me call your attention to the fact that our badge is the great American eagle," Lee said. "This is a fitting emblem for a division that will crush its enemies by falling upon them like a thunderbolt from the skies."

Known as "The Screaming Eagles," the 101st's soldiers set about creating a history for themselves. The division jumped into Normandy on June 6, 1944, and saw action across Europe, famously repelling a German siege at Bastogne during the Battle of the Bulge. The 101st stood down at the end of World War II, and was not reactivated as a combat division until 1956. Twelve years later, when deployed to Vietnam, the 101st morphed from an airborne (i.e., parachute) division to an airmobile (i.e., helicopter-transported) division. In 1974 the Army changed the division's "airmobile" designation to the more combat-oriented "air assault," and thus it had remained—not only the Army's sole air assault division, but unique among the world's militaries.

Used correctly, the 101st Airborne Division (Air Assault) was one of the most powerful divisions in the world. Its 72 AH-64 Apache attack helicopters and three battalions of 105mm howitzers could subject an enemy to withering firepower. But it was the 101st's massive complement of helicopters—two brigades' worth, or 234 aircraft, compared with the single aviation brigade of fewer than half that number in every other division—that made it unique. In addition to three Apache battalions, the division had three battalions of UH-60 Black Hawk transport helicopters, plus a CH-47 Chinook battalion for heavy lifting. This was all in addition to three superbly trained and equipped light infantry brigades. The combination of helicopters and light infantry created the air *assault*, capitalizing on the shock effect of helicopters appearing over the enemy's heads and depositing hundreds of troops in a matter of moments. The division could lift an entire infantry brigade into battle at once.

But the helicopters that gave the 101st its unique mobility were also its greatest vulnerability. The spread of sophisticated air defense weapons among America's enemies posed an increasing threat to helicopters. Even man-portable missiles like the widely available SA-7 spelled danger for the division's aircraft. And as the Somalis had shown in Mogadishu in 1993, a rocket-propelled grenade—among the most ubiquitous of Third World weapons—could down a Black Hawk. There was an inherent tension between these stark facts and air assault doctrine, which still clung to Lee's sixty-year-old vision of avenging eagles swooping from the sky to crush their enemies.

It was a quirk of the Army's arcane system for naming its fighting formations that divisions and brigades rarely shared the same history as their component battalions. Such was the case with the 101st. Wiercinski's brigade was composed of the 1st, 2nd, and 3rd Battalions of the 187th Infantry Regiment. Those battalions had only formed the 3rd Brigade of the 101st since 1987, but their glittering history stretched back to World War II, when the 187th Infantry Regiment saw a lot of action in the Pacific theater as part of the 11th Airborne Division. Reorganized as the 187th Regimental Combat Team, it performed magnificently in the Korean War, conducting two dramatic parachute assaults. By then it had gained its unusual nickname while on occupation duty in Japan, where the natives dubbed the unit *Rakkasan,* which translates loosely as "falling umbrella."

The legacy of valor Wiercinski inherited as the Rakkasans' commander gave him an advantage over commanders of less-storied units in fostering esprit de corps. Rakkasan veterans of earlier wars enjoyed almost unfettered access to the brigade in garrison, visiting frequently to share war stories and wisdom with their successors. "They're always at functions, and the soldiers always hear of their tales, and of the Rakkasan legacy, whether it be World War II, or Korea with the two combat jumps, or Vietnam—Hamburger Hill," Wiercinski said. "And then of course, Desert Storm, with the great deep air assault into the Euphrates River Valley. That all plays into combat power. It just does something to soldiers to feel a part of such a tight-knit organization. . . . You hear boys talk about it all the time, you know, 'We're keeping up the Rakkasan legacy, we've got to uphold the standards of the Rakkasans and the 101st, the Screaming Eagles.' All of that was such a great combat multiplier for us. We knew where we came from, we knew who we were, and we knew what we stood for."

The 101st's commander, Major General Dick Cody, a cigar-chomping, tobacco-chewing Apache pilot who had led the first helicopter attack of the 1991 Gulf War, resolved to ensure that if the Pentagon called on his soldiers to participate in the war that was starting to unfold, they would not be found wanting. He put every available infantry company through a series of rigorous combat drills. Most of his 2nd Brigade was deployed in Kosovo—one of those peacekeeping missions that continued to eat away at the Army's combat power long after most Americans had forgotten about them—and would not return until November, but the other two brigades knuckled down. No company was considered "qualified" unless it had successfully conducted a live-fire exercise at night. The training ran through October, November, and December in miserably cold and wet conditions, but the pace was unrelenting.

In early November Wiercinski lost a third of his infantry force when 1-187 was sent to guard the air base at Jacobabad, Pakistan, where U.S. aircraft were staging for missions over Afghanistan. The battalion was lucky to have gone through the exercises at Campbell, because training opportunities were very limited in Pakistan. Political constraints prevented them from even firing their weapons on the ranges at Jacobabad.

AS the Rakkasans braved sleet and rain to hone their skills at Campbell, the CENTCOM and CFLCC generals were discussing who should replace the Marines at Kandahal. CENTCOM initially planned to bring in another Marine task force. But Mikolashek was determined that this time the Army take the lead. "It was important to have the Army replace the Marines because we were making the transition into what the Army does, which is sustained land operations," Mikolashek said.

In early December the call came down from the Army Staff, via Forces Command in Fort McPherson, Georgia: Get the Rakkasans ready. (Cody had kept the Rakkasans on "black cycle" after September 11.) But for Keane, Mikolashek, and other Army leaders, the success in persuading Franks and others to deploy the brigade quickly became a case of "Be careful what you wish for."

WHEN a brigade was sent to war, particularly when it is deployed without its parent division, it usually went as a brigade combat team, or BCT. The brigade combat team consisted of the brigade itself—essentially the brigade's three "maneuver" battalions (i.e., infantry or armor, depending on the brigade type) and the brigade headquarters—plus the division "slices" that habitually accompanied the brigade. These slices were division-level units that did not fall under the brigade in garrison, but which were deemed essential for the brigade commander to fight according to Army doctrine and were always pushed down to him by the division commander during training and combat. In the 101st these slices typically included a battalion each of artillery, Apaches and Black Hawks, plus a Chinook company, an air defense battery, a military police platoon, engineer, signals, and military intelligence elements. The brigade commander and his staff, the commanders and staffs of the infantry battalions, as well as those of the "slice" units all trained together and expected to fight together. With all its components a 101st brigade combat team numbered around 5,000 soldiers—a formidable organization. But Franks didn't want a complete 101st BCT in Afghanistan, just a few of its parts. Now the "force cap" on the number of troops CENTCOM would allow on Afghan soil began to bite. Instead of asking for the 3rd Brigade Combat Team, CENTCOM gave Cody and Wiercinski a list of the pieces of the BCT they were to deploy. Missing was any mention of artillery or attack helicopters—the two most powerful weapons systems in Wiercinski's arsenal. The troop cap for the BCT was set at about 2,200, a number to which Mikolashek had reluctantly agreed in the belief that it was his only hope of persuading CENTCOM and the Joint Staff in the Pentagon to agree to the deployment. The cap meant Wiercinski could only take one infantry battalion into Afghanistan.

This news sat well with neither Cody nor Wiercinski, whose soldiers' lives were at stake. The Rakkasan commander had taken most of his brigade combat team to the Joint Readiness Training Center (JRTC) in Louisiana, and then had put it through another intensive train-up at Campbell. He was intimately familiar with the strengths and weaknesses of the commanders, staff officers, and troops. The trust and bonding essential to the cohesion of a combat organization had taken place. Now Wiercinski was being asked to break that organization apart for a real war. It was the only war the United States was fighting, and his was the only brigade the Army was deploying to take part in that fight, yet he was being ordered to leave over half his force at home. This made no sense to Wiercinski, Cody, or the colonels and generals higher up the Army chain of command. "The brigade commander [and] the division commander back at the 101st clearly wanted to provide more troops," Keane said. "At the Army Staff we were asking the same questions, because it makes sense to send the whole organization." Wiercinski appealed. "I said how about the rest of the brigade combat team, particularly the artillery and the rest of the aviation—can we take that?" he recalled. His division commander backed him to the hilt, recommending that the entire BCT deploy. An Apache pilot, Cody was incensed that CENTCOM's wish list didn't include a single attack helicopter. He sent a request through Mikolashek to CENTCOM to deploy at least some Apaches. It was denied. "Dick Cody went crazy, and we agreed with him," said Edwards, another helicopter pilot. "We all agreed we had to have attack helicopters—the Marines had attack helicopters there with them. There was no question over whether we should have them or not." The debate was still raging when the Rakkasans deployed in January. Wiercinski left Campbell without his Apaches.

Franks also made it clear that no requests for artillery would be entertained. Again, this ran counter to the wishes of just about every general between Wiercinski and CENTCOM. "Did Wiercinski ask for artillery in his package? Yes. Did Cody advocate sending artillery in? Yes," Edwards said. Another advocate for including artillery in the Rakkasan BCT was Major General Hank Stratman, an artillery officer and Mikolashek's deputy commanding general for support. "Hank very nobly said several times, 'Edwards, we need to get artillery in,'" Edwards said. "My answer was 'Yes, Hank, in a perfect world, we certainly do. But I can't get there.'"

The decision to deploy Wiercinski's brigade combat team—Task Force Rakkasan—to a combat zone with no artillery had major implications. Since the nineteenth century the Army had committed its infantry to battle as part of a combined arms team, capitalizing on the complementary capability of direct and indirect fire, maneuver, and, when it appeared in the twentieth century, airpower, to present an enemy with an overwhelming range of lethal threats simultaneously, giving him, as soldiers liked to say, multiple ways to die. The Army rarely if ever sought to maneuver large numbers of light infantry against an enemy beyond the reach of friendly artillery. But American commanders had already bent or broken so many rules in Afghanistan without suffering a reverse that leaving the Rakkasans' most reliable source of firepower behind didn't seem misguided. Dagger's unconventional war had relied upon fixed-wing airpower for fire support. That approach worked to spectacular effect when air-delivered precision munitions could be guided on to targets by Special Forces soldiers wielding laser designators. (The Taliban's military ineptitude didn't hurt, either.) CFLCC and CENTCOM generals thought bombers could fill in for TF Rakkasan's missing artillery. But artillery had unique qualities. Unlike aircraft, it could remain on the battlefield for more than an hour or two, and neither its availability nor its performance was affected by the weather. It might not—except in the cases of very expensive, specialized rounds—have enjoyed the precision of the Air Force's smart bombs, but an artillery battery could keep an enemy's head down merely by dropping lots of shells in his vicinity, even if they didn't blow his head *off*. Of course, another advantage for CENTCOM of relying on airpower was that the planes dropping the bombs were all flying from air bases outside Afghanistan, thus keeping Franks's force cap for Afghanistan low. The generals were sending mixed messages to Wiercinski. On one hand, Mikolashek was telling the brigade commander that one of his missions was to be prepared to conduct "full-spectrum operations," everything from peacekeeping operations through combined arms warfare; on the other, CENTCOM was forbidding Wiercinski access to what has historically been the biggest killer on the battlefield: artillery. It is hard to avoid the conclusion that Franks's and Mikolashek's orders to Wiercinski paid lip service to the need to be prepared for "full-spectrum operations," but did not equip him for such, and that the reason was that senior U.S. commanders thought the war was all but won, and that combined arms battles were not in the cards.

When TF Rakkasan deployed to Kandahar in early January, it included Wiercinski's headquarters, an infantry battalion, a signals package to enable the brigade to maintain communications in that far-flung, desolate part of the world, beefed-up engineer and military intelligence elements, ten Chinooks with their crews and maintenance troops, eight Black Hawks (including three designed for medical evacuations), and some support soldiers. Wiercinski was also given a military police battalion to run the prison camp being built at Kandahar to house Taliban and Al Qaida prisoners. The force package "was an effort to get the right amount of force for the type of missions we had envisioned," Mikolashek said. "Our philosophy was that this was an unconventional war that we were going to introduce conventional forces into, and they were going to behave more like unconventional forces than conventional ones, because that had been successful up to that point in time. . . . We saw a fairly depleted, defeated enemy, with some pockets that were out there." This view emanated from the highest levels of the Defense Department. "Rumsfeld's view was the war was basically over," Army Secretary White said. "There was this kind of mindset that this was going to be a low-intensity conflict against an enemy that was running away." (Rumsfeld fired White in April 2003 after they had disagreed over the Crusader howitzer program, which Rumsfeld terminated.)

Senior U.S. officers also excused the decision to strip the Rakkasans of so much combat power on logistics grounds. Both Kandahar and Bagram airfields had been mined during the Afghan civil war, they noted, and the mines had to be cleared to create space for incoming units. Space at Kandahar was at a premium in the early weeks of 2002, before all the mines were cleared. In addition, the more combat soldiers there were in Kandahar, the more support soldiers would be needed to feed them, run their shower and laundry services, and handle their mail. Faced with potholed and cratered runways in Kandahar and Bagram and a strategic air bridge creaking under the weight of supporting even the relatively small deployment to Afghanistan, CENTCOM and Joint Staff officers were keen to keep the numbers as low as possible.

They were doing so under extraordinarily close supervision by Rumsfeld, who took it upon himself to ensure that not a single soldier was deployed to Afghanistan unless the defense secretary considered that soldier's presence there absolutely necessary. "Rumsfeld came to the table with a view that commanders are sloppy about their use of manpower," White said. The defense secretary decided to personally vet each request for forces. To officers hanging on his decisions, this meant an agonizing wait every time a request went forward. "I've watched lots of deployments in my life, [and] I have never seen the pain of deployments like there was for Afghanistan," Edwards said. It usually took two weeks, and sometimes three, for Rumsfeld to approve a request. The defense secretary's "micromanagement" resulted in what White called a process of "nickel-and-diming" each request for troops. Task Force Rakkasan and Frank Wiercinski fell victim to this process.

According to a senior officer in the Pentagon, Franks was not acting under orders from Rumsfeld or anyone else when he set the force cap. But the CENTCOM commander decided to minimize the number of troops in Afghanistan knowing his boss, the defense secretary, was scrutinizing each and every request for forces. The urge to keep the Rakkasan numbers down was shared by "the services," including, presumably, some in the Army leadership, who were reluctant to pony up more forces for a war that seemed to be winding down, the senior officer said. This reluctance to a the concern in the Pentagon over the size of the Rakkasan headquarters, and CENTCOM's obsession—based partly on the tone emanating from Rumsfeld's office—with keeping the numbers down, all were factors in the decision to drastically limit TF Rakkasan's combat power. "With Rakkasan there's a little shame probably on both sides," said the senior officer. "All of the people had fingerprints on this." But another Pentagon official, who participated in VTCs with Rumsfeld and Franks, said the defense secretary put extreme pressure on Franks to minimize the number of conventional troops in Afghanistan. "The responsibility goes all the way up the chain," he said.

White was more willing than others to cut Franks a break. "Tommy did the best he could with a very hardheaded guy who walks into the room thinking he's right before the discussion's even started," White said. In the Army secretary's view, even if Franks had argued strongly for the deployment of a larger conventional force, he would have gotten nowhere with Rumsfeld.

Since the Army's training revolution of the early 1980s, one of the service's rules of thumb had been "train as you fight." Whatever the rationale behind the decision, by forcing Wiercinski to deploy with less than half his brigade combat team, CENTCOM was ripping that page from the rule book and tearing it into tiny little pieces.

OVER the course of the first three weeks of 2002, Task Force Rakkasan's soldiers kissed their loved ones goodbye and climbed aboard chartered airliners that flew them to Germany, where they boarded military transports for the flight to Kandahar. Behind they left a country whose wounds were still raw. The chartered flights passed over New York, and at least one pilot, after telling air traffic control that he was flying troops en route to Afghanistan, received permission to divert from his assigned flight path in order to give his passengers a chance to gaze down at the floodlit Ground Zero, where the World Trade Center had stood. It was a somber moment, reinforcing for each of the soldiers why this deployment differed from those to Somalia, Haiti, Bosnia, Kosovo, or the Sinai. They were being sent to Afghanistan as neither peacekeepers nor nation-builders, but as defenders of their country.

SITUATED several miles outside the city of Kandahar on the edge of a desert, the airfield that was to be the Rakkasans' home for the next six weeks was bitterly cold. The troops from Fort Campbell arrived to find that special operators had taken all of the prime real estate—the string of garages and compounds on the grounds of the airfield, which had served as both a military air base and civilian airport—and the Marines had taken most of what was left. But the Marines were on their way out, and the soldiers' khaki GP (for General Purpose) Medium tents, which could sleep about a dozen troops in reasonable comfort, soon replaced the Marines' tiny pup tents. The Rakkasans quickly assumed the perimeter security mission. The infantrymen filled hundreds of sandbags as they built bunkers and guard posts along the edge of the airfield to replace the rudimentary "hasty fighting positions" left by the Marines. A couple of Rakkasan platoons escaped the drudgery of Kandahar when they flew north to perform security for the pilot team safe house in Khowst. Others went to Zawar Khili, about twenty miles southwest of Khowst, to conduct sensitive site exploitation missions (combing through the debris left after enemy hideouts were hit from the air). But the vast majority of the Rakkasans remained at Kandahar. They repelled a few minor probing attacks of the airfield by unknown assailants but otherwise settled into a life of dreary routine. The exceptions to this rule were Wiercinski and his staff. Not only were they coordinating the steady buildup of their task force, they were also handling a new mission from Mikolashek, who had designated the Rakkasans as the quick reaction force for Task Forces K-Bar and 64 (the Australian Special Air Service). This meant the staff had to draw up a plan to reinforce or rescue the commandos every time one of the special ops forces launched on a mission, which was several times a night. The pace got so hectic in early February that the Rakkasan staff wrote seventeen plans in seventy-two hours. "The battalion and brigade staffs were literally pulling their hair out," recalled Lieutenant Colonel Jim Larsen, Wiercinski's executive officer. "We were dealing with a mission we'd never trained on, with people we'd never trained with, facing an ambiguous threat in a completely unknown environment. It was chaotic. We were all walking around in a state of sleep deprivation for the first month."

But because the Rakkasans never had to execute any of these missions, they remained transparent to Wiercinski's increasingly frustrated junior officers and enlisted troops. Every night the infantrymen watched K-Bar's SEALs and Special Forces operators fly off on secret missions. For the Rakkasans, eager for action after months of hard training and with a proud legacy to uphold, shivering in the sand at Kandahar watching tumbleweeds blow on the other side of the perimeter fence was less than they had bargained for.

AS the Rakkasans adjusted to their new environment, Cody, Edwards, and others continued their efforts to beef up the task force. Wiercinski asked again for his artillery, as well as more Chinooks and Black Hawks. The generals finally persuaded Franks to allow a single company of Apaches—eight attack helicopters, only a third of a battalion—to join TF Rakkasan in Kandahar. They also got permission to deploy another three Chinooks, although a crash quickly reduced the total number in the task force to twelve. But as far as U.S. troops were concerned, that was it for TF Rakkasan. Cody never received a straight answer about who had prevented his brigade commander from taking more combat power with him into a war zone. But at CFLCC the answer was clear. Tommy Franks "had at the back of his mind, just like Rumsfeld did, that the Army was too big, too slow, too unresponsive, and wanted too many things," Edwards said. (The reader may question why Franks, an Army general after all, and an artillery officer into the bargain, would take so many decisions that appeared to denigrate the value of the Army and of artillery. In this context, it is worth noting that Army leaders thought that Franks believed he owed his appointment as head of CENTCOM to the Marines, and to Marine General Anthony Zinni, his predecessor at CENTCOM, in particular. If the choice had been up to the Army's leadership, Jack Keane probably would have become CENTCOM commander. "It did give Franks some disgruntlement with the Army way of doing business," a general said.)

Wiercinski's force was also boosted by the arrival in late January and early February of a 900-strong battle group formed around the 3rd Battalion of Princess Patricia's Canadian Light Infantry. The Canadian formation was placed under Wiercinski's command and included three infantry companies and some reconnaissance elements. Wiercinski planned for the Canadians to take over the security mission at Kandahar, freeing the 101st troops for missions further afield. When he took the call from Bagram, Wiercinski knew Task Force Rakkasan didn't represent anything close to its usual killing power. Nevertheless, the colonel thought he had enough forces on the ground to conduct "full-spectrum" operations. After a month manning guard posts and conducting uneventful patrols, the Rakkasans were ready for some action. As he put the phone down, his heart started to beat a little faster. He wondered what challenges lay ahead. *Sounds like the pace is picking up,* he thought as excitement coursed through him. *It's time to go to work.*

12.

THE addition of Wiercinski's force drove Mikolashek to reexamine the forthcoming operation's command and control structure. What had started out as a plan for a fairly limited mission by Dagger and Zia's troops under Mulholland's command had more than doubled in size. Moreover, Mulholland and Wiercinski held the same rank—colonel—and would need someone above them to make decisions in the case of disagreement. Mikolashek realized he needed to install a tactical headquarters in Bagram to integrate the special operators and conventional forces. Mulholland had already come to the same conclusion. In early February he sat in one of Bagram's decrepit buildings discussing the evolving plans for the Shahikot with Haas and Blaber, who was still based out of the Ariana, but making frequent trips to Gardez, Khowst, and Bagram. All three officers were dressed in civilian clothes and their conversation was similarly informal. The chat turned to who should be placed in charge of the upcoming operation. "You should," Blaber told Mulholland, who was wearing his signature black-and-white Arab kaffiyeh headdress as a scarf. "How am I going to get the assets?" replied Mulholland, referring to the larger headquarters he believed was required to command and control such a complex operation. "Sir, you don't need the assets," Blaber said.

Blaber thought Mulholland, the Dagger boss, should command the operation because he alone of the various colonels and generals in Bagram had followed the operation from its inception, he had the most experience of operations in Afghanistan and his troops along with Zia Lodin were to be the main effort. Some special ops officers were wary of allowing command and control to pass out of their hands. Up to now, Afghanistan had been their battlefield. The introduction of an infantry brigade and a higher headquarters from the conventional Army would distinctly alter the war's character. To Blaber, the most critical part of the battle would be finding and isolating the enemy in the Shahikot. He knew the team of CIA operatives, Special Forces soldiers, and AFO operators at Gardez could accomplish that. Once battle was joined, tight coordination between allied forces would be vital. Since Mulholland's Dagger staff had worked with all of them and understood who was doing what and why, Mulholland was the ideal choice to command the operation, Blaber said.

Blaber welcomed an expanded role for conventional forces. But other special ops troops feared the arrival of the "Big Army" would stifle initiative and impose a rigidity from which the campaign had heretofore been refreshingly free. Mulholland understood these concerns. But as he watched the concept of operations for the Shahikot developing, the Dagger commander couldn't help but conclude that it was growing too big for his headquarters to handle on its own. He had already been sharing intel on the Shahikot with Hagenbeck, the Mountain commander. Now he took the conversations a step further. If Franks wanted to attack the valley, Mulholland told Hagenbeck, then the size of the enemy and the way they appeared to be arrayed argued for a higher-level headquarters on the ground. "Would you be willing for me to ask General Franks for you to command and control this?" Mulholland asked the two-star. Hagenbeck's answer was as immediate as it was predictable: "Absolutely."

Having secured Hagenbeck's approval, Mulholland took his suggestion up the chain of command. It met with a positive response from CENTCOM and

CFLCC. Mikolashek gave Hagenbeck an overview of the operation being planned, but without all the details, because Hagenbeck didn't have the clearances necessary to be read in on the compartmented intel. This was not as frustrating as it might have been for Hagenbeck. He had been in the Army for thirty years and was used to not being read in on every detail of an upcoming operation immediately. What *was* frustrating for him and his troops was the two months spent cooling their heels at K2 while a couple of hundred miles to the south, their country was at war. "We were really chomping at the bit to do something," Hagenbeck said. "We thought we'd gotten there at the tail end of the war in Afghanistan, and we weren't gonna see much action. So when we heard that there was some Al Qaida there, we wanted to be a part of the fight. When [Mulholland] extended that offer, we jumped at the chance." But Mikolashek said nothing at first to indicate any intent to send Hagenbeck's headquarters south. The Mountain staff continued planning their return to Fort Drum. Within a few days, those plans were shelved. In a video-teleconference around February 5 Mikolashek gave Hagenbeck as direct a hint as he could that his mission was about to change: "Start thinking about how to spell 'Bagram.'"

JIM Larsen, in Bagram to establish a Rakkasan quick reaction force, strode briskly along the 300 meters of muddy road that separated the Rakkasan tents by the runway from Dagger's advanced operating base in the middle of the base's cantonment area. The AOB building looked from the outside as if it might once have been a movie theater for the Soviet troops garrisoned at the base. But the large kitchen and sleeping quarters in the rear of the building suggested it had actually been a mess hall. Now it was occupied by 5th Special Forces Group's B Company, who had patched up the roof with some plywood to make the run-down building habitable. The work area was at the front of the building. This was the room where briefings were held, and it was full of people when Larsen climbed the steps leading up to the front door and disappeared inside.

The Rakkasan officer walked into a scene he found hard to fathom. About twenty Dagger personnel and at least one TF Bowie representative were discussing the Shahikot Valley. Most of the Dagger troops appeared to be NCOs, but it was hard for Larsen to tell, because none of the long-haired, bearded men wore a uniform, and all called each other by their first names. But Larsen didn't find this unusual. He'd gotten used to the sight of heavily armed commandos in ball caps and jeans. What surprised him was that Major Perry Clark, Rosengard's deputy, was leading this scruffy group—none of whom resembled an infantryman's version of a soldier, let alone an officer—through a textbook version of the Army's military decision-making process. This was the meticulous—some would say needlessly detailed—process by which Army doctrine says units should plan operations. It is the sort of thing that Ranger and other light infantry staffs pride themselves on, but not something that Larsen expected from Special Forces troops. Having taught tactics for two years at the Army's Command and General Staff College, Larsen knew good staff work when he saw it. He was seeing it now.

The reason for the meeting was clear. Mikolashek had ordered Dagger to draw up a plan for the Shahikot that relied on Special Forces and Afghans as the main effort. Clark was leading his staff through a "receipt of mission," in which they analyzed the task in hand, the intelligence on the enemy, the troops, the terrain, and the time available in order to arrive at an operational concept that had a good chance of success. Once the discussion moved beyond what was known or assumed about the enemy to the topic of what troops might be available, eyes turned to Larsen: What could TF Rakkasan contribute? Almost two full infantry battalions, he replied, so long as Wiercinski was allowed to pull most of 1-187 out of Jacobabad. Larsen didn't pick the two battalion figure just because that was all TF Rakkasan could spare. It also seemed to be the minimum needed to execute the role envisioned for the 101st troops: sealing the passes on the valley's eastern side. Larsen reckoned it would take about a company (90 to 100 men) to close each pass completely. "When you started doing the math, it quickly became a two-battalion operation," he said. That seemed to satisfy Clark and his colleagues. The Dagger guys hadn't specified how they wanted the infantry forces to get to their blocking positions, but to Larsen there was only one answer—air assault, the 101st's raison d'être. "This mission had the 101st written all over it," he said later. He was confident that the "psychological impact" of helicopters full of troops descending suddenly out of the sky would unhinge the enemy fighters. The meeting moved on, but Larsen's mind was already racing. *Two battalions!* That meant a brigade-level air assault, something that had only happened once since Vietnam. But would two battalions be enough? The intelligence on the number of enemy in the valley was vague. *We'll need a reserve,* Larsen thought. During a break, he dashed across the road to a tall gray building that housed the forward command post of 10th Mountain's 1-87 Infantry. Although most of that battalion was still at K2, in late November the battalion commander, Lieutenant Colonel Paul LaCamera, had moved his C Company and a small command element to Bagram, where his troops assumed the same perimeter security and other force protection missions they had been conducting in Uzbekistan.

Larsen and LaCamera had served in the 2nd Ranger Battalion together in the late1980s, and Larsen wondered if his buddy wanted to get in on the action being briefed across the street. As luck would have it, LaCamera was visiting K2. His operations officer raised him on the phone. Believing two Rakkasan battalions ought to be able to handle the couple of hundred enemy fighters thought to be in the Shahikot, Larsen was hoping LaCamera might spare a platoon that the Rakkasans could use as a reserve. But LaCamera told Larsen that he could probably commit a company to the fight. (By the next day LaCamera was talking about making his whole battalion available.) Larsen retraced his steps and sat through the remainder of the briefings. At the end of the evening Clark invited him to another meeting. This one was to be held the next day in the Dagger safe house in Kabul, and Larsen was welcome to hitch a ride with the Dagger contingent driving down the next morning. But there was a catch: He would have to wear civilian clothes, so as not to attract attention en route to the capital (as if a couple of vehicles full of well-armed American-looking young men in mufti would pass unnoticed by the locals).

Larsen didn't have any civilian clothes in his rucksack. But the Ranger old-boy network came through yet again for him. An ex-Ranger assigned to TF Bowie loaned Larsen a set of civilian clothes for the journey. Combined with an Afghan hat and scarf somehow procured for him by another Rakkasan staff officer, the civvies did the trick. No one would mistake Larsen for an Afghan tribesman any time soon, but at least the Dagger guys would let him ride in their pickup trucks.

The next morning the two-vehicle convoy assembled by the AOB. In addition to Larsen, the non-Dagger passengers included three CFLCC staff officers who had flown in specifically to attend the Kabul briefing: Lieutenant Colonel Andy Nocks, from the deep operations cell; Lieutenant Colonel Craig Bishop, who coordinated special ops activities in the CFLCC operations cell; and Commander Jim Markloff, a military intelligence officer. Larsen climbed into the back seat of a maroon Toyota pickup. As a Ranger company executive officer, he had jumped into Rio Hato airfield during the Panama invasion, and another Ranger job had taken him to Haiti in 1994, but this was a different level of adventure altogether. The soldiers crammed into the cabs of the two trucks had their weapons—M4s and 9mm pistols for each of the Dagger troops—locked and loaded. There were to be no refreshment or bathroom breaks. The full water bottles in the trucks were for drinking, the empty ones for pissing in. The trip lasted about two hours. Gazing out of the window as he rode, Larsen was awestruck by the Shomali Plain's lunar landscape, the rusting hulks of T-55 tanks and ZSU antiaircraft guns by the side of the road, the unexploded ordnance lying on the curb like traffic cones that a passing vehicle had casually knocked aside, and the cemeteries full of fighters who had fallen in battle, with black, green, and red Afghan flags fluttering in the winter wind above many of the graves. The Shomali Plain marked the northern approach to Kabul. The green flatlands had served as a battlefield during each of the last twenty-three years, and it showed.

The Toyotas pulled up outside the safe house at midday. Larsen, who had spent the last few weeks shivering in dusty tents in Kandahar eating MREs, walked into the safe house and discovered how the other half lived. Task Force Dagger and the CIA had been the architects of the triumph over the Taliban, and for those Special Forces soldiers lucky enough to be based in Kabul, the palatial safe house, which had served as a Taliban guesthouse, represented the first fruits of victory. "It was a beautiful mansion, four stories, each floor probably had 900 or 1,000 square feet. Just an amazing place, and they lived in that with a cook," said an envious visitor. "They were living good." Larsen was equally impressed. "The best thing about this place was the food," he said. "They had real food, not like Kandahar or Bagram. I mean real food—meat, rice, bread, and snacks with recognizable names on the wrappers."

Larsen's sense of arriving at some Shangri-la was only slightly disturbed by the odor of mildew that greeted his nostrils as he descended the stairs into the dank basement where the meeting was to be held. Several days earlier Dagger and Bowie had announced they would be holding a meeting to allow Dagger to present their concept for an operation to crush the enemy forces in the area south of Gardez known as Shahikot, and to figure out how best to fuse the various sources of intelligence. Representatives from K-Bar, the CIA, Task Force 11, CFLCC, the Coalition and Joint Civil-Military Operations Task Force, and Task Force Rakkasan had been invited. Now about forty-five people were crowding into the basement. A sense of expectation hung in the air. These men had known nothing but victory in Afghanistan, and now the opportunity to take a huge step toward completing the destruction of Al Qaida appeared to present itself. Larsen didn't recognize most of the attendees, and their civilian clothes made it hard to even hazard a guess which organizations they worked for. But he spotted a few familiar faces, including those of Pete Blaber and a major named Mark O. who ran the AFO operation in northern Afghanistan out of the Ariana. Larsen knew both from their time in the Ranger Regiment and was glad to renew acquaintances. "It was great to see their faces again, even with the beards," he said. "They were real warriors—true to the core." Among the others there were Gary Harrell, regarded by Larsen as "a legend," Commander Ed Winters—a SEAL who was the TF 11 operations officer—and Chris Haas, who served as the moderator.

Rich, the CIA chief of station, began by updating the group on the latest intelligence. His spies were reporting about 200-250 enemy fighters in the Shahikot, the only remaining Al Qaida concentration in Afghanistan. He urged action. History showed that Al Qaida and its allies did not like to fight in the winter, preferring to husband their forces for spring offensives. His conclusion was blunt: *We must take the battle to the enemy by attacking this winter, forcing the enemy to fight in conditions to which he is unaccustomed, when the passes are less accessible.* The experienced agent pressed for action by February 15, just a week away.

The senior AFO intelligence analyst, Sergeant First Class Glenn P., laid out everything that was known about the Shahikot. Human, signals, and imagery intelligence pointed to a concentration of between 200 and 1,000 Al Qaida, IMU, and Taliban fighters in the Shahikot, Glenn told his audience. There were also indicators that a high-value target was in or around the valley. Brian Sweeney, who had flown down from K2, presented a detailed analysis of how and why the enemy was gathering south of Gardez. He didn't have all the answers, but he used deductive reasoning to fill in the gaps as he outlined his "ratline" theory. "That was one of the best briefs I've ever heard," Blaber told him when he had finished.

The talks by Sweeney and Glenn P. complemented each other. Their analysis was founded on the assumption that the Al Qaida forces at Tora Bora had escaped via two routes: one straight into Pakistan and another southwest to the Gardez-Khowst region. Those who had taken the southwest route were now ensconced south of Gardez in some of Afghanistan's most defensible terrain. They had been joined by IMU fighters who had fled south through Logar and Paktia as the Taliban regime disintegrated. The Shahikot's proximity to Pakistan made it an even more attractive refuge to Al Qaida and their allies. Analysts present from other agencies, including the CIA and the Defense Intelligence Agency, agreed.

Perry Clark then outlined Dagger's concept for attacking the Shahikot. It was the same concept Larsen had seen the Dagger troops refining the night before, involving an attack from the west by Zia's troops and their Special Forces advisers, with the Rakkasans sealing the escape routes to the south and east. However, Clark and Glenn Thomas, the Texas 14 team leader who was also in the room, poured cold water on Rich's hopes of attacking within the next week. Zia's force would not be ready for another ten to fifteen days, they said. The

Dagger proposal was only a concept. No one beyond Dagger had approved it, and no other forces had been officially committed. Harrell became frustrated with the lack of commitment he perceived from some in the room. Task Force 11, represented by Winters, was particularly reluctant. Winters said his organization would consider participating in the operation, but wanted no role in the planning, for fear it would distract them from the hunt for high-value targets. Dagger and Bowie wanted to know who stood with them as they worked to turn this from a concept in a dingy basement in Kabul to violent, bloody reality at 9,000 feet in the Shahikot. "Okay, who's in?" Harrell asked loudly, as if he was rounding up a Wild West posse, not setting the stage for the biggest battle U.S. troops had fought in a generation. Blaber was first to respond. "We're in!" he said loudly and without hesitation. Sensing Blaber's confidence, "the rest of us followed suit," Larsen recalled.

Larsen's enthusiasm actually unnerved some special operators in the meeting. They became concerned when the Rakkasan executive officer stood up and told them: "The key to success here is the air assault. Throughout history the air assault has struck fear into the enemy's hearts." Larsen later said he was trying to repeat something he remembered from Trevor Dupuy's book *Understanding Defeat*: that most defeats in battle resulted when one side became unhinged by the prospect of an enemy maneuvering on its flanks or in its rear. But to the others his words might just as easily have been spoken by the ghost of Major General Lee using Larsen as a medium. Sixty years after he articulated it, Lee's vision of the 101st falling on its enemies "like a thunderbolt from the skies" still held the division's officers in its thrall. Larsen made no apologies for being an air assault true believer, but others in the room, particularly the special ops men, were not convinced that the air assault held the "key to success" in the Shahikot. After Larsen's outburst, "We kind of looked at each other and got worried," one attendee remembered. "'Uh-oh. What did we get ourselves into?'"

13.

IN the late morning of February 10, Wiercinski climbed aboard a Black Hawk at Kandahar and made the four-hour flight to Bagram with Major Michael Gibler, his operations officer, and Major Dennis Yates, his fire support officer.

When the helicopter landed at Bagram in midafternoon, Larsen and Lieutenant Colonel Ron Corkran, the 1-187 commander, were waiting. They took Wiercinski into the tent that housed their tiny headquarters. As Wiercinski tore open an MRE's brown plastic packaging, the officers huddled around Larsen's laptop. Over the cacophony of radio chatter inside the tent and helicopter engines just a few yards outside on the runway, Larsen ran through a slide briefing that enlightened the brigade commander on why he had been summoned to Bagram (security concerns had prevented Larsen telling his commander over the phone). "It's an operation in a place called the Shahikot Valley," Larsen said. "They're going to use us as blocking forces initially, in an air assault operation, I would assume. I don't have the full details about where we would be going [in the valley]—obviously that would be something we have to figure out. It's going to be a combination of Afghan forces, Task Force Dagger, Task Force Rakkasan, and even, potentially, some other elements." Wiercinski was excited. *Finally we're going to get to do a real full-up mission here,* he thought. But his enthusiasm was tempered by skepticism that there was a large enemy force in the valley. "So many of the targets that we and K-Bar had been in were cold," Larsen explained later.

That evening the Rakkasan officers walked over to the AOB to hear Dagger's ideas on how to tackle the large enemy presence they had apparently detected south of Gardez. Wiercinski sat down on a folding chair and glanced around. There were about thirty-five men in the room, including Mulholland, Rosengard, Haas and sundry other Dagger officers, as well as Bishop and Nocks from CFLCC, Blaber and Rich, the CIA Kabul chief of station. Out of the corner of his eye Wiercinski spied LaCamera, whom he knew from the Ranger Regiment and who had returned from K2. The meeting followed the normal pattern for an operational brief, with each principal Dagger staff officer speaking in turn. The task force's intelligence officer, Air Force Major Barry Leister, summarized the intelligence that had led Dagger to focus on the valley. Sweeney presented his "ratline" analysis. Then the irrepressibly flamboyant Mark Rosengard, also newly arrived from K2, took center stage. Dressed as he was in full Tajik garb, including a flat wool "pakhul" hat, with his thick black hair and mustache, many in the crowd assumed Rosengard was an Afghan until he opened his mouth and his broad Boston vowels rang out. Using the laser on his pistol to point to maps and overhead photos pinned to easels behind him, the Dagger operations officer laid out his concept of operation in detail. Wiercinski, Gibler, and Yates were hearing for the first time what the others in the room already knew: that intelligence sources had identified as many as 200 to 250 Al Qaida guerrillas in the Shahikot, but the fighters were thought to be living with and among their own women and children, as well as other civilians who were locals with no Al Qaida connection. This drove Rosengard's concept, in which Zia's men would identify the enemy fighters among the valley's civilian population, before either killing them or forcing them toward the passes blocked by the Rakkasans. (Rosengard referred to the notion of bringing a force to bear that would scatter the enemy fighters towards the valley exits as "splashing the puddle.")

Listening to Rosengard and looking at the maps, which were already overlaid with acetate sheets marked with colored arrows and lines drawn with alcohol pens, Wiercinski realized that Rosengard's team had already invested considerable time and effort in the planning. After Rosengard finished, Mulholland discussed what he hoped to achieve. By the end of the meeting the Rakkasan officers were eagerly anticipating the operation. "This is what we had been training for for years," Larsen said.

With the meeting about to end, Chris Haas and Rich pulled Blaber aside and recommended he give a quick briefing on the Shahikot, emphasizing the need for surprise and the downsides of using Chinooks. When Rosengard asked if there was anything else they needed to discuss, Blaber strode forward. He updated the audience on everything his teams had discovered about the people in the area, including the enemy, and said if anyone had any requests for information to let him know and AFO would do its best to answer them. He then discussed the terrain and environment, and warned the others that using helicopters did not obviate the need for smart tactics. "There are only two air approaches into the valley, and we should assume both will be covered by heavy weapons," he said. "Remember, every enemy on the planet expects the U.S. military to attack using helos, this enemy will be no different. The time it will take you to brake, flare, hover, and land will make you highly vulnerable to his antiaircraft weapons."

The briefing over, Mulholland and Wiercinski talked over the operation together. The two had never served together before being posted to Fort Campbell, but they and their wives had gotten to know each other at social functions, and Wiercinski knew of Mulholland's strong reputation in the special ops community. "I felt very, very comfortable with John Mulholland," Wiercinski said. To the Rakkasan commander, the tone of his conversation with Mulholland was one of mutual trust and support.

The Rakkasan officers strolled back to their tent. Larsen detected a lack of enthusiasm on the part of his boss about the role that LaCamera's battalion would play in the operation. The Rakkasan commander—often known by his radio call sign "Rak 6"—had only two of his infantry battalions, 1-187 and 2-187, in theater. CENTCOM's force caps meant 3-187 still languished at Fort Campbell. It seemed increasingly likely that LaCamera's battalion would fill the gap left by 3-187's absence. "Rak 6 wasn't really keen on the idea because we still had 3-187 back at Campbell and he really, really wanted to get them in the fight," Larsen said. "It was wearing on him emotionally not to have the entire brigade combat team together. Though Paul LaCamera and his command sergeant major, Frank Grippe, were highly respected within the Ranger community of which Colonel Wiercinski and I were longtime members, and we were convinced that 1-87 would perform well in combat, Rak 6 would have felt like a million bucks if he could get the Rakkasans' third battalion to Afghanistan."

Wiercinski, Gibler, and Yates returned to Kandahar the next morning. They now knew the mission. Their job over the next several days was to develop a plan for the Rakkasans that they could present to the other commands involved in the operation. Once back at Kandahar, the Rakkasan planning cell conducted a standard Army mission analysis, which required the staff to examine the mission, the enemy, the troops available, the terrain, and the time period in which the mission must be accomplished. Wiercinski told his planners to give the Apaches a forward arming and refueling point close to the Shahikot, to maximize the use of close air support from fixed-wing aircraft, and to ensure that a large reserve force was retained to conduct follow-on operations. "We thought that by striking hard in the Shahikot Valley, other enemy elements around there would start moving, and we wanted to be able to pounce on them quickly," Larsen said. Wiercinski told them to assign highest priority to ensuring the safest possible helicopter landing zones for the initial insertion of the infantry force. Without good LZs, an air assault mission would be an invitation to disaster.

MEANWHILE, Bishop and Nocks remained at Bagram as Mikolashek's representatives as the plan for the Shahikot developed. One evening a couple of days after the big meeting in the Kabul safe house, the two officers were sitting in the Bowie headquarters, talking about whether the operation in the Shahikot deserved a name of its own, and if so, what that name should be. They knew giving the operation its own name might be courting controversy. So far the guidance they had received was that "there was only one name for any and all operations—Operation Enduring Freedom," which was the name the U.S. government had given to the entire war against Al Qaida and the Taliban since September 11. But the operation in the Shahikot was shaping up to be the largest set-piece battle of the war. It seemed like it deserved a monicker of its own, so they decided to stick a name on the latest version of the plan and see if it stuck through the next round of briefings. The name Nocks had been using was Operation Shwack, a comic-book–style reference to the idea of suddenly bringing an overwhelming force down on the enemy. Amused, Larsen pointed out that if this operation came off, it would be on front pages all over the world, so it would probably need a "sexier" name than "Shwack." Nocks and Bishop went back to the drawing board.

Other elements were being added to the plan. In addition to the battle of envelopment conceived by Rosengard, in which Zia's force would attack from the west while the Rakkasans sealed the escape routes in the east, there was talk of using other G-chiefs and A-teams to create a wider perimeter around the Shahikot, in order to capture or kill any enemy fighters who slipped the noose being drawn by the Rakkasans and Zia's troops. Task Force K-Bar teams would be inserted to watch the passes that led toward Pakistan. The concentric circles of pressure around the enemy in the Shahikot reminded Nocks and Bishop of a snake crushing its prey in its coils. Each would later—politely—claim credit for the suggestion that followed, but what is beyond reasonable doubt is that by the end of the conversation they had decided on a name they thought fit the operation perfectly: *Anaconda.*

14.

THINGS were getting crowded—and sometimes a bit tense—at the Gardez safe house. Thomas and his Texas 14 team were scheduled to return home, but with the Shahikot operation just weeks away, they were told to stay put. Meanwhile, their replacements, ODA 372, a team from 3rd Special Forces Group led by Captain Matthew McHale, had arrived. With two A-teams and burgeoning CIA and AFO recon contingents, there was little space left in the house itself, so Thomas put the new team up in a tent in the yard. Initially neither A-team was comfortable with the new arrangement. Special Forces teams prefer—indeed are trained—to operate on their own, not with other teams. "It's like moving in with your brother," McHale said.

CONDITIONS were primitive. "It was wintertime, and it saps you. It snowed and rained almost every day," said an inhabitant. "The place was mud." At each of the compound's four corners was a guard tower that contained a room reached by ladders from the ground. The AFO operators used these as sleeping areas. There were two spacious rooms in the front wall, divided by the gate into the compound. The Dagger and AFO men worked in one of these rooms, the CIA in the other. Spread over a wall of the Dagger/AFO operations center were maps and overhead imagery of the Shahikot, including a 1:100,000 map of the area from the valley all the way back to Gardez and another map of the Shahikot on which all the past signals intelligence "hits" had been marked.

The upstairs was divided into bedrooms. There was no plumbing. "We were shitting in one hole," said a resident. Food and water were air-dropped regularly by MC-130s. The Americans fixed sheets of clear plastic across the window spaces in the mud walls. At night they used candles. They had a generator, but the need to conserve fuel meant it was used only to power the radios. (Candles also had the advantage of not silhouetting the men through the windows.)

DESPITE the spartan living arrangements, the Dagger soldiers felt they were making good progress in their primary mission: organizing and training the Afghan troops. Texas 14 had laid the groundwork with Zia. The team hadn't seen any combat with Zia, but they had forged tight bonds with him and his men. The G-chief was physically brave and, an operator said, "smart in a crafty kind of political way." Zia's second-in-command was his cousin, a fighter in his thirties named Rasul. Almost six feet tall, of slender build and dressed in a brown leather jacket he never took off, Rasul was a reserved man with an almost effeminate demeanor. But the U.S. soldiers soon realized he was also "super smart" and that they would do well to mark his words.

With Texas 14 having bonded so well with Zia's troops, it might have been difficult for McHale's team to make an impression with the Afghans. But an incident shortly before they arrived in Gardez led to a solution. The background to the episode was a power struggle between Pacha Khan Zadran, a local strongman, and the Gardez shura. The two sides fought a battle in which the safe house was caught in the crossfire. After Texas 14 sent some of Zia's troops to warn each side to stop, the Gardez shura decided to contribute some better troops to work with the Americans. So a new company of Pushtun fighters under a commander named Hoskheyar joined up with Texas 14 a few days prior to McHale's arrival. The U.S. officers settled on a logical division of labor: Thomas's team would continue working with Zia and Rasul, while McHale's team focused on organizing and training Hoskheyar's force.

Zia was now the equivalent of a battalion commander with two companies—Rasul's and Hoskheyar's—underneath him. (A third company was also organized under Ziabdullah, the Pushtun from Logar who had accompanied Texas 14 to Gardez. But the Americans considered Ziabdullah and his men less reliable than the others, and minimized their involvement in the assault on the Shahikot.) The A-teams organized each company into platoons and squads along U.S. lines, then held a ceremony to award the squad and platoon leaders and company commanders their rank. The rank insignia were no more than little silver-colored buttons that the Americans had bought locally.

Practices such as this were at the heart of the unconventional warfare approach Special Forces soldiers used to win over local militia forces. "You think it's a trivial thing, but they wore that on every single outfit," said a Dagger soldier. "If they took their coat off, they would take the pin off and put it back on their next outer garment. It means a lot to them. They were proud about their ranks. Just a little button on a safety pin. That gave them their status in that structure."

Of course, while silver buttons and mutual respect went a long way toward winning the Afghan fighters' hearts and minds, the cash the CIA doled out also helped. Although Special Forces were considered the United States' foremost unconventional warfare specialists, they were prohibited by law from actually passing out money or "lethal aid"—weapons and ammunition—to the forces they organized and trained. Only the CIA had that right. In Gardez, that meant that every few days a Soviet-built Mi-17 helicopter—one of a small fleet flown by a combination of U.S. military pilots and contracted foreigners—would land on the road beside the safe house and the CIA team's "money guy"—his entire job seemed to be to fetch and distribute cash—would run out of the compound and jump aboard. He would return with several holdalls full of U.S. currency, which he gave to Zia and the other Afghan commanders.

Like most men raised in the Afghan countryside, Zia's fighters took naturally to guerrilla warfare and were comfortable with firearms. Veterans of the war with the Soviets were sprinkled throughout the force. But they lacked the discipline and understanding necessary to combine mortar and machine gun fire with infantry maneuver. They would need these skills in the upcoming operation, and the Dagger troops had only a few short weeks to teach them. Hoskheyar's men appeared to be particularly raw recruits. The A-team members had to walk a fine line, avoiding the appearance of being too bossy and ordering Zia and his men about as if the Afghans knew nothing on the one hand, but not patronizing them on the other. In short, it required the U.S. soldiers to treat the Afghans with respect. A Dagger soldier said it helped to view the Zia's troops as the Afghan equivalent of the Minutemen of the American Revolution. "They're fighting for their country, and you're gonna organize them, treat them like soldiers, give them respect, to the point where, in the tents at night, when you start talking about how to fight, we do as much listening as we do talking," he said. "We don't tell them, 'You're gonna fight exactly this way,' it's 'Let's draw pictures in the dirt,' and 'How would you do this?'"

Despite the emphasis on developing mutual trust, however, the Dagger troops didn't breathe a word to the Afghans of the plan to attack the Al Qaida positions in the Shahikot. But the Afghans could tell something was up. The Americans weren't giving them brand-new weapons and clothing for the hell of it. The Special Forces operators told their Afghan partners that this was all in preparation for some training "up north." But whenever the conversation between the Dagger troops and the Afghans turned to Al Qaida, the Afghans would reply simply, "Shahikot."

THE CIA presence in Gardez grew to about fifteen or twenty personnel by the end of February, of whom maybe seven or eight were "shooters," with analysts and technicians making up the remainder. They were led by a six-foot-tall, fit, affable man with blondish hair and a thick beard. He was in his mid-forties and was one of the Special Activities Division's most experienced operatives. Unlike many other operatives in the division, he did not have a military special ops background, as far as the soldiers in Gardez knew, but he was a veteran of numerous covert operations, including those in Somalia and the Balkans, and had frequently worked with Delta. "He was brought in because they knew that they needed their best ground leader," said another safe house resident. Appropriately for someone with an outsize reputation for visionary combat leadership, this covert warrior went by not one but two *noms de guerre*: To some, he was "The Wolf," but most knew him only as "Spider."

Spider led a handpicked team whose level of expertise reflected the high priority that Rich, the Kabul chief of station, placed on the Shahikot. "They went with their first team," Haas said. "They pulled in their heavy hitters, their most experienced, trusted, successful paramilitary guys."

15.

WHILE the Special Forces soldiers put the Afghans through basic combat drills in the dirt outside the safe house, the CIA and AFO men were heavily engaged in what the military calls "IPB"—intelligence preparation of the battlefield, the business of building as accurate a picture as possible of the enemy's locations, force size, order of battle, intentions, and likely courses of action if attacked.

Blaber's decision to push his intel analysts and commo guys down to the safe house paid off in spades. Working closely with their CIA counterparts, and led by Glenn P. (described by a source as "the best of the best" of Delta's intel analysts), they collected all the available intelligence on activity in the mountains south of Gardez. Attempts to mine the U.S. intelligence community's databases came up dry. Before deploying to Afghanistan, Blaber had asked for any U.S. government information on Afghanistan based on debriefs of CIA operatives who had spent time with the mujahideen in the 1980s, but the search turned up little useful intelligence. And after ordering a lot of satellite imagery of the Shahikot, the Americans in Gardez were disappointed but not surprised to find that it revealed nothing. Any Al Qaida forces there were too lightly equipped and too adept at camouflage to stand out. This wasn't like looking for a Soviet—or even an Iraqi—tank brigade. The agency operatives and AFO troops realized they would have to rely primarily on human sources (HUMINT) and intercepted signals (SIGINT) to gain an understanding of what was going on in the valley.

The CIA controlled HUMINT collection in and around Gardez, a process that ranged from quizzing locals who approached the safe house looking to trade information for cash to hiring more traditional spies among the Gardez population. In general, the Americans treated the information gained from "walk-ups" as the least reliable. Because the locals thought the Americans wouldn't pay for vague tips, their reports often contained details they could not substantiate. But sometimes these reports seemed to pan out. On one occasion a local walk-in reported Arabs with vehicles in the Shahikot. Thomas sent a couple of Zia's men together with the walk-in toward the Shahikot in a vehicle to check out the story. Upon their return they told the Americans they had run into men manning machine-gun positions who blocked their path with a "semiplausible" tale about wanting to protect their herd's pasture.

In mid-February the CIA recruited a local doctor to drive toward the Shahikot and see what happened. The doctor, about forty to fifty years old, coaxed his beat-up sedan along the track that led east from the main Gardez to Zermat road, only to encounter Al Qaida roadblocks and surface-laid mines. He made it as far as the final turn around the southern end of the Whale before Al Qaida fighters dragged him from his car, beat him up, and stole his medical supplies before letting him go. His report gave the Americans at the safe house another vital piece of the puzzle they were assembling about the route the doctor had taken and what lay beyond it.

For signals intelligence, the team in Gardez could call on a six-man cell from the National Security Agency (NSA), the vast and secretive body that monitors the world's telephone and e-mail conversations. Led by Major Fred Egerer, a stocky Marine intelligence officer, the cell was the medium through which commanders in Bagram gained access to the U.S. government's vast panoply of signals intelligence technologies. Whenever a commander—particularly Harrell—was interested in enemy activity in a particular location, he would buttonhole Egerer and ask him, "What do you have on this?" Egerer would then check if any U.S. assets—satellites, airborne listening posts, or the U.S. military's ground-based voice intercept teams—were listening to transmissions from that part of Afghanistan. If nothing was focused on that patch of terrain, Egerer had authority to direct any element of the United States' signals intelligence apparatus to orient on the target area.

In Afghanistan, the communications systems used by America's enemies as well as by the general public ranged "from crappy walkie-talkies to the most advanced communications systems out there," a TF 11 source said. Ironically, the introduction of U.S. forces into Afghanistan so cluttered the ether that the NSA found it harder to collect signals intelligence once the Americans had arrived. Even when a signal was detected, that didn't equate to instant intelligence. "There's a false sense out there that if someone turns on their cell phone, we've got their name, just like that," said a special operator, clicking his fingers. "It takes hours for that stuff to be analyzed, and one of the things we worked on over there was getting the quickest 'flash to bang.'"

When U.S. forces began paying attention to the Shahikot, efforts to intercept enemy transmissions from the valley produced few results. This was partly due to good communications security practices on Al Qaida's part. "They used a lot of codes," said Lieutenant Colonel Jasey Briley, Hagenbeck's senior intelligence officer. "They would use code words like *wedding*. Normally that meant a meeting or something." But the dearth of SIGINT also resulted from the fact that there just weren't many radios, satellite phones, and other transmitters in the Shahikot at the turn of the year. Human intelligence thus played the key role in focusing U.S. attention on the Shahikot. But in January or early February, Blaber gave Egerer the Shahikot's coordinates and told him: "Crunch on this." This directive, along with the communications technology the enemy was bringing into the Shahikot as their forces built up, resulted in a stream of valuable intelligence. By the second week of February, the NSA was picking up enemy transmissions from the valley, as well as discussions between other individuals in Afghanistan and elsewhere about the forces gathering in the Shahikot.

This information was fed immediately to the pilot team in Gardez, who marked the spot where the SIGINT hit had been detected on the map of the Shahikot in their operations center. A few feet away, Glenn P. sat trawling classified intelligence databases for any mention of the Shahikot. "The intel databases now are just like the Internet," said a special operator. "You type in the name and out spit 400 technology reports, after action reports, anything that mentions the name, including overhead imagery [and] SIGINT hits that include the word *Shahikot*." Meanwhile, Spider worked to gain access to every CIA report that might shed light on what Al Qaida was up to in the valley.

As they gathered information, the Dagger and AFO troops in the safe house took time to digest it. Blaber wanted his men immersed in the history and topography of the area. If they had to conduct missions in the valley, he wanted them to know and understand the terrain as well as any Al Qaida guerrilla. In the evenings drinking coffee, tea, and cocoa and seated on wooden crates and MRE boxes around the small potbellied stoves they had brought with them, the operators read everything they could get their hands on that dealt with warfare in Afghanistan in general, and the Shahikot in particular. Before deploying from Bragg, the AFO guys had assembled a database of every known engagement of the Soviet war in Afghanistan. The safe house residents now pored over this, as well as both of Les Grau's books on the conflict. They learned that the mujahideen always sought to take and hold the high ground, and hid their artillery in creek beds. By knowing where the mujahideen had fought and how they had positioned themselves in the past, the operators hoped to figure out where the Taliban and Al Qaida would be most likely to set up ambushes now.

Around this time an old friendship bore fruit for Blaber. He had asked an intelligence analyst who had worked with Delta previously to look out for documents that could prove useful to AFO in Afghanistan. Back in the States, the analyst kept his eyes and ears open and came across a fascinating document that he forwarded to Blaber. It was the product of an interrogation of Ali Mohamed, an Egyptian-born Al Qaida operative arrested by U.S. authorities in September 1998, for his role in the bombings of the American embassies in Kenya and Tanzania on August 7 of that year. But his association with Al Qaida stretched back to the late 1980s.

Ali Abdelsoud Mohamed was born in Alexandria, Egypt, in 1952, and entered the Egyptian military, rising to become a special forces major. Along the way he became enchanted with radical Islam, secretly joining the Islamic Jihad organization that assassinated President Anwar Sadat in 1981. After his religious extremism led to his being forced out of the armed forces in 1984, Mohamed obtained a U.S. visa and traveled to the United States. Settling in California, he became a U.S. citizen after marrying an American woman he had met on the flight over. Bizarrely, Mohamed then joined the U.S. Army and became a supply sergeant at the John F. Kennedy Special Warfare Center and School at Fort Bragg, where he also lectured on Middle Eastern culture. Since his arrest, there had been published speculation that Mohamed was more than just a supply sergeant and was acting as a liaison between the CIA and the Afghan mujahideen.

Mohamed left the Army in 1989 and became even more deeply embedded in radical Islam. In the early 1990s he accompanied Ayman al-Zawahiri, the leader of Egyptian Islamic Jihad who would later become bin Laden's second-in-command, on a fund-raising trip—ostensibly for the Kuwaiti Red Crescent—to California. He also helped bin Laden set up shop in Sudan and Afghanistan. One of his duties was to train bin Laden's bodyguards. Mohamed also became a sometime informant to the Federal Bureau of Investigation, in 1993 giving American authorities their first insider's account of Al Qaida that has been publicized. Then he moved to east Africa to join the Al Qaida cell that would eventually bomb the embassies.

After the August 1998 bombings, Mohamed was one of five Al Qaida members arrested on charges related to the incidents. The U.S. government kept his arrest secret for eight months while it tried to negotiate a deal with him. Those efforts seemed to have foundered in May 1999 when he was publicly indicted. However, Mohamed's commitment to Al Qaida's cause apparently wavered when he was confronted with the prospect of spending the rest of his life behind bars. He cut a deal and pled guilty to five counts of conspiracy to kill American nationals and U.S. government employees on account of their official duties, to murder and kidnap, and to destroy U.S. property. The details of Mohamed's plea agreement were kept secret. But he divulged enough in his plea to suggest he had a very close understanding of Al Qaida's organizational structure, training, and operations in Afghanistan and elsewhere. No doubt some of the United States' best interrogators went to work to find out how much more he knew. The fruits of their labors now found their way into laptops in the Gardez safe house.

Mohamed told his interrogators that for hunting Al Qaida in Afghanistan, the best sources of human intelligence would be shopkeepers, shepherds, taxi drivers, and money changers. Shopkeepers, because the Arabs needed special spices for their food; shepherds, because the Arabs had to buy goats for their milk and lambs to eat; taxi drivers, because the Arabs didn't have their own cars and always hired Afghans to take them from town to town; and money changers, because the Arabs usually arrived with Pakistani rupees that they need to exchange for Afghanis. Mohamed also told the Americans that if he were searching for bin Laden, he would focus on the towns in and around Paktia—Khowst, Gardez, Jalalabad, Shkin, and Zermat—as well as in the mountains south of Gardez, in a valley called Shahikot. To the folks in the safe house, this was invaluable intelligence, even though they had heard nothing to suggest bin Laden himself was in the Shahikot.

Another document that found its way to the safe house was a debriefing of a Soviet officer who had fought the mujahideen around Gardez. This report mentioned Shahikot by name (although, curiously, the Soviet officer thought it was a village only seven kilometers south of Gardez), as well as several other villages in the area. The safe house residents paid special attention to what the officer said about how the mujahideen had used the terrain to their advantage, particularly in the Zhawar Ghar mountain range just east of the Shahikot. "Mujahideen retreating from Shahikot passed through the Zhawar Ghar mountain range, which was fairly easy to traverse, using a complex network of dry river and creek beds," the report stated. The description might have been taken straight from Sweeney's briefing. Clearly, the Arabs, Uzbeks, and Afghans fighting in Paktia had forgotten none of the lessons from their predecessors in the 1980s.

DURING this period Blaber was shuttling between Gardez, Khowst, and Kabul, where he met regularly with Rich and John. The more he and Spider read and heard, the more convinced they were that a sizable enemy force was coalescing in the Shahikot, and the more eager they became to mount more ambitious reconnaissance and intelligence gathering operations in that direction. It was increasingly clear to those in Gardez that getting full situational awareness of the Shahikot would require putting "eyes on the target," or at least getting much closer to the valley than any of the U.S. elements—CIA, AFO, or Dagger—had managed since Texas 14's aborted venture January 18. (Inexplicably, Blaber was unaware of Texas 14's foray into the Shahikot. Thomas later expressed surprise at this, and said he thought Blaber knew all about it.) The challenge the men in the safe house wrestled with was how to get close to the Shahikot without compromising the larger operation. Any heliborne insertion of reconnaissance teams ran a high risk of being seen by the valley's defenders. Even if the teams escaped, their very presence would tip the enemy off that something bigger was coming, with the likely result that many of them would disperse. Blaber was unwilling to countenance this risk. He announced there would be no helicopter infiltrations ("infils," in reconnaissance lingo) of AFO teams anywhere near the valley. If the AFO recce specialists were going to get close to the Shahikot, they would have to do it the hard way: walking through the mountains with everything they needed on their back, and without being seen.

Blaber began to talk to the others in Gardez about conducting a trial run by putting teams into the mountains to perform a "risk analysis." He wanted to see how far they could travel per night, how deep the snow was, and whether it was feasible to infiltrate the Shahikot unseen. In AFO this sort of trial run is called an environmental recon. But before he could begin to plan such a mission, Blaber had to overcome significant resistance from his chain of command related to two specific issues.

The first of these was what a special operator termed "the weird stigma" that senior U.S. commanders, including Blaber's bosses in Joint Special Operations Command, attached to winter operations in Afghanistan. February was still midwinter in Afghanistan, with deep snow clogging the mountain passes and temperatures well below freezing. Senior U.S. officers had read about campaigns in Afghanistan coming to a grinding halt during the Soviet war in the 1980s and the civil war in the 1990s, and were skeptical about the prospects of any operation in the mountains launched before spring. Most thought the mountains were impassable in summer, and wouldn't even consider attempting to traverse them in the winter.

The previous summer, while still in command of Delta's B Squadron, Blaber had taken thirty operators on an excursion to Montana's Bob Marshall Wilderness area. Inhabited by large numbers of gray wolves and grizzly bears, the "Bob" consisted of about 1.5 million acres of wilderness, with mountain ranges that rose over 9,300 feet. Blaber wanted to figure out "the art of the possible" in case Delta ever had to operate in such terrain. Split into teams of five, the operators walked cross-country over five mountain ranges to a pickup point almost 100 miles from where they'd set out five days earlier. They lived off what they carried in their rucksacks and what they caught in the streams. It was tough. The thin air at such altitudes magnified the effects of even the slightest exertion, leaving the extraordinarily fit men gasping for breath after the shortest movements. But they learned valuable lessons: They could walk over at least one mountain—and sometimes two—every day. With the right conditioning, a reasonable load, and by taking advantage of natural sources of water, the operators realized that a mountain was no longer the insurmountable obstacle it had appeared on a map, or when viewed from a distance. It was just another terrain feature.

At the time many in Delta had mocked the B Troop excursion. "What a boondoggle!" they had said. "That's a waste of time. You should be shooting." But eight months later Blaber's Montana adventure seemed prescient. Of course, Afghanistan in midwinter is colder than Montana in the summer, but the operators figured that one reason the Afghans, and, to a lesser extent, the Soviets, did so little winter fighting in the mountains was because they were ill equipped for it. For instance, Afghan fighters typically wore sandals or light shoes, even in winter—not the best choice of footwear for operating in the snow. By comparison, the special operators thought, U.S. troops were the best trained and best equipped in the world, and should be able to overcome whatever challenges they might face in the mountains. As one said, "That's why they give us $5,000 worth of winter clothing and boots—to actually use them."

Blaber also told the others in Gardez that his lifelong passion for backpacking and climbing had taught him that movement in the mountains would be easier in the winter than during the warmer months. In winter, streams that can impede progress are frozen over and at high altitudes the snow develops a thick crust that actually makes for a more level surface across which to walk than the undulating terrain underneath. The chances of a reconnaissance mission in the mountains running into an enemy patrol in midwinter were low, Blaber told them. Neither the Taliban nor their Al Qaida guests were nearly as well equipped as AFO to survive in the mountains. Unlike previous guerrillas the U.S. military had fought, these adversaries were not adept at living off the land. Even poor Afghans subsisted on flour, goat milk, and lamb, not wild animals and grubs. This was doubly true in the case of the Arabs and Uzbeks congregating around the Shahikot, who relied on a logistics umbilical cord to Gardez and Zermat to keep them supplied. "They're not hunting wild boar and digging up roots to survive" was Blaber's message to his troops. "It's not like fighting the Viet Cong."

As he argued the case for aggressive reconnaissance missions in the mountains south of Gardez, Blaber realized he needed more troops. In his opinion, three teams of four or five men were required to conduct those missions. But when he made the request in a Febrary 12 video-teleconference that linked him, sitting in the TF Blue headquarters at Bagram, with Trebon and his senior staff in Masirah and Dailey, who still appeared to be trying to micromanage the TF 11/AFO operations in Afghanistan from North Carolina, the JSOC commander again expressed skepticism about AFO's approach.

In fairness to Dailey, he was skeptical that any of the "big three" high value targets were in the Shahikot. Nevertheless, with the support of Kernan, the TF Blue commander in Bagram and Colonel Frank Kearney, JSOC's operations officer at Pope, Blaber got most of what he asked for. But Dailey's acrimonious reaction was indicative of how little trust the higher headquarters of both Spider and Blaber had in their assessments that a large enemy force was gathering in the Shahikot. It also reflected the strained relationship the introspective and inflexible Dailey had with the more open and engaging Blaber. "Their personalities are oil and water—they don't mix," said a JSOC officer who knew both men. "There's not a lot of love there." (A senior Army officer disagreed, claiming that Dailey considered Blaber "creative" and "innovative.")

Dailey thought Blaber and his AFO troops in Gardez were exceeding their authority with their ambitious plans for the Shahikot and their close coordination with the CIA and, when they arrived, the conventional forces. The JSOC commander found this frustrating. According to a JSOC officer, Dailey's frustration was compounded by his lack of confidence in either Trebon or Commander Ed Winters, the SEAL officer serving as TF 11's operations officer in Masirah. "You've got the CG [commanding general] not really comfortable with Ed, not really comfortable with General Trebon, and the perception is that Pete Blaber is running the show and running amok," the JSOC officer said. "I think that he [Dailey] was upset that they [AFO] were not following his instruction, which was to stay focused on the target and not do whatever the CIA wanted them to do," the officer said. "Pete was out doing things that General Dailey had pretty clearly told General Trebon and the teams not to do, which was to be strategic reconnaissance for the conventional guys." From the perspective of those in Gardez, AFO's actions clearly supported the mission to find the HVTs. They had followed a trail of facts and deductive logic that led to the Shahikot Valley as a likely location of a large body of enemy fighters. Wherever there were a lot of Al Qaida troops, there was a good chance they would be protecting at least one senior enemy leader, Blaber thought. This was particularly true when the enemy gathered in an almost inaccessible mountain redoubt close to the Pakistani border. Blaber put his thoughts in a daily report titled "AFO Commander's Comments" that went to the TF 11 headquarters and from there to CENTCOM and JSOC. But these reports failed to resonate with Dailey.

Either way, the perspective of those in Gardez was that neither Blaber's reports nor similar ones written by CIA officers in Afghanistan were being taken seriously at CIA headquarters in Langley, Virginia, in the Pentagon or, particularly, on Masirah Island and at JSOC headquarters at Pope Air Force Base. "There were a lot of skeptics [at Pope and Langley] saying, 'Why would they be concentrated? You're not going to find a pocket,'" said a Gardez source.

But from the point of view of those in Gardez, it was better to be ignored than to be micromanaged. They realized that only the safe house's sheer isolation prevented the generals in Masirah and Pope from interfering with the AFO element in Gardez. As it was, officers at TF 11's desert island headquarters mocked the independent role that Blaber had carved out by calling him "Peter the Great" and "Colonel Kurtz," a reference to the U.S. officer in the Vietnam War movie *Apocalypse Now* who cut all ties with his chain of command and went native. But to Chris Haas, the Dagger lieutenant colonel, the AFO commander's approach reflected his "bold and audacious" personality. "His concept was, we're gonna find that actionable intelligence, we're not gonna wait for actionable intelligence to come to us," Haas said.

Part of the reason for the skepticism at higher levels was the Shahikot's proximity to Gardez and Zermat. The valley seemed too far from Pakistan and too close to the towns, which on some maps resembled sprawling cities. (In fact, both towns were very concentrated, with just scattered compounds on their outskirts.) But to those in the safe house, the enemy's decision to base himself in the Shahikot was "simple genius." The valley was close to an urban area, giving the guerrillas access to food and other supplies, and was within a day's travel of Pakistan. But, crucially, the Shahikot represented all but inaccessible terrain. A force that held the high ground around the valley enjoyed commanding views of all likely approaches. "Once you got up there and you saw this, you realize what a perfect spot this is for a base camp," said an American in Gardez.

16.

THE dark gray shape of the Combat Talon descended steeply, a 100-foot-long piece of the night sky falling suddenly to earth, each of its four turboprop engines churning out the power of 4,910 horses as the plane's undercarriage landed with a short squeal of rubber on the blacked-out Bagram runway. The aircraft taxied to a halt, and an officer with an unusually long—for an infantryman—shock of brown hair that flopped across his forehead rose to his feet. In the luminescent green cabin "slime lights" it was just possible to make out two khaki stars on the desert camouflage fabric covering his helmet. The plane's ramp swung down, and the officer took his first deep breath of Afghan air. Finally he was here. The months of frustration in K2 melted away. Looking across the tarmac to the headquarters of the various task forces, he could see a few chinks of light escaping through window frames and tent flaps. Inside tumbledown buildings and GP Medium tents, bleary-eyed staff officers and NCOs on the night shift were typing on laptops, staring at map boards, and punching numbers into calculators, honing plans for Operation Anaconda (Nocks and Bishop's name for the operation had stuck). And the moment the general's feet touched the ground, he became the senior officer. Not just in Bagram, but in all of Afghanistan. It was 4 a.m. on February 17, and "Buster" Hagenbeck had got his war.

After finally securing Franks's approval, Mikolashek had notified Hagenbeck February 11 that the Mountain headquarters would be moving to Bagram to assume command of all U.S. conventional ground forces in Afghanistan, plus Task Forces Dagger and K-Bar. The only American military outfit in Afghanistan to remain outside Hagenbeck's command was Task Force 11, over which Franks retained direct command and control. Mikolashek directed Hagenbeck to change the name of his headquarters from CFLCC (Forward) to Coalition Task Force Afghanistan, once he had established himself at Bagram. Mikolashek made it clear to Hagenbeck that although his task force's lifespan was open-ended, its first order of business—and the catalyst for its deployment to Afghanistan—was to oversee the planning and execution of Operation Anaconda. However, he delayed issuing the order that granted Hagenbeck formal command authority over the other elements. (Mikolashek later said this delay was not deliberate.) While the rest of his staff began breaking down the headquarters at K2 in preparation for the move to Bagram, Hagenbeck sent several key members of his staff ahead in order to quickly gain some kind of control over the planning process that was already progressing apace. Among the first to arrive, in the early hours of February 13, were Lieutenant Colonels David Gray and Chris Bentley. Gray, a lean, youthful fair-haired officer, was the division's director of operations. Bentley, Hagenbeck's deputy fire support coordinator, was the man responsible for ensuring the command had all the "fires"—artillery and close air support—it needed to support its operations. Following hard on their heels later that day were Wille and Ziemba, the two officers whose brainstorming had first alerted the division's higher-ups to the potential for an operation in the Shahikot. Over the next several days the rest of Hagenbeck's headquarters loaded onto C-130 and C-17 aircraft and moved to Bagram. The 10th Mountain Division was going to war again.

THE 10th Mountain Division had existed in its present form only since 1985. Despite the division's name, its troops no longer laid claim to special expertise in mountain warfare. The division traced its heritage back to World War II, when it *was* a mountain warfare unit that distinguished itself in Italy in 1945. Disbanded that November, the division was reactivated in 1948 as a training organization called 10th Infantry Division. Inactivated again in 1958, the 10th did not reappear on the active rolls until the mid-1980s. The Iranian revolution and the Soviet invasion of Afghanistan in 1979 prompted the Army to design a "light infantry" division that could deploy quickly to crisis spots. One of four divisions activated or converted to the new design was the 10th, officially designated 10th Mountain Division (Light Infantry).

The 10th survived the cuts at the end of the Cold War and had the dubious privilege of being the most deployed Army division in the 1990s, serving in Somalia, Haiti, and the Balkans. (The deployments exerted a disproportionate strain on the 10th because, alone among the Army's remaining ten divisions, it had only two maneuver brigades, instead of the standard three.) In November

2001, when duty again came calling to Fort Drum, the division was already stretched thin by peacekeeping commitments long forgotten by most Americans. The 10th had about half its division headquarters plus a brigade combat team in Kosovo, a battalion task force in Bosnia, another battalion task force in the Sinai, and, of course, 1-87 already in Uzbekistan. But Hagenbeck and most of his principal staff remained available for deployment, and it was to them, rather than a more intact division like the 101st, that the Army turned to establish the CFLCC (Forward) headquarters at K2. This decision guaranteed that if the headquarters dispatched to Uzbekistan ever moved to Afghanistan to command combat operations, it would have few troops of its own in the fight.

WHEN Mikolashek, the CFLCC commander, decided to put a forward headquarters in K2, he did so fully aware that the headquarters the Army gave him might move to Afghanistan and oversee combat operations. For that reason he insisted the headquarters should be commanded by a general. He did not specifically request a division headquarters, but when the Army's decision-makers examined the request, they realized that a division command post most closely matched Mikolashek's requirements.

Once Forces Command decided a division headquarters was needed, the choice of division became a process of elimination. Forces Command oversaw only the Army's six divisions in the continental United States, not the four overseas. Of these six the three heavy (i.e., mechanized or armored) divisions were not considered suitable for Afghanistan's terrain, and anyway, the Army wanted to hold them in reserve in case of a war against North Korea or Iraq. That left the three light divisions in XVIII Airborne Corps: 82nd Airborne, 101st Airborne (Air Assault), and 10th Mountain (Light Infantry). The 82nd was disregarded because of its mission to maintain a brigade as a national reserve, ready to deploy on very short notice. That left a straight choice between the 101st and 10th Mountain. The 101st's combination of helicopter-provided mobility and light infantry strength should have made it the obvious choice for Afghanistan. Unlike 10th Mountain, whose troops were scattered around the world, the 101st was at home (except for the brigade returning from Kosovo and the battalion in Pakistan) and being put through an intensive training regimen by its commander, Major General Dick Cody, a former commander of Delta's aviation squadron who knew most of the special ops commanders in Afghanistan. The Army could have deployed Cody's headquarters to K2, knowing that if the headquarters later moved to Afghanistan to command combat operations, there would be three infantry brigades at Fort Campbell just waiting to be called forward to go to war with their division commander. But it was not clear to those making the decisions in the United States that the headquarters they picked to go to K2 would ever command a combat operation in Afghanistan. And they knew that once committed to Afghanistan, the 101st, a unique division, would not be available in case trouble flared elsewhere. "The 101st is on every war plan there is," said Major General Julian Burns, Forces Command's deputy chief of staff for operations.

The generals and colonels at CENTCOM and CFLCC were fully aware of the 101st's unique capabilities. In the weeks after September 11, they had worked on a plan called "Desert Viper" to put the 101st in a country close enough to Afghanistan that it could be used in the war that America was only just beginning to wage there. "We were hoping to get the 101st in theater," Mikolashek said. His planners considered positioning the division at airfields in either Turkmenistan or Uzbekistan, but ruled both out as "politically unfeasible," he said. A third option was basing the division in a remote desert airfield in Oman. This appealed because Oman was close enough to allow for flights into Afghanistan without having to negotiate overflight rights with any country other than Pakistan, but also provided easy access to other likely Al Qaida hiding places, like Yemen and the Horn of Africa. "We didn't know where Al Qaida was," Mikolashek said. "We thought we might have to go in and do an Afghanistan-like operation in Somalia."

Another plan, for which the 101st was considered "the force of choice," according to a senior officer, was for a limited war with Iraq. The response of the Pentagon's civilian leadership to September 11 had been to agitate for an immediate attack against Iraq, despite the lack of evidence linking Iraq to the terrorist attacks and the fact that a war in Afghanistan would strain the military's airlift capability all by itself. President George W. Bush rebuffed those initial urgings from Defense Secretary Rumsfeld and his deputy, Paul Wolfowitz. But in October the Pentagon asked CFLCC to draw up a plan to seize the southern oil fields in Iraq. Mikolashek's planners put together a plan involving two brigades of 1st Cavalry Division—an armored division at Fort Hood, Texas, that already had a brigade in Kuwait—and at least one brigade of the 101st. Mikolashek said the operation might have been launched as "a fairly early preemptive" attack if the United States received any intelligence indicating that Iraqi dictator Saddam Hussein was considering an attack on Kuwait or Saudi Arabia.

Burns was unaware of the plan to seize the oilfields, which was never executed, but others in the decision-making chain at CFLCC, Central Command, Joint Forces Command, the Joint Staff, and the Department of the Army surely were. Every senior officer knew his civilian bosses might order a war in Iraq sooner rather than later. "In the minds at the Defense Department and in the

CinC's [i.e., Franks's] staff, that was a real possibility," recalled Warren Edwards, Mikolashek's deputy commanding general for operations. "There was clearly a thought process that was being worked at the highest levels that said, 'We may want to do something else, somewhere, and a piece of that will probably be the 101st.'" One senior special operations officer who served in Afghanistan said Central Command was distracted from the war in Afghanistan by the need to plan for a "general war" in Iraq, which was originally scheduled for much earlier than March 2003, when it actually occurred. "It was supposed to go in October [2002]," he said. "That was the plan, that's what everybody was working for. . . . That's what CENTCOM was focused on. They believed that it was done in Afghanistan and that the 10th came in to do this civil goodwill, start to rebuild things."

At the recommendation of XVIII Airborne Corps commander Lieutenant General Dan McNeill, the Army passed on the 101st and instead selected Hagenbeck's headquarters—the most undermanned, stretched, and stressed division headquarters in the Army—to deploy to K2 in preparation for a move into Afghanistan. Asked if Forces Command was told that the 101st should be kept on the shelf for Iraq, Burns replied: "That was certainly implied in the message that we got to deploy the 10th Mountain." Burns and General John Hendrix, head of Forces Command, were frustrated that a division as obviously suited to Afghanistan as the 101st was being left on the shelf. "That was our frustration, but we were told continue to train," Burns said.

Again it bears pointing out that senior U.S. commanders had completely misread the situation in Afghanistan. They were already patting themselves on the back for a job well done and looking ahead to the next war, despite the fact that the Al Qaida leadership remained at large in Afghanistan and in command of hundreds, probably thousands, of well-trained, highly motivated fighters. The United States faced a stark choice: to deploy conventional forces into eastern Afghanistan and destroy those enemies or to allow them to escape and foment violence against America and her allies for years to come. But neither the opportunity—nor the risk of not seizing it—appeared uppermost in the minds of senior leaders who already had one eye on Baghdad. Shortly after the Mountain headquarters deployed to K2, Burns again asked Joint Forces Command and CFLCC, "What is the mission set for them?" "The answer I got back," he said, "was that they were going to return in early February because this war was over."

AS they would a few weeks later with the Rakkasans, CENTCOM's restrictions bit deeply into the force 10th Mountain was preparing to deploy. Franks's planners sent a message that all that was needed was a force smaller than a division tactical command post (a forward headquarters of about sixty-five to seventy people usually commanded by a brigadier general). By the time this message reached Fort Drum, it had been translated into an informal directive to deploy only fifty to sixty troops. The 10th Mountain staff knew such a skeletal headquarters would never be able to maintain round-the-clock operations, and they managed to negotiate a limit of about 160 troops. Roughly a third of these were augmentees from XVIII Airborne Corps and Forces Command, replacing division staffers deployed in the Balkans. The new troops—many of whom were assigned to Mountain's intelligence section—were good, professional soldiers. But for Hagenbeck, being forced to deploy with almost a third of his headquarters filled with unfamiliar faces was hardly an auspicious start.

ON February 14 Hagenbeck's staff assumed control of planning for Operation Anaconda. That was not a signal to give up for the Dagger and Rakkasan planners, whose work was already far advanced, but it was now the Mountain staff's job to oversee their planning and to add the *oomph* their larger headquarters could provide. The Mountain officers took to their new mission with gusto. A couple of weeks previously, they had been anticipating their return to snow-covered upstate New York. Now they were in charge of what promised to be "the culminating point" of the war. Their headquarters finally was getting a chance to prove its worth. They were determined not to waste the opportunity.

The draft plan for Anaconda had fixed D-Day—the day the attack would commence—for February 25. But first the Mountain staffers faced the challenge of forging a spirit of teamwork and understanding among organizations and units who rarely, if ever, had worked together before. They weren't helped by the fact that CFLCC waited a week after they got to Bagram to make Hagenbeck's command of the operation official. This frustrated the Mountain staff, who, in the meantime, could only ask, not order, representatives from other task forces to come to meetings or assume particular missions. At first some of the other units ignored their Mountain counterparts' requests. Nor did it help that TF Dagger's men considered themselves the experts on how to make war in Afghanistan, yet now had to take directions from conventional officers who hadn't spent a week in country. But day by day the cooperation increased as the SEALs and Special Forces soldiers of K-Bar and Dagger mingled with Rakkasan and Mountain light infantrymen, AFO's Delta operators, and CIA covert operatives. The Australian Special Air Service commandos—perhaps the hardest-looking men in Bagram—added an even more exotic, weatherbeaten aspect to the mix. As soon as the Mountain staffers established their tactical operations center (TOC)—the bustling, high-tech nerve center from which Hagenbeck would run Anaconda—by hooking together about eight modular olive drab tents, liaison officers from the other organizations began drifting in. The TOC soon resembled "the bar scene from *Star Wars*," said Major Lou Bello, an artilleryman on the Mountain staff. "[There were] guys with ballcaps and beards, and guys with turbans running in and out," he said. "It was a high-adventure place."

High adventure or not, invisible walls had to be broken down and cultural barriers breached before an atmosphere of cooperation and mutual trust could prevail. CENTCOM's insistence on making Dagger's little Afghan force the main effort and its refusal to countenance the deployment of the rest of the Rakkasans' combat power meant that from the start the command structure for Anaconda was jury-rigged from top to bottom. For a battle that would involve perhaps 2,000 allied troops—less than a brigade's worth—in combat, CENTCOM had cobbled together a force that drew elements from eight countries, two U.S. Army divisions, two Special Forces groups, a hodgepodge of aviation units, and a variety of clandestine organizations. Despite the enormous military skill and experience nested in most of these units, the operation's main effort was to be a few hundred Afghans drawn from different clans and provinces who had barely a month of semiformal military training under their belt. Their Special Forces spine was provided by two A-teams from different SF groups, led (eventually) by Chris Haas, commander of a battalion that included neither of the A-teams. Much of the special reconnaissance mission was the purview of TF K-Bar, a mishmash of units from half a dozen countries under the command of a Navy SEAL whose maritime background had better prepared him for reconnoitering enemy-held beaches than for keeping watch over mountain passes. The air assault/blocking force mission was the responsibility of TF Rakkasan's three infantry battalions, one of which was from not just a different brigade than the others, but another division entirely, and each of which was missing one of its three rifle companies. Within TF Rakkasan, units had been pulled from companies and battalions and cross-attached to others to such an extent that from the rank of lieutenant colonel down to lieutenant officers were working alongside and under commanders they had never trained with and in some cases barely knew. Even the Rakkasans' helicopter outfit, Task Force Talon, was a jumble of units from different commands: an Apache company from 3rd Battalion, 101st Aviation Regiment; five Black Hawks from 4th Battalion, 101st Aviation; two Chinook platoons from 7th Battalion, 101st Aviation; and another Chinook platoon from Bravo Company, 159th Aviation Regiment, an XVIII Airborne Corps unit that had spent most of the war in

Jacobabad. Perhaps the most tightly bonded, least rearranged unit in Anaconda was Task Force 64, the Australian SAS force whose mission would be to guard the Shahikot's southern approaches. But, of course, the Australians were all but an unknown quantity to the Americans.

The job of lashing this Rube Goldberg organization into a cohesive fighting force fell to Hagenbeck and his downsized staff (almost a third of which consisted of complete newcomers to the 10th Mountain headquarters). This was asking an awful lot of a staff for whom Anaconda would be virtually the first experience of war in Afghanistan. U.S. Army units were supposed to all follow the same doctrine, and the service's training and personnel systems were designed to allow the Army to take a soldier of any rank from one unit and drop him into another of the same type with minimal fuss. That, at least, was the theory. But the setup forced upon Hagenbeck and the troops under his command would put that theory to the most extreme of tests, with soldiers' lives on the line. The Mountain staff came up with a word for the organizing principle behind the force they were being asked to control: "ad-hocracy."

AS the new arrivals from K2 took the helm, their first order of business was to gain the confidence of the special operations forces. Given the mutual antipathy that had traditionally characterized the relationship between "the big Army" and the special operations community, this was no small task. "There were a lot of holy cows who had to be taken quietly out the back and sorted out before this could become a success," said Major Jonathan Lockwood, a British exchange officer posted to the 10th Mountain staff at Fort Drum who now found himself going to war with the U.S. Army. It was a credit to Hagenbeck and the other leaders at Bagram that the slaughter of holy cows was allowed to take place at all, he added. The common doctrinal grounding shared by the 101st and 10th Mountain troops was a huge asset in enabling LaCamera's 1-87 Infantry to blend with Wiercinski's Rakkasans in a matter of days, while the exchange of liaison officers and NCOs between conventional and special ops units helped bridge the divide between those two communities. Despite the best efforts of all involved, however, Hagenbeck and his team failed to create a seamless organization out of so many disparate parts. That was too much to ask in such a short space of time. To the extent the different elements were able to work together at all, most of the credit must go to a serendipitous alignment in key leadership positions of individuals who already knew each other.

The most obvious prior connection, and one of the most advantageous, was between Hagenbeck and Wiercinski. As a brigadier general, Hagenbeck had served as the 101st's assistant division commander for operations—a position with decision-making responsibility—when Wiercinski had been the division's director of operations, or G-3, in which position he would ensure that the general's decisions were carried out. Now they were together again. Knowing how his boss thought gave Wiercinski a comfort level he would not otherwise have enjoyed working for a division commander other than his own. "Having had a great relationship with General Hagenbeck when he was the ADC(O) of the 101st and I was the G-3 made it incredibly easier, because he understood air assault tactics and how we do things in the 101st," the Rakkasan commander said. "So I didn't have to do a lot of explaining. When I was giving my backbrief, he knew exactly what I was talking about, and I knew he did."

But it was the Ranger Regiment that provided the largest set of shared experiences that connected the leaders gathering at Bagram. The regiment falls under U.S. Special Operations Command but is really an elite airborne infantry force that links the light infantry and special ops communities. Unlike Delta or Special Forces, into which troops tend to disappear for the rest of their careers, soldiers often rotate between the Ranger Regiment and the Army's light infantry divisions. So it was that many Mountain and Rakkasan officers and senior NCOs had served together in the Rangers. This was a massive slice of good fortune. The 75th Ranger Regiment is a tight community of warriors whose ethos is summed up in the Ranger Creed. There are 241 words in the Ranger Creed, and every Ranger is required to learn them all by heart. But the Creed's essence is encapsulated in six of them: "Never shall I fail my comrades."

If the Ranger Regiment Association had opened a Bagram chapter, Wiercinski, Larsen, LaCamera, Grippe, and Nielsen would all have been members. Of these, only Nielsen had not fought with the Rangers in Panama. Other Ranger alumni included Blaber, Jimmy, and Rosengard, as well as Lieutenant Colonel Chip Preysler, who commanded 2-187 Infantry. Blaber and Grippe had served together in 1997 as the operations officer and B Company first sergeant of 2nd Ranger Battalion. When Grippe left the battalion, he bid farewell to Blaber with the prophetic words, "I'll see you on a distant battlefield."

Walking out of one of the many briefings held at Bagram in the prelude to Anaconda, another soldier whispered to Wiercinski, "Holy smokes! Look at everybody's right shoulder!" In the U.S. Army, soldiers wear their unit patch on their left shoulder. The space on their right shoulder is reserved for the insignia of a unit in which they have served in a combat zone. As Wiercinski glanced around, on right shoulder after right shoulder he saw the small black scroll-shaped patches of the Ranger battalions. It told him these were men who lived the values of the Ranger Creed, men who would not let him down.

For Wiercinski, still smarting from the refusal of generals far above his level to allow his third battalion to join him in Afghanistan, there was some solace to be gained from knowing that its place would be taken by a unit led by LaCamera, who had been the operations officer of the Ranger Regiment's 1st Battalion when Wiercinski had been the regiment's deputy commander. "I knew him very well—superb reputation, great soldier," Wiercinski said. "I know we all train to the same standards, but that would have been a little bit different, had I not known Paul LaCamera and served with Paul LaCamera before, and understood exactly how he trained and the kind of leader that he was."

Then Hagenbeck made an inspired decision. A division commander is normally supported by a pair of one-star generals who serve as his assistant division commanders, one for operations and the other for support (i.e., logistics). But neither of Hagenbeck's assistant division commanders was in Afghanistan. One was in Kosovo, where about half the division was stationed. The other had fully expected to deploy to K2 with Hagenbeck. But Forces Command ordered Hagenbeck to leave a general behind at Fort Drum, even though there were few troops left to command there, because the four-star headquarters felt more comfortable with a general available to handle any tasks assigned to the post as part of Operation Noble Eagle, the mission to secure key facilities in the United States after September 11. So Hagenbeck had to deploy to a war zone without either of his right-hand men. Once he got to Bagram, the Mountain commander realized he could use some general officer help, both to organize the various components of his new command into a cohesive whole and then to help him run the battle. There weren't many generals in Afghanistan to choose from, but the two Hagenbeck had in mind were perfect for the job. One was Gary Harrell. The other was Brigadier General Mike Jones, a six-foot-four Special Forces officer who was in Kabul as the military's liaison to the CIA. Both brought impeccable credentials as warriors with contacts throughout the special ops and intelligence communities. When asked by Hagenbeck, the two readily agreed to serve as his deputy commanding generals. Hagenbeck then got Franks to approve their assignments in that capacity. Harrell began working with Hagenbeck around February 22. Jones came on board several days later. Now Hagenbeck had two seasoned special ops generals—officers well known to many of the other leaders in Bagram—at his side. These weren't just experienced special ops officers, they were generals willing to use their rank to break bureaucratic logjams at CENTCOM and other higher headquarters. In the days and weeks ahead they would prove invaluable.

Harrell and Jones were also useful intermediaries between Hagenbeck and the two elements of U.S. force in Afghanistan over which he exercised no control: Task Force 11 and the CIA. That the CIA was beyond the control of the military commander in country was to be expected. But CENTCOM's decision to retain control of TF 11 in Tampa caused concern in Bagram, even though that too was par for the course in large military operations. Because of the covert nature of their specialized missions, the sensitive intelligence on which those missions were often based and the equally highly classified methods used to conduct them, black special ops units were rarely placed under conventional two or three-star commanders. But this didn't mean such circumstances met with the approval of the generals cut out of the command chain. Hagenbeck and his staff were preparing to fight the largest set-piece battle the U.S. military had waged since the 1991 war with Iraq, and yet American units over whom they exerted no control would be running around on the same battlefield. This was a clear violation of the military principle of unity of command—the idea that a single commander should control all forces involved in an operation. U.S. officials like to say that in circumstances in which unity of command is impossible, "unity of effort" is the goal. But this doctrinal sleight of hand only papers over the cracks left when two generals at the same base each command forces operating over the same patch of ground, yet neither is answerable to the other, or to another commander in the theater of operations. In the Mountain TOC, the situation made officers uneasy. "There's definitely some concern any time you've got two forces working in the same location, and there's so little known about what one of them is doing," Wille said.

To reduce the risk of friendly fire and to share situational awareness, Task Force Blue permitted a single liaison officer from Mountain to hang out in their TOC, located at the other end of the airfield from Hagenbeck's headquarters. But there was only one other exception to TF 11's "never the twain shall meet" policy regarding conventional forces: Pete Blaber's AFO. In keeping with his belief in "the power of combinations," Blaber had begun to work closely with the conventional troops soon after the basement meeting in Kabul. Although friction persisted between Blaber and some JSOC leaders, Blaber persuaded the TF 11 staff to support Anaconda and his participation in it. "Pete's arguments, and why we ended up going into Shahikot, is if you go to the places they have fought before, where the caches were, where they had a historical pattern, that's where the leaders will be, and that's what some of the signals [intelligence] supported," said a TF 11 staffer. "We were watching and supporting their operation because we believed that would flush the pheasants."

(Despite the lack of hard evidence that any of the "big three" HVTs were in the Shahikot, the very presence of a large number of enemy fighters in one place, combined with a spike in Arabic cell phone traffic and a concentration of

SUVs, suggested that one or more of them might be wintering there, protected by a large cadre of guards. This added to the widespread view among U.S. officers that Anaconda would prove to be the decisive operation in the Afghanistan. "It's safe to say that the intel community thought that there were some significant leaders potentially in the Shahikot Valley," Harrell said.)

Blaber installed Jimmy and his small command and control element in the Mountain TOC as soon as it was established in Bagram. The AFO officers decided there was no point in gaining knowledge only to keep it from the commanders whose troops would be at the tip of the spear, so Blaber fed Hagenbeck intel from Gardez and Jimmy ensured the AFO teams' locations were marked on Mountain's maps of the Shahikot and the surrounding area. Jimmy, who by now had about half a dozen operators working for him in Bagram, also attended every important rock drill and briefing that Mountain held. In the Mountain TOC Jimmy ran his operation from a table just five feet away from the table at which the three generals sat. Sitting on the AFO desk were enough radios, satellite phones, and secure laptops to keep a small electronics store in business. But the gadgetry and the proximity had a purpose. If Jimmy learned something important, he could immediately pass it on to the generals without even raising his voice.

THE first Mountain staffers to arrive in Bagram—Bentley, Gray, Wille, Ziemba, and Captain Shawn Prickett, an air operations officer—threw themselves into their work. February 14, the day after their arrival, marked the start of a two-day planning conference held by Rosengard in Dagger's AOB building. Mulholland and Rosengard gave the newcomers another detailed overview of the intelligence regarding the Shahikot, and how they proposed to attack the valley. The Mountain planners liked what they heard, and applied themselves to the painstaking staff work required to give such a complex military operation any chance of success. The work Wille and Ziemba had done sketching out a concept of operations for the Shahikot now paid dividends, drastically shortening the time the Mountain planners needed to get smart on the operation. By the time Hagenbeck arrived February 17, his advance party had a detailed concept of operation ready to brief to him. The nascent plan still clung to Rosengard's vision of attacking the valley from the west with Zia's troops and the two A-teams (a force now collectively known as Task Force Hammer) while air-assaulting TF Rakkasan—including LaCamera's battalion—to occupy blocking positions astride the escape routes out of the valley. Many *i*'s remained to be dotted and *t*'s to be crossed, but the basic elements were there.

With D-Day set for February 25, the planners needed the commanding generals at every level to sign off on the work that had been done so far. Those crucial briefings occurred February 17.

Hagenbeck was briefed first, by Gray and Smith, and gave his thumbs-up. Then Mikolashek flew in from Kuwait. His approval was vital for Anaconda to proceed, and represented the highest hurdle so far for the work into which Rosengard, Wille, and the other planners had been pouring themselves. All the assorted task force commanders—Hagenbeck, Harrell, Mulholland, Wiercinski, Harward, and even Trebon—gathered to hear Gray and Rosengard brief the CFLCC commander. Rich, the CIA chief of station, also came up to Bagram for the occasion. Gray outlined the conventional forces' role in each phase of the plan to Mikolashek, Rosengard described what Dagger would contribute. Mikolashek raised two issues. He was concerned that the operation was scheduled to begin on the last day of Eid ul Adha, the three-day Feast of Sacrifice that commemorates Abraham's willingness to sacrifice his son Ishmael to Allah. During the holiday Moslems around the world sacrifice a lamb or other animal and distribute the meat to relatives or the needy. Mikolashek told Hagenbeck and the others that they should not ignore the holiday: Either they should take advantage of it and attack during the festivities to catch the enemy by surprise—he cited Washington's Christmas 1776 crossing of the Delaware and attack on Trenton to illustrate what he meant—or they should delay the attack until the holiday had passed. Worried that some of their Afghan allies wouldn't show up for the fight unless the date changed, the Americans decided there and then to move D-Day from February 25 to February 28.

Mikolashek was also concerned that too many conventional forces were being committed to the fight, according to officers who heard him speak. Larsen, the Rakkasan executive officer, who was present at the briefing, said Mikolashek reflected CENTCOM's view that "the more targets we present to the enemy, the more he will kill." This was a curious approach to take to an operation in which the objective was to trap and kill the enemy. Wiercinski countered that "he didn't think we had enough force, because the enemy situation was too vague, and there were a lot of escape routes," Larsen said. There was, of course, no chance of CENTCOM providing more forces for the operation. Just getting eight Apaches into the country had taken a momentous bureaucratic struggle. But Wiercinski's argument at least persuaded Mikolashek not to tamper with the force already set aside for Anaconda. (Mikolashek took strong exception to this account. "I don't remember saying anything about 'too many conventional forces,'" he said.)

Finally, the leaders in Bagram held a video-teleconference with Franks and his principal staff in Tampa. The CENTCOM commander liked Rosengard's concept of forcing the enemy in the valley to flee toward Pakistan, which the Dagger operations officer referred to as "convincing the enemy to do what he already wants to do." Franks approved the concept of operations, but told Hagenbeck to give his task force a new name. "Don't call yourself 'Afghanistan,'" he said. "Call it anything else, but that has geopolitical implications." With CENTCOM apparently still gripped by the fear of appearing like an army of occupation, Hagenbeck renamed his organization Coalition and Joint Task Force (CJTF) Mountain.

Having gotten a green light, the planners redoubled their efforts. What Mikolashek and Franks had approved was a concept of operations—the broad brush outline of who would do what in Anaconda. There was still much work to be done to determine the hows, wheres, and whens of the operation. As C-130s and C-17s landed night after night on the airstrip and scores of tents went up to shelter the army gathering at Bagram, Gray, Wille, Rosengard, and Larsen toiled long caffeine- and nicotine-fueled hours refining the plan. There were plenty of devils left in the details.

17.

PETE Blaber had a rapt audience.

It was February 14. The B Squadron recce guys had arrived earlier that day, only forty-eight hours after Blaber had requested them in the tense video-teleconference with Dailey. (They had actually been warned several days earlier by others in Delta that Blaber wanted them in Afghanistan, forcing them to cut short a training exercise in Europe to return to Bragg less than a week before their arrival in Gardez.)

Blaber gathered the new men—the operators he planned to send on the reconnaissance missions—and explained why they had been called forward. The meeting, held in the big work room, was also attended by the Special Forces and CIA folks. Their mission was to reconnoiter the approaches to and—eventually—the interior of the Shahikot Valley, Blaber said. He repeated his guiding principles for operating in the enemy's backyard. First was the need to understand the enemy. Blaber told the new arrivals they should read everything about the Shahikot, talk to Zia's troops about the enemy, and ask themselves, "If I were the enemy, how would I defend this area?" Locking eyes with each man in turn, he told them, not for the last time, that the key to success was to follow Patton's three principles of war: "Audacity, audacity, and audacity."

Blaber had handpicked these men because he knew they were some of the very few in the U.S. military—in anyone's military—who could attempt the missions he had in mind with any hope of success.

The next day the reconnaissance effort began in earnest. The new guys got up to speed quickly, reading all the same books and intel papers the other guys had read, and familiarizing themselves with the surrounding area using maps and overhead photos. Helped by Glenn P., the AFO intel analyst, they looked for avenues of approach into and escape from the Shahikot, potential enemy lines of communication, evidence of enemy activity, and, crucially, places in and around the valley where they might be able to establish observation posts. It was busy, as they war-gamed numerous options for infiltrating teams into the valley.

The AFO operators were imbued with their commander's audacious spirit, but neither they—nor he—were blind to the dangers of operating in that environment. They were particularly concerned about the threat of mines, which had been strewn about the Afghan countryside liberally over the previous twenty-five years. These haphazardly marked minefields had cost many civilians their legs or worse. The maps and other intelligence documents identifying the area's minefields left a lot to be desired. The AFO troops turned for help to Hoskheyar's fighters, who, as locals in the pay of the Americans, were the best sources of intel on the mine threat. Prompted by the AFO operators, the Dagger troops at the safe house asked their Afghan allies a series of seemingly innocuous questions designed to elicit information about minefield locations without letting on that a big operation in the Shahikot was in the offing. The militiamen knew there were Al Qaida troops in and around the Shahikot, and the Americans were clearly building up the force in the safe house and paying, training, and equipping the Afghans for something, so whether the local fighters failed to put two and two together is open to question. However, they did give the U.S. troops valuable information about "thousands" of mines that lay along routes the AFO patrols might otherwise have taken.

Blaber envisioned an initial recon mission divided into two phases. The first would be a "vehicle recce," driving along and off the roads southwest and southeast of Gardez in order to determine the feasibility of moving deeper into the mountains on foot. Providing such penetration seemed possible, the second phase would be the true environmental recon, with two teams approaching, but not entering, the Shahikot Valley—one from the north, one from the south—and establishing observation posts, before returning to Gardez to prepare for a mission into the valley just prior to D-Day.

The troops who would take the lead were the recce experts newly arrived from Bragg. The B Squadron operators were divided into two teams: India and

Juliet. A Delta recce team usually consisted of four men, divided into two sniper-spotter duos, with the spotter being the senior man of each pair, but these teams had only five operators between them.

Juliet was the larger of the two. Its three men were led by Master Sergeant Kris K., a family man with golden blond hair and a boyish face from West Virginia. Kris was in his thirties and about five feet ten with a very athletic build. His work was characterized by precision and attention to detail. Second in command was Master Sergeant Bill R., an easygoing skydiver and technology wiz who could work miracles with computers. The team was rounded out by Sergeant First Class Dave H., the youngest of the five new arrivals who was also incredibly fit and another technology buff.

India had only two operators, less than the bare minimum for a mission with such a thin margin for error. But the two men could not have been better suited for the task at hand. The thirty-six-year-old team leader was Master Sergeant Kevin W. Short and tautly muscled, he grew up in the backwoods of western Kentucky, learning how to handle a hunting rifle by his eighth birthday. In addition to his hunting prowess, Kevin possessed a natural talent for running far and fast. He had been a competitive triathlete, and after he left his colleagues for dust in his first five-mile run during Delta's operator training course, he was nicknamed "Speedy." Every operator is assigned a nickname when he joins Delta. The names usually refer to a physical characteristic or personality trait, and are not always flattering or even completely accurate. But Speedy's was entirely appropriate. Speedy did everything—eating, driving, running—as if his life depended on being the first one to finish. His penchant for speed had actually forced him into the Army. When he was seventeen, police arrived on the scene during an illegal motorcycle race between Speedy and a friend. His buddy was arrested on the spot, but Speedy outran the law on his bike, only for the police to show up at his home soon after. The judge strongly suggested Speedy join the Army, and dropped all charges when Speedy did so. That was nineteen years ago. Western Kentucky's loss had been the Army's gain. Speedy had gone straight from high school into Special Forces as an "SF baby." He joined Delta in 1991. After doing his time in an assault troop, his hunting ability made him a natural for a spot in one of the reconnaissance and surveillance troops.

Speedy's thirty-eight-year-old second in command was another master sergeant, Bob H., a stocky six-footer from Austin, Texas, who functioned as a "pack mule" on patrols, carrying other operators' gear if they were having trouble keeping up. Bighearted and reliable, Bob's reputation was of a guy who just wouldn't quit. "If you're in a bad situation, there's nobody you'd rather have beside you, 'cause he's gonna be there," said another Delta NCO. Speedy and Bob were close friends and made a terrific recce team. Both were extraordinarily fit and avid outdoorsmen—expert trackers and game hunters. "If you needed two men to track a chipmunk in a 100,000-acre forest and kill it with one bullet, these are the two," said Blaber later. "Although two operators was less than I would have said were needed for these missions, these two were living proof of why you never say 'never' with regards to rules or guiding principles governing tactics. Having Speedy and Bob on a team together was like having Daniel Boone and Simon Kenton together in the frontier days—as hunters and athletes, they had no peer, anywhere."

Juliet had the northern reconnaissance. Their goal was reach a position from which the tri-cities area and the Ewadzkhal Valley, five kilometers to the Shahikot's east and the site of reported enemy activity, could be observed. The concept they developed was to drive southeast down the road that ran in front of the safe house and penetrate the Sate Kandow pass that led through the mountains to Khowst. The Americans knew all about the Sate Kandow from their homework. Throughout the 1980s mujahideen forces under Jalalluddin Haqqani held the pass, effectively blocking the main road from Gardez to Khowst. The Soviets only broke through once, in 1987, behind an artillery and air bombardment so powerful that the chemical residue from the explosives poisoned the mountain streams. Twenty-five years later the pass retained its reputation as a forbidding, treacherous gateway to eastern Paktia and Khowst. No U.S. or other allied troops had yet broached the Sate Kandow. According to the Afghans at the safe house, hundreds of old antitank mines lined the pass, so once between its sheer cliffs, the operators would leave the road and drive south via a trail to find a suitable site to drop off the recce team. In phase two of the mission Juliet team would either walk or ride on all-terrain vehicles (ATVs) to positions several kilometers northeast of the Shahikot.

The southern recce was India Team's responsibility. The first phase would be to drive to Zermat, which appeared to be a logistics hub for the enemy in the Shahikot. No Americans had driven down the Zermat road since January 20, after the CIA and Dagger higher headquarters had told their men in Gardez to limit operations in that area. Reopening the road would open the back door to the Shahikot, Blaber told his men. The second phase would involve a second vehicle recce, dropping India Team off at a point from which they could continue toward their observation posts on foot. An alternate plan involved a helicopter insertion south of Pecawul Ghar, Celam Kac and Jakangir Kot, the site of a suspected Al Qaida exfiltration network and headquarters. Intel analysts assessed this area as the main avenue of escape from the valley. From their LZ, the team would then hike to their observation posts. (Blaber did not want either of his teams to actually enter the Shahikot. That would have carried too high a risk of compromise, not only for the teams, but for the entire operation.)

The first phase of the northern recce was ready to go within a couple of days, but there were problems with the southern approach. The CIA was running local agents into Zermat and didn't want Americans driving in that direction and arousing local suspicions. Bad weather south of the Shahikot also argued for a delay. So while India Team refined their plan, the rest of the AFO contingent focused their energies on Juliet's mission. Glenn P., AFO's intel wizard, gave Juliet a briefing paper on the situation in the area they were about to enter. Their route was controlled by militiamen loyal to local warlord Pacha Khan Zadran. Although loosely allied with him the Americans had identified Pacha Khan as a troublemaker and begun to marginalize him. Pacha Khan's men had a checkpoint and billets along the Gardez-Khowst highway before it reached the Sate Kandow, and an observation post in the hills overlooking the road. There had been no report of enemy movement around the Sate Kandow since the end of December, when about 500 Al Qaida troops were supposedly in the area, as well as Taliban forces. The only reported enemy activity in the area was west and south of where Juliet hoped to emplace their observation posts. Those reports—of up to 100 Al Qaida fighters and sixteen tanks in the town of Menjawar to the west, and of "many Al Qaida" to the south in the Shahikot—were, of course, why the mission was being undertaken in the first place. The briefing included another unsettling detail: "According to mine maps, the infiltration road area is cleared of mines, meaning the area was mined in the past. Accuracy of the clearing is not known."

The reconnaissance mission began at 11 a.m. February 17. A Predator unmanned aerial vehicle (UAV) appeared in the cloudy skies above the safe house and began following the route toward the Sate Kandow. The Predator beamed back live television pictures to Bagram where Jimmy watched closely, relaying what he saw to the operations center in the safe house. (There were two types of Predator flying over Afghanistan: an unarmed version controlled by the Air Force and a CIA-controlled version armed with a Hellfire missile.) AFO had arranged for the Predator to fly the entire route before the patrol left Gardez, so the team would be forewarned of any obstacles or potential threats. The Predator returned within an hour, having spotted nothing untoward. It took up position overhead as Juliet's two Toyota Tacoma crew-cab trucks pulled out of the compound onto the main road, hung a right, and headed for the mountains.

The Toyotas trundled through Pacha Khan's checkpoints without incident.

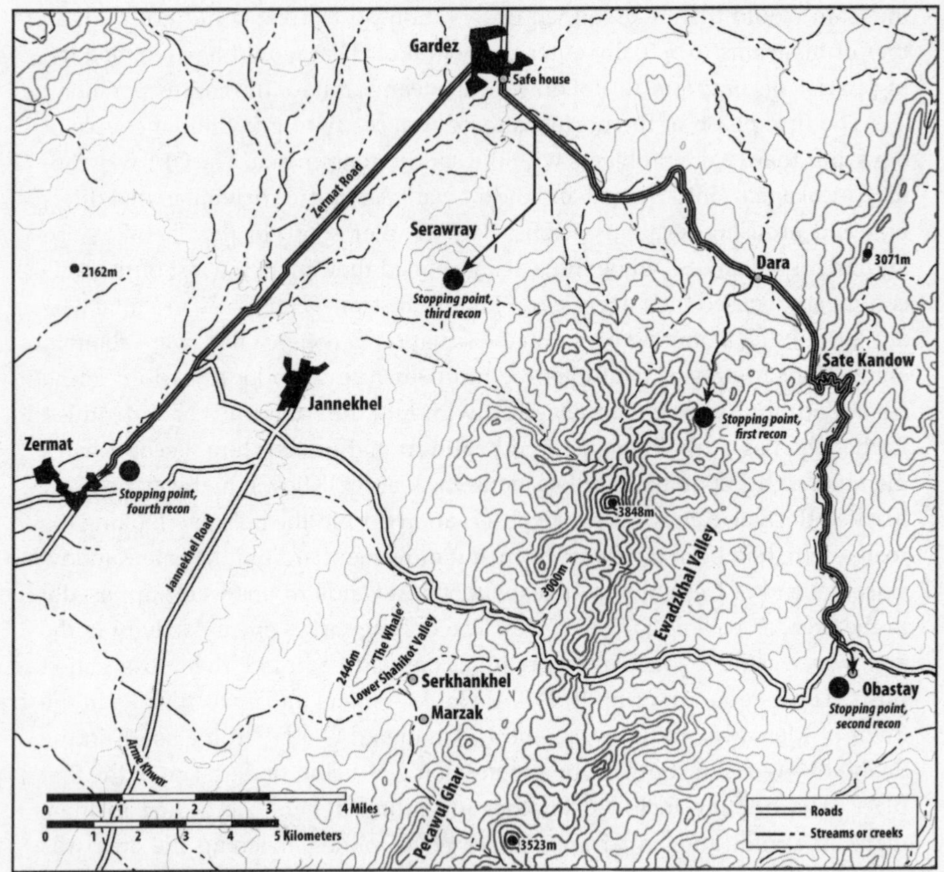

Juliet Team reconnaissance (expeditions begin from Gardez safe house)

The tiny convoy drove into the small town of Dara and turned south along a dirt trail that led into the heart of the dark mountains. The operators kept their eyes peeled for danger, bouncing in their seats as the bone-jarring ride took them past the snowline at 8,000 feet, higher and higher into the mountains. But there was no sign of Al Qaida, or any other human activity. The trail became a creek bed covered with deep snow. The truck engines labored as the drivers negotiated the increasingly rough and rocky terrain. The operators wanted to get far enough south to identify spots for future observation posts, but the route became impassable before that was possible. Juliet turned around and retraced their route back to Gardez. The Predator, which observed nothing alarming, monitored their progress until they reached the safe house.

That first recce taught Juliet several lessons. Most important, the rough terrain meant the northern routes toward the Shahikot were not viable avenues of approach or escape. The AFO troops found it harder than expected to negotiate the rocky mountain trails. In addition, communication and coordination with the numerous intelligence, surveillance, and reconnaissance aircraft that supported the mission needed more planning. On the plus side, the team's satellite radios with batwing antennae that could be attached to the roof or the bed of the truck worked well. For the first time the troops could talk securely over satellite from inside a moving vehicle. Overall, the operators were more than satisfied with the mission's planning and execution.

The next day the Americans got a big break when one of the CIA's sources gave up fresh information on Al Qaida positions in the Shahikot area. Once again the way Spider and his men treated the information validated the pilot team concept. Instead of the usual CIA practice—even in war zones where U.S. troops were fighting—of sending a report up the Agency's chain for editing and dissemination, which would have forced the AFO and Dagger troops working just yards away from their Agency colleagues to wait days before receiving the benefits of their wisdom, the CIA operatives gave the soldiers the raw report of their interview with the source immediately. As a result, the AFO men were able to order overhead imagery to confirm or deny the source's report, and share the pictures with Spider's men.

Meanwhile the operators continued planning further recon missions. They were still running into problems over the CIA's reluctance to sanction a road recce to Zermat, which in turn was delaying India's environmental recce of the Shahikot's mountainous southern approach. AFO considered several options, one of which was to land India by helicopter around the Zawar Ghar Mountains that ran southwest to northeast about twelve kilometers south of the Shahikot. In the meantime, Speedy and Bob decided to see if it was possible to ride ATVs down the Zermat road, leaving the road and outflanking each village to avoid being seen. They went about five kilometers before veering off ahead of the first village, only to discover that the ground was far too muddy. The transmission on Speedy's ATV broke and Bob had to tow it back to Gardez. So much for that idea.

Events were moving faster for Juliet. Blaber wanted them to penetrate deeper into the Sate Kandow than on the first mission, and to enter the Ewadzkhal Valley, which ran west from the Sate Kandow toward the Shahikot. To prepare for the mission, the team was introduced to Pacha Khan's son, who was an old friend of Rasul and who led a group of Pacha Khan's fighters manning a checkpoint on the Gardez-Khowst road between the safe house and the Sate Kandow. Pacha Khan's son declared himself more than willing to escort the team into the pass, which intelligence reports indicated was controlled by his father. The team members doubted the reports' accuracy, but nevertheless realized the value of a local guide who commanded some loyalty in the immediate area.

Juliet's reconnaissance patrol departed the safe house at 10 a.m. February 19. A Predator again led the way, but this time a manned spy aircraft—a Navy EP-3 Aries II with a twenty-four-person crew whose job was to intercept and analyze a wide range of signals, as well as to provide detailed moving footage of the ground from high altitude—was also on station overhead. AFO requested that the two aircraft check the entire route for potential ambush sites and gauge reactions in nearby towns to Juliet's probing.

This time Juliet took a more robust force into the Sate Kandow. Crammed into six pickups were all three Juliet members, plus Master Sergeant Bob H. from India, an Air Force combat controller called Jay, whose job was to call in air strikes if the team came under attack, two more AFO men from Gardez, and a dozen Afghan fighters. Also along for the ride was a signals intelligence soldier called Jason, who worked for one of the U.S. military's most secret organizations. The unit was code-named Gray Fox, but it had also gone by a smattering of other bland code names, including the Intelligence Support Activity, the Army of Virginia (sometimes amended to the Army of Northern Virginia), and the U.S. Army Office of Military Support.

Gray Fox was a strange animal. Formed in 1981, it specialized in gathering human and signals intelligence for the Pentagon under the most challenging of circumstances, often working with Delta's aviation squadron to get behind enemy lines. It had about 200-250 operators, divided into squadrons. Many, but by no means all, of the operators were drawn from Special Forces, because of SF soldiers' reputation for self-sufficiency and independence. During the war in Afghanistan, Gray Fox worked directly for CENTCOM, which attached Gray Fox personnel to AFO from the start of the conflict. Four of the six AFO teams in Afghanistan included a Gray Fox operator, which was how Jason now found himself sitting in a Toyota pickup truck with his secret equipment, concentrating intently as he scanned frequencies for any suspicious broadcasts from the mountains. Jason was a linguist, but his ability to track the frequencies of Al Qaida broadcasts was arguably more critical than his ability to translate them. Once he identified a frequency on which the enemy was broadcasting, it could be passed up the military intelligence chain of command so that spy planes and satellites with more sophisticated listening equipment could monitor it twenty-four hours a day, or help him triangulate the source of the broadcast. When a Gray Fox element joined a black special ops task force, it was known as Task Force Orange.

ONCE again the drive to the pass went smoothly. This time, instead of turning off at Dara, the convoy continued. Juliet's group became the first Americans to penetrate the feared Sate Kandow. The road was a series of hairpin bends once it entered the pass, the shoulders of which towered 1,200 feet overhead. It was perfect ambush country, but the villagers who waved from the side of the road appeared friendly. Once inside the Sate Kandow, the convoy linked up with another group of Pacha Khan Zadran's fighters, who guided the Americans to two places of particular interest.

The first was a small valley running north-northeast from the midpoint of the Sate Kandow. Pacha Khan's men said an enemy force of about 700 men had passed through this valley about four weeks previously, bound for the Shahikot through the Ewadzkhal Valley. Between ten and twenty "Taliban" had remained until about ten days ago, they added. That a significant force had come through was clear. The valley was covered in footprints and littered with syringes, empty tuna cans, and coupons issued by al-Wafa (a Saudi "humanitarian" agency long suspected of financing Islamist terrorists).

The convoy continued for five kilometers to the small town of Obastay, which lay about a kilometer to the southwest of the highway down a smaller road. Local militiamen told the Americans that "bad guys" had a base and an observation post near there, close to Al Kowt, where the Americans knew of some underground Al Qaida facilities. Pacha Khan's men were clearly worried about what their new American allies were getting them into, and refused to go down the side road that led to the observation post. With the Predator low on fuel because the patrol had taken longer than expected, the operators were preparing to return to Gardez when word came that they might already have overstayed their welcome in the Sate Kandow. The Predator had picked up suspicious activity at the western end of the Ewadzkhal Valley, about thirteen kilometers west of Obastay. About twenty men had arrived in seven vehicles, dismounted, and set up a checkpoint about 700 meters from the reported location of another suspected underground facility. The AFO operators questioned Pacha Khan's men about the report. The militiamen said the activity had nothing to do with them, and whoever it was could not be friendly.

That conclusion was reinforced by an intercept Jason made at 10:47 a.m., the best assessment of which was that someone in the Sate Kandow was warning fighters in the Shahikot of the AFO convoy, hence the blocking force's appearance in the Ewadzkhal Valley. (Intriguingly, the intercepted broadcast was transmitted on the same frequency bin Laden had reportedly used in Tora Bora, leading the AFO troops to believe there was a good chance a senior Al

Qaida leader was near the Shahikot.) With their access to UAVs, spy planes, and satellites, the AFO troops had a high-tech edge over their foes in the reconnaissance arena, but these events proved they did not enjoy a monopoly in the spying game. They, too, were being watched.

The AFO operators judged the patrol a success. The news of the 700 enemy fighters headed for the Shahikot buttressed earlier intelligence reports and illustrated that the "bad guys" were using the Ewadzkhal Valley as a route to and from the Shahikot. The Americans now also knew that the Al Qaida forces had a reasonably effective security network screening their operations in the Shahikot.

ON February 20, Blaber finally moved to launch his recce missions to the south and west of the Shahikot. With Anaconda's D-Day set for February 28 and bad weather approaching, the window of opportunity for India's environmental recon was closing. Blaber's only option was to infiltrate the team by helicopter. But to avoid compromising the mission, the team would have to insert far to the south of the Shahikot. AFO's plan was to insert India (Speedy and Bob plus Hans, a SEAL Team 6 operator from the Northern AFO element) south of Zawar Ghar. The trio would scale Zawar Ghar, then hike north to establish an observation post from which they could monitor several areas of reported enemy activity, including the villages in the Shahikot, and to assess the potential of the area south of the Shahikot for future AFO missions. The day was spent in a frenzy of planning and coordination as AFO lined up several intelligence, surveillance, and reconnaissance (ISR) aircraft as well as Navy F-14s and F-18s and at least one AC-130 Spectre gunship to provide on-call close air support if necessary. (The AC-130 was armed with a stabilized 105mm howitzer, as well as 40mm and 25mm cannons, and could deliver devastatingly accurate fire from thousands of feet above the ground.) The team took off in a 160th Chinook shortly after nightfall and, in order to avoid arousing suspicion, followed the route used by all helicopters to resupply the Khowst safe house. But again the men of India Team were to be frustrated. An impenetrable layer of cloud covered both their primary and alternate landing zones. At 7:31 p.m. the clouds parted for a long moment, allowing the EP-3E shadowing the mission to scan the countryside and report nothing unusual. But that was all the luck India was to have that evening. The mission was canceled. The team flew back to Gardez.

However, the night was not to be wasted. Juliet Team decided to take advantage of the ISR aircraft assembled in the sky for India's mission and instead embark on their environmental recce. Joining Juliet's three Delta operators in two Toyota pickups were Jason, the Gray Fox SIGINT NCO, and Jay, the Air

Force combat controller. Driving and riding shotgun were four other operators: Sergeant Major Al Y., a laid-back Alabaman and the senior NCO in B Squadron's recce troop, who had traveled from Bragg with India and Juliet; Captain John B., another Delta operator who was the northern AFO setup's impressive commander; Hans; another SEAL Team 6 NCO called Nelson. Together Hans and Nelson made up Northern AFO Team Two. The plan was for Juliet's five men to jump off at a predetermined drop-off point in the mountains and trek to their observation post on foot. They picked a spot on Serawray, a mountain five miles southwest of the safe house that overlooked the Gardez to Zermat road. Once ensconced there, Juliet's mission was to keep an eye on several "named areas of interest" (as the military refers to spots on the map that require particular attention), monitor the Zermat road and other trails, creek beds, and draws north of the Shahikot for patterns of enemy movement, and collect "technical information," or signals intelligence—all while surviving the elements and staying out of sight of the hundreds of enemy fighters thought to be in the area.

The small convoy pulled out of the compound and headed southeast toward the Sate Kandow. Driving with night-vision goggles instead of headlights, the operators coaxed the pickups off road and into the mountains. When they reached the drop-off point, Juliet's five men jumped out and said their goodbyes. As the trucks turned around, the handful of Americans slung their rucks over their backs and began climbing south up the mountain, their M4 carbines in their hands. They started at 7,733 feet, just below the snowline, and climbed steadily upward. The weather worsened by the hour. A blizzard engulfed them as they labored through the thick snow and thin air. Now their endurance—and their gear—would be put to the test.

The tough terrain, deep snow, and blinding storm eventually forced them away from their planned route. They descended to 8,300 feet to look for another path, but the steep slopes and awful weather persuaded them that the smartest course of action was to rest until daylight. While at least one man kept watch, the others huddled on the mountainside and tried to sleep. It wasn't easy. They had packed with survival, not comfort, in mind.

By daybreak almost twelve inches of snow had fallen. But the weather had cleared enough that they could plan another route to their desired observation post. They began their ascent. As they crept forward, Juliet saw no enemy guards. They concluded that the enemy's positions were oriented on the roads that led toward the Shahikot. The Arabs and Uzbeks apparently did not anticipate anyone—least of all the soft, decadent Americans—would hike in along the snowbound ridgelines. "They really didn't expect us to be walking anywhere," said an operator. "They all expected the helo, which is what the whole world expects America to come in on." Moving steadily, Juliet team reached its goal before sundown. The spot they picked faced southwest at 8,700 feet, just below Serawray's peak. From this vantage point, looking through their high-powered scopes, Juliet could see people on the streets of Jannekhel, a town six kilometers to the southwest on the Gardez to Zermat road. Turning south, they could see the western slopes of snow-covered ridgelines flattening out into a valley of terraced fields and mud-brick houses about eight miles (14 kilometers) away. They were finally gazing upon the Shahikot.

SHAHIKOT means "Place of the Kings" in Pushto, and the valley had a long history as a place of refuge, if not for kings, then certainly for warlords. It had been a stronghold for Pushtun guerrilla commander Jalalluddin Haqqani during the 1980s. A glance at the map made it easy to see why. The Shahikot's terrain strongly favored the defender. It was riddled with natural and man-made caves. Criss-crossing the valley floor were dry creek beds that doubled as trails into the mountains. The key terrain—that which, when held by either side, will provide a decisive advantage—was in the ridgelines: the Whale, the eastern ridge, and the Finger. From the Whale, the enemy enjoyed a commanding view of the approach from Gardez, and could see any vehicle approaching from several miles away. "You don't really have to do too much to get yourself seen," said a Dagger NCO. "It's a difficult area to get into without being observed. . . . You're only going to get so close before you either one, get seen, or two, start getting engaged. And once you've been observed and engaged, then the cat's out of the bag."

JULIET spotted little of note, observing only three vehicles, all traveling along the Gardez to Zermat road. They spent their second night in the mountains. They were at the limits of even their endurance, shivering on the edge of hypothermia. Their superior fitness and cold weather equipment saved them.

The next morning the team retraced their steps to where they had begun their trek into the mountains. The same operators who had driven them out the previous evening picked them up. When they had returned to the safe house and warmed up, they gave their report. The 1:100,000 maps they had been using were not good enough for navigation and planning, due to the fifty-meter contour level. This observation made the Juliet members the first—but by no means the last—U.S. soldiers to complain that their maps of the Shahikot did not match reality. Better resolution was offered by Soviet 1:50,000 maps that AFO had, as well as the FalconView computerized mapping program. Jason, the Gray Fox NCO, said he had been able to communicate well with the Air

Force RC-135 Rivet Joint aircraft that was supporting Juliet's mission. (The Rivet Joint is an extensively modified C-135 whose crew of thirty-two can detect, identify, and geolocate almost any electronic or communications broadcasts across the electromagnetic spectrum, and then forward that information in real time to intelligence consumers, be they national-level decision-makers in Washington or NCOs shivering on the side of an Afghan mountain.) The team also discovered to their dismay that batteries died very quickly in the mountains. This was a serious problem. The green, brick-sized BA5590 batteries powered their radios and laptop computers—their lifeline to Gardez and beyond. Under normal conditions two batteries would run a PRC-117 satellite radio nonstop for forty-eight hours, but the cold cut this time in half. This meant that when the teams returned to the Shahikot before D-Day, they would have to strike a balance between increasing their overall loads and sacrificing food and cold-weather gear in order to carry more batteries.

WHILE Juliet shivered on Serawray on February 21, India Team prepared for its long-delayed mission to reconnoiter the southern approaches to the Shahikot. The area around the valley was increasingly popping up in human, signals, and imagery intelligence reports, but at only five places did two of the intelligence disciplines indicate enemy activity. These were: a pair of DShK heavy machine gun positions on the Whale, where man-made structures had

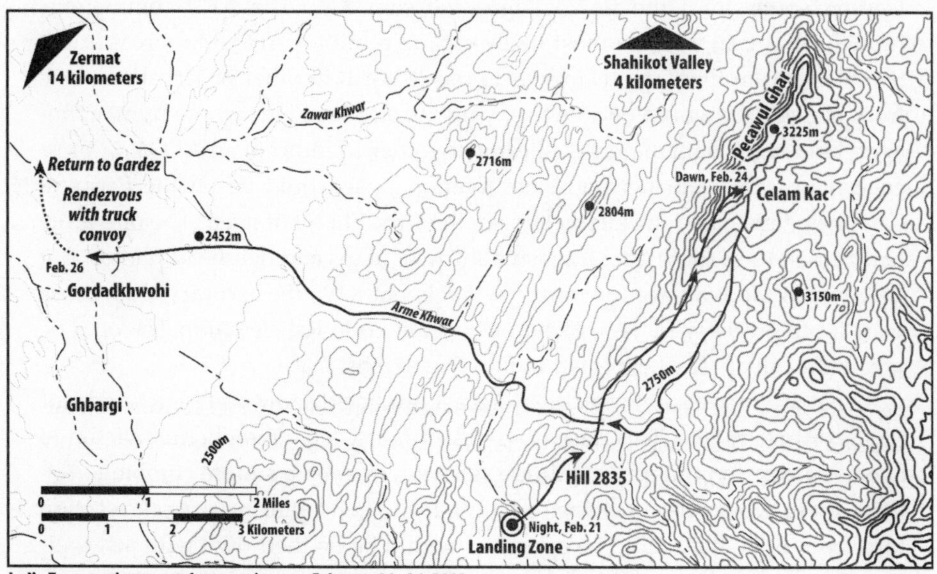

India Team environmental reconnaissance, February 21 - 26, 2002

shown up in overhead imagery; the Ewadzkhal cave area, where human intelligence and the Predator had identified enemy activity; a spot in the middle of the Upper Shahikot Valley where signals and imagery indicated activity; and at Jahangir Kot, six kilometers south of the Shahikot, where human intelligence and signals intelligence came together. There were only two locations where all three intelligence disciplines coalesced. The first was a cave along the Sorbuchi Khwar, a stream that ran south from the Shahikot to the east of the Finger. An overhead system had photographed a vehicle with personnel standing nearby on a road beside the stream. The CIA's agents reported a cave near there with many Al Qaida and Taliban forces. Intercepted transmissions also suggested this was an enemy hideout. The second location was an Al Qaida headquarters that spies said was just south of Celam Kac, a hamlet about five kilometers south of the Shahikot. The AFO troops got their hands on overhead photos that indicated three buildings at the location of the supposed headquarters. Signals intercepts supported this conclusion. All this information was fed to India Team to help focus their reconnaissance.

But time was running out. Anaconda was scheduled to kick off in less than a week. If India's mission was to be a "go," it had to be tonight. The plan was still to infiltrate the team by helicopter onto the southern slopes of the Zawar Ghar range about a dozen kilometers south of the Shahikot. The team was to move immediately to an observation post where they would spend the day watching a spot where the Arme Khwar stream that ran east to west met a trail leading south from the tiny village of Celam Kac. The AFO commandos thought that trail was the most likely escape route for Al Qaida forces in the Shahikot. From there the team was to move north to other observation posts from which they would be able to spy on the two locations where human, imagery and signals intelligence all came together to indicate an Al Qaida presence. The team's northernmost observation post would be on the Pecawul Ghar ridgeline, just four kilometers south of the Shahikot itself. The operators had chosen their route after intensive study of maps and overhead photos. But they weren't looking for the most navigable path. On the contrary, they chose their route precisely for its treacherous terrain and high elevation. It would be where the enemy least expected to find Americans.

That afternoon a new weather forecast predicted snow and high winds for the next three nights. This raised the stakes. If any team member fell victim to enemy attack, hypothermia, altitude sickness, or even a simple climbing accident, there would be no chance of a medevac helicopter or a quick reaction force coming to their aid. The operators would be on their own with just their weapons and their wits to protect them. For many commanders, whether or not to send the team on such a perilous mission would have been a tough call. But it was a no-brainer to Blaber. He had full faith and confidence in his troops' ability. Speedy and Bob had spent their lives stalking game in some of the most isolated parts of the United States. In Blaber's view they were uniquely qualified for the mission. He was taking a calculated risk, but the potential payoff in information was worth it. The mission was a go.

Four men would brave the mountains. The original India Team members—Speedy and Bob—were again joined by Hans the SEAL. Added to the mix was a quiet, black-haired NCO of medium build called Dan, a Gray Fox linguist in his mid-twenties whose job would be to intercept and monitor communications using a small piece of equipment that resembled a police radio scanner. In the darkness a pair of the 160th's MH-47E Chinooks landed outside the safe house. The four operators climbed aboard and the helicopters flew south into the night. But again, the preferred landing zone on the south side of Zawar Ghar was obscured by clouds. This time the operators decided to take a chance. They had the helicopters fly about ten kilometers west along the southern slopes of Zawar Ghar to a break in the mountains. There, the two Chinooks banked right and then right again, heading north and then east along the mountain range's northern face until they reached an alternate landing zone in Zawar Ghar's northern foothills. The four passengers jumped out at the bottom of a small mountain Speedy judged to be "Hill 2835" (so named because that was its height in meters), on top of which he planned to establish their first observation post. But as they clambered toward this initial destination, they realized, as Juliet had several days before, that the maps did not do the terrain justice. It was far more uneven and tougher to traverse than the team had anticipated. Again and again they had to descend into steep ravines and then attempt the backbreaking climb back out the other side. When they reached the peak, Speedy saw another small mountain about a kilometer to the northeast. It could only be Hill 2835. They had just spent hours climbing the wrong mountain. Speedy broke the bad news to his colleagues and they set off again, slipping and sliding in single file over a seemingly endless series of ridges and humps.

Delta's extensive mountain training in Montana and elsewhere had taught the AFO troops what equipment was needed to endure such a harsh environment. They would be walking for miles on end at high altitude, so their clothing and sleeping gear had to be warm enough to keep them alive and ready to fight, but not so bulky or heavy that it slowed them down. They wore black thermal underwear for warmth under desert camouflage Gore-Tex jackets and pants that kept them dry in the snow. Waterproof gloves protected their hands. Each team member wore his favorite brand of cold-weather combat boots. On their heads the operators wore Pro-Tek foam-lined plastic sports helmets that they modified by cutting off the earpieces and adding chinstraps and mounts for their night-vision goggles. The helmets offered no ballistic protection but weighed less than a pound and allowed the operators to avoid wearing the awkward face mounts for night-vision goggles. They also wore Peltor earmuff-style radio headphones, which blocked out loud noises like close-in gunfire while enhancing distant sounds like footsteps. The operators also carried Afghan scarves and blankets, so that if seen from afar as they picked their way along the ridgelines, they wouldn't stand out immediately as Americans. None of them wore body armor. Too heavy and bulky for their mission, it also prevented snipers from lying fully prone. In an effort to save weight, the operators carried just one cold-weather sleeping bag between them, to be used only in emergencies. "If a guy went hypothermic, we could at least stuff him in a bag and warm him back up," an operator said. Otherwise, they slept in "Norwegian sleeping bags" they had bought on a mission in Bosnia. These were little thicker than military poncho liners and could be rolled into tiny packages and stuffed in rucks. When bedding down, an operator would slip the Norwegian sleeping bag into a "bivvy sack," a Gore-Tex shell that kept the sleeping bag—and the soldier inside it—dry. Before moving out, the operators packed the sleeping gear, food, water, and communications equipment into civilian long-range mountaineering and hunting rucks designed to distribute weight evenly. The commandos spraypainted these in khaki and tan camouflage patterns, except for a couple that came with a preprinted camouflage design for civilian hunters.

Bob the "pack mule" broke the trail. As they ascended the real Hill 2835, this meant creating a path through thigh-deep snow that sucked energy from them at every step. The conditions were brutal. The effort required to hump eighty-pound rucksacks uphill through thick snow at high altitude forced the team to pause every half-dozen steps. It was a cloudless night. The temperature hovered around 20 degrees Fahrenheit, but the cold didn't bother the operators as long as they were moving. "You'd be sweating while you were climbing, and as soon as you sat down to rest, in about three or four minutes you'd be cold because the wind was blowing and you'd start to chill instantly," an operator recalled. "As soon as we started getting cold, we'd get up and start moving again." The slope became so steep that the operators were crawling up on their hands and knees. Dan, the linguist whose day-to-day job gave him the least preparation for such exertions and who might reasonably have been expected to complain or quit, just kept putting one foot in front of the other. Hans, the SEAL Team 6 operator, was a different story, especially as he realized how far Speedy expected the team to hike over the next several days. "This is bullshit," he complained. "We're never going to make it." It was a refrain he would keep up for the rest of the mission, but Speedy ignored him. The team leader was determined to gain the high ground, even if their calves, thighs, and lungs had to pay a terrible price to reach it. If the enemy spotted them, Speedy wanted to be on a ridgeline or a mountaintop, not down in a valley. He was sure that even though they were only four men armed with rifles, once on the high ground they could hold off any attack until close air support jets arrived.

The team reached the summit thoroughly spent and with daylight less than an hour away. From their perch they had a clear view down the northeast slope of Hill 2835 to the confluence of the Arme Khwar and the trail from Celam Kac about 1500 meters to the northeast, where signals intelligence had indicated some activity. The operators spent the rest of February 22 holed up behind some rocks watching the spot, taking turns to try to sleep. Using a small Panasonic laptop, Speedy wrote a report and sent it back to Gardez as a document over the satellite radio. The team saw nothing moving. When darkness fell, they pulled their rucksacks over their shoulders and set out again, heading for the slopes of Pecawul Ghar, the peak of which rose six kilometers to the northeast. They left Hill 2835 via a draw on its eastern side. Compared to the climb up, it was easy movement despite the sharp incline, because the waist-deep snow prevented them from falling when they lost their balance. Once at the bottom of the mountain the snow only came up to their knees, and they reached the Arme Khwar stream within two hours of setting off. It was a bright, moonlit night. While Dan and Hans rested, Speedy and Bob spent an hour reconnoitering farther upstream to the east. They saw nothing out of the ordinary, and, after locating a spot that could be used for an emergency helicopter landing zone, they rejoined the others. The team began climbing the southern slopes of Pecawul Ghar, which lay just across the creek from Hill 2835. Here the sun had melted the snow, but this actually made the ground more difficult and dangerous to cross. The loose shale underneath frequently gave way as the operators' feet searched for purchase on the steepest slopes. At one point their path was blocked by a sheer-sided 100-meter-deep ravine they knew they could not traverse, so they had to double back and around. The thin atmosphere again slowed the team's movement, and they had to stop to catch their breath every minute or two. They would start to climb again as soon as the wind chilled the sweat on their bodies to the point where they were shivering uncontrollably. This usually took no more than two minutes. Few words were spoken. They were too busy gasping for air. Only the sounds of their boots slipping on the rocks and their labored breathing broke the silence of the Afghan night. When they finally stopped before dawn, they had climbed to about 3,000 meters. They settled in for the day on the eastern side of Pecawul Ghar's long southern ridgeline. They had only traveled about three kilometers as the crow flies, but to their aching muscles and burning lungs it might have been thirty.

ON February 22 Blaber finally lost patience with the risk-averse attitude he perceived on the part of the CIA, TF Dagger, and other higher headquarters regarding the dangers of the Zermat road. He ordered an armed recce to proceed the next day. The CIA and Dagger personnel in the safe house tried to dissuade him. Their sense, reinforced by the "safety first" message broadcast by almost all higher headquarters, was that the roads were too dangerous to drive down. Blaber was incredulous. "Hey look, guys, I use deductive reasoning to make my decisions," he told them. "We've already driven the Sate Kandow Pass. I drove here from Kabul. I've driven almost every road in and around Kandahar. How can you tell me that the one road that sits right outside this fort, with [our] 300 Afghans, we can't drive down? I'm driving down it tomorrow."

Despite Blaber's confidence, Glenn Thomas, Texas 14's team leader, and his team sergeant continued their efforts to dissuade the AFO guys from driving down the road right up to when the vehicles pulled away, according to two accounts. (Thomas disputed this. "That absolutely did not happen," he said.)

The six-vehicle convoy consisted of Juliet's three Delta NCOs, the Northern AFO command element (Captain John B., Sergeant Major Al Y., and Master Sergeant Isaac H.), Nelson from Northern AFO Team 2, Jason from Gray Fox, Jay from the Air Force, and a group of Afghans led by Rasul, Zia's second in command. Texas 14 remained behind, ready to respond in case the convoy got into trouble. The trucks pulled out of the compound at 10:30 a.m. This time they turned left into the town of Gardez, then headed south. The snow lay thick along the roadsides, and the hair was standing up on the back of the operators' necks as they drove through what was, for them, uncharted terrain.

But once again Blaber's instincts proved correct. The convoy did not come under fire once as it drove south. The troops even threw candy at the wide-eyed children who ran to the side of the road to stare and wave at these strange-looking men. The recce was by no means uneventful, however. As the Americans passed a typical mud fort near Janekkhel, they came upon four men guarding a checkpoint. At the sight of the convoy the quartet took off running. In an act of loyalty that impressed the AFO troops, several of Rasul's men sprinted after them, while another, armed with a PK machine gun, took up position on a nearby knoll. Rasul's troops caught up with and captured the four checkpoint guards after a lung-busting 500-meter dash. The detainees were left at the side of the road with seven AMF fighters and a truck while the rest of the convoy drove on toward Zermat. Once there, the trucks turned around and headed back. After picking up Rasul's men and the detainees, they saw a pickup truck barreling toward them along the road from Zermat. The AFO men and their Afghan allies took up defensive positions, but the truck stopped and it quickly became apparent that its four occupants had come to negotiate, not to fight. A man stepped out of the vehicle and approached the AFO troops. He explained he was the commander of the four detainees and demanded their release. The AFO troops denied his request, but, thinking quickly, told him he was free to follow them back to Gardez and there discuss the matter further. He agreed and fell in trail behind the convoy. Once back at the safe house, the AFO troops got out of their vehicles, surrounded the truck, and detained the four men in addition to the four captives they had already taken. A search of the vehicle turned up a PK machine gun, several AKs, other small arms, and ammunition.

The Americans soon realized they had trapped a fairly big fish. The prisoners' leader was Mohammed Naim, the Zermat "police chief" and reportedly the main supplier of food and other necessities to Al Qaida forces in the Shahikot. He was quickly dispatched to Bagram for further questioning. The interrogations of the captured men revealed that Zermat was a vital source of logistical and moral support for the forces gathering in the Shahikot. This support emanated from the town's Islamic school, or *madrassa*. "The *madrassa* was obviously the mechanism through which the local population was coerced, required, indentured, whatever, to provide resources and support to this pile o' bad guys that occupied the Lower Shahikot Valley," Rosengard said, with what he acknowledged was 20/20 hindsight. "[Local] people were asked by the people that worked for the *madrassa*, 'Hey, it's your turn now, dude, you've gotta provide a goat and some cheese and some milk, and if you have some clothing . . . but you're gonna provide resources.'"

In a briefing to the Mountain TOC after the battle, Blaber said reopening the road was perhaps the most "mission critical" task AFO accomplished to facilitate the recon missions. For India Team it would turn out to be a lifesaver.

AS night fell on February 23, India continued north. They were now moving through treacherous terrain, sometimes having no choice but to walk along the crest of Pecawul Ghar, which in places was only two meters wide with a sheer drop on either side. With the wind gusting to forty miles per hour, it was no place for an attack of vertigo. The temperature was below freezing. Speedy coaxed his men beyond what they had thought were the limits of their endurance. Despite Hans's complaints, Speedy had no intention of canceling the mission just because it was tough going. As long as he had batteries and food, he was determined to continue. Quitting just wasn't in Speedy's vocabulary. He had broken both feet in Ranger School and still gritted his teeth and carried on to graduate. (It was a costly display of determination—foot problems plagued him for the rest of his Army career.) Here the risks were manageable, especially with the air cover the team enjoyed. There was always at least one aircraft scouting the route ahead reporting any potential dangers. During the daytime Predators and EP-3Es filled this role. At night the drone of an AC-130 could often be heard overhead. (Worried the aircraft noise would draw attention to the area, Speedy sometimes sent the planes off station once they had checked his route.)

India Team stopped before dawn on February 24 about 1500 meters southwest of the peak of Pecawul Ghar, and a similar distance directly west of Celam Kac, which appeared uninhabited. Down the slope to their right they could see the three structures south of Celam Kac where all three intelligence disciplines had indicated suspicious activity. Upon closer examination, it was clear that what had appeared in the imagery as possible buildings were actually ruins or fighting positions made of stones. There was no sign of recent human activity. Indeed, the operators had seen no one but themselves since bidding farewell to their buddies who had driven them down from Gardez. With the winter sun warming their chilled bones, it was hard to imagine there were hundreds of enemy fighters hidden nearby. *Maybe we're in a dry hole,* they thought. *Maybe there ain't nobody out here. Maybe we're on a wild-goose chase.*

Speedy's only concern was battery power. To stretch out the life of his last few batteries he shut down the radio when he wasn't using it. But he didn't like doing this, because it took a couple of minutes to power back up. If an enemy force spotted the team and suddenly attacked, those 120 seconds could spell the difference between close air support jets arriving in the nick of time or never even getting the call for help. On February 24 Speedy called Blaber and told him the team needed to be resupplied or pulled out within the next twenty-four to forty-eight hours.

That night they struck out for the peak of Pecawul Ghar. The balmy weather in which they had luxuriated a few hours previously disappeared. Just as the forecast had predicted, a ferocious blizzard blew up out of nowhere, reducing visibility to a few feet and driving snow into the operators' faces as they struggled to keep their balance. Each man concentrated on keeping sight of the figure in front of him, who shimmered like a greenish-white ghost in the night-vision goggles each member wore. The only advantage conferred by such godawful weather was that it reduced the chances of running into an enemy patrol to almost zero. Struggling to keep their footing, the operators finally reached the 10,578-foot peak and immediately sought shelter from the elements. The wind was from the east, but Pecawul Ghar's western side was a sheer cliff. There was no escape from the icy gale. The team's only option was to move a short distance back down the eastern slope to some rocks sticking straight up out of the mountainside. Squeezing into crevices, they used bungee cords to string their ponchos across the gaps between the rocks to protect them from the snow and wind driving sideways into the mountain. They hunkered down and waited for morning. The miserable conditions made real sleep out of the question. Their lightweight sleeping gear meant they were lucky to drift off for a few minutes before their own shivering woke them. By the time dawn cast its cold gray light across the jagged landscape, fourteen inches of new snow lay thick around the operators.

The location would have made an ideal observation post, but for the weather. A cloud layer blanketed everything below, completely obscuring the spots the team had come to observe. They were only three kilometers south of the Shahikot, and had proven that it was possible to infiltrate on foot from the south without being detected. But their batteries and their own physical energy were being sapped by the cold weather and frozen ground covered with deep snow. When they relayed all this back to Gardez, Blaber followed Speedy's recommendation and decided to exfiltrate the team.

(Additional factors contributed to Blaber's decision. Along with his intel analyst Glenn P. and Texas 14 leader Glenn Thomas, the AFO commander had driven to Kabul and attended a midday meeting February 24 with Rich, the CIA chief of station, and Lieutenant Colonel Chris Haas of TF Dagger. The meeting's purpose was to discuss the roles to be played by Dagger, the CIA, and AFO in Operation Anaconda. With D-Day set for February 28, Blaber needed to get his men back to Gardez from the side of the mountain quickly if he were to reinsert them for the recce mission inside the Shahikot prior to the Rakkasan air assault.)

After being told that one of the Mi-17s controlled by the CIA would pick them up at the emergency LZ that Speedy and Bob had located northeast of Hill 2835, the four members of India wearily climbed down Pecawul Ghar and began the five-kilometer trek south. This time they took a different, much easier route. Having seen no sign of the enemy or anyone else, Speedy felt confident enough to pick up a trail in the valley south of Celam Kac and follow it until it intersected with the Arme Khwar. Once on the trail, the four got their first indication that maybe this wasn't a wild-goose chase after all. The path was well worn, but how recently and by whom there was no way to know.

Again the weather interfered with their plans. Earlier in the day the solid bank of clouds above them had begun to break apart, but as the team closed on the LZ, the weather worsened again. A call to Gardez confirmed that the Mi-17 flight had been canceled. But because AFO had opened the Zermat road, there was another option: to drive south and pick up India. While AFO headquarters scrambled to put together an alternate plan for extracting India, Speedy marched his men west along the Arme Khwar stream, the direction they would have to take to meet a ground exfiltration force. When they passed the foot of Hill 2835, they found the first ominous sign that they were not alone in the area: two or three pairs of footprints in snow that had fallen since India had walked over the same ground on their way north a couple of days previously. Fighting positions that were little more than low stone walls lined both sides of the Arme Khwar. Having followed Blaber's orders to read up on the area's military history, Speedy realized these positions dated back to the 1980s. As with the trails north past Celam Kac, weather conditions at that time of year made the Arme Khwar route unsuitable for motor vehicles, but it was more than adequate for horses and donkeys, to judge from the hoofmarks and dung along the trails. The creek cut through the mountains, and rock walls rose almost sheer on each side of the streambed. Gazing up, the operators saw caves in the rock face, some clearly man-made with narrow trails leading up to them.

Physically exhausted and moving cautiously through the rough, potentially enemy-controlled terrain, the team had taken longer than Speedy had anticipated to make it back this far. Dawn had broken some hours ago, exposing the four to anyone staring down from one of the caves. Speedy began to second-guess his decision to trade speed for security by taking the low ground. For the first time on the mission, the India Team leader felt vulnerable. He opted to move the patrol up one of the trails and explore some of the caves overlooking the creek. Still unsure the exfil was going to happen that day, he decided to wait in a cave for word from Gardez. Most of the caves were small—barely large enough for one or two men. But the opening to one measured twenty feet by fifteen feet, and inside the floor was tiered. The operators found trash and firewood in the caves and along the trails, but it all looked several weeks old. Nevertheless, this evidence validated the ratline theory put forward by TF Dagger's Brian Sweeney. A sizable force had come through here this winter.

The team found a suitable cave and settled in. Looking around their temporary quarters, the operators contemplated how many other warriors had taken refuge in there over the preceding centuries. After a few hours in the most comfortable surroundings they had enjoyed for five days, the operators called Gardez, to be told a ground convoy would pick them up. But there was no precise pickup point established. Instead, Speedy told Gardez he would move west and try to find a good spot. As India resumed their march, four Toyota pickups pulled out of the safe house gate and headed south.

After seeing no humans during the entire patrol, India then spotted suspicious activity in the tiny village of Ghbargi, about 1.5 kilometers south of Gordadkhwohi, which was about seventeen kilometers southeast of Zermat. The village was inhabited. Outside a three-story building a knot of men wore dark clothing that seemed out of place among the other pedestrians' pale *shalwar kameez* suits. The team noted the building's grid reference, then moved to a deserted location just north of Gordadkhwohi that Speedy decided was the best place around for a dozen Americans to link up without being noticed. So it proved. John B.'s convoy made the rendezvous with no problems. After the briefest of greetings India climbed into the Toyotas. The trucks sped back to Gardez, where Speedy, Bob H., Hans, and Dan spent the afternoon thawing out and being debriefed by Glenn P., the AFO intel analyst.

Every member of India Team had reason to feel proud of what they had just accomplished. They had crept through a snowbound, frozen hell to penetrate deep into enemy-held territory unseen, proving the southern routes were a viable avenue of approach for future reconnaissance missions timed to precede the launch of Anaconda. Further, though Speedy remained unconvinced of a large Al Qaida presence in the area, they had found evidence suggesting the enemy was using the trails and wadis to the south of the Shahikot as routes into Pakistan, and they had been able to check several sites pinpointed by intelligence. Most important, together with Juliet Team they had proven Blaber's theory that the awful Afghan winter weather in the mountains actually gave superbly equipped athlete-warriors like those in Delta a clear advantage over their enemies. This was to prove a mixed blessing for India Team. While they had been scrambling through the snow and ice at 10,000 feet, events in Bagram and Kabul had been moving forward apace. The generals had set an H-Hour of dawn on February 28, less than two days away. India's prize for the near-perfect execution of their mission was to be handed a tougher one. There was no time to rest on their laurels. Out came the maps and the imagery. It was time to start planning.

18.

AS men and materiel flowed into Bagram, inside Dagger's AOB building where most collaborative planning took place, officers from all task forces were hashing out the final details of the Anaconda plan, often in tense debates tinged with acrimony and mutual suspicion.

The basic thrust of the plan that developed changed little from the concept that Hagenbeck, Mikolashek and Franks had approved February 17: TF Hammer—Glenn Thomas's and Matthew McHale's A-teams, plus Zia's 300–400 militiamen—would approach the Shahikot from the west, while TF Rakkasan sealed the trails and passes running east and south out of the valley; TF K-Bar's motley crew of SEALs, Special Forces, and allied special ops units would form an outer ring of security, together with some other Afghan militia forces; TF 64's Australian SAS troopers would keep watch to the south of the valley; and TF 11's door-kickers would remain at Bagram, ready to launch if one of the "big three" high-value targets was spotted.

What this plan was designed to accomplish was encapsulated in CJTF Mountain's mission statement for Anaconda:

CJTF Mountain attacks to destroy (capture or kill) Al Qaida vicinity Objective Remington (Shir-Khan-Kheyl), and to identify or disrupt Al Qaida insurgency support mechanisms and exfiltration routes into Pakistan. On order conduct follow-on operations to clear selected objectives and interdict Al Qaida movements in Area of Operations Lincoln.

The plan envisaged defeating the enemy in the Shahikot within three days, allowing Hagenbeck to make a decision the morning of the fourth day: whether to launch further attacks on fleeing Al Qaida forces and other enemy troops between the Shahikot and the Pakistan border (an area referred to as AO Lincoln), or, if no other targets presented themselves, to conduct civil affairs operations to help the civilian population around the Shahikot. Wille and Ziemba each told their bosses that they anticipated a two-week operation in and around the Shahikot, but they were rebuffed. "We were told, 'No, this is gonna be a three-day operation,'" Wille said.

Central to the plan were intelligence assumptions of enemy strength in and around the Shahikot, and of what the enemy's intentions were. There was broad consensus that there were 150-250 enemy fighters in the valley. The view of Jasey Briley, Hagenbeck's senior intelligence officer, based on intelligence from sources interacting with the enemy fighters and on Al Qaida's recruiting activity at local mosques, was that the guerrillas were waiting out the winter in their mountain fastness before launching a spring offensive to retake Gardez and Zermat with the support of local Taliban figures. Two tribal leaders had reported similar Al Qaida plans to the American contingent at Gardez.

Locals usually described the fighters in the valley as "Arabs and Chechens," but it is likely that many Uzbeks were referred to as "Chechens" because they shared the Russian language. The Americans believed these fighters would be vastly outnumbered in the Shahikot by the valley's civilian population, estimated at 800, as well as some of the fighters' own families. This assumption that they would be forced to distinguish between local civilians and hardened fighters was a driving factor in the Americans' planning. They geared everything to avoid the nightmare of a battlefield strewn with civilian corpses. The Mountain planners shared Rosengard's view that using Zia's force as the main effort would minimize the chances of needless civilian deaths. The Rakkasans focused much of their energy on how to discern enemy fighters among the civilian crowds expected to approach their blocking positions. (No civilians were to be allowed to leave the valley during the operation, however.)

As to the enemy fighters, the intelligence assessment was that they were concentrated on the valley floor around Serkhankhel. The Mountain intelligence staff expected the enemy to have observation posts just to the west of the valley "for early warning," and similar positions and air defense systems on the Whale and the eastern ridge. But much of this was little more than educated guesswork. For two months the United States had focused spy satellites, spy planes, and plain old spies on the Shahikot, but was finding it impossible to sketch out the enemy positions with any clarity. "We had just about every available intel asset focused on a ten-kilometer by ten-kilometer box around the objective, but we still had a lot of gaps that we had to fill, and we did that with templates and common sense based on what we had seen before, especially at Tora Bora," Ziemba said. (By templates, she meant a process by which intelligence analysts, in the absence of hard information, suggest the possible locations of enemy positions based on previous experience.)

The planners at Bagram were equally in the dark about the weapons enemy forces might use. Their biggest concern was anything that might shoot down a helicopter. Wiercinski, the Rakkasan commander, made it clear that his priority was to get his troops on the ground safely. He was confident in their ability to handle anything that came their way once on the valley floor, but the prospect of Chinooks tumbling out of the sky in flames filled him and the other officers with dread. Such an outcome would give Al Qaida a tremendous propaganda victory, and, in a war that had cost precious few American lives so far, would be viewed in the United States as nothing short of a disaster. Although there had been little use of shoulder-held air defense missiles in the war, and no U.S. aircraft had been shot down, the Mountain planners obsessed over the possibility of the enemy using man-portable missiles such as the Soviet-made SA-7, the American Stinger or the British Blowpipe against the Allied helicopters and fixed-wing aircraft involved in Anaconda. Their fear was based on the mujahideen's success using U.S.-supplied Stingers against Soviet aircraft. But in the case of the Stinger, this threat had almost certainly evaporated. Although the mujahideen had received thousands of Stingers in the 1980s, the missiles needed careful maintenance, and the chances of any still being useful fifteen years later were low.

Of greater threat were the DShK heavy machine guns Al Qaida was assumed to have placed around the valley. These simple yet lethal weapons could bring down a helicopter up to a kilometer away. Produced by the Soviet Union and China, thousands found their way into Afghanistan during the 1980s, where they constituted the mujahideen's standard air defense weapon until the Stinger's 1986 introduction. Overhead photos revealed a couple of possible DShKs on the Whale. These became the focus of much discussion in planning meetings, but otherwise there was little hard intel about the numbers or locations of these weapons. "We had no clarity on the enemy air defenses in that area," Hagenbeck acknowledged.

The Rakkasans and Zia's militiamen would be going into combat unprotected by tanks or other armor, but little attention was paid at Bagram to any indirect fire assets such as artillery or mortars that the enemy might use to devastating effect against light infantry caught in the open. Ziemba would later say she and the other intel officers had "expected some mortars" in the Shahikot and also identified an artillery piece of unknown type there. But neither the mortars nor the howitzer were emphasized at the Mountain or Rakkasan rehearsals in the final days of February. Ziemba and her colleagues were also concerned about the threat of mines, rocket-propelled grenades (RPGs), and booby traps, as well as a BRDM reconnaissance vehicle reported to be in the area. But the commanders' focus remained on the air defense threats.

Worries over antiaircraft weaponry aside, the bottom line was that at Bagram, as at CFLCC, CENTCOM, and, apparently, the Pentagon, the thinking was was that victory was assured before the battle had even begun. "The belief was that the enemy resistance had all but collapsed," Hagenbeck, the Mountain commander, said. The assessment of "virtually all" intelligence agencies "was that they weren't going to stand and fight," he added. "That once Zia's forces confronted the enemy inside Shahikot, that there would be a standoff for somewhere between twelve and twenty-four hours, in which any HVTs would try to negotiate their way out or escape by night. And then when the sun came up the second day, the fight would be on or they would surrender. But the important people that might have been in the valley would have tried to escape. Therefore it was important for us to get our infantry troops into the blocking positions . . . and to have the main effort [be] Afghans on Afghans and Afghans against the Al Qaida early on. In all of the fights leading up to this point, there had not been . . . fierce resistance."

(Rosengard, on the other hand, said later that in Dagger's view, the enemy leaders would try to escape—hence his plan to leave the eastern trail open—but the rank and file would fight hard to cover their leaders' withdrawal, albeit with nothing heavier than machine guns and RPGs. Ziemba's prediction, she said, was similar: once U.S. and allied Afghan forces appeared in the Shahikot, the enemy's priority would be to get their senior leaders out. Their next objective would be for as many fighters as possible to slip the noose tightening around their positions while some stayed to inflict U.S. casualties and, if possible, take an American prisoner. Finally, the enemy would try to get their remaining fighters out, in order to regroup elsewhere when conditions permitted. The enemy's center of gravity was its senior and mid-level leadership, the Mountain intel staff concluded. "It seemed that their loss would unhinge the defense," Ziemba said.)

Like other officers in Bagram, Hagenbeck noted that he and his staff had war-gamed several scenarios to ensure that if events didn't go quite according to plan, they had enough combat power in reserve to handle the unexpected. "We worst-cased it, but the reality was that the intel said there was 150 to 250 bad guys in the valley and we had more than enough troops and firepower—read air assets—to take care of that size of a force," he said. Asked what he felt in his gut prior to the operation, Hagenbeck replied: "I had no reason to doubt the intel."

To help with the fight on the ground, Blaber asked Trebon, the TF 11 commander, to permit TF Red's Rangers to be used as additional blocking forces in the Shahikot. If there was a large enemy force in the Shahikot and it decided to fight, Blaber knew even a couple of platoons of Tony Thomas's superbly trained and equipped Rangers could be invaluable. But Trebon refused to release the Rangers from their gate-guard and quick reaction force duties at Kandahar and Bagram unless Blaber could prove there was a high-value target in the Shahikot. Of course, there was no such proof. The Rangers remained in their guard shacks and TOCs, planning for missions that never came off. Then Blaber turned to Kernan, the commander of SEAL Team 6 and TF Blue, and suggested the Navy officer commit his entire squadron to help man the Shahikot passes. But Kernan also preferred to keep his force intact at Bagram, waiting for one of the "big three" to be located. (In such an event the entire operation was supposed to freeze while the Rakkasans cordoned off the patch of terrain the high-value target was in and TF 11's operators launched from Bagram, over an hour's flight from the Shahikot, to snatch him.)

Undeterred, the AFO commander asked Kernan to instead release just his twelve-man recce troop to Blaber's command. Blaber was thinking ahead to the recce missions he wanted to run into the Shahikot. He only had India and Juliet available. They were good teams, but they wouldn't give him all the coverage of the valley he desired. SEAL Team 6's recce troops had a good reputation. Blaber held them in high enough regard to figure he could send them into the valley with the two Delta teams. Blaber had worked extensively with several of the recce SEALs in previous operations. He not only had full confidence in them, but from conversations with them knew they were itching for the sort of mission he had in mind. Kernan compromised and gave Blaber one of his two teams. The five-man team's call sign was Mako 31. It was led by a lanky, gregarious senior NCO called Mike, but better known to all as "Goody."

NO sooner had the Rakkasan, Mountain, and Dagger planners gathered in mid-February to begin putting flesh on the bones of the operational concept for Anaconda than they found themselves deeply divided over a key issue: when and where the Rakkasans should conduct the air assault. Rosengard's original concept envisaged most of the Rakkasan force landing under cover of darkness in the Upper Shahikot, then walking west to stealthily occupy the blocking positions in the passes. Only the troops who were to occupy the southernmost blocking positions needed to land in the Lower Shahikot, near Marzak, he thought. He and Paul Wille, the lead Mountain planner, thought it imperative to leave open the most heavily used trail that ran out of Serkhankhel through the eastern ridgeline. Rosengard's vision was of Zia approaching to block the western avenue of escape and a Rakkasan element landing in the gap between the Finger and the eastern ridge, preventing any exit to the south. The enemy fighters in the villages would then, he thought, make a run for it via the trail that appeared open, only to be confronted and trapped by the Rakkasans who had landed in the Upper Shahikot and, unseen, marched west to block the pass out of the valley. Rosengard and Wille thought it might even be possible to land the helicopters far enough away that the guerrillas wouldn't hear them and the Rakkasans could reach the blocking positions before the Al Qaida fighters realized they had landed. (Wiercinski, the air assault expert, ridiculed this notion: "Everybody's gonna hear those helicopters coming in.") In all this, Rosengard and Mulholland were supported by the Mountain planners as well as by Blaber and Spider. All preferred a night air assault into the Upper Shahikot.

From the moment they became involved, however, Wiercinski, Larsen, and the other senior Rakkasans were fiercely resistant to this concept. They wanted the entire air assault to go into the Lower Shahikot in daylight. The Rakkasans put forward several arguments to support their position. By landing an element in the Lower Shahikot and the rest of the air assault force in the Upper Shahikot, Wiercinski would be separating his forces by a mountain range, making mutual support impossible if either or both of the elements came under fire in the battle's opening minutes. In addition, unlike the Lower Shahikot, where overhead imagery revealed numerous potential landing zones, the Upper Shahikot was entirely snow-covered, making it impossible to determine whether there were any suitable LZs, the Rakkasans said. Dagger and Mountain staffers strongly disagreed, pointing out what they thought were several good LZs. "We determined that the snow was not that deep and we could use them," Wille said.

But, the Rakkasans argued, even if it were physically possible to land a Chinook in the Upper Shahikot, doing so would dramatically cut into the number of soldiers in the air assault. If the air assault went into the Lower Shahikot, they said, each Chinook could be filled to the max with about forty-two infantrymen. But as the altitude got higher and the air got thinner, the amount each helicopter could lift got lower. Larsen said that the proposed LZs in the Upper Shahikot were at 11,000 feet, which would only allow the Rakkasans to half fill the Chinooks. Given the tiny number of Chinooks CENTCOM had given for the operation—Hagenbeck described the number of Chinooks as "the long pole in the tent" of the Anaconda plan—landing in the Upper Shahikot would therefore impose great constraints on how many Rakkasans could get into position at the start of the battle, according to Wiercinski and Larsen.

Wiercinski also expressed doubts about trying to land helicopters in the Upper Shahikot, particularly at night. The Rakkasans had already experienced a very close call trying to land a Chinook at night in difficult terrain. A Task Force Talon Chinook had suffered a "hard landing" on the night of January 28 while inserting a small infantry force into Khowst to protect the safe house there. No soldiers were killed, but sixteen were injured and the helicopter destroyed. Wiercinski had no desire to repeat the experience. His nightmare was losing a helicopter during the air assault, and he was willing to go to the mat to minimize that risk.

The Rakkasans thought they were putting forward reasoned arguments based on the professional opinions of Lieutenant Colonel Jim Marye, the TF Talon commander, and his senior pilots. "All the helicopter guys were saying, 'No way in hell can we get back up in there,'" Larsen said. But to everyone else, it appeared as though each time they knocked down one Rakkasan argument,

Wiercinski or his staff would raise another. Among the Mountain, Dagger, and AFO field grade officers, there was deep suspicion of the Rakkasans' motives. Everyone thought the Rakkasans—the Johnny-come-latelies to the planning process—were trying to elbow the others aside with the goal of redrafting the plan so that the Rakkasans, not Zia's force, would end up assaulting Objective Remington. The Rakkasans were using the safety argument in order to become the main effort, the Dagger and Mountain officers thought. "The real reason is Colonel Wiercinski wanted to get as close as he could to Serkhankhel, to the point that they would start taking fire from Serkhankhel and once they were taking fire they could use it as an excuse to take down the objective themselves, rather than letting Task Force Dagger with Zia's forces take care of Serkhankhel," said a Mountain officer who closely monitored the planning debate. Wiercinski flatly denied any such thought crossed his mind. "Never," he said. "We always knew our mission was as the support for this thing. . . . We weren't going in to attack or seize anything."

The conversations between Wiercinski and the Mountain and Dagger officers were "not very" strained, according to the Rakkasan commander. Other participants begged to differ. There was no shouting, but a lot of raw feelings were on display, they said. "There was a lot of emotion about who gets to take down the objective," said Wille. "[Lieutenant] Colonel Rosengard, Colonel Mulholland, and Colonel Wiercinski were very emotional on the issue." Rosengard was worried that by landing along the eastern ridge's western slopes, the Rakkasans would jeopardize his goal of "making the enemy do what he already wanted to do"—flee the valley via the trail deliberately left open. "We wanted him to think that's open," Rosengard said. Putting the first air assault in close to or astride that avenue of escape could "fuck up" the plan that sought to convince the enemy to enter the trap, Rosengard told Wiercinski.

Rosengard and several other Dagger personnel were convinced that the Rakkasans failed to grasp the plan's subtleties and were interested only in executing a magnificent air assault into the valley, killing everyone they could see and claiming victory. "I part company with the Rakkasans on the fact that they lost the vision of what we were trying to accomplish," Rosengard said. "To them it was an airmobile assault into this valley." To Rosengard, the Rakkasans seemed obsessed with air assaulting almost on top of the suspected enemy positions on the valley floor. "They were seeking—and I heard these words come out of their mouth—'the psychological impact of the appearance of helicopters on the battlefield,'" he said. "I respect them for the warriors that they are . . . but in my exposure to them their instantaneous reaction to this is 'We just need to do the air assault and get in there and kill 'em all.'"

The A-teams in Gardez who would accompany Zia into the valley were equally concerned. The Special Forces captains and NCOs thought the Rakkasans wanted to land far too close to Serkhankhel. Above all, the SF soldiers feared a friendly-fire incident between the Rakkasans and Zia's troops. "We had a good clear idea of where the 101st was gonna go, [and] that was a stupid, stupid, stupid thing, because they're landing right on an objective that I'm treating as a hot objective," said a Dagger officer in Gardez.

The constant references by Larsen and Wiercinski to "the psychological impact of helicopters on the battlefield" only reinforced the special operators' view that the Rakkasans were more concerned with their place in history than with fulfilling the supporting role assigned them in the original plan. "The 101st decided that this was a helicopter legacy mission," said a special ops officer who participated in the meetings. "They allowed that to overwhelm their own common sense." But Wiercinski said all he wanted was to ensure the plan minimized the risk attached to the few moments when his force was at its most vulnerable—when the Chinooks entered the valley from the south and flew north to deposit their troops near the villages. "You only get one shot at surprise and I wanted to get that first lift down, situated in a position where they could overwatch those three towns almost immediately." he said. "Our job was to block people coming out of these towns." Rosengard and Mulholland on one side and Larsen and Wiercinski on the other were talking past each other. Their TOCs were only fifty meters apart, but in their understanding of each other's approach to warfare they were separated by a yawning cultural chasm.

For instance, Wiercinski's assertion that assaulting Objective Remington was the farthest thing from his mind is borne out by the series of internal Rakkasan briefings, rehearsals, and rock drills in the days leading up to Anaconda, in which no one mentioned that course of action. The Rakkasans focused on establishing their blocking positions as quickly as possible. Despite Rosengard's fears of a Rakkasan "kill 'em all" attitude, in talks with his subordinates Wiercinski stressed the importance of fire discipline and safeguarding civilian lives. But the Dagger, Mountain, and AFO officers did not attend these briefings. They had only their perceptions formed in the planning sessions to go on. On the other hand, Rosengard's idea of leaving the main trail free of a visible American presence—a key element in his version of the plan—made little sense to Wiercinski. "My thinking was, we're going in here to set up blocking positions," the Rakkasan commander said. "That's why you have us. Why is it you want people to escape?"

MATTERS came to a head at a February 20 war game. Rosengard made a comment that another field grade officer took as a threat to take Dagger out of the operation. "I know that happened," the officer said. "I was there." Rosengard emphatically denied making any such threat. "None of us were about to walk away from our responsibilities—immaterial of the command and control relationships that necessarily existed, and despite the resultant friction points," he said. But the fact that another officer could—even mistakenly—perceive the Dagger operations officer to be threatening to withdraw his forces shows how fractious the meetings had become. Sergeant First Class Frank Antenori, a Third SF Group NCO whose A-team was assigned to TF K-Bar, recalled sitting in Dagger's AOB building one evening when Mulholland returned from a planning meeting enraged that his advice wasn't being taken. "He said no general in the history of the United States, if you have the advantage of taking the high ground, would start off on the low ground, and try to take the hill, but these guys were doing it," Antenori said. "He was fuming mad."

It appeared to special ops folk at Bagram that Mulholland was being sidelined. It made no sense to them. The gruff, beefy colonel had extensive special operations experience. In addition to his time in Special Forces units, he had commanded a squadron in the unit now known as Gray Fox and served as a Delta staff officer. And of course, he commanded the task force whose troops had been a major reason for the United States' victory in Afghanistan, which made the trouble he had getting his point across to the Rakkasans all the more puzzling to others. "This was a guy who basically took this country with twelve A-Teams . . . and they wouldn't listen to him," Antenori said.

(Not all Mountain officers at Bagram remembered the acrimonious discussions that made an impression on their colleagues. "I thought the relationships and the personalities that came together for that operation came together remarkably well," said Bentley, the senior fire support officer in Bagram. "There was never a time when I was there that there was any animosity or misgivings as to who was doing what. I was never present in any kind of sessions where there were issues and advice not being taken." Lieutenant Colonel Mike Lundy, the deputy operations director in Hagenbeck's headquarters, agreed. "There was very good cooperation," he said. "It was as close to one team as you could get.")

WITH Wiercinski and Larsen at loggerheads with their Dagger, Mountain, and AFO counterparts, it was left to Hagenbeck to make the final decision on the night of February 22. He sided with Wiercinski. The Rakkasans would air-assault into the Lower Shahikot, in daylight. Hagenbeck said he made the call based on the Rakkasans' assessment that flying in to the Upper Shahikot would be too difficult. "The discussions on the LZs had to do with the combat experience or lack thereof of the pilots, and the risk assessment that was made, and the risk management," Hagenbeck said. Jimmy from AFO went back to Hagenbeck to counsel against the daytime air assault. "Jim, we just don't have the experience here yet, that's why we've got to do this," Hagenbeck said. "Roger that, sir, got it," replied Jimmy. "We'll do everything we can to protect that." (Despite this, in one of their last meetings with Hagenbeck before D-Day, Blaber and Spider made a final, unsuccessful attempt to dissuade him from having TF Rakkasan air-assault into the Lower Shahikot.)

That the Mountain commander made his decision only after carefully considering all sides of the argument helped mollify those whose recommendations were not taken. "He deserves an incredible amount of credit," Blaber said. "I've got a lot of respect for his leadership and management techniques. He follows the number one rule of a solid combat commander—always listen to the guy on the ground. It doesn't mean you have to do exactly what he says, but always listen to him, and you'll have a much better chance of making optimal decisions for your men." Nevertheless, Hagenbeck's decision did not sit well with everyone. One Mountain officer felt the Rakkasans had cynically played the "safety" card to advance their own interests at the expense of the larger plan, knowing how difficult it is for a commander to order a subordinate to do something that the subordinate says is "unsafe." In the modern Army, the officer said, "as soon as we mention 'safety,' then it's all over with."

Wiercinski prevailed on another point. He disagreed with Mulholland and Rosengard that the trail east out of Serkhankhel was the most likely avenue of escape for any senior enemy figures. The Rakkasan commander thought a wadi-trail combination that led from the Whale's northeast corner across the top of the valley through a gorge in the eastern ridgeline was the route that U.S. forces should leave open, before using the second wave of the air assault to cut off any enemy leaders making their exit along it. The final version of the plan reflected this. The first lift of Chip Preysler's 2-187 Infantry was given the mission to block the trail out of Serkhankhel that the Dagger leaders wanted left open. The northern path was to remain untouched until later on D-Day, when the second wave of air-assault troops would arrive to "close the back door."

WHILE the Dagger and Mountain officers worried about the Rakkasans' perceived desire to become the main effort, the Mountain staffers joined their conventional Army brethren in the 101st in concern over whether Dagger could deliver on their promise to get Zia into the fight at the prescribed hour, which was now dawn on D-Day. The force of 300–400 Afghan militiamen accompanied by a couple of dozen SF troops was supposed to travel in convoy down the Zermat road, then veer onto a dirt track that ran east toward the Whale before turning south and then east again into the valley around the southern end of the Whale, a turn that became known as "The Fishhook." Zia's fighters and the A-teams—Task Force Hammer—were the main effort in the biggest battle U.S. troops had fought in over a decade. The conventional officers wondered if they were up to the task. "The big concern from the [Rakkasan] battalion and brigade commanders was that the Afghan forces would not do their job," said Wille.

Rosengard and Mulholland tried to put the conventional officers' minds at rest. They "flat guaranteed" that Zia would arrive at the chosen hour on the battlefield, according to Wille. "Rosengard said on a couple of occasions, 'Don't worry about Zia, we've got the Zia piece licked,'" recalled Major Lou Bello, a Mountain fires planner. Despite these assurances, Hagenbeck and Wiercinski had a fall-back option if Zia's forces failed to show up: air-assaulting the TF Rakkasan reserve, Lieutenant Colonel Ron Corkran's 1-187 Infantry Battalion, into the Fishhook.

This plan reflected an apparent contradiction: Zia's force was the main effort, but its presence on the battlefield—let alone its successful execution of its mission—was not deemed essential to the success of Anaconda. "We were going to go into the Shahikot Valley, with or without Zia," said Bentley, Hagenbeck's senior fire support officer. "We always knew that we weren't going to get full resolute cooperation from the Afghans," Bello said. "We had several discussions on this because we knew the Afghans were fickle, we knew that they may or may not cooperate. We knew that they at some point would decide, 'Hey we've got to go back to the farm now and tend goats,' so that was always factored in. The plan wasn't hinging on the success of that Dagger piece with Zia. . . . There was always that concern in the planning process that Zia and the boys might not be fully cooperative."

The conventional officers voiced their doubts about Zia in terms that left their Dagger counterparts shaking their heads in the belief that the Mountain and Rakkasan officers did not understand the "human terrain" in which they they were about to fight. "There were some open comments and discussions [about whether Zia could be relied upon], which increased the friction," Wille said. "The 5th Group [i.e., TF Dagger] guys were kind of insulted by . . . the regular Army guys saying, 'These Afghan units are not gonna do shit for us.' . . . It was a sensitive issue. I specifically heard several of the staff from Colonel Wiercinski's brigade discuss it. It was brought up when everybody was in the same room and frequently brought up separately. The 5th Group guys knew their concern and said, 'We will be there.'"

THE inclusion of Harward's Task Force K-Bar in the plan as the outermost ring of security for the operation injected more tension into the planning process. "TF K-Bar were a real pain in the butt to deal with as far as getting them to locations on the other side of the Shahikot Valley where we wanted reconnaissance done," Gray said. It took "three or four days of wrangling" before Harward agreed to put his units in the observation posts the Mountain staff had chosen for them, said another Mountain staffer. "It was like working out a divorce contract for each one of those positions," he added. "If CJTF Mountain tried to tell those organizations [i.e., K-Bar and Dagger] what to do, and they didn't want to do, then it became a big food fight—a polite food fight—in terms of getting them to do it."

That they had to negotiate with units that were supposed to be working for their commander was intensely frustrating for the Mountain staff. "I could never count on units actually doing what they were tasked to do in the operations order," Wille said. "I never knew for sure. The joke was that we were running a blue-light special, and commanders could sign up for a mission if they wanted to, but they didn't have to." Their difficulties were compounded by the fact that CFLCC's order formalizing Mountain's authority over the other task forces did not take official effect until February 20. Prior to that date, Hagenbeck's staff held a series of important synchronization meetings to ensure that everyone knew what was supposed to be happening on the battlefield at each stage of the plan, in order to minimize the risk of friendly fire. With no authority to compel other task forces to send representatives, the Mountain staff found the right people rarely showed up. "We never had everybody in the same room at one time," Wille said. "Even when we did have representatives there, they weren't always decision makers. They didn't always have the authority to speak for their commander." Only after February 20 did "the more competent people" start attending the meetings, he said.

The rancorous debates that blighted the final fortnight of planning would never have happened had most of the forces involved in Anaconda been part of the 10th Mountain Division (or if Major General Dick Cody's 101st Airborne headquarters been deployed instead of Hagenbeck's, along with one or two complete brigade combat teams of its own). Lieutenant colonels and colonels from the same division, who worked day in and day out for the same commander (who in turn exercised great power over their careers), would not have dared engage in such disruptive and divisive arguments while planning a major operation. But Central Command's enthusiasm for assembling the Anaconda force in piecemeal fashion from a grab bag of units was now paying predictable dividends. In theory, Hagenbeck and his senior staff officers should have quickly settled the arguments that arose. But that was easier said than done when the Rakkasan and Dagger officers had been in Afghanistan longer than anyone from 10th Mountain. Mikolashek had sent Hagenbeck to take firm command of all these task forces and lash them together. The Mountain commander did his best in difficult circumstances. "I met with the commanders of all of these disparate units at least once and many times twice a day about an hour or so at a time in my office," he said. "The whole purpose was to build this team . . . to war-game and make a determination on how each of us thought, so that we would at least have a sense of how people would react under given situations."

But until Harrell and Jones came aboard, no Mountain staffer outranked Wiercinski or Mulholland. This encouraged the colonels and their subordinates to continue their debates longer than necessary. David Gray, Hagenbeck's director of operations, said he and his colleagues had twelve days to bring together "a coalition of coalitions of coalitions." They were very sensitive to any perception on the part of Rakkasan or, particularly, Dagger that Mountain was now in charge, even though Mountain *was* in charge. "We didn't want to come across as 10th Mountain taking over," said Wille, a statement as extraordinary as it was undoubtedly accurate.

Through all the distractions, Wille worked tirelessly on a plan that would somehow take all these disparate parts—from Norwegian special operators to barely trained Afghan tribesmen to 10th Mountain infantrymen and 101st Airborne Apache pilots—and glue them together into a war machine that would not break apart the moment it came into contact with the enemy lurking in the Shahikot. His wife Karen e-mailed him a photo of their sons Pete, Jake, and Matt, ages eight, six, and two respectively. To motivate himself and remind others of their responsibilities, he printed the photo and pinned it on the plans bay door, together with a message he had added: "If these were your sons going down to the Shahikot Valley, would the plan be good enough?"

19.

AMIDST all the squabbling over the Rakkasans' landing zones and K-Bar's observation posts, one historically significant detail about the operation being planned went unnoticed: For the first time since the November 1942 invasion

of Papua New Guinea, the U.S. Army was sending a brigade-size infantry formation into battle against prepared enemy positions with no supporting artillery.

The Mountain and Rakkasan planners wanted artillery, but they had been told repeatedly by CFLCC and CENTCOM that they weren't allowed any. "We were told we were not going to get any more than what we had already," Wille said. "That was it, period. We could not have any more forces, and we really had to work to pull the forces we did from Jacobabad, K2, and Kandahar." Bello sat through a lot of video-teleconferences involving flag officers in Bagram, Kuwait, and CENTCOM's Florida headquarters. Whenever the subject of artillery came up, the senior leaders "tap-danced" around it. "I never heard a general officer say, 'Okay, here's why we're not bringing artillery,'" Bello said. "Nobody ever said, 'Because Don Rumsfeld said we can't have artillery,' or 'General Franks said we can't have artillery.' . . . It was a sensitive decision."

Bello was unaware that Franks had told Mikolashek to forget any thoughts of deploying artillery. But after repeatedly running into negative or evasive answers when he asked his chain of command in Bagram and CFLCC headquarters in Kuwait about the possibility of bringing over artillery, Bello concluded that artillery had fallen victim to the pervasive fear at MacDill and the Pentagon that if the United States deployed anything heavier than a few mortars to fight the war in Afghanistan, the locals would view the Americans as no better than the Soviets. "If you study the Soviet Afghan experience, you come away with learning that the Soviets indiscriminately used artillery, leveled cities and towns, and that was not the impression that we wanted to give," he said.

Hagenbeck knew his staff was asking their CFLCC counterparts about artillery, but felt he had no grounds to take the matter up at the general officer level. His planners had war-gamed several scenarios that predicated an enemy in the Shahikot with more strength than intelligence reports indicated. On each occasion CJTF Mountain had enough combat power to achieve victory. The two-star thought his mortars could handle any requirement for ground-based indirect fire. "In my view I didn't have any feasible or reasonable argument to go back up the chain to General Franks and say, 'I need more of this or more of that,'" Hagenbeck said. The result was that Mountain was "operating with reduced assets," Bello said. But in Bentley's view, their task was to figure out how to maximize what had been given to them. "The force package [for Anaconda] will be debated for years," he said. "Our job was to employ the assets that we had."

When it came to fire support, those assets were not insignificant. But most were airborne. If anything packing a bigger wallop than mortars was required to subdue the enemy, it would have to come from the sky. Few in Bagram had any concerns over this state of affairs. Airpower had worked wonders in the war up to this point, and there would be a wide variety of aircraft on hand to support the troops in the valley, ranging from Apache attack helicopters to F-15E Strike Eagle and F-16 Fighting Falcon fighter-bombers and B-52 heavy bombers. At night they would be able to call on AC-130 gunships whose sensors and rapid-firing cannons could track a man or a vehicle relentlessly from 15,000 feet in the sky. But close air support was not the equivalent of flying artillery. There were several key differences between the capabilities of the aircraft that would be over the Rakkasans' heads in the Shahikot and those of the artillery batteries they had been forced to leave behind. The standard bomb used by the Air Force and Navy jets in Afghanistan—the Joint Direct Attack Munition, better known as the JDAM—was much more precise than a howitzer round. Each JDAM had a Global Positioning System-updated inertial navigation system allowing a crewmember to program it to hit a particular grid reference point. But this precision was only useful if an enemy's exact location was known. At anywhere from $27,000 to $37,000 each, using JDAMs to blanket a hillside with fire to keep enemy fighters' heads down—what the military called "suppression"—was prohibitively expensive. Once on the battlefield, artillery could keep firing under almost any conditions unless it ran out of ammunition or was physically overrun by the enemy. Airpower could not always be relied upon. Bad weather often mitigated against the use of helicopters and jet aircraft, and the Air Force kept the slow-flying AC-130s out of harm's way during daylight hours and even brightly moonlit nights. Aircraft also had to fly away from the battle area to be refueled. Unlike artillery, which always belonged to the ground commander, Wiercinski and Hagenbeck would not "own" the fixed-wing aircraft providing their close air support. Those pilots answered to their own Air Force or Navy chain of command. If the commanders on the ground needed their help, they had to request it. They could not order it.

Bringing air power to bear was a more complex process of coordination than using artillery (itself a skill many battalion and brigade commanders in the Army found tough to master). If an infantry battalion commander spotted a target he wanted artillery to take out, he told his fire support officer, who ensured there were no aircraft due to fly through the space the artillery shells would pass through, made sure no friendly troops were in the area, and then called the artillery unit, gave them the target's coordinates of the target, and told them to fire the mission. The rounds should hit home within three to five minutes. In the case of close air support the battalion commander's air liaison officer (an Air Force officer attached to the unit) had to locate an aircraft capable of hitting the target, wait for the air component chain of command to approve the mission, then orient the pilot on to the target using visual reference points like mountains, bridges, or roadways. At lower echelons Air Force enlisted personnel called enlisted tactical air controllers (ETACs) did this. All the ETACs and air liaison officers in a division worked for an Air Force lieutenant colonel who commanded the air support operations squadron collocated at the division's home base. This officer headed up the air cell in the division headquarters and bore primary responsibility for coordinating all close air support missions through Air Force channels.

However, there was a significant gap between doctrinal theory and on-the-ground reality when it came to CJTF Mountain. In early November, while 10th Mountain was still at Fort Drum, the Air Force sent Lieutenant Colonel Louis Bochain, the division's air liaison officer, to K2 to command Task Force Dagger's fires cell. This left Hagenbeck without his air liaison officer when the Mountain headquarters deployed to K2. Not that it would have mattered if Bochain had still been at Drum, because Central Command denied Hagenbeck's request to bring his air cell to K2. At least, that was how 10th Mountain told the story. But Bochain said there seemed to be more to it. He noted that LaCamera's battalion deployed to K2 with an air defense company—hardly a top priority in a war against an enemy with no air force—and that it should have been possible to meet CENTCOM's force cap requirements by swapping air defenders at K2 for his eight- or nine-person air planning cell cooling their heels at Drum. From early December when Hagenbeck's headquarters arrived at K2 Bochain tried "daily" to get his team over to join the Mountain staff. But each time he asked, Mountain staffers told him "the force cap guys" wouldn't allow it. Bochain wasn't convinced the Mountain staff understood the handicap they would face if they were ordered to fight in Afghanistan without their air planners. "This frustrating bureaucratic bullshit was going on and we're just trying to convince everybody that you've gotta get these guys over here," Bochain recalled. It never happened. Thus when Hagenbeck moved to Bagram to command and control the U.S. military's biggest set piece battle in a dozen years, he went without his air cell. If Bochain had still been with Dagger, he could at least have helped his buddies in Mountain out. But several days before serious planning for Anaconda started, he returned to the United States to be with his seriously ill father. This deprived the staffs at Bagram of the officer with the most experience coordinating close air support in Afghanistan as they prepared to fight the biggest battle of the war.

But this wasn't clear to Bochain when he left. It appeared to him, as to so many others, that the war was winding down and he wouldn't be missed. "We hadn't dropped a bomb in quite a while in support of our ODA teams, a few weeks anyway, and it was sporadic before that," he said. "After Kabul fell there was very, very little kinetic activity going on." Bochain and the other Dagger staffers were already writing after-action reports and filling out "the standard paperwork that follows up an operation," he said.

In the absence of an air cell, the Mountain and Dagger fires cells put together the broad concept for fire support during the first week of planning at Bagram, assisted by Andy Nocks from CFLCC's deep operations cell. But once Mikolashek and Franks blessed the concept of operations February 17, Bentley knew they would need an air cell. He called CFLCC headquarters in Kuwait. On the other end of the line was Air Force Major Pete Donnelly, a man of average height and weight with thinning sandy blond hair framing a boyish face. Donnelly was working in the 18th Air Support Operations Group's Air Combat Center, an Air Force organization that functioned as a link between CFLCC and its Air Force equivalent, the Coalition Forces Air Component Command (CFACC, prounounced "see-fack") at Saudi Arabia's Prince Sultan Air Base. But in peacetime he worked under Bochain at Fort Drum and was on good terms with Bentley and Bello. Bentley explained why he was calling. He briefly outlined Anaconda, mentioning the operation's name, and asked if the Air Combat Center could send anyone to stand up an air cell in Bagram. Donnelly passed the request to his boss, Colonel Mike Longoria, and volunteered to lead the mission himself. Longoria agreed, and late February 19 Donnelly and a six-person Air Force team arrived in Bagram to set up an air cell.

It was apparent to Donnelly that the Army officers planning the operation did not anticipate a major fight that would stress the capabilities of the allied air component. "It was designed as a boots-on-the-ground operation, vice an intense air operation with ground support," he said. "It definitely wasn't a top priority [of the planners] to talk to the air planners and discuss what we're going to need." Coordination with the Air Force appeared to be done "almost as an afterthought." Even though Bentley had called Kuwait eleven days before D-Day to request Air Force assistance, Donnelly viewed the Mountain staff's attitude as one of "Oh by the way, we might need some air support."

But to Mountain staffers, Donnelly's team seemed too small and ill prepared to handle its responsibilities. A Mountain officer said Donnelly, who had spent two weeks at Bochain's elbow at K2 learning how Dagger's close air support was arranged, was "a squared-away guy," but added that the same could not be said for the rest of his cell. "Those guys didn't really know what was going on," the officer said. "It was clear to me from talking to the guys . . . that the crew that was sent to man that C2 [command and control] cell was not very well trained. They didn't really understand what was going on with the operation."

The Mountain staff read Donnelly and his team in on the plan and explained how they proposed to use airpower. The only air strikes they wanted prior to TF Hammer's arrival in the Fishhook and the Rakkasans' air assault were against about a dozen targets—mostly DShK machine guns—that threatened the Rakkasans' landing zones and Zia's approach from the west. These targets were to be hit while the first wave of air assault troops was in the air between Bagram and the Shahikot. Donnelly proposed a much longer and broader air campaign. He knew the villages on the valley floor were off limits because of the presumed presence of hundreds of civilians. But as D-Day approached and snippets of new intelligence suggested an enemy presence on the high ground above the LZs, Donnelly proposed two days of saturation bombing of the mountaintops and ridgelines that bordered the Shahikot. The Mountain staff rejected this on the grounds that such a bombardment would remove any element of surprise from the operation. "It was a risk they were willing to take," said an officer close to the debate.

BUT even as Donnelly pushed unsuccessfully for a massive bombing campaign, others in Bagram sensed reluctance on the part of senior CFACC and CENTCOM generals to permit any but the most limited air strikes. "Anaconda was the third war of three wars in Afghanistan in less than six months," Bentley said. "The first war was special operators supporting Northern Alliance forces fighting the Taliban and whatever Al Qaida forces there were in there. The second part of the war was sensitive site exploitation, where the Northern Alliance forces sort of stopped. There wasn't a direct ground-on-ground fight going on anymore." Anaconda marked the first introduction of large-scale American ground forces into combat. But the rules of engagement and targeting processes had not kept pace with events. They were still geared to pinpoint strikes against fixed targets, not killing large numbers of enemy fighters in close contact with U.S. and allied troops. This meant any targets struck prior to the air assault had to be confirmed by at least two of the three intelligence disciplines: human, signals, or imagery. But it was one thing to know—or strongly suspect—that a mountainside was riddled with caves and camouflaged fighting positions big enough for one or two fighters and maybe a machine gun. It was another to positively identify such positions, even with all the spy planes and satellites the United States brought to bear over the Shahikot. "It would have been great if we were looking at a Soviet motorized rifle regiment or some other large target set, but we were looking at a DShK on a hillside, in the middle of Afghanistan in the middle of the night," Bello said. "Very, very elusive targets . . . It really is like trying to find a needle in a haystack."

When the war in Afghanistan began, Lieutenant General Chuck Wald was the CFACC commander, the senior Air Force officer in southwest Asia. Wald flew F-15E Strike Eagles, which have a ground attack role, and he understood the complex business of close air support. But in November, in the middle of the war, the Air Force called Wald back to take a Pentagon job and replaced him with Lieutenant General T. Michael "Buzz" Moseley. "That was mistake one," said an Air Force officer who served under both men. "You're changing your key commander during a very complex, never-before-done operation in Afghanistan. And General Wald had done a spectacular job." Moseley was an F-15C air superiority fighter pilot with little experience in close air support. In this he had much in common with many of his staff, said an Air Force officer who flew missions in Anaconda. "The key staff members didn't support close air support," the officer said. Louis Bochain, the officer in charge of arranging close air support for Dagger's A-teams, disagreed. "I didn't get that read from General Moseley," Bochain said. "I had all the authority that I needed to execute the missions that they gave me."

The Air Force's policy of rotating almost all its personnel in the Central Command theater every ninety days meant that neither the staff in Moseley's Combined Air Operations Center (CAOC, pronounced "kay-ock") at Prince Sultan Air Base whose job was to coordinate air support for Anaconda nor the pilots who would be flying the missions had been around during the peak of the war against the Taliban. A personality conflict between Mikolashek and Moseley that filtered down to their staffs did not help. "The CFLCC and the CFACC were having trouble communicating because Moseley and Mikolashek did not have a strong working relationship," an Air Force officer said.

That Anaconda was coming and would require close air support was no secret to Air Force officials in Saudia Arabia and Kuwait. When Hagenbeck published his operations order for Anaconda February 20, it was sent to Moseley's headquarters. In addition, said an Air Force officer, "there were e-mails from Mikolashek to Moseley that didn't generate enough interest." But according to this officer the real blame for the problems that would hobble the ability of pilots circling the Shahikot to provide effective close air support during the opening days of Anaconda lay with CENTCOM, and in particular with Air Force Lieutenant General Gene Renuart, Franks' director of operations. "Renuart is asleep at the wheel," the Air Force officer said. "When big Army gets involved, you've gotta get close air support working, and working now, period. General Renuart's staff didn't see that this was going to be a close air support fight." While the staffs exchanged information, none of it trickled down to the pilots. "Those guys are having rock drills at Bagram," said the Air Force officer. "We, the guys who are going to fly the missions in support of it, aren't part of it. What the fuck? Over."

Word of the impending operation did not filter up to Brigadier General John Corley, the CAOC director, until February 23. CAOC officials felt blindsided and later complained that it was hard to get any specifics from their counterparts at Bagram about what was expected from the air component.

Donnelly acknowledged that his team did "very little" communicating with their Air Force chain of command in the run-up to D-Day. They held two video-teleconferences with Longoria in which they described the plan and their "issues" with it, and they got the CAOC to increase the number of planes in the sky over Afghanistan for a five-day period beginning forty-eight hours prior to D-Day. Donnelly asked for increased air coverage to start two days out for two reasons: in case Hagenbeck changed his mind and agreed to Donnelly's recommendation to conduct forty-eight hours of bombing prior to the air assault, and to have aircraft ready to come to the aid of Blaber's AFO teams in case they were compromised. The air coverage was scheduled to wind down three days after D-Day "because it was supposed to be a seventy-two-hour operation," Donnelly said.

Hagenbeck, Mikolashek, Franks, and Moseley held another video-teleconference February 26. Monitoring the VTC, Wille had his mind put at rest by Moseley. "I was always concerned because we don't have control over the Air Force guys until that three-star general in the VTC said that all air that they had in the AOR [area of responsibility] was prepared to support Anaconda to whatever degree we needed," Wille said. "Fire support was a big concern of mine. But when I hear a three-star Air Force general say, 'You've got the world,' then I think things are squared away."

Things were not squared away, but Wille was by no means alone in his optimism, which permeated Bagram and the higher echelons of command. Anaconda would be overseen by an ad hoc command and control setup and fought by units weakened by Central Command's force cap executing a plan that was a product of negotiation and compromise, but confidence was not in short supply in Bagram. "Originally people thought there was anywhere from 150 to 250 Al Qaida sitting right in Serkhankhel, right in the valley," Wille said. "It didn't look like it was gonna be that big of a deal."

20.

THERE was still no evidence any of the "big three" high-value targets were hiding in the Shahikot. But in Gardez and Bagram there was a lot of speculation about who *was* leading the enemy force hunkered in the valley.

There were reports Jalalluddin Haqqani was still pulling some of the strings in his old stomping grounds around the Shahikot. As a Pushtun warlord who had long been close to the foreign Islamists in Afghanistan, it was to be expected that he was at the very least helping support the force in the Shahikot with logistics, intelligence, and perhaps an outer ring of security. But as analysts worked feverishly to build the intelligence picture, one name was popping up repeatedly in the chatter: Tohir Yuldeshev.

A skilled organizer and passionate orator, Tohir Abdouhalilovitch Yuldeshev was a radical Islamist from Uzbekistan's Fergana Valley who had spent the 1990s traveling to Pakistan, Saudi Arabia, the Caucasus, and elsewhere forging bonds with pan-Islamic jihadi groups. Between 1995 and 1998 he was based in Peshawar, the dusty city in Pakistan's Northwest Frontier Province, where he was supported by Pakistan's Interservices Intelligence agency, the driving force behind the Taliban. In 1998 he and Juma Namangani, a fellow Islamic militant from his hometown, formed the Islamic Movement of Uzbekistan, dedicated to the violent overthrow of Uzbek President Islam Karimov's authoritarian government and its replacement by an Islamic state. Given refuge in Afghanistan by the Taliban, the IMU grew to a multiethnic force of at least 3,000 guerrillas from as far afield as Chechnya to the west and China to the east. It waged jihad across the Central Asian republics and fought for the Taliban against Massoud in Afghanistan. Yuldeshev was the political brains of the IMU. Namangani, a clever and charismatic guerrilla leader, provided its military muscle. When U.S. forces enlisted the Northern Alliance to drive the Taliban from power after September 11, the IMU staunchly defended their hosts. After a U.S. bomb reportedly killed Namangani near Kunduz in November 2001, Yuldeshev was thought to have assumed total control of the organization. As the Taliban was swept aside, IMU forces who survived the punishing bombardments in the north fled to the old mujahideen hideouts of eastern Afghanistan.

By late February a rough consensus had formed that Yuldeshev was the senior enemy figure in the Shahikot. "We had a fairly good idea that Yuldeshev was in there," said a TF 11 officer. "He was probably in there about a month or two before." The officer's analysis was based partly on his "gut feeling" and partly on intercepts of Yuldeshev's aides "chattering." However, U.S. SIGINT personnel never heard Yuldeshev himself. He and the other enemy leaders practiced very good communications security. "Those guys are really good," the officer said. "The senior Al Qaida guys are phenomenal. That's why it's so hard [to find them]. They're just smart in that way."

21.

OBSESSING over opsec was not the exclusive preserve of Al Qaida and the IMU. The Americans went to great lengths to conceal their plan to attack the Shahikot, which relied on achieving at least tactical surprise. If the enemy leaders knew hours or days ahead of Anaconda when and where they would be attacked, they would be unlikely to stick around. So U.S. forces took extreme measures to keep a lid on information. They decided to permit half a dozen journalists embedded with the Rakkasans in Kandahar to cover the operation. But the journalists they tapped were told only that a mission was in the offing, to have a rucksack packed ready to leave within an hour's notice, and to not breathe a word to anyone. They were forbidden to bring laptops or satellite phones when they boarded the C-17 that flew them to Bagram February 25, for fear one of them would discuss the mission in an e-mail or phone conversation with his editors, and that that information would find its way back to the Shahikot.

U.S. forces took other steps to shroud their future actions, but it is hard to believe their enemies in the Shahikot had no idea an attack was coming. Zia and his men were not told of the mission until the day before, but the fact that dozens of Americans were living in a compound in Gardez training and equipping an Afghan force would hardly have gone unnoticed or unreported. The enemy must also have been aware of the Predator drone flying over their positions in and around the Shahikot, which Ziemba acknowledged "sounded like a flying lawn mower."

The Rakkasans seemed more intent on achieving total surprise than the other elements grouped under Hagenbeck. This was to be expected. The Rakkasan air assault relied on surprise. If the enemy were waiting with DShKs and, perhaps, surface-to-air missiles pointed skyward when the first Chinooks flew into the valley, the chances of disaster were high. Dagger officers warned the Rakkasans such surprise might be difficult to achieve. The officers in Gardez thought that the moment that the TF Hammer convoy left the safe house, cell phones would be ringing in the Shahikot. "We believed that as soon as Zia got trucks lined up in Gardez . . . that that was going to be the call to arms for whoever was in that valley," Rosengard said. "We did tell them [i.e., the Rakkasans], 'Have no doubt in your mind, that when Zia moves out of Gardez south, that the boys in this valley are going to know something's coming.'" Nonetheless, U.S. officials remained upbeat about their chances of gaining a measure of surprise. "While we figured the enemy would be able to figure out in general the day of the attack by the AMF, they probably would not be able to [determine] when or where we would insert U.S. conventional forces," Ziemba said.

THE Rakkasan company-grade officers and NCOs kept their soldiers busy. Preparations focused on how to survive and prosper in the mountain environment, and how to set up blocking positions and distinguish "bad guys" from the civilians they expected to rush the positions in an effort to escape any fighting.

Anaconda would be the highest-altitude battle ever fought by U.S. troops. Bagram was at about 5,000 feet, which gave troops a few days to acclimate before going into the valley, the floor of which was at 8,000 feet. Some medical officers gave out altitude-sickness pills, others figured the risks of side-effects weren't worth the benefit. Sergeants major put their minds to figuring out what gear soldiers should wear and carry so that they could withstand the cold but not be too weighed down.

In battalion TOCs and around sand tables, battalion and brigade staffs refined their plans, making sure each officer and NCO understood his role in the operation. Outside, sergeants ran their troops through drills that focused on how to identify and apprehend enemy fighters. Space was at a premium, so if the drill required some soldiers to pretend to be Al Qaida leaders fleeing in an SUV, a John Deere Gator (akin to a lawn tractor) was used instead. Special Forces NCOs gave classes on how to subdue, search, disarm and flex-cuff enemy fighters. The special operators warned that Al Qaida troops might try to conceal hand grenades in order to blow themselves and U.S. soldiers up. These battle drills were the only collective training the TF Rakkasan companies could perform. There were no ranges at Bagram for them. They had done no maneuver or live-fire training since leaving Fort Campbell almost two months previously.

Platoons practiced getting on and off Chinooks. (Most infantrymen are used to riding in helicopters, but the use of Chinooks was unusual. Black Hawks are the Army's air assault helicopter of choice, but the Chinooks got the nod for Anaconda because their twin sets of rotors gave them more power in the thin mountain air.) In an exercise that was part rehearsal, part deception operation, the entire first lift of helicopters planned for D-Day took off with its assigned complement of soldier-passengers. But instead of flying south toward the Shahikot, the helicopters flew north before returning to Bagram.

22.

EVERY few days in the second half of February, an Mi-17 would settle on the Bagram tarmac and out would step Blaber and his CIA counterpart, Spider. After a short SUV ride from the flight line the bearded warriors would sweep into the hangar that held the overflow workstations that didn't fit in the Mountain TOC. Followed by the gaze of curious staff officers, the CIA operative and the Delta Force lieutenant colonel would stride into a closed-door meeting to brief Hagenbeck on their latest discoveries.

By now Blaber was working as much for Hagenbeck—albeit unofficially—as he was for Trebon and TF 11. The AFO commander had taken it upon himself to begin reporting to the two-star general, who, unlike Trebon and Dailey, took Blaber's reports seriously and hungered for more information from the Shahikot. Hagenbeck otherwise had little contact with TF 11, whose commander preferred to keep his distance. Without Blaber and Spider coordinating their operations with Mountain, Hagenbeck would have had no direct access to the intel being developed at Gardez. Such coordination was doubly important because Blaber was planning to send his teams into the Shahikot ahead of Hagenbeck's troops. With Hagenbeck enjoying no authority over AFO or any other TF 11 operators who might be running around in his Shahikot "battlespace," a close relationship between the Mountain commander and staff on one hand and Blaber and Jimmy on the other not only made sense, it was essential. Knowing that if the AFO teams made it into the Shahikot they would run into the Rakkasans, Jimmy, who usually wore black jeans, a bright blue polar fleece top, and jungle boots, even put on a fashion show for the Rakkasan leaders, dressing up in garb that the AFO troops would be wearing, so the Rakkasans would not mistake them for the enemy.

But when word of the close interaction between AFO and Mountain reached JSOC headquarters, it infuriated Dailey. The JSOC commander became so angry with what he considered Blaber's freelancing that he considered bringing the AFO commander home. This was in keeping with Dailey's reputation for disdaining interaction with or use of conventional forces. "In almost every case Dell Dailey was probably resistant to using any kind of conventional force," said Warren Edwards, the CFLCC deputy commanding general for operations, who participated in numerous video-teleconferences with Dailey.

But in Dailey's view, Anaconda could only divert TF 11's attention away from the mission to track down bin Laden, Zawahiri, and Mullah Omar. He had heard nothing to convince him any of the "big three" were in or around the Shahikot, and when Trebon told him that he had committed TF 11—principally AFO—to help out Hagenbeck, Dailey was not pleased. "Hey, Greg, we are in manhunt mode, and this is a conventional fight here," Dailey said to his deputy. "How did we get hornswaddled into this?" Trebon replied that AFO was only supposed to be "on the periphery" of the fight, not in the middle of it. This cut no ice with Dailey. "This is gonna blow up in our face, but if you've made the commitment, then we need to honor the commitment," he said. However, the perception remained that Dailey's attitude to AFO's role in Anaconda was one of grudging acquiescence at best, outright opposition at worst.

With Dailey trying to undercut Blaber's efforts, Gary Harrell's support was crucial in smoothing the AFO commander's path into Hagenbeck's office. When Harrell, the former head of Delta Force, urged Hagenbeck to take advantage of AFO's capabilities, his black special ops credentials gave his advice added weight. "He was a good sounding board, a good reality check, and I think he emboldened Hagenbeck as far as 'Damn right you should be using those guys [i.e., AFO], and damn right you should be a little more audacious,'" said an officer who watched the two generals interact in the Mountain TOC. Over the course of several weeks, Blaber and Hagenbeck developed a strong mutual respect, yet another example of a personal bond that helped paper over the cracks in the command-and-control setup.

BY late February the Gardez safe house was bursting at the seams with over 100 heavily armed commandos. This included the two A-teams; the AFO headquarters personnel plus India, Juliet, and Mako 31, and upward of 20 CIA personnel. But there were three new elements taking up residency in the little fort: a small Australian SAS command-and-control element from TF 64; a squad of 101st Airborne engineers, who were to clear mines or other obstacles from TF Hammer's approach to the Shahikot; and the fourteen-man tactical command post of Chris Haas's 1st Battalion, 5th Special Forces Group. Haas's February 25 arrival resulted in another confusing command-and-control situation. Haas saw his job as threefold: to provide a headquarters that could relieve the A-teams of responsibility for communicating with Mountain and Dagger in the run-up to and execution of the battle; to exercise command over the A-teams, eliminating the awkwardness of having one captain command another; and to show Zia Lodin that the Americans cared enough about the operation to put a lieutenant colonel in charge. But neither A-team in Gardez belonged to Haas's battalion, and they were confused about his role. Blaber, however, liked Haas's attitude and was glad to have a kindred spirit show up on his doorstep. "He was all over, cutting through the bureaucracy and working missions based on what the best solution was for America, rather than a particular unit or staff," Blaber said. The AFO commander's respect for Haas gave the SF officer instant legitimacy in Spider's eyes, bringing all three together as a team whose members happened to work for different organizations.

It was now time for Blaber to implement his plan to send three teams into the Shahikot itself. He gathered his men and told them it was going to happen. If they managed to infiltrate the valley unobserved, they had three tasks: to confirm or deny the presence of any senior enemy leaders; to check that the Rakkasan landing zones were usable and prevent enemy forces from concentrating near them when the air assault went in; and to call in air strikes on targets of opportunity. These were veteran Delta, SEAL Team 6, and Gray Fox operators, but what Blaber was proposing set their pulses racing: to sneak overland into a valley occupied by hundreds of enemy fighters without being seen. It would be the mission of their lives if it came off. "We were a reconnaissance unit and that's what we'd trained all our careers for," said an operator. They were due to depart the next night, February 27, but the members of India, Juliet, and Mako 31 were still skeptical that they would get a green light for such an audacious mission. "We thought this wasn't gonna happen 'cause it was too risky. You're not gonna send four guys into 700," said one team member. But it was slowly dawning on the AFO operators that they were working for an unusual commander, one willing to take calculated risks to achieve tactical, operational, and strategic gains, and more than willing to buck the system to make it happen. "Blaber is the first commander I've worked for willing to take the risk," said an AFO operator. "He's not risk averse. He leaves the tactical decisions to the guy on the ground, especially the enlisted guys. His officers he's pretty hard on." Of course, Blaber knew Delta was one of the few organizations in the Army in which the enlisted soldiers usually had far more experience than most officers. A captain in Delta might have eight years in the Army. Most NCOs in his troop would have double that. Indeed, some operators would tell you that all but the best troop commanders in Delta were "figureheads." It was the sergeants major who ran the troops.

The operators also respected the fact that by conducting a mission Dailey so clearly disapproved of, Blaber was laying his career on the line. "Blaber was leaning farther forward" than the TF 11 and JSOC headquarters realized, according to one operator, who said Blaber had not been his favorite officer back at Fort Bragg, but had won him over at Gardez. "He was taking career-political risks to get guys on the ground," he said. "That's why I changed my mind about him." Blaber gave each team a final mission brief. After walking the India Team members through the mission as he saw it, the AFO commander joined Speedy outside in the frosty, moonlit night. "Sir, now I know you don't really care whether I live or die," the team leader joked in his Kentucky drawl after hearing what Blaber expected of him and his men. "Speedy, your dying is none of my concern," Blaber replied with dry humor, but added shortly afterward, "Speedy, it's not that I don't care, it's just that I know how good you are, so I don't have to worry about you dying. You're uniquely qualified to execute this mission. It's your destiny."

THE two A-teams were less sanguine about their roles in the upcoming mission, and their concerns increased as they watched the plan evolve through the second half of February. Thomas and McHale, the A-team leaders, were particularly worried that the plan called for their ragtag force to conduct a tightly synchronized advance, crossing phase lines on the map at precise times. "That clearly showed us that nobody was giving a darn about how difficult it was going to be to get our guys down there," said McHale. They had not expected this when they had been told they were the main effort. The SF officers thought the sequence and timing of the preparatory strikes and the air assaults should be triggered by TF Hammer's movement, not the other way round. "Because if you're the main effort, everybody supports you," McHale said. With such an inexperienced force, it was hard for the A-team leaders to guarantee that Zia's fighters would be exactly where the plan required them to be, when it required them to be there. They had bonded with their militia brethren as well as could be expected, but were not blind to their weaknesses. Zia's men were hit-and-run fighters, but the plan called for them to behave like American light infantry, using tactics they had just learned and weapons they had only owned for a few days. This reflected a split between the Dagger leaders at Bagram, who promised their Rakkasan and Mountain counterparts that Zia's force would stick to the tight schedule, and the A-team leaders in Gardez. To McHale and Thomas, the planners in Bagram seemed to have lost touch with reality. The A-team leaders suggested that instead of landing along the eastern ridge, at least one Rakkasan company land behind their task force as it swung east into the Fishhook, to provide extra firepower in case they had to close with an enemy force in the villages. The suggestion got nowhere at Bagram.

Haas, McHale, and Thomas knew instinctively that just moving a few hundred Afghans and a few dozen Americans in the dead of night along rutted, washed-out dirt roads was going to present a significant challenge. The Americans would travel in a combination of Toyota pickups and a few armored Mercedes SUVs donated by Norway. But moving the 300–400 Afghan fighters was a challenge of a different scale. "We labored intensively trying to figure out how we were going to move all these dudes," Haas said. The Americans' preferred solution was to buy more pickup trucks. But the CIA couldn't find fifty pickups for sale on such short notice anywhere. In the end the CIA bought a couple of dozen "jinga" trucks—the gaudily decorated, seemingly top-heavy trucks that are ubiquitous in Afghanistan, Pakistan and India. But who would drive them? Hoskheyar had been a truck driver, and some of the other Afghans claimed experience in driving trucks. "So we thought okay, let's just have our own [Afghan] guys drive these trucks," McHale said. "Well, in their culture they hate to say no when they can't do things. So we ended up with some guys who weren't really truck drivers."

Haas shared his team leaders' concerns about moving hundreds of men into battle down poor roads in nontactical vehicles. "There were spots where we knew we were going to have problems," Haas said. "We said it's a risk, but it's the only way to get Zia's guys into the battle." If the SF officers felt a sense of foreboding, they weren't the only ones. Not long before D-Day an intelligence report reached the safe house that someone in Zermat, the local Al Qaida logistics hub, had placed an order for 165 coffins.

23.

THERE was an eerie feel to Bagram on those nights in late February. Tendrils of fog snaked around the tents and even on overcast nights the sky retained a ghostly pallor. A Rakkasan soldier making a nocturnal trek from the Mountain headquarters hangar back to tent city would have noticed the base was a little chillier than Kandahar and a lot wetter. Pools of water lay everywhere, surrounded by mud rutted with the tracks of Humvees and SUVs that plied the main routes around the base. Half-closing his eyes and gazing between the strands of barbed wire that surrounded the special operations compounds, the soldier could have imagined himself somewhere on the Western Front during World War I.

ON February 25, Wiercinski met with his commanders in a large tent erected inside the hangar that housed Hagenbeck's headquarters. On the floor was an eight-foot by nine-foot scale model of the Shahikot, surrounded by a map overlaid with operational graphics, and two large aerial photos that each measured about thirty inches by thirty inches. The officers gathered around, serious and attentive, but not noticeably nervous.

"You're making history here," Wiercinski told them. "You need to be proud of yourselves, you need to be proud of your soldiers." Leaders would have a critical role to play on the Anaconda battlefield, he told them. "Do not slacken up. . . . Our soldiers will do what we tell them. They always have." Then he reiterated his priorities: "The most important thing is surprise and opsec and getting 100 percent of the force on the ground."

The next morning Hagenbeck and Wiercinski briefed the handful of journalists who had flown up from Kandahar. Hagenbeck described the plan. Task Force Hammer would approach the Shahikot from the west, halting at daybreak at the Fishhook, just as the Rakkasans' first air assault wave landed along the eastern ridgeline. The plan counted on surprise to get the air assault on the ground safely, but it also hinged on the enemy fighters realizing that the Rakkasans had landed. The idea, Hagenbeck explained, was for the enemy leaders to know that Zia blocked the valley's western exits and the Rakkasans blocked the trails to the south and east. Hagenbeck anticipated a stand-off would then occur, as the enemy leaders pondered their options. The enemy had 150 to 200 fighters in Serkhankhel, the Mountain commander said. But even though "Zia really wants to get these guys," Hagenbeck said there was no intention for Zia to attack the villages on D-Day, still set for February 28. The enemy would probably try to slip their leaders out using the northeastern trail that the plan deliberately left open and inviting. To preclude that option, at dusk part of the Rakkasans' second air assault would set down in the northern end of the valley "to close the door," with the remainder landing in the south to reinforce LaCamera's 1-87 Infantry. This time, Hagenbeck said, the air assault in the north would probably be unseen by the enemy. "We think the action on D-Day will be completely minimal," he added.

On March 1, if the enemy forces had neither surrendered nor tried to escape, Zia would attack Serkhankhel. "He's willing to go house to house" to root out Al Qaida fighters, Hagenbeck said. He acknowledged that he had never met Zia, but appeared unconcerned that he was commanding a major combat operation in which the man at least nominally in charge of the main effort was an unknown to him. That John Mulholland, the Dagger commander, had faith in Zia was enough of a guarantee for Hagenbeck. "Our Special Forces guys are very, very confident," Hagenbeck said.

The Mountain headquarters at Bagram would function as Anaconda's command-and-control hub, but Wiercinski said he intended to fly with his forward command post into the valley behind the Chinooks, landing lower down the same Finger upon which Mako 31 planned to put their observation post in order to get a firsthand feel for how the battle was going. He planned to just stay for an hour or so and then return to Bagram. It would nearly cost him his life.

If the enemy chose to fight, Wiercinski predicted it would be in the villages—"That's where they have cover and concealment." In a statement that might have surprised Rosengard, who still believed the Rakkasans suffered from a "kill 'em all" mentality, the Rakkasan commander stressed his commitment to the rules of engagement, which only allowed his troops to fire at personnel they had "positively identified" as enemy fighters. "I don't want to kill women and children in this place," Wiercinski said. "I don't want to kill an innocent Afghan. Nobody does." The Rakkasan commander also noted that, contrary to the fears of the Hammer A-teams, his blocking positions would be located over a kilometer from the villages, so the Rakkasans would not be able to influence any small arms fight in the towns.

LATER on February 26 Wiercinski held a "confirmation brief" in which his subordinate commanders walked him through how they intended to execute their part of the operation. The meeting was held in "The Hunting Lodge," a GP Medium tent belonging to Ron Corkran's scout platoon that had a satellite photo of the Shahikot taped to the tent wall and a to-scale relief model of the valley, made out of dirt. Over forty soldiers clustered around the sandtable, going over the operation one more time. Their comments reflected a focus on distinguishing between civilians and enemy fighters, and their belief that firepower would not be a priority. Chip Preysler, the fresh-faced 2-187 Infantry commander, described how his companies intended to configure their blocking positions: Anybody approaching from the villages would first encounter a fence made from engineering tape with a sign in Pushto saying GO AWAY; if they ignored this warning, they would encounter a second sign indicating they were entering a minefield (even though the U.S. troops had no intention of actually laying a minefield); only if they ignored both warnings and continued to advance would the U.S. troops consider shooting at them. (Preysler was more concerned with the prospect of a vehicle approaching at high speed than with pedestrians, who would be easier to deal with.) Wiercinski approved of the false minefield, which fitted with his concept of applying an "escalation of violence" against people approaching the blocking positions.

In keeping with the overriding belief that any combat would be dominated by small arms and automatic weapons, Preysler said he would not bring any mortars in on the first air assault wave—or lift—and would take just one 60mm mortar team in on the second lift. As with LaCamera's battalion, only three Chinooks had been apportioned to carry his first lift—just enough to haul most of his C Company plus a twelve-man battalion command post. Preysler asked for another Chinook so he could bring in all of his C Company. But there were no more helicopters to be had. Wiercinski instead suggested that Preysler create space on the second lift by leaving his mortars behind, as LaCamera's battalion was bringing a 120mm mortar capable ranging of the entire valley.

Then Preysler voiced a concern heard frequently in the run-up to Anaconda: that Al Qaida leaders would try to escape disguised as women clad in burkas, the uniquely Afghan garments that covered women from head to toe, with just a gauzy latticed slit to see through. "Do you want us to actually take the burkas off?" he asked. No, Wiercinski replied. Special operators had told him the best way to handle the situation without offending Muslim sensitivities was to look at a person's feet to see if they resembled a man's or a woman's.

The discussion turned to the potential for friendly casualties. "When there's a casualty, nothing else matters at that time," Wiercinski told his audience. "Get the casualty to a location where we can bring him out without causing more casualties." If a Chinook was shot down, the brigade commander said, the other helicopters in the lift should land beside it to perform combat search and rescue, with the Apaches "laying down a wall of steel" between the troops and the enemy. "We go back to the old Ranger creed of never leaving a fallen comrade, hooah!" Wiercinski said.

After Dennis Yates, the Rakkasan fire support officer, briefed the group on procedures for calling in close air support, Wiercinski gave a prophetic final piece of advice. "Fight the enemy, don't fight the plan," he told his men as a series of explosions caused by soldiers blowing up captured materiel echoed in the background. "The second the first shot goes downrange, things are gonna change with the plan."

SHORTLY thereafter, Wiercinski convened the Rakkasan "maneuver rehearsal," also held in the Hunting Lodge, in which each commander repeated how he intended to conduct his mission. The Rakkasan commander again cautioned his audience that "a plan goes about as far as the first shot being fired," and he reminded them that Zia was the operation's main effort and TF Rakkasan the supporting effort. "For me, the decisive point of the fight is getting the force on the ground," he said. Once the troops landed, "the first five minutes of the fight is going to tell the story," he added presciently. Then he returned to the theme of taking care not to target civilians. "There's about 800 to 1,000 people in this town," he said, pointing to Serkhankhel on the terrain map on the floor. "About 10 percent of them are bad people and about 90 percent of them are good folks."

NEXT the senior Rakkasan officers joined the other task force commanders and the Mountain staff in the big tent in the hangar to brief Hagenbeck. About fifty-five personnel, ranging from clean-shaven, uniformed infantry officers to TF 11 representatives in jeans, beards, and ballcaps, crowded in. The more senior officers sat on folding chairs, generals and colonels in the front row. Others stood around the side. The atmosphere was tense, the mood serious. Nobody was expecting a bloodbath, but most attendees had enough experience to realize no combat operation could be taken lightly, even one in which the enemy was not expected to stand and fight. The commanders and planners were putting over a thousand soldiers' lives on the line, and that heavy responsibility focused their minds. There was little side chatter. Everyone paid close attention to the briefers.

Captain Eric Haupt, the Rakkasan intelligence officer, gave a short rundown on what he expected to find in the valley. Intelligence on the enemy was scant. "We're looking at approximately 200 to 250 Al Qaida and Taliban fighters," he said. But he had little solid information on how they were positioned and armed. From overhead imagery they had only been able to identify one DShK position, he said, adding that there must be more. After repeating the intel gurus' mantra that enemy leaders would probably try to flee, he warned that care must be taken with enemy captives, who were not above hiding hypodermic needles on their bodies. "What we've seen in the past is these guys will put grenades on their testicles," he said.

Gary Harrell added a warning that, in light of events a few days later, prompted surprisingly little discussion: An intelligence source U.S. forces had "picked up" in Khowst had said the enemy fighters in the Shahikot were not in the villages, but were living up in the ridgelines and coming down to the villages to get supplies. Hagenbeck listened intently. This was the first he'd heard of this intelligence report. Harrell said the intel folks thought the source was reliable. Given that the plan was predicated on the enemy being in the villages, it is noteworthy that when the general responsible for collating all the intelligence coming into Bagram indicated that that premise might be false, nobody suggested changing the plan. David Gray, the Mountain director of operations, later said that it was unreasonable to expect wholesale changes based on "single source" intelligence. But Paul Wille, his chief planner, acknowledged that writing the plan had been such a painful process of compromise and negotiation that nobody could face the prospect of tearing it up—or even significantly modifying it—at the eleventh hour simply because the enemy might not be where they were supposed to be. (However, Wille also said that the Rakkasans' refusal to land in the Upper Shahikot meant there was little that could have been done to change the plan anyway.)

As for engaging targets in the villages, Hagenbeck told the officers any target they wanted to strike with an Apache would be considered "a sensitive target," and Tommy Franks's approval was needed before attacking it. This illustrated a drawback of the digital age for tactical commanders: the requirement—absurd on its face—for an infantry battalion or brigade commander to relay a message from a battlefield in eastern Afghanistan to a four-star general in Florida requesting permission for an attack helicopter to take out a single target during a firefight. The requirement was a function of Central Command's desire to control as much of the fight in Afghanistan as it could from the United States, but it would not have been possible without a dazzling array of technologies that had given some generals the illusory perception that they could control a battle from thousands of miles away. In any case, Wiercinski seemed to dismiss the possibility of using the Apaches in such a situation, saying he wouldn't need them "in an infantry-on-infantry fight."

Once the crowd had drifted out of the tent, a smaller group strolled in. Most were TF Dagger members and were there for the TF Hammer rehearsal—a rock drill in which the officers at the spearhead of Hammer could run through their moves using the terrain board on the floor. Rosengard presided and the attendees included Jimmy from AFO, CIA operatives, and at least one 3rd Special Forces Group officer not based at Gardez. "I brought guys to that rock drill that no one else needed to know about," Rosengard said.

But segregating the special ops rehearsal from the Dagger-Mountain briefing to Hagenbeck meant the officers leading Anaconda's main effort were walking through their battle plan unseen and unheard by the Rakkasan and Mountain leaders. The opposite also held true. Neither Glenn Thomas nor Matthew McHale—the two A-team leaders charged with taking Zia's force into the valley—had even been to Bagram before, let alone attended any Rakkasan or Mountain-level briefings or rehearsals. They had no idea what the conventional troops expected of them. Had just one officer from the operation's "main effort" attended the walk-through of the operation with Hagenbeck, all participants would have been on the same page when it came to how events were expected to play out in the operation. The A-team leaders had not heard the latest version of the plan, but Rosengard's first words were not encouraging. "He starts out with a disclaimer, saying, 'You cannot argue over what the 101st is doing. This is done. This is the way it's gonna be. This is how you're gonna execute,'" McHale recalled, a memory seconded by Haas. (Rosengard said he remembered his opening remarks being along the lines of "The good-idea window is closed. . . . The course of action has already been determined.") Then Rosengard laid out the plan, with the Rakkasans landing along the eastern side of the valley. *This doesn't make any sense,* McHale thought. He and Thomas bit their tongues as Rosengard went around the tent calling on other officers to say their piece. Finally he asked the two team leaders for their thoughts. "Well, sir, I think what's gonna happen is, the 101st will land, and they're gonna take fire from the villages, and of course, they'll return fire, so they're gonna get in a firefight," McHale said. "And if that happens about the same time we're coming around through the south side [of the Whale], you're gonna have two American forces on either side of the objective attacking toward each other in close proximity, which hasn't been a good idea since, like, the Revolutionary War. Also, the 101st will be in contact, getting shot at, and they don't know what my guys look like. So I think we'll have an extreme chance of fratricide. And so it's gonna get all fucked up, sir. And that's what's gonna happen."

Haas was of like mind. "That's an infantry [force] that pride themselves on being meat-eaters, and they weren't going to sit in the blocking positions," he explained. "The minute they took fire, their training told them 'fire and maneuver, engage, close with, find, fix, finish the enemy.'"

Unbeknownst to McHale and Thomas, Rosengard had been arguing the same points unsuccessfully over the past two weeks. But there was no turning back from what had been agreed with the Rakkasans. "That's where they're going, so you've got to deal with it," he told the team leaders. Then a Texas 14 soldier asked whether TF Hammer was still considered the main effort. Rosengard said yes. "It was very clear that we were the main effort," said McHale. The young Special Forces officers left the meeting under the impression that as the main effort, they would enjoy "priority of fires"—first call on the close air support aircraft—until they had cleared the villages.

McHale and Thomas had some time to kill before their helicopter left for Gardez. As they chatted in a dark passageway that led from the main hangar bay to a side door, Rosengard walked up. "You guys the team leaders from down there?" he asked in his broad Boston accent. "Yes, sir," they replied. His next comment shocked them. "The best thing that can happen is [for you] to get around the south of that mountain [the Whale] and make contact with the enemy. Because if you're in contact, the 101st won't land in front of you." It took a moment for the implication of what Rosengard was saying to sink in. McHale recalled their confusion: "I remember Glenn and I looking at each other and saying out of frustration, 'You're telling us that this thing has to get screwed up for us to succeed. . . . I mean, that doesn't seem right.' And the colonel cocked his head and raised his eyebrows. Certainly, that's just what he was trying tell us." The captains suddenly understood they weren't the only ones with profound doubts about the plan. "It was clear to me at that point that it wasn't our chain of command that thought this was a great idea," McHale said.

BETWEEN all the rock drills, the task force commanders, and senior staffers in Bagram had to find time to attend three daily video-teleconferences that linked them with Mikolashek's CFLCC headquarters in Kuwait, Moseley's CAOC in Saudi Arabia, and Franks's Central Command headquarters in Tampa. Video-teleconferences were Franks's preferred tool for managing operations in central Asia from Florida, but they imposed a strain on staffs, especially because of the eight-and-a-half-hour time difference between Bagram and Tampa.

Some officers appreciated the opportunity for almost face-to-face contact with the senior leaders in Kuwait and Florida. On the evening of February 26, Wiercinski came away from a VTC with Franks with renewed self-confidence. "I got one of the greatest feelings when I talked to General Franks," the Rakkasan commander said. "It was one of the best things any general officer had ever said to me. Because I didn't know what he thought we could do. When he said, 'You all will know what to do on the ground. I have full faith and confidence. You will know when not to squeeze the trigger, you will know when to squeeze the trigger.' . . . It just gave me a sense that he trusted us and I had—we all had—his full faith and confidence. That did a lot for me personally as a commander, because to hear it from your big, big boss is important."

But others in Bagram and Kuwait saw CENTCOM's command-by-VTC approach as symptomatic of Franks's tendency toward micromanagement. Within twenty-four hours of the VTC in which Franks had imbued Wiercinski with confidence, Central Command ordered the Mountain staff to forward to Tampa a PowerPoint slide showing the proposed D-Day locations of TF Rakkasan troops in the Shahikot down to the platoon level. This extraordinary order—four-star generals and their headquarters are usually concerned with moving corps, not platoons, around a battlefield—sent a shiver through officers who feared CENTCOM's habitual reluctance to commit conventional troops to the fight was rearing its head yet again. "That created a lot of concern among us because at the last moment [we thought] they were going to start taking away forces that we had already gone through rehearsals with," said a Mountain staff officer. The attitude of those at CENTCOM who demanded the slide seemed to be: "Why do you need that many forces? Why can't you do it [with fewer]?"

Edwards, the CFLCC deputy commanding general for operations, said such behavior was par for the course from CENTCOM, but CFLCC tried to "filter" similar demands to avoid overloading the staffs in Afghanistan with petty requirements. However, not all the requests for information originated at CENTCOM, he said. "Some of this was driven by the insatiable need for detail in Washington because the SecDef was having a daily press briefing," Edwards said. "There are many things acceptable in Washington, but what's the one absolutely unacceptable answer in Washington, D.C.? 'I don't know.'

"When the SecDef started having a [press] briefing every day, it meant that for hours of the day you could not talk to the CENTCOM staff. It didn't matter what was going on. For hours of the day you were unable to get to a senior person to make a decision at CENTCOM because they were tied up prepping themselves for the SecDef's briefing. The SecDef called CENTCOM every morning. They had a morning telephone call and I believe they had an afternoon telephone call. And for a couple of hours before that telephone call you could not talk to the CinC, you could not talk to the deputy CinC, you could not talk to the J-3 [director of operations], you probably could not talk to the J-2 [director of intelligence], and therefore you couldn't get a decision. Numbers became so important that if the SecDef went to a briefing, and we had reported that we had captured fourteen Al Qaida, and it really turned out to be twelve or sixteen, then it would be easier to let two go or go back and capture two more than to go back and try to change the OSD [Office of the Secretary of Defense] number."

But many officers were too consumed with the frantic preparations for battle to ponder these issues. To them, the collaborative planning process between task forces, the standing-room-only backbriefs, and the video-teleconferences with higher headquarters were evidence that everything was proceeding as it should. This was particularly so after Mountain held its own VTC February 26 to discuss the fires plan. The VTC connected Gray, Briley, Yates, Bentley, and Donnelly at Bagram, CFLCC and CAOC representatives, and the commander of the aircraft carrier *John Stennis*'s air wing. "We discussed the pre-assault fires and the follow-on CAS [close air support] plan," Gray said. "Some minor issues arose and were dealt with, but we left that meeting feeling like everyone was on the same sheet of music."

This was an illusion. Everyone was not on the same sheet of music. That evening, when Hagenbeck briefed Franks, Mikolashek, and Moseley via VTC,

Moseley said he had only recently been made aware of the operation and had some issues with it. The staffs tried to iron out these differences, but events on D-Day would reveal significant command-and-control problems between Moseley's Air Force operation in Saudi Arabia and the Mountain staff at Bagram. Even more incomprehensibly, the rehearsals hid—or perhaps, because the Hammer A-team leaders did not attend the Rakkasan-Dagger run-throughs caused—at least three major communication breakdowns between Mountain's component task forces, two of which would have serious repercussions.

The first misunderstanding involved what TF Hammer—Zia's 300-400 tribesmen plus the two A-teams—was to do at dawn on D-Day as it reached the Fishhook. The conventional Mountain and Rakkasan officers thought the plan called for Hammer to halt at the entrance as the Rakkasans air-assaulted into the eastern side of the valley. The Rakkasans expected Hammer to hold at the Fishhook throughout the day and night in the open, while the enemy leaders in Serkhankhel pondered their options before surrendering or making a break for the open trail to the northeast. Only if the enemy was still hunkered down in the village on day two was Hammer to attack Serkhankhel.

That was not how the Hammer A-teams understood the plan. In their minds there would be no pause; they would round the Fishhook and drive into the villages. Only if they met heavy, sustained opposition would they pull back, in order to let close air support aircraft soften up the target. (However, Haas thought his force would only get as far as Babulkhel on D-Day, occupying that village and some of the Finger overlooking Marzak before halting. Attacking Serkhankhel on D-Day, he said, would have been "a village too far." It is possible the Mountain and Rakkasan officers misinterpreted this version of the plan as a pause at the Fishhook.)

The second major breakdown in communication between Gardez and Bagram concerned the airstrikes planned against suspected enemy positions on the Whale as Hammer was approaching from the west. The Special Forces troops thought Mountain's February 20 operations order specified that the Whale would be pummeled by fifty-five minutes of airstrikes. Mulholland, the Dagger commander, reiterated that to Haas, who was to command Hammer, telling him as early as mid-February that "the Air Force is gonna commit more assets to this fight than they committed to Mazar-i-Sharif and the Kabul campaign, they are on board and this is the main effort for the Air Force, and we're gonna have fifty-plus minutes, they're gonna be racked and stacked for you." This view persisted among Hammer personnel even after the February 26 special ops rehearsal at Bagram. "We were working off the assumption that we would get the fifty-plus minutes of air support," said Haas, who regarded that level of air support as essential if he were to push his convoy through the constricted terrain of the Fishhook under fire. The SF officers in turn told Zia and his men not to worry about Al Qaida forces on the Whale. Any DShK positions up there would be subjected to a fearsome barrage before the convoy of Toyota pickups and jinga trucks got within range, they told Zia. The awesome capabilities of U.S. airpower had achieved mythical status among Afghans, and the promise—delivered by Haas to Zia—calmed their fears. "Zia had seen what happened in Kabul, he saw what happened in Tora Bora, and that was the kind of air campaign that he expected for his fight, especially as I had been in both campaigns and explained to him how those things were run, and that's one of the reasons why I was there: to make sure that he had that kind of fire support," Haas said.

But the officers in Bagram who would have been responsible for planning and arranging for that sort of bombardment—Wille, Bello, and Bentley—said no plan to bomb the Whale for fifty-five minutes ever existed and were unaware their Special Forces brethren at Gardez were laboring under such a serious misconception. "I can tell you what was not going to happen along the Whale, and that was carpet bombing," Bentley said. "We didn't have enough assets in theater to plaster the Whale. It's a huge terrain feature. And . . . we did not identify an abundant amount of targets on the Whale." The fires planners at Bagram identified only five targets to be struck ahead of H-Hour in support of Hammer's movement from Gardez. Two of those were west of the Whale. Only three were on the Whale itself. The plan's final version called for thirteen targets around the valley to be bombed prior to H-Hour—the time the first Rakkasan helicopters were supposed to touch down in the valley. These bombs were to be dropped over a forty-minute period, ending five minutes before the first helicopters entered the valley. Bentley later speculated that at some stage in the planning process this series of "prep fires" was supposed to take fifty-five minutes, and that somehow the SF officers at Gardez misconstrued this figure and thought all fifty-five minutes would be devoted to a barrage of the Whale. Haas agreed with this assessment. "That's absolutely what happened," he said later. Rosengard, the lead TF Dagger planner, was also unaware that the troops in Gardez were expecting a fifty-five-minute plastering of the main terrain feature in their path. He suggested that perhaps they were confused by "fifty-five minutes of available B-52 [bomber] coverage." But whatever the source of the confusion, "I've gotta take the blame for that," he said.

The final misunderstanding between the Special Forces troops who would lead the charge toward the Shahikot and the conventional officers on the

Mountain staff concerned the seriousness with which Hammer's role as Operation Anaconda's "main effort" was viewed. In Gardez, McHale, Thomas, and Haas took this literally, and expected Mountain to treat them as such. In particular, they expected to enjoy priority of fires. Even Wiercinski repeatedly reminded his subordinates that the Rakkasans were the supporting effort in Anaconda. But some senior Mountain officers were only paying lip service to the notion that Zia and his SF advisers were the main effort. "Zia was the main effort for information operations perspectives," Bentley said. Bentley was implying that Zia's designation as the main effort had more to do with the propaganda value of having an Afghan lead the way into the valley than it did with any military necessity, and that Mountain's senior leaders would behave accordingly. The problem with this approach was that no one informed the Special Forces officers charged with coordinating Zia's assault on the Shahikot that they were only being referred to as "the main effort" for "information operations" purposes.

WHILE scores of officers and NCOs at Bagram filed in and out of briefing after briefing, VTC after VTC, Spider and his CIA team in Gardez reported startling news to the others in the safe house February 26. One of the CIA's local sources—a Taliban "squad leader" who claimed to command thirteen fighters—divulged a treasure trove of information that would have significantly changed the outlook of those huddled around the sand tables in Bagram, had they been made aware of it. It might have at least persuaded them that Gary Harrell's comments had the weight of authenticity.

The Taliban fighter told the CIA that 580 to 700 Al Qaida fighters were in the Shahikot area—triple the numbers those in Bagram were expecting to face—and they were not living in the villages, but higher in the mountains. The source based this estimate on his observation of thirty-five local residents who prepared food for the Al Qaida fighters. The guerrillas would descend into the villages, collect the food, and climb back into the mountains. The Al Qaida–Taliban force was divided into three tiers, the source reported. The Taliban were at the bottom of the hierarchy. Armed only with AK-type weapons, they provided an outer ring of security for the Al Qaida force in the Shahikot. Mostly, this meant manning a series of mobile checkpoints. Approaches not covered by checkpoints were seeded with mines that could be turned on and off. He said he was one of sixteen Taliban squad leaders to whom this task had been assigned, each of whom commanded between twelve and fifteen fighters. Most of the Taliban fighters had families nearby and had been "forced" into providing security for Al Qaida, the source said.

Occupying the enemy hierarchy's middle tier were fighters the source described as "Chechens," equipped with small arms and DShKs. At the top of the pecking order were Arabs, armed with mortars, sniper rifles, and two "Stingers." The mortars had preplanned fire plans—they were already set up to fire at certain targets in and around the valley. The mention of "Stingers" caught the Americans' attention, as there was still a concern among U.S. forces that their aircraft would fall victim to the very weapons they had provided the mujahideen in the 1980s. The source assured the Americans that he knew the difference between Stingers and similar weapons systems. Even more disturbingly, the Taliban fighter said the Al Qaida force was arrayed in small groups in fortified positions around the valley and prepared to resist to the bitter end. "They are described as being dug in and not going anywhere," an account of the source's report stated. The Arab fighters would not allow the Taliban to talk to them, the source said, but nevertheless he said he knew that the Al Qaida forces were aware of the Americans' presence in Gardez.

None of this information made it to Hagenbeck, to Wille, his chief planner, or to the Rakkasans. David Gray and Jasey Briley, Hagenbeck's operations director and senior military intelligence officer respectively, each said he might have heard the gist of the agency report, but not the fine details. But at the time each was reluctant to place much fath in "single source" intelligence. Gray remembered a report that said "there are more in there than we think . . . and more in the high ground than down in the villages," but he was never told the source of the intelligence. "At my level there's no way of knowing who these characters are," he said. Gray assumed it was coming from Pacha Khan Zadran, the local warlord with a reputation for dishonesty. No one in the CIA, Task Force Bowie, or the Mountain headquarters bothered to brief Eric Haupt, the Rakkasans' senior intelligence officer, on what the Taliban squad leader had said. "I wish to hell I had had that report," he said later in bitter frustration. The failure to share such crucial intelligence among the different task forces was another symptom of the patched-together operation at Bagram, where some officers seemed so busy congratulating themselves that they were able to work together at all that they neglected to consider what might be falling between the cracks that separated the different components of the allied effort. "I just didn't get anything from Mountain," Haupt said. Briley, whose job it was to pass such intelligence down to Haupt, acknowledged that the system did not work as smoothly as it might. How such a detailed CIA report could have escaped wider dissemination—especially to the commanders whose troops would soon be in combat—may never be fully established. But with D-Day fast approaching, the Anaconda plan appeared to have built up so much momentum that intelligence that ran counter to the premises on which the plan was based was all but ignored.

24.

ON the morning of February 27, a forecast of bad weather for the next day forced Hagenbeck to postpone Anaconda forty-eight hours. H-Hour was now set for 6:30 a.m. on March 2. Few would openly admit it, but there was a lot of relief in TF Rakkasan, which had been sprinting flat out to be ready in time for February 28. Now they could draw breath, refine their plans, and make other final adjustments. Wiercinski used the time to conduct a full-up flyaway rehearsal for his task force. On February 28 all soldiers slated for the first lift into the valley climbed onto six Chinooks in exactly the order prescribed for Anaconda, but instead of flying south toward the Shahikot, the helicopters flew north before turning around and returning Bagram. The rehearsal not only allowed the Rakkasan aviators to fly a full load of soldiers into the mountains and see how the helicopters responded, but because the troops were carrying exactly what they intended taking into combat, it gave senior NCOs a chance to assess the "soldier load" for the mission—the amount of gear each soldier was bearing. The rehearsal proved the troops were overburdened for high-altitude infantry combat. "We had guys who were huffing and puffing just getting off the aircraft, dragging these humongous packs," Wiercinski said. Horrified, the three battalion sergeants major overhauled their soldiers' packing list before D-Day.

Of all the non-American forces involved in Anaconda, it was the Australians who inspired the most confidence among the U.S. officers. Paul Wille found the Aussies' commander, Colonel Rowan Tink, "a pain in the butt sometimes," but overall considered Task Force 64 "very cooperative and extremely effective," more so than the rest of the American-led Task Force K-Bar. "K-Bar was a joke, compared to TF 64," Wille said. "They were a bigger pain in the butt to work with, and they were nowhere near as effective as 64 was. I loved to work with those guys." Ed Burke, Mountain's deputy director of logistics, had a similar impression of the tanned, grizzled Australian warriors. "They rarely needed anything," he said. "They were pros."

The Australian SAS was designed along the same lines as the British SAS and Delta Force, with three line squadrons, each of which had three troops. Task Force 64 was built around 1 Squadron and included three troops—A, B, and C—plus headquarters and support elements for a total of about 100-150 soldiers. When the Aussies first got to Afghanistan in early December they fell under the operational control of Marine Task Force 58. When the Marines left in January, tactical control of the Australians shifted to TF K-Bar, which left the Australians less than perfectly happy. The Aussies regarded themselves as the equivalent of Delta or the British SAS and felt K-Bar's missions were neither challenging nor prestigious enough for a unit of their capabilities. They were not alone in this perception. U.S. special operators observed that K-Bar seemed to exist as much for public relations reasons—the need to find missions for allied special ops units—as it did because of any military necessity.

By mid-February the Australians were on the verge of going home. Then they got word of Anaconda and asked to participate. The Australian operations officer said to Craig Bishop, the special ops coordinator in Mikolashek's CFLCC headquarters, "Craig, if there's any way you can get us involved in what's going on, we want to be involved." Bishop supported their request and suggested to Mulholland that TF 64 be used to plug a gap in coverage southwest of the Shahikot. The Aussies could be used to watch for "squirters," as the Americans referred to enemy personnel who might escape the dragnet thrown by Hammer and Rakkasan, and as a quick reaction force, Bishop said. He suggested this because the Australians enjoyed an advantage over K-Bar's other non-American special ops units: They had their own vehicles—four- and six-wheeled sand-colored Long Range Patrol Vehicles that looked like Land Rovers on steroids and were all but indestructible. "One of the reasons why we didn't employ the other nations' special operations forces to a greater extent is that nobody but the Australians brought their own transportation," Bishop said.

AT the Gardez safe house February 27 was a day of last-minute preparations for the AFO recce missions: weapons cleaning, radio checks, and preparing and loading the trucks that would take the teams to the drop-off point. Jay, the Air Force special ops combat controller, gave a class on how to "rack and stack" aircraft for close air support operations. This was particularly important for India Team, which was not taking a combat controller into the valley this time.

After further analysis of maps and imagery, the three teams had settled on locations for their observation posts and the routes they would take to reach them. Juliet would travel around the northern tip of the valley to occupy a spot high in the eastern ridgeline from which they could overwatch Serkhankhel and the northern half of the valley. They would not be walking. After examining the northern approaches to the Shahikot on the environmental recce mission to Serawray Mountain, Kris K., the team leader, had hit upon the idea of using ATVs to penetrate the valley and climb up the eastern ridge. Juliet Team would be riding to battle.

India and Mako 31, on the other hand, would approach the Shahikot on foot from the south. India had picked an observation post in high ground south of the Fishhook, from which they could observe the southern end of the Whale and TF Hammer's route toward the valley. The SEALs of Mako 31 intended to occupy a position on the Finger that poked into the southern end of the valley. Together, these three positions would allow Blaber's teams to observe the entire valley, except for some dead ground between the mountains on the eastern ridgeline.

Goody and his SEALs hadn't had time to conduct an environmental recon, so they were naturally a bit wary about the task ahead. "At first Goody was very apprehensive about taking this mission," said a source in the safe house. "His guys didn't have the benefit of either Montana or those environmental recons, so Blaber had to make sure they knew how confident he was in them. . . . He just told them, 'I wouldn't send you in if I didn't think you could do it, and I think you can do this.'" As the teams prepared to depart the safe house, Blaber held a last face-to-face, heart-to-heart talk with the Mako 31 team leader, whom he regarded as "a true warrior and a great guy."

"Goody, the success or failure of your mission will predicate the success or failure of the entire operation," the AFO commander told the SEAL NCO. "You have to make it to that OP [observation post] before H-Hour." Neither man could have known how true Blaber's words were to prove, but Goody was determined not to let his new boss down. "Sir, I'll make it to my OP come hell or high water," Goody replied. "If we're hurting on time, I'll drop our rucks. If we're still having problems, I'll keep dropping gear until five naked guys with guns are standing on the OP at H-Hour." *Where do we get such men?* Blaber thought as Goody walked away.

JUST after 7 p.m., two Toyota pickups pulled out of the safe house and turned left. The trucks were mounted with MAG-58 7.62mm and Squad Automatic Weapon machine guns. On board were the eight operators of India and Mako 31, plus the four members of "the infil team"—Captain John B., Master Sergeant Isaac H., Sergeant Major Al Y., and Hans—plus about fifteen of Zia's fighters in the backs of the trucks. Behind them on four ATVs rode Juliet's five commandos—Kris K., Bill R., and Dave H. from Delta, each on his own ATV, with Jason from Gray Fox sharing a ride with Jay, the combat controller.

Some of the ATVs were Delta's and had been provided by Task Force 11 and some were loaned to Juliet by ODA 372. The Delta ATVs had been exten-

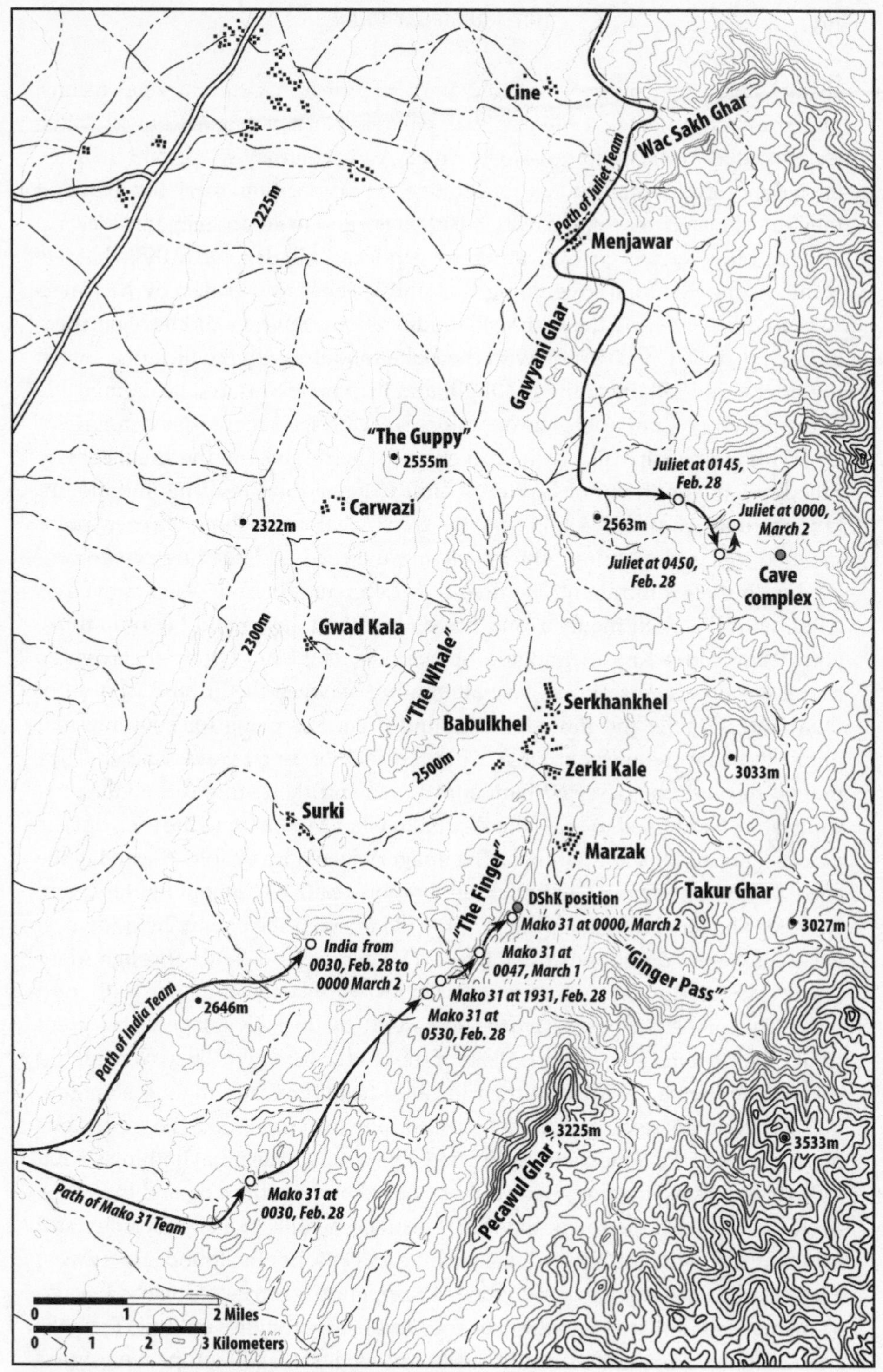

India, Juliet and Mako 31 reconnaissance, February 28 - March 2, 2002

sively—and expensively—modified with reinforced axles and suspensions, plus special mufflers that silenced their exhausts. "They're really quiet," said a Delta source. "I mean, impressively quiet. And then they're spec'd out. They have the proper torque and engine horsepower capacity to carry the load that they're supposed to carry—a heavy load—fast, and to go up steep hillsides. . . . Our mobility gurus go out, bring in vendors, tell them exactly what we want . . . [the vendors] love doing that shit." The ATVs loaned by McHale's A-team didn't have all the high-tech modifications, but they did have one neat piece of gadgetry in common with the Delta models: With the flick of a switch the rider could kill the white headlight and turn on an infrared beam invisible to the naked eye, but not to the operators wearing their night-vision goggles.

With the pickups also being driven with their lights off, the small convoy rolled quietly south out of Gardez, a family of shadows heading into the unknown. Juliet's four ATVs split from the convoy before reaching the checkpoint manned by Gardez shura fighters, leaving the road and heading east to proceed with their infiltration. The time was 7:45 p.m. The four ATVs moved as pairs, with Bill R. in the lead, and Dave H. second. Jason and Jay rode third, with team leader Kris K. bringing up the rear. The team bounced across the rough terrain, the operators' gaze alternating between the ground in front of them and the hills and mountains around them, searching for anything that might threaten the mission, be it a hidden rock or an Al Qaida sniper. They moved through the deserted hamlet of Kwas and then around the village of Cine. They had hoped to cross the Wac Sakh Ghar Mountain to the east, but the passes that had looked inviting on the imagery were impassable. Ahead lay the small town of Menjawar, in which intel reports said 100 enemy fighters were billeted. The team had no option but to ride through the enemy-held town. It was half past midnight when the four ATVs zigzagged silently through Menjawar's deserted streets, which were just a few yards wide and lined with mud walls. The solid cloud cover gave the operators a distinct advantage as they crept under their enemy's nose in the dead of the cold, dark night. They were all but invisible to the naked eye, but their infrared headlights and night-vision goggles gave them perfect vision. They saw nothing to alarm them. The special ops mechanics had done their jobs well: The ATVs were so quiet that nothing stirred in Menjawar, save the dogs that could be heard barking from behind the walls.

Once through the town, the team breathed a collective sigh of relief and motored on, jouncing toward the Shahikot. They finally found a way east through the Gawyani Ghar ridgeline. The operators navigated using FalconView maps loaded into laptops that they carried in pouches on the ATVs' gas tanks, where the operators could easily access them. The laptops were fitted with GPS receivers, so the team members were able to trace their own movements on the digital map in real time. They were tracked by a Joint STARS surveillance aircraft designed to spot moving vehicles. The crew on the Joint STARS, one of several spy planes supporting the recce missions, reported to the team that they could see additional movement in the area. The Juliet operators were in an area where an enemy bunker with a DShK had been reported. They rode south with their senses on high alert, but the only things moving were a few dogs. As they neared the Shahikot, Bill raised his hand quickly to signal "Stop!" He had made a heartstopping discovery—around them the rocks were painted with red Xs—the symbol for mines. Despite the care with which they had chosen their route, they had ridden into a minefield. If just one ATV hit a mine, it would mean mission failure. The explosion would alert enemy fighters for miles around to their presence and would almost certainly kill or maim the unfortunate rider of the ATV that triggered it. Kris evaluated his options. Sixty meters to the south a sloping rock face rose steeply from the ground, paralleling their route and offering a potential avenue of escape. The operators pointed their vehicles toward the outcropping and then rode for several hundred meters along the exposed rock with their ATVs tilted at a gravity-defying 45-degree angle until they were safely out of the minefield.

As Juliet Team approached the Shahikot's eastern wall, the terrain began to rise. Giant rock shelves jutted menacingly over the plain. Bill scrutinized the dim silhouettes ahead of him with a practiced eye and again calmly raised his arm to halt the team. Kris drove up to ask him what he'd seen. Bill pointed upward. There, 4,000 feet above them, was an enemy fighter standing beside a DShK smoking a cigarette. Then Bill indicated another DShK position 200 meters away from the first. Of course, they were too far away to be seen by the enemy gunners. Kris lased the two positions and recorded their locations. Then the team drove directly under the machine-gun posts, moving more slowly to ensure they wouldn't be heard. A few minutes later they came to the draw they had selected as their route toward their observation post. Pointing their vehicles up a dry creek bed, they began their ascent into the mountains. They climbed slowly through increasingly deep snow. Suddenly Bill felt his ATV beginning to tip upright into the "wheelie" position. He flung himself off just before the vehicle rolled backward end over end down the slope. There was remarkably little damage done. The team members had packed to minimize the risk to any sensitive equipment if the vehicles rolled over. When they clambered down the slope, they realized they had been successful.

Poring over the maps and photos at Gardez, Juliet had picked two possible locations for their observation posts in the Shahikot. Their plan was to reach the first by daybreak, spend all day there, and then move to the second after dark. They made good time, but found the first location unsuitable. Kris decided to press on to the second observation post. This was the most dangerous stage of the infil. At any moment an enemy fighter could spy them as the ATVs crawled forward through the snow, the operators scanning their surroundings for the smallest hint of an Al Qaida presence. It took the team three hours to cover the last 1,000 meters, but they made it. This spot was much better and afforded good views of the Whale, Serkhankhel, and the valley's northern end. The operators hid the ATVs behind a ten-foot embankment and camouflaged them with netting. They put up a tent right behind the ATVs, then walked about 100 meters up to the observation post. This way they could have three guys in the OP and two sleeping in the tent. Once they reached the OP, they took off their helmets to get a sense of what an operator called the "sights, sounds, and smells" of their surroundings. This was a key part of the recce concept. "Whenever you get in a new place, you want to stop, take off your helmets, and get used to the environment," an operator said later. At 4:47 a.m. Kris called back to Gardez and reported that the team was beginning operations. It had taken them nine hours to drive about twelve kilometers, but Juliet Team had made it in.

AFTER watching Juliet's ATVs disappear into the darkness, the two pickups continued south for about 15 kilometers then left the road and headed east for about 4,500 meters before stopping at 10:15 p.m. This was the drop-off point for the remaining teams. As soon as the trucks came to a halt, the AMF fighters jumped out and ran to the nearest high ground, throwing a secure perimeter around the Americans in a matter of seconds. The small force was deep in territory that, if not enemy-held, could certainly be considered enemy-controlled. There was no time for long goodbyes. The teams had far to walk to reach their observation posts before dawn. The eight operators of India Team and Mako 31 jumped down from the cabs, shouldered their packs, and marched into the night.

John B. kept his team sitting at the drop-off point for about thirty minutes after the recce teams departed, ready to come to their aid if they ran into trouble immediately. Then he called the Afghan pickets down from the high ground, mounted up, and headed back toward Gardez. This was the riskiest part of the operation for the infil team. Any enemy elements they might have surprised on the way in would by now have been alerted to their presence and waiting in ambush for their return. The infiltration team's job—to drop off and pick up the recce teams—was not glamorous, but John B., who usually led such missions, earned the recce operators' respect for the way he applied himself to the task. "He's the best troop commander I've ever worked for," said an operator. "He displayed a lot of physical and moral courage." John would need to call on his reserves of courage and coolness under pressure on the nerve-jangling drive back. First, the operators spotted two or three vehicles behaving suspiciously near a small town west of their route. The infil team stopped and observed the vehicles, which eventually left the area. Continuing north, the two Toyotas were shot at by militiamen manning the Gardez shura checkpoint. Equipped with night-vision goggles, perfectly zeroed M4 rifles, and years of shoothouse training, the four operators in the vehicles—three from Delta and one from SEAL Team 6—were infinitely superior marksmen to the tribesmen at the checkpoint and in all likelihood could have killed every one of the militiamen without even calling on the AMF fighters in the back of the trucks. But John decided the checkpoint guards probably fired more from sheer fright at the sight of the two pickups emerging from the darkness than from any ill will they bore those in the vehicles. Eager to avoid what one account of the episode described as "unneeded killing," he told his troops to hold their fire and outflank the checkpoint. They did so and arrived at the safe house without further incident.

THE men of India Team and Mako 31 walked east together at a steady pace, following the Zawar Khwar creek. After three kilometers India Team turned north up a smaller creek bed. For this mission Speedy had cut his team down to the bare minimum of three men: himself and Bob from Delta plus Dan, the Gray Fox operator who had proved himself on the environmental recce. Neither Speedy nor Kris, the Juliet Team leader, had been keen on taking Hans or Nelson on this most vital of missions. The pair's negative attitude counted against them when it came time for the team leaders to pick the warriors they would take into the mountains. "Hans and Nelson were naysayers the whole time," a Delta operator said.

The weather—clear in Gardez—turned foul as they pushed into the mountains. The operators fought their way through rain, sleet, and intermittent snow flurries. It wasn't comfortable, but the weather wrapped the trio in its shrouds, shielding them from the prying eyes of any lookouts in the mountains. Nevertheless, the three walked with their weapons at the ready. Speedy and Dan each carried an M4, but Bob had armed himself with his prized SR25 Stoner sniper rifle, which is modeled on the M16, but is designed for extraordinary accuracy and fires a 7.62mm round instead of the 5.56mm bullet fired by the M16 and M4. India faced a seven-kilometer hike to their observation post, but compared to the grueling trek they had endured during the environmental recce, this was an easy movement with just a few short climbs up rocky stream banks interrupting an otherwise gentle ascent, albeit in freezing temperatures carrying over 80 pounds of gear per man. But none of the three was relaxing, physically or mentally. As they trudged uphill, the smell of smoke drifted into their nostrils. Someone had lit a fire nearby. Dogs were barking off to their right in the distance. On a normal patrol the operators might have been tempted to investigate, but tonight making it to the observation post by daylight was all that counted.

After more than six hours of movement, they knew they were getting close. Because the site they had picked for their observation post was only two kilometers from the southern tip of the Whale, they were even more careful than usual about staying hidden, though it was still dark. Dropping their rucks, they crawled the final 200 meters to the position, which was behind some large rocks. Once they had clambered down, they realized they had chosen well: from their aerie they could observe the Fishhook, the southern end of the Whale, Hammer's route into the Shahikot, and the southwestern corner of the valley.

At 5:22 a.m. Speedy called back to Gardez with a simple message: India Team was in.

MAKO 31's operators were less experienced in this terrain than the two Delta teams, but they had been handed the toughest movement. The five-man team included three SEALs and an Air Force combat controller called Andy, but also, incongruously, a Navy explosive ordnance disposal expert. Once India Team had split to the north, Goody and his men faced a daunting eleven-kilometer walk over jagged 8,000-foot ridgelines to reach their observation post. Because the goal was to arrive in the valley unseen by the enemy, Goody's men did not take the most direct or obvious route to the Finger. Instead, they took a roundabout approach, heading south for at least 1,000 meters before turning north again. Knee-deep snow, rocky terrain, and driving rain, snow, and sleet that slashed their faces made it heavy going. With Blaber's exhortations fresh in his memory, Goody drove his men forward just as Speedy had done a few days earlier under similar conditions. "He did a great job, too," Blaber said of Goody. "They had a really tough movement." But despite their best efforts, as the night wore on, it became clear Mako 31 would not make it to their observation post before daylight. Exhausted, they stopped about a thousand meters southwest of their desired position. Their present location was just west of a 9,400-foot ridgeline that stretched north to become the Finger and blocked

Mako 31's view of Marzak and the landing zones designated for Paul LaCamera's 1-87 Infantry. However, they enjoyed good sight lines down to the Fishhook and across to the Whale. At 5 a.m. the team called the AFO operations center at Gardez to report their location and their intention of staying put until the next night, when they would move forward to occupy the observation post.

As the gray dawn broke over the Shahikot Valley, Blaber and his men had reason to feel proud of what they had accomplished. Two of the three teams were already in position, with the third just a thousand meters away. They had moved from the safe house—whose location was undoubtedly known to all Taliban and Al Qaida leaders in the area—overland through harsh weather and harsher terrain into the heart of the enemy without being seen. Through a combination of meticulous preparation, tactical boldness, personal courage, and a professionalism honed by years of rigorous training, AFO had given the generals in Bagram an extraordinary advantage. There were now thirteen pairs of American eyes watching the Shahikot. How the generals used this gift would go a long way toward determining the course of the operation.

25.

THE satellite radio in the AFO operations center in Gardez crackled to life at 9:20 a.m. on February 28. On the line was Speedy, the first of the three team leaders to report in. He had had an interesting start to his morning. The site India had picked for their observation post could accommodate one person, but was too exposed for the entire team to spend days on end there. The hillside dropped away just behind (i.e., to the south of) the observation post, so the operators moved their rucks and communications gear about twenty-five meters back to a small nook out of sight of the Fishhook and the Whale. Then Bob crept back down behind the rocks, while Speedy crawled to a ledge about 200 meters to the east. With the team separated, the early morning silence was broken by the unexpected—and definitely unwanted—tinkling of small bells.

Speedy froze then turned his head away from the valley to look behind him where the noise seemed to be coming from. Below him a couple of hundred meters to the north he saw an old Afghan man, unarmed and alone except for the small herd of goats he was tending. Speedy shrank back. The man hadn't seen him yet. Grabbing his small handheld MBITR (pronounced "embitter" or "M-biter") radio, he whispered the news to the others, then squeezed himself further into the crack between two rocks where he had been hiding and lay still. He was well hidden, not only by the rocks but also by the camouflage outfit he was wearing. Designed for hunters and snipers (Speedy and Bob were both), the gear was little more than netting overlaid with artificial leaves, hence its trade name: Leafywear. The two had chosen suits of grayish brown, the same color as the rocks in that part of Afghanistan, topped with soft tan "boonie" hats. Speedy and Bob were virtually impossible to spot as they crouched between the rocks. They hadn't worn the gear on the way in, but whenever either of them moved forward from where they'd stashed their rucks, they put on the Leafywear, which was less bulky than the traditional "gillie suits" worn by snipers. To Speedy, wearing Leafywear was second nature. He wore the same sort of outfit hunting wild turkeys in his native Kentucky.

The other two operators were hidden by rocks, and Speedy was confident he hadn't been seen, but he was still very concerned. The goatherds in these parts had probably been grazing their livestock on the same land for years, and would notice if something seemed out of place, he figured. His mind raced through his options if the goatherd stumbled upon him. He couldn't think of many. There was no way he would shoot an unarmed civilian, and if they took the man prisoner, his family would probably come looking for him within twenty-four hours. Speedy's only course of action would be to let the man go and immediately call back to Gardez with the news his team had been compromised. That would probably mean immediate extraction or an order to sneak back out of the valley. It could jeopardize the entire operation. Very fortunately, the wizened Afghan led his goats away. Speedy breathed again and turned his attention back to the valley.

OVER the next several hours the AFO teams gathered the first empirical evidence of a large-scale enemy presence in the Shahikot. Using Schmidt-Cassegrain spotting scopes, each team methodically scanned as much of the landscape as its members could see from their perch. (The scopes allowed an operator to follow a man and know he was carrying a Kalashnikov rifle from six or seven kilometers away.) The clouds lifted for the first part of the morning, giving India a clear view of the Fishhook, the village of Surki just outside the valley entrance, and the route planned for Hammer's approach along Whale's western base. There were no signs of mines, and Surki and the Fishhook appeared deserted, save for a white Jeep CJ5 circa 1980 a few hundred meters northwest of the village.

Juliet, meanwhile, spotted movement on the Whale—the first confirmed activity on the huge humpback mountain or in the valley. Kris moved his team a short distance to a position that afforded better views of the valley and the Whale.

Mako 31 had yet to make it to their designated observation post, but they managed to sneak into a position from which they could observe a good road that led south from Marzak and then turned east into a valley. The road was lined with white rocks, a local sign that indicated it was clear of mines. The movement on the Whale that Juliet had seen was the only activity any of the teams spotted during the morning. But their ears told them Blaber's hunch had been right. Dan and Jason, the Gray Fox operators with India and Juliet respectively, set up their monitoring equipment. Soon each was picking up cell phone or radio traffic from the immediate area. And at 12:10 p.m., Mako 31 heard gunfire coming from the direction of Marzak. It didn't sound like somebody hunting. It sounded more like marsksmanship training.

Then, from their new observation post in a narrow valley about 3,500 meters northeast of Serkhankhel, the Juliet operators watched an unnerving episode unfold before them. To their east they spotted five men walking in single file toward them from the direction of a cave complex the operators knew about from examining the overhead imagery. Bin Laden had supposedly stayed at the cave in December. Three of the five were armed with AKs. The other two had RPGs. Their facial features were those of local Afghans. All wore turbans and earth-tone clothing. To the Juliet operators' great concern, they appeared to be following the tracks left in the snow by the ATVs. There were a lot of tracks muddled in the snow, but if the enemy fighters found the ATVs, Juliet would be in big trouble. Kris used his MBITR radio to warn Bill and Dave, who were sleeping in the tent. They took up defensive positions, but the embankment at first prevented them seeing the enemy troops.

Step by step the turbaned warriors inched toward the hidden ATVs. Juliet Team watched and waited as the quintet stood and scratched their turbans, talking among each other and looking at the strange tracks in the snow with bemused expressions. Infrared dots danced around their torsos as the operators took aim and curled their index fingers around their triggers. Kris whispered to his men to hold their fire until the last possible moment, while he juggled the possibilities in his mind. The five fighters might be the lead element of a larger force, and if Juliet shot them the operators would be on the run, on foot. Killing them would also compromise the mission. But if Juliet didn't kill them, they might raise the alarm and return with more enemy fighters. Or they might be confused and just let the tire tracks pass unexplained. But the AK-toting militiamen were getting closer and closer to the ATVs. Kris was on the verge of giving the order to open fire when they paused, talked to one another for a few moments, and then turned around and walked away. One man turned back toward the ATVs. "It was bothering him, the tire tracks," an operator said later. "But he's looking at tire tracks at 10,000 feet on the east side of the valley, with the north being impassable due to terrain and minefields, and the south—you've still got the long axis of the valley [to traverse], so how could there be these tire tracks up here, and who could've ridden the thing that made it up here? He was probably wondering, what sort of spaceship was able to get up here?" Again, Kris got ready to fire at the confused fighter. Then, "at what would have been his last moment," as a military report of the incident put it, the inquisitive Taliban fighter appeared to reconsider before turning around and rejoining the group.

In a turn of amazing good fortune, a blizzard suddenly appeared out of nowhere. Gale-force winds whipped snow into the small knot of guerrillas. As if of one mind, the Afghan fighters apparently decided that in this case discretion was the better part of valor and continued west toward the shelter of the village. Thinking the five enemy troops might be back with reinforcements, the operators broke down the tent and hauled the gear up to the observation post. They set a trip wire with a grenade by the ATVs to give them early warning. The snow fell for the next two hours, smothering the area. After it stopped, Kris looked around and realized this would be their final observation post. He had planned on possibly pushing further south to establish the team on Takur Ghar. But if the team were to move now, the snow would provide what an operator called "a cookie-crumb trail" for the enemy to follow. Of equal import, they now had superb overwatch of the valley and the Whale, and the blanket of snow would give them an accurate indicator of any enemy movement in the area.

(Juliet sent a data message reporting their close call back to Gardez via satellite. Blaber read it and immediately forwarded it to Hagenbeck, Harrell, and TF 11's Masirah headquarters. Displaying his renowned flair for the dramatic, he introduced Kris's report with three words—"We're in business"—a line taken from the moment in the movie *Saving Private Ryan* when U.S. troops pinned down on Omaha Beach use a Bangalore torpedo to make a breakthrough.)

After their brush with catastrophe, Juliet turned their attention back to the Whale. The weather abated long enough for them to spy four "possibly armed" individuals on the east side of the mountain. A few hours later they spotted three enemy positions on the Whale. One was an observation post occupied by a single guerrilla at the top of the ridgeline facing west. Two other fighters sheltered nearby in a rock shack with a cloth cover. Fifty meters below them were concealed fighting positions. Shortly thereafter Juliet identified another observation post and four fighters moving between a pair of bunkers on the eastern side of the Whale. Kris and his men were starting to realize the Whale was honeycombed with fighting positions. Looking south, they could see a portion of Marzak a little over five kilometers away and reckoned that at least five or six buildings in the town were active.

The weather worsened as the day wore on. The cloud ceiling descending to 7,000 feet and visibility was restricted to 400 meters. Speedy repositioned India a little lower down their hillside to get under the cloud cover. He and his men were momentarily alarmed to hear gunfire from the direction of Juliet, but quickly concluded it was the same sort of marksmanship training Mako 31 had reported earlier. The Gray Fox signals interceptors became the main effort. They reported every intercept they made quickly back to Gardez. From there the information was sent to Bagram, where Fred Egerer used it to task the NSA's spy planes and satellites for further collection.

Later that afternoon Mako 31 also spotted enemy positions on the Whale. Once darkness fell, Goody and his troops struck out for their OP. A thick blanket of fog covered their movement, but the going was even tougher than the previous night's efforts. With snow and sleet stinging their faces, the five men picked their way carefully along the steep, jagged ridgeline, only too aware that the slightest misplaced step could send them tumbling hundreds of feet into the dark crevasses below. It took them six hours to cover about 1,000 meters. They halted at about 2 a.m. on the morning of March 1 in a depression about 250 meters southwest of the Finger's highest point. This would be their mission support site where they would stash their rucks and rest. The next morning they would push out and establish the observation post a little farther along and on the eastern side of the crest. That night the AFO operations center passed a message to the teams in the valley: H-Hour was set for 6:30 a.m. March 2, less than thirty-six hours away.

BY the evening of February 28 word was seeping into the Mountain and Rakkasan final rehearsals that the enemy might not be concentrated on the valley floor after all. At 8.30 p.m. the senior officers and NCOs from Chip Preysler's 2-187 Infantry gathered in a dark GP Medium tent where Captain Denis Holtery, the battalion's intelligence officer, told them the focus was turning to the mountains that surrounded the valley. "The change is we're not so much worried about taking rounds from the town," Preysler then explained to his men. The threat to the platoons conducting the air assault was more likely to come from the mountains on the Shahikot's eastern side. "We may have an uphill fight," in which case the plan was to send the Apaches against the enemy positions in the mountains, he said. There was also new thinking on when the air assault's second lift would be committed, Preysler told them. Originally scheduled to touch down in the valley at dusk on D-Day, the plan now was for the second lift of infantry to arrive within three hours of the first lift, he said. (The reason was that the planners now considered it impossible to seal all the blocking positions without those additional forces.) However, despite the reports reaching Bagram of an enemy presence in the ridgelines around the valley, no effort was made to change the plan to accommodate these new facts.

The focus for most Rakkasans that day had not been on new intelligence from the Shahikot, but on the flyaway rehearsal Wiercinski used to tailor his load plans for the aircraft. The extra forty-eight hours they had gained courtesy of Hagenbeck's weather call also gave the battalion commanders and command sergeants major more time to focus their soldiers' minds on the mission. Their messages reflected the curious dichotomy that existed at the higher levels of command. On one hand, the plan and the forces used to execute it were a function of the expectation that the enemy would not put up a big fight. Hence the focus at the small unit level on how to screen crowds of civilians for the presence of guerrillas trying to escape. On the other hand, in the world of the infantry officer or NCO, it was considered almost criminal to allow your soldiers to go into a "real-world" mission without mentally steeling them for combat. Nowhere was this more apparent than in the meeting Preysler held with his subordinates that evening. Mark Nielsen, Preysler's wiry sergeant major who commanded enormous respect among the battalion's enlisted men, personified this hardheaded, combat-oriented mentality. His eyes sweeping the tent, he told the company first sergeants to scrub their lists of soldiers heading into the Shahikot and leave behind those they thought couldn't cut it physically or mentally. "I don't want any pussies going on this mission," Nielsen said, glowering like a bulldog in the weak electric light. "There's no pop-up targets this time, boys; there's fucking real flesh and blood out there. Let's get 'em on the ground, meet the enemy, and destroy him."

Major Rick Busko, Preysler's operations officer, reminded the infantrymen that the eyes of President Bush and everyone else in their chain of command would be on them in the Shahikot. "At the National Command Authority-level . . . this is the only game in town," he said, adding that company commanders and first sergeants needed to tell their soldiers "now is the time to perform." The message was getting through to the soldiers. As he stood in line outside the chow tent waiting for dinner, Sergeant David Dedo of 2-187's Charlie Company reflected on the mission to come. "Osama bin Laden made a comment that U.S. soldiers are 'paper tigers,'" he said. "Well, now he's got a chance to find out." But, he added, displaying the hard-boiled realism of an infantry

NCO, "I don't think this is going to be the new-age Normandy the 101st is looking for."

The Rakkasans also used the extra time to give some last-minute instruction on how to fight and survive in the frozen conditions they expected to find in the Shahikot. Standing on the hood of a Humvee on the edge of tent city, Staff Sergeant John Hodges, a squad leader in 2-187 Infantry's A Troop, gave a cold-weather operations class to a walk-up crowd. Hodges had been stationed in Alaska for three years and had gone through cold-weather training at the Army's Northern Warfare Training Center at Camp Greely. He ran through the basics that might never have occurred to soldiers unused to operating in subfreezing temperatures. "In the cold it's going to take two to three times as long to do anything," he said. A simple task like loading a magazine could take ten to fifteen minutes in extreme conditions. It was vital to keep eating and drinking water, particularly at high altitude, Hodges said. Then he explained the three types of cold weather injuries—chilblains, hypothermia, and frostbite—and how to avoid them. Finally Hodges gazed around the crowd and asked whether there was anyone who had never seen snow before. Two soldiers raised their hands. "If you've never seen snow, don't worry about it," Hodges told them. "Here's your chance, and the Army's picking up the tab."

26.

SHORTLY after dawn on an overcast March 1, Goody sent two Mako 31 snipers up the Finger to scout the location the team had selected for their observation post. The two SEALs inched forward for 500 meters along the rocky ridgeline until they could put eyes on the exact spot Goody and Blaber had agreed on. As they poked their heads above the rocks to get a good look, they got the shock of their lives. Someone had beaten them to it. There, in the lee of a large, jagged outcrop, on the very patch of ground on which they intended to establish their observation post, sat a gray-green tent big enough to sleep several people. As the commandos digested this unexpected turn of events, their eyes fastened on an even more unsettling sight. About fifteen meters up the rock-strewn slope, they discerned the outline of a tripod-mounted DShK wrapped tightly in blue plastic. The discovery was momentous. The position dominated the southern end of the valley—that, after all, was why the AFO operators wanted to occupy it—and overlooked the 700-meter gap through which TF Rakkasan's helicopters were to fly between the Finger and the eastern ridge. With an antiaircraft range of 1,000 meters, the DShK was ideally located to shoot down the infantry-packed Chinooks due to fly into the valley in less than twenty-four hours. It would be Frank Wiercinski's worst nightmare come to horrifying life.

The loss of even one Chinook full of Rakkasans would be a disaster from which Operation Anaconda might not recover. Troops would have to be dispatched from their previously assigned missions to secure the downed helicopter, all while enemy fire poured down on them from the mountainsides. Any reserves flown in would have to brave the same gauntlet of fire that had precipitated their arrival in the first place. But the DShK was positioned to deal an even more devastating blow to the operation. Wiercinski planned to bring his forward command post, containing himself, Savusa, Marye, Corkran and Air Force Captain Paul "Dino" Murray, the Rakkasans' air liaison officer, into the valley on two Black Hawks and land just a few hundred meters farther north along and a little farther down the Finger from the DShK. At such close range it would be hard for the Al Qaida gunner to miss. As he emptied his weapon into the two American helicopters, even he would not have dreamed that the Black Hawks cartwheeling to the ground were carrying to their deaths not only the commander of the entire air assault force but also the commanders of his aviation task force and his only reserve, as well as his senior NCO and the officer responsible for coordinating close air support for the troops who survived the initial air assault. In the opening minutes of Anaconda a single heavy machine gunner would have dealt the operation a shattering blow.

"The success or failure of your mission will predicate the success or failure of the entire operation," Blaber had told Goody. The AFO commander learned how truthfully he had spoken at 10:02 a.m., when India Team relayed a message from Mako 31 to the safe house stating the bare facts of their discovery: an unmanned DShK and a tent sitting on the observation post. The news validated Blaber's bold decision to risk an infiltration of the Shahikot before D-Day. Without the audacity displayed by the AFO commander and his three recce teams, the staffs at Bagram would have remained ignorant of the DShK's existence until the moment Task Force Rakkasan flew into a buzz saw of high-caliber bullets. This was a lesson for anyone who thought the U.S. military's billions of dollars' worth of spy satellites and surveillance aircraft obviated the need for ground reconnaissance. Despite the boasts at Bagram that "every national asset" was being focused on the valley, none of the satellites or spy planes—not even the Mi-17 helicopter the CIA had flown over the Shahikot the previous day with an operative filming the valley floor—had revealed either the tent or the weapon that could have spelled defeat for the Americans in the battle's opening moments. Lou Bello, the Mountain fires planner, compared searching for a single DShK on a mountainside from the air to "looking for a needle in a haystack." In the giant haystack that was the Shahikot Valley, Mako 31 had found a needle and it was pointing straight at the heart of Operation Anaconda.

The SEAL snipers used a Nikon Coolpix digital camera equipped with an eight-power telephoto lens to snap a few photos of the DShK and the tent. They marked the position's coordinates with a Global Positioning System receiver then slipped away as low clouds and a sudden snowstorm appeared to cover their withdrawal. Once the weather cleared, they returned for a second look and were rewarded with an extended sighting of two fighters manning the position. One was a short, dark-haired, and bearded man with Mongol features—possibly an Uighur Chinese. The other, clearly in charge of the DShK, was a tall, clean-shaven Caucasian with reddish-brown hair—most likely one of Yuldeshev's Uzbeks. They were well equipped for the elements. A blue five-gallon gas can just outside and a pipe protruding from the roof indicated that their tent was heated. The shorter fighter wore a pale tunic, a sleeveless jacket, and what appeared to be a wool hat. The taller man wore a thick red Gore-Tex jacket, a Polartec fleece jacket tied around his waist, Russian-style camouflage pants, and Adidas sneakers. Each fighter appeared fit and healthy. The Uzbek-looking guerrilla would shadow-box in his spare time. Strolling between machine gun and tent with his hands in his pockets, he would not have looked out of place on any main street in Western Europe or North America.

The SEALs clicked off a few more photos and crept back to the mission support site, about 200 meters northwest of the DShK. From there, Goody sent several photos and a report back to Blaber using a Toshiba Libretto mini-laptop hooked via a USB port to the satellite radio. To emphasize the importance of the material, Goody labeled the photos and the report "eyes only," his way of saying they were for Blaber alone. The SEALs had alone seen two enemy fighters, but they reckoned as many as five might be occupying the position. Mako 31's leader also had an urgent question for Blaber, prompted by the machine gunner's European features: "Are there Brits up here?" He wanted to make sure he wasn't about to get in a firefight with the SAS. "It was so fantastical seeing this guy with no beard and red hair and Gore-Tex [and] BDU pants, they had a hard time believing that's what the enemy was," recalled an operator. "And the guy did look like he could have been British. He could have been American, too. But they figured they knew where all the American special ops guys were." Blaber assured Goody there were no Brits in the area, then he forwarded the photos to Jimmy in Bagram, who in turn sent them to Hagenbeck and to Masirah. Blaber followed up with a call to Hagenbeck. The AFO commander underlined his view that the fighters seen by Mako 31 and Juliet were proof the enemy was in the mountains. But despite the enemy presence, Blaber told the Mountain commander that with the three AFO teams occupying dominant terrain, "we are in a position to control the valley." "Good job," Hagenbeck replied.

Using point-to-point digital messages similar to e-mail sent via satellite, Blaber and Goody discussed what to do about the DShK position. It clearly had to be eliminated before H-Hour. Goody asked Blaber what he thought Goody should do. Blaber typed a response that turned the question around, asking Goody what *he* thought he should do. "I think we ought to wait until H minus two [hours]," Goody wrote. "At H minus two I start moving; I engage at H minus one, and then follow up with AC-130. I understand that you have to make the decision on this and I'll support any decision you make." Blaber sent him a two-word reply: "Good hunting."

Goody was relieved. Not used to being given such latitude, he was worried someone higher up the TF 11 chain of command would veto any suggestion that Mako 31 take out the DShK team on their own. (His fears were not entirely misplaced. After quoting from *Saving Private Ryan* in the wake of Juliet's close encounter with the cave-dwellers, Blaber chose *Apocalypse Now* as his inspiration for another message up the chain of command, in which he said that he planned to tell Goody, "Terminate with extreme prejudice." The message caused some angst at Masirah. E-mails pinged back and forth saying AFO shouldn't jump to conclusions and Mako 31 didn't have enough men to engage the tent and DShK position. At least one TF 11 staffer complained that such direct action missions were not in AFO's bailiwick.)

While Goody and his men focused on the DShK position, India and Juliet continued their observation of the valley. As the day lengthened, they reported more evidence of a significant enemy presence. India Team, a couple of hundred meters south-southwest of the Fishhook, monitored three SUVs driving around Babulkhel, the village closest to the valley's western entrance and into which the road that passed through the Fishook ran. The vehicles would stop at the village's westernmost house—a two-story adobe structure with a walled-in compound—before proceeding further. When three horsemen with AKs approached the village, six armed men came out and greeted them about 100 meters from the village. India concluded the house was an enemy checkpoint.

Speedy and Bob also spotted an antenna mast protruding from a compound in Serkhankhel, and another walled compound with what appeared to be a guard at the gate and ten to fifteen people milling inside. In an ominous sign, at noon they observed a family below them hurrying out of the valley on foot with their belongings loaded on a camel. Other than a sighting about half an hour earlier of two women in Babulkhel, the family represented the only report of civilians in the valley by any AFO team before H-Hour.

The low clouds prevented Juliet, whose observation post was higher than India's, from seeing much of anything during the morning. But once the weather lifted, Kris and the other operators in the northeast observed plenty of suspicious activity in Serkhankhel. They saw six men meeting at a mud-walled compound in the village. Two pickup trucks were parked beside the fortlike building, and when a Predator drone flew overhead, the six scattered. Once the Predator had passed, an armed man came out and circled the compound as if on patrol, before going back inside. Later that afternoon Juliet reported seeing more vehicles and armed men in Serkhankhel, as well as six men with rucksacks walking south into Serkhankhel from a position about a kilometer southwest of Juliet's observation post. Meanwhile, Jason, the Gray Fox operator, intercepted a call indicating the enemy would be holding "a group meeting" the next day.

By afternoon's end the operators realized Blaber had been right. There was a large enemy force in the valley. How large they didn't know, but India and Juliet had each observed dozens of fighters moving in and around the Shahikot. Their observations also told them that the enemy occupied the high ground around the valley on the Whale, the Finger, and the eastern ridge. These facts were included in the reports they sent back to Gardez that were immediately forwarded to Bagram. Mako 31's reports and photographs of the DShK position were particularly telling: the Uzbek machine gunner was no amateur; he took meticulous care of his weapon, wrapping it in plastic to shield it from the elements; he had arranged his 12.7mm rounds around the weapon ergonomically, for easy access; and he had built a small brick platform that he could rest the barrel on, with other bricks beside it that could be added or removed depending on the desired elevation. He also had less professional habits that the AFO operators pointed out: He and his colleagues walked around without their personal weapons, sometimes with their hands in their pockets. It was as if they felt completely secure on their mountain perch.

The AFO reports supported the recent intelligence from Gardez and Khowst that had received such limited attention and distribution in Bagram: The Al Qaida force in the Shahikot was almost certainly larger than the Americans were anticipating, and the enemy was well-armed, well-trained and ready to fight. But again, there was little alarm in Bagram. Officers there had been encouraged by the Mi-17 flight over the valley, which revealed no significant enemy troop concentrations or weapons and helped refine the selection of the landing zones in the low ground. (That Mi-17 flight was itself controversial: AFO, who had no advance notice of it, and Dagger officers disapproved, believing it was bound to tip off the enemy; but Wiercinski and Larsen were grateful for the opportunity to view film of their objective taken so close to D-Day.) Not until late that night did Hagenbeck started to comprehend the significance of AFO's discoveries (beyond the obvious importance of the DShK position). "I had no reason to doubt the intel until about six to eight hours before we launched," he said. "I got a call back from a special operator [Blaber] who said they believed there were up to 400 in the valley," Hagenbeck said. By then there was little time to adjust.

The reports from the AFO teams in the Shahikot were also notable for what they did not include: any mention of civilians, beyond the two women seen by India and the family fleeing the valley with its possessions piled on top of a camel. The operators noticed the difference between the Shahikot villages and those they had observed during the environmental recces, in which women and children had been clearly visible. "This place was nothing but a bunch of men, and they weren't going about daily life," said an operator who was watching the valley floor. But the fact that the AFO teams had seen virtually no civilians—something completely at odds with Wiercinski's expectation of a valley in which 200 enemy mingled with 800 civilians—never reached the Rakkasans, whose plan was geared around the civilians.

Why not? Much like Sir Arthur Conan Doyle's Sherlock Holmes story of a "dog that didn't bark," the absence of any mention of civilians from the AFO reports was a negative clue no one in Bagram picked up on because they weren't looking for it. The Mountain and, particularly, Rakkasan officers were intently focused on the air assault and scoured the AFO reports for any information suggesting a threat to the landing zones. "The sit temp [situation template] we got asked to confirm or deny was weapons systems, enemy concentrations," said a special operator. "No one ever said to us, 'Hey, are there civilians out there?'" Not having been asked to report on the presence of civilians, the AFO teams made no mention of the fact that they weren't seeing any. "We're trained to report what we see, not what we don't see," said an operator who was in the Shahikot.

One officer in Bagram who was reading the reports from the valley with growing concern was Jimmy, Blaber's deputy and AFO's liaison to Hagenbeck. The DShK on the Finger, the fighting positions on the Whale, the intel reports that said most of the enemy was in the mountains, not in the villages—none of this sounded good. On March 1 Jimmy went back a final time to Colonel Joe

Smith, Hagenbeck's chief of staff. "Sir, do not land those helicopters [there]," Jimmy said. "The current plan is not going to work out for you." "I know, Jim," Smith replied. "But it's too late to do anything about it.'"

AT 12:30 p.m. Wiercinski met with the pilots and staff officers from TF Talon, his helicopter task force. The briefing was held in Bagram's pitifully small chow tent. Over sixty soldiers stood shoulder to shoulder, most of them pilots wearing tan one-piece flight suits. Even though it was midday, the tent was dark and the electric lights made it seem more like a nighttime gathering. This meeting was crucial for Wiercinski. The aviators' role was central to the operation. The Chinook crews had the vital job of ferrying the Rakkasan infantry into enemy-held territory and the Apache pilots would provide the only heavy firepower under Wiercinski's direct control. The Rakkasan commander wanted to look them in the eye and tell them he believed in them.

As usual, Wiercinski's intelligence officer, Eric Haupt, briefed first. He told the crowd, which was swollen with representatives from the other task forces, that as recently as January there had been an estimated 700 to 800 enemy fighters in and around Serkhankhel, but they had mostly departed. All that remained, he said, were 150 to 200 "remnants" of that force. Seventy-two hours had passed since the report from Gardez casting grave doubt on that assertion, and fewer than eighteen hours remained before the first Chinooks were due to land in the Shahikot.

A few minutes later Wiercinski spoke, his comments alternating between efforts to bolster the aviators' confidence and more cautionary wisdom. He said he had told the infantry commanders they were going into battle with the best crews and the best helicopters in the world. "Not every helicopter and not every crew could do this," he said. "You've got the equipment, you've got the people, this is going to be a great mission." But then he gave his first indication that the AFO reports were worrying him. "I'm mostly concerned with any threat to the aircraft from the east ridgeline," he said. Turning to the pilots who were to fly the half-dozen Apaches into the valley a couple of minutes ahead of the Chinooks, he told them to "service" any targets they saw on that ridgeline "immediately." Chief Warrant Officer 2 John Quinlan of Bravo/159 could sense the Rakkasan commander's tension as the weight of responsibility bore down on him. "Colonel Wiercinski—excellent commander," Quinlan said. "But even on his face you could see a dire amount of concern."

Wiercinski let other officers brief, then resumed where he had left off. Again he locked eyes with the dozen pilots charged with flying the hornetlike Apaches into combat the following dawn. Normally his brigade would be able to call on a full battalion of twenty-four Apaches and thunderous barrages from a battalion of howitzers to pummel the enemy into submission. Tomorrow, these twelve men in their six helicopters would be all he had. He needed them to know he was counting on them. "Apaches, protect the force," Wiercinski said. "Protect them. Give them everything you've got."

To underline the importance of good fire discipline, he cited tales of America's Wild West in which the cowboy who shot six times quickly never hit anything, but the cool customer who took careful aim before pulling the trigger always hit the target. He also wanted it understood that he would be in control of fires. "It will be on my word that we unleash hell," he said, a quote from the movie *Gladiator* that showed he yielded nothing to Blaber in his ability to draw on Hollywood for melodramatic inspiration.

Then his speech wandered down a rhetorical path that, to the ears of the 101st troops in the tent, did not sound out of place. But had some AFO and Dagger officers been there, Wiercinski's words probably would have confirmed their fears that he was letting the potential legacy of Task Force Rakkasan and his place in air assault history overrule his best tactical judgment. "When they wrote the book on air assault, this is what they were talking about," Wiercinski said. "You will make history. You've got to be very proud of yourselves, and very proud of your unit. No other unit in the world could do this. . . . Go out there and give them hell, guys."

The soldiers streamed out into the cold afternoon, but Wiercinski had only been warming up. Next on his agenda was an eve-of-battle speech to his entire 1,700-soldier task force. It was quite an occasion. Each battalion lined up in formation on an empty patch of ground in tent city, colors fluttering in the breeze. A public address system was rigged up for Wiercinski and Savusa, his command sergeant major, to address the troops from the hood of a Humvee. Savusa clambered up. "You guys are fixing to go in and do exactly what you get paid for," he reminded the soldiers, before continuing the historical legacy theme where Wiercinski had left off in the chow tent. "Be proud of yourselves because you're part of history right now," the sergeant major said. Alluding to the composite nature of TF Rakkasan, which included LaCamera's battalion from 10th Mountain standing proudly before him, he drove home a message of unity: "We're going in all of us together." Then he added a touch of humor. After the operation, he told them, "You can go back home and tell all the lies you wanna tell. And if I see you in a bar anywhere telling stories, I will back you up." To cheers he yielded the Humvee to Wiercinski, who delivered his speech in a clear, confident voice that held every soldier's attention.

"It's Friday night and every soldier here's been invited to the party!" the brigade commander said by way of introduction. Then he turned serious. Every American generation had been called on to give something for their country, he told the serried ranks. Their generation was no different. "Every man, every woman has certain defining moments in their life," he said. "Today is one of those defining moments." They would be going into battle to avenge the firefighters, police, and other emergency workers who had gone into the burning Twin Towers of the World Trade Center to save others, he added.

"A lot of you are thinking, 'I've never been in combat, I don't know how I'll do,'" the colonel continued. Experience had nothing to do with it, he said. "I guarantee you there are a lot of people out there that drive cars every day that are shitty drivers. . . . You will be good in combat for a lot of reasons. The first one is because of who you are. You volunteered. You've got it in here," he said, pounding his chest. "That's what makes you good in combat." Great training and equipment would also help, he added. "And you'll be good in combat because of comrades. . . . You will do it for each other. . . . We have two missions tonight. One is to defeat an enemy. The second one is a goal: to bring everybody home. Never leave a fallen comrade."

"There are two kinds of people out there tonight," he said, again touching on the subject of the civilians he expected to find in the Shahikot. "There are innocents who don't want any part of this fight, and there are those out there who want nothing better than to kill an American or kill a coalition partner." This time Wiercinski's message was that he didn't want any hesitation when the time for killing those in the latter category arrived. "Do not be afraid to squeeze that trigger," he told the young soldiers. "You will know when, you will know why."

"We few, we happy few, we band of brothers," he continued, channeling Henry V via Shakespeare and Stephen Ambrose, before closing with references to the 10th Mountain and 101st Airborne mottos. "I wouldn't want to be anywhere else, anywhere else in the world today, than right here with you. Today is your 'Climb to Glory,' today's another chapter in Rakkasan history, today's our 'Rendezvous with Destiny.' You should all be proud of yourselves. God bless each and every one of us. I'll see you when we come back. Remember *our* motto: 'Let Valor not Fail.' Rakkasans!"

Wiercinski departed the makeshift stage to cheers. The chaplain led the troops in prayer and the Mountain and 101st troops sang loud, if somewhat off-key, renditions of each division's song before the units walked back to their tents. The infantry companies on the first lift would be getting up in the middle of the night. Most soldiers hit the chow tent one last time, made sure their rucks were packed and ready, and then racked out. Who knew when the next opportunity for sleep would present itself?

LATE that afternoon Hagenbeck took part in a video-teleconference with Central Command and CFLCC. Hagenbeck explained that the AFO teams now had eyes on previously unknown enemy positions. He requested additional preassault air strikes the next morning to destroy them. "General Hagenbeck said, 'Hey, bomb these frickin' things,'" recalled Mikolashek, who was also in the VTC. This request provoked what Mikolashek described as "a little consternation" on the part of the CENTCOM participants in general, and Renuart, the Air Force general who was Franks's director of operations, in particular. "Hey, you guys said you wanted this many targets bombed, and now it's all of a sudden this many. What are you doing?" was how Mikolashek characterized Renuart's response. Another officer who witnessed Renuart's outburst was more graphic. "The J-3 [Renuart] went crazy on the VTC, bitching and moaning and yelling, 'We can't do that, we can't adjust,'" he said. "He showed himself big time."

In the end Renuart and Central Command said they would try to arrange the additional air strikes. But Renuart's initial reaction suggested that Central Command was not postured to quickly adapt to changing battlefield circumstances. "CENTCOM, in their defense, had not been exposed to this kind of close combat heretofore," Mikolashek said. It promised to be a steep learning curve for all concerned.

AS the infantry slumbered, a single pair of Vietnam-style jungle boots squelched through the mire of tent city. Jimmy was dog tired after a twenty-hour day monitoring the radios and keeping the senior members of the Mountain staff updated on the latest revelations from the AFO teams in the Shahikot. But before he crashed he had a personal commitment to fulfill. Jimmy was a "prior service" officer, meaning he had entered the Army as an enlisted man. As a young specialist in 1st Ranger Battalion's B Company he had come to know and respect a staff sergeant in A Company, even though the hard-as-nails NCO would drop him for push-ups for parking his motorcycle in A Company's parking area. By strange coincidence, after Jimmy obtained a commission via a Reserve Officer Training Corps scholarship at the University of Pennsylvania and was given a platoon in 2nd Ranger Battalion at Fort Lewis, Washington, his mentor, now a sergeant first class, was assigned as his platoon sergeant. At first the NCO couldn't believe his bad luck—taking orders from a kid you used to drop for push-ups is a hard adjustment for a grizzled non-com to make. "But he turned out to be one of the best platoon leaders I've ever had," the NCO said many years later. Jimmy had learned a lot about soldiering from his platoon sergeant. Now, after twenty-eight hard years in the Army, that NCO was preparing to lead men in combat for the first time and Jimmy wanted to help out in any way he could. That's why he found himself splashing through the mud peering at one tent after another at 2 a.m. on March 2. He found the right tent and pulled the flap back. The light was on inside and he easily picked out the leathery face of his old platoon sergeant, now Command Sergeant Major Mark Nielsen. Jimmy bent over Nielsen's cot and shook him gently awake. The sergeant major was alert in a nanosecond, looking up at Jimmy inquisitively. The Delta officer whispered a short, potent message: "The LZs are clear. Watch the high ground." Then he was gone.

REACTION TO CONTACT

1.

ON the road outside the Gardez safe house, Task Force Hammer got ready to roll.

Exhaust fumes from over three dozen trucks mixed in the night air with smoke from scores of cigarettes as drivers idled their engines. Dozens of SF soldiers, AFO operators, and CIA personnel mingled with about 400 Afghan troops, whom the Americans were trying to group in their new squads, platoons, and companies as they climbed onto the trucks. The Americans had only told their Afghan allies about the impending attack on the Shahikot earlier that day, but Zia's men were not in the least surprised. "We've been telling you about the Shahikot for a long time," they said.

Finally the last militiaman pulled himself up into his assigned truck. The Special Forces NCOs walked down the line of vehicles, checking everyone was where he was supposed to be, then climbed into their pickups. Inside the Americans' Toyota Tacomas, radios crackled to life. At 11:33 p.m., three minutes behind schedule, the column of vehicles pulled away from the safe house, heading west into Gardez and then south along the Zermat road. After two months of planning and preparation for Operation Anaconda, it was showtime.

The Americans had done their best to organize the convoy vehicles into a logical order of march. At the front in a couple pickups rode Glenn Thomas, the Texas 14 commander, and "Engineer," the English speaker who was the most tactically astute Afghan "platoon leader." Behind them was a four-vehicle element led by Chief Warrant Officer 2 Stanley Harriman, McHale's second-in-command, known to his men simply as "Chief." With Harriman were a couple of his teammates and thirty-five to forty Afghan fighters led by Ziabdullah, the local commander in whom the Americans placed less faith than they did in Zia Lodin. Harriman's mission was to split from the convoy several kilometers northwest of the Whale and position his little force so that it could guard a narrow gap that separated the Whale from the ridgeline just to the north called Gawyani Ghar. Their purpose there was to block anyone from escaping out of the Shahikot to the northwest, preferably by calling in close air support. If Harriman's force saw an enemy element heading their way, they were to "bomb the snot out of it," McHale said. Joining Harriman's force of two pickups and a jinga truck was a third pickup carrying Hans and Nelson (the AFO SEALs) and Thor, a recently arrived Gray Fox linguist. This trio's mission was to meet Juliet Team as they rode back down out of the mountains on their ATVs and escort them back to Gardez.

Next in the order of march came McHale and the rest of his men with Hoskheyar's company of local fighters. Behind them was the Afghan mortar platoon, followed by Chris Haas, the lieutenant colonel who had arrived with a small command cell only a few days previously, and his operations officer, Major Mark Schwartz, each in his own pickup. (Haas's role was a little fuzzy. Even though Haas outranked Thomas and McHale by two pay grades, Thomas felt in command of the column. "Our teams had the leeway of making the calls on the ground," with the understanding that Haas or Schwartz could impose their authority at any time, Thomas said.) Haas was leading the second half of the column, which included Zia Lodin, the overall AMF commander, his deputy, Rasul, and the hard core of thirty militiamen recruited with Zia by Texas 14. The Afghans rode in jinga trucks, slightly smaller vehicles, and, in the case of a few senior men, pickups. The Dagger guys had tried to keep the Afghans in their squads and platoons as they got in the trucks. Each Afghan "platoon" had been assigned a Special Forces NCO as the platoon's principal instructor. Now the trucks carrying each platoon were together in the column, with the platoon's associated SF sergeant in a pickup directly in front of them. That way, Thomas and McHale figured, when orders needed to be given, the Afghans would be hearing them from the American they knew best.

Somewhere in the middle was the Rakkasan engineer squad. There were also a handful of Australian SAS troopers, who were Task Force 64 liaisons, relaying information between Hammer and the Australians south of the Shahikot. Bringing up the rear was another AFO element, consisting of Captain John B., Sergeant Major Al Y., and Master Sergeant Isaac H. in two pickups. Their job was to extract India and Mako 31 after linking up with them at the Fishhook. There were also three empty trucks at the end of the convoy to be used as spares in case of breakdowns.

As they drove down the Zermat road toward the turnoff to the Shahikot, the task facing the men of TF Hammer was clear. They were to drive east to the

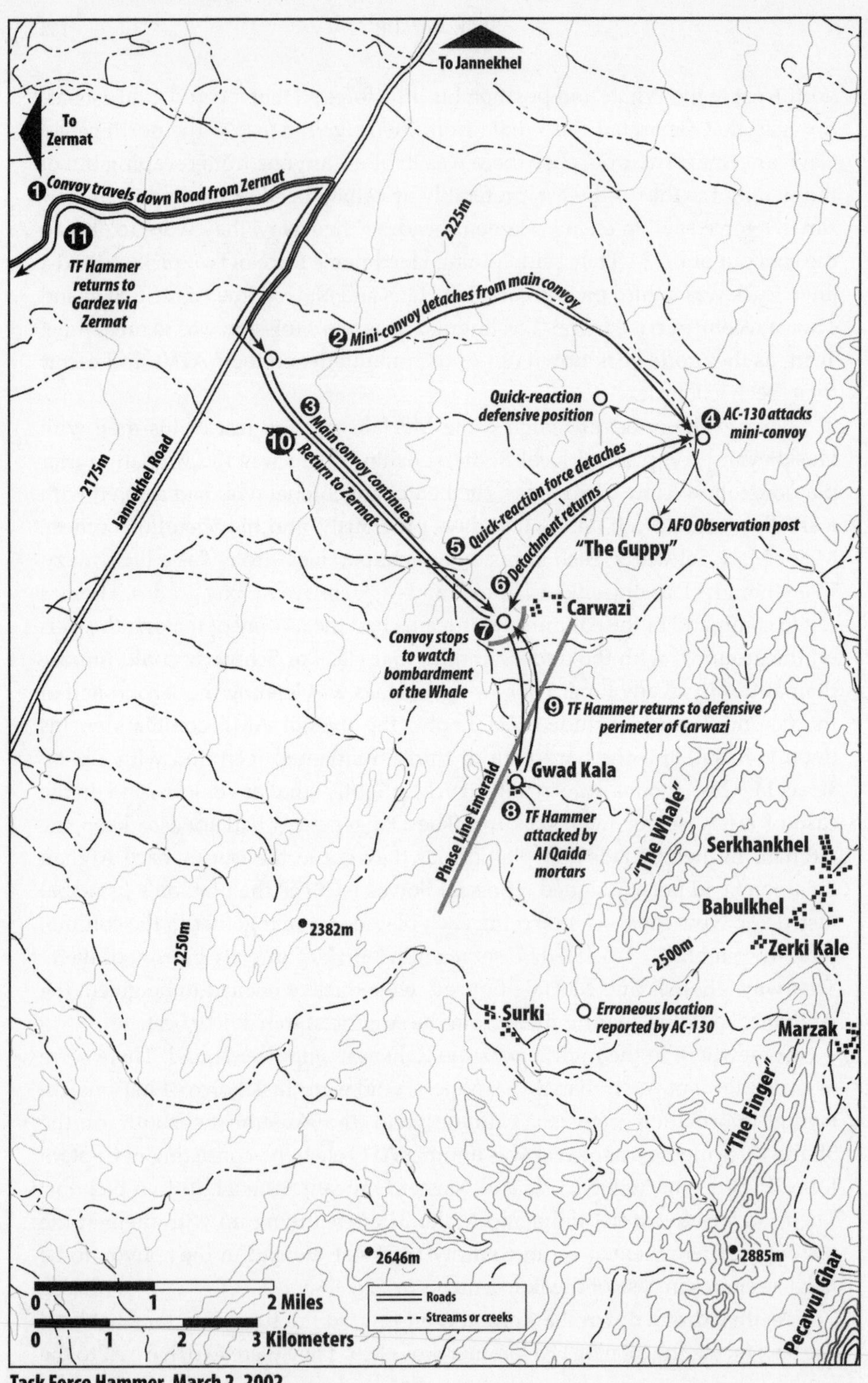

Task Force Hammer, March 2, 2002

Whale, then south until they reached the Fishhook. Once through that potential ambush point, most of Texas 14 and the company of Afghan fighters under Zia Lodin and Rasul would charge into the valley, clearing the villages from south to north, starting with Babulkhel. Meanwhile, Hoskheyar's force with McHale's team (minus Harriman's element but plus a couple of Texas 14 sergeants) would move into a position on the lower, northernmost reaches of the Finger that Mako 31 had selected for their observation post. From there they would support Zia's men with mortar and machine-gun fire if necessary as they wheeled into the valley.

It is a military cliché that no plan survives first contact with the enemy. But in TF Hammer's case, the plan for Anaconda didn't even last that long. Things began to unravel within an hour of the convoy departing Gardez. The problems stemmed from the fact that the plan to load several hundred Afghan fighters into top-heavy jinga trucks driven in the middle of the night with no lights by inexperienced drivers along a "road" that was no more than a dirt track on a tight timeline was fundamentally unsound.

The Zermat road was in awful condition. It wasn't really a road, but a muddy track that in places was completely washed away, forcing the drivers to cross wadis the floors of which were up to fifteen feet below the surface of the road. To make matters worse, two days of rain had softened the ground. It would have been hard to drive a jinga truck along such a treacherous route in broad daylight, let alone at night with all lights off, as the Special Forces officers had ordered for tactical reasons. The Americans quickly realized they had underestimated how challenging their drivers would find this route. For the U.S. troops in their pickups at the head of the convoy, driving with lights out posed few problems. Their night-vision goggles enabled them to choose a safe path, and, of course, their four-wheel-drive Toyotas were inherently more stable than the jinga trucks. But the Afghans enjoyed no such advantages and were forced to negotiate the treacherous passage with only the moonlight to guide them. The SF troops belatedly realized their mistake in assigning driving duties to Afghan militiamen who had volunteered for the job out of a desire not to let the Americans down, not because they knew how to drive trucks. "We should have gone somehow with truck drivers that drive all the time," McHale acknowledged. Haas also admitted he had "underestimated" the difficulties they would face on the road. Some drivers became visibly nervous in the perilous conditions, unsure of how to control the jinga trucks that swayed this way and that, their short chains jangling against the sides of the vehicles. First a jinga truck became irretrievably stuck, tilted over at such an angle that half of its wheels spun uselessly in the air. A few minutes later, just after midnight, another jinga truck driver completely lost control of his vehicle as he drove over a log bridge that covered a four-meter gap in the road. The heavy truck tipped over on its side, spilling its load of Afghan fighters onto the ground. The Special Forces soldiers could sense their allies' morale plummeting as militiamen with injuries of varying severity lay wailing beside the tipped-over truck. Thinking quickly, an SF medic announced through an interpreter that the most seriously injured fighters should climb on a nearby truck. As several guerrillas roused themselves with suspicious speed and clambered onto the truck, he turned to treat those too badly hurt to move. Three were no longer fit for combat—their injuries included broken ribs and a punctured lung—so they were evacuated on two small trucks to a local hospital.

No sooner had the SF soldiers dealt with that crisis than another truck got stuck fast. The "friction of the battlefield"—first described as such by the nineteenth-century Prussian military theorist Carl von Clausewitz in a phrase that has become a cliché—was rearing its ugly head. Something close to chaos descended along the length of the stalled column as Afghan fighters milled around in the dark trying to find their colleagues. Shouts and curses flew as the SF soldiers tried to bring some order to the situation against a backdrop of revving engines as drivers tried to free their trapped trucks or maneuver the spares forward from the back of the line. Only too aware that they were falling behind schedule, the Special Forces troops got most of the Afghans who had been riding on the three disabled trucks to climb onto the reserve trucks, but in the darkness it proved impossible to keep each truck's contingent of fighters together and load them all onto the same empty truck. Neither the extent of this mix-up nor the fact that some Afghans were jumping onto the backs of the American pickups so as not to lose contact with their own buddies was immediately clear to the U.S. troops.

The two A-team leaders conferred. The rule about driving "blacked-out" was hurting their cause more than helping it and so the two captains gave the order to turn on the headlights. Three dozen pairs of yellow-white lights flashed on. If the Al Qaida pickets on the Whale had been in any doubt about the convoy's location up to that point, now they knew for sure. With some Afghan fighters running beside the trucks because there was no room for them anymore, the convoy moved on. Task Force Hammer was the main effort, but the tight timeline for the opening hours of the operation revolved around the supporting effort—the Rakkasans' air assault. The convoy had to reach the valley in time for the air assault. The Rakkasans were not going to wait for them. The Special Forces soldiers spurred the Afghans on. They were painfully aware that they were "a little bolloxed up," as McHale put it later, and "racing time."

Nevertheless, the convoy was moving again. It turned east off the Zermat "road" and drew ever closer to the Shahikot. From their perch just south of the Fishhook, India Team reported seeing lights approaching the Whale from the west. The time was 2:55 a.m. Maybe Task Force Hammer would make it after all.

2.

SHORTLY after midnight, at about the time Task Force Hammer's trucks were getting stuck and rolling over, Goody and the other four men of Mako 31 left the hollow they had used as a hide site and crept toward the enemy observation post. Goody moved ahead of the others, scouting a site where they could drop their rucks about 500 meters from the enemy position. The explosive ordnance disposal expert assigned to Mako 31 and Andy, the team's Air Force combat controller, remained with the rucks to minimize the chances of the enemy overhearing them as they arranged AC-130 and P-3 coverage of their assault on the tent position. Trying hard to keep to the long shadows cast by a full moon, the three SEAL Team 6 snipers advanced toward a small ridgeline on the other side of which sat the tent. They could hear the low drone of the AC-130 overhead.

Once they reached the ridgeline, their plan was to wait until H minus one (i.e., 5:30 a.m., an hour before H-Hour) and then assault the tent, coordinating their attack with the AC-130. Not long after they had found cover behind some rocks on the reverse slope of the ridge from the tent, an enemy fighter appeared on the ridgeline like a ghostly apparition in the moonlight. He looked around, then turned and retraced his steps without noticing the nearby SEALs. Goody and his men settled down to wait. But at 4 a.m. the same fighter appeared, again walking up from the tent (which the SEALs could not see from their vantage point) and gazing west. Perhaps he was looking for the approaching TF Hammer convoy, word of which was undoubtedly circulating on the enemy's radios and cell phones by now, or perhaps he was merely seeking some privacy to relieve himself. Either way, it was a fateful decision. Glancing up, the enemy fighter caught sight of the SEALs before they had time to duck behind the rocks. Yelling a warning, he sprinted back to the tent, his body's "fight or flight" mechanism pumping adrenaline into his bloodstream.

For the SEALs, it was now or never. Goody gave the order to attack. The commandos charged over the ridgeline and down toward the tent twenty meters away. From inside the tent an Al Qaida fighter fired off an entire magazine in the general direction of the Americans, who could see the Kalashnikov's muzzle flash between the tent flaps. The SEALs dropped to their knees to return fire. A SEAL fired a single round into the tent from his M4 before the rifle jammed. Goody fired next, but he, too, got off only one round before his rifle jammed. The two SEALs worked frantically in the frigid night air to clear their weapons as the third sniper kept the enemy at bay. Five Al Qaida fighters poured from the tent as the SEALs cleared the jams and began picking them off. The first guerrilla sprinted straight at them. In a split second a commando put the red dot of his laser sight in the middle of the fighter's chest and squeezed the trigger. Several bullets slammed into the fighter's body and sent him tumbling lifelessly to the frozen earth. The next man out of the tent broke right but got no more than a couple of steps before he was felled by another SEAL fusillade. A third tent occupant tried to escape over the backside of the ridge, only for the SEALs to put their long hours of marksmanship training to good use yet again.

The SEALs leveled their rifles and emptied their magazines into the tent, then pulled back. Goody decided to let the AC-130 take care of any enemies left alive. Andy, the combat controller, had already alerted Grim 31, the AC-130H Spectre orbiting overhead. The aircraft reported seeing two bodies just outside the tent and a third, wounded, enemy fighter trying to crawl to safety. Grim 31 also spotted the two remaining enemy fighters, who had apparently escaped the firefight outside the tent unharmed and were now trying to outflank the SEALs. From a range of 75 meters—almost point blank for a machine gun—one of the Al Qaida survivors fired a long burst of 7.62mm bullets from a PK machine gun at the SEALs, who hadn't noticed their maneuver. The rounds missed. It was to be the last opportunity the two Islamist fighters would have to kill in the name of Allah. Grim 31 requested permission from the SEALs to engage the enemy fighters at "danger close" range, a step required of any aircraft crew about to attack a position in such close proximity to friendly forces that they might be hurt by the airstrike. The SEALs gave their okay. Within a couple of seconds the AC-130 poured 105mm rounds down upon the mountainside, killing both enemy fighters instantly. Then the Air Force gunners adjusted their fire and opened up on the tent and the wounded fighter outside. The explosions shredded the tent and sprayed its contents across the mountainside. When the echoes had faded away, five Al Qaida corpses were left cooling on the mountainside.

The sound of the AC-130 firing alerted every Al Qaida position around the valley. As they gazed upward, searching the night sky for the source of the attack, many fighters made a fatal error—they tilted their weapons skyward and fired blindly into the air, sending tracer rounds arcing into the darkness. Doing so revealed their positions to the three AFO teams, who quickly noted the location of each source of gunfire, to be passed to aircraft later that day as targets to be engaged.

The SEALs moved back to the Al Qaida observation post, which they intended to occupy themselves. What they found as they searched the debris confirmed how vital their mission had been. The DShK was in great condition, clean and well oiled with 2,000 rounds of ammunition arranged neatly within arm's reach. The guerrillas had built a rough-and-ready traverse and elevation mechanism that, in the opinion of a special operations source, would have allowed the gunner to hit targets up to 3,000 meters away and to cover "easily" the routes to be taken by the helicopters that were shortly to enter the valley. It was fortunate that the SEALs had been able to take the guerrillas by surprise, because the Al Qaida fighters had been well armed. In addition to the DShK, the five tentmates were equipped with a Soviet-style SVD Dragunov sniper rifle, AK-series assault rifles, at least one RPG-7 launcher with several rounds, a PK machine gun, and several fragmentation grenades.

Scattered around were several handwritten documents. The fact that most were in Cyrillic script—suggesting at least one or more of the fighters were Uzbeks or Chechens—with a few in Arabic, when coupled with the different ethnicities of the five fighters who had been killed, was the first indication that enemy commanders had divided at least some of their force in the valley into cross-cultural teams. (Blaber speculated that the enemy did this to prevent one ethnic group—Arabs, Uighurs, Uzbeks, or Chechens—from leaving the others in the lurch.) The documents included what appeared to be a range card for an artillery system, as well as a notebook that included sketches and instructions on how to build homemade bombs and blow up bridges, buildings, buses, and cars. But as one special operations account of the notebook's contents later put it, "The one chapter it didn't have was how to defend against Americans who infil over 11,000-foot peaks."

3.

RISING from their cots in the early hours of March 2, the dozen Apache pilots at Bagram were almost oblivious to the nerve-stretching tension felt by their infantry colleagues.

Despite Wiercinski's melodramatic "give them everything you've got" comments of the previous evening, the pilots were anticipating "nothing out of the ordinary" from Anaconda. They had flown several missions since deploying to Afghanistan, all uneventful. Today, they expected, would be no different. "We were just there to make sure that Rak 6's guys got on the ground," Chief Warrant Officer 2 Stanley Pebsworth recalls thinking. "Zia's forces were gonna come in. It was gonna be their show." "For us," said Chief Warrant Officer 4 Jim Hardy, "it was just another operation."

The pilots pushed the green canvas flap of their tent aside and walked out into the night. Before them, infantry platoons were assembling in the cold darkness, nervous soldiers making last-minute adjustments to overstuffed rucks and awkward, bulky web gear. Sergeants with stress and determination etched on their faces shouted final roll calls before marching their troops to the airstrip. The contrast with the jovial atmosphere inside the pilots' tent the previous evening could not have been sharper. "We were sitting around the pot-bellied stove, laughing, joking, making fun of each other," Pebsworth said.

The Apaches were parked at the north end of the runway, almost one-and-a-half miles from tent city, and the pilots hitched Humvee and Gator rides down to the aircraft. Nary a butterfly stirred in their stomachs. The Apache drivers and their ground crews felt prepared for the mission. They had grounded the helicopters for the previous 48 hours in order to allow the crew chiefs to get them in perfect working order for D-Day, and TF Rakkasan had given them a detailed plan that seemed to leave little to chance.

That plan called for the six Apaches to fly from Bagram to the Shahikot in three flights—or "teams"—of two Apaches. The first flight consisted of Apache 203 (the helicopter's serial number), flown by Chief Warrant Officer 3 Keith Hurley and Chief Warrant Officer 3 Stu Contant, and Apache 299, with Chief Warrant Officer 3 Rich Chenault as the pilot in command, and Captain Joe Herman—Ryan's executive officer and 2nd Platoon leader—as his copilot gunner. They were to take off ten minutes before the first Chinook serial and get to a spot about five kilometers southwest of Serkhankhel five minutes before Air Force jets bombed the preplanned targets around the valley. In the aviation phrase book, this spot is called the release point. It marked the place where the Apaches were released from the fixed route they must fly to the edge of the battlefield and could begin to move tactically into the engagement area. Once the bombs had gone in, the two Apaches were to swing into the valley and check each landing zone for crew-served weapons or enemy troops. They would then fly north into a position from which they could overwatch 2-187 Infantry's landing zones at the foot of the eastern ridge. It would be Team 1's responsibility to make the call as to whether the LZs were "hot" or "cold." A "hot," or "cherry," LZ meant that the air assault probably would be met by enemy fire, a "cold," or "ice," LZ meant no enemy activity could be observed.

Team 2 was led by Captain Bill Ryan, the commander of 3-101's A Company—"the Killer Spades"—and the senior officer on the Apache mission. His pilot was Chief Warrant Officer 3 Jody Kilburn. Ryan's wingman was Chief Warrant Officer 4 Bob Carr, the most experienced Apache pilot in Bagram. Flying with Carr was Chief Warrant Officer 2 Emanuel "Manny" Pierre. Their orders were to take off immediately after the second serial of Chinooks, which would depart Bagram ten minutes after the first serial. The Apaches would follow the second serial—carrying the 10th Mountain troops—into the southern end of the valley, covering them as they established their blocking positions.

Team 3 included the Apache flown by Hardy and Pebsworth, along with another flown by Chief Warrant Officer 2 John Hamilton and 1st Lieutenant Gabriel Marriott, the 1st Platoon leader. This team was Ryan's reserve force. Their "on order" mission was to escort the reserve task force built around 1-187 Infantry if it had to be launched south. Otherwise they were to remain on standby at Bagram for any other missions that might arise. However, to give himself maximum flexibility in case he needed to change the plan at the last moment, Ryan had all six sets of pilots head to the tarmac together about an hour before takeoff, run through their preflight checklists and start their engines together.

The Apaches of Team 1 and Team 2 were to remain on station for two hours and thirty-five minutes, then make the thirty-minute flight back to the forward arming and refueling point (FARP), code-named Texaco, about eighty kilometers to the north, roughly halfway between Bagram and the Shahikot.

At about 4:37 a.m. the pilots cranked their auxiliary power units (APUs). These are small fuel-saving engines that provide enough juice to run the Apache's electronics systems without having to start the helicopter's two large turbine engines. As each APU powered up, going from a whine to a roar in a matter of seconds, the pilots ran through their checklists. Ryan had just gotten into his aircraft when he spotted a couple of maintenance troops running over—never a good sign with a mission less than thirty minutes away. Sure enough, they were the bearers of bad news: Carr's 30mm cannon had sprung a hydraulics leak. It could still fire, but it might get stuck as it slewed from side to side or up and down. It was a small glitch, not a serious break, but with take off only twenty-five minutes away, there was no time to fix it and stick to the schedule. Helicopters often launch on combat missions carrying minor technical ailments that would keep them grounded in peacetime. But there was no way Ryan was going to let one of his Apaches fly into a potential gunfight without its cannon working. Instead, the captain adapted his plan on the fly, switching from three teams of two aircraft to a first flight of two and a second flight of three by combining Team 3's aircraft with Team 2's remaining Apache. Team 1's composition and mission would remain the same. Team 2's three Apaches, under Ryan, would execute Team 2's original mission of covering La-Camera's troops as they set up their positions. Carr and Pierre would remain behind until the crew chiefs fixed the leak, then fly forward to join their comrades at Texaco. If Wiercinski had to launch the reserve force, Ryan figured he would have five Apaches either over the battlefield or at the FARP and he could detach a couple of helicopters to link up with the inbound Chinooks en route.

At 4:47 a.m., Hurley and Chenault turned the keys that enabled their turbine engines to crank up and flicked the switches to turn their number one engines on. They spooled up with a roar, the increasing turbine speed powering the transmissions, which in turn powered the rotor systems. The number two engines followed immediately. As the pilots turned off the no-longer-needed APUs, each helicopter's four rotor blades slowly began to turn, scything faster and faster through the darkness until they became a blur. At 5:07 and fifteen seconds Contant's voice came over the radio: "Lift off in ten," and at 5:07 and twenty-five seconds, exactly on schedule, the two high-tech birds of prey lifted into the air, then banked and turned south, heading for their hunting ground in the Shahikot Valley.

AS Wiercinski had made clear in his emotive comments the previous evening, the Apache drivers bore a heavy responsibility, however lightly it might have rested on their shoulders. They were the only source of heavy firepower that Wiercinski controlled, other than a couple of mortar tubes in the hands of the first wave of air-assault troops. Of course, in theory there would be "fast-movers"—Air Force and Navy bombers—available overhead to rain precision-guided munitions on the enemy, but ground commanders prefer to depend on firepower they control, rather than that which they must request from another service. For Wiercinski and the rest of Task Force Rakkasan, that meant relying on Bill Ryan and his six Apaches.

Designed to destroy Warsaw Pact tanks on Europe's central plains, the Apache had been a controversial weapons system since it was fielded in 1985. At its best, it was a supremely capable killer of men and machines. Each of its stubby wings had two pylons, which could each carry a rack fitting up to four Hellfire antitank missiles or a pod containing nineteen 2.75-inch rockets. The Hellfire could destroy a tank or any other vehicle at a range of up to 8,000 meters.

The rockets came in a dozen types. In addition, slung under the helicopter's fuselage was a cannon that fired 30mm high-explosive rounds as big as a child's forearm out to a range of 4,000 meters. Fired at targets in the open, the 30mm round would kill anyone and disable any vehicle within five meters of where it hit. Thus the cannon was an ideal weapon for engaging unprotected enemy troops and other "soft" targets like mortar and air defense weapons and crews, or the SUVs that formed the Al Qaida logistics fleet. Before a combat mission pilots had to preset their cannon to fire a certain number of rounds each time they pulled the trigger. This setting could not be changed from inside the cockpit. For Anaconda, the Killer Spades set their cannons to fire ten-round bursts.

Such a variety of killing mechanisms packed into a highly maneuverable helicopter made the Apache an extraordinarily complex machine to operate; so complex, in fact, that it required two pilots, sitting one behind the other. In the rear seat, the higher of the two, sat the pilot-in-command. Typically the more experienced pilot, his primary responsibility was flying the helicopter and making radio calls. In the front seat was the copilot gunner, whose primary jobs were to navigate and to identify and engage targets with the Apache's suite of weapons. Each pilot, however, could perform the functions necessary to pilot the aircraft and fire most of the weapons systems. (An interesting quirk of Apache crews was that the pilot-in-command might be outranked by his copilot gunner. This is because an Apache unit's most experienced pilots were its warrant officers, who had often spent their entire careers flying helicopters. The commissioned officers, who commanded platoons, companies, and battalions, on the other hand, had to spend much of their time in schools, or flying nothing more than a desk in a staff job. Therefore, although Ryan, as a captain and company commander, was the senior man on the mission whose job it was to give orders to the other pilots regarding their overall mission, he was not the pilot-in-command of his own helicopter.)

To be survivable on the battlefield, a weapons system must combine lethality with mobility and survivability. The Apache possessed the latter qualities in spades. It could perform all manner of acrobatic maneuvers that could enthrall air show audiences at air shows and confound enemies in combat, but it had also been designed by the McDonnell Douglas Helicopter Company to take a lot of punishment. It had dual redundant engines and hydraulics systems, and its critical systems, such as the rotors and driveshaft, were built to be "ballistic tolerant," meaning they could be hit—even shot through—by anything up to a 23mm round without causing the helicopter to crash. The pilots themselves were protected by the Kevlar sidings fitted to their seats and by the flak vests each had to wear. But when the Army fielded the Apache in the mid- to late-1980s, its advertisement of these capabilities seemed only to whet the appetite of some in the media and Congress eager to find fault with a weapons system they correctly identified as part of the Reagan defense buildup.

The limited but successful role played by the Apache in the December 1989 Panama invasion was canceled out by stories claiming the helicopter couldn't operate in the rain. A 1990 General Accounting Office report cast further doubt on the helicopter's reliability and maintainability, and formed the basis for a November 18, 1990, CBS Television *60 Minutes* report highly critical of the Apache, as well as newspaper articles that followed a similar theme. Many issues identified in the reports were teething problems of the type that often occur shortly after weapons systems have been fielded. But to critics, they implied that the helicopter could not bear up to the strain of combat.

Much of the criticism dried up after the Apache's superlative performance in the 1991 Persian Gulf War. The Apache units deployed for that conflict achieved good operational ready rates despite the additional wear and tear the sandy conditions imposed on the helicopters, and the aircraft was credited with destroying many Iraqi tanks and other armored vehicles. In one famous encounter Iraqi soldiers actually surrendered to a hovering Apache.

But the Gulf War marked the last time that the Apache had seen combat. The U.S. military spent much of the 1990s deployed in Somalia, Haiti, and Bosnia. Of these, the Apaches had deployed only to the peacekeeping mission in Bosnia, where they were never called on to engage an enemy. This pattern was reflected in the experience levels of the pilots flying on March 2. Of the twelve pilots penciled in for the mission, only three—Carr, Hardy, and Hurley—had flown in combat. All were Desert Storm veterans, but in that war each flew a different aircraft. The dozen pilots on the mission varied in experience from Marriott, who had only about 350 flight hours, to Carr, who had over 5,000. But all shared one thing in common: None had ever flown an Apache in combat.

Each pilot placed his faith in the Apache's combination of high-tech weapons, maneuverability, and ruggedness. But so much capability came at a high price, not only in dollars, but in the man-hours needed to keep each bird mission capable. The Apache's maintenance-intensive profile continued to earn it a reputation as an expensive yet unreliable weapons system. In 1999 that reputation sunk to a new low when General Wesley Clark, NATO's supreme military commander, wanted to use Apaches to attack Serb targets in the Kosovo war. In response to his request, the Pentagon deployed Task Force Hawk, an ad-hoc outfit designed around twenty-four Apaches, from Germany to Albania, but withheld permission from Clark to use it in combat. Diplomatic problems held the helicopters up in Italy for ten days, but to outside observers it seemed the helicopters themselves were at fault. That view gained strength when two Apaches crashed in the Albanian mountains during mission rehearsals, causing the deaths of two pilots. To the immense frustration of Task Force Hawk's pilots and commanders, not to mention Clark himself, the Pentagon never allowed them to be sent into battle.

The damage to the reputations of the Apache and the Army itself was significant. Within six months the Army reacted by announcing its high-profile "Transformation" effort to design new combat units that are easier to deploy, yet no less lethal and mobile than the tank-heavy force that was victorious in the 1991 Gulf War. But the Apache could not "transform." It was what it was, and had to stand or fall on its own merits. To many in the media, the Task Force Hawk experience raised new doubts about the helicopter. THE APACHE: AERIAL KILLING MACHINE OR "HANGAR QUEEN"? asked *USA Today* in a headline. The negative press—and the Pentagon brass's implicit lack of faith in the aircraft—stung the tight-knit Apache community, which felt the helicopter had been unfairly maligned by people ignorant of the facts regarding the Task Force Hawk fiasco. It may not have been uppermost in the minds of Bill Ryan and his Apache drivers as they climbed into their cockpits and cranked their engines on that chilly March morning, but the reputation of a weapons system was riding on their performance.

4.

AFTER the chaos of the first hour, TF Hammer's ragged convoy was back on track if not on schedule, driving east along a dirt trail toward the Whale, which they expected to see erupt in flame soon from the "fifty-five-minute" bombardment. About seven kilometers northwest of the Whale, Harriman's four-vehicle mini-convoy split off and headed east-northeast. For about fifteen minutes the trucks carrying Harriman and the others bounced and rattled in a lazy arc that curved back southeast to connect with a wadi running northwest to southeast through the gap between the Whale and the Gawyani Ghar ridgeline. Leading the way was a small truck full of Afghans, followed by Ziabdullah, the untrustworthy militia leader, in a silver Toyota pickup. Next came Harriman's pickup, which also contained Staff Sergeant Caleb Casenhiser, one of the A-team's medics, and Staff Sergeant Larron "Larry" Wadsworth, one of the team's engineers. The AFO pickup carrying Hans, Nelson, and Thor brought up the rear.

A quietly religious father of two, Harriman, thirty-four, had been sent to Kuwait in late 2001 to work in the office of Lieutenant Colonel Craig Bishop, the special operations coordinator on Mikolashek's CFLCC staff. The warrant officer made an immediate, positive impact on those he worked with in Kuwait—"He was a super, super guy," Bishop recalled—but he yearned to be closer to the action. When word came in January that McHale and the rest of ODA 372 were headed to Afghanistan, Harriman pleaded with Bishop to be allowed to rejoin them. The lieutenant colonel relented.

Now the short, serious warrant officer, a steadying influence on his team who enjoyed huge respect from the Afghans, was bouncing up and down in a Toyota pickup in a wadi en route to the biggest battle of the war, about as close to the action as it was possible to get. As they turned south toward the Whale, some Afghans dismounted and walked ahead of the trucks, scouting the route. The moon emerged from behind its veil of clouds to light their way. Harriman called in reports to the main body every five minutes in a matter-of-fact tone of voice: He wasn't lost; there were no problems.

Both Harriman's convoy and the main column were moving in a southeasterly direction toward Phase Line Emerald, a line planners had drawn from southwest to northeast about 1,500 meters west of and roughly parallel to the Whale. TF Hammer was to pause at Emerald while the air strikes went in against targets on the Whale and the eastern ridge. But soon the main column's progress stalled again as several of Zia's trucks got stuck in the sandy, desert-like terrain. The convoy was strung out along several kilometers west of the Whale, making it difficult for the U.S. officers and NCOs to keep track of everyone. As the Hammer troops struggled to free the vehicles, Thomas grew concerned about the threat of ambush in the Fishhook, where the convoy would have to pass through a narrow wadi between two rocky hillsides. Knowing Grim 31, the AC-130 that had just shot up the DShK position for Goody's SEALs, was available overhead, Thomas asked the aircraft's fourteen-man crew to check out the area and report what they saw. (Special operators of all branches placed great faith in the AC-130's two sensors—televisionlike cameras, one geared to the infrared spectrum, the other working from the same image-intensification technology as night-vision goggles—and often used the lethal attack aircraft for reconnaissance.)

Grim 31 had arrived on station over the convoy at 2:04 a.m., taking over from another AC-130H in the first of a series of late night–early morning missions during Anaconda that would earn the crew its nickname of "The Dawn Patrol." At first clouds had obscured the aircraft's view of TF Hammer, but the sky cleared and the crew was able to track the convoy's progress. However, when it flew south in response to the SEALs' call for support during their assault on the DShK position, Grim 31 lost visual contact with the convoy. After shooting up the tent and its occupants, the AC-130 answered a call from Juliet to destroy an enemy observation post and bunker they had spotted on top of the Whale from their hideaway on the eastern ridge. Again, Grim 31 was more than equal to the task, scoring several direct hits on the positions at 4:44 a.m. Below them, the pilots saw the crude structures obliterated in bright yellow-orange flashes that blossomed and faded almost instantly.

Mako 31 then asked the AC-130 to fly back around the Finger to ensure there were no enemy survivors from the DShK position lurking in the rocks. The Grim 31 crew spotted nothing, and it was then that they received Thomas's request to reconnoiter the Fishhook. Onboard the aircraft, the crew members knew they were getting close to "bingo" fuel—the point at which they would have to turn for home. But even had they had a full tank, dawn was barely an hour away, and that meant their time over the battlefield was drawing short. The AC-130 was the vampire of the Air Force's fleet of attack aircraft, extraordinarily lethal at night but incredibly vulnerable in daylight. The gunship community was haunted by the memory of *Spirit 03,* an AC-130 brought down by an Iraqi SA-7 antiaircraft missile during the January 1991 battle of Khafji. *Spirit 03* had stayed on station until 6:35 a.m. to help some embattled Marines, allowing an Iraqi air defender to use the early-morning light to line up the slow-flying aircraft in his sights. The AC-130 community was determined to never again lose a plane to daylight, and prior to Anaconda the rule was that all AC-130s had to be out of Afghan airspace by dawn. Those rules had been relaxed to give the troops on the ground more coverage during Anaconda, but Grim 31 was still required by the Task Force Dagger leadership to be clear of the Shahikot area before sunrise.

The crew of Grim 31 had other problems, the extent of which they were as yet unaware. The plane's computer systems were acting up. Both had failed totally earlier in the flight. The crew thought they had solved the problems by rebooting the computers. But although the systems seemed to be up and running, hidden problems remained. Most seriously, the inertial navigation system, which told the navigator and pilots where they were flying, was giving incorrect readings. Believing they had fixed the trouble, Grim 31's crew, one of the most experienced in the 16th Special Operations Squadron, based at Hurlburt Field, Florida, did not raise them as a major issue with the TF Hammer personnel on the ground. (Although they did hint at it: When asked by Texas 14 to reconnoiter Serkhankhel, they sent possible target coordinates that were ten kilometers off to the convoy. When TF Hammer pointed this out, the aircrew replied that their "systems" had problems that evening.)

Investigators would later suggest that Grim 31's inertial navigation system failed again before they turned back to perform the "cleanup" reconnaissance for the SEALs. Under this hypothesis, the AC-130 never actually returned to the Finger from the Whale, but instead unwittingly flew in a more easterly direction and reconnoitered a portion of the eastern ridgeline believing it was the Finger. Then, at the direction of the navigator, regarded by his fellow officers and airmen as the best in the squadron, the pilot flew about three kilometers northwest to a position which appeared to match the Fishhook's terrain as it was depicted on his 1:100,000 map. It was now about ninety minutes since Grim 31 had left its station over Hammer to support Mako 31, and the crew no longer had a firm grasp of the location of the convoy, from which Harriman's element had already split off. Instead of scanning the wadi that ran around the southern tip of the Whale, they were actually about eight kilometers off course, flying over a streambed that curled around the *northern* end of the Whale, just to the south of the Gawyani Ghar ridgeline. Looking down, the crew saw several vehicles driving in the wadi, including two with their headlights on, with twenty to thirty personnel walking ahead of them. Based on an examination of the map, Grim 31 passed what they thought was the location of the convoy to Glenn Thomas's enlisted tactical air controller, Air Force Master Sergeant William "Buddy" McArthur, with the message that if Texas 14 wanted the target attacked, they had to speak up soon, because Grim 31 only had five minutes' station time left.

McArthur told Grim 31 to stand by and passed the grid reference the crew gave him to Thomas and Haas to verify there were no friendly forces in that location. With McArthur present, Thomas read the grid to his driver, Sergeant First Class Charles "Todd" Browning. All three agreed there were no friendly vehicles at that grid, which was squarely in the Fishhook. Thomas figured the vehicles and personnel being reported were an enemy force trying to make their escape from the valley westward via the Fishhook. But whatever their purpose, they appeared to be on a collision course with Task Force Hammer and needed to be taken care of. Thomas called Mark Schwartz, Haas's operations officer, seeking approval for Grim 31 to engage the target. Schwartz passed the information straight to Haas. Meanwhile, Harriman, by now heading south toward the Whale, was concerned. He had heard Grim 31's radio call about the small truck convoy with dismounted personnel and was worried that it sounded a little too much like his. As a precaution he broadcast his grid coordinates over the radio. They were over six kilometers from where Grim 31 was saying they could see a possible target.

The Grim 31 crew was also concerned that they not inadvertently attack a friendly force. They knew that to prevent nighttime "friendly fire" attacks from the air, all Hammer vehicles were supposed to be marked with several strips of "glint" tape—adhesive tape that brightly reflects light within the spectrum for which night-vision goggles and the AC-130's low-light television sensor are optimized. So Grim 31 "glinted" the convoy for several minutes, illuminating the vehicles with an extra-bright beam in a portion of the spectrum that was invisible to the naked eye but would appear like daylight to anyone wearing night-vision goggles, as the Americans in the convoy were. In one of several unsolved mysteries from the incident that followed, not only did the crew see no sign of glint tape on the vehicles, but no one on the ground reported being "glinted." Nor could the Grim 31 crew see any sign of VS-17 panels—large orange and purple pieces of cloth that U.S. troops use for identification from the air, and which all Task Force Hammer vehicles were supposed to have fixed to them. Grim 31 called Texas 14 with the news. To Thomas and the others in TF Hammer, the vehicles reported by Grim 31 represented a big threat: a potential roadblock or ambush right in the middle of the Fishhook, a natural choke point through which they had to pass to gain entrance to the Shahikot.

It took a few minutes for the officers and NCOs in the convoy to confirm there was no chance of any Americans being at the spot at which Grim 31 was reporting activity. Thomas verified the grid three times. Onboard the aircraft, the discussion turned to whether to shoot at the vehicles or the dismounted personnel first, and what sort of 105mm howitzer ammunition to use: point detonation or proximity fuse. "If we're going after the vehicles, let's go with the PD," one of the crew said. The crew's navigator, a major, asked the Air Force Special Tactics Squadron commando who was serving as Dagger's liaison officer onboard the plane whether he thought the vehicles below were "a good target, and not friendlies," and the liaison replied in the affirmative. A minute after Grim 31 called Thomas again with a reminder that they would have to leave in a couple of minutes, Schwartz radioed Thomas and said Grim 31 had permission to engage. Thomas told McArthur, who immediately called Grim 31. "Those vehicles can be engaged," McArthur told the crew at 5:30 a.m. "Cleared hot on those vehicles."

Harriman's four-vehicle convoy was inching south, about a kilometer northeast of a hill that confusingly bore the same Pushto name—Tergul Ghar—as the Whale, and so had been nicknamed "the Guppy" by the Americans, when McArthur told Grim 31 it was "cleared hot" to fire. Within sixty seconds the world around the four trucks flew apart as 105mm shells rained down, spraying clods of frozen earth and baseball-sized chunks of shrapnel in all directions. The first round hit about ten feet in front of the lead vehicle with a loud boom, sending a shower of sparks upward. Riding in the Special Forces pickup two vehicles back, Casenhiser thought the lead truck had hit a mine. But as he opened his door intending to run over and check whether everyone was okay, another explosion went off nearby. He and Wadsworth thought they must be getting mortared. In a desperate maneuver to evade the devastating fire, the three trailing vehicles in the convoy were wheeling around to reverse course when a round fell in the bed of the Special Forces truck. Casenhiser felt something hit him in the shoulder and right hip.

Inside Grim 31 the crew pressed home the attack with a ruthless efficiency honed to a razor's edge in thousands of hours of training. As the pilot, Major D. J. Turner, slowly circled about 10,000 feet above the target, the 105 gunner—who functioned more as a loader; only the pilot and the two sensor operators could fire the howitzer protruding from the aircraft's belly—opened the gun's breech after each round was fired and pulled the spent brass casing out, dropping it to the floor and kicking it out of the way. Then he hoisted another fifty-three-pound round into the weapon, slammed the breech shut, and hit the button that let the hydraulics reactivate the gun mount. The whole process took five to seven seconds, at the end of which he yelled "Gun ready!" into his helmet microphone. After the flight engineer had repeated the "Gun ready!" shout, one of the sensor operators aligned the sights on his head monitor over a new target and pressed his "consent" button with his left hand to fire another round.

Again and again the earth around the little column of vehicles erupted as Grim 31's crew repeated the process, chasing the troops on the ground as they frantically tried to escape the rain of fire. Caught in the midst of the terrifying maelstrom, Wadsworth noticed there were none of the telltale whistles that announce incoming mortar rounds, just a series of sudden explosions. He was not alone in his suspicions. As they raced down the wadi at forty miles per hour trying to evade the barrage, the other special operators realized the rounds that followed their every twist and turn were raining down far too accurately for mortar fire.

"I'm taking incoming! I'm taking incoming!" Harriman yelled into his radio, a transmission monitored by the rest of TF Hammer and in Dagger's operations center at Bagram, but not by Grim 31. Then a shell exploded with a vicious *boom!* right beside Harriman's truck. A racquetball-sized lump of shrapnel punched a hole through the right passenger side door and hit the warrant officer in his lower back. Another piece of shrapnel, this one about the size of a golf ball, just missed Harriman but angled up and caught Wadsworth's hand as he twisted the steering wheel, skinning his fingers to the bone. The truck stopped moving as the other vehicles kept trying to outrun the murderous fire. Despite his wound, which was critical, Harriman got back on the radio and, with a weakening voice, requested support. On board Grim 31, the crew chatted in a businesslike fashion as they lined the targets up in their gun sights. "They're un-assing the area," said one crewmember, as the troops in the convoy tried desperately to evade Grim 31's merciless pounding. "That last one is trying to boogie," replied another. "Scanners keep your eyes peeled." "The first one is stopped." "Second one hit." "Get out in front of that lead vehicle and lead 'em." Soon all the vehicles in the little convoy had stopped and anyone who could walk was taking cover behind rocks. Above them, Grim 31 had made one-and-a-half orbits of about a two-kilometer radius. The crew had fired between eight and ten rounds and could see there were still targets left to engage. But they were at "bingo" fuel and dawn was coming, and so D. J. pointed the aircraft north. Two minutes and thirteen seconds after the firing began, it was over.

As soon as the rounds stopped falling, Casenhiser and Wadsworth ran back to their truck, where Harriman remained, his breathing labored and his blood spilling onto the seat. Casenhiser checked his pulse, then began CPR on him. Meanwhile Wadsworth grabbed the PRC-148 radio and called up the chain to say they were receiving fire and that Harriman was badly wounded. "Chief is dying! Chief is dying!" Haas heard a clearly rattled Wadsworth yell over the radio. Their colleagues in the main column, which had only just started moving again, had heard muffled gunfire in the distance but didn't make the connection between the AC-130 mission and the tragedy that had just befallen the smaller convoy. "Looks like our northern OP is now taking on mortar fire," one of the special operators said over the radio. At first, ironically, TF Hammer asked Grim 31, who they believed was still engaging targets in the Fishhook, to fly north and attack the enemy mortar position presumed to be firing on Harriman's element. But a faint pink-yellow glow along the eastern horizon announced the impending dawn. "Uh, we gotta leave," Grim 31's navigator reported. "It's daylight. We are ordered to leave." Instead, they would get an inbound flight of F-15E Strike Eagle fighters to come to the rescue, the aircrew told TF Hammer as they flew north.

Meanwhile, in Gardez, Blaber, Glenn P., and the other operators in the AFO operations center had been monitoring the radio exchanges and were now scrambling to figure out what Grim 31 was engaging. Because they could combine the reports from the three AFO teams in the valley with all the other message traffic, they had a better sense of what was happening in the valley than any other headquarters, a fact which would become increasingly apparent over the next seventy-two hours. None of the teams had reported an enemy convoy in the Fishhook, and when they heard Grim 31 report they had disabled at least two vehicles, Blaber and Glenn P. became worried. Then, a minute or two later, at about 5:35 a.m., John B.'s three-man AFO team with the main body of TF Hammer radioed back to Gardez that the northern convoy, including Hans, Nelson, and Thor, was being mortared. Blaber and Glenn P. immediately made the connection. "Cease fire! Cease fire! Cease fire!" Blaber yelled into the satellite radio hand mike. Glenn P. shouted the same into a hand-held MBITR as he ran outside to get better transmission on the line-of-sight radio.

The Grim 31 crew members never heard the "Cease fire!" call. It would have been irrelevant anyway, as they were already heading home. But Glenn P.'s next transmission from the Gardez safe house got through. "We have friendly force receiving mortar fire, break," the AFO intelligence NCO said. "We hope that's not you firing on them." The stark message was the first chilling indication anyone on the AC-130 had that they had been shooting at Americans. "Who is this?" Grim 31's navigator replied in what one special ops account described as an "audibly shaken" voice. "Ultra 01," Glenn P. replied, giving Blaber's AFO call sign.

A few kilometers away in the main column, Schwartz had been monitoring Harriman's transmissions and told Haas that Harriman's element had taken casualties. Haas halted the main column and began organizing a quick reaction force to go to the assistance of Harriman's convoy. Meanwhile, Schwartz continued communicating with Harriman until the badly wounded warrant officer could no longer talk on the radio. At that point Wadsworth, who could barely operate the radio himself because of his badly wounded hands, took over communications duty while simultaneously struggling to get the Afghans to set up a security perimeter. Schwartz asked Wadsworth a series of questions: *What is your location? What is the friendly and enemy situation? What are the numbers of U.S. and AMF wounded? Can you identify an exfil HLZ?* Schwartz also kept the TF Dagger command post at Bagram updated on the situation.

BACK at the site of the attack on Harriman's convoy, the scene was one of devastation. One of Ziabdullah's fighters lay dead and another dozen had been wounded, one mortally. Nelson, one of the AFO operators, had suffered superficial cuts to his face and head and a scratched cornea. All three Special Forces soldiers were hurt, but Harriman's wounds were easily the most severe. He now had a fist-sized hole in his back through which his life was quickly ebbing away. Ignoring his own wounds, Casenhiser worked feverishly to try to save his friend's life.

About twenty minutes after the main column ground to a halt, a four-vehicle quick reaction force took off for Harriman's position. In the two lead vehicles—an armored Mercedes SUV and a pickup—were Texas 14's second-in-command, Chief Warrant Officer 2 Sean Ballard, McArthur, Schwartz, and a couple of Special Forces NCOs, including ODA 372's other medic, Sergeant First Class Brian Allen. The third vehicle was a truck containing Engineer's thirty-strong platoon—among the best of the Afghan fighters—and the fourth vehicle was an AFO pickup containing John B. and Isaac H. It took the rescue party about ten minutes to drive north to Harriman's stricken little convoy. A little more than halfway there, roughly 800 meters from Harriman's position, they thought they heard the crackle of small arms fire. Ballard charged ahead in his armored SUV. The other vehicles stopped and established a hasty perimeter, with Engineer's fighters orienting their weapons to the north and northeast. After a short pause Schwartz determined that they weren't receiving effective fire and couldn't see any enemy fighters, so he had everyone get back in the vehicles and continued north. While still en route, Ballard heard over the radio that one of the U.S. casualties was going into cardiac arrest.

It wasn't yet 6:30 a.m. The Rakkasan air assault had yet to land, but Task Force Hammer was already in the grip of Clausewitzean friction and had ground almost to a halt well short of its objective. The first mutterings of dissension were being heard from the Afghans, and the NCOs in the quick reaction force found themselves already arranging a medevac for their stricken colleagues. Operation Anaconda had not begun auspiciously.

(A Central Command investigation into the attack on Harriman's column found that it had been mistakenly engaged by Grim 31. The major factor in the friendly-fire incident was the failure of the aircraft's inertial navigation system, which led the aircrew to believe they were over the Fishhook when in fact they were flying over very similar terrain just north of the Whale, the investigators concluded. However, their report left several questions unanswered: Why, if the navigation system had failed after Grim 31 engaged Juliet's targets on top of the Whale, and Grim 31 had flown back to the eastern ridge, as investigators speculated, rather than to the Finger, the aircraft's crew reported that the flight time to the next target did not match how long it would have taken them to fly to a position above Harriman's convoy at the northern tip of the Whale; why the

crew saw no sign of "glint" tape on the vehicles they engaged; why the U.S. troops who were attacked didn't notice when Grim 31 "glinted" their position; and why the navigation system seemed to work perfectly in the immediate aftermath of the attack on Harriman's column, steering Grim 31 home to K2 through bad weather exactly as it should have. What the investigation did make clear was that, not for the last time in Operation Anaconda, in a situation in which every individual involved was doing his best to secure victory, tragedy resulted.)

5.

DESPITE the best efforts of the SF officers and NCOs to hold things together, chaos now engulfed TF Hammer, which was spread out over five kilometers west of the Whale. Some trucks were still advancing, others had stopped, while the SF troops, still believing Harriman's convoy had been hit by enemy mortar fire, looked to their own defenses and sent AMF fighters out to establish a perimeter around the convoy. It was "a very confusing time," recalled McHale, who was one of those who had stopped. Glenn Thomas had driven off in his pickup with the quick reaction force, but he only accompanied the other vehicles far enough to ensure they were headed in the right direction. While Thomas was gone, Haas told McHale to move to the front of the column and continue driving southeast to Gwad Kala, a collection of ruins less than two kilometers west of the Whale. Phase Line Emerald ran through Gwad Kala, and McHale was to pause there and wait for the bombing runs against the Whale. Not realizing that Thomas was only accompanying the quick reaction force part of the way to Harriman's convoy and then returning, McHale understood Haas's order to mean that he—McHale—was now in charge at the head of the column. The ODA 372 leader did as he was directed, gathering a half-dozen U.S. and Afghan vehicles and moving out smartly. But this only added to the confusion, because when Thomas returned to the main column and resumed movement southeast, he assumed he was still in the lead element and didn't realize there were seven or eight friendly vehicles ahead of him. "He thought he was in the front, and I thought I was in the front," McHale recalled.

The original Task Force Hammer order of march had long since been discarded. McHale had told his team's senior engineer, Sergeant First Class James Van Antwerp, to lag behind the main column and "keep pushing vehicles forward." In fact, Van Antwerp ended up in the middle of the convoy, which was where Glenn Thomas ran into him when the Texas 14 leader rejoined the main body of TF Hammer. Elements of the two A-teams were intermixed at the front of the column. Worried there might be unmarked minefields ahead, McHale put one of Texas 14's armored Mercedes in the lead and drove through a narrow gorge just west of Carwazi, a small village about two kilometers west of the northern tip of the Whale.

It was about 6:15 a.m. when the first few vehicles from McHale's element emerged from the defile, still two-and-a-half kilometers north of Gwad Kala with the rest of TF Hammer stretched out for several thousand meters behind them. Behind him, Haas looked at his watch and congratulated himself on being almost on schedule, despite all the catastrophes that had befallen his task force. Haas's Toyota bounced through the defile, and then up onto some nearby high ground. Raising his gaze, Haas took in the awesome size of the Whale, looming dark and forbidding in front of him. "Holy shit!" he gasped. For the first time he fully understood the dominance the rocky massif exerted over the Shahikot's western approaches. He looked back at his watch. This was when the bombing was supposed to start. The Americans and their Afghan allies cast their eyes toward the heavens, waiting for the promised fifty-five-minute bombardment to begin. The Afghans, nervous about the enemy they expected to find on the Whale, set great store by the Americans' ability to deliver death and destruction on command from the air. For their part, the Americans knew their ability to cajole their allies rested on their ability to deliver on their promises. Both parties were about to be sorely disappointed. In an underwhelming display of American firepower, a single B-1B bomber hurtled through the predawn sky, and a grand total of six orange explosions blossomed along the humpback ridgeline. And that was that. The ballyhooed "fifty-five-minute" bombardment had in fact lasted less than a single minute. The Whale was over six kilometers long and, at its broadest point, two kilometers wide. The Air Force had dropped less than one bomb per kilometer on the massive terrain feature.

At first neither the Americans nor their Afghan allies could believe that they had just witnessed the entire bombardment. As the first bombs erupted along the spine of the Whale, Zia Lodin jumped with his harms raised aloft in a universal gesture of triumph. "All the Afghans are screaming 'Yay!'" Haas recalled. When Zia was done with his premature victory jig, Haas called him over and explained that as soon as the bombing finished, in about an hour, they had to be ready to move forward. Then they looked back toward the Whale expectantly. "And I'm waiting, and I'm waiting, and I'm waiting," Haas said. Nothing happened. *Where's the rest of the bombs?* McHale wondered. The bombs, of course, had been lost in the miasma of miscommunication in the days preceding the operation. Apprehension among the Afghans deepened. Zia Lodin, upon whose troops the Anaconda plan revolved, turned to Haas and said, via an interpreter, "Where are the bombs you promised us? Where are the planes?"

THE events surrounding the air strikes that were supposed to hit the valley prior to H-Hour remained clouded in mystery two years after the operation. The plan called for thirteen preplanned targets to be struck by a B-1B bomber, a B-52 bomber, and two F-15E Strike Eagle fighter-bombers in the hour prior to H-Hour. Some of these bombs went in as planned, including a thermobaric bomb that struck the cave complex that Juliet had identified two days previously and the JDAMs dropped on the Whale. But others—the exact number and location of the targets involved is still debated, but there is general agreement that they included targets in the southeast of the valley—did not.

Two factors lay behind the failure to drop these bombs. The first is that the B-1B had a bomb get stuck in its bomb bay. It requested permission from the Combined Air Operations Center in Saudi Arabia to jettison the bomb over the target area and then waited for several minutes for permission to be granted. Meanwhile, the B-52, which had three bombs left to drop (fewer than the B-1B), waited for the B-1B to finish its bombing run. Before the CAOC could come back with an answer for the B-1B, the aircraft all heard what they interpreted as a "knock it off" call from a special operations reconnaissance team—presumably one of the AFO teams, as these were the only teams in the valley at the time—that felt the bombs were falling too close to its position. This was reported by the crews of one of the F-15Es and the B-52, but without any specifics as to the call sign or location of the recce team. Blaber, who was monitoring all three teams' radio transmissions, said that he was unaware of any of his teams making such a call. It is possible that the air crews misinterpreted a radio call from the ground, or even that they had heard the "Cease fire!" calls directed at Grim 31 by Blaber and Glenn P. in Gardez. (Major Richard Coe, the weapons systems officer on the lead F-15E, acknowledged that it might have been the "Cease fire!" calls from Gardez that he heard.) Whatever the source of the "knock it off" call, the result was that no more bombs fell before the Chinooks entered the valley.

WITH Task Force Hammer stalled in the sand west of the Whale and the Chinooks carrying the first wave of Rakkasan infantry already skimming the mountaintops en route to the Shahikot, Hagenbeck faced a critical decision: Should he abort the mission? If he did, surprise would have been lost, and the episode would doubtless be portrayed by the press as a significant military setback. But if he continued with the air assault, he ran the risk of having his supporting effort land in Shahikot with no main effort to support. The Rakkasans could occupy their blocking positions, but with no Task Force Hammer to drive the enemy into those positions, the Rakkasans would be nothing but static targets for enemy gunners. But Hagenbeck was not concerned with the delay to Hammer's movement, which he considered temporary, and he thought the notion of turning the air assault force around to try again later was unrealistic. "We can get 'em moving again," the Dagger leaders in Bagram told Hagenbeck and his staff concerned about Hammer's lack of progress. "Colonel Mulholland and Colonel Rosengard were very confident that they could get the Zia forces to move," said Bentley, Hagenbeck's senior fires officer. "It was just as much a surprise to them as to anybody that they were not moving." However, among the Mountain leaders in Bagram, there was a determination to put Task Force Rakkasan into the Shahikot, even if the main effort failed to show up for the fight. "We weren't going to wait on Zia to dictate to us what the plan was going to be," Bello said.

WHEN Ballard reached the site of the friendly-fire incident, he found the vehicles and the casualties in a streambed that was seeded with six rows of mines. The AMF fighters were hiding behind rocks looking very scared. Casenhiser, suffering from significant wounds himself, was still working urgently on Harriman. Wadsworth brought Ballard quickly up to speed on what had happened. The warrant officer directed that an HLZ be marked out so that one of the inbound TF Rakkasan Chinooks could pick up the casualties after dropping off the infantry and take them back to Bagram. The Chinooks were supposedly already inbound, but Ballard couldn't raise them yet on his radio.

THE helicopters' flight south to the Shahikot was difficult. Low clouds hid the moon and pockets of fog obscured the ground. Dawn was almost an hour away when the Apaches took off, so the pilots used their helmet-mounted thermal night-vision sights to penetrate the haze as they flew between the snowcapped peaks. Chenault and Hurley kept an altitude of at least 150 feet above ground level for most of the flight down. But after an hour, as they were closing on the Shahikot, they hit a cloud bank that forced them to rise to over 500 feet above ground level—far higher than they would usually fly on the approach to an engagement area. Behind them, Team 2's pilots dealt with the fog differently as they raced toward the Shahikot, preferring to hug the earth. The three helicopters bounced and swerved over and around the ridgelines at 125 miles per hour, sometimes just a couple of dozen feet above the ground. The

Team 2 aircraft lost visual contact with each other several times. An Apache's instruments did not allow for easy flight through clouds, and the pilots discussed turning around. But in their hearts they knew that wasn't an option. Their colleagues in Team 1 were already over the Shahikot, having taken a different route. More important, the infantry-laden Chinooks ahead of them had avoided the worst of the weather and were nearing the Shahikot. The plan called for the second flight of Apaches to arrive on station just as the 10th Mountain troops were establishing their blocking positions. If Team 2 turned around now, the infantry would land and move to their positions, only to find themselves bereft of their primary means of fire support. Peering into the gloom, the pilots flew on.

IN fact, the weather had already played havoc with the aviation plan. Somehow the first three Chinooks, carrying the 2-187 troops, had gotten ahead of the Apaches and were already turning into the valley. The two Apaches of Team 1 followed hard on their heels, but they couldn't catch them in time. The Chinooks would have to do without the benefit of the "cherry/ice" call.

The smoke from the air strikes had barely dissipated as the Chinooks swooped into the valley. The three helicopters spread out as they selected their individual landing zones along the foot of the eastern ridge. At the controls of chalk number three were Chief Warrant Officer 3 Loyd Blayne Anderson and Chief Warrant Officer 2 Jeff Fichter. Anderson was the more experienced and higher-ranking pilot, but was acting as copilot that morning. "I told Fichter I'd fly with him that day, 'cause he's got a little girl coming in May, and so my job was to keep him alive," Anderson said. About fifty miles north of the Shahikot they and the other first serial Chinooks had received a call from the Air Force E-3 Airborne Warning and Control System (AWACS) aircraft that was controlling the airspace for Anaconda. The AWACS—call sign Bossman—needed them to divert from their flight path home to pick up the casualties taken in Harriman's column and fly them back to Bagram. Now, as they lowered themselves to the valley floor to deposit their precious cargo of soldiers, the two pilots were already making the mental adjustments to their flight plan. Within two minutes they were airborne again.

THE medevac mission interfered with Apache Team 2's flight. The second serial of Chinooks was due soon, carrying the 1-87 troops whose establishment of blocking positions was to coincide with Team 2's arrival. But as the three Apaches in Team 2 approached the Shahikot, they were forced to slow down to allow the first serial of Chinooks that had just dropped off the 101st troops to divert from their flight path in order to land and pick up the casualties. The delay put Team 2 several minutes behind schedule, but otherwise the bad news caused remarkably little alarm among the pilots. "We still weren't expecting much resistance when we got there," Hardy said. "There wasn't a lot of adrenaline pumping."

By the time Team 2 got to the release point, the weather had improved slightly. As the second serial of Chinooks flew into the Shahikot, the three Apaches turned north and tucked in behind them. The attack helicopters circled as the three Chinooks landed and disgorged their infantry without incident.

Once all five Apaches were on station, each team began flying "racetrack" patterns in its half of the valley, using Serkhankhel as the north-south dividing line. For Team 2, this meant flying clockwise in an oval no more than two kilometers long and one kilometer wide. The idea was to keep at least one aircraft with an eye on the infantry and Serkhankhel at all times. They flew in this pattern for several uneventful minutes, watching the infantry gather themselves on the ground. *Okay, here we go again, nothing's going on,* Chenault thought. "Then all hell broke loose."

BY the time Schwartz arrived at the site of the attack on Harriman's column, all three Chinooks in the first serial were attempting to land at the landing zone that had been marked out. Schwartz told his radio-telephone operator (RTO), Sergeant First Class Eric Navarro, to get on the radio and help the Chinooks land, then opened his door to step out. As he did, someone yelled to him to watch out, the creek bed was mined. Looking down, Schwartz saw an antipersonnel mine right where he was about to put his foot. Sidestepping the mine and breathing a sigh of relief, he walked carefully up to where he could see several personnel performing CPR on Harriman. As soon as the Chinooks landed, Schwartz helped carry Harriman to the nearest helicopter, which was the one piloted by Anderson and Fichter. Looking at Harriman's glazed eyes and ghostly pallor, Ballard thought it was already too late for his counterpart from 372.

Once Harriman had been lifted aboard, Casenhiser, Wadsworth, and Nelson climbed in, along with several of the more badly wounded AMF soldiers, two of whom had taken shrapnel to the head. (Ziabdullah told Ballard that all his wounded had been taken care of, but that wasn't the case. Some had been too scared to get on the helicopters, while others who had jumped on the Chinook were not wounded, but were looking for a way to get out of the fight.) Fully aware that a fellow soldier's life hung in the balance, Fichter and Anderson wasted no time on the ground. By 6:47 a.m. they were in the air again, en route back to Bagram.

After the helicopters took off, Ballard set about "sterilizing" the site, recovering sensitive items—especially cryptographic gear—and placing them in his vehicle. But some equipment wouldn't fit on the remaining trucks and had to be left behind. About fifteen minutes after Anderson's Chinook had left, half a dozen rounds variously assessed as RPGs, mortars or recoilless rifle rounds whistled over the heads of the troops who remained at the site. The fire, which caused no casualties, was probably aimed at the Apaches flying about 500 meters in front of the U.S. and AMF troops, but it served to focus the Americans' minds on the task in hand. Nevertheless, it still took them almost an hour to recover all the mission-essential equipment and bandage up the AMF walking wounded.

John B. and Isaac H., the AFO personnel who had accompanied the quick reaction force, stayed behind to establish an observation post on a hillock just to the north of the Guppy. Ziabdullah moved his forces south to link up with Haas and the main convoy just west of Carwazi, while Schwartz, Ballard, and about twenty of Engineer's fighters remained at the site and established a hasty defensive position, waiting for Afghan reinforcements to be sent up to provide security for the AFO observation post. Upon their arrival, Schwartz moved them forward and told their leader where to position his forces. As he was driving back to the main convoy, Schwartz got a call from Ballard saying that the AFO guys had left some "mission essential equipment" in their vehicle at the base of the Guppy, and they wanted the AMF troops to bring it up to them. The major returned to their vehicle, secured the equipment, and told a pair of AMF fighters to bring it up to the observation post. Then Schwartz went back to the hasty defensive perimeter, gathered all the U.S. and AMF forces, and proceeded to link up with Haas and the main body.

ONBOARD Anderson's Chinook, Casenhiser ignored his own wounds, which were soaking his pants leg in blood, and worked frantically to keep his buddy alive. Blood slickened the floor as he knelt over Harriman. "Go faster! Go faster!" he yelled desperately at the pilots. Fichter and Anderson were already pushing the helicopter as hard as they could, squeezing every last knot of speed from the shuddering airframe as the Afghan landscape flashed below them. They received permission to break formation, leaving the other two Chinooks in their wake as they made a beeline back to Bagram, flying far closer to the ground than they had on the way down. "I didn't want to waste the time pulling up to gain altitude," Anderson said. "We didn't care if we got shot at or not." The pilots threw all caution to the wind in their efforts to deliver Harriman alive. "We decided to pull everything we had and see what she would do," Anderson said. They watched the air speed indicator creep up from 130 knots per hour, past 140, 150, 160, then 165, the equivalent of about 190 miles per hour. Fichter had 1500 hours flight time under his belt, while Anderson had 2600. Neither had ever flown a helicopter this fast before. "We just decided we were going to tear it apart to get him there," Anderson said. The airframe was shaking so violently they couldn't read some of the instruments. "We were sucking the guts out of the aircraft to get back," recalled Fichter. As they roared over Kabul less than 100 feet above the ground, the two bubble-shaped windows in the cabin popped out and sailed to the ground. "Somebody in Kabul got a new salad bowl," Fichter remarked dryly.

With Casenhiser working full-time on Harriman, Sergeant Jonathan Gurgel, the flight engineer, passed out blankets and used the aircraft's medical supplies to dress the wounds on the walking wounded, some of whom were going into shock. About ten miles from Bagram, the pilots radioed the airfield tower with the message that they were inbound carrying a litter-urgent American casualty receiving CPR. Only thirty minutes after they had taken off, Fichter and Anderson brought their Chinook hurtling over the mountains surrounding Bagram airfield at 170 knots. With Anderson at the controls, they tore up another page from the rule book by using a banned maneuver called an "Australian decel" to land the aircraft at high speed. Anderson barely slowed the aircraft before suddenly tilting it on its side, pivoting, and almost slamming it to the ground in a move that took no more than a couple of seconds. A small convoy of cargo Humvees that served as ambulances for the elite medical professionals of the 274th Forward Surgical Team raced out to meet the helicopter and unloaded Harriman immediately.

As the Humvee with Harriman in the back sped away, Casenhiser, at last relieved of his medical duties, turned to one of the Chinook crew and asked casually, "Is there blood on my leg?" There was. "He had blood all over his thighs," said Anderson, who marveled at the SF medic's ability to put his own pain out of his mind in order to focus on treating Harriman.

Once the casualties were unloaded, the crew realized how much blood there was on the floor. Knowing they were due to fly another load of infantrymen—"Joes"—down to the Shahikot soon, they started throwing dirt on the seats and the floor to soak it up. "Nothing will degrade morale more than to have blood on the floor and seats when you're picking up forty-three Joes," Fichter said.

Later that day Anderson walked over to some Special Forces soldiers and asked how Harriman was doing. A warrant officer told him Harriman had died. The news hit Anderson and his crewmates hard. They rehashed the flight, trying to figure out if they could have saved an extra few seconds anywhere along the route. Anderson was so troubled by these thoughts that he went back to the forward surgical team's doctors in the medical center that they had established in the airfield tower building. They told him Harriman had been beyond help, and that a few minutes here or there wouldn't have made any difference. It was cold comfort to the air crew. "We wanted to tell his wife we did it as fast as we could," Anderson said. "I don't think any other helicopter or any other crew could have done it any quicker. . . .We just wanted to make a difference."

MCHALE'S ragged formation of seven or eight vehicles, including three jinga trucks, an armored SUV, AFO's Sergeant Major Al Y. in his truck, an AMF Toyota pickup, and McHale in his pickup, continued south to Gwad Kala. (When Thomas came through the defile believing he was at the front of the column and then caught sight of McHale's element up ahead, he was confused, but did not fire at them.) McHale halted and dismounted the troops at Gwad Kala with the intention of sending the trucks back to the main body of the convoy, which was still north of the defile. He needed to do this because so many trucks had broken down, rolled over, become stuck or been dispatched north with the quick reaction force that, despite starting the night with three spare trucks, Task Force Hammer was now running out of vehicles, so there were more fighters back west of Carwazi than the vehicles there could accommodate. The steady attrition of the convoy's trucks also caused the system of squads, platoons and companies into which the A-teams had carefully formed their 400 Afghan allies to completely break down. This became clear to McHale the moment he alighted from his truck at Gwad Kala and watched the Afghans dismounting. "They were looking at each other like 'Who are you?'" The Afghan "platoon leader" McHale had placed in charge of the three AMF trucks in his advance force was nowhere to be seen. "It became apparent that their command and control was lost," McHale recalled. It was now daylight, and the Al Qaida fighters on the Whale had a clear view of the straggling column. McHale and the other SF soldiers pointed to a nearby wadi and motioned for their Afghan colleagues to seek cover there. As the Afghans walked over, the Al Qaida mortar crews nestled in the Whale's rocks let fly. With a *boom!* the first round landed among the one-story adobe ruins about 200 meters from the column. McHale, under indirect fire for the first time in his life, thought briefly that it wasn't as loud as he expected. He didn't have much time to chew on that thought, however, because a few seconds later another round exploded, this time about 150 meters on the other side of the column.

As mortar rounds bracketed their vehicles, the Afghans' nerve broke. "They started scattering like cats," McHale said. Now the disruptive effect of the cross-loading of personnel precipitated by the earlier truck accidents came into play. Task Force Hammer might have stood a chance if the Afghans had retained unit integrity, with each Afghan platoon grouped together under its original platoon leader. But that was not the case. The Afghan force had become hopelessly mixed up, and under the stress of sustained incoming mortar fire, it broke. McHale looked in vain for an Afghan commander of any rank that he recognized. But because the column had become so intermingled and Engineer's platoon—the best of the Afghan fighters—had been dispatched with the quick reaction force, the ODA 372 team leader recognized none of the Afghans around him.

To McHale's horror, not only were the Afghans running away, but they were running straight toward the ruins where the first round had landed, and which the mortar teams on the Whale had obviously used as a target to register their tubes. McHale ran to the three AMF trucks, only to find that their drivers had abandoned them and taken the keys with them. The A-team leader jumped back into his truck with his commo NCO, Sergeant Bill Guthrie, and an American Pushto interpreter, then raced after the fleeing Afghans. With mortar rounds raining down, he tried to rally the Afghans and persuade them to get back on the trucks so that they could withdraw in good order. It was a hopeless task. "They were more in the self-preservation mode at this point," McHale said. But although the incoming fire had spooked the Afghans, it wasn't effective enough to inflict any casualties. "If you were organized you could have sustained and continued the maneuver under it," McHale said. "The difficulty being you can't just stand there and continue to have those guys running around like chickens in an open valley where you're clearly being observed."

McHale realized quickly that the mortar rounds seemed to follow his truck. The guerrillas on the Whale were obviously more interested in killing U.S. troops than they were in killing the Americans' local allies, and it didn't take long for them to zero in on him. When a round landed close enough to shower him with dirt, he knew it was time to beat a retreat. But for the first time Task Force Hammer's men had "eyes on" their enemy. Staff Sergeant Christopher Grooms of Texas 14, who had been a mortarman in the regular Army before joining Special Forces, spotted the puffs of smoke from the tube firing at them. Meanwhile, Sergeant Major Al Y. and a Special Forces medic attached to the CIA were taking shelter in a ditch and thought they could see the Al Qaida mortar crew's observer popping up from behind cover. Guthrie and Sergeant First Class John Southworth (Texas 14's commo sergeant) raised the Apaches on the radio, hoping they could take care of the problem.

Hearing the calls for help, the two Apaches in the northern part of the valley broke from their racetrack pattern and flew up the west side of the Whale. Spotting the mortar pit's location using the vague directions they had received seemed an impossible task. At that hour the Whale's west side was still bathed in shadow. "It was like trying to see fleas on a dog," Hurley said. But there it was, in a wadi at the base of the southwest side of the Whale, manned by eight enemy fighters wearing traditional Afghan brown woolen pakhul hats, with brown scarves around their necks. After one pass over the enemy position to positively identify it, the Apaches wheeled around and came diving in. Chenault took the lead, struggling to keep his crosshairs on the mortar as his helicopter closed on the target at a speed of about 115 miles per hour. At 1,000 meters from the tube, his left index finger squeezed the trigger and the pods on his aircraft's stubby wings spat a pair of high-explosive rounds at the target. The rockets sped toward the target, short yellow flames trailing from their motors. Chenault squeezed again and again, each pull on the trigger firing another two rockets, walking them closer and closer to the mortar pit. At 200 meters from the enemy position, he yanked on the controls and broke to the left. Five rotor discs behind him, Hurley flew in firing three rocket bursts to suppress any enemy to the right of Chenault's target area. Then he also broke left. Out of the shadows leaped two streams of tracers, arcing under the nose of Hurley's aircraft. Making a mental note of the spot where the tracers had been fired, Chenault and Hurley turned and barreled toward the target yet again. Both pilots put their rockets right where they remembered the tracers coming from. Bull's-eye. The mortar position blew apart in a cloud of dust.

That at least persuaded the enemy fighters on the Whale's western slopes to keep their heads down long enough for McHale and his colleagues to get back in their vehicles and beat a retreat north to the security perimeter that the remainder of the column had established just south of the defile. One of the Afghan drivers returned to his truck, but most of the Afghans chose to walk back in ones and twos. "There was nothing organized about it," McHale recalled. Over the cacophonous din of incoming mortar rounds, men shouting in two languages, and the static bursts from several radios, McHale's ears caught another sound drifting over the Whale from the Shahikot valley: automatic weapons fire, and lots of it.

6.

SERGEANT Scotty Mendenhall's feet hit the ground and he peeled left to take up position at the Chinook's three o'clock. Behind him the rest of 2nd Platoon fanned out and formed a perimeter around the battalion and company command post personnel as the helicopter took off. Raising their heads as they lay on the scrubby grass and hard-packed dirt, some soldiers were stunned to see a walled compound just 150 meters to the north. Frank Baltazar, commander of 2-187 Infantry's C Company, wasn't surprised. In the days leading up to D-Day he'd seen overhead photos of the compound that indicated it was empty, nothing to worry about. He'd told his battalion commander, Chip Preysler, he'd clear the compound—run his troops through it to check it out—before moving into the blocking positions. Staff Sergeant Chris Harry, one of Baltazar's squad leaders, knew his first mission was to clear the compound. Within three minutes of landing, seven of his men were "stacked" to the left of the doorway along the outside wall. Sergeant David Dedo approached the door-way from the right and peered into the courtyard. "One American dead!" Harry heard him shout. The soldiers had been briefed that TF 11 troops—the AFO recon teams—would be in the valley. They feared the worst. "One American dead?!?" Harry exclaimed. "No, one American TENT!" Dedo replied, explaining he'd spotted a U.S. military-style tent in the courtyard. Relieved, the troops surged through the doorway.

But as Harry's troops stormed in, bullets ripped over the men still sitting exposed on the LZ, fired from a position about 400 meters to their west on a low east-west ridgeline that ended just short of the compound. Machine gunners Mendenhall and Specialist James "Fred" Thompson returned fire as their buddies sought cover. A running battle ensued as soldiers maneuvered down and up the banks of a creek between the LZ and the compound, exchanging fire with a dozen enemy fighters. Preysler and Baltazar moved their command posts to a nearby bluff. "Look out!" Baltazar's RTO yelled. Foolishly the captain raised his head to see an orange fireball hurtling straight at him. He slammed his head down as the RPG flew over and landed harmlessly fifty meters behind Preysler. The leaders waited the ten minutes it took Harry's squad to clear the compound, then they and the rest of 2nd Platoon went inside, where they encountered a scene reminiscent of an Al Qaida Marie Celeste. Someone had left in a hurry moments before the Americans burst in. The teapot was still warm, as were the half-eaten breakfasts of goat meat and the bedclothes for thirteen to fifteen men strewn on the floor of the compound's one-story main building. The place was an arsenal that proved the guerrillas were better armed than the Americans had expected. They found several recoilless rifles, 82mm mortar tubes and rounds, dozens of AK-style assault rifles and RPGs, Dragunov sniper rifles, three sets of U.S. PVS-7 night-vision goggles, binoculars, and handheld ICOM radios that Sergeant First Class Anthony Koch, the troops' platoon sergeant, said "were better than ours." There was also a sports bag from a Nike store in Beaverton, Oregon, full of blasting caps and prayer beads, plus Middle Eastern currency and a notebook full of Arabic writing on military tactics, including a diagram on how to shoot down an aircraft. Fifty alarm clocks, a number of Casio watches, and books on digital electronics suggested a bomb-making operation. "These guys weren't taking an electrical engineering exam in that compound," Wiercinski said. Human hair lay on the floor, as if beards had been hurriedly shorn.

Outside, Baltazar's troops were trading fire with Arab-looking fighters in the hills dressed in lightweight black garb and armed with AKs and RPGs. Thomson dropped two with his machine gun. Koch looked south and suddenly realized the extent of the combat. RPGs flew in all directions, all fired with the same goal: shooting down an Apache.

AS Apache Team 1 obliterated the mortar position on the Whale, Team 2 was encountering enemy fire in the south of the valley. Hardy was making his first turn through the valley when he felt the helicopter "bounce." "It sounded like somebody just took their bare hand and slapped the side of the aircraft," his copilot-gunner Pebsworth remembered. Like most Apache pilots, he had never been shot at and failed to recognize the sound for what it was. "You're always on the delivering end of a round, you're never on the receiving end," he said. "It just wasn't in my mind, or any of our minds, really, that we were going to be getting shot at."

"What was that?!?" the two pilots asked each other. Hardy was one of the few pilots who might have been expected to correctly identify the sound. With Bob Carr still back at Texaco getting his cannon fixed, Hardy's 3,400 flight hours made him the "highest time" pilot over the battlefield. As A Company's maintenance test pilot, the rangy forty-year-old was, in Hurley's words, the unit's "maintenance god," responsible for the upkeep of the helicopters and for test-flying those that had been fixed. He knew all the Apache's quirks yet had no idea what had just happened to his helicopter.

A few confused seconds after feeling the bump, Pebsworth realized his symbol generator—the electronic device that allowed him to read data such as compass heading, altitude, and air speed by converting it to graphics in his helmet-mounted display—had died. This made the pilots think the "pop" they'd heard was a fuse or some other electrical failure. Pebsworth started pulling the circuit breakers to reset the electronics. But as he did so, he realized other displays had also gone dark. Nothing connected to the electronics bay on the left side of the fuselage was working. Frantically flicking switches and pushing buttons, the pilots tried to isolate the problem's source. Then reality dawned in the form of urgent radio traffic from the other Apaches. "We started to realize that we're being shot at, all the aircraft are being shot at," Pebsworth said.

The two pilots assumed an RPG had exploded close enough to shower the left electronics bay with shrapnel. *How in the world could one bullet cause that much damage?* Pebsworth thought. But in fact a single Al Qaida bullet was the cause of their difficulties. That bullet had entered the electronics bay and sliced neatly through sixty wires zip-tied together in a bundle as thick as a man's wrist, knocking out the weapons and target acquisition systems. The pilots could still fly the aircraft, but were unable to shoot back at the enemy. The Apaches' battle in the Shahikot was less than fifteen minutes old, and already the most experienced pilot in the fight had been rendered impotent.

Having recovered from the initial shock of a couple of hundred U.S. soldiers air assaulting into their stronghold, the Al Qaida fighters were directing a fusillade of RPG, machine gun and Kalashnikov fire at the helicopters. None of the pre-mission briefings had focused on the RPG threat to helicopters, even though it was no secret that Al Qaida and other Islamist guerrilla organizations had grown adept at using RPGs to down helicopters. An RPG gunner can set his weapon either to fire in a point-detonating mode, meaning the round explodes when it hits something, or in an air burst mode, meaning it detonates in midair after a preset distance. In the wars against the Soviets in Afghanistan and the Russians in Chechnya, the Al Qaida fighters had honed their expertise at using RPGs in the air burst mode to down helicopters, setting the rounds to explode close enough to an aircraft to shred its hydraulic and electrical innards—and, perhaps, its pilots—with a lethal shower of shrapnel. The pilots were not ignorant of the risk posed by the shoulder-fired weapons. "Every pilot in the tent talked about the RPGs and how they've been used in Somalia," Hamilton said. "Everyone knew that potential might exist, even if it had not been briefed as part of the threat."

TEAM 1 was breaking a cardinal rule of helicopter combat. The two Apaches were racing north up the Whale hunting another reported mortar position on the ridge's northeast corner. Chenault was in the lead, almost 2,000 meters ahead of Hurley. Figuring "altitude was gonna help us," as Hurley put it, both aircraft "rode the backbone of the Whale," flying along the crest of the ridgeline for its entire length. The pilots were trying to put themselves between the enemy and the sun, to blind any Al Qaida fighters trying to track them with the naked eye. But this silhouetted the aircraft against the sky—a tactical no-no. Chenault reached the Whale's northeast tip and began a wide right turn. Hurley was preparing to follow suit when from the front seat Stu Contant screamed a warning: "I have a man, 3 o'clock, RPG!" Looking down, Hurley spotted a brown-clad figure 400 feet below. He had an RPG launcher over his left shoulder and was aiming it at the tail of Chenault's aircraft. Flying about 100 feet lower than Chenault, Hurley banked his Apache into a tighter right turn. He knew the danger was imminent, but his speed had carried him past the enemy. He needed to be facing a target to destroy it with rockets or Hellfires. The cannon could be more flexibly employed, by "slaving" it to the movements of the pilot's helmet, but at this stage the small brown figure was too far behind them for Hurley to swivel the cannon around to fire at him, even by craning his neck. There was nothing to do but complete the turn. Then, facing the gunner at a range of 800 meters, he squeezed off a ten-round burst. It was too far away for such a small target. The rounds dispersed too widely. Hurley cursed the decision to set the burst limit at ten rounds. *Twenty would have been better,* he thought. *We're not getting enough steel in the box.*

Hurley flew farther east into the valley, then turned to make another run at the Whale, this time flying out of the sun. He could see five brown spots running from right to left across the ridgeline, all except the RPG gunner carrying AK-style assault rifles. Their brown woolly coats blended perfectly with the rocks and weeds. *No wonder these bastards are so hard to spot when they're not moving,* Hurley thought. He fired three or four pairs of rockets at the elusive guerrillas, walking the rounds in toward the scattering brown figures. "We're almost out of rockets," Contant cautioned. Hurley switched back to cannon and fired two more bursts of high explosive 30mm rounds. *It's time to switch tactics,* he thought. *We keep turning to the right. We've got to do something different.* He made a split-second decision to turn left and head south along the Whale, reasoning that they'd already cleared that route a couple of minutes earlier flying in the opposite direction. But "clearing" a 6,000-meter ridgeline by flying 400 feet above it at over 100 miles per hour is not an ideal method for ensuring it is free of enemy, as Hurley and Contant were about to discover. In the shadows of a crevice at what soldiers would call the Whale's "military crest"—about twenty-five meters below the actual top of the ridge—an Al Qaida gunner shouldered his RPG launcher, sensing opportunity. He might even have been the same gunner they'd observed a couple of minutes previously. Although they'd seen him aiming at Chenault's aircraft, they hadn't seen him fire. Maybe he'd been waiting for a better chance. Having decelerated to ensure greater accuracy, Hurley was just low and slow enough to allow an expert RPG gunner to line the Apache up in his launcher's metal sights. As Hurley turned left and pulled abreast of the Whale, the gunner pulled the trigger. Unseen by Hurley and Contant, a small puff of smoke marked the launch point as the rocket-assisted projectile hurtled toward their aircraft. It detonated as it struck the helicopter's left Hellfire launcher, destroying all three missiles on the pylon. Shrapnel tore through the adjacent rocket pod. The helicopter bucked with the force of the explosion. Before Hurley had time to process what had happened, bullets were smacking against the airframe. One burst through the left side of the cockpit at the same moment that the RPG hit. Whizzing inches in front of Hurley's knee and hand, the bullet lodged in the console. A small piece of metal debris hit him in the leg. For an awful moment he thought he'd been shot.

A dozen bullets hit the helicopter's fuselage, but Hurley didn't hear or feel them. "What got my attention was the bullet that came through the cockpit," he said. "I'm hit, but I'm okay!" he yelled to Contant. Momentarily confused, he wondered how the impact of one small bullet could make the aircraft rock so much. Leaning forward and peering out of the cockpit to his left, he saw a Hellfire's seeker head hanging down from the pylon. The rest of the missile was missing. It began to dawn on him that he'd been hit by something larger than a bullet. As he straightened the helicopter out, he heard the *Whoop! Whoop! Whoop!* of an alarm in his headphones. The master caution light—a big light on the left of the dashboard designed to draw attention to smaller warning lights that indicate problems with individual systems—flashed an ominous red. Hurley scanned the array of sixty caution lights to see which were on. The first to flash was the fail light for the helicopter's back-up control system, a fly-by-wire system for use in case of problems with the main controls. One of two main transmission oil lights was flickering, as if hesitant to announce bad news, and the helicopter was handling sluggishly. Hurley's gut told him he wasn't going to be able to keep the Apache aloft for much longer.

He keyed his mike. "Hey, Rich, I'm hit," he said to his wingman. "I need to know, where do you guys want me to put this?" But Chenault was now on the northeastern side of the Whale, putting the ridgeline's rocky bulk directly between the two helicopters. The Apaches' radios operate on a line-of-sight principle. Chenault might as well have been on the dark side of the moon. All Hurley heard was the hiss of static. As he reached the southern tip of the

Whale, both transmissions' oil pressure lights flashed on. Low on ammo, the weapons stores on his left wing destroyed, and with oil and smoke pouring from his aircraft over enemy territory, he figured now was a good time to call his maintenance god.

At that moment Hardy and Pebsworth were dealing with a few problems of their own. Unable to shoot, Hardy fell back on a game he had learned as a young AH-1 Cobra pilot. Back then it involved sending an unarmed OH-58 Kiowa scout helicopter out ahead of his Cobra. The idea was that the Kiowa would draw fire by offering such an inviting target that the enemy was compelled to engage it as it flew by. The enemy having revealed his position, the Cobra, following close behind, would move in for the kill. The game was called "hound and hare," and it involved an obvious risk to the crew of the Kiowa. Now Hardy was putting himself and Pebsworth in that unenviable position. With the damage his helicopter had sustained, no one would have questioned his right to withdraw immediately to Texaco to get his aircraft patched up. But he chose to remain on the battlefield, drawing fire for his colleagues as the Apaches circled the valley.

Drawing fire was easy. Avoiding it was tough.

The pilots were for the most part blissfully unaware of the DShK and Kalashnikov bullets peppering their aircraft. The RPGs were harder to ignore. The guerrillas were firing them at a rate of about one every minute, and each round's relatively slow velocity and short smoke trail meant the pilots could visually track the grenades as they flew through the air and exploded with a puff of black smoke that reminded Hamilton of World War II flak. "They're shooting RPGs at you," Hamilton told Hardy as the two helicopters flew along the ridgeline. "I don't want to hear about it. Just shoot them!" Hardy replied. Then Hurley called. He read off the cockpit warnings. Hardy listened with growing alarm. Hurley and Contant had to leave the battle and return to the FARP immediately. That much was clear. Normal practice called for the damaged Apache's wingman to leave with him. But Hurley's wingman was Rich Chenault, whose Apache was holding up relatively well in the maelstrom of RPG and DShK fire. "We need to go with that aircraft, because we can't shoot anyway," Pebsworth told Hardy. "It doesn't make any sense to send a good aircraft out of the fight."

His backseater agreed. "I've gotta go back to the FARP," Hardy told Hurley over the radio. "Fall in trail and follow me, and we've got to go quick." But first the two helicopters had to find each other—usually no easy task when all Apaches look alike and four of them were swarming like bees in a one kilometer by three kilometer slice of sky. The risk of a fiery midair collision was high. "Somehow we stayed away from each other," Pebsworth said. "That was amazing to me."

Hardy and Pebsworth easily identified Hurley's aircraft by the smoke streaming from the burning oil, and flew up beside the stricken Apache. "I'm dipping my nose so you can identify me," Hardy said over the radio. "I've got you," Hurley replied. The two Apaches flew out of the valley's southwest corner at high speed, turned north toward the FARP and scooted along the western side of the Whale. Hardy had Hurley take the lead, so that if the latter's Apache caught fire, the pilots in the trailing aircraft would be able to spot it and alert Hurley and Contant instantly. But no more than two kilometers northwest of the Whale more lights started blinking insistently in Hurley's cockpit. Their message was blunt: You have no oil left in your transmission. Hurley called off the lights to Hardy as they flashed on. The maintenance pilot knew there was no choice about what had to be done. He needed to assess the aircraft's condition immediately. "You've got to land, and you've got to land now," he told Hurley.

Spotting a wadi below them that might offer a little protection from any enemy in the area, the pilots steered their helicopters toward it and landed almost simultaneously on a dirt road that ran through the middle of the creek bed. It was a rough landing for Hurley. He had lost the system that stabilizes the aircraft as it lands, and the helicopter rocked forward and backward as he brought it in. As soon as he set the helicopter down in the 100-foot-wide river bed, the extent of the damage it had sustained became vividly apparent. "It was like a hunter when he guts a deer," Pebsworth said. "He set it down and all this stuff falls out from underneath it. Transmission fluid was leaking from that aircraft from nose to tail."

Although the pilots' position was perilous—they were within sight and weapons range of Al Qaida positions on the Whale, and they could still hear the din of the battle raging in the Shahikot—Pebsworth hadn't lost his sense of humor. "I think he's got a transmission fluid leak," he told his backseater with more than a hint of sarcasm.

Jumping out of his cockpit, Hardy told Hurley to shut his engine down. As the rotors slowed, the maintenance pilot opened the cowlings and began to inspect the engine, much like a doctor conducting a triage examination of a patient. The damage to the Apache was shocking. In addition to the torn and dented rocket pod and the mangled Hellfires, the Apache had a cracked rotor blade and almost three dozen bullet holes, out of which the last of its transmission fluid was leaking. It was a testament to the helicopter's sturdy design that it was still flying at all, and that neither pilot had been hit.

Hardy had a tough decision to make. It was a decision that could prove fatal if he chose wrong, and he had to make it fast. One option was to try to fly the helicopter back to Texaco, about thirty minutes' flying time away. Thanks to engine bearings that have a felt wicking designed to collect and hold oil, helping to lubricate an otherwise dry engine, the Apache is supposed to be able to fly for thirty minutes with no oil. That, at least, was the manufacturers' claim. But it had never been done before, and this was a hell of a time to put the theory to the test. The alternative was to fly back to Texaco with Hurley and Contant strapped to the wings of his helicopter. This was not quite as dangerous as it sounds, and—although never done in training—is an approved method for evacuating downed pilots in such situations. Each Apache carries nylon ropes with a metal D-ring attached for just such a purpose. However, it would mean abandoning Hurley's damaged Apache. Such an outcome held no appeal for Hardy, a plainspoken man who had grown up on a farm in Alabama and now raised cattle for market on a farm of his own.

"It would have been a superior victory for these guys to shoot down one of those Apaches, and that was something we couldn't let happen, something I wasn't going to let happen," he said. As A Company's maintenance test pilot, Hardy viewed all the aircraft as "his." Of the four pilots in the wadi, his maintenance background, and long years of flying gave him the best "feel" for the Apache, a fingertip sense of the nuances required when flying a badly damaged bird to safety. His thoughts drifted back to a promise he had made Jim Marye the previous evening. "I told Lieutenant Colonel Marye that if an aircraft went down, instead of sending more guys out there to get shot at, if it could crank, I'd fly it out of there."

Hardy told Hurley to trade seats with him, and that he was flying the leaking Apache back to the FARP. The distinctive sound of the other Apaches' 30mm fire could be heard over the roar of his own aircraft's engine as he announced the decision—a reminder of how close to the enemy they were. "There wasn't time for a committee decision," Hardy said. "The bad guys were just on the other side of the hill." Hardy set a clock in the dashboard so he could keep track of exactly how long he had been in the air. "Don't dick around," he told Hurley. "When I get it started, I'm going."

Each Apache carried three spare one-quart cans of oil for emergencies. Well, this qualified as an emergency under anybody's definition, so Hardy grabbed all six cans and emptied them into the leaking transmission, then hoisted himself up to the cockpit. When he saw Hardy climbing into 203's backseat and realized what that meant, Contant, who had stayed in the aircraft, was alarmed. "He didn't want to go at first," Hardy said. "I was called 'stupid' along with some other adjectives to go along with it. But the airplane wasn't going to be left there. I was flying with him or without him. He sucked it up, and we took off." Pebsworth, who had also remained in his aircraft, with the engine running and rotors spinning, was just glad to be leaving. "I was scared," he said. "I was paranoid." The only Al Qaida-held position from which the helicopters could be seen was the top of the Whale. Pebsworth's eyes were glued to that ridgeline, watching for any enemy fire or movement. *We're sitting ducks if they come over the top,* he thought. But the guerrillas failed to notice that two of their most highly prized targets were located so vulnerably just two kilometers away, and less than ten minutes after the Apaches landed, they were airborne again.

Any margin for error that might have existed evaporated when the helicopters took off and immediately flew in the wrong direction. One of the three dozen bullets that hit 203 had lodged in the computer that took Doppler and GPS information and put it into the navigation system, with the result that the electronic compass had stuck on a heading of due north—the direction they needed to fly in. Not realizing this, Hardy, flying lead, thought he was heading north toward the FARP when he had actually pointed the aircraft east-northeast toward Pakistan. In the trailing aircraft Pebsworth's navigational equipment was also barely functional. Information that should have been flowing into the system was being held up at the severed wire harness, like a vital of convoy of supplies stuck on one side of a collapsed bridge. Dispensing with the high-tech approach, Pebsworth got out his map and spread it on his lap, using the basics of time flown, distance covered and heading to navigate. He quickly realized they needed to turn around, and relayed the information over the radio to Hardy, who reversed course.

Now it was a race against time. Hardy was flying four or five rotor discs ahead of the Apache now flown by Hurley, so that the pilots in the rear helicopter would be able to warn him early if his engine caught fire or any other visible problem developed. But visibility was proving tricky for Hurley and Pebsworth. The oil Hardy had poured into 203's transmission was spraying out through the bullet holes and coating the Plexiglas canopy of their cockpit. The 140-mile-per-hour flight was the ultimate white knuckle ride. Pebsworth had plotted a flight back to the FARP that took them over the lowest ground he could find, in case Hardy had to put the helicopter down. But the initial wrong turn out of the wadi put paid to that plan. Now the pilots counted down the minutes as the refigured route took them over snow-covered mountain passes in which, were 203's engines to fail, there was nowhere to make an emergency landing.

After twenty minutes the Apaches crested a 7,000-foot mountain range. Spread before them was a flat brown plain. By Pebsworth's reckoning, somewhere ahead in that dun expanse of semi-desert lay the FARP and salvation. After several increasingly tense minutes the pilots spotted the green hulk of a Chinook sitting on the ground less than two miles ahead. It was Texaco—nothing more than a patch of sand dotted with a few helicopters and tents, and soldiers nervously scanning the sky. Hardy eased his aircraft down to the ground, no easy task with the flying dirt and sand creating "brown out" conditions that can disorient a pilot. With immense relief, he shut down the engines. It was twenty-six minutes since he had taken off from the wadi. Then Jim Hardy jumped out of the cockpit, and into Army aviation history.

"There are not a lot of folks out there who would have taken that aircraft off the ground," Ryan said. "It was an incredible action by Mr. Hardy."

AS sounds of battle echoed around the compound, the 2-187 leaders conferred. They were with C Company's 2nd Platoon. Baltazar's other two platoons had landed in other LZs along the eastern ridge and were also taking fire. *Today is not going to be like it was planned,* Nielsen thought. Preysler also realized everything had changed. It didn't look like anyone was trying to escape the valley. The enemy was trying to kill Americans, not run away from them. But over the radio he heard that Task Force Hammer was still on its way, so his mission remained to establish the blocking positions as soon as possible. The fire his troops were taking from enemy positions all around the compound only heightened his sense of urgency. *We need to get out of this area,* he thought. *It's too hot. We need to fight our way up to the high ground, to our original blocking positions.*

The southernmost of those blocking positions was Diane, on the slopes of a mountain known as Hill 3033 (its height in meters) directly east of Babulkhel. Responsibility for setting up Diane fell to C Company's 3rd Platoon, led by Sergeant First Class Kelly Jack Luman. Also on his Chinook were a handful of soldiers from Preysler's scout platoon, under the command of 1st Lieutenant Glen Helberg, twenty-four, whose mission was to establish an observation post directly west of Diane on a hilltop halfway between the eastern ridge and Serkhankhel. Pilots Fichter and Anderson executed a difficult landing in a narrow ravine that sloped down to the valley floor. As the helicopter hovered with only its rear wheels barely touching the ground, the troops jumped off the ramp. As soon as they hit the ground, the scouts split from Luman's platoon and headed north-northwest, up a shale-covered hill, down into a draw, and then up again, struggling to keep their balance as their feet slid in the snow. The altitude hit the scouts hard. Each was carrying roughly 140 pounds of gear

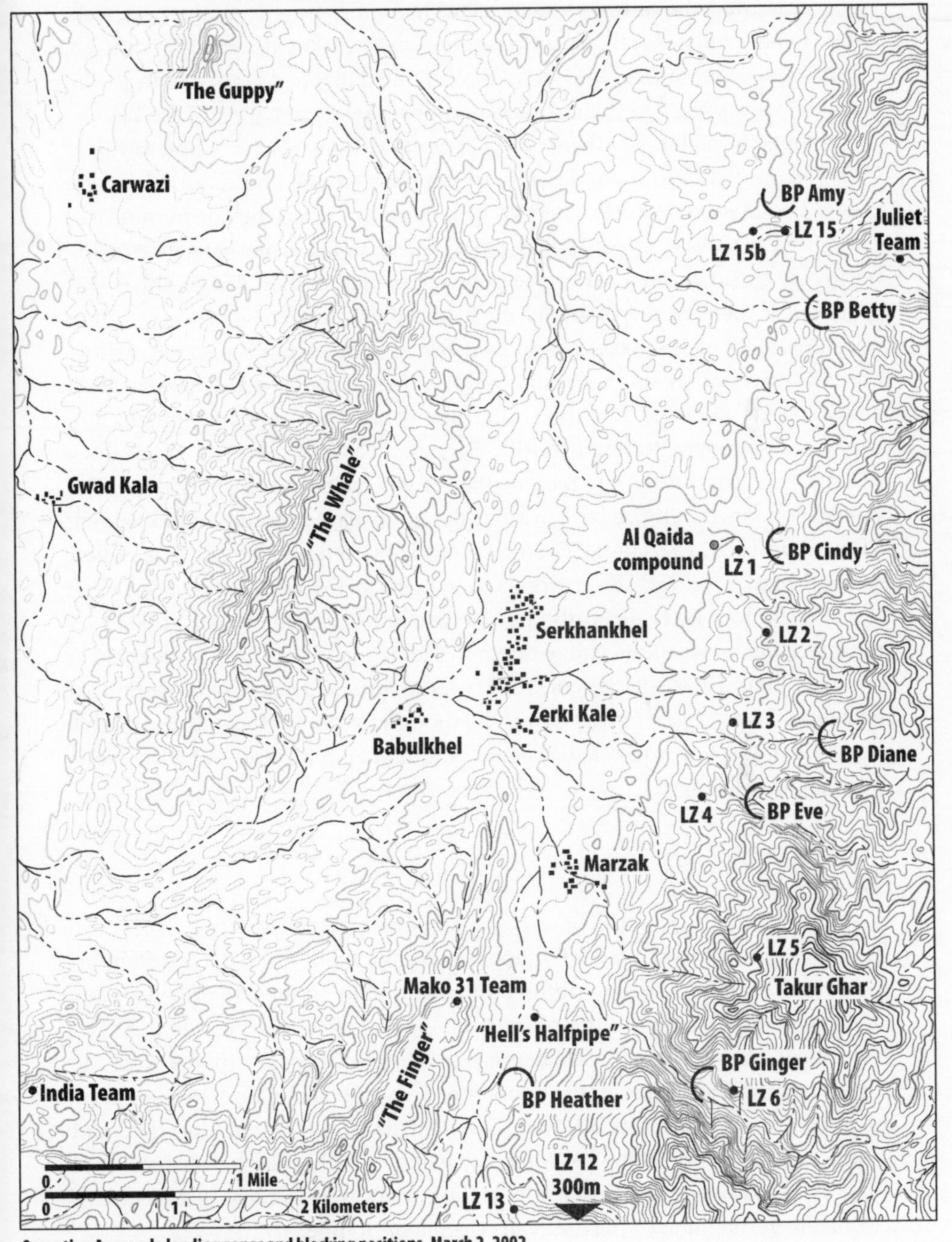

Operation Anaconda landing zones and blocking positions, March 2, 2002

that seemed to bear down on their shoulders more heavily with every step. After Helberg took a brief detour to talk to—and get shot at with—Rick Busko, 2-187's operations officer, who led a small element that had landed with 1st Platoon, the scouts reached their observation post, 400 meters west of the LZ.

About 750 meters southeast of Helberg and Luman's LZ, Captain Roger Crombie landed with a similar mix of infantry, scouts, and assorted attachments. Crombie commanded 1-87's A Company. His job as the northernmost of LaCamera's chalks was to establish Blocking Position Eve astride a pass on the north side of Takur Ghar. After deciding not to land in their assigned LZ—LZ 5—because there were personnel on it, the pilots landed in a wadi farther north, only about 100 meters from Eve. But after releasing the scouts, whose objective was farther south, Crombie and his men faced a back-breaking climb a steep slope to get to Eve. En route they spotted two enemy fighters in a crevice 150 meters to their north. Sergeant Reginald Huber fired three M203 40mm grenades at the pair, neither of whom looked over eighteen. The grenades bounced off the back wall of the guerrillas' position and exploded. "They didn't stand a chance," Crombie said. They continued to climb as bullets cracked high overhead, fired from somewhere to the north. When Crombie reached the top, he realized the two-hour climb had been worth it. He had commanding views of the valley down to Marzak, and was only vulnerable to fire from Takur Ghar, the peak of which was about 1,800 meters to the southeast on a map. *This is a good piece of terrain,* he thought. *We can defend this.* He got his satellite radio set up and called the 1-87 command post to find out how things were going elsewhere.

7.

THE scene on board the three Chinooks carrying about 120 10th Mountain infantrymen into the Shahikot differed little from that on the trio of helicopters that had landed their brethren from the 101st a few minutes earlier. The men aboard these aircraft had been away from home longer than any of the other conventional troops in the operation. They had spent long, boring hours guarding the perimeter at K2, and, like their division commander, they had resigned themselves to the likelihood that they would return home without having the chance to fire any bullets at the enemy. Now, almost unexpectedly, they were getting that opportunity. It was payback time.

Frank Grippe, the troops' sergeant major, detected "a feeling of elation that we're actually finally going to go in and do the overt offensive operations that we're so well trained in." But the strapping non-com ensured that his NCOs didn't allow their enthusiasm to overwhelm their professionalism. He made sure every one of his sergeants going into the Shahikot understood that the mountainous terrain would break battalions, companies, and platoons into squads and sections. This was going to be "a sergeant's fight."

One of the sergeants most frustrated with the way the battalion's war had turned out so far was a trim twenty-nine-year-old squad leader with short, spiky blond hair riding in the second helicopter. Little in Staff Sergeant Andrzej (pronounced Andr-zhey) Ropel's early years suggested he would one day be leading American infantryman in combat. Born and raised under Communist rule in northeast Poland, where he and a friend taught themselves English in their spare time, Ropel had evaded compulsory military service in his homeland by having a doctor who was a family friend sign a form saying Andrzej had a spinal problem ("which of course was fake").

Ropel's life changed the day his mother won a visa lottery that allowed her to move to the United States with her family. Andrzej's parents moved to New York, but, unsure whether he wanted to leave Poland, their son accompanied them over to help them settle, but stayed for only ten days. That was all it took. "I loved New York City," he recalled. "That was the city for me." He returned to Europe, but only to settle up his affairs there. A few months later he stepped off a plane at New York's JFK Airport, this time with the goal of making a new life for himself in America. The sort of fellow who always lands on his feet, Ropel worked a series of jobs in construction, personal care for the elderly, and upscale commercial decorating. All the time he improved his English and fell slowly in love with the United States, where, as he put it, "starting from basically nothing, by working hard you can actually achieve something."

But by the mid-1990s Ropel felt he needed a new challenge. He was thinking of going to college, but couldn't see how he could make that leap straight from his decorating job. He decided to join the Army, a decision many young Americans in his position make, but a curious choice for a man who had been so determined to avoid entering the ranks in Poland. However, Ropel discerned a stark difference between the U.S. military and what he had seen of the military in Poland. "In the U.S. Army a soldier has dignity," he said. "Over there he didn't."

In March 1996 he entered basic training after enlisting as an 11 Bravo—an infantryman. Possessed of a sharp, technically oriented mind, Ropel could have had his choice of less combat-focused Army jobs that might have prepared him for a lucrative career after his service, but he never had any regrets about becoming a grunt. "I think the infantry is the best school of life," he said. "I cannot even imagine myself working for ten hours a day like we do and just sitting behind a desk doing paperwork." A four-year stint in Hawaii with the undermanned 25th Infantry Division (Light) gave him the opportunity to learn a variety of infantry positions—from rifleman to antitank gunner manning an obsolescent Dragon missile launcher to company armorer to mortarman—treating each as an opportunity to expand his knowledge. He earned his Expert Infantryman Badge and after four years left Hawaii as a sergeant for the distinctly chillier climes of Fort Drum. There he found the pace of training slower than in the Pacific, as a result of the harsh winters, but the unit cohesion stronger.

September 11, 2001, found Ropel halfway through an eight-week course for young sergeants at Fort Benning, Georgia. Stunned, he watched in a television lounge filled with silent soldiers as the news replayed again and again the destruction of the World Trade Center, a complex he had helped decorate for Christmas 1992. At Fort Drum, 1-87 Infantry was alerted for possible deployment within days. Ropel called his unit and pleaded in vain to be allowed out of the course so he could deploy with them. But his senior NCOs told him the course was important for his career, and that if they left before he graduated, he could follow them over. The rest of the battalion deployed for K2 a few days before Ropel graduated as a distinguished honor graduate from his course. As soon as the ceremony finished, Ropel, still wearing his Class A dress uniform, jumped in his car at midday and started the long drive to Fort Drum, sleeping for three hours in a truck stop before arriving on post at 4 p.m. the next day. He drove straight to the battalion headquarters, where he ran into the absurd lengths to which the military sometimes goes in order to convince itself that it is dutifully protecting operational security. His own chain of command wouldn't tell him officially that the unit had deployed to Uzbekistan. "It was a joke," he recalled. "You could find out more from TV sometimes than from your own commander." It was an open secret that the battalion had gone to K2, and all Ropel was concerned with was catching up with them as soon as possible. But to his immense frustration, the date of his deployment was repeatedly delayed. He finally left on November 21.

But at K2 he found only more frustration. "We did everybody else's job, but not ours," he said. The infantrymen—trained to close with and destroy the enemy—were put to work cleaning latrines and functioning as military police. Only those elements designated as the quick reaction force had a job that fell within the mission profile of an infantry unit. Ropel's squad got to spend a few weeks conducting security missions for Task Force Dagger in Mazar-i-Sharif and Sheberghan in northern Afghanistan. That was better than sitting around the airfield at K2, but when they returned to Uzbekistan they embarked on an emotional roller coaster that was to last a month. First they were told they were headed back to Fort Drum. Then the news changed: They were going to Bagram instead. At first morale plummeted, as would be expected when troops who have made the mental switch from "going to war" to "going home" are told they aren't going home yet after all. But soon after they arrived in Bagram, it became clear that they had not been brought down for more of the same sort of glorified gate-guard duty that they had been performing at K2. A real mission was in the offing. For Ropel, the sergeant who loved leading soldiers, but hated the monotony of guard duty, the prospect of a combat mission was a godsend. He was not alone. "Morale went up because we were actually going to do something," Ropel said. But the briefing they received February 25 made the chances of seeing combat during Anaconda seem remote, and the last few days' training before D-Day had focused almost exclusively on the procedures for properly apprehending and searching detainees, not on combat. As his Chinook turned into the southeast corner of the Shahikot, Ropel, who had to put his application for U.S. citizenship on hold when he deployed, was anticipating little more from Operation Anaconda than a break from the tedium of camp life. "We did not expect we were actually going to have any [enemy] contact," Ropel said. "I don't think anybody expected that."

Scrunched into a seat in the back of the lead Chinook was another young sergeant whose path into the ranks of the infantry's NCO corps had been less than straightforward. Like Ropel in the helicopter behind his, thirty-year-old Staff Sergeant Randel Perez was a squad leader in Charlie Company, 1-87 Infantry. But unlike his Polish counterpart, this grandson of Mexican immigrants hadn't envisioned himself leading troops in combat when he joined the Army. Far from it. Born and raised in the small Texan town of San Benito, twenty minutes from the Mexican border, Perez joined the Army in 1991 to escape the drudgery of life in the Rio Grande Valley. But the infantry's life of mud, blood, sweat, and tears was decidedly not what he was looking for. "When I joined the military, I was gonna come in, do two years, get some college money, and get out," he said. At the insistence, of his father, a senior Border Patrol agent who exerted a strong influence on his early life, Randy avoided the combat arms—infantry, armor, and artillery—and opted for a job as a supply clerk. His father's stated aim was to ensure his son's time in the military set him up for a job in civilian life, which he thought would be less likely if Randy chose a position in the combat arms. But Randy's father was also concerned about his son's physical safety in a branch like the infantry. "I think the fact that it was dangerous had a lot to do with it, too," Perez said.

Perez began his Army career at Fort McClellan, Alabama, a sleepy Southern post where his biggest challenge was confronting the racist attitudes that remained entrenched in the Deep South. He was called "half-breed" to his face in one restaurant. His black friends were, if anything, treated even worse. In the mid-1990s he was posted to Germany just as the Balkan peacekeeping missions were looming. Unlike McClellan, where he had worked in a large headquarters, in Germany he was assigned as the supply clerk for a mechanized infantry company, a job that entailed a much faster pace than he was accustomed to. "I wasn't really used to getting up early in the morning and doing PT," he said. "I wasn't used to going to the field." But he decided he liked the more soldierly approach of what he termed "the go-go-go Army."

A tour in Bosnia opened Perez's eyes to the possibility that greater job satisfaction could be found in the Army, but outside the supply corps. His company was undermanned, so he was pressed into service on raids as a makeshift infantryman. He noticed the sergeants in a combat unit had a responsibility he had never experienced in his "soft skill" job, and the infantry platoons had a cohesiveness missing from the noncombat organizations he had observed. "There was thirty-odd guys, and they were like one big family," he recalled. *This is pretty cool,* he thought. *I could do this for a living.* The soldiers' role on the raids reminded him a little of that of police officers. Perez had always suspected that his father wanted him to follow him into the law enforcement world. *Maybe this ain't following exactly in his footsteps, but it's close to it, and it'd probably make me happy,* he thought. Perez made up his mind to become an infantryman. He knew he'd make a good one. Now he just had to persuade the Army to allow him to make the switch from supply clerk to infantry sergeant.

The Army in the 1990s had a chronic shortage of infantrymen, but it was still the Army—a large impersonal bureaucracy in which common sense often went missing in action. What should have been straightforward—keeping a soldier in the Army by permitting him to enter a field that was short of men and which he wanted to join—instead became tied up in red tape. In Germany, Perez argued in vain to be allowed to follow his dream. The reaction of those above him veered between bemusement at why anyone would want to become an infantryman several years into their career and intense pressure to reenlist as a supply clerk. He reluctantly did so, adding only a year to his current enlistment, and was reassigned to an air traffic control unit at Fort Campbell. There he took up the fight again, only to run into similar resistance (although his commanders, former infantrymen themselves, tried to help).

The breakthrough came when a Pentagon bureaucrat visited Fort Campbell to find out why the post's reenlistment numbers were down. Perez's superiors put the two together and Perez again pleaded his case. He noted that people are always trying to get out of the infantry, and that hardly anyone ever tries to get into the infantry, a point with which the suit concurred. Then Perez made his pitch: He was willing to forgo any resigning bonus, to reenlist for six years (the longest reenlistment allowed) and, to top it all off, he was willing to relocate to Fort Drum, one of the coldest, snowiest, and, in most soldiers' eyes, least desirable posts in the Army. "Are you serious?" the bemused bureaucrat asked. "Are you really willing to do all this?" Assured that Perez was indeed serious, the bureaucrat went to work. Not long afterward, Perez was headed to Fort Benning, where all new infantry recruits are trained. But his trials had only just begun. Due to a paperwork screwup, he was forced to go through basic training again, this time as a sergeant among a horde of teenage privates. It was a couple of weeks before the drill sergeants realized the mistake and pushed him straight into advanced individual training—the infantry-specific course that follows basic training.

After completing AIT, Perez headed straight to Drum, assigned to 1-87 Infantry. By now he was a staff sergeant, the rank of a squad leader. But he encountered a marked reluctance on the part of the battalion's senior NCOs to entrust the lives of nine men to a squad leader who'd never spent a day in an infantry platoon before. Initially told there was a squad leader position for him in A Company, he headed to the company headquarters, where he met with the company first sergeant and one of his platoon sergeants. They asked Perez to wait outside the door, but it stayed open a crack, and he had to endure the indignity of overhearing the two NCOs talk with each other about how they didn't want a "supply guy" running one of their squads. They emerged from the meeting and told him there was no job for him in the company. The battalion sergeant major of the time sent him to C Company instead. Again he was made to wait in a hallway while others discussed what to do with him. But his luck changed when Sergeant First Class Thomas Abbott, the platoon sergeant for 1st Platoon, ran into him sitting there. "You're the new staff sergeant?" Abbott said. "We'll take you." Conditioned to disappointment, Perez explained his background to Abbott, expecting the platoon sergeant to change his mind. "Who gives a fuck?" Abbott said. "Come on in here, we'll take you." And just like that the supply guy became a light infantry squad leader.

Recognizing that Perez's enthusiasm and determination more than compensated for his lack of infantry experience, Abbott took the new squad leader under his wing, helping him climb the steep learning curve he needed to ascend in order to earn the respect of his men and his fellow NCOs. Perez applied himself fiercely to the task, burning with ambition to make all those who had doubted him eat their words. "I didn't want to fail, because I didn't want nobody to come back and say, 'Well, of course he's fucked up; that's the former supply guy,'" he said. His efforts earned him a gradual acceptance into the infantry fraternity, but inevitably some questions remained. Frank Grippe took over as the 1-87 command sergeant major a few weeks after Perez arrived, and was surprised to find out that one of his squad leaders used to be a supply clerk. *What a ballsy individual,* the former Ranger thought after his first meeting with Perez, *but I hope he knows what he's getting himself into.*

What Perez was getting into at dawn on March 2, 2002, was exactly the situation his father had hoped he would avoid. As the Chinook made the final turn into the valley, Staff Sergeant Randel Perez, infantry squad leader, was about to jump into the middle of the fiercest battle U.S. troops had fought in a generation.

Perez was flying on the first of the three helicopters carrying 10th Mountain troops. The troops on his helicopter—collectively known as Chalk 1—included 1-87 commander Paul LaCamera, his command sergeant major, Frank Grippe, the Charlie Company commander, Captain Nelson Kraft, plus the men of 1st Platoon, led by 1st Lieutenant Brad Maroyka. Riding into battle on the second helicopter were LaCamera's operations officer, Major Jay Hall, an eight-man squad from the battalion's mortar section, plus 2nd Platoon. Together these men were known as Chalk 2. The third chalk was led by Crombie and was headed for a landing zone 2,000 meters northeast of the other two. The LZs for Chalks 1 and 2 were only 500 meters apart between Takur Ghar and the Finger, about a kilometer south of Marzak. From there 1st Platoon was to move a few hundred meters southwest to set up Blocking Position Heather, cutting off the valley's southern exit, while 2nd Platoon hiked a similar distance southeast to establish Blocking Position Ginger overlooking the deep gorge that ran to the south of Takur Ghar.

Like almost everyone else onboard the helicopters, Kraft, thirty, from Toledo, Ohio, was glad to finally have the opportunity to get into the fight. His company was the battalion's main effort. Setting up the blocking positions struck the ROTC graduate of Ohio's Bowling Green State University, as "a simple 'defend' task." But he had also paid attention when LaCamera reiterated one of his favorite phrases—"The enemy gets a vote"—an Army saying that means that no matter how good the plan is, the enemy will seek to make his decisions count on the battlefield. "The enemy has a vote and he will make sure that he places it, so be ready," LaCamera had told his subordinates.

A stocky figure with a long history in the Rangers, LaCamera was hard to get to know, with a reserve easily mistaken for hostility. But those who had fought with him swore by him. LaCamera heard over the radio on the flight down that TF Hammer was meeting heavy resistance. *Okay, these guys are fighting.* The battalion commander was prepared for that. He'd made sure his first lift of Chinooks was "heavy on the trigger-pullers," while holding the psychological operations troops assigned to him and the few journalists embedded in his battalion back until the second lift.

He was confident in his men. Since taking command in May, he had focused 1-87 on the "four basics": battle drills, physical training, marksmanship, and medical skills. LaCamera took the last item very seriously. Light infantrymen often fought far from the nearest field hospital and had to rely on whatever and whomever they brought to the fight to provide lifesaving medical care. He had almost succeeded in his goal of getting each of his soldiers qualified as a combat lifesaver, a step between the Army's "buddy aid" and the platoon medic, and he had sent his medics to train with emergency medical technicians in New York City, treating gunshot wounds. As for marksmanship, to LaCamera, it was a case of simple logic. He told his soldiers there were only two sorts of people on a battlefield—marksmen and targets. Left unsaid was that sometimes it was impossible to avoid being both.

8.

CHALKS 1 and 2 touched down almost simultaneously at their LZs 13A and 13 respectively. The soldiers rushed down the ramps and set up their perimeters around the helicopters, ducking instinctively as they ran under the giant rotor blades. So far so good. Wiercinski had achieved his overriding goal of getting all six Chinooks on the ground safely. Now it was up to the infantry to do their job. The first Chalk 1 soldiers off the bird looked up from behind their rucksacks and took the measure of the battlefield. They were in the southeastern corner of the Shahikot. Takur Ghar rose ominously to the east, its saddled peak 750 meters above the valley floor. A few hundred meters to the west the Finger pointed straight at the Shahikot's heart, its northernmost slopes almost reaching the village of Serkhankhel. From where the soldiers lay or kneeled, the valley rose gently toward the south. Less than a kilometer to the north sat Marzak, a collection of single-story adobe buildings. The light brown soil between the troops and the village had been divided into terraced onion fields. Patches of snow covered about thirty percent of the valley floor, and all of the upper ridgelines and mountainsides. Like the AFO operators before them, the Mountain troops quickly realized that their maps bore only a vague resemblance to reality. The contour lines only reflected differences of fifty meters or more.The rolling hillocks and small ridgelines that crisscrossed the valley did not appear on them.

The first thing Sergeant Jerry Higley noticed was the dead silence that reigned after the Chinooks flew away. It lasted only a few moments, barely enough time for the twenty-six-year-old heavyset squad leader in Kraft's 1st Platoon to get to his feet and start moving. Then the first bullets zipped over the troops' heads. *Welcome to the Shahikot.* For all but a few of the men who'd just flown in, getting shot at was a new experience. It took some getting used to. Despite LaCamera's admonition in the run-up to Anaconda that the enemy had a vote, Kraft still had to mentally adjust to the fact that someone was trying to kill him. Brad Maroyka, the 1st Platoon leader, had already begun moving to Blocking Position Heather. He called Kraft with a statement of the obvious: "We're taking direct fire." "Roger, so are we," Kraft replied. "Continue with your mission."

The rest of the troops at the LZ moved out. As the first sporadic bursts of gunfire echoed round the mountains, Grippe looked up, trying to identify the source. Unable to spot the enemy locations among the rocks and crevices on the eastern ridge, he instead had the soldiers shoot at trees and boulders he considered the enemy's most likely hiding spots.

Higley and his platoon sergeant, Thomas Abbott, moved southwest with half a dozen men to a snow-covered ridgeline no more than ten feet high. Sergeant Bill Sakisit, walking point, crested the ridge and was pointing to what looked like a trail on the western side when a mortar round exploded several meters in front of him, causing him to duck. As the others got to the top, they saw black-clad figures moving about on the Finger, several hundred meters ahead of them. Abbott and Higley quickly arranged their men in pairs of marksmen and spotters. Higley began squeezing off rounds. The private first class acting as his spotter saw an enemy fighter crumple and get pulled away by one of his buddies. He let out an ecstatic yell. "You tagged his ass!" he whooped. Higley didn't share the private's enthusiasm. Before that moment the sergeant hadn't viewed America's enemies as human beings. That changed when he shot his first man. "Then you realize these are people, too," he said. "You don't really feel sorry for them, but you realize this is this guy's friend that just got whacked. You start thinking about it the way that someone outside the military might." *Okay, I'm kinda done here, I'd like to take off now,* he thought. But he kept firing.

Kraft's plan was to stay with 1st Platoon at least until 2nd Platoon had established Blocking Position Ginger. But 1st Platoon hadn't moved more than about 100 meters when there was a dramatic increase in the small arms fire cas-

(l to r) Brigadier General Gary Harrell, Lieutenant General Paul Mikolashek and Major General "Buster" Hagenbeck discuss plans at Bagram. *(Joe Raedle/Getty Images)*

The courtyard of the Gardez safe house where AFO planned the most audacious U.S. special operations mission in many years. *(U.S. Army)*

Dinner in the Gardez safe house. Seated at the table are (l to r) Hoskheyar, Zia Lodin, a U.S. Special Forces officer, and Rasul. Zia was the "G-chief" in whom Task Force Dagger placed so much faith. *(U.S. Army)*

Frank Wiercinski gives his eve-of-battle speech to his troops in Bagram. "Remember our motto: 'Let valor not fail.' *Rakkasans!*" *(Photo by Warren Zinn, copyright Army Times Publishing Co.)*

Pete Blaber, whose ethos was "audacity, audacity and audacity." *(U.S. Army)*

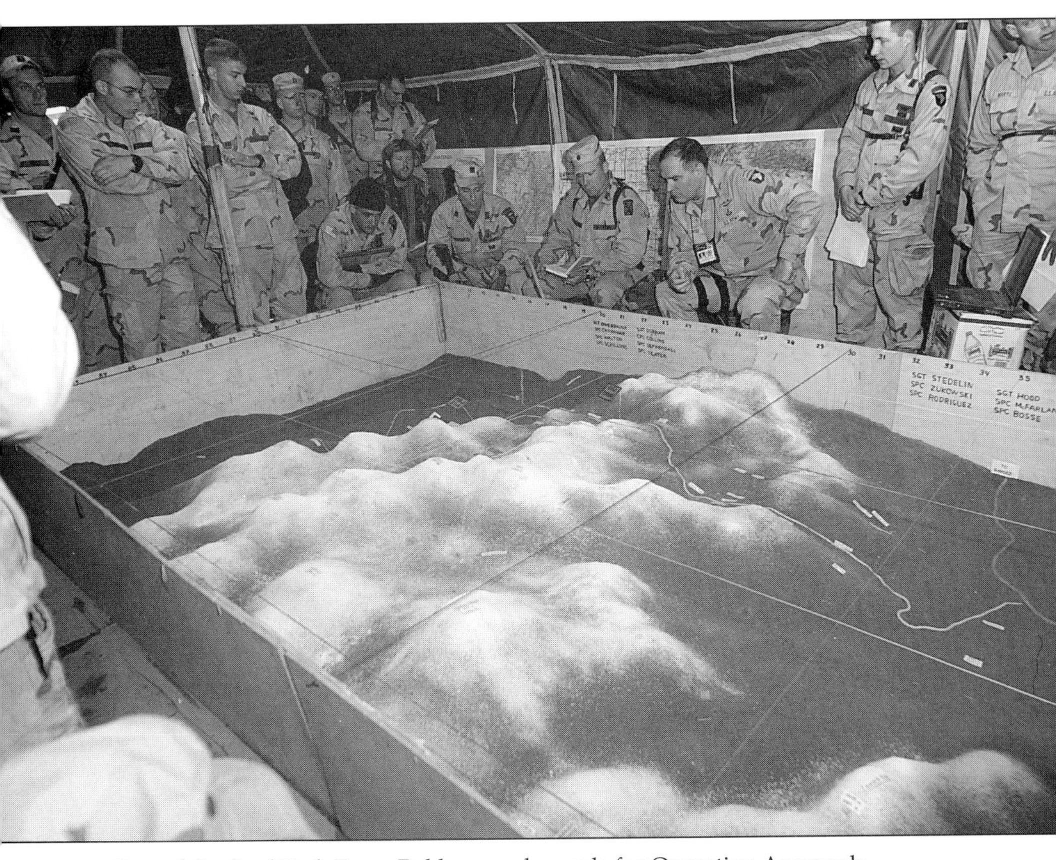

One of the final Task Force Rakkasan rehearsals for Operation Anaconda. Seated around the sand table are (l to r) Lieutenant Colonels Chip Preysler, Ron Corkran and Paul LaCamera, and Colonel Frank Wiercinski. The author of this book is seated between and behind Preysler and Corkran.

(Photo by Warren Zinn, copyright Army Times Publishing Co.)

The enemy position that the SEAL Team 6 commandos of Mako 31 discovered March 1, 2002. *(U.S. Navy)*

The DShK machine gun that would have wrought havoc with the Task Force Rakkasan Chinooks, had Mako 31 not dealt with it. *(U.S. Navy)*

The DShK gunner who took such good care of his weapon. Note his Caucasian appearance. *(U.S. Navy)*

The aftermath of the attack on the enemy position by Mako 31 and an AC-130 gunship a couple of hours before the Task Force Rakkasan air assault landed in the valley. *(U.S. Navy)*

Private First Class David Brown, a 10th Mountain Division mortarman, crawling up the outer slope of "Hell's Halfpipe" on the first day of Operation Anaconda. *(SFC Michael Peterson/U.S. Army)*

Perilous moments on "Rak TAC Ridge." From his position on the Finger, Frank Wiercinski (second from left) coordinates the larger battle as his tiny band of men hold off the enemy. Furthest from the camera is Mako 31's Air Force combat controller, Andy. *(U.S. Army)*

The Al Qaida compound seized by Chip Preysler's men on D-Day. Takur Ghar looms in the background. *(U.S. Army)*

Andrjez Ropel, the Polish sergeant who earned a Bronze Star for valor fighting for the U.S. Army in Operation Anaconda. *(U.S. Army)*

Kevin Butler's mortar section fires a round from the wadi near Landing Zone 15. Their superb shooting helped knock out an Al Qaida mortar position that had harassed U.S. troops all day. *(Photo by Warren Zinn, copyright Army Times Publishing Co.)*

Chip Preysler (l) and Mark Nielsen (r), after a couple of days fighting and moving in the Shahikot valley. *(U.S. Army)*

Gregory Trebon, the Air Force pilot who placed himself in charge of a close-in gunfight on top of a mountain. *(U.S. Air Force)*

Razor 01 shot down on top of Takur Ghar—a photo taken by a Ranger in the heat of battle. *(U.S. Army)*

TSgt. John Chapman *(Courtesy of Lori Longfritz)*

Nate Self, whose Rangers endured a hellish fight on Takur Ghar. *(U.S. Army)*

Anthony Miceli during the fight on Takur Ghar. He is holding Specialist Aaron Totten-Lancaster's SAW light machine gun after his own was shot in four places as he ran off the helicopter. *(U.S. Army)*

Looking down the barrel of Randy Pazder's machine gun during the fight on Takur Ghar. The intensity of the battle can be gauged by the pile of brass in the snow. In the middle distance is the ridgeline from which Al Qaida launched the counterattack that killed Jason Cunningham. *(U.S. Army)*

The wreckage of Razor 01 lying on Takur Ghar a few days after the battle, when most of the snow had melted. *(Photo by Department of Defense; notations by Chris Broz and Sean Naylor.)*

The "bonsai tree" and the shallow trenchline dug by Al Qaida on top of Takur Ghar. *(U.S. Army)*

The Al Qaida command tent hidden in a rock cleft on top of Takur Ghar. *(U.S. Army)*

A Chinook makes a tricky landing on a ridge in the Shahikot. *(U.S. Army)*

C Company, 2-187 Infantry, moves east to reoccupy Blocking Position Amy on March 4, 2002. *(U.S. Army)*

One of the CIA's Mi-17s at Bagram. The metal stakes in the foreground mark a minefield. *(Photo by Warren Zinn, copyright Army Times Publishing Co.)*

Jonathan Blossom stays low during the mortar duel.
(Photo by Warren Zinn, copyright Army Times Publishing Co.)

Tommy Franks congratulates 10th Mountain troops on March 18, 2002—the last day of Anaconda. *(Joe Raedle/Getty Images)*

Task Force Rakkasan troops returning to Bagram from the Shahikot March 12, 2002. *(Joe Raedle/Getty Images)*

David Brown (l) and Jason Ashline (r) of 1-87 Infantry fire a 120 mm mortar at Al Qaida positions March 9, 2002. *(Joe Raedle/Getty Images)*

cading down from the eastern ridge. As the guerrillas woke up and became aware of the enemies in their midst, the caliber of weaponry aimed at the Americans increased. The *whoosh* of RPGs was added to the din, to be followed by the deep thump of a mortar tube firing. No Americans were hit in these initial volleys, but Kraft could sense the plan slowly sliding away. "At that point, just because of the amount of fire they were throwing at us, it was obvious to me that we had to execute Battle Drill Two—React to Contact," he said.

Kraft and all the men around him dropped to the dirt. At that moment an RPG flew over their heads and hit the ground but failed to explode. Kraft's radio operator, Specialist John Ogilvie, looked at the warhead stuck in the ground making a buzzing noise, then turned to the captain with eyes as big as bowling balls. "Holy shit, sir! That one was close."

"Roger, we need to drop rucks and get the hell out of the kill zone," Kraft replied. That was no small decision the captain was announcing. Other than their weapons, water, and basic loads of ammunition, which they carried on their person, the soldiers' rucks contained almost everything they needed to fight and survive for a few days in the mountains. Inside the rucks were sleeping bags and other "snivel gear" to help them stay warm, as well as ammunition for the M240B machine guns (this was far too heavy for the two-man machine-gun teams to carry alone, so it was divided up so each soldier packed 100 rounds). Some soldiers had even stashed their night-vision goggles in their rucks, although others had worn them around their necks. But this was way more resistance than Kraft and his superiors had expected, and the rucks weighed about eighty-five pounds, not an inconsiderable load when you're trying to outrun bullets. Those 1st Platoon soldiers close enough to take cover behind rocks or dips in the ground began returning fire, allowing everyone else—the battalion and company command post personnel and the rest of 1st Platoon—to sprint to a bowl-shaped piece of terrain that seemed to offer some protection, leaving a trail of rucksacks all the way from the landing zone.

Once in the bowl—later dubbed "Hell's Halfpipe" by Specialist Brian McGraw—Kraft felt better. As a defensive position, it wasn't perfect, but it would certainly do. About 300 meters west of the lower slopes of Takur Ghar and a similar distance east of the Finger, Hell's Halfpipe was shaped like an enormous dugout canoe. It was 100 meters long and six meters wide at its base, with fifteen-meter slopes at its northern end and its western and eastern sides. Its southern end was open. (Jay Hall said its shape resembled that of a football stadium enclosed on three sides.) The problem was that to fire at the enemy on the eastern ridge, the soldiers had to crawl up the Halfpipe's eastern slope to its rock-strewn tip, exposing them to fire from the Finger. Soldiers engaging the

Al Qaida fighters on the Finger faced the same situation in reverse. Nevertheless, Hell's Halfpipe was eminently defensible and gave both the company and battalion command posts somewhere to set up their radios and allow the commanders to take stock. LaCamera established himself with his radio operator and Grippe at the northern end of the Halfpipe, about seventy-five meters north of Kraft's command post. Kraft was relieved that somehow none of the thousands of bullets that had been fired at his men had found their mark. As his men clambered up the slopes and began returning fire with a vengeance, the captain focused on his three priorities: getting Blocking Position Heather established, making contact with 2nd Platoon at the other LZ, and figuring out how to get the rucksacks back. He called Maroyka, the 1st Platoon leader, who was still taking cover near the LZ with a squad's worth of soldiers. The captain told him to press on and establish Heather. Then his 2nd Platoon leader, 1st Lieutenant Aaron O'Keefe, reported that his troops were also receiving fire.

O'Keefe's men had only moved about thirty meters from the LZ when the first RPG flew in with a sound Ropel described as "a deep whistling combined with static." "Incoming!" he yelled, diving to the frozen ground with the others. Again the 10th Mountain troops' guardian angel was watching over them as yet another RPG fizzled in the dirt without exploding. The soldiers got to their feet and shouldered their rucks, only for the unseen enemy nestled into crevices in the eastern ridgeline to open up on them with mortar and small arms fire. This time it was 2nd Platoon's turn to drop their rucks and sprint for cover. Immediately a pair of Apaches zoomed overhead. The pilots had spotted one of the enemy positions shooting at 2nd Platoon, and they subjected it to withering rocket and cannon fire, providing the troops on the ground with welcome relief in the process. The infantrymen were already realizing the drawbacks of landing on the valley floor. "You can only see so much from the ground," Ropel noted. And they could also only do so much with the light weapons they had brought to the fight—M4 assault rifles, SAWs, and M240B medium machine guns.

Task Force Rakkasan's limited number of Chinooks had forced Kraft to make hard decisions about what to bring in on his first lift. He had chosen to leave his 60mm mortars behind to make room for more riflemen. It was a decision he'd regret, but at the time it seemed justified. He knew LaCamera was bringing one of the battalion's 120mm mortars in on the same Chinook as 2nd Platoon. Between that, the Apaches, and fixed-wing close air support, Kraft figured he was covered for any fires he needed.

The man in charge of the only ground weapon more powerful than a medium machine gun that Task Force Rakkasan brought to the battle on March 2 was Sergeant First Class Michael Peterson, 1-87 Infantry's mortar platoon sergeant. "Sergeant Pete" had seven men under him: four to man the huge mortar tube and three to provide security. LaCamera had brought the 120 in on his first lift because it had a greater range and killing power than the battalion's 81mm mortars. The mortar had a range of 7,200 meters, long enough to support the 2-187 troops farther north if need be. And if it had to be brought into action, its shells could slice apart a man standing within seventy-five meters of their impact. But all that firepower carried a high price in mobility. The weight of the tube plus the ammunition Peterson brought with him was 1,500 pounds. The weapon was ideal for sitting in a protected area firing missions for troops a couple of thousand meters forward, but it was not the perfect system for the running battle in which Task Force Rakkasan now found itself, a fact Peterson well understood, but could do little about.

Peterson and his men got their weapon up and running in no time. The enemy had fired the first round in the mortar duel, but the Americans were about to fire the biggest. First fielded in 1994, the 120 mortar had never been fired in combat until Sergeant Raul Lopez, who had never even fired it in training, sent the first round looping toward the enemy with a loud *whoomph.* Within moments the mortar crew was working in a smooth rhythm, with Peterson the main gunner. The Al Qaida fighters quickly realized the 120 was their greatest threat and therefore their highest priority target. Within a minute or two, bullets were zipping and cracking past the American mortarmen with steadily increasing intensity. Then the enemy mortars found their range and began walking rounds in toward Peterson and his men, who were running in circles trying to find cover in between returning fire. It was clear they had to move, so with difficulty they broke the mortar down under fire, loaded it and the ammunition on a series of sledlike devices called Skedcos, and hauled them 200 meters west to a wide ditch or wadi beside where Maroyka was setting up Heather with Higley's squad.

The new position offered only slightly better protection than the last. As enemy fire dogged their every step, a combination of Peterson's mortarmen and riflemen from Sergeant Thomas Finch's fire team ran back and forth ferrying the rest of the ammo between the two positions. Just as Peterson and his team seemed to have found their rhythm again, the ears of Maroyka's RTO, Private First Class Kyle McGovern, picked up an odd whistling sound. A split second later his world turned black as a mortar round exploded with a loud, cracking *thud* inside the ditch three meters from where Peterson stood with Maroyka. The explosion knocked a dozen soldiers to the ground. As they came to their senses, they checked themselves for wounds. Peterson and Higley were unscathed, but glancing down they realized the enemy had finally done some real damage. No soldiers were dead, but at least half a dozen were wounded. McGovern seemed to be bleeding from his head to his toes (two of which were now missing), and the platoon's two senior figures, Maroyka and Abbott, were also hurt. Looking at the faces of the wounded men, Peterson saw fear in American eyes for the first and only time that day. He and Higley went to work, Peterson directing the men, Higley bandaging Abbott's arm, where shrapnel had left a hole in his tricep big enough for Higley to stick his pinkie in. McGovern came to and started yelling, thinking from the pain that his legs had been blown off. Deciding this wasn't the time for sympathy, Higley screamed right back at him. "Get the fuck up!" The RTO gritted his teeth and staggered to his feet. Everyone realized they had to move before another round caught them in the same place.

Kraft had heard the mortar round detonate near Heather. Concerned, he picked up the hand mike. "Cobra 1-6, Cobra 1-6, sitrep, over," he said. In a calm voice Maroyka relayed the bad news. "Cobra 6, this is Cobra 1-6, still taking mortar fire, and I have been hit, over." With the able-bodied supporting the wounded, the soldiers stumbled across 100 meters of open terrain between Heather and the Halfpipe. Glancing back, they saw a mortar round detonate at the spot they'd just left. By the time they got to the Halfpipe, Kraft had set up a casualty collection point—a place to put and treat casualties—on the outside western slope of the Halfpipe. (He put it there because there were too many people running around inside the Halfpipe.) The battle was now at its most chaotic. Most of the 10th Mountain troops were in the Halfpipe, but small groups were scattered elsewhere on ridgelines and in wadis, taking and returning fire. For those in the Halfpipe, the noise of battle was almost deafening. "You've got major explosions from both RPGs and mortar rounds," Kraft said. "You've got the enemy direct fire from both west and east, you can hear it zipping past our heads and cracking into the rocks. Then you've got my machine guns, my small arms fire returning fire in both directions. It was pretty much like any war movie you ever see, how loud it is, with smoke and dirt in the air." Mortar rounds would land every thirty seconds. The prevalence of the enemy's mortars came as a shock to every American. No one had focused on mortars as a threat at Bagram. LaCamera and his mortarmen were particularly impressed with the speed and accuracy with which the enemy mortars were able to target their locations. As if that wasn't enough to focus the Americans' minds, Peterson heard a new threat whistle through the air: the unmistakable sound of an artillery round. Somewhere in the draws and wadis of the Shahikot, Al Qaida had hidden the equivalent of a battery of towed howitzers. Now one or more of them were letting loose. Fortunately, the flat trajectory of artillery fire made it tough for the enemy gunners to drop the rounds into the Halfpipe.

Peterson's 120 tube was still sitting no more than 100 meters away, but he had fired all thirty-five of his high-explosive rounds, so there wasn't much point risking anyone's life to retrieve the tube. Instead the mortarmen became riflemen manning the Halfpipe's northeastern corner, which had none of the rocks that offered protection along the rest of the rim of the bowl. Peterson was the first to crawl up to the lip, to make sure his men wouldn't become instant casualties. His leadership by example left an impression. "His leadership skills were just unbelievable," said Private First Class Jason Ashline. "He was just so calm during the whole thing. He didn't show any fear whatsoever."

9.

AS the Al Qaida fighters in the mountains ran to their fighting positions and aimed the first RPGs at the American troops below them, two Black Hawks flew low and slow over the Finger. They carried Wiercinski's tactical command post (known as the TAC), which sounds like a big headquarters but in reality consisted of only a handful of men and radios. The Rakkasan commander's aim was to land on the Finger, stay for thirty to sixty minutes, long enough to get a sense for how the operation was unfolding, and then fly back to Bagram. The first challenge, however, was to find somewhere to land. The ridgeline looked like a knife edge from the air, a thin sliver of rocky terrain pointing into the heart of the valley. For several minutes the pilots circled, searching for a flat space wide enough to land in. Every second spent over the valley made them more vulnerable. Both helicopters were flying with external fuel tanks on their wings in order to allow Jim Marye, the air mission commander, to stay aloft long enough to oversee the first phase of the operation. These tanks were not bulletproof. A single bullet or shard of shrapnel would turn one into the equivalent of a torpedo-shaped firebomb strapped to the side of the helicopter. Mako 31 had taken care of one DShK that would have spelled certain death for the men on the two helicopters, but other threats remained in the shadows of the Shahikot.

Trying not to think of the dangers lurking below, the men on the birds concentrated on finding an LZ. Savusa, Wiercinski's stalwart sergeant major, thought of his family and said a silent prayer. *If this is it, then let it be so.* Wiercinski spotted a bowl-shaped gap in the rocks that looked just big enough to accommodate a Black Hawk. "Put us down there," Wiercinski told the pilots, pointing to the location about halfway up the ridge's spine. But the pilots of his Black Hawk had a hard time trying to put the bird down in the narrow strip of land between large rock formations the colonel had identified. After not making it the first time, they opted to fly around the valley and try again.

The pilot of the other helicopter (which carried Savusa, Corkran, plus a captain and two lieutenants from Corkran's battalion, who were there to provide security for the TAC and get the lay of the land, in case they were called forward as the reserve) then gave it a shot, and succeeded in deftly maneuvering his aircraft into the space. The soldiers in the back held their breath as the whirring blades flashed no more than two feet from sheer rock walls as the helicopter settled on to the Finger. They jumped out but, with no space to run, just kneeled as the helicopter took off in cloud of dust.

Meanwhile, Wiercinski's aircraft, which also carried Michael Gibler, Dino Murray, Jim Marye, and Specialist Brandon Hall, circled around the valley. Unseen by those aboard the Black Hawk, who were distracted by the first radio calls from the valley floor reporting fierce enemy resistance, an Al Qaida fighter below them shouldered his RPG launcher and took aim. The rocket-assisted projectile shot upward, exploding just beneath the chin bubble of Wiercinski's Black Hawk and hurling a big piece of shrapnel into its underbelly. Another fighter pointed his Kalashnikov at the same aircraft and pulled the trigger. His aim was even better, but not quite good enough. The bullets peppered the helicopter's tail rotor hub, one of the rounds nicking a push-pull rod in the tail rotor assembly. "If that thing had severed, we'd have lost tail rotor control, and we'd have been gone," Marye said. "It was by the grace of God that that didn't happen." A lone AK-47-wielding guerrilla firing a bullet that cost pennies had come within millimeters of downing a multimillion-dollar Black Hawk helicopter and consigning the brigade commander, his air mission commander, operations officer, and air liaison officer, as well as an RTO and the air crew, to their doom. Such a disaster in the opening minutes of the battle would have left Operation Anaconda hanging by a thread.

Unaware of how close they had just come to catastrophe, the pilots arrived back over the precarious LZ on the Finger and again attempted a nerve-jangling landing. This time they got it right, sliding the helicopter down perfectly between the rocks.

The first thing Murray did as he jumped off the helicopter was chamber a round in his M4. This was an altogether new experience for the Rakkasan air liaison officer, an F-16 pilot who had always imagined experiencing combat from behind a joystick, not dodging bullets with a rifle in his hand. The nine men who jumped from the aircraft (Marye's role as air mission commander required that he stay airborne) realized they were being shot at even before the helicopters pulled away. Bullets cracked and popped over their heads. "Is that sound bullets going by?" Murray asked innocently, a comment that was to pass into legend in the Rakkasan headquarters. Assured that it was, the twenty-nine-year-old Air Force Academy graduate from Chicago's South Side tensed up. *Man, what did I get myself into?* But Wiercinski had chosen the site well. The bullets that weren't flying overhead were pinging off the boulders that lined the eastern edge of their position. Nevertheless, no one on the ridge was happy about being taken under fire. "Guys, I've heard this sound before. I didn't like it then and I don't like it now," said Wiercinski, his mind flashing back to that dark night in Panama in December 1989.

Bullets or no bullets, there was work to be done. Moving north down the ridge a little way, Corkran and his scout platoon leader, 1st Lieutenant Justin Overbaugh, established an observation post from which they saw about ten enemy fighters maneuvering toward them from the direction of Serkhankhel along a low ridge that ran east of and parallel to the Finger. After the Rakkasan TAC troops took them under fire, the enemy squad sought cover behind some rocks on a low ridgeline about 200 meters to the northeast. Those members of the TAC not consumed with command and control responsibilities on the radio then traded fire with the enemy squad for about thirty minutes, killing at least one of them with rifle fire. The fight ended when the TAC called in some help from a pair of Apaches, which fired several rockets and bursts of 30mm at the position, silencing it. Meanwhile, Wiercinski, Gibler, and Murray began to work the radios, talking to Preysler and LaCamera on the valley floor, the aircraft overhead, and the different headquarters at Bagram. The ferocity of the battle and the difficulty of landing at the LZ forced Wiercinski to postpone the TAC's departure from the Finger. He sent the Black Hawks back to Bagram so they could refuel and return with the second lift of Chinooks. That would make them available to pick Wiercinski and the TAC up, but the Rakkasan commander only planned to use that option if he knew his forces and TF Hammer had total control of the valley. Otherwise, he would send the Black Hawks back empty.

Several hundred meters up the slope of the Finger, the TAC personnel could see the corpse of one of the guerrillas killed by Mako 31 and the AC-130 earlier that morning. The SEALs now occupied the DShK position and they signaled their presence by laying a brightly colored VS-17 panel on the ground. The Rakkasan TAC personnel signaled back using their own VS-17 panel. Having already been mistakenly engaged by LaCamera's troops, Goody decided to link up with the TAC to reduce the risk of a more serious friendly-fire incident.

He and his men walked down the slope, calmly introduced themselves to the soldiers as "recon and surveillance snipers," and quickly went to work expanding the TAC perimeter and applying their expert skills to the job of killing the Al Qaida fighters maneuvering to gain positional advantage over Wiercinski's tiny band. Savusa, who hadn't even been aware of the DShK's existence until he had landed, now realized the significance of what Goody's men had accomplished. "I owe my life to those guys," he said. "If it wasn't for them taking out that machine gun, who knows what would have happened to us."

In addition to beefing up the TAC's security element, the arrival of Mako 31 also provided Murray with invaluable assistance in the shape of Andy, the combat controller from 24th Special Tactics Squadron, the Air Force special ops outfit that worked most closely with Delta and SEAL Team 6 (and was known as Task Force White when it did). Andy and Murray quickly formed a team. Andy used his Viper laser rangefinder to get the precise coordinates for the targets that Murray then arranged to have bombed by talking directly to the pilots of the fast-movers. The young Air Force officer stayed glued to his radio throughout his time on what later became known as "Rak TAC Ridge," so much so that he was the only man on the ridge who didn't fire his weapon. So engrossed was he in his duty that he failed to notice when the enemy fire was creeping dangerously close to his location. "Dino, get down before you get your fucking head blown off!" Wiercinski yelled at him.

The TAC withstood three distinct mortar barrages consisting of three or four rounds. On each occasion the first round landed a safe distance away, but the subsequent rounds would walk closer and closer to the TAC, stretching nerves to breaking point. The next attack would begin closer than the previous one, but otherwise the pattern would be repeated, leading Murray to conclude that the Al Qaida mortar crews had at least one observer calling in the fires. There was little the Rakkasans could do about the attacks, because they had no idea where the enemy mortar positions were located. After one round landed less than fifty meters away, Wiercinski and Savusa looked at each other. "Okay boys, it's time to pack," Wiercinski said, and troops gathered up the radios and moved a short distance along the ridge in an attempt to escape the enemy mortar crew's attentions. Back in the Rakkasan TOC in Bagram, Jim Larsen listened as his commander signed off with the words, "We're in contact, we're moving." For an hour Larsen sat by the radio waiting nervously until the TAC reestablished communications. "There was a certain helpless feeling," he said. "You couldn't do anything about it, they were on their own."

Murray's own nerves were calmed somewhat by the coolness under fire of Wiercinski and Savusa. Not many colonels, even in the infantry, got to engage in direct firefights, and Murray speculated that the engagement "brought back some memories" for the brigade commander. "He was in his element," the Air Force captain said. "He looked like an infantryman at some times and at others he looked like a guy in command of hundreds of men that were in a tough dogfight. He looked drained and stressed at times, but most of the time he looked like he was in his element. I'd go back on the mountain with the guy anytime."

The sporadic small arms fire aimed at the TAC began to morph into a more concerted attack. "Whenever you want bombs, just let me know," Murray told Wiercinski, aware that the situation was getting worse. A short while later there was a brief lull in the calls for fire from the valley floor, and Wiercinski took the opportunity. "Dino, let's get some bombs in there," the colonel told his air liaison officer. "What can you do for me?" Murray wished Wiercinski had asked a little earlier, as the enemy was now within "danger close" range of the TAC. Because of the guerrillas' proximity, the captain issued a request for any aircraft equipped with laser-guided bombs. Two F-16s were vectored in. Murray crawled to a little ridgeline to get the coordinates for the target area. "We've got troops in contact," he told the pilots. "We're taking fire from the north." He described where they were on the Finger, and used a mirror to try to signal his location to the pilots overhead. But the pilots couldn't identify the Rakkasan TAC on the ground, which raised the tension level a notch or two. "When you're dropping that close, you'd really like him to know where the friendlies are," Murray said. So Murray first had one of the F-16s drop a bomb outside of the danger close range. The bomb hit exactly where Murray had asked for it. "You see where the bomb hit? Now I want you to come up that ridgeline about halfway and tell me what you see," he said to the pilot. "I see some guys maybe running around in there, and certainly I see a little cave entrance and stuff like that," the pilot replied. "That's where I want the next bombs." "All right, how close to the friendlies?" "Three hundred meters." "All right." Murray then passed the ground commander's initials, in this case, "FW," for Frank Wiercinski—a necessary step whenever a force on the ground asks an aircraft for a "danger close" air strike.

There was a brief pause as the bombs fell to earth, then an orange explosion was followed by an earsplitting boom as the bombs detonated right on target. "There's nothing left down there," one of the infantry officers told Murray. "Thanks, you guys saved us," Murray told the F-16s as they prepared to leave. But he had no time to bask in the satisfaction of having solved the immediate problem to his north. The battle around the Halfpipe demanded his attention.

WITH the departure of the two stricken Apaches, Ryan consolidated his remaining aircraft in a team of three helicopters. The fight in the south was becoming even more chaotic. Communications problems hindered the pilots' ability to get a good read on the location of friendly and enemy forces at that end of the Shahikot. Having to fly straight into the early-morning sun didn't help matters. The pilots knew that LaCamera's troops had taken refuge in the hollow that became known as Hell's Halfpipe, but they were having a hell of a hard time locating it on the ground. They had to take several turns on the racetrack pattern around the valley before they saw it, and every time they flew past the Whale, they would get shot at.

It was around this time that Chenault unleashed the only Hellfire missile the Apaches fired that day. His opportunity arose when an urgent call for help came over the radio from Chip Preysler, the 2-187 commander. He and several of his soldiers were still in the compound, but were pinned down by Kalashnikov and RPG fire raining down on them from an Al Qaida bunker only 150 meters to their west on a plateau a little to the north of Sherkhankhel, and just to the east of the Whale. Chenault was closest to the target, and responded immediately. First he located the 2-187 soldiers on the valley floor, picking out their VS-17 panel. Then they gave him the heading and the range from which they were taking the fire. Chenault flew off in that direction. Within a couple of seconds he and Herman spotted the bunker underneath them. It was no more than a hole in the ground, fortified by some loose rocks around the rim, with no overhead cover. Looking down, the pilots saw two enemy fighters. One was firing a Kalashnikov at the Apache, the other had an RPG launcher on his shoulder. Two backpacks lay beside them in the dirt—one blue, one orange. Realizing their peril, the guerrillas scrambled out of the bunker and sprinted for their lives as Chenault circled back around. As the fighters ran down the side plateau, he let loose with his last twenty cannon rounds. One fighter dropped, but the other survived, and decided his best hope lay in the bunker's protection. He clambered back up the hill, perhaps hoping to get an RPG off before the Apache could attack again.

Out of rockets and 30mm rounds, Chenault's only recourse was his Hellfires. He wheeled to face the bunker again. (Unlike the cannon, neither the rocket pods nor the Hellfire pylons are slaved to the pilot's helmet, so Chenault had to point the helicopter toward the target in order to engage it with these weapons.) He could see the target clearly—too clearly. The Hellfire has a minimum range of 500 meters—if it is fired any closer to the target, it wouldn't arm in time, and would fail to detonate on impact. Chenault was too close, so he held fire. Wheeling around, he again lined up the Apache with the bunker. The Hellfire was not a true "fire-and-forget" missile—it was guided onto its target by a laser beam that had to remain pointed at the target until impact. Rather than passing over the enemy again without firing, Chenault pulled the controls back and put the Apache into reverse. At 520 meters from the target, the laser rangefinder finally locked on. Herman fired immediately. The missile sped off the rail on a flat trajectory, its motor trailing smoke as it rode the laser down.

At the very moment that the Al Qaida fighter reached the top of the plateau and dived for cover into the bunker, the missile exploded dead on target with a white flash and a cloud of smoke and dust. It was a classic case of bad timing on the guerrilla's part. Chenault and Herman flew over the position one last time. "It was gone," said Chenault.

Still the remaining three Apaches wheeled and swooped around the valley, trying to be everywhere at once, keeping the enemy's attention diverted from the infantry. Ryan and Kilburn were making an engagement run on an Al Qaida position just north of Ginger. They had just put a 30mm burst on the target, by now only 200-300 meters in front of them, and were about to break left when the captain was startled by a loud bang, as if a firecracker had exploded just outside the cockpit. Tiny pieces of Plexiglas showered him, collecting on his lap, on the radio console, and on the floor. With a sickening feeling, he noticed blood on his flak vest. "I'm hit!" he yelled to Kilburn, his heart racing as he checked himself for wounds. With relief he found that all his fingers and toes were still attached and intact, and he had no other obvious wounds on his arms, legs or torso. He turned his attention to his head, checking his face in the cockpit's small mirror, which he usually used to observe his backseater. There was blood running from a small cut on his chin, where a bullet had nicked him after deflecting off the right door frame. After giving Ryan the closest of close shaves, the bullet had exited through the canopy. Al Qaida had come within a couple of inches of killing the commander of Task Force Rakkasan's Apache force. It was another in the extraordinary series of close calls enjoyed by the task force's soldiers. Ryan would later wryly refer to the incident as "a significant emotional event"—Army slang for something that scares you shitless.

"I was very lucky," he said. "It was my day, I guess."

By then the remaining Apaches were almost out of fuel and ammo. At about 7:50 a.m. Ryan gave the order to return to the FARP, and the three helicopters flew out of the valley.

10.

AFTER helping the battalion mortar troops move their ammo away from the LZ, Ropel linked up with the rest of his squad, who had been on Chalk 1, and together they moved south in a wedge formation. But as he crested a small rise, an Apache flew in behind them and shot a pair of rockets that hit only thirty feet away from Ropel—one to his left rear, another to his right front. Ropel didn't even realize he was being shot at until the two explosions sent shrapnel whistling past him. With no enemy in his immediate area, it was clear the pilots had mistaken his men, who all escaped unscathed, for the enemy. Other 1-87 troops who witnessed the near-tragedy quickly spread VS-17 panels on the ground. "We actually got a little bit nervous about the Apaches," Peterson said. O'Keefe told Ropel to pull his men back to the Halfpipe.

Ropel and his men spent the next ninety minutes in the Halfpipe, but he felt uncomfortable in such a static role. As the Al Qaida mortars rained down, he felt the urge to do something about them. Ropel turned to a Marine NCO attached to the battalion as an interpreter or military intelligence role. "We need to get the hell out of here," he said. "Damn right!" the Marine said. After clearing his plan with O'Keefe, Ropel led his squad and the Marine about 100 meters south from the Halfpipe to a knoll roughly four feet high, twenty feet long, and twenty-five feet wide. They took up position on this hillock, becoming LaCamera's southernmost outpost in the process. They remained there for a couple of hours, just observing, before Ropel's instincts again told him to take more assertive action. He was sure that somewhere in the eastern ridgeline there was at least one Al Qaida observer adjusting the enemy's mortar fires. As he looked east he realized that the eastern wall of the valley was divided into a ridge system. Immediately in front of him was a lower ridgeline that he thought he could scale with his men. He decided to give it a try. Leaving a machine-gun team on the knoll for security he led the rest of his men up the slope. But after only a few minutes he got a call on his ICOM radio from O'Keefe to come back down, because an air strike was inbound for close to his position. This sequence repeated itself several times over the next couple of hours—Ropel and his men would start clambering up the ridge, only to be called back down. On his fifth or sixth attempt Ropel succeeded. Urged on by Ropel in his thick Polish accent and using dead space to hide from the enemy gunners to their south and east, the soldiers gradually climbed the ridgeline, their breathing becoming increasingly labored as the air thinned. The rocks they were moving behind offered less and less cover the higher they climbed, forcing the men to drop first to their hands and knees and then to crawl the last few yards to the crest on their bellies.

Ropel, second from last in the group of seven or eight troops in the assault, found a trail lined by stones that protected him so long as he kept himself flat. *Zing!* A bullet ricocheted off a large flat rock beside him. Then he heard other ricochets, and the distinctive crack of a bullet breaking the sound barrier as it whipped over his head. But at first he couldn't tell where the rounds were coming from. He pushed himself a couple of feet back down the hill and looked over his shoulder to see the ground "popping" around the feet of Private First Class Steven Henderson, the "skinny-as-a-finger" soldier bringing up the rear who was standing upright. With a start Ropel realized the troops in the Halfpipe were engaging his squad. Thinking quickly he pulled a green smoke canister from his protective vest, pulled the pin, and rolled it down the hill, hoping the smoke would both conceal his men from the Halfpipe and signal that they were American. Almost simultaneously he yelled, "Cease fire! Cease fire!" into his ICOM radio, then told Henderson to get his ass up to the top of the ridge and lay flat behind the bushes there. The men ahead of him had already crawled out of sight, but now the enemy fighters in the mountainsides spotted Henderson and Ropel inching their way upward and opened fire. For a few moments the pair took fire from their front, their right and their left rear, until the troops in the Halfpipe realized their mistake.

Once he was behind cover on the crest, Ropel realized that the ridge fell away in a sheer cliff. He was looking across a gorge to the eastern wall proper of the valley. He and his men settled down between the rocks and scrubby bushes searching for targets that they could engage themselves or bring air strikes in on. Their elevated position meant they had could see further south and east than anyone else who had flown in with LaCamera. Holding the high ground, separated from the static defense of the Halfpipe, and looking for the enemy, Ropel was at last in his element.

HELBERG'S scouts focused their binoculars and scopes on Serkhankhel and soon reached a startling conclusion: The village appeared completely empty. Before they'd fully comprehended the implications of this, they heard gunfire behind them and bullets cracking overhead. They seemed to be coming from the direction of Diane.

Luman's small force had moved 200 meters east when fire erupted from a position 300 meters ahead of them. Luman, who had begun the deployment to Afghanistan as 3rd Platoon's platoon sergeant, but been made the platoon leader when Preysler removed the weak lieutenant who had held that position, was disappointed with some NCOs' slow reaction when the bullets started flying. "Get the fuck up and lead your fucking men!" he yelled, and called up a pair of snipers and a 240 team led by Sergeant Henry Schmitz. The machine gunner spotted two armed men in a U-shaped position built into a crevice. One fighter was standing, visible from the waist up. Schmitz lined the man up in his iron sights. "I got eyes on, can I take him?" he asked. "Take the motherfucker down," Luman said. Schmitz fired a burst at the fighter's waist, chest, and head. The man in his sights "splintered," Schmitz said. "There was stuff going everywhere." Schmitz fired a burst at the other guerrilla. Forty rounds silenced the position.

Luman's men began a punishing climb up a steep ravine toward Diane. In the rarefied air even the fittest young 11 Bravos felt their thighs and lungs burning. With every step the air got thinner and the rucks seemed to get heavier. As the column of men crossed the snowline, a few of the signals intelligence troops Dagger had attached to Rakkasan units to conduct radio intercepts struggled to keep up. Luman was losing patience. A final ridgeline stood between the platoon and Diane. The rock face was as smooth as it was steep. No ledges or goat paths offered themselves as routes to the top. They would have to make the ascent the hard way: straight up, hand over hand. The men scrabbled up the slope as best they could, but they were close to total exhaustion. Every potential handhold was slippery with ice, every toehold hidden by snow. Again and again, soldiers made it halfway up before losing their grip and sliding back down. They'd grit their teeth and try again, but often with the same result. "By textbook standards it was no-go terrain," Schmitz recalled. One by one, however, the infantrymen finally hauled themselves to the top with a supreme effort. But the linguists weren't making it.

Luman, almost at the top, heard a shout from the bottom. "We've got a guy down." *I don't need this shit,* he thought. *We always got told "March or die." I don't want my boys to die today. It's not a good day to die.* He retraced his steps to find a linguist totally spent at the bottom of the slope. Schmitz came down to help. One by one Schmitz carried the linguists' rucks up the slope. Then he pushed and pulled the linguists up. Luman got the platoon moving again. After another 300 meters he announced they were at Diane. The troops set up the blocking position using white engineer tape and other materials they had hauled up the mountain. They started with a sign about 300 meters from their position that said TURN BACK, THERE ARE MINES! At 200 meters a second sign read TURN AROUND NOW! LAST WARNING. Anyone who proceeded past both signs would run into a wall of lead from Schmitz's 240.

It was 8:45 a.m. Luman had heard little from 1st and 2nd Platoons. The radio was quiet. The soldiers caught their breath and began digging fighting positions. "Then all hell broke loose," Luman recalled. The soldiers sent down to set up the blocking position had just returned when the platoon started receiving small arms fire from several directions. Luman believed the most accurate fire came from caves near the top of Hill 3033. He called Baltazar and asked permission to move out and "clear" the caves. Baltazar restated Luman's task and purpose—"to establish Blocking Position Diane in order to prevent enemy escaping from AO Remington"—and told him to stay put. A fusillade so intense that Luman compared it to the fire on the Normandy beach depicted in the movie *Saving Private Ryan* rained down from Hill 3033. Luman strode to the edge of the perimeter, where his men were sheltering from the bullets. Holding his M4 by his side like a pistol, he pointed out the enemy positions to his troops, directing their fire. If they couldn't see the enemy, he told them, they were to rake the hilltop and the ridgelines to the left and right with fire. Third Platoon began giving it back to the enemy in spades. Within a couple of minutes the 240 gunners had fired about 400 rounds of 7.62mm, the SAW gunners between 200 and 400 rounds of linked 5.56mm ammunition, while those firing M4s were also emptying magazine after magazine of 5.56mm ammunition.

For thirty minutes Diane reverberated to the crackle of automatic weapons fire and the occasional boom of an exploding RPG. Then the enemy fire faded away briefly. Luman walked over to his RTO. A couple of extra medics who had been attached to 3rd Platoon were there, also, huddled with their aid bags. "Welcome to combat, motherfuckers!" Luman barked. The stunned medics looked at him, he said, "like I was smoking crack."

By 10:30 a.m. Baltazar's three platoons were all in their blocking positions. Only Luman's was still in heavy contact. Preysler and Baltazar had moved their command posts up to Betty, which was occupied by Baltazar's 2nd Platoon and was the northernmost of the three blocking positions set up by Preysler's first lift of troops. The battalion's leaders monitored the urgent radio traffic between Wiercinski and LaCamera. It was clear 1-87 faced a significantly larger force in the south than had been predicted. A glance at the map told the 2-187 leaders that the enemy attacking the Halfpipe could easily move up the eastern ridge to assault them. Preysler and Nielsen figured the Al Qaida fighters would back off at night and then use hit-and-run tactics against their troops on the eastern ridge the next morning. Someone in the Halfpipe pleaded for close air support over the radio and the mood at Preysler's command post turned somber. *Holy Christ, they're taking a pounding,* Nielsen thought. *That could be us tomorrow.*

LACAMERA called Kraft up to his location soon after the casualties arrived. Usually a company commander doesn't want his battalion commander 75 meters away when he's trying to execute his mission. But Kraft realized there were two big advantages to having LaCamera there. First, the 1-87 commander could use his rank in the struggle to coordinate timely close air support from the fixed-wing jets overhead. Second, LaCamera's calmness filled his subordinates with confidence. "Up until that point I really didn't know my battalion commander," Peterson said. "I thought he was kind of aloof. But in the crunch he showed his true colors. He's a warrior." Kraft appreciated the fact that LaCamera let him control his own fight, rather than reaching down and micromanaging it for him. "Think of how easy it would have been for him to just take over," Kraft said. "He didn't. He is one of the big reasons why I want to have a career in the Army."

When Kraft arrived at the battalion command post, LaCamera was talking to Wiercinski on the radio. When the conversation ended, he turned to Kraft. It was time to "relook the plan," LaCamera said. They had anticipated a few "leakers" trying to escape along those routes, but not the entrenched, heavily armed force that surrounded them. "Okay, here's what I'm thinking, Nelson," LaCamera said. "We can keep what we're doing we're doing here, and strongpoint this area, or we can try to move back to the south a little bit and establish our blocking positions back there. What do you think?" "Well, based on the number of casualties I've got right now and the number of rucksacks I've got out on the LZs, we ought to strongpoint this," Kraft replied. His boss agreed. "Hooah, sir," the junior officer said. "I'll make it happen."

Kraft called O'Keefe and told him to move his men into the Halfpipe. Leaving Ropel's squad on their knoll 100 meters to the south, the rest of 2nd Platoon moved to the Halfpipe in a "bounding overwatch"—in which one element provides covering fire while another moves. En route they were struck by mortar fire that wounded several men. When they reached the Halfpipe, Kraft had about a squad from each platoon in the bowl. He gave O'Keefe's men to man the western side while the Peterson's mortarmen and the remnants of 1st Platoon engaged the enemy on the eastern ridge.

O'Keefe's casualties joined the others at the casualty collection point, where Major Thomas Byrne, the battalion surgeon, presided over a bloody scene. The soldiers' Kevlar helmets and body armor had stopped a lot of shrapnel, meaning there were few life-threatening injuries but lots of wounds to soldiers' limbs. Soldiers' pants legs had been torn off so their wounds could be dressed. No one was panicking. Even the worst off, Specialist James Burkins, a SAW gunner, and Kyle McGovern, Maroyka's twenty-one-year-old RTO, were stable. Burkins, it would transpire, had a shrapnel wound to his heart (the shrapnel had entered through the unarmored side of his vest) and was drifting in and out of consciousness. McGovern seemed to have been hit almost everywhere not protected by his helmet and body armor. In addition to their protective gear, the wounded men owed their stable conditions to two factors. One was the priority LaCamera placed on training his medics and getting every soldier qualified as a combat lifesaver. The other was "Doc" Byrne, who, under fire for the first time, impressed every soldier in the Halfpipe. When the shout of "Incoming!" went up, he covered the wounded with his own body. When casualties were taken outside the Halfpipe, he ran to treat them with no concern for his own safety.

Grippe credited Byrne with giving the battalion's leaders very professional, unemotional status reports on the casualties that helped LaCamera make decisions. No commander likes to see his men suffer, but after discussing the status of the casualties with "Doc" Byrne, LaCamera decided not to request any medevac aircraft until after dark. He did so knowing that the casualties could survive until then and that if the enemy shot the medevac helicopter down it would change the battle. Even so, the final decision on whether or not to attempt to medevac LaCamera's wounded rested with Hagenbeck. After talking to Wiercinski, who had in turn been talking to LaCamera, Hagenbeck made what he described as the "excruciating" decision to hold off on trying to evacuate the wounded from the Halfpipe until after dark. "I was hesitant to send them in because RPGs and everything were flying around the valley and I was quite certain we'd have helicopters shot down trying to extract them in daylight," he said. "In fact I turned some around in midair that were going in." Kraft said this was the right call. "The soldiers knew going into the operation that we would have to sustain our own casualties until the battle allowed us to evacuate them," Kraft said. "Every soldier knew that going in. It didn't cause any leadership problems [with the troops] whatsoever."

Among the wounded soldiers Byrne was treating were Maroyka and Abbott, the 1st Platoon leader and platoon sergeant respectively. Maroyka had shrapnel wounds "just about everywhere," but especially to his calf, Kraft said, while Abbott's upper arm had been torn up by the same round. When the two arrived from Heather with the rest of the casualties, Kraft realized neither was in a condition to lead troops in combat. Randy Perez, the supply clerk turned infantryman, was now the senior healthy man in 1st Platoon. Kraft was about to hand him an awesome responsibility, but there was no time for pleasantries. "Hey, you're the 1-6," the captain told him over the radio, using the 1st Platoon leader call sign. "Roger that, sir, I got it," Perez said. Kraft told him that 1st Platoon was going to be responsible for the eastern side of the strongpoint. "You've got from twelve to three to six." And just like that, "the supply guy" was given command of a platoon of grunts in the toughest battle U.S. infantry had fought in a decade.

Perez's first thought was for the men who'd just been placed under his command. *I want to get these guys safe, and I want to get them outta here,* he thought. To that end, he immediately ordered them to spread out as they crawled up to the lip of Halfpipe. Then he scanned the ridgeline in front of him, trying to spot the enemy fighters who continued to rake the Halfpipe with Kalashnikov and DShK bullets, RPGs, and mortar rounds. He could see a few in what looked like black uniforms, but they were easier to spot on the Finger than the eastern ridge. Then two Apaches flew over his head from west to east, hammering positions on the eastern ridge with rockets and cannon fire. Perez exulted. *These guys are fixing to fuck these guys up.* But then a hidden DShK spat fierce resistance in the shape of 12.7mm bullets. The Apaches wheeled about and were gone. Perez was amazed at the enemy's defiance. *It's gonna be a long fucking day,* he thought, gazing up at the ridge. *What the fuck is up there?*

The Army's newest platoon leader slipped into his command role as if born for it. Throughout the day, he walked the line of his men, making sure everyone had enough ammo, handing out magazines to those who needed them, and checking on the casualties. His men were handling their challenges as well as he was handling his. *Nobody's freaking out, nobody's hugging their weapon, nobody's in the fetal position, so I have no problem,* he thought. Abbott, who had mentored Perez for long hours back at Drum, teaching him everything he needed to survive as an infantry NCO, now got to witness the fruits of his labor. Perez could sense his wounded platoon sergeant monitoring his progress, but he resisted the temptation to lean on Abbott. *This is my test and I can't run to him and ask him what to do every two minutes,* he told himself. He needn't have worried. Six or seven hours into the fight, Abbott, in one of his more lucid moments, told him, "You're doing a good job." As the day wore on, Grippe, who had questioned if Perez knew what he was getting himself into when he chose to become an infantryman, watched in awe as Perez proved he had what it took and then some. "He kicked ass as if he was a combat vet from numerous firefights," Grippe said. "He just did a spectacular job that day." "He [Perez] was all over the place," Kraft said. "Sergeant Perez acted as a seasoned platoon leader. If I were to write down the perfect platoon leader in a combat situation, that was Sergeant Perez."

Up and down the length of the valley, a pattern was emerging that would have been familiar to veterans of every clash of arms from Gaugamela to Gettysburg. At every point in the Task Force Rakkasan fight, as young soldiers looked for leadership, noncommissioned officers were providing it. The chips were down and Randy Perez, Andrzej Ropel, Michael Peterson, and their brethren were stepping up. Grippe's prediction had been on the money. It was a sergeant's fight, all right, and the sergeants were giving it everything they had.

Their soldiers didn't let them down. Pinned down and surrounded by an enemy that outnumbered and outgunned them, and who were fighting with a ferocity that no one had predicted, the young infantrymen responded to the chaos and confusion with a courage that surprised even their NCOs. "I was just amazed watching these young guys under fire for the first time, the way they were moving around and returning fire, they looked like seasoned combat veterans," Grippe said. "My guys weren't freaking out. There was no one that thought we weren't going to get out of there."

But as the AK-47 rounds richocheted off the rocks and the RPGs exploded with an orange burst and a puff of black smoke, not everyone in the Halfpipe kept their cool. "You could see a few people starting to fray," said Peterson. He was referring to one or two members of the signals intelligence team that had accompanied the infantry into the fight. These troops had abandoned their high-tech listening gear with their rucksacks in the mad dash to the Halfpipe. Now unable to perform his job, a staff sergeant lost his nerve during a particularly intense mortar barrage. "We need to get outta here!" he yelled. "We're all gonna die!" "Where the hell are you going to run to, bud?" Peterson replied. "Just stay here and fight." The plan was shot to hell, they were pinned down by enemy fire, and their double-figure casualty list would have prevented them from maneuvering their force anyway, but LaCamera and Grippe were not disheartened. Their casualties were stable, their troops were fighting well, and they were in little danger of being overrun. On the rare occasion that enemy fighters tried to maneuver toward them from Marzak, they were killed or driven back by M4 and machine-gun fire from the Halfpipe. The enemy's unexpected strength in the high ground around Ginger and on the Finger had prevented Kraft's men from occupying Ginger and forced them out of Heather, but in LaCamera's opinion his troops controlled each of those positions "by fires." This point is debatable, but the larger truth is that the rationale for the blocking positions—to prevent the enemy on the valley floor from escaping—

had been superseded by reality. Most of the enemy was in the high ground and no one was trying to escape through the passes that were to be blocked by TF Rakkasan. Nevertheless, LaCamera's preferred course of action was to wait until nightfall, then evacuate his casualties and move the rest of his force to a new position under cover of darkness. When Hagenbeck decided to "reinforce success" in the northern end of the valley while pulling LaCamera's force out of the south, it frustrated the two ex-Rangers in the Halfpipe. "We didn't want to leave," Grippe said. "Higher made the decision to evacuate us. . . . We had these guys freakin' fixed."

11.

THE FARP had been a hive of activity from the moment Hardy nursed Apache 203 safely home. When he and the other three pilots climbed out of their cockpits, the adrenaline pumping through their veins began to get the better of them. "Everybody's talking loud, talking like we were out there catching bullets with our teeth," Pebsworth said. "I don't think any of us at that point realized that we could have died. At that point we're just flexing our muscles, so to speak, and just saying, 'Wow, we made it.'"

The other three helicopters arrived back about an hour later. Once they were on the ground, Hardy and Pebsworth, who was studying to become a maintenance test pilot, walked among them, assessing the damage. What they saw stunned them. Each aircraft had been repeatedly hit, in most cases far more times than the pilots flying them had known. Hamilton, for instance, returned to the FARP believing his was the only helicopter not to have been hit. But closer inspection revealed that, in addition to several bullet holes in his rotor blades, his Apache had also taken a bullet to the power-available spindle, which connects the power lever to the engine.

Also walking among the aircraft was a handful of ground-crew mechanics and armaments soldiers, who were having a busy day themselves.

When the helicopters launched from Bagram a couple of hours previously, there had been no cheering from the ground crews. They watched the Apaches disappear into the gloom to the south, and then—except for a couple of soldiers laboring on Carr's cannon—turned and headed back to their tent. Like the pilots, the ground crews began the day underwhelmed by the significance of the threat the Apaches would face. That mood didn't last long.

"They hadn't been gone for long when somebody ran into our tent and said they needed all the ammo we had," recalled Staff Sergeant Chad Bardwell, who was in charge of the maintenance crews for all eight Apaches. The plan was to load the ammo on a Black Hawk or a Chinook and fly it down to Texaco. "After they started asking for all the ammo and sending back reports of the aircraft being hit, it got real—real quick," said Bardwell, who had been in the Army for seven years, half as a cavalry scout, and half as a helicopter crew chief.

Bardwell and his soldiers went down to the ammo supply point at the north end of the runway and loaded cases of rockets, Hellfires, and 30mm ammo on to Gators and Humvees before driving the loads half a mile back down the flight line to where the Chinooks were parked. As the reports of damage and casualties filtered back to Bagram, Bardwell got a team of three soldiers together. Their mission would be to head to the FARP and patch up the Apaches so the helicopters could return to the fight as quickly as possible. They loaded fifteen cases of 30mm ammo (110 rounds per case) and two cases of four rockets each on to a Black Hawk. Then Bardwell and his three-man team climbed aboard and flew to the FARP at about midday. When they got to Texaco all six Apaches were waiting for them.

Bardwell walked down the line of aircraft, inspecting each one. His reaction to what he found was a mixture of relief and shock. Relief that, although the aircraft had taken a lot of hits, some of the more dramatic accounts of damage that he'd received over the radio were not accurate. No helicopter had taken an RPG in its nose, or in its transmission. "I was expecting to see stuff just blown to bits, from some of the reports we were getting," Bardwell said. Not for the first or last time, the reports reaching Bagram from the battlefield were shown to be significantly wide of the mark. But Bardwell and his troops still were shocked that some of the helicopters had made it back from the Shahikot. Almost all the rotor blades had bullet holes through them, as did several drive shafts, which ran down the Apaches' tail booms and up the vertical fins to the tail rotors. "That shocked me," Bardwell said.

Under Hardy's direction, Bardwell's team got to work. "Basically we were looking to see what we could do to get as many birds as we could flyable," Bardwell said. The crew chiefs tried to patch up the blades by spreading Hysol, a glue-like substance, into the holes to prevent any cracks from spreading and the blades from debonding. Meanwhile the armament guys worked feverishly to repair the damage to the Apaches' electronic systems.

The toll the fight was taking on the attack birds, and their superb performance under fire, persuaded Wiercinski to order the one remaining airworthy Apache in Afghanistan to fly up from Kandahar to join the battle. The two pilots—Chief Warrant Officer 2 Randy Huff and Chief Warrant Officer 2 Sam

Bennett—were sleeping when the call for help came in. "They woke them up and said, 'Hey, we've had two shot down, you've got to go up there,'" Bardwell said. Together with Carr's Apache, which had only taken forty-five minutes to fix in Bagram and which had then flown on to the FARP, there were now two undamaged attack birds ready for combat.

Within an hour of his getting to Texaco, Bardwell and his maintenance team had two more ready to return to the fray. But Ryan decided to risk sending only one of these—that piloted by Chenault—back into the valley. A couple of the others could have been readied for combat if necessary, but neither Apache number 203—the one Hardy had flown back bone dry—nor number 304—Hardy's original bird, which had lost almost all its electronic systems, were going to be combat ready soon.

After refueling the Apaches, there was one more task the ground crews had to perform: rearming the helicopters. In particular, they had to replace the MPSM rockets with the point detonating variety. The pilots found the MPSM rockets to be next to useless in the Shahikot, because they were designed to be fired from a hover. The troops were frantically pulling twenty-seven-pound MPSM rockets off the helicopters and replacing them with twenty-two-pound PD rockets, many of them pulled from the four helicopters that weren't set to go back out that day. The process was repeated throughout the day. "Every time somebody came back to the FARP, every person in this company, regardless of rank, was walking rockets that we could use from the bad birds up to the good birds," Hurley said.

The three good Apaches flew several more sorties through the valley that day, but none came close to matching the intensity of those first ninety minutes in the cauldron of the Shahikot. That evening all the Apaches flew back to Bagram (the other four all having been patched up enough for noncombat flight). At the airbase they were able to conduct a more thorough review of their helicopters. The amount of damage they had sustained was truly extraordinary. In addition to the three most obviously damaged Apaches, the others had all sustained numerous bullet holes, and damage that would have sent lesser helicopters tumbling from the sky.

There was at least one bullet hole in all but one of the Apache force's twenty-eight rotor blades. Several had bullet holes to their Robertson fuel tanks, none of which self-sealed as they were supposed to, the pilots were quick to note. One Apache had taken two bullets to the stringer, the main support beam that holds up the tail boom. Other bullets had shredded tires, damaged landing gear, and punched holes in cockpit Plexiglas.

Of course, the fire hadn't all been incoming. The Apaches had fired 540 cannon rounds, several hundred PD rockets, four MPSM rockets, and one Hellfire. They had also saved countless lives, according to the testimony of the grunts below them, and of the commanders watching the battle from nearby hillsides and monitoring the fight from the headquarters in Bagram. "Captain Bill Ryan and his guys were absolutely magnificent," Hagenbeck told a press conference March 6. "They really made a difference for us. Any other helicopter in the world would have crashed." Wiercinski went even further, saying the Apache "clearly saved the day" for his task force on March 2.

The Apache itself emerged as a hero from that first day's combat, dispelling the awkward memories of Task Force Hawk and surprising even some of the soldiers who know it best. "The aircraft took a lot more damage than I thought they would, and they all kept flying," Bardwell said. "Some of the components they hit, I didn't think the aircraft would still fly and it did." "It was billed as something that was very combat survivable, and regardless of what we say about the airframe, it did exactly what it was billed to do for the last two decades," Hurley said.

A couple of days later twenty-three-year-old Senior Airman Stephen Achey showed up at the Apache drivers' tent at Bagram, looking for Chenault. His face streaked with tears of gratitude, he explained that he had air assaulted into the Shahikot as the enlisted tactical air controller for Charlie Company, 1-87 Infantry, but had become separated from the others on his chalk almost immediately. He had taken cover behind his rucksack in a small dent in the ground. When he turned around, everyone else had sprinted to the Halfpipe. Al Qaida troops had spotted him, pinned him down with machine-gun fire, and were steadily walking mortar rounds toward him. They had already shot up the huge satellite radio in his ruck and almost hit him with an RPG. Seeing no way out of his predicament, he had given up hope when out of the clear Afghan sky Rich Chenault's Apache came spitting fire at his attackers. As the Al Qaida fighters shifted their attention, and their fire, to the new threat that seemed to have materialized out of nowhere, the young airman made good his escape. Now he had come to pay his respects to his saviors.

The pilots knew they also had much to be grateful for. "Luck was on our side that day, no doubt about it," said Ryan, who had cheated death by a couple of inches. "It definitely could have been a lot worse."

ROGER Crombie's men spent most of the day in a gunfight with a dozen guerrillas gathered around a forty-foot-high hill 1,000 meters to the northwest. The skirmish began when two of the fighters, whom the Americans had been tracking as they walked north from Marzak, advanced from the hill until they were only 800 meters from Eve. At that point 240 gunner Private First Class Mark Henry opened fire on the lead man. His first burst was high. The pair dropped to the ground and returned fire. But within moments Henry killed them both. For a couple of hours the two sides exchanged fire harmlessly. Then the scouts returned after hearing they and everyone else would be pulling out. The scouts, who had worked their way farther south along the base of Takur Ghar, had spent two hours watching one of the very few female enemy fighters observed by U.S. forces during Anaconda. The woman, in her mid-thirties, wore her hair in a ponytail, a long scarf that draped all the way to her knees, and an AK-47 on her back, said Sergeant Jorge Alcaraz. The scouts watched as she sat on a ledge at the foot of Takur Ghar cooking. Enemy fighters, some of whom had been sniping at the scouts, would come down to eat and then return to their positions. As the scouts picked up to move, a mortar attack they had called in from Peterson's men in the Halfpipe pulverized her position.

When the scouts arrived back at Eve, Crombie pushed Alacaraz's two-man sniper team to the perimeter to engage the enemy fighters behind the knoll. Scanning the hillock with a forty-five-power scope, Alcaraz spotted a person moving in a gully at its base. His sniper couldn't identify the target, so Alcaraz took the rifle and lined the man up in his sights. He aimed just above the target's left shoulder to compensate for the slight breeze and squeezed the trigger. "I hit him right in the gut," Alcaraz said. The man doubled over, tottered a few steps, and fell to the ground. The other fighters came out to retrieve him, but they were moving too fast for Alcaraz to double his tally.

LYING on their bellies behind rocks that hid them from all but the most prying of eyes, Speedy and Bob watched through their spotting scopes in mounting frustration. For half an hour they had been observing an Al Qaida mortar crew send round after round arcing toward the 10th Mountain troops in the Halfpipe from a spot on the southeastern tip of the Whale. From their vantage point 3,500 meters to the southwest, the AFO recon experts could clearly see the guerrillas' position, which included a machine gun that was well positioned to shoot at anyone foolhardy enough to drive through the Fishhook. The two Delta operators hidden on the south side of that bottleneck had tried repeatedly to call in an air strike on the mortar team, to no avail. First they had attempted to get the Apaches to destroy the position, only for Jimmy, monitoring their efforts from his table in the Mountain headquarters at Bagram, to tell them the Apaches were tied up on other missions, and to use fixed-wing aircraft instead. But none of the fast-movers was answering their calls.

Finally a B-52 with the call sign Stiletto came up on the net and agreed to attack the mortar. But as it was about to release its bombs, a female voice—presumably from the AWACS—aborted the strike, for reasons that no one on the ground could understand. India team got back on the radio. They asked why the strike was aborted and reported that the enemy mortar was still firing at U.S. troops. After a while an F-16 was vectored onto the target. But this time India was unable to talk to the jet directly, and watched as its bombs sailed harmlessly wide of the target. At 8:41 a.m., over ninety minutes after India had first called for fire on the mortar position, a pair of Apaches finally rolled in and destroyed it with a lethal combination of 30mm cannon fire and a salvo of rockets. Speedy and his men said this was the most impressive close air support strike they witnessed during the operation. "The aircraft was able to shoot the target from a short distance and was able to fire until the target was destroyed," one written account of the air strike said. "This was something aircraft at 18,000 feet could not do."

But the entire episode was typical of the problems with which all three AFO teams had to grapple as they tried to convert their positional advantage into killing power. The core of the problem was that although AFO's awareness of their surroundings in general and of the enemy's disposition in particular was far superior to that of the TF Rakkasan troops on the valley floor, the Rakkasans enjoyed "priority of fires," meaning if a Rakkasan element and an AFO team were each requesting an air strike, the aircraft would be vectored to answer the Rakkasans' call first. This situation was compounded by the lack of timely information the AFO teams were getting about where all the U.S. infantry elements were on the battlefield. The AFO operators sometimes found themselves talking to the Task Force 11 fires officer over a thousand miles away in Masirah in their efforts to get an aircraft overhead to strike a target only a couple of thousand meters in front of them. The result of this confused and confusing situation was that 10th Mountain and 101st troops were filling the radio nets with calls for close air support, but were often only able to give the strike aircraft a vague description of where they thought the target might be. The AFO teams, meanwhile, could identify the mortar positions and machine guns firing at the infantry, but sometimes had to wait over an hour to arrange for an air strike on the target. All the while the enemy mortars continued to prosecute punishing attacks against the TF Rakkasan soldiers in the Shahikot. "Listening to the AFO teams ask for any aircraft to drop JDAMs on enemy mortar positions without execution for hours, while hearing hearing [Rakkasan] calls for medevac was very frustrating," a special operator wrote.

In Gardez and Bagram, Pete Blaber and Jimmy worked aggressively to unscrew the situation. With Blaber deep in discussions with Jimmy, Glenn P. monitored all the radio traffic from the valley in order to stay abreast of the friendly and enemy situation. Back at India's observation post, while Speedy and Bob wrestled with the inadequate system for calling in close air support, Dan, the Gray Fox operator, was listening to enemy transmissions and relaying the most important info that he was able to translate to the others. A consistent theme running through Al Qaida's radio chatter was the enemy fighters' fear of the Apaches, whose presence over the battlefield they had not anticipated. Jason, Dan's counterpart in Juliet, who spoke Arabic and Pashto, was also enjoying some success. He managed to intercept several enemy communications and identified the frequency Al Qaida was using to control its mortar fires.

Juliet initially enjoyed more success than India, probably because the team had two satellite radios, enabling them to streamline their calls for fire, compared with India's single PRC-117F. A few minutes before 9 a.m., Juliet team leader Kris and his men saw Al Qaida forces move into position on a plateau about 1,300 meters east of Serkhankhel and only 1,000 meters away from Chip Preysler's 2-187 command post. From Juliet's observation post less than a kilometer away in the eastern ridge, Dave H. watched through his scope as six enemy fighters armed with RPG-7s, AK-type assault rifles, and one PK machine gun with six boxes of ammunition occupied three fighting positions on the plateau. All six wore black turbans, greenish shirts, and black or brown blanket wraps. They also wore military webbing and carried duffel bags or small rucksacks. The leader was a short, stocky fighter with black hair and a medium-length beard who directed his men with hand and arm signals and, in a bizarre touch, carried a big silver flag with Arabic writing on it.

Realizing the Al Qaida fighters were setting up to engage Preysler's troops, Juliet called in a "bomb box" on the enemy positions. (A bomb box is a rectangular patch of terrain—expressed as width, length, direction, and elevation—given to a bomber crew, who then drop enough bombs to destroy all targets within the area.) The team contacted a B-52, and within minutes six JDAMs rained down, killing four of the fighters, including the commander. The two survivors, one of whom was mortally wounded, got to their feet and dragged the commander's body down to some nearby low ground. The air strike alarmed the Rakkasan troops, who angrily voiced their concern until they were informed that it had saved them from being ambushed. Al Qaida fighters reoccupied the same position twice, and each time Juliet arranged a similarly devastating bombing run. In a testament to the enemy's motivation, after each air strike, even the wounded would assist in carrying off the dead.

As the day wore on, the AFO teams gradually overcame the systemic obstacles in the close air support process. The result was a series of air strikes that pulverized Al Qaida mortar positions, command and control buildings and troops in the open, but also highlighted the weaknesses of a plan that relied almost exclusively on air power for indirect fires. For every air strike called in by AFO that resulted in a destroyed enemy position, there was a bombing run that couldn't be arranged before the target had moved, that missed the target completely, or, in some cases, that hit right where it was supposed to, but failed to kill the enemy. Typical of the last scenario was India's experience of chasing three enemy fighters around the battlefield with JDAMs. The team called in a bomb strike on the guard tower they had noticed the previous evening on the southwestern edge of Babulkhel. The bombing destroyed the structure and killed two of the five guerrillas in the building. The three survivors ran from the ruins to a small building just south of Babulkhel. Again India called in an air strike, but this time the bomb missed by fifty meters and the trio escaped and hid in a rock crevice outside the village. Speedy and Bob kept their eyes on them and called in more JDAMs, but the enemy fighters had found a perfect hiding spot to protect them from the flying steel shards. Then, to the astonishment of Bob and Speedy, the three militants emerged from the gap in the rocks that had been their salvation, laid out their prayer mats, and kneeled to begin their prayers. That was all the invitation the AFO men needed. Another air strike was quickly arranged. When it struck, it killed two of the kneeling men. But the third, apparently unharmed, stood and raised his hands to the sky in a gesture of helplessness before walking off to the north.

Together, the thirteen men of India, Juliet, and Mako 31 (with the assistance of the jets and Apaches overhead) were almost certainly responsible for killing more enemy fighters during daylight hours on March 2 than the rest of the U.S. forces in the Shahikot put together. It is impossible to assess the exact number of enemy killed by the air strikes called in by the AFO operators, but a conservative estimate based on the recorded observations of the teams would put the number at several dozen. By identifying a series of Al Qaida mortar and machine-gun positions and command posts so that the jets and Apaches could destroy them, AFO kept the enemy from bringing even more fire to bear on the embattled TF Rakkasan troops in the Shahikot. It is not much of a stretch to state that some of the U.S. infantrymen—who knows how many?—owed their lives to Pete Blaber's men.

By occupying positions high above the valley floor, the AFO teams had given themselves a near-perfect situational awareness that the Rakkasans could not hope to achieve from either the valley floor or their blocking positions. The special operators also enjoyed a territorial advantage that made up for their lack of numbers. "I was comfortable so long as I held the high ground that I could hold off a hundred of them," one of the men on the teams said. Their achievements represented a total validation of Blaber's decision to push the envelope with his chain of command in order to contribute what AFO alone could provide to Operation Anaconda. His belief in "Patton's three principles of war"—audacity, audacity and audacity—and his trust in the ability of his well-trained, superbly motivated men to make the right calls had been proven right.

By early afternoon three distinct views of how the operation was going were emerging among U.S. commanders. The views of the Special Forces officers associated with Task Force Hammer, which had failed to deliver on the promises made by Mulholland and Rosengard, were unremittingly negative. Their force was in retreat, having been beaten back by an enemy arrayed in more depth than they had been led to expect. The chain of command in Task Forces Rakkasan and Mountain was similarly downcast. Almost half the force they had air-assaulted into the valley was pinned down and had taken heavy casualties. Like Task Force Hammer, they had been shocked at the enemy's strength and resilience. Nothing was going as planned. Hammer's ongoing withdrawal had allowed the enemy to focus almost his entire attention on the Rakkasan forces in the valley. Already senior officers were discussing a complete withdrawal from the Shahikot. Only at the AFO command post in Gardez, where Blaber had the most complete picture of the battlefield, courtesy of the reports from his three teams, and fully understood the damage being inflicted on the enemy, was the mood confident and upbeat.

WHEN Lou Bello, the Mountain fires planner, walked into the TOC not long after LaCamera's troops had landed, it was clear something big was going wrong. The headquarters tent was more crowded than usual, and there was a distinct tension in the air. "Ashen-faced" officers clustered around the screen showing feeds from the Predator while Hagenbeck and Harrell talked earnestly on the radio and telephone.

Already the plan had gone wildly off course. The strength of the opposition that confronted Zia surprised Hagenbeck, who had expected Anaconda to proceed along the same lines as earlier battles in Afghanistan, with little actual combat in the early stages. Hagenbeck thought Zia would be able to proceed into the Shahikot's villages and conduct "negotiations" over the enemy's surrender. "There might be a few shots fired" during the "negotiations," he said, but otherwise he thought TF Rakkasan would be able to land relatively unhindered along the eastern side of the valley to establish the blocking positions.

Task Force Hammer's failure to gain entrance to the valley presented Hagenbeck with his first critical decision of the day: whether or not to proceed with the supporting effort—the air assault—when his main effort had been stymied. Believing that Task Force Hammer would get back into the fight quickly, he decided to press on with the air assault. Zia's attack meant there was little chance of achieving any tactical surprise by delaying the rest of the operation. "To think we could come back and do this twenty-four or forty-eight hours later was just not realistic," he said.

About two hours into the fight, Hagenbeck spoke for the first time with Wiercinski, whose location on the Finger afforded him a ringside seat from which to observe the action on the valley. The Rakkasan commander also had good communications with Preysler and LaCamera as they fought their pieces of the battle. Hagenbeck was coming to the realization that Marzak was a nest of enemy fighters, rather than a village full of civilians, as much of the intelligence had claimed. He asked Wiercinski whether he saw any signs of civilians there. Wiercinski replied in the negative. Hagenbeck was getting similar reports from the AFO teams via Jimmy, who, he said, "was like a shadow, always whispering in my ear, telling me what was going on." Convinced there were no women or children in the village, the two-star general decided to use the Air Force and Navy jets to "level" Marzak.

Hagenbeck then faced a decision about where and when to insert the second lift of six Chinooks carrying the remainder of Wiercinski's force into the valley. The 250-plus soldiers spent the day sitting on the tarmac by their helicopters waiting for the word to launch. As the Mountain commander considered various courses of action and different flight routes to get the lift into the valley, some of his staff officers, trying to get ahead of the game, indicated that a "go" was imminent. As a result, some of the chalks climbed aboard their Chinooks three times, thinking they were about to go into combat. Each time they they were ordered back off the helicopters, their frustration mounted. Finally Hagenbeck decided to delay the second wave indefinitely, in the belief that the LZs were too hot and that LaCamera and the other commanders had the situation well in hand. "I didn't want a shoot-down, and we were pretty well stabilized by early afternoon," Hagenbeck said.

But as frantic reports of troops in heavy contact along the length of the eastern ridge poured in to Bagram, it appeared to observers in the Mountain headquarters that Hagenbeck was on the verge of pulling everyone out of the Shahikot and "recocking," i.e., trying again. Hagenbeck acknowledged that was an option he seriously considered. Perhaps anticipating an official order to that effect from Hagenbeck, his subordinates directed all the Rakkasan forces in the Shahikot to prepare for extraction that night.

By early afternoon TF Rakkasan radios were crackling to life throughout the Shahikot with orders from Bagram to pull out of the valley. The details changed as the afternoon wore on, but the essence of them was that helicopters would land after dark near the Halfpipe to evacuate LaCamera's troops who were pinned down there. All others, including Crombie's element, were to march north to LZ 15 at the top of the valley and prepare for extraction. This meant a tough movement of up to six kilometers through difficult, possibly enemy-held terrain at night. Up and down the eastern ridge, exhausted TF Rakkasan soldiers who had fought hard to gain their blocking positions now prepared to abandon them. When he heard the order come over the radio at Blocking Position Betty, Mark Nielsen was shocked at what such a directive implied about the enemy strength. *There must be thousands of 'em here,* he thought.

But then, after listening in to a radio conversation in which Hagenbeck and Wiercinski appeared to reach a decision to pull their forces out, at 3:27 p.m., Pete Blaber made the most important radio call of Operation Anaconda. Speaking to Jimmy, who sat just a few feet from Hagenbeck and the other generals, Blaber said that pulling out would be a huge mistake. The three AFO teams held much of the key terrain in the valley. The enemy was being decimated by the air strikes they were calling in. Regardless of the actions taken by Wiercinski and Hagenbeck, Blaber said the AFO teams would stay in position at least until the next day. This was "the battlefield opportunity of a lifetime," he told Jimmy, and he intended to keep on killing the enemy until there was no more killing to be done.

Jimmy walked over and recounted the conversation to Hagenbeck. After hearing him out, the Mountain commander gathered his three most senior advisers—Harrell, Jones, and Joe Smith, his chief of staff—and pulled them outside to discuss the situation. They considered three options: pulling everyone out, holding what they had, or doing something else. Hagenbeck's assessment, he said, was "we were being extraordinarily successful, except in one place," an almost exact rendition of the sitrep Blaber had delivered via Jimmy minutes earlier. The outcome of the huddle was a decision to "reinforce success" by putting the next lift into the northern end of the valley, with the intention of having the troops then fight their way south, while extracting the troops pinned down in the Halfpipe and on Rak TAC Ridge after dark.

To Hagenbeck, these decisions reflected the best options left to him. But some of his subordinates viewed them as the products of vacillation and a plan that was flawed to begin with. These officers were dismayed when the initial decision was taken to pull TF Rakkasan out. "The reaction [in the TOC] was 'What?! You don't take ground and then give it up!'" recalled a field grade officer. The same officer was cutting in his criticism of the way Hagenbeck "piecemealed" his forces into the valley without enough mortars, then pulled the Rakkasans out of their blocking positions and evacuated LaCamera's troops from the Halfpipe (a decision, he said, which taxed the limited number of Chinooks at Bagram). "It put the operation a couple of days behind," the officer said. Pulling out of the blocking positions "gave the enemy twenty-four to forty-eight hours to reinforce," he added. Instead, he said, "We could have moved forces to the Upper Shahikot Valley and gotten on the other side of the enemy. If I were making the decision, we would have gone there initially."

But D-Day afternoon was no time for Hagenbeck to dwell on what could or should have been done previously. His planned main attack element, the Afghan forces organized by TF Dagger, was withdrawing without ever having reached the mouth of the valley. The prevailing wisdom in Bagram had been that the Al Qaida forces in the valley numbered no more than a couple of hundred, and that they were living among 800 civilians in the villages. Now it appeared the enemy's strength was substantially larger than that, and there was no sign of any civilians. There were indeed enemy fighters in the villages, but there were also hundreds dug in on the eastern ridge and the Whale—the same high ground the special operators and CIA had been concerned about. The prediction that the enemy would try to either escape or negotiate a surrender now looked silly. The enemy was fighting hard and well, with high-caliber weapons—mortars, recoilless rifles, and howitzers—that no one in Bagram had warned of. Wiercinski and LaCamera had cautioned their troops before D-Day that "the enemy always gets a vote." Well, now the enemy was voting and the turnout was high.

12.

AS Ropel scanned the face of the ridgeline opposite him, he saw a black shape moving about 175 meters away. Peering through a three-power scope that he'd removed from a set of night-vision goggles and fixed to his M4, he realized that what he'd seen was the head and torso of an enemy fighter. The figure was in a bunker made by building a stone wall to connect a boulder to the side of the mountain. It was through a little window in the wall that Ropel could see the enemy. Because Ropel's ridgeline sloped down to the north, the bunker offered an excellent view of the Halfpipe as well as the spot where the VS-17 panels marked the location of some of the 1-87 rucksacks. Ropel immediately surmised the figure he could see was the observer who had been causing them so much trouble. But killing him proved difficult. The guerrilla knew he was being watched and seemed to enjoy the attention. He teased Ropel by popping his head up for a split second, then ducking before Ropel squeezed the trigger. After each shot Ropel fired, his target would yell *"Allah U Akhbar!"*—"God is great!"

Ropel quickly tired of this "cat-and-mouse game." He couldn't afford to waste the ammo, and so slunk back out of sight and waited for his adversary to lose patience. By now his men were also eyeballing the guerrilla's hiding place. Ropel told them not to fire. He had a better line of sight. "I did not want to scare him so he would go away," Ropel said. "I wanted him to think that we were gone." Sometimes the enemy fighter would lift his AK over his head, poke it through the window, and let off a burst without looking where he was firing. Ropel and his men watched and waited. Finally, as Ropel had figured he would, the figure raised himself for a couple of seconds to look around, exposing his head and upper torso. That was all the Polish NCO needed. He lined up the man in his sight and pulled the trigger. "I don't know if I hit him or killed him, but I didn't hear any more 'Allah U Akhbar!'" Ropel said. There was also a pause in the mortar fire, lending credence to Ropel's suspicion that his target had been calling it in.

The troops on the ridgeline with Ropel took only one casualty that afternoon—Sergeant Thomas Finch, who was shot in the foot. Finch later told his buddies that the bullet pulled from his foot was a 5.56 round, the caliber of the Americans' M4s and SAWs, but not of Al Qaida's AK-47s. Finch had almost certainly been hit from a bullet fired from the Halfpipe.

As the sun sank toward the western horizon, O'Keefe tried to call them back down off the mountainside, but Ropel's ICOM was attached to his vest and he was lying on it, inadvertently muffling it. Unable to reach Ropel by radio, about ten minutes after Ropel took his last shot at the Al Qaida observer, O'Keefe sent a single soldier scurrying up the mountainside to pull Ropel's team back down. They returned to their knoll and spent the rest of the evening helping with the casualties and retrieving whatever they could from the abandoned rucksacks.

As the afternoon lengthened, the Apaches and fast-movers vanished from the sky. The Americans prayed for nightfall, when they knew their night-vision equipment would give them an edge. The Al Qaida fighters must also have realized this, because after a lull in early afternoon, they raised the intensity of the fire they were aiming at the Halfpipe. Every weapon Al Qaida could bring to bear opened up on the Americans. Automatic weapons fire raked the Halfpipe from one end to the other. Volleys of RPGs flew overhead. Then the mortars started walking in, *crump! crump! crump!* "This was probably the enemy's biggest push to try to kill us," Kraft said. Even as the mortar rounds whistled in, his men were scrambling back up the slope to return fire. It was a sight Kraft would never forget.

Bullets suddenly chewed up the ground inches in front of the mortarmen in the northeastern corner of the rim. "We're moving," Raul Lopez said. Ashline raised his torso off the ground, only to feel a massive thud against his rib cage that spun him backward. "I'm shot!" he yelled. Fearing the worst, Lopez took hold of the handle on the vest's collar and dragged Ashline to the floor of the Halfpipe. Ashline slid his hand under his vest, looking for blood, but found none. His bulletproof plate had done its job perfectly. The round's impact had done no more than knock the wind out of Ashline and put a slight dent in the plate. He wasn't even bruised. "Get your ass back up there, there's nothing wrong with you," Lopez told him as Ashline scampered back up the slope.

Others were not so lucky. At about 3 p.m. those in the Halfpipe heard a thump as another enemy mortar round left the tube. Someone yelled "Incoming!" and everyone put their heads down. This time the Al Qaida gunners got it right. Buzzing "like a big bee," the round hit the battalion command post, wounding six soldiers. LaCamera ordered the troops to move to a safer position. As they did, two more rounds hit, but this time no one was hurt. It was the last effective mortar fire aimed at the Halfpipe. (Sergeant First Class Robert Healy, 1-87's operations NCO, suspected that this was because an air strike seemed to score a direct hit on the mortar position shortly after those rounds fell.)

In the dirt of the Halfpipe, sodden with piss and blood, the troops' heaviest weapon, the mortar, had long since run out of ammo. Now their machineguns were running low. Because M240B ammo was so heavy, it was shared out. Most infantrymen carried at least 100 rounds. Unfortunately, all that precious lead was in the rucks that littered the free-fire zone between the landing zones and the Halfpipe. In addition, the graphite powder that troops had been told to pack instead of oil as a lubricant for the weapons wasn't working and the guns were seizing. They could do nothing about the lack of oil, but soldiers sprinted in pairs to the rucks, frantically foraging for ammo and warming gear for the casualties as bullets nipped at their ankles.

Unlike Preysler's second lift of helicopters, which sat on the tarmac at Bagram all day, LaCamera's took off in late afternoon in an effort to give him some reinforcements. The 1-87 commander had made some long-range adjustments to the chalks, calling back to Bagram to order the rest of Peterson's platoon and every 60mm mortar section in the battalion to load into one of the Chinooks. He wanted to turn the Halfpipe into a firebase and hammer away at the enemies in high ground. The three Chinooks appeared over the Shahikot at dusk, carrying Kraft's 3rd Platoon in addition to the mortar reinforcements and ammo for Peterson's 120, which had been silent for seven hours. But the intensity of the battle raging on the valley floor prevented them from landing and they diverted to the FARP. Then they flew back to the valley, but were still unable to find a safe spot to put down. To the intense frustration of the troops on board, who knew that their buddies below were in a fight for their lives, the Chinooks turned and headed back to Bagram.

Lying in the dirt, Kraft glanced around and made a quick assessment. The enemy was throwing everything they had at the Halfpipe, but his men were still holding their own. They had 360-degree security, they were returning fire, and they had put the casualties in as safe a location as the Halfpipe offered. Still, one thing gnawed at his mind. Here they were, several dozen American soldiers pinned down under heavy fire in an operation that had been in the pipeline for weeks, yet there hadn't been an aircraft over the battlefield for half an hour. *Where the hell is our close air support?* he wondered.

WHERE the hell, indeed. No issue to emerge from Operation Anaconda has generated more heat and less light than the question of why the airpower upon which the TF Rakkasan troops were forced to rely for indirect fire did not deliver the results they expected. The debate began raging within the commands that had responsibility for Anaconda before the end of the operation. It then broke into the public eye in September 2002 with an interview that Hagenbeck gave *Field Artillery* magazine, the official journal of the Army's field artillery branch, in which he complained that it "took anywhere from twenty-six minutes to hours" for air strikes to go in. Air Force officials responded by saying they had been largely left out of the planning for Anaconda, and that what advice they had offered had been ignored.

Lost in all the vitriol was the fact that for long periods in the early stages of Anaconda, fixed-wing aircraft provided critical fire support to the troops on the ground. When the first wave of air assault troops ran into far greater resistance than they anticipated, the first thing they did was call for close air support. Often those calls were answered quickly with supremely accurate bombing that hit right where the young sergeants and captains asked for it, knocking out mortar positions and machine-gun nests, and slaughtering advancing enemy fighters. But at other times the wait for salvation from the sky seemed interminable to infantrymen like Kraft, facedown in the dirt dodging bullets. LaCamera complained of long periods during D-Day when there seemed to be no aircraft available to help his beleaguered men. But Stephen Achey, the senior airman whose job it was to arrange close air support for Nelson Kraft's C Company, and who was stuck in the Halfpipe just a few yards from LaCamera, saw things completely differently. "I don't know what he's talking about," Achey said of LaCamera's comments. "We were turning aircraft away because there just weren't enough targets."

By seizing the low ground, TF Rakkasan had put itself on terrain from which it was hard to identify the enemy positions from which it was receiving fire. The allied forces with the best awareness of the enemy's layout were the AFO teams, but TF Rakkasan took precedence over them when it came to whose calls for fire were answered first. The AFO teams and the TF Rakkasan units on the valley floor nevertheless managed to kill scores of enemy fighters using close air support on March 2, using everything from JDAMs dropped by B-52 bombers to F-15Es strafing enemy positions with their cannons, which were designed for air-to-air combat. However, many other targets went begging, despite Achey's protestations to the contrary. Officers and NCOs from Hammer, Rakkasan, and AFO all told similar stories of opportunities to kill enemy fighters missed because their calls for close air support went unanswered.

The problems that plagued the provision of close air support during the opening days of Anaconda would be argued over between Army and Air Force generals long after the last round had been fired and the last bomb dropped in the Shahikot. Inside the Beltway the problem was discussed exclusively in "Army versus Air Force" terms, but in reality it was a subset of other, wider problems afflicting Anaconda: CENTCOM's decision to treat the operation as a pickup game and its failure to establish a clear, tight chain of command for the operation; the reliance on aircraft to provide almost all the heavy firepower; and the overriding belief in all higher headquarters that the war was virtually over. Although Al Qaida's forces remained in the field and the leaders who had planned the September 11 attacks were still at large, much of CFACC commander Buzz Moseley's staff had been sent back to the United States, many to work on war plans for Iraq. During the critical last week of February, when his command should have been working closely with Mikolashek's and Hagenbeck's headquarters to prepare for Anaconda, Moseley was not at his desk at Prince Sultan Air Base, but was touring capitals in the CENTCOM region laying the diplomatic groundwork for the war with Iraq.

There were also specific problems that hurt the relationship between ground and air forces during the planning and execution of Anaconda: The small, enclosed battlefield meant the calls for fire often outnumbered the number of aircraft that could safely fly bombing runs over the valley simultaneously; the icy relationship between Mikolashek and Moseley, who should have been working hand in glove, trickled down to their staffs; the Mountain staff's failure to anticipate the likelihood of ferocious resistance on the enemy's part meant they had given only cursory attention to close air support issues; and the Combined Air Operations Center staff had grown used to controlling air strikes from their base in Saudi Arabia, rather than yielding that authority to the ground commander, as called for in joint doctrine. As ever in combat, it was left to captains and sergeants to bear the consequences of mistakes made by generals.

13.

BACK on the west side of the Whale Task Force Hammer was getting nowhere. By now they should have been sweeping through Serkhankhel, but instead they were hunkered down five kilometers short of the Fishhook under sporadic mortar fire. To make matters worse, they were discovering how little their designation as Operation Anaconda's main effort really meant. The February 26 special ops-only rock drill at Bagram had left McHale in no doubt Task Force Hammer would have first call on the close air support aircraft overhead. "It was very clear that we were the main effort," he said. "We had priority of fire all the way up until the point where we had cleared the valley." But now, with the shit well and truly hitting the fan in the Shahikot, those guarantees were revealed as nothing more than empty promises. During the hours of darkness, Hammer had been able to call on Grim 31 for support, but once dawn broke they were dependent upon staff officers at Bagram to line up conventional jets to provide close air support, and it wasn't happening. "We couldn't get another aircraft to drop bombs to save our lives," McHale recalled. "Nobody would drop a bomb on our side of the hill."

"Fires priority was, first and foremost, troops in contact," said Chris Bentley, the senior fires officer on the Mountain staff. "Then high payoff targets—those targets that must be engaged for you to have success; an example would be a heavy machine-gun. We knew we had to at least neutralize that target for our helicopters to have success coming in to the helicopter landing zones. And then the third category became main effort vice supporting effort. So to say the main effort would always have fires isn't always going to be true, because sometimes the main effort is supported by supporting the supporting effort, to allow the main effort to maneuver. So when 1-87 came under fire down in the southern part of the eastern ridge we simply provided them assets." When questioned whether, using his own criteria, the fact that Hammer was not only the main effort but was also in contact with the enemy meant it, rather than TF Rakkasan, should have enjoyed priority of fires, Bentley expressed skepticism that the accounts from Hammer personnel of being engaged by the enemy were accurate. "Did they ever take enemy fire?" he asked rhetorically, many months after the battle. Whether Bentley doubted the honesty of the Hammer officers or was merely misinformed about the opposition they encountered on D-Day, the fact that the senior fires officer in Bagram was making decisions based on such a serious misunderstanding of events on the battlefield tells its own story about how information was being shared between the different components of CJTF Mountain.

BY the time Texas 14 leader McHale had pulled back to the perimeter at Carwazi, Hoskheyar's troops, under the guidance of a couple of McHale's fourteen sergeants, had set up four of their own 82mm mortars. They oriented one tube towards Carwazi, another to cover the Fishhook, while the remaining two went straight into action, firing back at Hammer's tormentors on top of the Whale. Even though the mortar rounds aimed at his troops in the perimeter were falling short, Haas was determined not to just sit and take fire from the Whale without returning it. He already was fending off Zia's entreaties to be allowed to assault the Whale. "We're firing back," Haas recalled. "That gives Zia at least something to be happy about." This exchange of mortar fire continued sporadically for the next several hours, with Southworth convinced that the Hammer mortars put at least one enemy mortar crew out of action within thirty minutes. The overall Task Force Hammer situation had become so confused that the Special Forces soldiers decided to call formation in an attempt to count and then organize their remaining AMF fighters. In between shell bursts the SF troops got the Afghans lined up in platoons and counted heads, a process that took half an hour. The results were mildly encouraging. Although many of the AMF fighters appeared to have run off during the convoy's travails, almost all had made their way back inside the perimeter west of Carwazi. Once the formation broke up, at about 9 a.m., McHale finally sat down and tore open an MRE.

While the SF officers put their heads together to come up with a new plan, they sent some of Zia Lodin's men into Carwazi to see what was there. The AMF troops went through every building in the village and found no enemy fighters but about twenty women, old men, and children, all of whom they detained for a few hours. The Hammer leaders also expanded their security perimeter, putting Afghans on the Guppy and other high ground around Carwazi.

McHale and Thomas then communed. Things were falling apart, and they decided to come up with a common position to present to Haas on what would be required for them to continue the attack. The fire taken by TF Hammer to the west of the Whale had come as a shock. No-one in Bagram or Gardez had expected Al Qaida's defenses to extend that far west, but the volume of fire indicated that the convoy was already inside the enemy's defensive belt. That meant one thing for certain: driving through the constricted terrain of the Fishhook would be a hard fight. The Americans correctly surmised that their enemies would have DShKs pointing down into that defile, which was only wide enough to allow a single vehicle to pass at one time. "They had that place laced pretty tight," said one TF Hammer NCO. Task Force Hammer had been left with no good options. Even if they made it past Carwazi and Gwad Kala, attacking through the Fishhook with such a loosely controlled force and without close air support held few prospects for success. The wadi at the southern tip of the Whale was a natural ambush point. All the Al Qaida gunners would have to do to stall the convoy and turn the passage of Task Force Hammer into a turkey shoot was knock out the lead truck.

The two A-team leaders told Haas that they were willing to press ahead into the Shahikot only if they could get close air support to destroy or suppress the enemy they were sure would be waiting for them in the high ground overlooking the Fishhook. "If you start dropping bombs in and around Surki, no problem, we're gonna attack," McHale told Haas. But getting that sort of close air support required a detailed understanding of what was happening in the Shahikot in general, and the locations of the TF Rakkasan forces in particular—all information that the Task Force Hammer officers lacked. "We never had a good clear picture of what was going on with Task Force Rakkasan," McHale said. "We knew they were in contact, but we didn't know exactly where they were, or from which direction they were drawing fire. Continuing to fight a plan that was not very well conceived to begin with seemed foolish. Our greatest fears could have been realized, fighting right into a fratricide incident." Under these conditions, the captains saw little point in proceeding into the valley. "Clearly, we are not the main effort right now," McHale told the lieutenant colonel. Haas agreed. Nevertheless, all three officers started drawing up contingency plans in case they received the close air support.

Haas called Mulholland, who told him the situation for Task Force Rakkasan on the other side of the Whale was bad and that all available jets were being directed to help the infantry in the Shahikot. TF Hammer was getting similar reports from the AFO recon teams above the valley. Looking south from his position just south of the defile, Haas agreed with the A-team leaders that the "bowl" beside Gwad Kala and Surki would be a death trap for his trucks unless he received some serious fire support. With that looking less and less likely, he planned instead to maneuver Zia's forces on foot towards the Fishhook, using the high ground just west of Gwad Kala as cover.

Task Force Hammer was finally given a lone F-15E Strike Eagle, but this only resulted in more exasperation. Despite the assistance of TF Hammer's two Air Force enlisted tactical air controllers and one Air Force combat controller, the pilot flew back and forth for forty-five minutes but couldn't locate the task force on the ground and was reluctant to drop his bombs, even when told to just drop them anywhere on the enormous mass of the Whale. He continued circling above Hammer until he was "bingo" fuel, at which he point he left without delivering his ordnance, a tremendously frustrating experience for the troops on the ground who had been waiting hours for an aircraft. *How can you not find this mountain?* Haas thought. "We had mirrors out shining up at him, thirty-seven vehicles with VS-17 panels on top of them, and he could not find us," McHale recalled. "My only explanation is the battlefield was too confusing by that time, with too many elements on the ground, and he wasn't comfortable enough to drop a bomb." Other than a French Mirage jet that missed its target by over 2,000 meters, this was the only fixed wing aircraft apportioned to Task Force Hammer after the initial bombing of the Whale.

Soon, the enemy brought more firepower to bear against the troops hunkered down outside Carwazi. At 10 a.m. a BM-21 rocket flew about 100 feet over their heads with a loud buzzing sound before burying itself in the ground without detonating. (The rocket was almost certainly not fired from a launcher, but from a leaning position against a rock, a technique the mujahideen had used against the Soviets.)

Shortly afterward, as McHale was walking the perimeter, the quick reaction force sent to assist Harriman's convoy rejoined the main column. A few minutes later ODA 372's team leader strode back to the cluster of vehicles at the center of the position where Master Sergeant John Deane, aka "JD," his senior NCO, was waiting with tears in his eyes. "Did you hear?" JD said. "What are you talking about?" McHale replied. "Chief didn't make it," JD said. It was a crushing blow, but the team leader's initial response to the news of his second in command's death was a numb disbelief. "You spend your whole career in the Army saying, 'There's a potential to lose guys in this business,'" McHale said, recalling the moment. "But when it actually happens . . ." his voice trailed off. For a few moments the numbness remained, and then the thought of

Harriman's two fatherless children hit him like an emotional sledgehammer and the tears flowed. The others left the two alone to grieve together for several long minutes.

IN the early afternoon what had been relatively desultory mortar fire aimed at the Hammer position suddenly intensified after the fog that had obscured the top of the Whale for about an hour cleared. The increased range and caliber of whatever was shooting at them led Haas to believe that the enemy had brought "at least one" D-30 122mm howitzer in Babulkhel into action, using spotters on top of the Whale to radio target information to the gunners in the village on the valley floor. (U.S. troops later found a map in Babulkhel with target reference points plotted all along Hammer's route west of the Whale.) As the shells rained down, Spider had a lucky escape. Seconds after he wandered away from his Toyota 4Runner to confer with Haas, an incoming round showered his side of the vehicle with shrapnel. The whistle of the dropping artillery shells was punctuated by the occasional sizzle of a recoilless rifle round flying overhead. With rounds exploding thick and fast around them, the SF officers realized they were sitting ducks. They had to move somewhere that was hidden from the enemy observers on the Whale. Their sense that action had to be taken soon was heightened at 1:50 p.m. when Schwartz reported that about twenty enemy fighters were moving along nearby ridgelines trying to outflank his position.

Haas called Zia over to brief him on his plan to push the Afghan forces south using the high ground as cover. He also gave the order to move the trucks out of sight behind a low ridgeline nearby. But when they heard that, the Afghans decided enough was enough. Their morale was already low as a result of the fratricide incident, the truck accidents, and being on the receiving end of mortar, rocket, artillery, RPG and automatic weapons fire all day. One or two drivers decided that if they were going to move the trucks, they would instead pull them back through the defile northwest of Carwazi. On board the trucks were the Afghan troops' duffel bags, containing all the highly prized gear they had received from the Americans. As soon as he saw the truck with his duffel bag disappearing, one of the Afghan officers left his position and sprinted after it. Inevitably, his men followed, turning a misunderstanding into a pell-mell retreat. Haas' perimeter was collapsing as the Afghans ran back to the defile. "They didn't panic, but they started withdrawing fast," McHale said. So fast, in fact, that they abandoned their mortars and ammunition. Two Texas 14 men, Sergeant First Class Maurice Golden and Staff Sergeant Greg Sabus, were having none of that and pulled some of the Afghans out of the trucks to police up their equipment. Haas sent an American truck to chase down and halt the lead Afghan trucks, but the Afghans didn't pause until they were several hundred meters west of the defile. Meanwhile, the rest of Task Force Hammer was still in headlong retreat through the defile, with men outrunning vehicles as the convoy bunched up at the eastern entrance to the pass.

It was there, in the mass of men and machines just east of the choke point, that a mortar or artillery round detonated ten to fifteen meters to the right of the silver Toyota truck driven by Sergeant First Class James Van Antwerp and the truck in front of it. The blast shattered the windows and punctured the tires on the silver truck, which carried four special operators, and blew the bed off the other truck. Van Antwerp tried desperately to restart the smoking engine, but nothing happened when he turned the key. As other rounds followed, all of them far too close for comfort, Master Sergeant John Deane, ODA 372's senior NCO, who was riding in the back, gave the order to abandon the truck. Ditching the Toyota, which carried not only all their personal gear but also much of the material recovered from Harriman's vehicle, the four troops ran for their lives, carrying only their weapons, ammunition, GPS receivers and a couple of radios. There they didn't stop until they reached a wadi about 1,000 meters from the truck. They met up with other U.S. and AMF fighters there, and rejoined the main body of the convoy farther west. Meanwhile, the silver truck quickly became a target for the enemy mortars, with rounds landing all around it, and therefore all around the Hammer troops still stuck at the choke point. One of the rounds hit home, killing an AMF fighter instantly and wounding several others, three of whom "got screwed up pretty bad," McHale recounted. Haas had brought along his battalion surgeon, Captain Robert Price, a young doctor new to the Special Forces world, for just this sort of situation. The doc told Haas three of the wounded Afghans were "litter urgent" and several others were less badly hurt but still needed a medevac. But Haas knew that no U.S. military helicopter would land on what was a hot LZ with incoming mortar and artillery rounds. He turned to Spider. Not for the first or last time, the CIA operative came through. The veteran agency paramilitary fighter called his higher headquarters in Kabul. Within 45 minutes one of the CIA's Mi-17s was kicking up dust as it picked up the wounded Afghans. The medevac mission restored a little of the Americans' battered prestige in the eyes of Zia. "It showed that we were willing to accept risk to our aircraft to come get his wounded," Haas said.

Then RPGs started whooshing over the heads of the men of Task Force Hammer, an indication that the enemy fighters Schwartz had seen earlier had now penetrated the loose cordon of AMF troops on the nearby hilltops to get within a few hundred meters of the vehicles. All this happened as the AMF fighters manning that perimeter were running back along the high ground parallel to the main body of the convoy. The Special Forces troops managed to halt about half of the convoy west of the defile on a dirt track bounded on either side by sand that was too loose for the trucks. They rounded up as many AMF fighters as they could, counted heads again and tried to link all the Afghans up with their commanders and vehicles. But as they did so some of the older Afghans—battle-scarred mujahideen in their forties and fifties—began to take out their frustrations on their younger brethren. "They're so upset that they've left the battlefield that they're dragging guys out of the backs of the trucks and kicking the shit out of them," Haas recalled. "Talk about chaos." Like military policemen, the SF troops had to jump into the melee to break up the brawls.

With fistfights raging around them, Haas and Zia looked west and saw several jinga trucks still barreling towards the Zermat road. Zia sent several subordinates to chase the trucks down and Haas turned his attention back to the headcount. But while Haas was distracted, Zia decided to take off after the errant vehicles himself. Then one of Hammer's CIA operatives delivered an alarming message to Haas: Zia was planning to attack Zermat. Haas quickly concluded his attempts to reorganize the convoy and ordered it to move out in the direction Zia had taken. The Special Forces lieutenant colonel finally caught up with his G-chief on the outskirts of Zermat, where Zia was walking down the line of vehicles talking on the radio.

The G-chief in whom the Americans had placed so much faith was becoming unhinged. "Zia is just beside himself now," Haas recalled. "He's embarrassed by his guys, he didn't get the fifty-five minutes of [close air support] like he thought he would, he's taking casualties, and he feels like he's been let down by his guys, by me, by everybody." Again the Afghan leader walked up to Haas and, with a face like thunder and his hands raised to the heavens, screamed "Kojast planes?!?" ("Where are the planes?!?") "He didn't speak much English, but he understood 'planes,'" Haas recalled.

In his frustration and desire to redeem himself in the eyes of the Americans, Zia confirmed his patrons' worst fears. "I am attacking Zermat!" he told Haas through an interpreter. "The enemy is there, I can't get to the valley, so I am attacking Zermat—there are enemy there." "No you're not," said Haas, appalled that his G-chief was even proposing this course of action. "I am attacking Zermat!" Zia reiterated. "They are all traitors. They told everybody we were coming. We are attacking Zermat!" With that he turned and began rounding up his men.

The SF officers at the heart of TF Hammer knew everything had changed. They were no longer being treated as the main effort—if they ever had been—and events in the Shahikot were now playing the decisive role in the decision-making at Bagram. They needed to know what role Mountain headquarters foresaw for them. "Were we counter-attacking? Were we relieving pressure? It was now a totally different ball game," McHale said. But the SF officers couldn't even get a clear picture of how the battle was unfolding elsewhere. "We were not getting good feedback on that—where were the 101st? How far had they gone?" McHale recalled. The confusion and chaos had reached "the point where our attack didn't make sense. . . . Nobody likes going backward, but where are we going to go to? What piece of terrain are we going to go seize and what support are we going to get to get there? If you can slice us something [in terms of air power], and it's effective and useful, then put us somewhere. But there was no mission given to us. . . . There wasn't a good, solid FRAGO [fragmentary order] that came out from any one headquarters that said, 'Okay, break, break, break, here's the situation, this is what we're gonna do,'" McHale said. "None of that was coming down. Nobody had another plan for where do we go from here." There was no way Hammer was going to stay where they were. "We needed to get out of there, because staying right there outside of Zermat and camping there that night was bad juju," McHale said. The morale of their Afghan allies had sunk to new lows. "They were pissed, they'd taken casualties, yet they didn't feel like they were getting any air support," McHale said.

For Hammer's remaining Afghan fighters, the Americans' inability to deliver their vaunted air power when it was needed was the final straw. They had suffered chaos, confusion and casualties in the drive from Gardez, then been attacked by an American aircraft, killing and wounding more of their colleagues, seen the promised "fifty-five-minute" bombardment of the Whale turn into something closer to a fifty-five-second bombardment, and when the enemy fighters left undisturbed on that massive humpback mountain turned their guns and mortars on the convoy, the Americans had no response.

Now Task Force Hammer was back on the road where its problems began over twelve hours previously. They were out of range of the mortars on the Whale, but their new location wasn't making the SF officers feel much more secure. Many of the trucks were parked just fifty meters from a compound where anyone could have stuck their head over the wall and sprayed the line of vehicles with AK fire. "Zermat was not a friendly town, we were standing out in the middle of the desert, we couldn't drive off the road, so we were really not in a defendable place right there," McHale recalled. "It was just a horrible place to be."

Haas eventually dissuaded Zia from attacking Zermat, but the price was high. The furious Afghan leader decided to pull his troops off the battlefield altogether. "I'm not staying here," he said. "If I can't attack Zermat, it's stupid for me to stay, because I will be attacked from Zermat. You let me down. I am going back to Gardez." At the same time, Mulholland called, urging Haas to get Zia back into the fight. Haas, who felt that his force had already "taken an ass-kicking," tried to explain why that wasn't possible. "I've got a serious problem here," the lieutenant colonel told his boss. "Zia's unloading." "You've gotta stop him," replied Mulholland, who had promised the Mountain planners that his G-chief would not let them down. "You've gotta keep him in the fight."

"We were attempting to encourage them not to fall back, but instead to hold what they had, to stay in the field," Rosengard, the Dagger operations officer, said. "We knew that to be a stretch, but we wanted it to occur." While Haas spoke with Mulholland on the Dagger command net, Zia paced up and down the line of trucks talking to his subordinates on his own hand-held radio. Haas was caught between a rock and a hard place. His boss was ordering him to prevent Zia from leaving the area, but the Afghan leader had other ideas. Haas struggled to explain the reality on the ground to the TF Dagger commander while keeping Zia close enough to ensure that the G-chief didn't take off on his own again. After a few minutes Zia had had enough. He climbed into his pickup, gave the order to move and the Afghan convoy began heading toward Gardez.

Haas spoke bluntly with Mulholland. "This is the deal," he said. "Zia's leaving." If Hammer had to retain a presence near the Shahikot, Haas suggested concentrating his U.S. troops with the AFO guys at their observation post by the Guppy. Mulholland wasn't interested. "You've gotta get Zia to stay," he insisted. "Zia's not staying," Haas replied. "In fact, Zia's driving down the road right now. We can either lead him, or follow him."

The time for a hard decision had come. To Haas, it was crucial that the Americans stick with Zia, even in retreat, in order to maintain some semblance of rapport with the G-chief. "Had we left him, it would have been, 'Okay, they cut me loose, I'm not gonna play with these guys anymore, they're untrustworthy," he said. "I explained to Mulholland that I could no longer debate the situation or options—I needed his approval to lead Zia home. Despite what I am sure was intense pressure on Mulholland not to give me that approval, he relented anyway and supported me, the on-scene commander. It was a tough call, but the right call." At about 2:30 p.m. Schwartz told Rosengard that Task Force Hammer was returning to the safe house. The depleted convoy drove north, and by nightfall all surviving members of TF Hammer were back in

Gardez. There, Zia Lodin and Hoskheyar denigrated the Americans for letting them down.

HAMMER'S retreat resulted in mutual recriminations between some Mountain staff officers, who had always doubted the Afghans would show up for the fight and now felt vindicated, and those in TF Dagger who had guaranteed that the AMF fighters wouldn't let the Americans down, but felt that by not arranging for close air support TF Mountain had not kept up their side of the bargain. The Special Forces officers were particularly infuriated when, in the days following Hammer's withdrawal from the battlefield, Mountain officers made disparaging comments about the Afghans. "They wanted to turn around and bad-mouth the jundees and 594 and 372, because they fell back," Fletcher said in exasperation. "Why'd they fall back? Because they were out in the open, coming up to the Whale in that big open area, and they were just getting pounded by mortars. They had nothing to fight against the indirect fires that they were taking, because they couldn't get any CAS [close air support] in there to take it out. And they had no artillery. So they were left exposed. They would have been able to push into that little gap there no problem, if they had the CAS." But to Bentley, who said he didn't recall ever not providing a close air support asset to Hammer, the cause and effect were reversed. It was Zia's failure to reach the Shahikot that resulted in close air support being devoted to Task Force Rakkasan, not the other way around. "There was no intent or malicious effort to empty the sky for Task Force Hammer at all . . . I was never under the impression that our lack of bombardment of the Whale was a contributing factor to Zia not fulfilling his piece of the plan," Bentley said. "Once Zia's movement ceased and we knew it wasn't going to happen, we were going to go into the Shahikot valley, with or without Zia."

"The bottom line is the attack failed," Rosengard said. "The attack was turned back by the enemy, and the commanders on our side, rather than having caused that to happen by a decision, accepted that as the imminent reality, and then went back to reorganize, to live to fight another day."

14.

NIGHT finally cast its protective cloak over the beleaguered soldiers in the Halfpipe. The enemy fire died down as the guerrillas lost sight of the troops in the darkness. Then the most effective weapons system the United States was to employ against Al Qaida forces in the Shahikot arrived overhead—the AC-130 Spectre. The grunts in the Halfpipe quickly figured out the best way to use the gunship. They would identify enemy positions using their night-vision goggles and fire at them, causing the enemy to fire back, inadvertently confirming their position. Then the Americans would point their rifles' laser sights (invisible to the naked eye) at the enemy locations as the Spectre arrived overhead to pummel the enemy with 105mm howitzer fire, each round sending a shower of sparks into the night sky. "A lot of the enemy would go into the caves, but the AC-130 was pretty damn effective," Kraft said. "It caught a lot of them with their pants down." For the first three hours after the sun went down, he said, "We handed the enemy their ass."

Then, during another lull, LaCamera finally got the chance to medevac the worst of his two dozen casualties, some of whom had been lying in pain on the cold ground for fifteen hours. The agents of their salvation were the crew members of an Air Force HH-60 Pave Hawk helicopter that flew into the valley with an Apache as its escort. When Kraft heard the birds were inbound, he ordered Staff Sergeant Robert Brault to establish an LZ about 200 meters west of the Halfpipe, marking the LZ with infrared "chem lights" and strobe lights. The medevac helicopter found Brault's LZ. As it landed, the guerrillas in the ridgelines awoke to the fact that an American helicopter was hovering tantalizingly within range. An RPG flew out of the darkness and exploded in midair behind the Pave Hawk's tail. *Oh, no, now we have a helicopter down,* thought Ropel, watching from the top of his knoll. *Something else to worry about.* But with relief he realized the helo had survived and was making a 90-degree turn before landing. Once it was on the ground, the 1-87 troops detailed to help the casualties rushed the most seriously wounded aboard. They weren't the only ones making a dash for the helicopter. A lieutenant who had not been wounded, but was clearly shaken by the day's combat, was seen to throw his weapon away and run toward the bird as it sat on the ground with its rotors turning. As he tried to jump aboard, Brault grabbed him by his webbing and threw him away from the helicopter. "This bird is for wounded!" he shouted at the terrified lieutenant. ("Some people just weren't meant for combat," Brault said later.) The fighters in the mountains weren't done. A DShK gunner fired two ten-round bursts at the helicopter as it sat still and vulnerable on the valley floor. Healy's heart sank. *They're gonna hit the medevac bird with our guys on it,* he thought. But again, the enemy's aim had been off. The 240 gunners in the Halfpipe returned fire furiously, while Ropel's men pointed their lasers at the spot where they thought the DShK was. Moments after the Pave Hawk had pulled away with the casualties on board, the AC-130 opened fire and the DShK position disappeared to cheers of "Yeah, motherfuckers!" from the troops in the Halfpipe.

Knowing they were due to be pulled out of the valley in a couple of hours, the 1-87 leaders focused their efforts for the rest of the night on two goals: killing as many of the enemy as possible with close air support, and retrieving as much gear as possible from their abandoned rucksacks. Kraft sent fire teams from 1st Platoon to retrace their steps to their LZ, searching for dropped gear, while 2nd Platoon fire teams did the same to their LZ. By now enemy fire was minimal. The AC-130 had done its job well, and for the first time all day the soldiers were able to search for abandoned rucksacks without having to dodge bullets. Priority was placed on retrieving complete rucksacks (many had been torn apart by Al Qaida fire) and sensitive items like night-vision goggles. LaCamera was keen to avoid taking risks in order to salvage items of dubious importance. He didn't want to have to write a letter that said, "Dear Mrs. Jones, your son was lost because he was going to get a set of binos."

Word came that the helicopters were inbound. 1st Platoon remained in the Halfpipe, rifles aimed at the eastern ridge, providing cover while the rest of the force moved to a new LZ Brault had set up about fifty meters from where the medevac bird had landed. (Chinooks, being larger aircraft, needed a bigger LZ.) Peterson and his mortar troops recovered their tube and the rest of their gear and moved to the LZ with 2nd Platoon. Despite the pain he was in from the dozen pieces of shrapnel lodged in his legs and buttocks, Grippe had stayed on the battlefield rather than be medically evacuated. Now he carried his own ruck as he limped away from the Halfpipe. 1st Platoon then withdrew from the Halfpipe, followed by Kraft and Hall. The arrival of the two Chinooks led to one last adrenaline rush as the troops piled aboard and then sat for what seemed an eternity waiting for takeoff, bracing for an RPG or mortar round to hit them on the brink of their escape. But none came. Exhausted from a day of battle, cowering in fear of the AC-130, or dead, the enemy had shot his bolt. The Chinooks lifted off. After they had been airborne for a couple of minutes, the soldiers breathed a little easier. The battle of Hell's Halfpipe was over and they had all lived to fight another day.

What LaCamera's force achieved March 2 was not what they had set out to accomplish. When the Chinooks carried them away from the Shahikot, there were no blocking positions in the southeastern corner of the valley. But those blocking positions, so important in the Anaconda plan, had been made almost irrelevant by the enemy's disposition and determination to fight a fixed battle. There's an old Army saying, "Don't fight the plan, fight the enemy." The eighty-six soldiers Paul LaCamera took into LZs 13 and 13A had fought the enemy damn well before withdrawing without losing a single man. Kraft took issue with descriptions of the battle as "an eighteen-hour miracle." He told his troops, "It wasn't a miracle, guys, it was you." Peterson was equally proud of the soldiers' performance, but he was under no illusions that things might have turned out a lot worse. "We were blessed," he said. "We were fucking blessed."

THE night also brought a respite for the nine men of the Rakkasan TAC stuck on the Finger. (Mako 31 had long since taken their leave of the TAC to reoccupy their original observation post. "I've killed enough for today," one of the SEALs told Savusa before walking off.) Under cover of darkness the junior officers Corkran had brought with him as a security team left the position to scout out a new LZ for the Chinook being sent to extract them. They found what looked like a good spot about 500 meters to the west and returned to collect the rest of the TAC. This time Savusa walked point as the short column descended to the valley floor. But when they reached the spot picked out by the security team they realized it was too rocky. They walked over 1,000 meters to a more suitable location. Once there Gibler got on the radio to direct the inbound Chinook to their location. He did this based on the direction the noise of the Chinook's engine seemed to be coming from, because the helicopter pilots couldn't see the green chem light being held aloft by one of Corkran's captains. It was about 3:30 a.m. when the Chinook finally landed. "That was an awesome sight," Murray said. "It had been a long day." Even before the helicopter took off, enemy fighters were swarming over the position on the Finger that the TAC had just vacated. As he had on the flight into the valley, Savusa said a prayer as the helicopter carried him back to Bagram. This time he prayed for the soldiers who remained in the valley. Murray's thoughts reflected those of Peterson sitting on another Chinook. The Air Force officer knew they had ridden their good fortune hard and put it away wet. "We were," he said not long afterward, "the luckiest sons of bitches."

WHEN darkness fell all Rakkasan units along the eastern ridge except for those with LaCamera began one of the most difficult movements in Anaconda. The plan was for all elements to link up west of Betty and then move north to LZ 15, which lay on some fairly flat ground about 750 meters west of the eastern ridge and 2,000 meters east of the north end of the Whale. But things started badly and only got worse. Preysler pulled his men off their blocking positions. Baltazar's 2nd Platoon moved down to the link up point to await the others. The next closest unit, C Company's 1st Platoon, joined up with them.

The temperature plummeted, freezing clothes that were drenched with sweat from the movement down the slope. A soldier became hypothermic and stopped breathing. The medics resuscitated him with CPR and put him in a sleeping bag, but to Nielsen it was a warning sign. "Hey sir, I don't think we're going to be able to move as a team tonight," the sergeant major told Preysler. "We've got some guys going down." The two leaders agreed to secure the site they were at and move on at first light.

Helberg's scouts linked up with Luman's platoon and established a perimeter in a wadi about 1,000 meters west of Diane and settled in for the night, waiting for Crombie's force. The temperature was 17 degrees Fahrenheit. Luman created a rest plan so everyone got a couple of hours sleep while others stood watch.

After lightening their load by dumping all but the most essential equipment and supplies from their rucksacks, Crombie's men embarked on a torturous march west and then north, aiming for the infrared strobe light marking the link-up point. Every painful climb uphill preceded a slipping, sliding descent down a snow-covered north-facing slope. The ground was so jagged and rock-strewn that there seemed to be nowhere flat enough to place a foot. Winded, Crombie pushed himself forward, driven on by adrenaline and a sense of responsibility. Aware that they were "moving through Indian country at night," he applied "a lot of asshole leadership" (his words) to get troops to pull security when the column paused to rest. But eventually he had to acknowledge his men were smoked. He halted the march 300 meters from the link up point and, like Luman, established a rest plan so half his men stood guard while half slept. Overhead an AC-130 circled protectively.

While the colonels and generals in Bagram tore up plan after plan and the Rakkasan infantry marched this way and that along the eastern ridge, Pete Blaber's thirteen NCOs hidden in the mountains kept on killing. Some of the air strikes they called in were spectacular, all were ruthless; none more so than the bombing of a mud compound that appeared to be a field hospital, or at least a casualty collection point, for wounded Al Qaida fighters. Speedy and Bob had patiently watched and waited, biding their time as they observed more and more enemy casualties being brought to the little fortress 200 meters northeast of Zerki Kale. Once the sun had set and the target appeared ripe, with between ten and twenty personnel inside, India added it to a list of four other targets they wanted struck. At about 10:15 p.m. a B-52 with the call sign Mummy 21 high overhead released a stick of JDAMs from its belly that flew unerringly to their targets, hitting each in quick succession with a series of explosions that rumbled down the valley with a sound like nearby thunder. "He hit all five of those targets dead-on," said an NCO who watched the strike. Three bombs hit the casualty collection point alone, completely destroying it. "This was a devastating hit," stated another account. "No survivors were seen."

The reality was now dawning at the TF Blue TOC in Bagram, the TF 11 operations center in Masirah, and the JSOC headquarters in North Carolina that Blaber had been right about the Shahikot and that there was a real battle going on there. In the Blue TOC, where TF 11 commander Trebon was monitoring the operation, having flown to Bagram from Masirah shortly before D-Day, there was a flurry of planning activity underway to try to capitalize on AFO's success. Trebon's phone was ringing off the hook with calls of congratulation on what Blaber's—and by tenuous extension, Trebon's—teams had achieved. Even Central Command chief Tommy Franks called to compliment Trebon on the success of India, Juliet, and Mako 31. Trebon forwarded several of these calls to Blaber. Then, after discussing the situation with Joe Kernan, the TF Blue commander, Trebon placed a call to Gardez himself. But Trebon's call in the afternoon had a sting in the tail. "Pete, wonderful job," he told Blaber. "Look, we can't ask you guys to continue this, you're not set for that. What I want to do is turn this over to TF Blue, let them command it; and let them continue prosecuting the fight." Blaber and his AFO organization should be out looking for "the next battlefield," rather than continuing to fight on this one, he said. "I want to send some [Blue] guys down and I want you to get these guys in there as quick as possible." Blaber asked whether this meant TF Blue was going to conduct direct action missions, their supposed forte. No, Trebon replied, their initial missions would be recon missions just like the three teams already in the valley had been conducting.

To the AFO personnel in Gardez and in the valley, Trebon's move to have TF Blue take over the operation was ill-considered and appeared to be motivated by professional jealousy. After pooh-poohing Blaber's contention that there was a large enemy force in the Shahikot, the other TF 11 elements had been left on the outside looking in when events had proven him correct and his thirteen men were the only JSOC forces on the battlefield. The TF 11 elements in Bagram and Masirah seemed to have no appreciation for the thousands of man-hours the AFO teams had invested in understanding the Shahikot. To those who hadn't spent time in Gardez, the formula for success in the Shahikot seemed simple: put some operators in the high ground and have them call in air strikes on the enemy. They had been listening to India, Juliet, and Mako 31 doing that all day. Now the SEALs wanted in on the action, and Trebon was only too happy to help.

Realizing that even with logic on his side he had no hope of winning this argument, Blaber tried to compromise with Trebon in an attempt to ensure that the TF Blue teams weren't sent in blind. He recommended that the Blue teams follow the same routine as the three teams already in the valley; i.e., that before infiltrating, they spent some time at Gardez studying the history and geography of the Shahikot, talking to the CIA, Special Forces and Afghan militiamen who had been working in the area, and reviewing all the relevant intelligence. Blaber said he had always considered himself as working for Kernan, the TF Blue commander. He went on to suggest that TF Blue send an officer down to Gardez to work underneath him and help integrate the new SEAL teams into the operation, with Blaber reporting to Kernan, the TF Blue commander. Trebon's response was noncommittal. Trebon told Blaber that Kernan would be calling him soon with further guidance.

Next to call was Kernan. Blaber again made his pitch to stay on in Gardez working directly for Kernan, but with any SEAL teams sent into the Shahikot reporting to Blaber as the AFO commander. Kernan said that instead he would send an officer down to Gardez sometime in the next couple of days to take over command and control of the operation, and asked that Blaber help ease the new guy into the job. No problem, said Blaber, adding that in his opinion Tony Thomas, the Task Force Red commander, or the Blue operations officer would make excellent choices. Kernan said he'd discuss it with his subordinates in Bagram and get back to Blaber with a decision. He also asked Blaber for his recommendation on when the official turnover of command and control to TF Blue should be. Blaber suggested the moment the first TF Blue team lifted off from Gardez en route to the Shahikot. But the conversation ended without a firm decision on when the handover should be.

Then TF Blue's operations officer in Bagram got on the radio. He wanted to use a helicopter resupply flight to send one of his SEAL teams into the valley to relieve India. The teams' need for resupply *was* becoming critical. All three were low on food, water, and batteries, and Mako 31's SEALs were also low on ammo after all the shooting they'd done at the DShK position and protecting Wiercinski's command post. Juliet's resupply would be flown in to LZ 15 in the north of the valley after the Rakkasans had secured it. For India and Mako 31, who were due to link up after dark, AFO had planned a "speedball" method of delivery—stuffing a duffle bag full of the needed supplies and kicking it out of a helicopter as it flew close to their positions. This was a far different proposition from landing a team in the valley, which would break Blaber's strict "no helicopter infiltrations" rule.

"You can't send a team in on a resupply helicopter that hasn't been through Gardez," Blaber told the Blue operations officer. "They're coming from Bagram, they have no idea what's going on on the battlefield." "Well, that's the guidance we got," the Blue operations officer replied. "We briefed it to General Trebon and he approved it." "That is not going to work," Blaber protested. Speedy, monitoring the conversation from his perch in the Shahikot, came up on the net and backed Blaber to the hilt. "It's unsafe, it's unsound, it makes no sense," he said. Trebon called Blaber back. "That team's got to go in," he said, trying to make it sound as if pulling the three AFO teams out in the middle of the fight was somehow doing them a favor. "We've got to relieve you guys, you're getting smoked," the general said. Blaber again tried to reason with Trebon, but to no avail. Sending fresh Task Force Blue teams in without first giving them time to prepare for the Shahikot environment would amount to "setting guys up for failure," the AFO commander said. He had no idea how prophetic his words would be, and of the price that would be paid in blood for that failure.

15.

AT midnight on March 2 a Chinook descended out of the night sky to land on a gentle slope at the snow line in the north end of the Shahikot Valley. Forty-three men rushed out to establish a perimeter around the aircraft. As soon as the last soldier had run down the tail ramp, the twin-engined helicopter flew away, leaving utter silence in its wake. Lying behind their rucks in the treeless, moon-washed landscape, the men felt under a spotlight. Their senses were on high alert, straining to capture the first sign of an enemy attack. At any moment, surely, the silence would be broken by the staccato crackle of automatic gunfire, the report of a D-30 howitzer or the hollow *whoomph* of a mortar round leaving the tube. But there was nothing but silence.

Captain Kevin Butler, commander of 2-187 Infantry's A Company, was suspicious. *Where is the enemy? Is he setting a trap?* The enemy in the Shahikot was now fully alert to the possibility of American helicopters landing in their midst. Butler had therefore expected to fly into a hot LZ, and warned his men to mentally prepare themselves accordingly. Two other Chinooks bearing the rest of his company had also landed safely just to the east and the eighty-six troops they carried were making their way to him. The thirty-year-old Pattenburg, New Jersey, native was impatient for their arrival. He knew his luck, if that's what it was, wouldn't last. The company needed to find cover.

A bright orange flash illuminated the northern end of the valley for a split second. Moments later the boom of an explosion reached the ears of Butler and his men. The soldiers turned their heads southwest to see a cloud of smoke rising from the dark, hulking mass of the Whale. A few minutes later they heard the dull *Crump! Crump! Crump!* of an AC-130's 105mm gun hammering the Al Qaida guerrillas harassing LaCamera's men in the Halfpipe. Another AC-130 droned overhead, but the only other noise was the regular beeping of the SINCGARS radios and the harsh whispers of young officers and sergeants giving orders.

The other two chalks walked quietly up to Butler's perimeter, and he immediately got the company up and moving. They marched south down a gradual incline for about 1,000 meters until they reached a narrow wadi that carved a ten-foot deep furrow from the northeastern corner of the Whale across the north of the Shahikot. This wadi was the same egress route over which Wiercinski and Rosengard had argued during the planning sessions, and led straight to the pass on which Butler was to establish Blocking Position Amy. But Butler had been unaware of its existence until he stumbled upon it. Now that he'd found it, however, he realized it made a perfect spot to establish his command post and bed some of his men down for the night. Even after a day that began long before dawn and had been spent getting on and off the helicopters in the sun, he wasn't too tired to see that the wadi offered complete protection from the enemy's direct fire weapons—recoilless rifles and machine guns—and almost complete protection from his mortars and howitzers. It would take an extremely good, or lucky, mortar crew to land a round inside the wadi, the floor of which was only about five feet wide in places.

A trim officer of average height with short, stubby hair that was already flecked with a steely gray, Butler was relieved to have made it this far without a hitch. The repeated delays in getting his company into the fight had discouraged him, and he had not been able to get a clear picture of the enemy's disposition from the Rakkasan chain of command. Communications problems and the continued—albeit often inadvertent—compartmentalization of information meant the Mountain and Rakkasan staffs were having a hard time building a comprehensive picture of the enemy, even though the information required existed at various echelons and locations, particularly at the AFO headquarters in Gardez. He ordered the men to assume 50 percent security. In other words, half of his force unrolled their sleeping pads to get a couple of hours sleep while the other half maintained watch along a perimeter about 500 to 1,000 meters from his command post. Tired out as much from the nerve-stretching tension of their day on the Bagram runway as from the high-altitude hike from the LZ, the soldiers soon fell asleep to the sound of AC-130s and fast-movers "rearranging the countour lines" of the Whale and the eastern ridge. It was a lullaby every infantryman in the Shahikot quickly learned to love.

IN the middle of the night Preysler, the 2-187 Infantry commander, relayed the latest change in plans to Baltazar. Instead of being extracted, Baltazar would instead be reinforced by Kevin Butler and A Company. Nevertheless, the C Company commander and his men still had to move north to secure some high ground east of LZ 15. So in the predawn darkness, Baltazar got his company up and moving.

BUTLER'S men were out of their sleeping bags before 6 a.m. The first thing they heard as they heated water for coffee and cocoa was the rumble of more air strikes. Convinced by now that the only people in Marzak were Al Qaida guerrillas, Hagenbeck had directed that the village be "leveled." High overhead a lone B-52 traced lazy contrail arcs in the azure sky. As it passed over Marzak, the village was shaken by a series of explosions so powerful that Butler's troops 5,000 meters to the north felt the concussions in their chests.

By 8 a.m. Baltazar had linked up with Butler. Preysler also met with Butler and passed on the latest version of the plan: Wiercinski's reserve, Ron Corkran's 1-187 Infantry, was to fly in to LZ 15 and then attack south down the eastern ridgeline toward Takur Ghar and the gorge just below it, with Butler's company following. Baltazar was to divide his company between Blocking Positions Amy and Betty in the northeast of the valley. Butler told his NCOs he expected plenty of "contact" before the day was done, and that their day would consist of walking through the hills and having enemy fighters pop up from behind cover, fire an AK-47 or an RPG at them, and then run away as they returned fire.

ROGER Crombie and his men were also on the move before first light, covering the final 300 meters that separated them from Luman and Helberg. With a few hours' rest under their belts, they found the going much easier. They were walking over terrain that was merely rolling, rather than jagged. As the sun rose, Crombie and Helberg used VS-17 panels to signal each other before finally linking up. Helberg's scouts were to lead Crombie's men to Butler's position. That would mean a march of about 7,000 meters, but the scout platoon leader explained to Crombie that they would be covering gently rolling terrain instead of the harsh, rocky slopes he had encountered thus far. Moving through easier terrain with double the men he had had up to that point was a source of great relief to Crombie. Nevertheless, this wasn't a walk in the park.

They still had to rest every 800 to 1,000 meters. In addition to their lack of oxygen and sleep, Crombie's men were now on their last reserves of stored energy. The decision to dump so many supplies from their rucksacks meant they hadn't brought any food. By midmorning most of the troops were approaching twenty-four hours without having eaten anything.

As it snaked its way north along the eastern ridge, Crombie's column was spread out over about 300-400 meters in four separate platoon-size groups, with about seventy-five meters between each element. Every gully forced the troops into single file—always a vulnerable formation in such terrain. By the time the column had hiked about 1,400 meters and was marching through a creek bed about 300 meters east of the compound seized the previous day by Preysler and his men, Crombie had become concerned that his troops weren't pulling security properly. He got on the radio and reminded his platoon leaders of the passage in *We Were Soldiers Once . . . and Young* (a book about the Battle of the Ia Drang Valley in Vietnam read by every infantry officer), in which a column of U.S. infantry is ambushed and cut to pieces when it doesn't look to its own defenses. The captain knew his troops were tired and that exhaustion bred complacency. "My concern was we still had a good ways to go, and the guys were only going to get more fatigued," he said. This was "a leadership issue," he said. "If you're a leader, you need to be out there enforcing the standard." The lead elements of the column—Helberg's scouts—began following a trail. Crombie cut them loose, not wanting to follow the trail with his own troops, whom he pointed northwest towards his link-up point with 2-187 just south of LZ 15. He was already in contact with Preysler. The 2-187 commander told Crombie to just get to the northern creek bed. Preysler would guide him in from there.

Crombie's troops pressed on, gasping and sweating as the altitude and the heat of a forced march wearing heavy body armor took its toll. About 1,000 meters from the northern wadi, the column stopped again. A 1st Platoon soldier had collapsed. He had become overheated from his exertions, despite the chill mountain air. As the medics attended to him and the other troops sat down, gasping for breath, they heard mortars landing somewhere to their north.

BALTAZAR had just left Butler's command post a few minutes after 9 a.m. to return to his 1st and 2nd Platoons in the high ground when a mortar round exploded with a massive boom not 200 meters from Butler. Another followed within seconds as soldiers dove for cover. From their knoll-top positions on the perimeter, his troops scanned the mountainsides for any sign of the enemies who had taken them under fire. It wasn't long before the eagle-eyed infantrymen spotted two mortars firing at them: one on the crest of the Whale, about

4,000 meters to Butler's southwest, the other about 5,100 meters directly to the south. But mortar rounds weren't the only ordnance being hurled toward the troops in and around the wadi. Someone somewhere was firing a 57mm recoilless rifle at them, as well as a DShK and RPGs set to airburst mode. Those soldiers not manning the perimeter scanning for targets hunkered down in the wadi and listened as the fat DShK rounds zipped harmlessly over their heads.

To Baltazar, who was en route back to his men after visiting Butler's command post when the mortar attack commenced, the DShK fire was scarier than the mortars, because he couldn't hear the heavy machine-gun firing, just the bullets as they flew by. He hunkered down for about thirty minutes until a break in the firing gave him an opportunity to run back to his platoons, which were split between a couple of wadis.

As the incoming mortar rounds continued to crash in, making a lot of noise but doing no damage, Butler had one option that hadn't been available to most of his fellow Rakkasan leaders on D-Day. Alone of the company commanders who air assaulted into the valley on March 2, he had opted to bring his company's 60mm mortar section in with him. Standing on the Bagram runway the previous morning as news came in of the pounding the first wave was taking from Al Qaida mortars, he was unworried. "We're taking ours, and I'm willing to bet that our guys are better than their guys," he'd said. Now his mortarmen had a chance to back up the captain's boast. "It's all fun and games until the *other* guy has a mortar, too," Butler half-chuckled as he strolled down the wadi looking cool and unperturbed checking on his men.

(Butler's pride in his mortar section was grounded in reality. Specialist Tim Ouditt, one of his mortarmen, had once received a commander's coin—a prized keepsake in the Army—from Dick Cody, the 101st Airborne commander, for landing a mortar round directly on a truck at a range of 1,500 meters during training at Fort Campbell.)

As Butler's mortars went to work, with the soldiers on the perimeter calling in adjustments, Baltazar worked the radio to line up some close air support. None of Butler's soldiers had been wounded, but it appeared only a matter of time before that situation changed for the worse. At 10:15 a.m. a mortar round landed just 100 meters from Butler's command post. "They've got us bracketed," said Staff Sergeant Chris Harry, the squad leader from Baltazar's company who was standing nearby. At 10:21 a.m. a series of explosions marked the arrival of the close air support. But continued bursts of automatic weapons fire and more incoming mortar rounds told their own story of how successful the bombing run had been. "If they want the mortar situation sorted out, they'd better have a whole lot of CAS stacked up," Butler commented. "It was such a nice morning, too," his first sergeant, Jonathan Blossom, added dryly.

Watching the mortar duel from the top of a hillock about 600 meters to Butler's south were Specialists Justin Musella and Justin Celano, a sniper team from 2-187's scout platoon. They could see one of the enemy mortar positions firing at them, but it was 1,500 meters away, almost twice the effective range of their Remington 700 sniper rifle. By noon Al Qaida's mortarmen apparently had spotted them too. Mortar rounds began landing near the sniper team's position, kicking up clods of dirt. Each round fell closer than the last. The enemy had their range. As they saw another puff of smoke from the Al Qaida position, Musella and Celano knew they had to move, but decided to wait until the next round landed. This one was going to be close. Pressing themselves to the dirt they heard the shriek as gravity pulled the round down from the cloudless heavens. Then, to their horror, they saw the round's shadow on the ground beside them, growing larger by the instant. Each realized that in a split second the high-explosive shell was going to land in their midst and there was nothing they could do. They braced themselves for the inevitable.

Then, with heart-stopping drama, it hit a rock just four feet from them with a metallic *ding!* and bounced away. It was a dud. Without pausing to contemplate their immense good fortune, the pair sprinted back to a safer position as another round exploded less than 100 meters away. As soon as they reached the fall-back position, a round hit their old position about a minute after they'd vacated it. This time it exploded. Musella and Celano beat a hasty retreat all the way back to the wadi.

There, Kevin Butler was getting frustrated. The combination of close air support and his own mortars appeared to have silenced one of the enemy mortar positions, but the other continued to fire intermittently at his command post. Butler had had enough and hit upon an off-the-wall plan he thought might work. His spotters had told him that whenever the enemy mortar crew heard the roar of an inbound jet or the thump of one of Butler's mortar tubes firing, they would disappear into a cave or bunker, only to reemerge after the bomb or mortar round had exploded, waving defiantly at the Americans they knew would be watching. Butler's fire support officer, 1st Lieutenant Steve Leonhart, told him F-15s were inbound to strike the Al Qaida position. Knowing his mortar rounds had a thirty-two-second flight to the target on the Whale, Butler told his mortar crews to fire several airburst rounds in quick succession when they saw the bomb explode. The crews did exactly as they were told. As before, the enemy mortarmen ducked into their hiding place as soon as they heard the jet, which dropped its bomb close—but not close enough—to the enemy position, while Butler's mortar section hung round after round. And just as before, the four-man Al Qaida mortar crew reemerged once the dust had cleared, laughing and waving. Only this time, just as Butler had planned, they had been too distracted by the bomb to notice the sound of his mortars firing. As they waved mockingly at the Americans, seven 60mm mortar rounds exploded over their heads, blowing them apart.

Butler was quick to pass the credit to his mortarmen. "That was a phenomenal performance from everybody in that mortar section," he said shortly afterward. But the episode also validated his decision to bring the mortars in the first place—a choice that cost him seats on the Chinooks for several riflemen—and was an extraordinary example of cool, calculated thinking under fire for a young officer experiencing combat for the first time. The ROTC graduate of Mansfield University in Pennsylvania had spent the entire ride in on the Chinook "war-gaming" how he would act in front of the men and what he would do in the event they came under fire on the LZ. They didn't, but that only delayed his trial by fire by a matter of hours. When the bullets did start flying, Butler was surprised at how naturally command came to him. "You experience an epiphany out there," he said. He saw things that needed to be done, ordered people to do them, and everything worked out.

The efforts of both the mortar crews and the captain had not gone unnoticed by their fellow soldiers. "We've got the best mortarmen in the battalion," a soldier was overheard telling a buddy later in the afternoon. "And the best company commander," his pal replied.

BALTAZAR'S 3rd Platoon, under the command of Kelly Jack Luman, bore the brunt of the barrage of DShK, mortar and RPG fire. The platoon was crossing a creek about 400 meters south of—and within sight of—Baltazar when the Al Qaida gunners opened up. "They were lighting our ass up," Luman recalled. Luman ordered Schmitz to stay on the lip of the wadi to cover the platoon's movement with his machine gun. As Schmitz and his twenty-year-old assistant gunner manned their weapon, DShK rounds chewed up the ground inches from their faces, spewing dirt into Schmitz's mouth. Luman gave the order to drop rucks and take cover in the wadi. As his soldiers scrambled for cover, an RPG flew in, exploding beside Sergeant Earl Beaudry, Jr., who was lying on the ground trying to identify the source of the enemy fire. The explosion blew the chest plate clean out of Beaudry's body armor and sent shrapnel tearing into his legs and buttocks. "That's when it really became real for me," Schmitz said. Soldiers descended on Beaudry and dragged him to cover in the wadi. "My AG [assistant gunner] is going crazy: 'Sergeant, what are we gonna do? What are we gonna do?'" Schmitz said.

Watching his men getting slammed by mortar fire, Luman felt helpless. "My heart sank," he recalled. He had called for close air support, but the jets were still twenty minutes out. There was nothing to be done but hope Luman and the other leaders down in the wadi system could hold the men together.

As the mortar rounds landed closer and closer, the company executive officer, a lieutenant who was moving with Luman's platoon, completely lost his nerve. "We're gonna die! We're gonna die!" he shouted as he curled into the fetal position. Luman was infuriated with the officer's behavior. "Shut the fuck up!" the sergeant shouted at the lieutenant cowering in the dirt. "It was affecting my men," Luman explained. As he moved down the wadi telling his guys everything was going to be fine, Luman heard a report over the radio that the 10th Mountain company following him was also taking heavy fire.

AS his men took a breather and his medics treated the heat casualty, Crombie's ears detected the sound of a mortar tube firing from a flat ridgeline to his south. This round wasn't aimed at Butler's troops up north, but at Crombie and his men as they weaved their way toward them. The mortar rounds were quickly followed by small arms fire. As the young Americans sought cover, bullets cracked over their heads and ripped holes in the rucks they had temporarily laid aside. Crombie, like Butler, assessed that his column was being engaged from three sides.

"This becomes one big battle drill—reaction to contact," Crombie recalled. In most cases, reaction to contact requires a soldier to do two things: seek cover and return fire. Training kicked in and Crombie's soldiers did exactly that. "Our fire was far more effective than the enemy's fire was," Crombie said. Nevertheless, the captain had no desire to just sit and trade fire with an enemy who controlled the high ground. He told his platoon leaders to disentangle their troops from the fight and continue north. Crombie led a small element—his command post, half of his 1st Platoon and a couple of scouts—down into some low ground from which they could engage the enemy on the ridgeline to their right. From there they called in fire from Butler's mortar section. Meanwhile, at the back of the column, half-a-dozen soldiers remained in the kill zone, holding off the enemy to their rear in order to allow the rest of the force to maneuver north.

Crombie ordered his men to drop their rucksacks. His men were too exhausted to move under fire while carrying the heavy rucks, he thought. They were only about 700 meters from Preysler's position and could always return for the rucks at a quieter time. The fatigue was even getting to the company commander. Like many of his troops, his canteen had run dry. His tongue felt twice its normal size. More incoming mortar rounds signaled the enemy's intention to keep the pressure on Crombie and his men. But for once the Al Qaida mortar crews were off their game. The rounds fell 200 meters away from the Americans, and served only to irritate Crombie. *This is unbelievable,* he thought. *We are the United States Army, and somebody is firing mortars at us. Why aren't we destroying these mortars?* He was convinced that at least one of the mortar tubes was located inside or right behind the compound seized—and then vacated—the previous day by 2-187.

But, like their brethren elsewhere on the battlefield, Crombie and his men were surprised by the enemy's use of a weapon system no one had mentioned in the run-up to Anaconda. "It's like, 'Mortars? This wasn't in the brief,'" he said after the battle. "We never thought they'd have so many mortars." The incoming rounds at least had a salutary effect on the heat casualty. "He recovered real quick," Crombie said. "He got his clothes and gear on very quickly once that first mortar round landed."

The last element to move back was the tiny rearguard led by Sergeant Reginald Huber, with Specialist James Brossoie keeping the enemy's heads down with his 240. "This was a coordinated ambush that we walked into," Crombie said. "I was just amazed that there were no casualties."

Crombie's men spent the rest of the day keeping a low profile in the creek bed. When night fell, they moved out to try to recover the gear they had dropped. "It's a much easier movement now," he joked later. "We don't have rucksacks." They got to a point about 300 meters from the rucksacks, when they spotted an enemy fighter in a position overwatching their gear. The U.S. troops ceased their movement and directed an AC-130 to the guerrilla's position. Crombie's men put out infrared strobes to mark their own position just as the medevac Chinook for Beaudry was flying in. The helicopter crew saw the strobes and landed, thinking that Crombie's element had the casualty. Confused and worried about the attention that the helicopter would draw to their position, one of the infantrymen ran up to the helicopter. "What do you want?" he shouted at the crew. "Where's the casualty?" a crew chief asked. "We don't have any yet, but if you don't leave, we're going to have some," the grunt told him. The troops moved back to the creekbed. They would wait until the next day to recover the rucksacks.

BALTAZAR'S 2nd and 3rd Platoons and Helberg's scouts also spent the rest of the day hunkered down in the wadis, before linking up with Baltazar that night. In the meantime the captain sent a team down to Luman's platoon to collect the wounded Beaudry and carry him up to Baltazar's position, from where soldiers from Butler's company carried him down to their wadi to prepare him for medevac. Baltazar told his men they would occupy Blocking Position Amy the following day, at a time to be synchronized with 1-187's attack south. Butler's men held the position in *their* wadi, with Preysler's command post about 100 meters to the east in the same creek bed.

Hagenbeck had intended his reserve—a task force built around Ron Corkran's 1-187 Infantry—to fly into LZ 15 in midafternoon. But the reports of heavy enemy fire in the north end of the valley caused him to abort the mission and reschedule it for after dark. However, the order to abort only got through to three of the six Chinooks. As a result, 1-87's B Company, parts of 1-187's C Company plus 1-187's engineer platoon all landed (safely) at LZ 15 at about 3:10 p.m. and spent the rest of the afternoon waiting for their colleagues to show up.

THE day had been another learning experience for the infantrymen. Their enemy still showed little sign of withdrawing or losing heart, and had again pounded them with an arsenal of crew-served weapons. But the U.S. troops had more than held their own tactically, responding to each attack with accurate firepower from their own weapons and from the aircraft overhead. Incredibly, despite the thousands of bullets and hundreds of high explosive mortar rounds, artillery shells, and rocket-propelled grenades Al Qaida forces had fired at them, the Americans hadn't yet lost a man. Task Force Rakkasan's luck was holding.

MARCH 3 began frustratingly for the AFO teams. At about 2:25 a.m. an MH-47 that had flown straight from Bagram on a resupply mission dropped off Mako 22, another Task Force Blue team, a couple of kilometers to the south of India's position. Mako 22's mission was to take over India's observation post so Speedy, Bob, and Dan could return to Gardez to refit and rearm before being reinfiltrated elsewhere in the Shahikot. Speedy had not had prior warning that Mako 22 was inbound, but wasn't alarmed when he saw the SEALs walking toward his observation post. The new team quickly explained they were his relief. But Mako 22 was a five-man assault team, not a reconnaissance and surveillance team like Mako 31, and hadn't brought all the right gear needed for their mission in the Shahikot, forcing Speedy to leave some of his own equipment behind for the SEALs to use. (Mako 31, which didn't make it all the way to India's location south of the Fishhook during the night, was also due to leave with India.)

The Chinook crew on which Mako 22 flew in also kicked out India Team's "speedball" resupply duffel bag, which burst and spread its contents over the mountainside. When India had finally gathered the batteries, water and MREs, Speedy, the quintessential hunter and carnivore, got on the radio and said he would like to personally thank whoever packed him twenty-four vegetarian MREs. "Thanks a lot. Out."

As their radios buzzed and crackled with different plans to resupply or relieve them, the teams spent the morning trying to call in air strikes on enemy positions on the Whale, in Babulkhel and on Hill 3033. Several of these positions included mortars or machine-guns firing on the Rakkasans. Others consisted of enemy fighters building new defensive positions in the valley. But in almost all cases during the first half of the day the teams could not arrange for aircraft to strike their targets. To the NCOs sitting in their observation posts around the valley watching enemy fighters shooting at U.S. troops with virtual impunity, the close air support system seemed completely gummed up.

Exceptions to this pattern included a series of air strikes that Mako 22 called in at about 6:40 a.m. on targets in Babulkhel, a B-1 bombing run on the Whale arranged by Juliet, and an impressive Apache strike on a two-man position spotted by India on the southeast corner of the Whale. On other occasions bombs were dropped, but missed their targets. The situation improved somewhat as the shadows lengthened. At 6:04 p.m. a B-52 dropped seven JDAMs on an Al Qaida observation post and bunker complex on the Whale where Juliet had spotted an enemy fighter peering through binoculars at the Rakkasan troops. The mission was a complete success, scoring a direct hit that obliterated the enemy positions and almost certainly killed all nine enemy fighters seen there. About thirty minutes later Juliet finally got the bombing runs on Hill 3033 for which it had been waiting most of the day. A B-52 conducted two bombing runs, one for each of the 400-by-1000-meter bomb boxes Juliet had sketched out on the mountain. The first bombing run made seven guerrillas, a mortar tube and a DShK "disappear" and the second killed one of four "support personnel" nearby, the team reported.

One of the more successful air strikes in the valley wasn't carried out by the military, but by the CIA's Predator UAV. Both the Air Force and the CIA were flying Predators in Afghanistan, but unlike the Air Force's version, code-named Pacman, the mission of which was pure reconnaissance and surveillance, the CIA's Predator, code-named Wildfire, was armed with a couple of the same Hellfire missiles fired by the Apache. The CIA was also free of many of the bureaucratic processes that were tangling up the business of close air support in the valley. At 5:15 p.m., after observing enemy fighters moving in and around a Zerki Kale building that signals intercepts suggested was a possible command and control facility, the CIA Predator fired a Hellfire into it.

Shortly after dark India and Mako 31 left their positions and walked southwest out of the Shahikot to meet the three-vehicle exfil convoy led by Captain John B., Sergeant Major Al Y. and Hans. As they marched, they heard another B-52 emptying its bomb bay onto the Whale. It sounded as if the entire mountain was exploding. The teams' departure meant that of the original thirteen operators who had ventured unseen into the Shahikot, only the five men of Juliet remained. The dynamic of the operation was changing, nowhere more so than in Gardez.

TAKUR GHAR

1.

AS dawn cast faint shadows across the Gardez safe house courtyard on March 3, the AFO headquarters personnel went to sleep for the first time in over two days. They awoke two hours later to be greeted by a sea of new faces. A slew of Task Force Blue operators had arrived via road and helicopter while the AFO men were asleep. The new arrivals included two SEAL teams code-named Mako 30 and Mako 21, a Gray Fox operator named Thor, and in charge of them all, a TF Blue officer named Lieutenant Commander Vic Hyder.

The selection of Hyder to command and control the SEAL elements in Gardez was a strange decision on the part of Captain Joe Kernan, the Task Force Blue commander. Hyder had already been involved in two incidents in which he had displayed, in the view of many people familiar with them, extremely poor judgment. On New Year's Eve he had been the senior man in a group of SEALs who had "violated instructions," according to a TF 11 officer, by taking an armored SUV that belonged to TF Bowie and driving it down the Bagram to Jalalabad road on what Hyder described as an "area familiarization" reconnaissance outing. The TF 11 officer said it could also be described as "a joyride." Against the advice of the others in the vehicle, Hyder, who hadn't been in country long, had the driver blow through a couple of checkpoints manned by Afghan militiamen loosely allied with the U.S. forces. When they tried the trick a third time the militia fighters fired at them. The SEALs must have thought they were safe in their armored cocoon, but a bullet pierced the rubber seal between the bulletproof glass and the armor at the back of the SUV, went through the backseat and the driver's seat before striking the driver. He was not badly wounded, but had to pull over. The SEALs were traveling with their rifles stashed in the back of the vehicle, not on their persons. So rather than fight their attackers off, they meekly surrendered to the tribesmen, who took whatever they wanted from the vehicle. (The joke around the rest of TF 11 was the episode resembled the scene in the movie *Stripes* in which Bill Murray's hapless American troops surrender their weapons to the Czech police.) The only long-range communications system the SEALs had was an Iridium satellite telephone. But they had neglected to bring the number for the TF Blue TOC in Bagram. Hyder was left with little choice but to call the SEAL Team 6 headquarters in Dam Neck, Virginia, and ask them to call Bagram for help. Pulling the SEALs out of that sort of jam would usually be a job for the Ranger quick reaction force. But Hyder had picked the very evening that one Ranger force was departing Bagram and another arriving, and the gear for both elements was stowed on pallets when the plea for help came in. In the end a British force stationed at Bagram sent one of its helicopters down to pull the SEALs' chestnuts out of the fire. The SUV episode reflected "bad judgment" on Hyder's part and alerted JSOC commander Dell Dailey to a potential problem with the SEAL lieutenant commander, according to a senior Army officer. But other than being "counseled" by his chain of command, no further action was taken against Hyder.

The second of what came to be known in Joint Special Operations Command as "Vic Hyder's three strikes" occurred on a dark Afghan night when he had led TF Blue troops on what turned out to be a "dry hole" mission. While they were waiting, hidden, in the dark, Hyder and his men saw an unarmed old man approaching through their vision goggles. The man was unable to see them in their hiding positions. Hyder ordered him—in English—to stop. When he failed to do so immediately, Hyder shot him through the eye and killed him. An investigation apparently cleared Hyder of criminal wrongdoing in the matter, but the incident left a very sour taste in the mouths of many of his TF 11 comrades. The senior Army officer, who was familiar with the repercussions from Hyder's actions, defended Kernan's decision to keep giving Hyder missions that carried huge responsibilities, adding that SEAL Team 6 handled their internal discipline issues "at least as well" as Delta. "Hyder got as much of a fair hand as any other person would who ultimately showed, probably, not the right judgment," the general said. "You can't pick out a lousy judgment type guy right off the bat."

So Hyder was still around to take charge of the SEAL force in Gardez. His third "strike" was yet to come.

THE AFO operators in Gardez were stunned to see the new arrivals. It was the first time any TF 11 personnel had shown up at Gardez without first giving them a heads-up. "What are you doing here?" they asked Hyder. The SEAL officer told them he was there "to C2 [command and control] the Blue guys," and had orders to infiltrate the two SEAL teams into the Shahikot as soon as possible to support the fight. Blaber and Glenn P. assumed that Trebon had acted upon Blaber's suggestion to place a TF Blue officer under his command at Gardez to help integrate more SEAL elements into the battle. But the SEALs' first priority appeared to be establishing their own communications with TF Blue at Bagram and TF 11 in Masirah. It was becoming clear that Blaber would have no say in which teams were inserted into the valley, and that his strong recommendation that the Blue teams take time to familiarize themselves with the region was being ignored. Someone—AFO—had finally found the enemy, and now everyone wanted a piece of the action, especially TF Blue, which had seen almost none so far. "Once Blue realized there was a fight going on they were gonna get their guys in the fight come hell or high water," said another TF 11 operator.

In Bagram a satellite call came in for Trebon. On the other end of the line was Blaber. "What's going on, sir?" "Same thing I told you," Trebon replied. "I want these guys in the fight. Vic is in charge of the Blue guys, you just stay in charge of the AFO guys, and when do you think you can turn them over to TF Blue?" Trebon was telling Blaber he would no longer even be in command of the non-Blue AFO teams—India and Juliet—and perhaps not even the other AFO personnel at Gardez. Blaber said he didn't know when he could turn everything over to TF Blue. He was planning to accompany Chris Haas and the rest of TF Hammer as they tried to get Zia Lodin back to the Shahikot that night. To Blaber, the Zia mission was the most important thing going in the next twenty-four hours. He, Chris Haas, and Spider all planned to accompany Zia, for two reasons: to reduce the risk of friendly-fire incidents, and because they thought from the ferocity of Al Qaida's resistance that there might be a high value target trapped on the Whale. "I can't give you a time," Blaber told Trebon. But the general was insistent. "I want you to come back to me when the exact time is that you're transitioning this to Blue," he said.

Blaber and the other AFO personnel assumed that until he officially "transitioned" command of TF 11 forces in the Shahikot to Hyder, he remained in charge. But as the day wore on, the Delta operators in the safe house didn't realize that from the tent the SEALs had erected in the courtyard, Hyder was communicating directly back to the Blue TOC at Bagram. Command and control of what had been the most successful part of Operation Anaconda was now starting to fray.

In the Gardez TOC a small crowd of SEALs, AFO operators, and TF Dagger troops began scrutinizing maps looking for the best places to put observation posts that night. Among the men scanning the maps and overhead photos was the Mako 30 leader, a skinny senior chief petty officer with reddish blond hair and beard nicknamed "Slab." Blaber had worked closely with Slab on missions in Bosnia and considered him one of the most proficient operators he'd ever known. The Delta officer took Slab aside. "I'm really uncomfortable with you guys going right in," he told the NCO. "I want to make sure you get all the advantages that the other guys had." "I totally agree," Slab replied. "But I do what I'm told, and we're being told to go in tonight." Blaber didn't understand the urgency. The prospect of a couple of nights without as many AFO/TF Blue recon teams in the valley didn't overly worry him, because TF K-Bar was planning on inserting over twenty recon teams around the Shahikot. Trebon's phone in Bagram rang again. Blaber was calling. Were the SEALs to go in that night? he asked. They were, Trebon replied. The Air Force general, who had never commanded a ground combat operation before, was now making tactical reconnaissance decisions. "Back here it looks like you need guys up on the mountains. Those other guys need to be replaced. . . . You've got to pull them out." This time, Trebon spoke as if to leave Blaber in no doubt. He was to put both SEAL teams straight into the fight that night. That was an order.

2.

WHILE the SEALs began planning their infiltrations, the rest of the safe house's residents were consumed with trying to get Zia's Afghan force back into the fight. Task Force Hammer's retreat had left the CIA and Special Forces men involved—both in Bagram and Gardez—by turns angry and despondent. Blaber was determined to fix that. He had gathered them around him the previous night when they got back to the safe house and told them they had accomplished their mission by sealing the western avenue of escape from the Shahikot and forcing the enemy fighters to expose themselves by firing at the Hammer column. This in turn had allowed the AFO teams to identify the enemy positions and call in air strikes on them. He had told them to get some rest and then get ready to go back out. A plan was in the works to send TF Hammer back down the same route with the aim of resealing the western approaches to the valley.

That plan evolved throughout March 3. In its final form it involved Task Force Hammer, which now included a third A-team, ODA 394, bringing a smaller Afghan force under Zia back toward the Shahikot. But this time, instead of moving south past Carwazi, Gwad Kala, and the Whale and then east through the Fishhook, they would move north and seize the Guppy. In essence, the plan was a variation of what Harriman's mission had been: to establish a blocking position and observation post near the Guppy. The plan was dubbed "Operation Payback."

Mulholland flew in to the safe house to talk to the SF guys, instantly earning their respect. "He was the only guy to ever come talk to our guys," McHale said. Sad and somber over Harriman's death, the Dagger commander was the first to tell McHale that Casenhiser and Wadsworth were going to be okay. He listened to his troops' assessment of the situation and was briefed on Operation Payback. He also told them the folks at Bagram were not "talking bad" about them. "That was important and good to hear," McHale said. Meanwhile, Brigadier General Mike Jones, the military liaison to the CIA also serving as one of Hagenbeck's deputies, and Rich, the CIA Kabul station chief, each visited Spider and his men. The lack of close air support for Hammer on D-Day had left Spider as angry as the other leaders in the convoy. "He was pissed because the Agency thought they got left out to dry, too," Haas said.

McHale, the ODA 372 leader, decided he had to return to the States to represent the team at Harriman's funeral. He flew back to Bagram with Mulholland. During a quiet moment in Bagram, the captain spoke with the colonel, obtaining the Dagger commander's approval to put Harriman in for a Silver Star. McHale also obtained the colonel's commitment to keep the remainder of his team in the fight. McHale knew anything other than a return to battle would cripple their morale. "My analogy was, you can't let the guys feel like they lost the last game of the season," McHale said. His men's attitude was "We need to see this through to the end now, let's get back in there," said one of them. "We don't run from anybody."

But the Americans had to persuade the Afghans to step back into the furnace with them. As it turned out, the AMF fighters were more willing to follow the Americans into combat than they were many of their own leaders. A senior CIA interpreter at the safe house spoke to Haas. "I want to let you know that all the [Afghan] troops are talking about the bravery and the courage of the Americans during the battle," he told the officer. "They don't trust their leadership, because they all freaked out, but the Americans were calm and cool and came and picked them up when their vehicles left them. They're all talking about it around the campfire, that they will follow the Americans anywhere they want them to go." The SF troops built on this goodwill by holding a ceremony for the AMF fighters that day in Gardez, both to hand out individual medals and to commemorate the Afghan fighters who had been killed. The awards, which the Special Forces guys had designed and ordered ahead of the operation, included the Afghanistan Order of the Wounded Lion (the equivalent of the U.S. Purple Heart, for those wounded or killed in combat), the Afghanistan Commendation Medal, the Afghanistan Legion of Merit, and the Afghanistan Meritorious Service Medal. When the ceremony was over, the SF troops had a message for the militiamen: "We're going back in, tonight."

WITH Trebon and Kernan insisting that Mako 21 and Mako 30 go into the Shahikot that night, the only issues remaining to be settled were how the teams would be infiltrated and where they should establish their observation posts. Hyder asked the AFO guys for their recommendations. The AFO planning cell in Gardez received no guidance from the Blue TOC in Bagram, so Glenn P. put together folders on possible reconnaissance targets. By 3 p.m. Blaber and the other TF 11 personnel in Gardez had decided Mako 21's six operators would fly to LZ 15 at the north end of the valley—the same LZ into which Butler's troops had air assaulted at midnight—and from there move east to link up with and resupply Juliet. After receiving a situation update from Juliet, they were to move farther east to establish an observation post overlooking the Upper Shahikot Valley. The plan for Mako 30 was more ambitious. Unlike Mako 21 and 22, which were assault teams that specialized in direct action, Mako 30 was a SEAL Team 6 reconnaissance outfit. Its leader, Slab, was the most experienced SEAL sent from Bagram, and his team, with six SEALs and one Air Force combat controller, was the larger of the two. Blaber wanted to get Slab's team onto the most dominant piece of terrain in the valley: the peak of Takur Ghar. Anyone on top of the 10,469-foot mountain would enjoy a commanding view of the entire valley, as well as the Upper Shahikot Valley to the east. That was where the AFO commander had intended Juliet to establish their observation post, until the snowfall had forced them to remain in their position to the north. Along with the other U.S. commanders in Anaconda, including Hagenbeck, Blaber was keen to get an observation post on the mountain. But he didn't feel a need to do it that night. He didn't want to break his "no helicopter" rule, and there was no way to infiltrate the team overland in time to get them to the top of the mountain before dawn. But the decision was out of his hands. Trebon, Kernan and Hyder had decided Mako 30 was going in tonight, and if that were the case, they were going to have to fly in. (Despite repeated requests, Trebon, Kernan, and Hyder were not made available for interview for this book by U.S. Special Operations Command.)

An examination of maps and overhead imagery in Gardez revealed what looked like a suitable LZ on a spur about 1,300 meters east of Takur Ghar's peak. The operators in Gardez called it "LZ 1" (ignoring the fact that the

Rakkasans had already named another patch of the Shahikot "LZ 1"). There had been no enemy activity reported at the spot. Mako 30 was to be ready on the rough airstrip by the safe house at 10:30 p.m., with insertion planned for 11:30 p.m. The SEALs knew it was important to give themselves plenty of time to scale the mountain and set up their observation post before first light. They thought the climb would take about four hours.

Glenn P. gave the SEALs a detailed briefing on what to expect in the Shahikot. For Mako 30 he could refer to extensive, detailed overhead photographs of Takur Ghar, which he had ordered when it looked like Juliet would end up on top of the mountain. His briefing should have been a red flag to the Navy men. The intel NCO told Mako 30 and Vic Hyder that there was a high likelihood that the enemy already occupied the top of Takur Ghar. He based this conclusion on several factors: human intelligence reports had indicated the enemy was there; an overhead photo appeared to show a man-made trench or fighting position on the peak with what appeared to be a DShK; and the enemy had already demonstrated a determination to occupy the other high ground around the valley, such as the DShK position Goody's team had discovered on the Finger and the numerous mortar and DShK positions on the Whale. There was no reason to suppose the enemy's approach to Takur Ghar—the valley's most desirable terrain—would be any different.

In and of itself, this information should not necessarily have dissuaded Mako 30 from launching on their mission. By landing at the base of Takur Ghar at night and climbing up the mountain, Slab's team could ensure that any contact they made with the enemy would be in the form of a "meeting engagement"—an unexpected meeting between two opposing forces—and not an ambush. In a meeting engagement, the SEALs' night-vision goggles, superior marksmanship and the air power they could call upon would likely enable them to break contact and get away.

But already the SEALs were thinking of avoiding the tiring slog up the mountain that a landing at LZ 1 would entail. During the afternoon Slab proposed a couple of alternatives to Blaber, one of which was to land halfway up the mountain. Blaber tried to steer Slab back to the original logic of landing at the offset LZ, and believed he had dissuaded the SEAL from doing anything other than that. Then at 10 p.m. Hyder approached Blaber in the busy AFO TOC and asked the Army officer what he thought of having Mako 30 land on top of Takur Ghar instead of at LZ 1. Any Ranger or Special Forces soldier would have been able to tell Hyder that he was proposing a huge tactical blunder. It is a reconnaissance axiom that a recce team should never infiltrate by helicopter directly onto its observation post, because doing so essentially signals the team's location to the enemy. But this apparently had not occurred to Hyder. Blaber told him he didn't think the 160th pilots flying the mission would go for it. But Hyder said that he lived next to the pilots at Bagram, and he thought he'd be able to persuade them. Shortly thereafter, both SEAL teams moved to the airstrip.

IN Bagram, Hagenbeck greeted TF 11's decision to put a recce team on top of Takur Ghar enthusiastically. Because TF 11 worked directly for Central Command, Hagenbeck had no authority to task any of its operators, including AFO, to do anything, and he was not part of the discussions that led to Trebon ordering Blaber to transition command and control of the recce missions in the valley to TF Blue. But the Mountain commander had made his desire for more information about the southeast corner of the valley clear to Jimmy and Blaber, the two TF 11 operators with whom he worked most closely. The Halfpipe battle had revealed the area south of Takur Ghar to contain perhaps the heaviest concentration of Al Qaida forces in the Shahikot, while the deep gorge—now dubbed "Ginger Pass"—that ran along Takur Ghar's southern edge was likely a major supply route. That evening Jimmy passed the plan to get Mako 30 into position on top of Takur Ghar to Hagenbeck. "Hey sir, we think we can put guys right there," the bearded special operator told the general. "Jimmy, if you can do that, you're the man," Hagenbeck replied. Outside, two 160th—or Task Force Brown, as the 160th was known in TF 11—MH-47E helicopters, call signs Razor 03 and Razor 04, lifted off at 10:20 p.m. bound for Gardez where a dozen men waited by a dirt airstrip, shivering in the night air that retained an Afghan winter bite.

3.

THE two Chinooks touched down in Gardez at 11:23 p.m., picked up the SEALs and flew off again. But six minutes later, as they approached the Shahikot, word came that the infil for each team would now be delayed fifteen minutes in order to allow an AC-130U gunship to get into position. The 160th pilots wanted the gunship crew to use their high-tech optical systems to search the landing zones and, in the case of Razor 03 and Mako 30, the top of Takur Ghar for signs of enemy activity. This was not unusual. To an alarming degree, special operators had become psychologically dependent on the presence of aircraft like the AC-130 "clearing" their landing zones and objectives. "The special ops community has gotten so that we can't go in now unless a UAV is looking at it or an AC-130 is looking at it," an operator in Afghanistan said. The

Task Force Brown pilots considered the AC-130U, call sign Nail 21, essential to the mission. At 11:41 p.m., with the Chinooks finally inbound to their respective LZs, Nail 21 reported that it could not get "eyes on" Mako 30's LZ because of an ongoing B-52 strike. The senior Chinook pilot, a chief warrant officer 4 called Al, Slab, and the Mako 21 leader decided to return to Gardez. The air strike would not have stopped the Chinooks from flying to their LZs. Only the AC-130 was affected, because of its wide turning radius. However, so firm was the pilots' conviction that AC-130 coverage was a sine qua non, that despite Mako 21 and Mako 30 being only six and nine minutes out respectively from LZs at which no enemy activity had been spotted, they aborted the mission.

Their plan was to sit on the ground at Gardez for a few minutes and then fly back to the valley as soon as the B-52 strike was over. By then Nail 21 would have left the area and they would have to work with a new AC-130U, Nail 22. Once they had landed at Gardez, however, Razor 03, which was due to fly Slab's team to the foot of Takur Ghar, developed an engine problem. Al, the flight lead (the pilot in charge of getting both helicopters to their destinations), called Bagram to request a replacement helicopter. The 160th always flew in pairs in Afghanistan, so the TF Brown TOC's solution was to dispatch a pair of MH-47Es from Bagram to replace the two on the ground at Gardez. The two helicopters duly arrived. Razor 04 was low on fuel by this point, so the air mission commander (a 160th captain) and the pilots from Razor 03 and Razor 04 got into the new aircraft (the Razor call signs transferred with the pilots), with the incoming pilots taking their places in the helicopters that had been sitting on the ground in Gardez. (The new pilots included a maintenance pilot for Al's original aircraft. After checking it out he flew it back to Bagram alongside the original Razor 04.) The crew chiefs in the back all remained on the helicopters on which they'd flown to Gardez. But the repeated delays were eating into the precious hours of darkness. As Razor 03 and Razor 04 were about to launch, the pilots were told they would have to wait a little longer while a 101st helicopter mission went into the valley. This final delay slammed Mako 30's window of opportunity shut. The pilots told Slab the earliest they could land him at LZ 1 was 2:30 a.m., too late to allow the team to climb to the mountaintop in darkness.

Mako 30 and its chain of command faced a choice. They had two good options: They could abort, and delay the mission until the next night; or they could fly to LZ 1, go to ground in a hide site until it got dark the next evening, and then move up to the mountaintop. Slab's recommendation was to "bump" the mission twenty-four hours. But the lack of clear guidance about who was in charge of the recce missions being launched from Gardez now began to reap disastrous results. In theory Blaber was still in charge, because no firm time had been set for turning the mission over to Hyder and Task Force Blue. But from the moment they arrived at Gardez that morning, Hyder and the two SEAL teams had behaved as if the transition of authority had already occurred. This critical moment in Operation Anaconda was to be no exception. Just 1,000 meters away at the safe house, helping coordinate the preparations for Operation Payback (not scheduled to launch until 2:20 a.m.), was Pete Blaber, a man whose entire career had prepared him to make the sort of decision Hyder now faced, a decision upon which would hang the fates not just of Hyder's men, but of others as well. Blaber had spent weeks immersing himself in the tactical situation that confronted recce teams in the Shahikot. He was also still—officially—the officer commanding the reconnaissance effort in the valley. But Hyder chose to ignore him and instead seek guidance from the Blue TOC, which was almost 100 miles away and staffed with Navy personnel who had never been anywhere near the Shahikot. He used Razor 03 to relay his message on the TF Blue satellite frequency, which he knew Blaber would not be monitoring. "The earliest infil time possible is now 2215Z to 2230Z [2:45 a.m. local to 3 a.m. local]," the Blue TOC was told. "Mako 30 requests to bump twenty-four hours. What would you like to tell the team?" The message back to Razor 03, Hyder and Slab from the Blue TOC was clear and unequivocal: "We really need you to get in there tonight." (Task Force Blue officers tried to pin this decision on an enlisted man who had been manning the radio at the time, but the call sign used, according to the TF 11 Joint Operations Center log, was that of the TF Blue operations officer.)

With explicit orders from Kernan's headquarters (where Trebon had established temporary residency) to continue with the mission, Hyder revisited the idea of flying to the top of the mountain. Again he chose not to consult with Blaber. Instead he spoke with Razor 03's pilot-in-command, Chief Warrant Officer 4 Al, and the air mission commander, about whether it was technically possible to land the team directly on their observation post. Al calculated the effect of flying a couple of thousand of feet higher than the original LZ. "I can get you there, but I don't know that there's a suitable LZ at your OP," the pilot told the Navy officer. "It should be no problem," Hyder replied. "I've seen imagery." The pilots, Hyder and Slab, then decided among themselves to change the LZ at which Mako 30 would be dropped off from LZ 1 to the top of Takur Ghar. They relayed their change of LZ back to Bagram, but not down the road to the AFO TOC, where it would certainly have been countermanded. "The problem was no one was talking to AFO," said a special operator. "They were making all these calls back to the Blue TOC and Trebon. They weren't telling the guys they were fighting for."

Of course, not only would the SEALs' decision force them to break a cardinal rule of reconnaissance by infiltrating directly onto their observation post, it also would require them to fly straight onto a mountaintop that Glenn P. had told them not a few hours previously was likely occupied by the enemy. Slab would imply to the official U.S. Special Operations Command investigator that Glenn P. never included this in his briefing to Mako 30. "There were no significant indicators that the mountain was occupied," he told Colonel Andrew Milani. ". . . [I]t is incredulous that anyone would believe that we would have gone up to the mountain had our intelligence analysis indicated the presence of enemy personnel." Other sources flatly contradicted Slab's version of events. (However, in one respect at least, Slab was speaking accurately. After being informed of the SEALs' decision to head straight to the mountaintop, Nail 22, the AC-130 working for the Blue teams, flew over Mako 21's and Mako 30's LZs. Its fire control officer and navigator scanned both landing zones with their sensors and pronounced each LZ secure. That apparently satisfied Slab that the risks his team was being ordered to take were minimal.)

But the realization that the enemy, with weeks to prepare, had likely occupied the Shahikot's most dominant piece of terrain wasn't confined to Gardez. Earlier that day Jimmy and one or two other TF 11 personnel visited the TF Mountain military intelligence staff and asked where good landing zones might be found for the night's missions. In response an intelligence officer pointed to the top of Takur Ghar. "Anywhere but here," the officer said. Then, less than an hour before the two Chinooks lifted off from Gardez for the second time en route to the Shahikot, a report came into the Mountain TOC from the intel staff that enemy fighters were on the top of Takur Ghar. "They'd seen 'em," said a Mountain TOC source who saw the report. "They'd gotten some sort of IMINT [imagery intelligence], probably from the Predator, that there were bad guys running around that hilltop." When a battle captain passed the report to Jimmy, whose job it was to keep the AFO TOC apprised of this sort of intel, Jimmy's response was along the lines of *we've got it under control,* according to a source in the TOC. Of course, what Jimmy didn't know, because Hyder and Slab had stopped communicating on the AFO satellite net that Jimmy monitored from his desk in Bagram, was that the SEALs had decided to fly straight to the mountaintop. Neither the TF Blue TOC in Bagram nor the TF 11 operations center in Masirah bothered to call Blaber and Jimmy on the AFO satellite net to keep them abreast of the decisions. Yet again in Anaconda, senior leaders' failure to establish a tight, unified chain of command was adding unnecessary friction to that which is inevitable in any combat operation.

AT 2:20 a.m. on March 4 the Task Force Hammer convoy pulled out of Gardez and drove down the Zermat road headed for the Guppy. The convoy included about a dozen vehicles the CIA had acquired that were more suited to the mission than the jinga trucks had been: old Soviet gun jeeps and newer (but not brand-new) Toyota pickups and Mitsubishi trucks. Blaber was in AFO's command and control pickup, equipped with an x-wing satellite antenna that allowed him to talk to any U.S. military headquarters, anywhere. Hyder was now the only officer left in Gardez. When India and Mako 31 returned aboard the three trucks driven by John B., Al Y., and Hans, one of the operators was surprised to find Hyder in charge. "I got the feeling Hyder was now running the show on the ground," he said. "Of course, he was out of his league."

As the trucks drove out of the compound, Razor 03 and Razor 04 took off from the Gardez airfield, also headed toward the Shahikot. Razor 04's mission was still to fly Mako 21 into LZ 15 in the north of the valley. Razor 03 would fly Mako 30 to the top of Takur Ghar. Razor 03's crew included two pilots, an air mission commander sitting in the "jump seat" just behind the pilots, two door gunners at the side of the helicopter, and two gunners at the back. Mako 30 apparently consisted of eight personnel: six SEALs, led by Slab; Thor, the Gray Fox operator; and Technical Sergeant John Chapman, the combat controller from the 24th Special Tactics Squadron. As the helicopters approached the Shahikot, Nail 22 was no longer on station to cover their infil, having been called away a few minutes earlier to cover U.S. troops in combat elsewhere. In an ironic twist, the faith the SEALs had placed in the AC-130's ability to confirm or deny the presence of enemy fighters on the mountaintop with its sensors meant they did not consider the gunship's presence overhead necessary when they actually landed there.

At 2:38 a.m. Razor 04 landed at LZ 15. Within three minutes it had dropped off Mako 21 and was airborne again, flying back to a holding point over Gardez, where it was to wait for Razor 03 if the latter helicopter hadn't already caught up with it after dropping off Mako 30. Razor 03 flew on, the black helicopter gaining altitude as it got closer to Takur Ghar. The proposed LZ was a saddle on the southwestern side of the snow-covered mountaintop. As the helicopter made its final approach, with Al's copilot at the controls, the crew noticed footprints in the snow. This was not uncommon, even at that altitude, and since the AC-130 had already declared the site to be enemy free, Al wasn't that worried. He told Slab about the footprints. The Mako 30 leader raised no objections so the pilots brought the aircraft down carefully. The team got ready to jump off as soon as the ramp came down. Closest to the ramp was Petty

Officer First Class Neil Roberts, a thirty-two-year-old SEAL with a wife and eighteen-month-old son at home in Virginia. But as the Chinook settled onto three feet of snow, its rotors furiously churning the thin mountain air, Al's voice crackled over the intercom. "Team leader, you've got a DShK, unmanned, 1 o'clock." (This was exactly where Glenn P. had predicted a DShK would be.) "Yeah, roger," Slab replied. Then, with the ramp starting to fall, another crewman reported a donkey tied to a tree at 3 o'clock, and the left door gunner, Jeremy, saw a figure duck behind a knoll at the Chinook's 9 o'clock. Skinned goat or lamb carcasses hung from nearby trees. Nail 22's high-tech sensors had picked up none of this. The right rear crew chief, Dan, held his arm up, signaling the SEALs to stay put while Al discussed the situation with Slab over the intercom. "You've got a guy at 9 o'clock, stuck his head up, and disappeared," Al told Slab. "Is he armed?" Slab asked. "I don't know," Al replied. With his SEALs poised at the ramp hinge, Slab paused for a moment, then said, "Roger, we're taking the LZ." As Dan dropped his arm and stepped aside, Jeremy saw a bright orange flash to the left of the Chinook.

4.

IN Bagram, Hagenbeck had retired to the cot in his office less than an hour previously for his first sleep in three days and nights, leaving Harrell and Jones in charge. As Razor 03 flew south toward Takur Ghar, Jimmy was kneeling beside the generals' desk, talking to them about the next stage of the operation. The AFO radios were crackling in the background, but because he was unaware that the SEAL teams were communicating only on the Blue frequency, Jimmy still had no clue that Mako 30 had decided to land on the mountaintop. However, his RTO was sitting just a few feet away monitoring a radio conversation between the crew of Razor 03 and the Brown TOC in Bagram. "Hey, sir, they're one minute out," the RTO called out. "Roger that," Jimmy replied. As the AFO second-in-command continued chatting with Harrell and Jones, his RTO typed the grid that Razor 03 crew had just broadcast for their landing zone into a laptop computer, which instantly plotted it on a digital map of the Shahikot. The RTO did a double take. He didn't like what he saw. "Hey, boss, *boss,* isn't this the OP?" he said, pointing at the screen. "Hey, I'll be right with you," Jimmy replied over his shoulder. The Delta major concluded his chat, stood up, and turned around. His RTO pointed again to the top of the mountain on the digital map. "Here's where their LZ is plotted," the RTO said. Almost a hundred miles to the south, the black Chinook slowed to a hover over the top of Takur

Ghar. *"What?!"* Jimmy said. "That's where their LZ is plotted," the RTO repeated. "There's no way, redo it," Jimmy said. As the RTO hurriedly reentered the numbers into the computer, Razor 03's wheels sank into the snow on the mountaintop. Again the computer told Jimmy something he had hoped it wouldn't. The grid Razor 03 had given was not for LZ 1, the off-set location where he had been told they were going. It was for the very top of Takur Ghar, where no one in their right mind would ask a helicopter to land. Alarmed, he grabbed the radio hand mike to call the helicopter off. Too late. At that moment an Al Qaida fighter at the highest point of the Shahikot Valley raised his RPG launcher to his shoulder and took aim at the big, juicy target that had landed virtually in his lap. He couldn't miss.

The RPG slammed into the electrical compartment in the left side of the helicopter, the only place in the aircraft where all the otherwise redundant electrical systems came together, before plowing through the left ammo can and exploding, punching a hole in the Chinook's *right* side, hitting the right side electrical compartment, wounding Jeremy in the right leg and blowing his M4 rifle in half. The helicopter instantly lost all AC electrical power, knocking out the M134 miniguns that were its principal means of self-defense and jamming the ramp in the down position. Also out of action were the pilots' multifunctional displays, navigation and automatic flight control systems, as well as all the radios except part of the intercom. A moment later another RPG fired from the same area hit the ground in front of the aircraft, showering the multimode radar pod with shrapnel as bullets peppered the aircraft, slicing through hoses to send hydraulic fluid spraying across the floor. Acrid smoke filled the cabin. The door gunners had lost their intercom connection, but those in the rear could still talk to the pilots. The SEALs were still on the aircraft. "Get us out of here!" yelled Slab over the intercom. "Fire in the cabin! Rear ready!" shouted Dan to Al, also over the intercom. "Pick it up! Pick it up! Go! Go! *Go!*" As he finished yelling at Al that it was okay to take off, Dan, the senior crew chief, fired a bust from his M60 machine-gun mounted in the right aft cabin window.

Al's copilot had been flying the helicopter, but he wasn't moving fast enough. Al could see men off to his left with guns and wasn't prepared to wait a second longer. He took the controls and prepared to take off. In the back, Dan felt a jolt and thought another RPG had hit the aircraft, but in fact what he'd felt was a bullet slamming into his helmet. The Chinook had been on the ground no more than forty-five seconds when Al lifted it off the ground. With almost all his instruments blacked out the veteran pilot was flying by feel. But not everyone in the back had got the message that they were leaving the mountaintop. As the helicopter lurched from side to side, Roberts, who was closest to the ramp and, like the rest of his team except Slab, not plugged into the intercom, made as if to jump out the back. (Al speculated that Roberts, who was standing beside Dan, may have misinterpreted the senior crew chief's shout of "Go! Go! *Go!*" as a directive to get off the Chinook.) Noticing Roberts's movement, Dan tried to stop him, but was restrained by his safety harness. It's unclear whether Roberts realized that he wasn't supposed to get off, but slipped in the oil and hydraulic fluid coating the floor as he tried to stop himself, or whether he never got the message. Whichever is the case, he went flying toward the back of the ramp, which the power loss had stuck at about a fifteen-degree slope. Realizing what was about to happen, the left rear gunner, Alexander, tackled Roberts in a desperate attempt to prevent him falling out of the aircraft. He caught the SEAL by the ankle, but had no hope of holding on to Roberts, who was a beefy six feet two wearing a 150-pound ruck and carrying a SAW. The helicopter shuddered again, breaking Dan's hold. Alexander slid off the end of the ramp and fell about three feet before his safety harness jerked taut, leaving him dangling under the ramp. Roberts flew ten feet and landed in the snow.

The impetus of the takeoff carried the helicopter over the edge of the peak. Beneath the aircraft the mountain fell away in a 3,000-foot drop, over which Alexander was now dangling in his tether as tracer rounds from the Al Qaida positions chased the helicopter. In the cockpit Al was unaware that Roberts had been left on the mountainside and that one of his crew was swinging helplessly underneath the Chinook, but he knew he was in a life-and-death struggle to keep his aircraft aloft. The helicopter was already shaking violently when someone in the back yelled over the intercom, "We lost an engine! We lost an engine!" That was very bad news. Al knew he couldn't fly the helicopter at that altitude on a single engine, and immediately lowered the thrust to begin autorotation to the valley floor. In the back the severed hydraulic hose had filled the air with a red mist. Everyone was lying on the wet floor. Dan got on the intercom to report that both engines were in fact running, then got down on the ramp and pulled Alexander back on board. Al leveled the helicopter, which he said was "shaking and shimmying like a washing machine out of balance." Then an even worse report came in from the back: one of their own was still on the LZ. Al felt sick, thinking one of the team must have deliberately gotten out of the helicopter and been left behind in the rush to get off the mountain. "No, he fell out, he fell out!" his crew corrected him. "Where is he?" Al asked. "He's back on the hill," one of the crew chiefs said. "Okay, we're going back, any objections?" Al replied. There were no dissenting voices. *Never leave a fallen comrade.*

As Al banked to the right, he felt the flight controls vibrating so strongly they were becoming difficult to move. He was losing cyclic control, losing the ability to turn the aircraft. Dan, returning fire with his M60, also felt the helicopter shaking and saw hydraulic fluid continuing to spray the cabin. He realized the hydraulics system was failing. When it completely ran dry, the helicopter would drop from the sky like a twin-rotored stone. He looked at the three hydraulics gauges by his crew station. All three were at zero. Dan kept four spare cans of hydraulic fluid in the back. Using a can opener dangling on a string, he began opening them and pouring the contents into the hydraulic fill module, a device that allowed crew chiefs to replenish the hydraulics system in flight. As soon as he had emptied each can, he grabbed a hand pump and began manually pumping the fluid into the system. Al felt the cyclic controls return. "Okay, we're still going back," he announced. But as soon as Dan stopped pumping to open a new can, the controls locked up again. It was a simple race. To give Al a chance of keeping them all alive, Dan had to pour and pump hydraulic fluid into the system faster than it was spraying out of the shredded hose. Even with Dan pumping vigorously, however, Al was unable to gain enough cyclic control to turn the helicopter all the way back toward Takur Ghar. There would be no going back for Roberts aboard Razor 03. Al knew he had to put the helicopter down very soon. "I aborted the rescue in order to save the aircraft," he said. He leveled the helicopter and descended, aiming for LZ 15. Meanwhile his copilot monitored the backup attitude indicator, which was the only working flight instrument, and called out the helicopter's airspeed, altitude and direction to Al. "You're at 90 knots, 700 foot a minute," he said. Al may not have realized it, but he was flying over Kevin Butler's command post at the northern end of the valley. He couldn't descend fast enough to put the helicopter down at LZ 15, so he picked out a spot about 1,000 meters to its north. Al coaxed and cajoled the Chinook into an acceptable landing attitude and steadied it over a gently sloping smooth piece of terrain. As he brought the helicopter down, the crewmen called out how far they were from the ground. At ten feet Al felt the controls lock up. They were out of hydraulics fluid. The helicopter fell to earth with a bump. It settled at a precarious angle, but to the crew's surprise and relief didn't roll over. The time was 2:58 a.m. They had flown just over seven kilometers from Takur Ghar.

The landing had been hard, but no one was hurt. Al shut the engines down. Slab had his men drop their rucks, exit the aircraft and position themselves on nearby knolls. He counted heads to confirm what he already knew: Roberts was missing. The pilots collected their maps and other classified materials and jumped out, while the crew chiefs stripped 7.62mm ammo from the miniguns for their two M60s, which they carried out of the helicopter to join the SEALs. The air mission commander, an officer new to the 160th, turned on an infrared red strobe light to mark their position. Despite their superb performance in avoiding what could easily have been a catastrophic crash, the crew members were feeling down about having to crash land the helicopter, until Chapman piped up. "Aw, don't worry about it," he said. "I've felt harder PLFs [parachute landing falls]." Then Chapman set up his radio beside the Chinook and went to work.

About fifty miles to the east, in Pakistani airspace, Grim 32, an AC-130H, was just turning back toward Afghanistan after an air-to-air refueling when it received a frantic call: "Any Grim, any Nail, this is Mako 30. We've just had a crash landing and need some perimeter security." Grim 32's crew was the same one involved in the Harriman incident less than forty-eight hours previously. Now fate had cast them in a key role at another critical juncture in Operation Anaconda. But they would have a steep learning curve to climb. The delays to the SEAL teams' infil meant the AC-130s that had been briefed on Mako 30's mission—Nail 21 and Nail 22—had left the area by now. Grim 32 was just arriving on station. Through no fault of their own the crew members knew nothing of Mako 30's mission and lacked the coordinates for Takur Ghar. Chapman's call was the first inkling that pilot D. J. Turner and his crew had that anything had gone awry that night in the Shahikot. Grim 32's crew noted Mako 30's location and flew straight there, a flight that took about fifteen minutes. The crew saw no sign of any enemy within 2,000–3,000 meters of the downed Chinook. "It looks like we lost somebody at the LZ," Chapman told Grim 32. "Which LZ?" someone on the aircraft replied. Chapman passed the grid coordinates of the Takur Ghar peak, as well as a description of the LZ, told them Roberts would have an infrared strobe and an MBITR radio, and gave them his call sign and the frequency he was probably using. "They asked us if we could go and check on him and see if we could locate him," Turner recalled. "We were all in a CSAR [combat search and rescue] mode at that time . . . Everybody still thought the odds were, he was alive."

Thinking the Chinook had only flown to the foot of Takur Ghar before crash-landing, Slab began planning to march up the mountain to rescue Roberts. Chapman contacted Jimmy in Bagram at 3:06 a.m. and relayed a message to that effect. (Unlike Army special ops units, SEALs routinely use their Air Force attachments as their primary communicators.) Although Slab quickly realized his error and abandoned the plan, that 3:06 a.m. transmission, monitored by Grim 32 and several headquarters, created a false impression that Roberts was within walking distance of friendly forces.

At this time another AC-130H, Grim 33, arrived over the Shahikot, with even less awareness than Grim 32 of what had transpired. The Grim 32 crew coordinated with Grim 33 for the latter to take up position over the downed helicopter while Grim 32 went to search for Roberts. As they turned south, the Grim 32 crew easily identified the peak of Takur Ghar. Not only was it the highest point around, but at that moment it was also marked by an infrared light winking at them through the darkness. They could see a person holding the strobe, and several individuals around him. The crew kept their eyes on the flashing strobe as they flew south, reporting what they saw to K-mart (the CAOC), Bossman (the AWACS), and Mako 30.

ONCE Slab understood how far they'd flown he knew his team's only hope of getting back to the top of Takur Ghar in time to save Roberts was to jump on another helicopter. The quickest way to do that was calling Razor 04 back to pick them up. Hearing Grim 32's report of a strobe on Takur Ghar only heightened Slab's impatience to return to the mountaintop. He asked Razor 03's crew if they could remain by the downed helicopter while the SEALs returned to Takur Ghar on Razor 04 to look for Roberts. Al told him he felt comfortable doing that so long as Slab left one SEAL to help in their defense. But when that plan was relayed to Jimmy, the Delta officer recommended everyone fly back to Gardez on Razor 04 and come up with a plan before returning to an LZ where they'd already had one helicopter shot up. (Much of this conversation occurred between Jimmy and Al. Slab seemed reluctant to get on the radio.)

Slab called Blaber, his old battle buddy from Bosnia. The AFO commander was on the Zermat road, about to turn off toward the Guppy when Slab's first call came through. Blaber stopped, talked for a moment with Slab, digesting the info that one of Slab's men had fallen out of the helicopter "at the LZ," and drove on. A short while later, as the convoy passed a little ruined fort near the Guppy, Blaber pulled the convoy over again. With Zia, Haas, and Spider standing around him, Blaber got a more detailed update from Slab. It was only when Slab told Blaber that he wanted to go back "up" to get Roberts that the awful reality of what had transpired sank in with the AFO commander. *Fuck, they tried to land on top of the mountain,* he thought.

As they soared closer to Takur Ghar, the Grim 32 crew kept their high-tech "eyes" fixed on the infrared strobe light flashing on the mountain peak. Whoever the personnel surrounding the individual holding the strobe were, the fact that it was on at all gave everyone hope. But after thirty seconds it disappeared forever.

5.

BATTLEFIELD friction was now swamping headquarters from Gardez to Bagram to Masirah. As each TOC tried to figure out what had happened, officers drowned each other out on the satellite nets and misinterpreted the messages they were getting. The official Special Operations Command investigator summed the situation up thus:

As each of the separate headquarters attempted to sort out exactly what was happening, there was considerable confusion as to: 1) where Roberts had fallen off the helicopter, 2) where Razor 03 actually had set down in relation to Takur Ghar, 3) on which landing zone Razor 03 had attempted to insert Mako 30, 4) what the enemy and friendly situations were near Razor 03, 5) what the friendly and enemy situation was in Roberts' vicinity, and 6) whether the IR strobe light with personnel around it was at the Razor 03 site, at Mako 21's linkup point [with Juliet], or on top of the mountain.

Other than Slab's men and the Razor 03 crew, the individuals with the clearest picture of what was happening were Pete Blaber and Jimmy. Blaber had excellent line-of-sight communications with the men from the downed helicopter as well as Grim 32 overhead, while his satellite radio allowed Jimmy to relay to him any information from the Predator feeds. Both Jimmy and Blaber understood that Roberts had fallen out on top of Takur Ghar, that there were no friendly forces near him, and that Razor 03 had landed in the far north of the valley, only a couple of thousand meters north of Chip Preysler's command post. Blaber also knew from his deep reading on the behavior of the various enemy forces, especially the Uzbeks and the Chechens, that unless action to rescue him was taken immediately, Roberts would soon be dead, if he wasn't already. By contrast, in the Blue TOC just down the road from the Mountain headquarters and in the TF 11 Joint Operations Center off the coast of Oman, confusion reigned. In those headquarters officers still believed that the individuals Grim 32 had spotted on the top of the mountain around the person holding the strobe were friendly troops rescuing Roberts. The TF 11 and TF Blue operations centers also appear to have mistaken Chip Preysler's men for an enemy force moving toward the little knot of aviators and SEALs.

BLABER and Slab put a plan together on the fly. Blaber knew the personnel that Grim 32 reported walking towards the strobe on Takur Ghar could not possibly be friendly. He told Grim 32 that as soon as they were over the mountain, they were to fire as close to the group around the strobe light as possible without hitting them. Then, if the AC-130 crew saw someone break away from the group, to assume that was the missing American and use their fires to protect him. Meanwhile, Mako 30 would get on Razor 04 and fly back to the top of the mountain immediately. That was also what Slab recommended, and Blaber believed in trusting the guy on the ground. Razor 04, reached at its holding station over Gardez, was inbound.

Colonel Joe Smith, the Mountain chief of staff, walked into Hagenbeck's office and gently shook the general awake with words no commander ever wants to hear: "Sir, we've had a helicopter shot down." Hagenbeck quickly walked the few yards to the tent housing the Mountain TOC, which was becoming filled to capacity as word spread that another crisis was brewing in the Shahikot. Staffers and hangers-on strained to see the Predator screens as other officers and NCOs focused their attention on the radio traffic. Few of these people were in a position to make any difference to the events unfolding before them. Because this was a TF 11 mission that had gone sour, only folks in TF 11's chain of command were authorized to fix it. This was the inevitable result of the bifurcated chain of command the Pentagon and CENTCOM had imposed on U.S. forces in Afghanistan. The only guy inside the Mountain TOC whose job entitled him to issue orders to the men in the Shahikot was Jimmy. He was standing on his bench with a radio mike to his face, towering above the crowd in an effort to make himself heard and to keep his eye on the Predator screens as he coordinated events on the battlefield.

Suddenly another voice came on the radio, that of Brigadier General Gregory Trebon, the TF 11 commander, who was a few hundred meters away in the TF Blue TOC. "We don't need you getting all worked up on the radio," the Air Force officer told Jimmy condescendingly. "Get off the net, we've got it." "Goddamn!" said Jimmy, stunned and furious, as he ripped his headset off in bitter frustration and hurled it—with the cord still attached—in the direction of the generals a few feet away. It hit the bench between Jones and Hagenbeck, narrowly missing the latter. "Jimmy!?" Harrell exclaimed, turning around in his seat. "Sir, he just took me out of the fight," Jimmy explained. "What!?" the one-star replied in amazement. "Sir, he says they're going to fight it from there," Jimmy said. Harrell, who did not enjoy a good relationship with Trebon, fumed. In deciding to remove command and control of events in the Shahikot from the AFO leadership—Blaber and Jimmy—and manage it himself, Trebon was making a decision he would come to regret. He was taking the two men whose professional backgrounds and current situational awareness best qualified them to organize the rescue operation in the Shahikot out of the loop, and replacing them with staff officers in the TF Blue and TF 11 TOCs, roughly 100 miles and 1,100 miles away from the battlefield respectively. Trebon took this action in the belief that simply having access to the satellite radio nets and, especially, the Predator feeds gave the officers in Masirah as much understanding of events in the Shahikot Valley as they needed to run things from there. His faith in the power of technology trumped the principle of trusting the guy on the ground.

Perhaps acknowledging that his own background hardly qualified him for the situation in which he had placed himself, Trebon told his staff in Masirah, "I have command, you have control." JSOC officers would debate the meaning of these words long after Anaconda had ended. Command and control usually go together in military operations, but a Trebon supporter said the Air Force general's decision to separate them made perfect sense. "Command is the decision-making, control is the mechanism that supports the decision-making," this officer said. Few others agreed. In the space of a few seconds, Trebon had ensured that what was about to bubble into the fiercest close-range firefight U.S. troops had waged since Mogadishu, a close quarters, take-no-prisoners battle fought on a frozen Afghan mountaintop, would be "controlled" by officers watching video screens on a desert island and "commanded" by a man who had made his name flying transport aircraft.

IT took Razor 04 about half an hour to fly to Razor 03's position at the north end of the Shahikot. The Chinook landed 60 meters from its stricken sister aircraft at about 3:45 a.m. Shortly thereafter a signals intelligence element aboard Grim 32 intercepted an Al Qaida transmission that suggested enemy forces were aware a helicopter had crashed and were preparing to assault it. Grim 32 passed the intelligence to Grim 33, which was still circling over the two helicopters. Grim 33 in turn relayed the message to the men on the ground and scanned the area around the Chinooks for any sign of the enemy. When its crew saw a couple of mortar tubes and about forty personnel an estimated 1200 meters from the helicopters, they were convinced this was the enemy force getting ready to assault the small group of Americans by the helicopters, and they called down to the air crewmen and SEALs to warn them. Of course, what Grim 33's crew was looking at was Kevin Butler's A Company, 2-187 Infantry, including the mortar section that had performed so magnificently the previous day. Fortunately for those 101st infantrymen, the confusion in Bagram and Masirah meant Grim 33 was not given permission to open fire. But the combination of the radio intercept and the erroneous report about enemy troops on the ground spelled doom for the plan formulated by Slab and Blaber to leave the Razor 03 crew on the ground while Mako 30 flew back to Takur Ghar to find Roberts. With enemy fighters apparently closing in, the priority became getting everyone away from the crash site on Razor 04. Instead of flying them to the Rakkasan position just to the south, Razor 04's pilot wanted to get out of the area altogether. The extra seven men from Razor 03's crew would make the helicopter too heavy to fly to the mountaintop. There was no option but to fly them back to Gardez before setting off for Takur Ghar with Mako 30. Razor 03's crew set about stripping all the sensitive items—such as the miniguns—from their helicopter and loading them aboard Razor 04. Grim 33's message about enemy troops approaching caused a moment of panic as Razor 04 flashed its lights in a failed attempt to alert two crewmen making a final sweep of Razor 03. Finally Razor 04 took off and flew over to land right beside the downed Chinook in order to get their attention. The two men climbed aboard and at 4:10 a.m. the helicopter lifted off and flew north, away from Takur Ghar. Had the TF 11 personnel in Masirah and the Blue TOC been more closely tied in with TF Mountain, they could easily have put together a plan in which the Rakkasan troops with Preysler and Butler secured Razor 03 and its crew, allowing Razor 04 to pick up Mako 30 and fly back to Takur Ghar immediately, as Blaber had urged. Instead, the confused staffers and the Razor 04 pilot unwittingly scratched the last, best chance they had of saving Neil Roberts.

Razor 04 landed at Gardez about 4:34 a.m. The helicopter had lost radio contact with Bagram and Masirah and was relaying messages through Grim 32. (The satellite radios on all MH-47Es were notoriously unreliable. This problem would plague TF 11 for the rest of the Takur Ghar fight.) Hyder drove out to meet Razor 04. The Razor 03 crew got off, as did Thor, the Gray Fox operator. The air mission commander and the remaining six members of Mako 30 remained aboard. At 4:45 a.m. Razor 04 took off, headed at last to Takur Ghar.

It took Grim 32 only a couple of minutes to get on station over Takur Ghar. The strobe had disappeared, but between five and ten people were visible on the mountaintop. From the north of the valley, Mako 30 inundated Grim 32 with questions: *What can you see? Can you tell if he's alive? Can you tell if they've got him?* Grim 32 told the SEALs that they couldn't answer most of their questions. Mako 30 told the aircrew they were going to go back to the top of Takur Ghar. At 4:10 a.m. Blaber asked Jimmy if he could identify Roberts on the top of the mountain from the Predator feed. Jimmy said he could not. Ten minutes later Blaber, who by now was in sight of Takur Ghar himself, asked Grim 32 what they were seeing on the peak. They told him they couldn't see any strobe light or glint tape that would identify Roberts, but they could see about eight personnel who were almost certainly enemy fighters. Blaber decided a variant of the plan he'd drawn up hastily with Slab was still the only chance of saving Roberts. He told Grim 32 to fire into the middle of the group of eight enemy personnel when Razor 04 was between one and three minutes out from landing Mako 30 (i.e., before the enemy fighters heard the inbound helicopter and took cover). If one person broke away from the group, the AC-130 crew should use their judgment and if they decided he was Roberts, to continue to fire on the others. The AFO commander emphasized the importance of killing as many enemy fighters as possible while they were in the open and vulnerable. Razor 04 made a similar request to Grim 32, asking the AC-130 to put prep fires on the LZ when the helicopter was a couple of minutes out.

But unbeknownst to Blaber, Trebon's insistence on taking command and control away from him and Jimmy meant the satellite radio frequency on which much of the operation was being managed had also changed. Blaber was talking on and listening to the AFO satellite net, up to that point the frequency on which all TF 11-related action in the Shahikot had been discussed. But now the TF 11 operations center in Masirah and the TF Blue TOC in Bagram were trying to run things on their frequency (known as SAT-A or Tiersat), which Blaber wasn't monitoring, because TF 11 didn't bother telling him of the change. As a result, he was powerless to provide corrective guidance when interference from Masirah, based on the TF 11 staff's misreading of the situation, put paid to his plan. Instead of going ahead with Blaber's suggestion, Grim 32's crew received a welter of contradictory directions from Masirah, where Marine Corps Major Chris Naler, the TF 11 fire support officer, had been placed in charge of events in the Shahikot. Naler's directions veered between telling Grim 32 to "waste" everyone on the top of the mountain, then seconds later ordering them not to fire, telling the crew, "Don't worry, our good guy has been picked up by a friendly team," and informing Turner, Grim 32's pilot, that he, Turner, was now the on-scene commander (a message contradicted minutes later). This was maddening for the AC-130 crew. From their vantage point they could see the group on the peak getting larger and larger. Somewhere below them an American might be fighting for his life. Of all U.S. elements in the area, only they had the ability to help him and yet no one was giving them clear guidance on how to do that.

(Turner expressed sympathy for the TF 11 staff officers with whom he was speaking. "They had a lot of heat, a lot of general officers and colonels pumping them for information and offering advice, and they had the least SA [situational awareness] down there in their cave," he said. At this point the TF 11 staff in

Masirah still thought Roberts had fallen out somewhere near where Razor 03 had crash landed. It would be hours before they realized this was not so.)

When Razor 04 was about five miles out, Masirah refused Grim 32 permission to fire on the mountaintop. Razor 04 moved into an orbit waiting for the prep fires to begin, only to be called by Grim 32 with the news that Masirah had denied the request for prep fires because the gunship crew couldn't positively identify Roberts. The men on Razor 04 decided to risk landing on the mountaintop anyway. Masirah asked Grim 32 to "glint" the mountaintop instead of killing the personnel the gunship crew could see gathered there. But "glinting" a snow-covered landing zone only blinds pilots flying with night-vision goggles, and Razor 04's pilots told the AC-130 crew to stop it as they neared the peak.

6.

ROBERTS hit the snow with a thump. He must have realized instantly that he was in mortal danger. Alone and heavily outnumbered, he had landed in the middle of an enemy command post whose occupants had almost certainly seen him tumble from the helicopter. The SEALs' decision to proceed with their infil without AC-130 coverage deprived him of the protective fires from the sky he would otherwise have enjoyed in the first minutes after his fall. He would have to fight the enemy by himself, armed only with a SAW and a pistol. He also had an MBITR radio, but it wasn't powerful enough to communicate with his teammates 7,000 meters away. Grim 32, flying toward him, did not have his frequency. TF Green (Delta Force) and the recce AFO recce teams always loaded the line-of-sight frequency to Bossman, the AWACS, for just such emergencies, in case they needed the command-and-control aircraft to arrange immediate close air support. It was the sort of step the SEALs might have taken had they had the time in Gardez to fully integrate themselves into the AFO operation. But in the haste to push the teams into the Shahikot, it was apparently overlooked. Roberts's radio was therefore useless. He activated his infrared strobe, but the enemy had seen him. Within minutes they were firing at him. He fought back fiercely, returning fire with his SAW, trying desperately to buy himself some time. But while his would-be saviors were being held back by the confusion that paralyzed the TF 11 command setup, an enemy bullet to his right upper thigh struck him down. Bleeding in the snow, he continued firing, his blood dripping onto the bullets as they were fed into the weapon until it jammed. Within about thirty-five minutes of falling out of the helicopter, his wound had weakened him to the point where he was probably too weak to fire the heavy SAW anyway. Al Qaida fighters walked over to him, dragged him to his feet, and moved him up the slope to a tree and bunker complex. No one knows exactly what transpired between the American warrior and his captors, but at 4:27 a.m., the enemy fighters clearly decided Roberts was of no more use to them. One of them raised a gun to Roberts's head and fired a single round, killing him instantly. An Al Qaida fighter straddled his body for a couple of minutes, probably stripping it of any useful gear, and then walked to a nearby bunker. About an hour and a half after falling from Razor 03, Neil Roberts was dead.

RAZOR 04 was a minute out from Takur Ghar. The men on board braced for what would surely be a hot LZ. In Masirah, the TF 11 staff was desperately trying to get through to the helicopter with orders not to land on the mountaintop, but to set down at an offset location and wait for the Ranger quick reaction force, which was getting ready to launch from Bagram. This directive was based on the recommendation of Grim 32, which was looking directly at the peak, and could see it was "crawling with people." But again the decision to control the operation from Masirah exacted a toll. The message never got through on the satellite frequency (or, according to Turner, the Grim 32 pilot, the message got through but was disregarded by the SEALs because landing at the alternate LZ would have left them with too much of a climb). Anyway, from the SEALs' point of view, they had no option but to land at the top. If Roberts was still alive now, he was unlikely to survive the two hours it would take his teammates to climb up the mountain. Landing on top of Takur Ghar again "was not the smartest idea, but it was all we had," Slab said. But the staff at Masirah thought their message had gotten through, and told Grim 32 to start "glinting" the offset LZ. The AC-130 crew members did as requested and became confused when neither Razor 04 nor Mako 30 checked in as they approached the mountain, which was standard procedure in that situation. Those aboard Grim 32 were further confused when no helicopter appeared over the LZ, about 800 meters to the south of the peak. Then one of Turner's sensor operators glimpsed a Chinook approaching the top of the mountain. "Holy shit," the crewman said. "They're going back to the original LZ." Razor 04 was descending over the southwestern portion of the snow-covered peak. The time was 4:55 a.m.

Before the helicopter's wheels had touched the ground the pilots saw a DShK spitting flame and lead at them about 100 meters off their nose. *Oh, this is going to hurt,* thought the lead pilot. "Forward and down! Forward and down!" the air mission commander told the pilot. They nudged the aircraft a little farther forward to find a more level spot in the snow. There was a machine-gun about fifty meters to their front left, behind a rise. Both pilots pushed the thrust down together to lower the helicopter and keep the terrain between the machine-gun and the aircraft. "We're taking fire from eleven o'clock," the left door gunner yelled as the aircraft was forty feet above the ground. "Is it effective fire?" one of the pilots asked. "Hell yes!" the door gunner replied as bullets pinged against the left side of the aircraft. "Then return fire," the pilot said as he saw more muzzle flashes at the top of a nearby knoll.

The whirling of the two giant sets of rotor blades created a mini-blizzard around the Chinook as it settled onto the snow, but the crew could still see tracers flashing over the aircraft. The six members of Mako 30 stormed down the ramp, fanning out and stopping just long enough for the helicopter to take off. Slab tripped and fell flat on his face, but immediately picked himself up. As Razor 04 rose above the team, the left door gunner fired a few rounds from his minigun before it jammed. The right rear gunner fired a long burst from his M60 at a DShK he'd spotted at the helicopter's one o'clock position. Then, fearing that the SEALs had bitten off more than they could chew and might need immediate extraction, Razor 04's pilots began flying an orbit around the mountaintop. Despite losing radio contact with the SEALs as soon as they ran down the ramp, Razor 04 stayed in orbit until its fuel level dropped below 1,000 pounds. Then the helicopter returned to Gardez. By the time it landed, the fuel gauge was at zero. When the crew climbed out they saw why: Bullets had holed the left fuel tank in several places. A bullet had also sliced through the cluster of wires that controlled the left engine. The damage rendered the helicopter nonmission-capable, and until it was refueled, the aircraft was also nonflyable.

As the helicopter lifted off, the six men of Mako 30 split into three pairs and began assaulting the high ground to the north, where a large rock formation and a tree offered the closest cover to their position. Unfortunately, and for the same reason, the enemy was already there. The next few moments were a blur of bloody, violent action. Slab and Chapman were closest to the tree. Chapman saw movement under its branches and fired his M4 instinctively. Within seconds Slab was next to him, shooting at two men the Mako 30 leader saw under the tree. By the time he had emptied his magazine, both guerrillas lay dead. But now Slab and Chapman were taking fire from both north and south. A hail of belt-fed PKM machine-gun bullets burst from another bunker under a tree twenty meters beyond the position they'd just silenced. Slab could see the sparks and hear the ricochets of the 7.62 slugs hitting off the rocks around him. Then, according to Slab, one of the bullets found a target. Five feet to Slab's right, Chapman fell to the ground. As Slab and the two SEALs to his left kept firing at the position ahead of them, the team leader glanced down at Chapman. The Air Force man had fallen on his M4, Slab said. Slab could tell that his finger was jammed on the trigger, because he could see the aiming laser that shot from the rifle whenever the trigger was depressed. The laser wasn't moving an inch, which Slab said he took to mean Chapman wasn't breathing. "I realized at this point he was dead," Slab said. "He would be moving if he were alive." It was a decision made in an instant. Slab didn't even reach down to take a pulse or otherwise physically confirm Chapman's death. There was no time to dwell on it. He had four other men to lead, and the bullets and RPGs crisscrossing the mountaintop weren't going to pause to let him collect his thoughts. Turning from Chapman, he fired two 40mm grenades from the M203 grenade launcher on the underside of his M4. One burst harmlessly in the trees, but the other detonated in the bunker.

To Grim 32, now orbiting overhead, the battle below was nothing but chaos—"the proverbial firefight in a phone booth, with laser pointers and tracers going in every direction," Turner said. Even in such a close quarters battle, Grim 32 might have been able to help. But it had no way of knowing who was who down below. Masirah was supposed to have called the AC-130 crew back with the frequency that Mako 30 would be using. But Grim 32 never got the call. As they took up a new orbit over the mountain, the AC-130 crew tried three different frequencies they thought Mako 30 might be using, all to no avail. The team's main radio was the one Chapman had carried in his rucksack, which was now lying useless in the snow beside him. But the SEALs also carried MBITRs. Perhaps because they spent so much time in the water, SEALs were not as obsessive about radio communications as Army special operators. This was a time when lack of attention to that particular detail would cost them. On the ground they were taking casualties. The best close air support aircraft in the world was circling overhead, yet they weren't using it. On Grim 32 there was more excruciating frustration. "The hardest thing for us is to be zoomed in with a front-row picture of this event, watching good guys take bullets, and feel like you're helpless to do anything about it," Turner said.

Another SEAL climbed up on a rock beside the bunker and fired his M60 machine-gun into it at almost point-blank range. The fire from the bunker stopped. Slab turned and fired his last 40mm grenade at the bunker to the south. By now at least two SEALs were standing exposed up on the rock. Then more fire burst from the northern bunker. A SEAL threw two grenades into it.

Each detonated and the fire stopped. The SEAL with the M60 kept pouring fire into the position regardless. But as the SEALs prepared to flank the bunker, a grenade flew out, wounding one of them in the left leg. The machine-gun in the bunker resumed firing, the bullets smacking off the rock on which the SEALs were standing. Then a bullet caught the SEAL who'd already been wounded, this time in his right leg. He rolled off the rock, trying to evade the wave of murderous fire coming from the bunker. By now an enemy position to the west had opened up on the SEALs as well. Having lost one man already, and with another seriously wounded, Slab decided to break contact. They were outnumbered and outgunned and there appeared to be no sign of Roberts. Slab wanted to put enough distance between him and the enemy that he could use Grim 32's firepower. He ordered the two men with him on the rock to peel right, throwing two more grenades at the position under the tree as he did so. They almost certainly didn't realize in the darkness and the chaos, but as they jumped off the rock to get away, the SEALs ran right over Neil Roberts's corpse. Fifty meters away, the other two SEALs had been exchanging fire with a machine-gun position to their south, killing two Al Qaida men who had popped their heads over a knoll for a second too long. They realized Slab was disengaging.

Slab and another SEAL ran over to where Chapman had been hit. He was still lying there, in what Slab described as "an unnatural position." By now another SEAL had been wounded. In Slab's view, with a SEAL badly wounded in both legs and another less seriously hurt, he could not afford the manpower or the time to carry Chapman's body off the mountain. More fire erupted from a bunker. It was time to get off the top of Takur Ghar. "One at a time we jumped, ran, and slid over the crest of the mountain," Slab said. The two SEALs who had been separated from Slab's trio of survivors provided covering fire and then launched themselves over the northeast side of the mountain themselves, with the first three hiding behind rocks and trees and covering them in turn. Then machine-gun fire from the northern bunker wounded another SEAL in the left leg. Once the Al Qaida men looking over the side of the mountain had lost track of them, Slab moved his men a little farther down, until they were about fifty meters from the top. Only then did he pull out his MBITR and ask Grim 32 to cover their retreat. "Grim, Grim, are you up?" Slab said, breathing heavily. "Yeah, we've been trying to contact you," Grim 32's navigator replied. "Where are your guys?" Slab turned on an infrared strobe to identify his position for the AC-130, and then had the aircraft fire its 105mm howitzer at the Al Qaida positions above him. The SEALs were still receiving machine-gun fire, but it was ineffective. However, the only radio on which they could talk to

Bagram and Masirah was the satellite radio in Chapman's rucksack, which was still up on the mountain. But Slab used his MBITR to contact Juliet at their observation post 4,000 meters to the north. At 5:23 a.m. Juliet relayed a message to Bagram from Slab: Mako 30 was requesting the quick reaction force.

7.

AT 3:45 a.m., as Razor 04 was landing beside the downed Razor 03, Gregory Trebon alerted the Task Force 11 quick reaction force. He didn't fully understand what had happened in the Shahikot, but he wanted his quick reaction force ready to go. Responsibility for providing that force rotated between the three platoons of A Company, 1st Ranger Battalion, which formed the core of Task Force Red. On the night of March 3-4, the QRF was 1st Platoon, led by Captain Nathan Self.

Born and raised in Waco, Texas, Nate Self was an all-American kid who had realized his mother's worst fears when he entered West Point as a cadet in 1994, seeking a challenge and a way to serve his country. Two weeks after graduating from the military academy in 1998 he married his high school sweetheart, whom he had known since elementary school. In October she had given birth to their first child, a son, but Self had only two months to get to know him before A Company deployed to Afghanistan. As with other echelons of command in the Ranger Regiment, platoon command was a second command for the officers who received it, making the lieutenants who became platoon leaders slightly older and more experienced than their counterparts in the rest of the Army, because they had already been platoon leaders elsewhere. Self was no exception. He was twenty-five and in December had been promoted to captain, a rank more often associated with company command. When Anaconda kicked off, Self had led 1st Platoon for almost seventeen months. He knew the men, their strengths, and their weaknesses.

By the time Trebon gave the order to alert the quick reaction force (QRF), Self had anticipated the move and was well ahead of him. The captain had been sitting in the Blue TOC, where the Rangers had a corner to themselves, when he heard a message come across the radio saying a TF Brown helicopter had gone down. It was unclear whether the helicopter had crashed due to enemy fire or a mechanical failure, but in either case, Self knew it probably meant his men would be getting the call. Securing a downed helicopter was on the list of missions for the QRF. He hustled down to the two GP Mediums that housed his platoon and told his troops to get up. At first, few took him too seriously.

He'd already woken them up once that night when another possible mission had popped up—reinforcing the safe house in Khowst after a rocket attack. That had blown over, but here the captain was again getting his troops out of bed in the middle of the night. There was a sense of the boy crying wolf. "Yeah, sir, we got it last time," said Staff Sergeant Arin Canon half-jokingly. "No, get up," Self said, his voice turning serious. "One of our aircraft is down." That was all he needed to say. In a heartbeat the men were out of their sleeping bags, pulling uniforms and combat gear on, reaching for and checking weapons. The Rangers' standard was to be at the airfield ready to fly within thirty minutes of being alerted. They had rehearsed this over and over again, working through each possible contingency—*What if there's only one helicopter available? Will we need vehicles?* In each case every man was assigned a role and had it down pat.

Since arriving in Bagram in the last week of December, portions of the platoon had launched on several missions, but none of the men had seen combat. However, they had kept themselves on a razor's edge of readiness by training at Al Qaida's enormous Tarnak Farms facility near Kandahar. Using live ammunition they had rehearsed combat scenarios all the way up to platoon-level assaults in what Self described as "the best training I've ever seen in the Army." He and his men particularly relished the opportunity to "push the envelope" regarding safety restrictions further than they might have been allowed in the United States. "Bad for Al Qaida, lucky for us," noted Canon, the platoon's weapons squad leader. One of Self's squads plus a machine-gun team, a medic and his platoon sergeant were still down there, leaving him with a little over half the platoon in Bagram: two line squads, two two-man machine-gun teams, and himself. When Canon realized that this time they were really launching, he ran over to 2nd Platoon's tents and grabbed their medic, Sergeant Matt LaFrenz, to accompany them on the mission.

Self returned to the TOC. Word was coming in that someone had fallen out of a Chinook. On the Predator screen he could see Razor 04 on the ground beside Razor 03, although he didn't know exactly what he was looking at, or where it was. The captain assumed that his mission would be to secure the downed helicopter. He was confused by the references he kept hearing to a guy falling out of a helicopter. "Sir, what are we doing? Where are we going?" he said to his battalion operations officer, Major Jim Mingus. With Tony Thomas in Kandahar, Mingus was TF Red's senior officer in Bagram. Mingus told Self to go to the helicopters and then call the TOC for guidance.

Self headed to the airfield, only to encounter more problems. The QRF mission always involved a three- or four-man Air Force special tactics team, made up of pararescuemen, or PJs, trained in emergency medical skills and the swift rescue and evacuation of casualties, and combat controllers, whose job it was to conduct air traffic control and coordinate close air support. When his platoon had first been assigned the QRF mission, Self had been given a special tactics (STS) team to whom he had explained the nuts and bolts of how the platoon conducted its missions—simple but essential things like who would run to what position off the back of the helicopter, and what everybody's radio call signs were. But tonight that team was on another mission. When Self got to the airfield a four-man special tactics team he didn't know was waiting for him. This troubled Self and Canon. Neither man was comfortable going into what could be a combat situation with a team they'd never even met before, but Self ran through the platoon's standard operating procedures as clearly as possible with the airmen.

Then another issue reared its head: there were two TF Brown Chinooks on the tarmac, but only one was rigged to accommodate his men. The other was going to carry a fuel blivet to the airstrip in Gardez. Self couldn't understand why fuel was taking a higher priority than getting his men to the downed helicopter. He had about twenty-five men at the airfield, and he wanted to take as many Rangers as he was allowed. He called Mingus and told him about the four-man special tactics team. The platoon leader told the major that he couldn't take all four, especially as the 160th pilots were telling him that only one aircraft was available to carry his troops. If this were the case, Self would be restricted to taking only thirteen men. "There's no way I'm taking four of these [special tactics] guys and only nine of my own," Self told Mingus. Self would definitely be taking his enlisted tactical air controller, Staff Sergeant Kevin Vance. If all four special tactics men came along as well, it would leave room for only a seven-man Ranger squad. If Self took a two-man machine-gun team, that squad would be cut to five men. Mingus told him he could cut one of the special tactics guys. "Why don't we just not take 'em at all?" Self replied. "We know the aircraft is stable, we're not going to have cut anybody out of it, there's no casualties there. What are they going for? I'd just rather take thirteen of my own, so we can fight." Mingus told Self he needed to take the special tactics men in case his helicopter went down. They debated the issue back and forth, but Self wasn't getting anywhere. He was left with a load of ten Rangers and a three-man STS team. Self did some quick thinking about who he should take. He decided on Staff Sergeant Ray DePouli's squad ("because it was the best squad in the platoon," he said), scaled down to six men, plus himself, Vance, and a two-man machine-gun team. The six-man squad consisted of DePouli as the squad leader, a three-man fire team consisting of a team leader, a SAW gunner, and a 203 gunner, and a two-man fire team with a team leader and a SAW gunner. Calling back to Mingus, Self explained how limited his options would be with such a small force on the ground. "You're just going to secure a downed bird," Mingus responded. What about the guy who fell out of the helo? Self asked. "We're still working on it," Mingus said, an indication of just how little situational awareness the Blue and Red staffs in Bagram had.

A captain from the TF Red staff approached Self on the tarmac. "You've got launch authority, you can go," he told the platoon leader. "What's our mission?" Self asked for the umpteenth time. "We've got to get you guys in the air and get you down in that vicinity, fly you to Gardez and put you on the ground," the battle captain said. "When you get down to Gardez come up on tacsat and we'll give you further instructions. We just need to get you prepositioned and get you moved, because it's about an hour's flight." As he was speaking another two Chinooks—the original Razor 03 and Razor 04 that had just flown up from Gardez—landed on the runway about 200 meters away. A crew chief for one of the helicopters Self had thought he'd be flying on gestured at the Chinooks that had just flown in and told him those were the helicopters he'd be going in on now. Before he headed over to them, Self turned back to the other Ranger captain. "Get me another aircraft," he implored. "You've got to get some more people down there." Just then the special tactics team that usually worked with Self's platoon turned up, back from their mission. Self filled them in on what was going on and told the team he'd just met that he'd be taking the airmen he already knew. Then he and the rest of his chalk ran over to the helicopters that had just landed. When he got to the helicopter he was supposed to be riding on, a special tactics team was already onboard. "Who's the team leader," Self asked. "I am," replied Technigal Sergeant Keary Miller, 31. "You're off," Self told Miller. "I got my own guys." Then he moved forward, plugged into the intercom and spoke with the crew as the Chinook taxied down the runway to fuel up. When he turned around, he saw Miller and his teammates were still there. The two special tactics teams had run into each other on the ramp and agreed that the team already on the aircraft should stay, because their gear—specialized equipment for pulling people from helicopter wreckage—was already loaded on the helicopter. Self wasn't happy to be stuck with a team that he'd never even seen before that night. He'd have preferred to go in with the first team from the evening. At least he'd had fifteen minutes with them to explain how his platoon did things. But there was nothing to do now but make the best of it.

"Here's what's gonna happen," Self told them. "He's gonna be my RTO," he said, motioning towards Vance. "Who's the combat controller?" The special tactics guys pointed at Staff Sergeant Gabe Brown. "You're gonna control fires," Self told Brown. Self wanted Vance as his RTO because he knew Vance knew all the call signs and frequencies for talking to the Blue TOC. Brown, with less experience than Vance, would be responsible for calling in close air support if necessary.

Meanwhile Canon had gone to the TOC in the hope of arranging another aircraft. When he got there Mingus told him there was another helicopter waiting and to go get on it. He went back down to the airfield, collected his men and got on the Chinook, call sign Razor 02. On Self's aircraft, Razor 01, the platoon leader was on the intercom with the crew as they prepared to take off. He had no idea that the other half of his force was coming along until he heard the Razor 02 crew on the radio say they had Rangers on board. It was a huge relief to Self. Now he had the people he needed: nineteen Rangers, an ETAC, and a three-man special tactics team.

Shortly after 5 a.m. the helicopters took off. There were twenty-one men on Razor 01: two pilots, the air mission commander, four crew chiefs, one medic from the 160th, three special tactics men, one enlisted tactical air controller, and nine Rangers. Razor 02 carried sixteen men: two pilots, four crew chiefs, and ten Rangers. No one on either aircraft had more than the vaguest idea of what awaited them at the other end of their flight. Self and Canon each believed they were going to land at Gardez, get a more detailed briefing and then fly in to the valley to secure the downed helicopter. Seated toward the front of his helicopter, Self had the aircraft intercom plugged into one ear—allowing him to listen to the radio transmissions being sent and received by the pilots—and his MBITR plugged into his other ear, so he could talk to DePouli at the other end of the aircraft. The crew was tuned in to the TF 11 satellite frequency. Self recognized some of the call signs, but the only voice with which he was familiar belonged to Pete Blaber. The captain tried to piece together what was happening from the disjointed radio calls. When he heard a Mako call sign mentioned, Self inferred that somehow the SEALs had managed to secure whoever it was that had fallen out of the helicopter. Two and a half hours after Roberts had dropped into the snow on top of Takur Ghar, Self was still laboring under the misconception that the man who'd fallen out was probably some unfortunate private from the 101st. However, one thing was clear from listening to the radio chatter: Everyone wanted to know when the QRF was going to arrive. Self hoped they would all show some patience. *We've got to stop in Gardez first and figure out what's going on,* he thought.

On Razor 01 the three 160th warrant officers in charge of the flight—the air mission commander, a chief warrant officer 5 called Don, the pilot-in-command, a chief warrant officer 4 named Chuck, and the pilot, a chief warrant officer 3 called Greg, thirty-seven, from Louisville, Kentucky—were on their third mission of the night and having the devil of a time figuring out what was supposed to be happening. They divided up the radio responsibilities among them, with each monitoring different nets. Sitting in the jump seat, Don was trying with great difficulty to talk with Bagram. There wasn't much getting through directly from the Blue and Brown TOCs. Most of what the air mission commander heard was coming from a Navy EP-3 aircraft, which was relaying messages to the inbound Chinooks from Masirah and Bagram.

As they flew through the mountains north of Gardez, the helicopters lost radio contact with each other. Aboard Razor 01, Don was talking to the EP-3, which was trying to pass the grid coordinates for the Chinooks' LZ. Don made the EP-3 repeat the numbers three times before he was sure he and the others listening on Razor 01 had heard them right. "We almost wrote down the wrong grid," Self recalled. Given what followed, he acknowledged, such a mistake "might have been good." Self was doing his best to follow along and keep his men in the loop. He took a lightboard (a piece of Plexiglas taped on one side to give a white background and illuminated with a chem light) from his pocket and using a grease pencil wrote down the basics of what he could make out from the garbled radio transmissions, then passed it around. He wrote that "SEAL snipers" were near the man who'd fallen out of the aircraft, that they were "possibly in contact" and were requesting the QRF. It became increasingly clear the Chinooks weren't going to stop in Gardez. One of the few orders that got through from Masirah and Bagram was to head straight into the valley to help the SEALs.

It was almost three hours since Razor 03 had been shot down, but the commander of the quick reaction force en route to the Shahikot still had no appreciation of the SEALs' location relative to the downed helicopter and continued to believe that the helicopter crash-landing because of enemy fire or a maintenance problem (he still didn't know which) and the serviceman falling out of a helicopter were unrelated incidents. On Razor 02, Canon had heard nothing about the change in plans. He was familiar with Gardez from a previous mission and as the helicopter soared overhead he looked out of the window, recognized the town below and realized they weren't landing. *Something has obviously changed,* he thought.

The helicopters entered the north end of the Shahikot. The night had faded and the crews were flying aggressive nap-of-the-earth techniques, hugging the ground to avoid presenting a target to any Al Qaida gunners. Glancing out, they were surprised to see they were flying over the dark form of Razor 03.

Until that moment they had all assumed that they were flying to that crash site. Don asked the EP-3 if they were sure of the LZ coordinates, because they'd just flown over the crashed helicopter. "No, this is a different location," the man on the EP-3 said. "It's on top of a 10,000-foot mountain." "Are there friendlies or enemy there?" The EP-3 told Don there would be friendly troops on top of the mountain. "Are they stationary, moving, what?" Don asked. "They're moving," the EP-3 replied. By now the two Chinooks had flown back out of the valley and were in a holding pattern while Don, Self, and the pilots tried to get the details straight.

Meanwhile, in Bagram and Masirah, at 6:08 a.m., staff officers were trying to get through to Razor 01 and Razor 02 with no success. The satellite communications were failing them just when the special operators sitting beside banks of radios in the operations centers and behind controls in the Chinooks needed them most. The message the TF 11 staff was trying to deliver was a simple, important, lifesaving message: do not land on the mountaintop, where Razor 03 and Razor 04 had already taken fire; land at an offset LZ farther down the slopes of Takur Ghar. These instructions were never received on the helicopters, who were still acting on the orders they'd received via the EP-3. Again, the decision to take Blaber out of the command chain was revealed to be a terrible mistake. As the official Special Operations Command investigator wrote: *"Here the [AFO] commander on the scene would clearly have made a difference. At the least he would have insisted that Razor 01 use an offset landing zone. He would also have been in a position to give this direction personally, using the more reliable line of sight radios, which would have significantly reduced the chances of misunderstanding."*

As Razor 01 bucked and swerved, the men in the back held on. There were no seats in the cargo area, so they were sitting on the floor, trying not to get tossed around. Bracing himself, Nate Self scrutinized his map by flashlight, trying to figure it all out. He was still confused, but somehow he managed to deduce—and tell his men via the lightboard—three things: they were going to land "in the vicinity of the enemy"; the SEALs were in contact with that same enemy; and the SEALs were also not far from the man who'd fallen out of the helicopter. Self wrote his troops that they were going to do "a hot extraction on a possible hot LZ" (something the pilots had failed to pick up on). Speaking to each other over their MBITR radios, Self and DePouli established a game plan, the essence of which was that they were going to run off the back of the helicopter, secure the immediate area, link up with the SEALs and, maybe, the guy who'd fallen off the helicopter, get them onto their Chinook and fly away as quickly as possible. "Watch your fires coming off, there's friendlies in the area," Self wrote on the lightboard. At the very least he wanted his men to understand that there was a high likelihood of combat on the LZ and that the SEALs they were picking up would be breaking contact with the enemy as they ran toward the helicopter. He refocused his attention on the radio. The call signs were all from Bagram. Then he heard Blaber's voice, urgent now. Everyone seemed to be talking about the AC-130.

8.

ON the side of Takur Ghar, Mako 30 was in trouble. Slab and his four teammates who had made it off the mountaintop had managed to hustle and hobble down to a hiding place beneath a rock overhang that protected them from the fire that had chased them off the peak. But the only thing preventing the guerrillas up top from coming to look for them was Grim 32's presence overhead. Every time either the SEALs or the gunship crew saw the enemy trying to outflank Mako 30's position, the AC-130 would open up with a few of its trademark 105mm rounds. ("We felt like the 40s just weren't making a big enough boom to keep heads down," Turner said.)

But there was a limit to how long Mako 30 would be able to count on Grim 32's support. Air Force rules required the AC-130 to be out of the combat zone by dawn, less than an hour away. In the gunship's cockpit, Turner looked at his watch and then called Bossman to make sure there were some fast-movers available to support the SEALs once he had to break station. At the same time Grim 32 called back to its higher headquarters, the Dagger air component at K2. "We are in a firefight with these guys [i.e., Mako 30] for their lives," Turner told K2. "We're requesting permission to stay later." Dagger's answer was: "No, you will return to base." This sat well with neither the gunship crew nor a host of other officers monitoring the call. Radio and phone calls flew between Bagram, Masirah, K2, Bossman (the AWACS), and the Shahikot as these officers engaged in a high-level tussle with a few Air Force officials over who "owned" the AC-130. An unclear chain of command was again playing havoc with the effective control of the operation.

On the side of those arguing to keep Grim 32 on station were Blaber, Harrell, Mulholland, and Trebon. Putting up stubborn resistance, however, was Colonel Ray Kilgore, who had replaced Frank Kisner as Mulholland's deputy at Task Force Dagger and the commander of Joint Special Operations Air Component

(North). Kilgore was apparently gripped by the fear of a daylight shootdown that has haunted the AC-130 community since Spirit 03's demise over Khafji. The dispute led to some fierce telephone arguments with Mulholland.

The folks most worried when they heard the radio calls about the Grim 32 being pulled off station were the SEALs of Mako 30. "Hey, guys, don't leave me," Slab said to the gunship crew. "If you leave, we're dead." Grim 32 told Slab not to worry. "Until you have somebody else that can take care of you, we're staying," one of the aircrew told him. "We're just trying to work through this ROE [rules of engagement] crap." They continued shooting. To the SEALs and the crew of Grim 32, the argument for keeping the gunship on station beyond dawn was straightforward: the SEALs needed its firepower to keep the enemy off their backs. But to the others arguing in favor of keeping the AC-130 on station, its importance to the inbound quick reaction force was at least as important. One of the loudest advocates for holding Grim 32 over Takur Ghar was Pete Blaber. As soon as he heard Turner talk about breaking station, Blaber came up on the net. "Negative," he said. "I am ordering you to remain on station and support these guys. You're going to be the fire support when the QRF comes in."

This argument would have made perfect sense to Turner and his crewmates, except that they were running out of fuel as well as darkness and no one seemed to be able to tell them when Razor 01 and Razor 02 were going to show up. The best estimate Turner got from Task Force 11 was "within the hour." The pilot knew he didn't have an hour's worth of fuel left, if he was to make it back to K2. Then, from a ridgeline about five miles to his south, a shoulder-fired antiaircraft missile arced upward toward his aircraft. Through Turner's night-vision goggles it looked like the space shuttle was zooming toward him. The missile fell well short of Grim 32, but it was a wake-up call that reinforced their fears of their own vulnerability once the sun rose. "In daylight an AC-130 looks like a blimp overhead at a football game," Turner said. At least the base back at K2 wasn't bothering them any more with calls to return to K2. In fact, K2 had been surprisingly quiet. Turner called back to his electronic warfare officer, who controlled the radio channels that the aircraft listened to. "Hey, I haven't heard anything from Dagger for a while now," Turner said. "What's going on with them?" "Boss, it's just too busy up there, you guys are making the right decisions, I turned them off," the officer replied. He had a strong relationship with Turner and knew the pilot would remain on station until he ran out of gas or someone arrived to replace them, whichever came first. Under those conditions, there was no point listening to the increasingly frantic calls from K2 for them to return to base. "He turned them off so we couldn't hear them ordering us to come home anymore," Turner said.

Dawn broke over the Shahikot. From Masirah Chris Naler continued to urge Grim 32 to remain on station until the QRF arrived. But Turner still couldn't get Naler to tell him when that would be. The reason for this was simple: Masirah had lost track of Razor 01 and Razor 02. In a further sign of how little situational awareness the TF 11 staff enjoyed, Naler, call sign Champ 20, told Grim 32 to "glint" the LZ to enhance the effects of the QRF's night-vision goggles when the Chinooks arrived. "Hey, Champ, it's daylight out here," replied Turner, who was wearing sunglasses by that point.

Shortly after that, a nearby EP-3 with the call sign Toolbox asked Grim 32 if they'd seen the antiaircraft missile that had just been fired at them. They hadn't. The missile had been launched from a similar location to the earlier one and had also fallen short, but Turner was much more worried this time, precisely because he hadn't seen it. "If you look at all the aircraft that have been shot down since the invention of antiaircraft missiles, the vast majority of them were shot down by the missile they never saw," he explained. Just then two F-15E Strike Eagles flew through Turner's field of vision, letting him know that they were ready to take over the responsibility for close air support. The gunship pilot now knew that if he departed, the SEALs wouldn't be left defenseless, even though no other aircraft in the U.S. inventory came close to being able to replicate the constant, precise pounding that an AC-130 could deliver.

The sun was getting higher and Grim 32's fuel gauge was getting lower. The Strike Eagles were on station and there was no sign of—or word from—the quick reaction force. Turner got on the radio to the F-15Es and filled them in on what he knew, orienting them to Mako 30 and passing them the frequencies for the SEAL team and the TF 11 operations center in Masirah. Then, at 6:01 a.m., Toolbox reported a third antiaircraft missile had been launched at Grim 32. Unlike the two previous launches, which gained so much altitude that there was no doubt they were missiles, Turner conceded that the EP-3 might have mistaken an RPG for a shoulder-launched air defense missile on the third occasion. Nevertheless, the incident helped make his mind up. The Strike Eagles, being much faster than the AC-130, needed more space to operate in; it was broad daylight; his chain of command had already ordered him home; he'd been shot at twice and maybe just now a third time; and no one seemed to know when the QRF was coming. *It may be time to get out of the way,* he thought. Grim 32 asked again when Razor 01 was due. "We're figuring that out now," was the response. No one even passed the Chinooks' frequency to the AC-130. Grim 32 passed the Strike Eagle call signs to Mako 30, talked to Bossman, which had been telling the gunship to leave for at least thirteen minutes, and then turned for home. "There really was nothing else we felt like we could do,"

Turner said. One of his last calls from the Shahikot was to Masirah on the subject of the QRF. "Whatever you do, don't send them back to this same LZ," he told Naler. "It is absolutely hot." It was a message that was sent from Masirah, but never received.

Ten minutes later Razor 01 flew into the same hot LZ that Grim 32 had warned Masirah about. By now almost everyone in the TF 11 chain of command had belatedly realized that the top of Takur Ghar was not a good place to try to land a Chinook, except for the crews of Razor 01 and Razor 02. Had the men on board Grim 32 known that the two Chinooks were only 10 minutes out when they made the decision to leave, they would have stayed. "If we'd have known they were coming in, there is zero question in my mind we would have stayed there," Turner said. "That is what we train for and that is the bond we have with those guys. We train with the Rangers daily for that kind of thing. . . . We'd disobeyed our orders for an hour. Another fifteen minutes wasn't going to get me in any less hot water." The AC-130 had less than thirty minutes' worth of fuel left in the tank beyond what was required to get to K2. However, had they chosen to divert to Kandahar or to conduct an air-to-air refueling over Pakistan they could have circled Takur Ghar for another hour, more than enough time to destroy any enemy forces the Rangers might run into. Yet again, the problems inherent in trying to run a combat operation from over a thousand miles away based only on a couple of overcrowded satellite frequencies and the "soda-straw" view provided by the Predator were making themselves felt in the Shahikot.

As the AC-130 flew away from the valley, Blaber made one last effort to persuade it to stay. "If you pull off station before the QRF come in," he said, "we will have a helo knocked out of the sky."

AT 6:07 a.m. Razors 01 and 02 were about to break from their holding patterns outside the Shahikot and fly toward Takur Ghar. Slab and four of his Mako 30 teammates were sheltering under a ledge on the side of the mountain. But on the peak something curious was happening. At a time when there were supposed to be no Americans alive up there, a fierce firefight was underway.

The fight, captured by a Predator, was vicious and brief. At 5:52 a.m., an Al Qaida guerrilla wearing a pair of desert camouflage Gore-Tex pants he had looted from Neil Roberts's corpse or rucksack emerged from a concealed position and spent the next fifteen minutes slowly and methodically flanking the bunkers that Mako 30 had engaged at point blank range. As he moved, another fighter fired an RPG at one of the bunkers. Both guerrillas were clearly attacking someone in one of the bunkers. At 6:07 a.m. the Al Qaida fighter who had spent quarter of an hour maneuvering to the side of the bunker opened fire at it, only to be killed by rifle fire from the bunker. The fighter who had fired the RPG then assaulted the bunker, killing whoever was inside.

The burning question remains: Who was inside that bunker, putting up such fierce resistance? There are only two possibilities. The first is that an Al Qaida fighter reoccupied the bunker and then mistakenly fired upon his colleagues to the south, thinking them to be elements of Mako 30 who had remained on the mountaintop. Under this scenario, the Al Qaida fighters who had been fired upon returned fire and assaulted the bunker, thinking that the man inside was an American, when really he was one of their own. Colonel Andrew Milani, who conducted an exhaustive investigation of the entire Takur Ghar battle for U.S. Special Operations Command, noted two weaknesses with this explanation for the events seen on the Predator tape. The first is that there was already enough daylight at that hour for the enemy fighters to quickly realize their error. The second is that the AK-style assault rifles with which enemy fighters were armed sound distinctly different from the Americans' M4 rifles, so much so that any experienced fighter would immediately recognize it if his assailant was using an AK-47 or one of its many variants.

The second possibility, one far more troubling for U.S. Special Operations Command, is that the man in the bunker, fighting on alone against insurmountable odds on a frozen Afghan mountaintop, was Air Force Technical Sergeant John Chapman, who had been left for dead by Mako 30 less than an hour previously. Slab had been convinced that Chapman was dead, but he never physically confirmed that by taking his pulse or otherwise examining his body. There had been no time for that in the heat of battle. Chapman's body was not found where Slab said he left it, however, but twelve feet away in the bunker the two Al Qaida men had assaulted at 6:07 a.m. Slab said that before he and his men scrambled off the mountaintop, he'd briefly checked where he thought Chapman fell, and had seen Chapman's corpse "in an unnatural position." But the location cited by Slab is in fact the exact location at which Roberts's body was later found. It is possible that Slab took his eyes away from Chapman when Chapman was shot, or shortly afterward, then looked back in that direction, noticed the body lying there, and assumed it to be Chapman's, when it was in fact Roberts's. Meanwhile, under this scenario, Chapman had climbed into the bunker to continue the fight.

Nate Self, who became very familiar with the top of the mountain and the Predator footage, said the video shows the person in the bunker firing at the enemy while the SEALs were still on the mountaintop. The SEALs then pop at least one smoke canister to cover their withdrawal, while the man in the bunker continues fighting. There is no break in the film, and the man can be seen in the bunker until the fight at 6:07 a.m., when several Al Qaida fighters assault the bunker from two different directions and he is killed. Self also noted that the rifle shot from the bunker that killed the enemy was a very difficult shot that he doubted an Al Qaida fighter could have made. (Many U.S. troops remarked on their enemies' poor marksmanship during Anaconda.)

Chapman sustained wounds to his upper and lower body. The lower body wounds would not have killed him and might well have allowed him to fight on after coming to his senses and crawling into the bunker. The upper body wounds would have been almost immediately fatal. It goes without saying that someone standing and fighting from a bunker would be more likely to receive wounds to his upper body than his lower body. Counting against this theory, however, is the fact that no calls were recorded from either of Chapman's radios (his big satellite radio and his MBITR) during this period. A man fighting for his life who was an expert radio operator might have been expected to use his communications know-how to call for help in that situation.

Milani was unable to reach a decision as to which of the two scenarios represented reality. But other sources who had seen the tape and were otherwise familiar with the events on Takur Ghar were sure the man fighting from the bunker was Chapman. An officer who watched the fuzzy Predator feed live in the Mountain TOC was convinced that Chapman fought on after the SEALs ran off the peak. "I remember clearly seeing that blob still shoot after the other two blobs broke contact," he said.

If the man holding off Al Qaida from the bunker was Chapman, he held out almost long enough to give himself a fighting chance of survival. A mere forty-five seconds after his resistance was finally ended, the attention of every Al Qaida fighter on top of Takur Ghar was drawn to the rhythmic thunder of two giant sets of rotor blades as the dark shape of Razor 01 appeared over the mountaintop.

9.

THE Razor 01 pilots circled the mountain three times looking for a place to land. They saw footprints in the snow, but no SEALs. Chuck, Greg, and Don talked among themselves. None of them felt comfortable with this situation. Chuck called Razor 02 and told them to return to Gardez and wait. *Better to have only one aircraft shot down, not two,* Chuck thought. In the back Self paused his examination of the map for a moment to glance at his men. Their faces reflected a natural anxiety that any men in that situation would feel—"the fear of the unknown," as Canon, on Razor 02, described it—but that fear was mingled with confidence. The training at Tarnak Farms had honed their skills to something close to perfection. Their weapons were zeroed. The more religious among them had attended a church service the previous day, which was a Sunday. They were combat ready. They were at the top of their game.

Dave, the staff sergeant who was the left door gunner, turned and gave a thumbs-up to Sergeant Phil Svitak, the right door gunner, then yelled at everyone in the back, "Get ready!" Self leaned over and squeezed the shoulder of Specialist Marc Anderson, a 240 gunner, and gave him a thumbs-up as a sign of assurance. Anderson turned to his assistant gunner, Private First Class David Gilliam, slapped him on the back and shouted in his ear, "Today I feel like a Ranger."

After a brief discussion with the other pilot and Self over where they should land, Greg, the right seat pilot at the controls, picked out a spot on a gentle slope about seventy-five meters from the very top of the mountain peak and brought the helicopter in on a normal approach. *Well, this is it, make it a good one,* he thought. Below him at the 2 o'clock position he saw three men about sixty meters away aiming weapons at his helicopter. Before he had time to react the right windscreen shattered, his right multifunction display went out and two bullets hit him square in the chest, thudding against his body armor. Another bullet pushed his helmet to the left. "Taking fire at 2 o'clock!" he yelled.

Svitak also saw the men shooting at the helicopter. He turned to Cory, the sergeant first class who was the crew's medic. "Doc, you'd better move back," Svitak told him. Then he fired a one-second burst from his minigun—*whiiirrrrrr!!!!!*—and slumped over with two bullets in his stomach. He was dead within seconds. The right rear gunner, a sergeant called Shawn, fired four rounds from his M60 machine-gun—*dum!dum!dum!dum!* At that moment, as the Chinook slowed to a hover about eighty feet off the ground, one of the enemy fighters who had just killed the mystery figure in the bunker under the tree climbed up on a boulder and fired an RPG at the helicopter. It hit the right engine and exploded. Instantly there was a loud whine from the left engine as it picked up the load to compensate for the right engine being knocked out. Dave, the left gunner, was hit in the thigh as the Al Qaida fighters raked the helicopter with fire. The round struck his knife, shattering it and embedding pieces of it in his left leg. He felt as though a sledgehammer had hit his thigh, from which blood was now spraying. Angry, he swept his minigun from left to right, fighting fire with fire. Beside him Cory was hit by several rounds, none of which penetrated his body armor or his helmet.

In the cockpit a bullet caught Chuck's left leg just above the knee. Another hit his helmet, knocking his head back. But Greg, unaware that his colleague was wounded, still had control of the helicopter. Greg's first instinct was to repeat Razor 03's exploits of a few hours earlier and try to nose the helicopter over the edge of the mountain and fly away, except he'd have to manage it on a single engine. But very quickly he realized that if he tried to gain airspeed he'd lose altitude and wouldn't make it over the peak. He brought the nose back up into a landing attitude and slowed the helicopter to put it on the deck. His left seat pilot and flight lead, Chuck, reminded him that he was landing on a slope. He brought the helicopter down fast. The rear wheels hit first. Then the forward landing gear came down with bump. "It was probably the best damn landing I've ever made in my fourteen years of flying," he said. Given the circumstances, that was almost certainly the case, but to Nate Self and his Rangers in the back, the Chinook seemed to just fall out of the sky.

As they hit the ground another RPG flew in through the right cabin door. It didn't explode, but it hit an oxygen tank above the left window, sending sparks flying around the cargo area and starting a small fire. Bullets shredded the insulation and soundproofing material in the ceiling and it fluttered down like confetti. The bump when they fell to earth knocked everyone in the back to the floor. Now they were either still lying there or scrambling on their hands and knees to get out the back of helicopter. Self had been prepared for a hot LZ, but not this hot. He had no idea they'd just tried to land on an LZ at which two helicopters had already been shot up. Lying on the floor as machine-gun fire cut holes in both sides of the helicopter, he tried to make sense of the situation. *Somebody screwed us big time,* he thought. It was 6:10 a.m.

Shawn hurt his knee in the landing but got to his feet and dropped the ramp. The first Ranger to run down it was DePouli. As he got to the bottom a bullet hit him in the back, a fraction of an inch above the bottom of the rear bulletproof plate in his vest, spinning him around. Seeing an enemy fighter at the helicopter's 8 o'clock position, he fired an entire magazine from his M4 at the guerrilla. Behind him two bullets hit Sergeant Joshua Walker's helmet. He didn't even notice the impact. Spotting a bunker to his right he too fired off a full clip at it then headed left. Specialist Aaron Totten-Lancaster followed him out, wading into the knee-deep snow and then diving into the prone position by the airframe's lower right corner. Gilliam picked up Anderson's 240 and crawled off the right of the ramp on his knees and elbows. Vance, the ETAC, dropped his rucksack, heavy from the weight of the big radio in it, off the ramp and jumped out. But as Self crawled across the floor and onto the ramp he realized that not all his men had been as lucky as DePouli and Walker. Specialist

Matt Commons lay face up on the ramp, his eyes open but unseeing and a neat bullet hole in his head. His blood was dripping off the ramp, staining the snow red. Sergeant Brad Crose was lying dead facedown in the snow at the bottom of the ramp. Like their Ranger forefathers who landed on Omaha Beach, Crose and Commons had stormed down the ramp only to be cut down in a hail of machine-gun fire. Anderson, who only moments earlier had been telling Gilliam that he felt "like a Ranger," didn't even make it to the ramp. He was hit in mid-cabin and fell to the floor. Senior Airman Jason Cunningham, the PJ medic, crawled over and did his best but couldn't save him.

Sitting in the companionway, Don saw bullet holes appearing in the windscreen. He'd been in the Army twenty-six years but this was the first time he'd been shot at. He unbuckled his seat belt, grabbed his rifle and ran a couple of steps toward the back, only to encounter a scene of devastation. It seemed as though everyone had been shot. The troops were either on the floor or already outside, so he ran out the back.

As soon as the helicopter was on the ground, the same men Greg had seen firing on the approach advanced toward the aircraft. Still holding the cyclic stick in his left hand he grabbed his M4 with his right and fired a couple of bursts at them out of his sliding side window, forcing them back behind the rock. Greg's company commander had made his crews practice this exact scenario "ad nauseam," the pilot said. "At the time, I thought, *Oh my God, do we have to do these shootdown things again?*" he said. "It was like he could see into the future and knew exactly what was going to happen. So everything I did was kind of muscle memory. I attribute it to training. I don't attribute it to heroics or anything like that. It's just what I was taught to do."

Bullets flew into the cockpit, putting holes in and then shattering what was left of the windscreen and, in a couple of cases, skidding off Greg's helmet. The circuitbreaker panel to his right front was smoking. Chuck leaned over and slapped Greg on the shoulder. "I'm outta here!" he yelled as he grabbed his M4. Then he reached up with his left hand, grabbed the yellow and black emergency exit handle at the top of his door, rotated it down, kicked the door out, and dived out into the snow. That seemed like a smart idea, so Greg did the same, reaching up with his left arm across his head to pull the handle while holding the grip of his M4 with his right. But the instant he kicked his door out into the snow, his left arm flew backward. Confused, he tried to move his left hand to grip the stock of his M4, and missed the weapon completely. He looked down to see his left hand hanging limply at almost a 90-degree angle from his forearm, spurting arterial blood across the cockpit. He pulled his hand up and examined it. The flesh seemed to be glowing and smoking. Greg immediately realized why. There was a tracer round stuck inside his hand, burning away. He pulled it out and put it in his sleeve pocket. A good 60 percent of the circumference of his wrist was gone. A couple of tendons and a stick of bone were all that attached his hand to his arm. He fired one more burst from his M4 to cover himself, but diving out of his right-hand door no longer seemed an attractive proposition. He twisted around in his seat, laid his weapon on the center console and then wriggled through the companionway toward the rear of the helicopter, taking care to keep a pressure point below his wrist to stem the flow of blood somewhat. Part of his flight gear got caught on the jump seat as he tried to squirm through. Lying on his belly, his arms stretched in front of him, he kicked with his feet trying to free himself. Straight ahead he saw Cory working on a Ranger casualty. He yelled to Cory that he was stuck. Another explosion shook the aircraft as an RPG hit the nose, and Greg felt a "thumping" in his legs as shrapnel spattered them. The aircraft's armor-plated seats protected his torso from getting hit. By now his head was sticking into the back of the helicopter and he got his first good view of the carnage there. He looked left to see Phil Svitak crumpled on the floor. Greg kept shouting at the top of his voice, forgetting that he still had his helmet on and earplugs in. Turning his head right, he saw Dave, pale and sitting down, wrapping the lanyard from his Beretta 9mm pistol around his leg as a tourniquet. Dave looked up to see what all the yelling was about. "Take your fucking helmet off!" he shouted. Greg reached back with his good hand and yanked it off.

Finally Cory came forward, grabbed Greg by his survival vest and, after a couple of attempts, pulled him into the back of the helicopter. There was still a "fusillade" of rounds puncturing holes in the side of the aircraft and whizzing over the heads of the men lying on the floor. The bullets made a *tick, tick* sound as they punctured the side of the aircraft. "It sounded like hail hitting your car," Greg said, "but you'd see sunlight stream through the holes." By now Greg, who spent his first six years in the Army as a medic, had his bleeding under control. "Go check on Phil, he's not moving," he told Cory as soon as the medic had pulled him through. "I don't think Phil made it," Dave said. "How are you doing?" Cory yelled to Dave. "Fine," replied Dave. Cory and Jason Cunningham then went to work on Greg. Cory put on a tourniquet and stuffed bandages and curlix into the wound. When the medic held his arm up, it gave Greg his first opportunity to survey the damage the bullets had done. He stared at what remained of his wrist in disbelief, amazed at how much "stuff" Cory could pack into the hole in his arm. Then Cunningham applied an oximeter—a device that measures the oxygen in a patient's blood—to Greg's finger. It didn't seem to be working. Frustrated, Cunningham held the device up and discovered why: A bullet had severed one of the wires, probably while it was still in his bag. "Has anybody seen Chuck?" Greg asked. He was still unaware that Chuck had been wounded before he dived into the snow. No one in the back of the helicopter knew where Chuck was. "He went out the left door," Greg told them.

Greg was lying on his back in the rear of the aircraft, with his feet toward the cockpit. His M4 magazines, which he carried in the rear pockets of his survival vest, were sticking into his back. Cory was kneeling between his legs, Cunningham was on his right side. Since everyone else was fighting, he told the survivors in the back to pile the PRC-112 survival radios beside him and he'd use them to try to make contact with the outside. Greg grabbed the first one and spoke into it. "This is Razor 01, down, we are taking heavy fire, engaged, numerous casualties," he said, and gave the latitude and longitude reading for the helicopter's position. "Enemy engaging us from the 2 o'clock and 9 o'clock positions." He repeated that transmission on every radio, left each radio on, and turned two of them to send out a beacon signal.

Then the pain kicked in. Fierce, excruciating pain.

10.

SELF rolled left off the ramp and quickly got his bearings. The helicopter had landed in a saddle with the ground rising up on both the left and right sides. An RPG gunner lay dead on the high ground fifteen meters to the helicopter's right, killed either by Svitak's minigun burst or Walker. Another RPG gunner occupied the rise thirty meters to the left, along with at least one other enemy fighter armed with an AK. Sixty meters ahead of the helicopter at about the 2 o'clock position guerrillas armed with a machine-gun and multiple RPGs held the same tree and bunker complex from which Mako 30 had taken so much fire. Enemy fighters there and on the high ground to the left and right were now pouring fire down on the Rangers as they came off the ramp and stumbled and slipped in the snow. Specialist Anthony Miceli's SAW was hit in four or five places as he exited the helicopter. The gun was destroyed but Miceli was unharmed and headed up the left side of the helicopter.

DePouli fired at the enemy fighters on the high ground to the left, dropping at least one of them. Self told Totten-Lancaster to move farther up the Chinook's right side toward the nose. The captain's attention was now focused on the position under the tree. He had no idea it was a bunker, he just knew that a machinegun under that tree was firing a steady stream of bullets at the helicopter. *We're going to be here all day,* he thought. *No one's gonna send a helicopter in here until it gets dark.* Then an RPG flew out of the same position and over Self's head before skipping off the ramp. Another RPG exploded about ten meters off the helicopter's right side, spraying shrapnel into the platoon leader's leg, Totten-Lancaster's lower left calf, and Vance's arm. Totten-Lancaster was virtually immobilized, no longer able to walk properly. Self kept quiet about his own wound. The shrapnel had hit his thigh at a steep angle and gone through and through. The wound was bleeding, but not enough to soak through his long underwear and combat pants. He could still move, and he worried that at this critical stage of the fight, with several men dead and several others wounded, his men might lose heart if they knew their platoon leader was hit.

But the RPG gunner was careless and allowed the top of his head to remain visible above the boulder as he reloaded. DePouli removed it with some well aimed fire. The semidecapitated gunner fell, leaving his RPG launcher on the top of the boulder. That ended the RPG threat for several hours.

Firing as they went, Walker, Self, Vance, and Totten-Lancaster moved behind a boulder off the right side of the helicopter, from where they exchanged fire with the guerrillas under the tree. Walker ran back toward the helicopter. Brian, the left rear crew chief, picked up Commons' M203, the only one the Rangers aboard Razor 01 had brought, and carried it to Walker under fire. When Walker returned to the boulder he gave his M4 to Totten-Lancaster and fired several 40mm grenades at the enemy position. The first rounds shot over the hilltop because he was firing uphill. It took him a while to get his aim in. Self fired three or four rounds from his M4 before his extractor broke. He tried to use his cleaning rod to ram the stuck round out, only to have the rod break off in his weapon, rendering it temporarily worthless. He, too, ran back to the aircraft to retrieve Crose's M4. When he looked through the optical sight to aim the weapon, trying to place the red dot on his target, he was momentarily confused. There was more than one red dot in the sight. The battle was only a few minutes old and already Walker and Self were firing weapons covered in the blood of their comrades.

Self and his men were functioning automatically now. The long hours of training paid off. They were shooting and moving without stopping to think. They knew how to do this. "We really turned the fight around in about a minute," Self said.

Meanwhile, Gilliam and DePouli moved the 240 machine-gun to another boulder to the right and slightly behind Self's position as the others laid down covering fire. When they got there they found a dead enemy fighter there. The fighter was wearing Neil Roberts's jacket and had Roberts's night-vision goggles around his neck. The goggles had been shot through. Gilliam, not recognizing either item, yelled down to Self that the enemy fighter had a pair of binoculars (because they weren't the monocular type of night-vision goggle Gilliam was used to). He tossed them to the captain. Self recognized them as night-vision goggles, but didn't make the connection to their mission. *How does the enemy have NODs [night optical devices] like this?* he thought, and wondered what other captured U.S. gear the enemy might be using. *We must have landed in the wrong place,* he thought. *There's no sign of the SEALs.*

Self wanted to flank the enemy position under the tree. He sent Miceli and DePouli back down the slope with orders to double back around the right side and try to assault the enemy position from the side or the rear. They realized quickly that the plan was not practicable because the mountain fell away in a cliff on just the other side of the rock formation that Self and the others were on. But they found two enemy sleeping positions dug into the mountain about 130 meters behind the helicopter. DePouli called up to Self on the interteam radio. "Sir, I've found a sleeping position, I'm going to clear it." "No, don't clear it," Self said. Then he heard gunfire from that direction. *Oh, no, what's going on?* the platoon leader thought. But it was just the two Rangers shooting into the positions to make sure no one was there. When they searched the hideout, they found Roberts's rucksack. It had been ransacked, with its contents laying everywhere, including a Nalgene water bottle and an MBITR radio. They brought the radio back to Self. *What is going on?* he wondered. *Why does the enemy have an MBITR? This makes no sense.* Self, still unaware that he was on the same mountaintop where the missing U.S. serviceman had fallen out of a helicopter, began to suspect that he was the victim of an elaborate enemy trick. *They knew we were coming. Somebody speaks English here and was calling us in here on this radio,* he thought. *We got set up.*

Then Gabe Brown, using his MBITR radio, made contact with Mako 30. "They're down there on the right hand side," he reported to Self. "Their batteries are low. They'll call us back on the hour for radio checks." At least that settled the question of where the SEALs were. But because their radio batteries were so low, and they needed to save what battery strength remained for the exfil or emergencies, the SEALs weren't able to bring the Rangers up to speed with what had happened before Razor 01 landed on Takur Ghar.

When Don, the air mission commander, came out of the helicopter he hit the snow and rolled left, the way he'd seen the Rangers do it. Technically he was the second-highest ranking American on the helicopter, but once on the ground and in a fight, the seasoned pilot knew it would be better for everyone if he let the Rangers take control. "What do you guys want me to do?" he asked them. "Cover the left side of the helicopter," they answered. He rolled a few feet until he was about five feet behind the Chinook's lower left corner, lying perpendicular to the airframe, and scanned the left flank. He knew they'd received fire from that side, but he couldn't see any enemy fighters. He thought Dave might have wounded the guerrillas who'd been firing at them when he swept his minigun back and forth as they landed.

The sun was rising, shining off the snow that Don was peeking over. He worried about getting snowblind. Because the flight had begun at night, he hadn't brought any sunglasses. It wasn't long before the cold began to bite. He was wearing a tan two-piece flight suit, a black fleece jacket, body armor with front and back plates, and a Gore-Tex jacket. He had taken his flight helmet off when he left his seat and was wearing just a black stocking cap on his head. Now the snow was soaking through his pants. Cory came back and asked how he was doing. Don told him he was doing fine. It was only then that Don noticed the tip of his gloved finger had been shot off by one of the bullets that had smashed into the cockpit. The same bullet had ripped several holes in his jacket sleeve. Cory grabbed some soundproofing and insulation from the helicopter and brought it out for Don to lie on.

On the left side of the helicopter Chuck lay where he'd fallen in the snow. He could see blood dripping onto the snow through the drain holes in the floor of the Chinook. He yelled to one of the Rangers that he needed a tourniquet for his leg. "Can you cover the left side for us right now?" the Ranger asked. "Yes," Chuck replied. He improvised and used the strap from his kneeboard (a board that pilots use to write calculations and examine maps while flying) as a tourniquet. He wasn't sure if his leg was going to make it. He imagined himself living the rest of his life without it. A Ranger shouted to Don that Chuck was still lying in the snow by the cockpit. Don and Keary Miller went up to the left-hand side of the helicopter and asked him if he was okay. He said his leg was hurt. Don and Miller grabbed him by the shoulders of his survival vest and dragged him to the rear of the ramp. To Chuck's annoyance they strapped him into a litter and put his M4 on safe. Then Miller went to work on his leg wound.

Don and Brian were multitasking: covering the left side of the aircraft, occasionally firing when enemy fighters showed themselves, helping the medics and collecting ammo from the wounded and the dead. The two aviators piled most of the ammo by the ramp, but on several occasions they ran through the snow across the open ground ferrying belts of 7.62mm rounds from the miniguns to the Rangers, who needed it for the 240. "We tried to free up the Rangers to do other things," Don said. He also tried to raise help using the PRC-112 survival radios, but with no success. After trying several, he threw one to the floor. "What's the point of carrying these things if they don't work?" he asked angrily.

INSIDE the helicopter Cory had set up a casualty collection point, where he treated the wounded with Miller and Cunningham, the two PJs. Shawn, the right rear crew chief who hurt his knee in the hard landing, also stayed inside to help the medics. It wasn't a perfect location to be making life-and-death medical decisions. The enemy in the bunker under the tree could see through the right door into the helicopter and would shoot anytime they noticed movement inside. But if the men inside stayed less than two feet off the floor, the armor protection provided by the bulletproof fuel tanks on either side of the Chinook meant they were safe.

Cory, a veteran of the 1989 invasion of Panama and the 1991 Gulf War, was in his element working on the casualties. But the small fire burning had now ignited some of the rucksacks. Cory had to decide whether to stand up and risk getting shot in order to put the fire out, or just let it burn. Shawn tossed him a fire extinguisher and Cory stood up quickly and put out the fire without incident, much to his relief. He told Cunningham to start an IV on Greg, but Greg had lost so much blood that Cunningham had a hard time finding a vein. After several unsuccessful attempts, Cory took over and got it done.

Greg and Cory discussed the tactical situation, and in particular, whether they should leave the aircraft. Greg's first suggestion was to get out of the helicopter. Anytime anyone moved or poked their head up, a burst of fire would come in. But no one was getting hit. The self-sealing fuel tanks protected them. Greg began to feel fuzzy and get tunnel vision as he fought to stay awake. Cory decided to remain in the helicopter.

The flight medic told Dave he was going to put a splint on his leg. "This is going to hurt," he said to the crew chief. It did hurt, so much so that Dave asked for morphine. "No, not at this altitude," Cory told him. "It'd slow your heart rate." After they splinted his leg Cory and Cunningham put Dave on a Skedco. By now Greg was lapsing in and out of consciousness. Cory took one of the helicopter's portable oxygen systems and put the mask over Greg's mouth to keep him awake. Greg went into shock several times. On each occasion Cory's response was cool, calm, and professional. "He's the reason Greg is alive," Don said.

HAVING staved off the immediate threat of the RPG gunner, Self began to worry about having his tiny force outflanked. Gilliam was focused on the tree

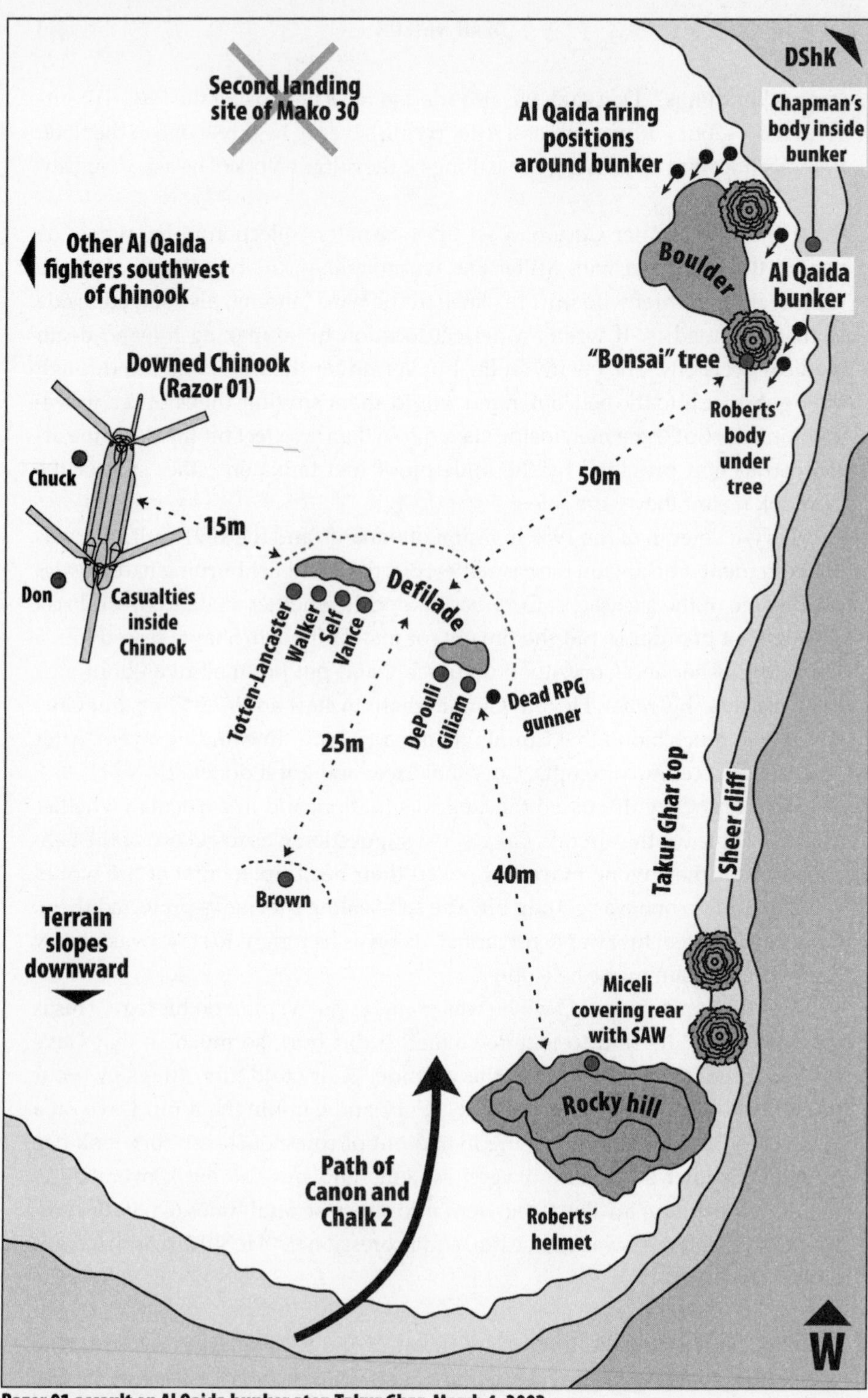

Razor 01 assault on Al Qaida bunker atop Takur Ghar, March 4, 2002

bunker. DePouli was watching the right flank. Miceli had taken up position with Totten-Lancaster's SAW about thirty meters behind him and was covering the entire rear area. Self, Walker, Vance, and Totten-Lancaster covered the helicopter's frontal arc. Don and Chuck (until he was moved inside) watched the left flank. Self also was getting word from Cory and the PJs that they needed to get the casualties medevaced as soon as possible.

After the enemy fighters on the left and right high ground had been killed in the battle's opening minutes, the only fire the Americans were taking came from the bunker under the tree (which soon became known as "the Bonsai tree"). The Al Qaida fighters would emerge from behind the tree, fire off an AK burst or hurl a grenade, and then pop back down. The Rangers behind the boulder with Self were protected from any direct fire unless they raised their heads to shoot. The enemy hurled grenades at them, but they all landed in the snow with a pathetic *poof.* Some Rangers carried their own grenades, but every time they tried to throw one up the hill at the bunker, it landed short. Walker's 203 seemed a more logical weapon in that situation, and he fired grenade after grenade up at the bunker, trying—often successfully—to detonate the grenade off the tree so that the shrapnel blew down onto the enemy position. Usually DePouli's squad carried bazookalike AT-4s, but they'd forgotten them on this occasion. Self cursed himself for neglecting to check for them on the tarmac at Bagram, but he knew that the upward angle of fire would have made it almost impossible to employ them from their current position.

Self thought that if he could just suppress the enemy's Bonsai tree position, perhaps with close air support, he and the other healthy Rangers could assault it, seize the hilltop, and then Razor 02 could come and pick them up. Although he had feared from the start of the fight that they wouldn't be able to leave until night fell, he was coming under pressure from the medical personnel to bring a medevac in for the wounded.

Normally Vance would be trying to arrange close air support and talk to higher headquarters. But Vance had left his radio in his rucksack sitting in the snow beside the ramp. Even if he'd had it with him, it would have taken time to attach the satellite aerial and then figure out the correct azimuth in which to point it. "That wasn't gonna happen anytime soon," Self said. Anyway, with so few able-bodied men, Self felt he needed Vance's help in holding off the enemy. The captain used Gabe Brown, the Air Force combat controller, as his RTO and to call in close air support. Brown was sheltering behind a rock in a tiny, shallow depression twenty meters behind Self's position. Self and one or two of the other Rangers yelled back at him to get on the radio and see what planes were available. Oddly, the Rangers had somehow gotten the impression that

Brown's first name was Jeremy, and that is what they called him until, about an hour and a half into the fight, between radio calls he told them, "That mission'll be here in about five minutes, and oh, by the way, my name is Gabe."

For this first mission of the day, a pair of F-15Es was inbound. Brown asked Self whether he wanted them to strafe the enemy position with their cannons or to drop bombs on it. Vance and Self talked. Vance yelled down to Brown to tell the planes to only use their cannons. It was just before 7 a.m. when the first F-15E came in on a dry run, popping flares. Vance, the more experienced coordinator of close air support, didn't like the angle of approach and told the pilots to adjust it. They zoomed in on another dry run. "That's good," Vance said. "Bring them in, guns hot." Every American put his head down. The jets swooped down firing their 20mm cannon into the tree position. To Don it sounded like someone stepping on bubble wrap. The tree branches flew apart. The planes went around and rolled back in. Somewhere an enemy antiaircraft gun opened up, and black clouds burst behind the jets. The gun run was accurate. The tree top was shredded. But after a couple of passes, the Strike Eagles were out of ammo. They tried to persuade the Americans on the mountain to allow them to drop JDAMs, but Self resisted. His impression was that fast-movers were always trying to "push" JDAMs on their close air support customers, but he wasn't ready to take that risk just yet. Sitting about sixty meters from where the bombs would land, his position just about defined "danger close."

THE Americans on the mountaintop were fighting for their lives, and dying, in large part because their satellite communications had let them down when they needed it most. Commo problems continued to hamper them throughout the day. Brown was having no luck on the frequencies TF 11 should have been monitoring. He tried using his own call sign—Slick 01—as well as those of Vance and Self. No one in TF 11 answered him, except for Juliet, the one AFO team left in the valley from the original three that had trekked in. From their OP Juliet had an excellent view of Takur Ghar. They told Self that they could see several enemy fighters milling on the back side of the mountain (i.e., just below and behind the bunker).

When Razor 02 landed at Gardez at 6:25 a.m., Canon went up to the cockpit to talk to the pilots. They told him they were awaiting instructions from higher headquarters. As calmly as he could, the NCO explained that his chalk accounted for half of the QRF, and the other half needed them to get back to the valley as soon as possible. Canon went back to the rear to tell the others what was happening, at which point Vic Hyder walked up. "Hey, I'm Vic Hyder," he told Canon. "Those are my guys out there." Together the SEAL and the Ranger NCO went forward to talk to the pilots. The aviators had a new set of grid coordinates for an offset LZ on the slopes of Takur Ghar and were cleared to return to the Shahikot. They also told Canon that Razor 01 had been shot down on its LZ and there were casualties. At 7 a.m. Razor 02 took off. The men oiled their weapons and got their game faces on. Halfway to the mountain Mako 30 called on UHF and told the aircrew the LZ was hot, a bombing run was beginning (the first F-15E dry run) and that Razor 02 needed to hold off. They flew to an adjacent valley and waited for the Strike Eagles to finish their gun runs. Then Mako 30 called back and vectored them in to an LZ close to the SEAL team. As they approached the LZ, together the Rangers in the back recited the Ranger Creed.

The landing was unopposed. The Rangers poured out of the back and assumed a security perimeter while the helicopter lifted off. Canon was pleased to find the snow hard-packed and firm underfoot. *This isn't gonna be that bad,* he thought, pulling out his compass, his GPS and his map to figure out exactly where he was. The NCO could hear Self and DePouli talking on the platoon radio net. He grabbed his MBITR and told the captain he was on the ground. But he still didn't grasp the scale of the mountain or the magnitude of the task ahead of him. Hyder pointed to where Mako 30 was sheltering several hundred meters away. "Let's go over and get my guys and then we'll go to the top." Canon, who could hear the sound of automatic weapons fire from the valley, spoke to Self. "I've got Vic Hyder with me," he said. "He wants us to go exfil his guys." Self wasn't surprised to hear that Hyder was with Chalk 2, but he was infuriated that the SEAL officer was trying to take the Ranger reinforcements away from the battle. "No, I need you up here," Self told Canon. "He can go and get with his guys, they're not in contact. We are in contact and have casualties. You're coming here." Canon told Hyder he was taking the Rangers up the mountain. The SEAL officer later said his impression was that the Rangers on the top of the mountain "had their situation under control" and that the "immediate need" was to assist the two badly wounded SEALs. He struck out alone in Mako 30's direction. The spectacle of the senior ranking officer on the mountain—and a special mission unit member at that—not heading to the sound of the guns himself did not disappoint Self as much as might have been expected. "I didn't want him to come up," Self said, explaining that he thought a SEAL officer showing up in a Ranger gunfight might just have confused the situation. "They're Navy. They do things differently. We knew that from working with them previously."

With Hyder out of the picture Self and Canon spoke again. Self thought

Chalk 2 had landed just southwest of the mountaintop. He told Canon that they should just assault up the mountaintop and through the bunker position while the men from Razor 01 suppressed the enemy. "You can just wipe right through them and we'll be done," he told Canon. He fired a star cluster to give Canon a fix on his position. Canon couldn't see it. Only then did they realize Canon had landed much farther east, away from the mountaintop. Self told Canon to move south to a draw, and then walk up the draw toward the top, meaning Chalk 2 should crest the mountain immediately behind the Ranger position. The captain asked Canon how long he estimated it would take Chalk 2 to hike up the mountain. About forty-five minutes, Canon said.

WHILE he waited for Chalk 2, Self opted to just keep his men pulling security and not try any more gun runs from the fast-movers. They weren't worth the risk, now that reinforcements were on the way, the captain reckoned. But his men were still taking sporadic fire from at least one enemy fighter under the Bonsai tree. Then mortar fire started raining in on them from the higher reaches of the mountains on the eastern side of the Upper Shahikot Valley, about 3,000 or 4,000 meters to the east. "Here we are on the side of a snowy mountain with a big, huge black helicopter on it—it's kind of an easy target," Self said later. The first mortar salvo landed about fifty meters off the nose of the helicopter, which was tremendously accurate for a first round. (The Al Qaida gunners clearly were not too worried about the risk of fratricide.) The next set landed behind the Rangers, farther down the mountain. The enemy had them bracketed. Self worried these opening salvos would be followed by rounds falling in between where the first two had landed; in other words, right on his men. *We're in trouble,* he thought. He began to get extremely impatient about getting his men off the side of the mountain. *The enemy might be firing these mortars in preparation for an assault,* he thought. He had been on the ground less than two and a half hours.

Worried that the enemy would get lucky, hit the aircraft in a vulnerable point and blow it up, Don recommended moving the casualties from the helicopter to a little depression in the rocky slope at about the Chinook's 5 o'clock position, close to Self's command post. Cory countered that the helicopter had already withstood RPGs and machine-gun fire, and moving the casualties outside could induce hypothermia. But Cory changed his mind when another mortar round fell far too close for comfort. Don, Cory, Cunningham and Brian carried the patients over one by one, Chuck and Greg on regular stretchers and Dave on a Skedco. The distance was little more than twenty meters, but the movement was extremely hard, even with four men carrying each casualty. By now the altitude had sapped their reserves of energy. They were exhausted. As they prepared to move Dave, Cunningham tripped and lost his grip. The Skedco, designed to move fast on snowy terrain, skidded away. "Dave was on a toboggan ride," Don recalled. Fortunately for all concerned, Dave's Skedco ran into Chuck's stretcher, allowing Brian and Don to grab it before it slid another 800 meters down the mountainside. "Sorry, are you alright?" Dave said to Chuck. "Yeah, as soon as you get off my leg," Chuck replied dryly.

Greg decided to do what little he could to make himself more comfortable and used his good arm to cut the chest straps and loosen the leg straps on his litter. Lying on his back he looked up to see a Predator high in the sky circling the mountaintop. *If only that were an AC-130,* he thought.

11.

ONCE they left the LZ, the consistency of the snow under the feet of Canon's men turned from hard-packed to dry powder, and it was no longer "underfoot," but knee-to-mid-thigh-deep. So much for the easy hike the squad leader had anticipated. His mens' route required them to move 800 meters laterally and to ascend 2,000 feet up a 70-degree slope. The loose rock under the snow only added to their problems. Slipping, falling and stumbling, they were soon spitting up blood from the effort demanded of their lungs. The Rangers had dressed in preparation for a static mission—securing a downed helicopter—not mountaineering. Many were wearing light or medium-weight thermal long johns and tops under their fatigues. With their body armor weighing them down, the men were overheating in the sun. Within fifteen minutes Canon stopped the climb and told the men to remove some clothing. But he still wasn't optimistic about their rate of progress. *There's gotta be something else we can download,* he thought to himself. He called Self and asked for permission to get rid of the back plates in the troops' bulletproof vests. The captain, impatient for his reinforcements, readily agreed. Canon told the men to dump the plates. They hurled them onto rocks below in an attempt to break them. "Have fun," the squad leader joked. "It's the most expensive Frisbee you're ever gonna throw."

WE just can't sit here and take mortar rounds, was the thought going around and around in Self's mind. *We've got to assault.* He called DePouli over to his position. Then he told DePouli, Vance, and Walker that the four of them were going to assault the enemy position at the top of the mountain, which Self thought was little more than a couple of guys hiding behind the Bonsai tree. None of the Americans had realized they were up against a well-entrenched bunker. With Brian, the left rear crew chief, serving as his assistant gunner Gilliam hammered the enemy position with 240 fire. But from that angle the machine-gun could do little damage. The bunker's aperture was facing down the slope towards where Self and the others were assaulting. They didn't realize it, because they couldn't see how the enemy had built up the position under the Bonsai tree, but the 240 was aimed right at the bunker's thick wooden wall. The Al Qaida fighters had constructed the bunker by digging away at the base of the tree, and then surrounding and reinforcing the pit with logs, with more branches covering the roof of the bunker. It was undetectable from the air and almost impenetrable from the ground. The four men in Self's little assault team struggled manfully up the slope, with their weapons up and firing as they went. Even if they hadn't been tired out from the altitude and their exertions so far, the knee-deep snow would have made it impossible to run. DePouli was ready with a hand grenade clutched in one fist while he shot his M4 with his other hand. One of the enemy fighters emerged from behind the tree and fired his AK at the Americans, then ducked back down. Only thirty meters away and closing, Self saw the guerrilla was standing in a waist high fighting position. The captain realized the extent of the fortifications he was assaulting. He knew there was a machine-gun in there somewhere. In training, it always took a full platoon of more than thirty men to take down a machine-gun nest. Here he was trying to do it with four guys at 10,000 feet stumbling uphill in the snow. "Bunker! Bunker!" the captain yelled. "It's a bunker! Get back!" The four turned and staggered back down the slope to their original positions in the rocks.

SELF asked Brown whether any strike aircraft were on station. A pair of F-16s was available, but they only had "dumb" 500-pound bombs, not JDAMs, Brown said. Self told him to have the jets drop the first bombs on the other side of the mountaintop, and then walk them up the slope onto the bunker. This worked, up to a point. The first bomb landed close enough to shower the bunker with debris. The next hit even closer. The fire from the bunker stopped briefly, and then restarted. But Self did not feel comfortable having unguided bombs dropped any closer. Then more mortar rounds fell. Canon reported that the Chalk 2 soldiers climbing the mountain were also receiving ineffective mortar fire. Miceli, covering the eastern side of the Chalk 1 position, spotted a couple of men walking around the valley to the east, pointing up at the Americans on the peak of Takur Ghar. Self concluded they were enemy observers calling in the mortar fire. They were beyond the effective range of any of the weapons the Rangers had at their disposal. Miceli harassed them with his SAW fire, trying to push them away, but they continued advancing slowly toward him.

Again, Self felt he had to take action to hasten his men's departure. He knew Brown had been talking to Wildfire, the call sign for the CIA's Predator, for much of the morning. He asked Brown to find out if the Predator was armed. Brown didn't know what he was talking about. "Armed?" he said. He had no idea there was such a thing as an armed Predator. "Yes, some of the Predators have Hellfires on them," Self said. Brown queried the Predator operator. "Yep, it's got two," he reported to Self. "Get ready to use it," the platoon leader told him. But Vance was nervous. "No sir, we're too close," he told Self. "Don't use the Hellfires." Yielding to his ETAC's advice, Self decided to hold off. But thirty minutes later more mortar rounds landed. Self pulled a little card out of his pocket that told him the "minimum safe distance" ranges for every indirect fire weapon system. Nothing he read suggested that the Hellfire would pose an inordinate risk. "We're good," he said, knowing his men enjoyed the protection of a defilade position, with the rocks sheltering them from any blast. He told Brown to call in the Predator strike. "Put it in the bunker," the captain said. But Brown told the Predator to do the same thing he'd done with the bombs: to fire the first one a safe distance away. That's exactly what the Predator did. Self was surprised to see the missile explode "way off" target to the north. Canon, on the other hand, immediately got on the radio. "Hey, whatever that was, don't do that again, you almost hit us," he said. "We're a lot closer to it than you are," Self told him. Then he turned to Brown. "Look, there's only one [Hellfire] left," he said. "Put it right in it." The men put their heads down. The second Hellfire shot was perfect. Rocks, dirt and branches flew over the Rangers' heads. They cheered. When the smoke had cleared from the top of Takur Ghar, the bunker had collapsed and part of the tree was missing. They took no more fire from there.

AFTER forty-five minutes had passed since he had spoken with Canon, Self called the squad leader again. "What's your ETA?" he asked Canon. Another forty-five minutes, was the answer. When that time elapsed with no sign of Chalk 2, Self's patience was wearing thin. *I've only got so much time before the enemy decides to counterattack,* he thought. *I've gotta get these guys off the side of the mountain.* He called Canon back. "Look, you've gotta move faster," he said. "We're moving as fast as we can," Canon replied.

They marched on in single file, Staff Sergeant Harper Wilmoth and Staff Sergeant Eric Stebner leading the way. They received ineffective mortar fire, almost certainly from the same enemy 82mm tubes that were bracketing the Rangers on the mountaintop. Canon could hear the air strikes going in up ahead. *What in the hell is at the top of this hill that is requiring us to bring this much firepower to bear?* he wondered.

At about 10:00 a.m. the Chalk 1 Rangers fired another star cluster in the air. Canon and his men still didn't see it. *How could they not see it if they're as close as they think they are?* Self wondered. It was half an hour later, just past 10:30 a.m., when Canon finally spotted Miceli and DePouli, the two men closest to his approach. "I think I see you all," Canon said over the radio. Miceli and DePouli weren't sure. Canon told them to pick up snow and throw it. They did. "Yeah, that was you," Canon said. "We're moving into your location now." It took another twenty minutes to make the linkup, but when it happened, Self's tiny force on the top of the mountain had doubled.

(DePouli and Miceli made a grim discovery as they came down to meet Chalk 2: a helmet with a bullet hole in it. From the state of the inside, it was clear the last person to wear it had been shot in the head. That person was Neil Roberts.)

IT took Hyder nearly an hour to link up with Mako 30. The first member of the team he encountered was gray-faced, shivering, and leaving a trail of blood behind him. Hyder gave him his coat and swapped his wool mittens for the bedraggled SEAL's wet gloves. The wounded man told Hyder that Chapman was dead, Roberts had not been seen, and a third team member had been shot in the legs and was seriously wounded. This was the first time Hyder realized how serious Mako 30's situation was. The terse radio conversations had barely hinted at it. There was no way to execute his initial plan, which had been to get the team to retrace the route he had just taken from the LZ. The upward climb was beyond the abilities of the SEALs, who would have to carry one man and help another. Instead Hyder decided to follow the draw downward toward a known LZ, in the hope that another potential LZ might offer itself up en route. They began the trek. Hyder and another SEAL carried the most seriously wounded man between them. The stricken operator was able to put weight on his right foot, but his left leg was shot clean through just above the ankle. The six men moved slowly, pausing every seventy-five meters. At one point Hyder moved up the slope to provide overwatch. He spied a bearded, dark haired man coming down the north face of the mountain into a draw parallel to the one the SEALs were traveling along. Hyder kept his eyes on the man for about five minutes, noting that he was wearing pants and a long jacket. The SEAL officer was waiting for a chance to shoot him. That chance came when, about 175 meters away, the target fell forward and then kneeled up. Hyder put his sight on the man's torso and pulled the trigger. His first shot hit the man in the chest. The bearded figure dropped to his left side. Hyder shot him again in the chest and the man fell onto his back. Hyder fired again but probably missed. He watched the man lying there for several minutes.

MORTAL combat doesn't stop the body's natural functions. As the reinforcements arrived, Walker realized he had to take a shit. He did so where he was lying, just pulling his pants down and rolling on his side. A moment after he was done. Eric Stebner and Sergeant Patrick George arrived beside him. George went to lie down where Walker had just taken a shit. Walker warned him just in time, but Stebner didn't hear and dived straight on top of it, which resulted in George then having to try to clean the mess off his buddy with handfuls of snow.

When Chalk 2's men had all made it up, Self walked down to the big rock outcropping and gave them a brief overview of events, then told them they would take the lead in assaulting the top of the mountain. DePouli's squad was going to secure the flanks. He had Chalk 2's machine-gun team of Specialists Randy Pazder and Omar Vela position their 240 next to the one manned by Gilliam and Brian (who also had 2,000 rounds of 7.62mm ammo retrieved from the Chinook). The platoon leader assembled his assault team: Walker, Stebner, George, Wilmoth, and Specialists Jonas Polson and Oscar Escano. He divided them into two three-man fire teams.

Now that he had extra manpower, Self decided neither he nor Vance were needed as riflemen. He told Vance to get his radio and start calling up the chain. The rest of the force, poised for the assault, gave Self a quizzical *What's the signal?* look. "Just start shooting," he told them. Both machine-guns opened up as the assault began. The two teams moved in "bounding overwatch" fashion, one team standing and shooting while the other fire team was moving and shooting. It only took them a couple of minutes to assault up the slope and then turn right toward the boulder and the tree. They shot a man on the back side of the bunker. Then Stebner noticed an American body laying facedown by the boulder. "Hey, we have a Blue casualty up here," Canon told Self. Again, the captain was confused, thinking Canon was using the word "blue" as the U.S. military uses it to denote friendly forces, not realizing he meant Task Force

Blue, the SEALs. *Not good,* Self thought. *We just shot one of our own guys.* "How do you know?" Self said. "It's obvious," Canon replied. "You need to come up here and look at this."

Self told him to finish the assault first. They had discovered several bunkers on the back side, and he wanted them cleared. The Rangers went through, tossing grenades and firing shots. Canon tossed a grenade, not realizing the position held a pile of RPG rounds. The RPGs cooked off, knocking him down. Then they went to the other side of the saddle, which had been cratered by Grim 32 earlier that morning. The Rangers shot and killed another guerrilla there.

Self walked over to look at Roberts (he still didn't know his name). The dead SEAL was wearing a U.S. desert combat uniform, but had a big beard. Self continued to suspect trickery. He wondered if this operator had been on a joint observation post with Afghans who turned on him. The RPG gunner who DePouli had killed with a shot to the head was bizarrely still half standing, leaning backward but held up at the knees by the snow. His hat lay a meter behind him where DePouli's bullet had carried it. Meanwhile Wilmoth's team went into the bunker and found two more dead enemy fighters and another dead American—John Chapman. Mako 30 finally came up on the radio again and settled things. "No, those are our guys," a SEAL told Self. "One of them's the guy who fell out of the helicopter." Still Self didn't understand. *Okay, he fell out of the helicopter down there in the valley. They captured him alive and forced him to call us in. They baited us and then they killed him anyway.* It took one more radio call with Mako 30 for the Rangers to finally understand what had transpired on Takur Ghar. It was 11:15 a.m.

12.

AT 8.30 a.m. two more TF Brown Chinooks took off from Bagram bound for Gardez with 35 TF 11 commandos, mostly from TF Blue. After take off the helicopters got a message to rendezvous with Razor 02 at FARP Texaco. The helicopter force gathering at Texaco to insert the new quick reaction force to pull the Razors 01 and 02 personnel plus Mako 30 off the mountain included three MH-47s and two "Killer Spade" Apaches. The air mission commander, flight leads and SEAL officers huddled to plan the extraction. TF Rakkasan Chinooks landed, ferrying fuel to the FARP. Meanwhile, Commodore Bob Harward's TF K-Bar caught wind of events on Takur Ghar and began planning to send reinforcements. In Kandahar, B Company of the 160th's 3rd Battalion was alerted at

10:30 a.m. The company had only arrived in Afghanistan a week earlier and had yet to conduct a mission. As K-Bar officers planned, the 160th officers in Kandahar woke their men up and prepared to fly the special ops troops to Bagram in four MH-47D Chinooks.

SELF brought Vance and Brown up to the crest and set up his command post behind a boulder. Brown finally got through to the TF 11 operations center and told them Takur Ghar was secure and the LZ was cold. Self's next priority was to move the casualties up and over the crest onto the reverse slope, partly because the most obvious LZ was up there and partly to keep the casualties out of sight of whoever had been directing the mortar fire against them. But just as Shawn, Stebner, and two other Rangers had begun this process, dragging Dave halfway up the slope on the Skedco, Al Qaida counterattacked. Bullets flew across the hillside. "Take cover!" someone yelled. The four stretcher-bearers dropped Dave into the snow. He had to reach out and grab a small bush in order to keep himself from sliding away for a second time that morning. *This is bad,* he thought. "Don't worry, Sergeant, we're coming to get you!" Stebner yelled at him. "You don't have to," Dave replied. "You fight." Despite Dave's bravado, Stebner tried twice to run out into the open and pull Dave to cover, but on each occasion he was driven back by fierce enemy fire. "Just leave me alone!" Dave yelled. "Shut up, I'm not gonna leave you there!" Stebner shouted back. On his third attempt, Stebner made it all the way to Dave and pulled him back behind cover as bullets bit into the snow with a *pffftt! pffftt!* sound.

The enemy was hurling a furious barrage of RPG, machine gun, and AK fire at the Americans from positions high on a ridge 300 meters to the southeast. On maps the enemy's location appeared part of the Takur Ghar peak, but in reality it was separated from the mountaintop by a saddle. Looking across, the Rangers could see what looked like a couple of cinder-block bunkers on the ridge.

Self watched an RPG fired from the opposite ridgeline skip on the lower part of the slope the helicopter was on and then soar up to the top of the mountain, close to where he was. It exploded harmlessly, but the enemy was really pouring it on. The captain could only see five or ten enemy fighters, but they were fighting as if they had several times that number. "That was some of the most intense gunfire that we had all day," he said. Self ducked back behind a boulder as bullets chewed up the snow and dirt. "It was like in the movies," he recalled. "The ground was just exploding around me." The enemy was below them, which didn't help in this situation, because the guerrillas' fire was "grazing," raking up the slope endangering everyone. Self and Canon repositioned their men to adjust to the new, potent threat. DePouli told Gilliam to turn his machine-gun around so he could take the enemy behind them under fire. Gilliam did so and began firing long bursts at the enemy fighters. The biggest problem was going to be the casualties. Greg and Chuck were still strapped into their stretchers on the rock face. With them were Cory, Don, and Cunningham. They were all directly in the line of fire. Self knew he had to get his wounded to the top of the hill fast.

It didn't take Don and the others long to realize how exposed they were tending the casualties. Bullets snapped past their ears and cracked against the rocks. Don returned fire, the muzzle of his M4 barking its resistance just eighteen inches from Chuck's head. For some reason, Don's weapon seemed louder than the others, and Chuck let him know it. With his arms strapped to his sides, unable to cover his ears, he could only yell "Ow! Ow!" as Don leaned back against the rock face and fired round after round at the enemy fighters moving back and forth between boulders and bunkers. *What do you want me to do, Chuck?* Don thought. *Quit firing?*

The natural human instinct for Don and the others would have been to take cover behind nearby rocks. But that wouldn't have helped Chuck and Greg. Everyone stayed. Cunningham had just started another IV on Greg. *We're not leaving these guys* was the attitude. *We're gonna stay here and shoot it out.* Cory was distinctly unimpressed with the enemy RPGs. *They're nothing compared to the 500-pounders,* he thought. The three noncasualties tried to move Greg, but didn't have the strength. After several minutes of fruitless effort, Don decided to go to the top of the hill to get the Rangers to help move the casualties. As he got up to run, the enemy opened up again. Within the space of two seconds, Cory and Jason were hit. "Uh! Uh!" each grunted as the bullets hit home. For the next few seconds they lay there moaning. Neither of them knew how badly they'd been wounded. Cory knew he'd been hit twice in the belly, just below the edge of his body armor. "It felt like somebody hit me as hard as they could with a sledgehammer," he said. There are no good places to get shot, but the belly's one of the worst. Cory had been married for ten years, with a seven-year-old son and a two-year-old daughter. As he came to his senses he thought how unfair it was on them that he was going to die on that mountain. He was scared to reach down and feel where he'd been shot. *This is really gonna suck,* he thought. But when he put his hand down he could feel wetness but not too much bleeding. The bullet had torn up his bladder, but he didn't know that at the time. He just hoped he wasn't bleeding too badly internally. Cunningham was in worse shape. He'd been shot in the pelvis and suffered heavy internal bleeding. He was in a lot of pain. Cory checked his watch. It was 11:30 a.m.

THE ratio of healthy medical personnel to wounded troops was getting worse. With Cunningham and Cory out of action, that left only Miller and Matt LaFrenz, the Ranger medic who'd arrived with Chalk 2, to care for the casualties. LaFrenz crawled over to the casualty collection point and began treating Cory and Cunningham. Meanwhile, the Rangers, and particularly the machine-gunners, kept up a murderous rate of fire to suppress the enemy. The Al Qaida men on the opposite ridge would pop up from behind cover, fire, and then drop down. But one of them exposed himself for a second too long. Pazder shot him. The Rangers saw more guerrillas maneuvering toward them. Canon told Vela to go back to the Chinook for more 7.62mm ammo. Vela sprinted as fast as he could in the snow towards the helicopter, 150 meters away, but on his way back came under fire and was forced to take cover with Stebner behind a rock. He crawled over to DePouli and put the ammo in a spare barrel bag that he then heaved halfway back to Canon. The squad leader ran out, grabbed the bag, and helped Pazder fire the 240 at the advancing Al Qaida troops. The Ranger 203 gunners kept up a rain of 40mm grenades. This was to be their fight for the rest of the day, keeping the enemy from moving closer or engaging them from the ridgeline. The Al Qaida forces broke into smaller and smaller teams in an effort to close with the Americans. Navy F-14s arrived carrying 500-pound bombs. Vance guided them in, but a bomb fell short and exploded seventy-five meters away from the Rangers, blowing DePouli's helmet off and hitting Wilmoth's helmet with shrapnel. Walker looked around with a *What was that?* expression for a moment and then resumed shooting. By that stage, little could have surprised the Rangers. Another JDAM hit the front slope of the enemy-held ridge and Self watched a three-foot long, eight-inch wide piece of shrapnel rotating through the air about thirty meters above him. The ridgeline they were aiming at had trees along the top. Brown called in more bombs—1,000-pound and 2,000-pound JDAMs. Soon the trees had gone. So had many of the enemy. The U.S. troops cheered as one bomb tossed three guerrillas' broken bodies through the air like rag dolls. That all but ended the battle. From then on, the enemy was only able to offer intermittent, ineffective mortar and AK fire.

The effort to move the casualties continued. The loss of Cunningham and Cory as active participants forced Self to rotate two more men out of the perimeter to help out. It was a sign of how physically spent the men were that it would take four men in superb physical condition twenty minutes to move a man eighty meters, albeit under fire. Every time the teams reached the top of the slope, they had to rest for a couple of minutes.

When the casualties—six dead and six wounded—were collected at the top of the hill, Miller and LaFrenz redoubled their efforts to save those still alive. LaFrenz's assessment was that both Cory and Cunningham were "urgent surgical" casualties—a phrase used to describe only the most extreme, life-threatening cases. He was particularly worried about Cunningham, whose condition was rapidly worsening. The Ranger medic had stopped the external bleeding, but he couldn't discern the extent of the wounded PJ's internal bleeding. At 1 p.m. Vance called Masirah and told them an urgent medevac was required. In the TF 11 operations center and the TF Blue TOC in Bagram, where the staffs suffered from the worst situational awareness of just about anyone involved in the operation, there was extreme reluctance to send any more helicopters to the top of Takur Ghar. As if to reinforce their fears, just as Vance answered their question about whether the LZ was hot or cold with the word "cold," a mortar round landed nearby. The time was 1:30 p.m. and at Texaco the elaborate, massive rescue operation was ready to launch.

AFTER being wounded Cory could no longer work on casualties himself, but despite the pain he was in, he directed the others, in particular telling Don how he could help. The first thing he asked Don to do was run back through the field of fire to fetch his aid bag, which was still sitting on the rocks where he had been shot. Don was reluctant. "Look Cory, it's too hot down there right now," he told the flight medic. But a little later, when the enemy fire died down, Don grabbed another soldier and together they ran down to retrieve the bag. (The troops felt more secure moving across open ground in pairs.) Once he had returned, Cory's directions continued: "Get in my first aid bag, get in the second pouch, reach down a third of the way, pull this out, and give it to 'em, they're gonna need it." LaFrenz renewed his pressure to get a medevac in for Cunningham and Cory. "These guys have to have surgery," he told Self. "They're urgent, a couple of them may die." LaFrenz got on the radio and told whatever RTO or staff officer was on the other end, "We have three urgent-surgical casualties." (In the TF 11 after-action review of the battle, someone said that no one in Masirah knew what "urgent-surgical" meant.) The platoon leader, who had been relaying most of his messages to Masirah and Bagram through Vance, got on the radio himself. He told the headquarters that he had three casualties who would lose limbs or die if they were not taken off the mountain immediately. The rest of his force could wait until after dark, Self added.

TF 11 told him a seventy-man enemy force was moving toward him but that TF 11 was dispatching seventy reinforcements to his position. "We don't need the [seventy extra] bodies," Self told them. "We've got no room for 'em. We just need aircraft to get out." The platoon leader told Masirah there was an

LZ on a reverse slope that offered good protection from enemy fire. "We're working on that," the staff officer in Masirah told him. Self sensed that the operation had changed, and that getting his casualties out was no longer TF 11's highest priority. "I got the impression we were being patronized with the exfil," he said.

IN Masirah and Bagram, Trebon, Kernan, and their staffs pondered their options. From their perspective, they were in a no-win situation. Listening to Self, LaFrenz, and Vance discuss the casualty status, knowing that if they chose to delay the medevac until nightfall at least one and maybe more of their men would die, must have been excruciating for Trebon and the other leaders. But the equally harrowing experience of watching four men die in a few seconds live on the Predator feed as Razor 01's complement of Rangers ran off the back of the Chinook was also fresh in their minds. Trebon decided not to risk another helicopter flight to the top of Takur Ghar in daylight. He thought his decision would cost Cunningham and Cory their lives and he called back to JSOC headquarters in North Carolina to get some moral support from Dailey, who was tracking the operation closely. "Sir, I just need some moral confidence here," Trebon told his boss. "Greg, I've monitored all this, you have made absolutely the right decision," Dailey responded. "It will be tough. You've already identified who the guys are who will possibly die on that mountainside. But you've made the decision, it's the right decision so drive on." Meanwhile, Hagenbeck called Franks. He asked for and received command and control over TF 11 for the duration of Anaconda. This belatedly conferred unity of command of the operation.

At 2:30 p.m. all the medevac/QRF helicopters at Texaco, which were sitting with engines running ready to launch on the mission to Takur Ghar, received the order to stand down. Plans were made for an elaborate operation to exfil Mako 30 and the Rangers starting at 7:45 p.m. (later bumped to 8:15 p.m. due to the late arrival of aircraft). The plan involved A-10 ground attack aircraft, AC-130H and U-model gunships, three MH-47E Chinooks, an MH-47D Chinook and two Apaches.

Self learned of the decision at 3:30 p.m., when he again pleaded his case for a medevac. "I need an aircraft for three urgent surgical casualties," he told Masirah. "We understand the nature of your casualties," a voice on the desert island replied. "The exfil will happen after dark." The time they gave him was 8:15 p.m.

The platoon leader understood where his bosses were coming from. They had flown three helicopters to the top of that mountain in the previous eleven hours. Two had been shot down and a third badly shot up. From the perspective of Masirah or Bagram, it probably seemed a huge risk to fly another Chinook to the top of Takur Ghar, and in broad daylight at that. But Nate Self had better situational awareness than anyone in the TF 11 or TF Blue operations centers. The three helicopters that had flown up there before had all been shot at by enemy fighters on the peak of Takur Ghar itself. Now those fighters' corpses littered the mountaintop, which was firmly in the control of Self and his men. They were only receiving poorly aimed, ineffective fire from one direction now, and he had an LZ that was protected from that. In addition the two helicopters that had been shot down had flown to the top of the mountain with no idea of the danger. A rescue operation now would be mounted by men with a full understanding of the risks. A few bombing runs by fast movers probably could have kept enemy heads down long enough to effect a successful medevac. This wasn't just the view of those on Takur Ghar. Juliet Team, who watched and listened to the entire battle, also reported up the TF 11 chain of command that the LZ was secure and the casualties could be medevaced. But it was not to be. At least, not until it was too late for one more brave airman.

DOWN beneath the Rangers, Mako 30 and Hyder continued their torturous march. By now they could only drag the SEAL who had been shot in the legs by his arms. "[He] displayed incredible physical strength, determination, and sheer guts each time we asked him for his hands," Hyder told the official Special Operations Command investigation. "He would ask how much farther, give a sigh, and grab our hands requiring all his concentration and energy. He was exhausted, near hypothermic, and falling into shock." After six hours of movement the SEALs had traveled roughly 1,500 meters. They stopped where two draws intersected. Hyder saw day-old tracks along a trail he had intended to follow that led to the LZ. He decided to hold in place and hope that a 160th Chinook could squeeze down to pick them up. His wounded men were in a bad way. The four less badly wounded moved the casualties under cover and then settled into positions from which they could watch all avenues of approach. The draw was wooded. Hyder cut branches from the evergreen trees around them and stripped bark in order to give one or two of the SEALs a place to sit insulated from the snow and frozen ground. In less than an hour both of the men he was worried about began to regain some color in their cheeks.

ON Takur Ghar, the shadows lengthened, the wind picked up and the temperature dropped. Soldiers stripped clothing from their buddies who'd been killed in action in order to keep the wounded warm. To supplement the clothing they went back to the helicopter in two-man teams and tore more soundproofing and insulation from its sides to pile on top of the wounded. While there they scavenged among the rucksacks left inside looking for food and water. They also "sanitized" the aircraft, removing all the sensitive items, such as weapons and night-vision goggles. On the mountaintop they prepared the bodies of Chapman and Roberts for exfil. This involved the grim task of tying a rope around each man's feet and pulling him to ensure the corpse wasn't booby-trapped.

At the casualty collection point, LaFrenz and Miller were making fifteen-minute rounds among the six wounded, changing their dressings. "Hey, guys, they're going to come get us," LaFrenz repeated over and over to the casualties. "We're going to be out of here soon." He crammed IV bags under his shirt to keep the fluid warm. As darkness settled over the valley Jason Cunningham began to slip away. Don held a pressure bandage to him for forty-five minutes, during which time Cunningham pulled Don to him and whispered a last message to pass to his wife. For thirty minutes LaFrenz and Miller did nothing but work frantically on the dying PJ, inserting a breathing tube and performing CPR. It was no use. Shedding bitter tears, LaFrenz walked over to Self at 6 p.m. "You can tell *them* our KIA total is seven," he said angrily.

A few minutes past 8 p.m., the troops at Kevin Butler's command post in the wadi south of LZ 15 glanced skyward as helicopter after helicopter flew overhead. On the mountaintop there were cheers as the sound of rotors reached the ears of the men who'd been waiting to hear it all day. Self radioed that the LZ was secure, but that his exhausted men would need assistance moving the casualties to the helicopters. Razor 02 was the first helicopter to land. The pilot mistakenly put his nose toward the casualties. The QRF—almost all SEALs—got out and kneeled in a perimeter formation. To the Rangers' anger no one who had just arrived made any attempt to assist them as they carried the eleven most seriously wounded men the forty meters to the helicopter. Loading the casualties aboard took nineteen minutes. When the first Chinook departed, another landed, this time facing the right way. Again the SEALs made no offer to assist as the Rangers, aviators and Air Force special operators carried their dead to the ramp and then climbed aboard themselves. A third Chinook landed and the SEAL QRF got on and flew away.

ANOTHER Chinook flew down the draw that Mako 30 had holed up in, searching for the men. The helicopter had no radio contact with the team and moved slowly down the valley from the east. The SEALs attracted their attention using a strobe light and a laser designator. Aware the SEALs were not able to move because of their wounded, the helicopter descended straight down in a hover beside them, blades spinning just feet away from granite walls on three sides of the aircraft. Only the rear wheels touched down as the SEALs limped aboard and the helicopter ascended into the night sky.

All the casualties were flown to Gardez, where an MC-130 Combat Talon specially equipped for in-flight surgeries waited. But the MC-130 got stuck in the dirt at the airfield, so the casualties were transferred to a pair of Chinooks, including a similarly outfitted British helicopter, and flown to Bagram, where they were delivered straight to the 274th Forward Surgical Team. There, surgeons labored all night on the most seriously wounded. Everyone who left the mountain alive survived. One member of Mako 30 had to have his leg amputated below the knee. But Cory lived to see his kids and to return to duty, and Greg not only kept his hand (albeit fused to his forearm), but by the summer of 2004 was ready to fly Chinooks again.

WINDING DOWN

ON March 3 TF Rakkasan commander Frank Wiercinski committed Ron Corkran's 1-187 Infantry to the fight. Like everything else in Anaconda, this didn't go entirely to plan. The air assault into LZ 15 was postponed due to the mortar fire Kevin Butler's men had taken near there that day. But half the helicopters didn't get the word to abort, so B Company, 1-87 Infantry, which had been attached to Corkran's battalion, had to wait on the ground until the rest of the force was inserted after dark.

Corkran's battalion, which was Wiercinski's reserve, received orders to attack south along the eastern ridge to Takur Ghar—a daunting prospect even after aerial pummeling had steadily ground down Al Qaida forces for the past forty-eight hours. As they moved south they noticed the same compound Preysler's troops had landed beside on D-Day. U.S. forces had abandoned it and Corkran's troops saw a mortar tube in there. While clearing the compound (again) they got orders to occupy Blocking Positions Cindy and Diane instead of assaulting down the eastern ridge. That night (March 4) they engaged in an intense firefight, receiving small arms and mortar fire from various positions, but sustaining no casualties.

The change in orders reflected a decision in Bagram to allow "fires"—i.e., bombers, mortars, and attack jets and helicopters—to shoulder the load in Anaconda. This decision was never announced or acknowledged, but it is clear from the static approach employed by TF Rakkasan after March 3. The U.S. Air Force's premier conventional ground-attack aircraft, the A-10 Thunderbolt (more commonly known as the "Warthog"), deployed to Bagram, as did Marine AH-1 Cobra attack helicopters and the other sixteen Apaches from the 101st's 3-101 Aviation. (The Apaches arrived from Fort Campbell just sixty-eight hours after being alerted—an interesting contrast with the gnashing of teeth at CENTCOM that accompanied the deployment of the first eight attack helicopters.)

The demonstrated value (to allied and enemy forces) of mortars in the Shahikot was underlined when Sergeant First Class Michael Peterson's 1-87 mortars were ordered back into the valley twenty-four hours ahead of the rest of the troops who had air assaulted into the south of the Shahikot on D-Day. The platoon spent March 3 catching their breath after their ordeal in the Halfpipe, then went straight back into the battle. No one was complaining. "Every soldier wanted to go back out," Peterson said. "At this point it was very fucking personal."

Things were different this time. The platoon was working directly for the Rakkasan brigade headquarters for one thing. And for another, this time around they went out forewarned and forearmed. They took two 120mm mortars, two 81mm mortars, about sixty 120mm high explosive rounds, ten 120mm white phosphorous rounds, 150 81mm high explosive rounds, and twenty 81mm white phosphorous rounds. The mortarmen also brought along a Gator to help them carry it all.

They landed at the Rakkasans' LZ 1 and took over the same compound 1–87's Bravo Company had recleared earlier that day. The infantry established security on the knolls around the compound. Peterson set his 120s up inside the walls and moved the 81s to a defilade position about 300 meters away. From the moment they screwed the tubes into the baseplates, "We were firing mortar rounds like it's going out of style," Peterson said. "At this point we had so many units out there, so many eyes, that we were whacking the enemy left and right. . . . Once mortars got inserted, we started owning the battlefield. There was nowhere they could go where we didn't have eyes on." (Kevin Butler's mortar position in the wadi near LZ 15 also expanded into a "firebase" like Peterson's at the compound.)

Taking a page from Al Qaida's tactics manual, Peterson's mortarmen put the baseplates in or around the compound and registered the guns, then unscrewed the tubes and remained out of sight until they received a fire mission. Then they would run out to the plates, screw in the tubes, fire the mission, and then run back to their hiding place carrying the tubes. After each mission they would displace to a different location, although they never moved more than 300 meters from the compound. The 120s stayed in the compound, the 81s moved a little up the road, behind a hill in a defilade position.

In the days that followed the 120mm mortar proved its worth. "It's awesome when you're not in direct fire contact all the time, and you're launching rounds in relative safety," Peterson said. They fired so often that they ran short of 120 ammo and had to fall back on the 81s. "We were getting target descriptions like, 'Two flatbed trucks with personnel loading equipment on them,'" Peterson said. "We would just hit them with HE and white phosphorous and burn that shit up." They were firing into Marzak, Babulkhel, and Serkhankhel, which had all been declared essentially free-fire areas (Marzak had been flattened by air power.) The Rakkasans' forward observers had reported that the mortars accounted for over thirty enemy killed and eight vehicles destroyed. They even killed a horse. "I felt bad about the horse," Peterson admitted.

Such was the demand for mortars that to conserve 120 ammunition, Peterson imposed a rule that the higher-caliber tubes were only to be used against targets consisting of over six personnel. Otherwise, the 81s would get the mission. As 120 rounds ran low, Peterson upped the criteria to a minimum of ten personnel or one vehicle.

Peterson's mortarmen had a lucky escape shortly after their return to the Shahikot. On March 5 or 6, a jet dropped a dud JDAM that landed 800 meters south of the compound and ten meters from a mortar platoon observation post. The bomb's arming mechanism switched off automatically because it was falling in an unguided fashion, but it still raised a huge dust cloud when it hit the ground. Peterson watched it fall from the sky, thinking *My God! These guys have the largest artillery piece that I've ever fucking seen in my life!* "It just looked like a huge Volkswagen coming down," he recalled.

AFTER the Takur Ghar battle Trebon's plan to have Hyder take over the recce missions launched from Gardez was put on hold while the SEAL officer returned to Bagram to take part in the postmortems of the operation. Blaber remained in command. He still had three teams in the Shahikot: Juliet, in their observation post to the east of Preysler's command post; Mako 21, about 2,000 meters east of Juliet in the same valley; and Mako 22, which had occupied India's observation post south of the Fishhook.

Mako 22, despite having shown up without some essential gear, went on to impress some of AFO's Delta troops with the work they did in the valley. "They did a fantastic job calling in air strikes and killing the enemy," said one account. The team was credited with calling in air strikes on Surki, the Whale, and the tri-city area that killed between twenty and forty enemy personnel. Mako 21 fared less well. They also arrived unprepared, and needed an immediate resupply because they had left important gear behind. Their mission was to watch the Upper Shahikot Valley to confirm or deny whether enemy forces were using it as an escape route. The team established an observation post, but soon reported back that they could see no enemy activity, and requested extraction. But when the operators in Gardez checked Mako 21's reported location, they found the team was 600 meters short of where they were supposed to be, and could not possibly have eyes on the portion of the Upper Shahikot it was their mission to observe. The SEAL team was resistant to all suggestions from Gardez about other possible observation posts they might occupy. After a lot of coaxing from Blaber, the team repositioned, but still failed to get their eyes on the Upper Shahikot. "It was apparent they were experiencing a difficulty but were not willing to express it," a special ops account of the operation said. Unbeknownst to the AFO personnel in Gardez, Mako 21 was sending reports back to the Blue TOC in Bagram complaining of being cold and tired and wanting to be pulled out.

Juliet Team left their observation post on March 5 to check out a cave and building complex compound at the eastern end of the pass they had been located in that had been hit by multiple airstrikes. They found the cave destroyed by a thermobaric bomb dropped into it the morning of D-Day, but two D-30 howitzers and several buildings were relatively unscathed, despite repeated AC-130 poundings. The next day Juliet straddled their ATVs and conducted a passage of lines with the TF Rakkasan elements near LZ 15. At dusk they rode up the ramp of a TF Brown MH-47E Chinook and flew back to Gardez, the last of Blaber's magnificent thirteen to leave the Shahikot.

U.S. commanders' apparent belief that fires trumped maneuver in the Shahikot was not the only reason TF Rakkasan's force remained so static. There remained a desire at higher headquarters to give Afghan forces pride of place in Anaconda, at least from a public relations point of view. So instead of sweeping through the villages on the valley floor, the Rakkasans stayed around the edges of the valley. There was little direct fire contact with the enemy after March 4, and no friendly casualties. "We could have taken that town [Serkhankhel] any time we wanted to, but that would not have helped in the overall purpose of legitimizing that [Afghan] military," Lieutenant Colonel Jim Larsen, TF Rakkasan's executive officer, said. "So that's why we just sat there and waited, and waited."

Encouraged by Spider, Chris Haas, and Pete Blaber, Zia's troops occupied the Guppy on the night of March 3, but didn't use it as a base to attack into the valley. Much of the steam seemed to have gone out of TF Hammer. However, U.S. officials were determined to put an Afghan face on the battle. So in the days following Zia's initial retreat, Rosengard, the Task Force Dagger operations officer, mediated in delicate negotiations between Zia and Gul Haidar, a the one-legged Tajik commander from Logar Province offered up by Fahim Khan, the head of the Northern Alliance who was the new Afghan defense minister. Haidar brought tanks, which the Americans now thought were important, even though the valley was emptying of enemy by the third or fourth day.

When Zia and Gul Haidar were brought together to discuss how their forces would work alongside each other in the Shahikot, it was clear that they had a history, and not a good one. "You didn't know the specifics, but you could tell," Rosengard said. The meeting occurred in the howling desert east of Gardez in Zia's tent. The two warlords met with Rosengard, Haas, and a couple of assistants in the middle of the night in a big dust storm. Zia's tent was a low-slung, rotting canvas affair with an arthritic stovepipe sticking out of the middle of it, belching smoke as Zia's deputy threw hunks of wood in to keep it alive. "It had Afghan carpets around the side, and a couple of pillows, and we're drinking chai and smoking cigarettes," Rosengard recalled. "Then you bring in Gul Haidar, a previous some kind of sort of enemy to Zia, here in his tent to negotiate how these two motherfuckers, who don't like each other, don't trust each other, are going to [enter] this valley with some effort to coordinate armor and infantry."

The meeting strained the Dagger negotiators' patience. They would tell Gul Haidar the attack was "the day after tomorrow," and that "tomorrow" was the prep day, and his reaction was, "Okay, I go tomorrow." The issue of deciding who would be first into the valley also caused problems. Each warlord took the position, "Oh, I don't want to be in front of him, because if he's behind me, he'll shoot me." All the meeting participants were armed, and none of the Afghans ever let their trigger fingers move too far from their weapons. "This was the Wild, Wild West at its finest," Rosengard said.

WHILE the Rakkasans waited for the Afghans, other units belatedly arrived to offer assistance. Canadian troops were brought in, as were more 10th Mountain soldiers, these ones from 4th Battalion, 31st Infantry Regiment. But there was no fighting to match the intensity seen on March 2, 3, and 4. U.S. commanders seemed largely content to sit in their positions in the mountains and let fires kill as many enemy fighters as possible.

Afghan forces finally swept into the Shahikot on March 12, accompanied by the Gardez triumvirate of Blaber, Spider, and Haas. The attack took the form of a pincer, with Gul Haidar's column of rusting T-55 tanks advancing through the gap north of the Whale. Haas escorted the Northern Alliance commander and was impressed by the one-legged Afghan's leadership style. Gul Haidar, with his eight-man personal security detail spread out ahead of him, insisted on doing his own "leader's recon" of the route along which his tanks were about to drive. Hobbling on his peg leg, the Afghan commander proved equal to the challenge of the terrain, climbing onto the high ground to get a good view of the battlefield. Then, inexplicably, he sat down and started "bawling his eyes out," Haas recalled. "Why are you crying, sir?" the bemused SF officer asked him. "Because General Massoud should be with me at this historic time," Gul Haidar replied, turning to embrace Haas in a bear hug as he continued sobbing. "Hey, sir, we've got to get moving on," Haas said.

When they entered the pass, Gul Haidar gave the Americans an object lesson in leadership by example. After finding a handful of antitank mines half-buried in his tanks' path, Gul Haidar called for rope and grappling hooks, with which his men traveled for just this purpose. As the Americans watched in horror, the Afghan commander and one of his aides hurled the grappling hooks at the mines, expertly catching their sides with the hooks. "No, no, no! You're a general, you're going to get yourself killed!" Haas yelled. Gul Haidar gave the American officer an almost condescending glance. "I know how to do this," he said calmly before walking back behind a rock, the rope still in his hand, and yanking the first mine out of the road. Then he walked over to the mine, knelt down, unscrewed the bottom and pulled the fuse out, all as Haas continued to plead with him to stop. To cap his remarkable performance, Gul Haidar picked up the mine, walked over, and handed it to the American officer. "Here, no problem," he said. The Afghan repeated the process four or five more times. "Then he calls his tanks forward," Haas recalled, clearly impressed with what he had seen. "How many armor generals actually get out there and clear the mines for their tanks? Well, Gul Haidar did. Then he's standing there like Patton, waving his tanks through. It was something to see."

Unfortunately, when Haidar's tanks rolled into the valley, the first thing they did was fire at the Rakkasans on the mountainside. A T-55 crew put a main gun round right through a 2-187 Infantry pup tent. Luckily for all concerned, no one was hurt and frantic radio calls soon corrected the mistake. "That's exactly why we wanted to pull out of there, because we had not trained with these guys," Larsen, the Rakkasan executive officer, said.

Meanwhile, Blaber was rounding the southern end of the Whale in an SUV with Zia's troops. This time the Afghans were given free reign to fight as they saw fit. It made a big difference. "They were on fire at this point because they were actually using their own tactics," Blaber said. Everywhere the AFO commander looked, he saw friendly Afghans manning crew-served weapons on the high ground. "You just knew that whole valley was clear," he said.

This was it, the moment of official victory for the allied forces in Anaconda. It was something of an anticlimax. The battle had been all but over for a week.

Rather than the original concept of Zia's men confronting Al Qaida troops in the villages, the U.S. operators and Afghan militiamen drove through ghost towns on the valley floor. Using the grid references passed to him by his teams, Blaber went to several sites at which his operators had directed air strikes. The bombs had done their job. He photographed over thirty enemy corpses.

Blaber and his men discovered five working artillery pieces (four 122mm howitzers and a 152mm howitzer) in the riverbeds, as well as an explosives laboratory. But what they didn't find were people. There was no sign of life, and no sign of civilian death either—none of the corpses in the villages were those of women or children. "I didn't even see a dead animal," Blaber said. No one fired at them. The enemy was gone. But where?

Many never made it out of the Shahikot alive. But just how many were killed is hard to nail down. Senior U.S. commanders described numbers of enemy dead as high as 800 publicly and over a thousand in private. However, they offered no evidence to back up their claims. "Ginger Pass," the gorge just south of Takur Ghar, was a key logistics route into the valley for Al Qaida forces and hence one of the most heavily bombed parts of the Shahikot. Yet a walk through the gorge on March 18, the last day of the operation, yielded no tangible proof that anyone had been killed there. The sides of the pass were scorched brown and black by high explosives. Shards of shrapnel big enough to cut a man in two littered the ground. There was even an unexploded bomb in the waters of the creek that ran through the gorge. But there were no corpses, bloodstains, shallow graves, or body parts. Bodies were found in other parts of the Shahikot, but usually in ones and twos and threes, not dozens. Some of this can be explained by good guerrilla tactics—no irregular army leaves its dead in the field of battle if it can help it, precisely because removing the bodies confuses its enemies about how many they have killed. But it is hard to imagine 600 or 700 bodies being spirited out of the Shahikot without anyone noticing—even America's imperfect eyes in the sky. (Interestingly, estimates of enemy dead in the Shahikot tended to rise the further the officer making the estimate was from the battle.) Some observers put the numbers as low as the double digits. But there are enough firsthand accounts of enemy fighters being killed—and enough bodies—to suggest this is too low. A better estimate—and one more in keeping with the number of bodies and body parts that were found, and the numbers mentioned in Al Qaida documents obtained by U.S. intelligence—is between 150 and 300. Given the size of the enemy force in the Shahikot—estimated by U.S. commanders in the first week of the operation as upwards of 1,000—one is forced to conclude that at least as many Al Qaida fighters escaped the Shahikot as died there.

ON March 13 Blaber again drove south from Gardez to the Shahikot, this time to drop off India Team, who he wanted to track the fleeing enemy. Speedy again put his hunting skills to good work. Following footprints, trash, and discarded clothes, he soon picked up the trail, which traced the route that AFO had long suspected the enemy would take from the Shahikot: east through Ginger Pass or the next gorge down into the Upper Shahikot Valley. From there some enemy fighters moved east to Obastay. Others traveled south to Celam Kac, before following a track southeast through the mountains to the Neka Valley, about seventeen kilometers southeast of the Shahikot. The Afghan forces who were supposed to be watching these routes with U.S. Special Forces had apparently abandoned their positions. "There was no one to stop the Al Qaida from escaping Shahikot south, southeast, or southwest," a special ops source said. From Neka, the guerrillas took old mujahideen routes into Pakistan, where they headed for Miram Shah, a wild town in the North West Frontier Province where Jalalluddin Haqqani had made his headquarters during the 1980s. Signs of distress India discovered along the way—a bloody hat here, a used bandage there—led AFO to refer to the route as "the trail of tears."

Over the next several weeks AFO and CIA personnel moved through the towns and villages on this route, talking to local leaders. "We really got a great forensic autopsy of what happened," Blaber said. The warlords and tribal elders told the Americans that Al Qaida had been building up for months in the area, preparing a spring offensive. The locals said they were glad Al Qaida—"the Arabs"—had left, because they treated their hosts poorly.

But "trail of tears" or no, the U.S. failure to fight a successful battle of encirclement in the Shahikot meant several hundred experienced Al Qaida fighters—Arabs, Uzbeks, and Chechens—escaped to Pakistan. Undoubtedly some senior enemy leaders were among them. Just how senior is a matter of conjecture.

The only enemy leader known to have been killed in the Shahikot was Saif Rahman Mansour, an Afghan who led the Taliban force in the area. He may have been the banner-carrying leader killed by an air strike called in by Juliet on D-Day. By contrast, Islamic Movement of Uzbekistan leader Tohir Yuldeshev was known to have slipped the United States' clutches in the Shahikot. Over the next two years the couple of hundred Uzbeks he commanded who made it out formed the core of the Al Qaida force in the North West Frontier Province's tribal areas. Yuldeshev became the day-to-day commander of Al Qaida's skirmishes with Pakistani security forces.

No intelligence surfaced that bin Laden had returned to the Shahikot since

December. But there were persistent, although unconfirmed, reports that his second in command, Ayman al-Zawahiri, had been in the Shahikot, and might have been wounded before making his escape. In this regard it is interesting to note that on March 6, an Australian SAS team covering the Arme Khwar stream about eight kilometers south of the Shahikot saw thirteen armed personnel moving through the area. The Aussies said the force consisted of an advanced element of four men, two to three men providing flank security on each side, and a main body of five men. In the center of the group walked a man with a cane who appeared older than the others. "All twelve security personnel wore black balaclavas," said a report of the episode. The Australians called in an A-10 strike on the group, which split into two elements. The A-10 attacked, but, frustratingly, no allied forces were able to conduct any bomb damage assessment. There were unconfirmed reports Zawahiri suffered a head wound during this period. If so, he survived and was still releasing audiotapes rallying the faithful to Al Qaida's cause in 2004.

THE Pentagon declared Operation Anaconda over on March 18, but in reality it had been all but done for well over a week. The Rakkasans returned to Kandahar. But for AFO, there was to be no heading back to the relative luxury of Bagram or Kabul. The Delta operators were already hunting the enemy ever closer to the Pakistan border. Blaber was quietly agitating for cross-border missions. To him the Pakistan border already resembled the Cambodian border during Vietnam conflict—a barrier to U.S. troops behind which their enemies found succor.

It was going to be a long war.

NOTES

PROLOGUE

1. The description of the scene on the lead Chinook is based on interviews with the following soldiers: Baltazar; Blair; Edwards; Fichter; Harry; Koch; Marye; Mendenhall; Moore; Nielsen; Preysler; Thompson; and Wahl, as well as on Combat Camera footage and photographs taken by some of the soldiers. The description is also informed by my participation in a very similar air assault into the valley later the same day.

IPB

Chapter 1

1. **. . . the hotel . . . ugly.** This description comes from the article "Losing the Peace?" by Michael Massing, *The Nation*, May 13, 2002.
2. **And so it was . . . Afghan cuisine.** The description of the Ariana is drawn from interviews with numerous U.S. sources who visited the hotel in early 2002.
3. **On this frigid . . . S-H-A-H-I-K-H-O-T.** The account of the meeting is drawn from an interview with a participant; a U.S. military source who attended other meetings in the same room helped with the description of the surroundings. The word *Shahikot* has several possible spellings. I was assured that John spelled it with three *h*'s, so I have spelled it that way here. However, in the rest of the book, it will be spelled *Shahikot.*

Chapter 2

1. **Two weeks earlier . . . "Buster" Hagenbeck.** Wille, Hagenbeck; Ziemba (from a presentation by Major Francesca Ziemba at the Fire Support Conference, October 3, 2002, Fort Sill, Oklahoma, which I attended).
2. **A native . . . of taking command.** CJTF Mountain "Operation Anaconda" Command Briefing; Hilferty.
3. **By late December . . . defeating the Taliban.** Hagenbeck.

4. **He was by no means . . . spring offensive.** Edwards; Task Force Dagger source; remarks by Robert Andrews at the Military Reporters and Editors annual meeting in Alexandria, Virginia, October 3, 2003. Andrews was acting assistant secretary of defense for special operations and low-intensity conflict during the war in Afghanistan.
5. **When, against all expectations . . . by U.S. commanders.** A senior U.S. officer with knowledge of the plan.
6. **So instead . . . December 1.** Hagenbeck, Mikolashek, Gray, Edwards.
7. **When Franks . . . Hagenbeck's fingers.** Edwards, Hagenbeck.
8. **But he wasn't about . . . to do something."** Hagenbeck.
9. **He knew there were still . . . puddles of resistance."** Edwards.
10. **Hagenbeck gathered his . . . to head up.** Hagenbeck, Wille.
11. **Wille and Ziemba . . . rough plan.** Wille.
12. **Their job was made . . . return to Fort Drum.** Hagenbeck, Wille, Edwards.

Chapter 3

1. **Within forty-eight hours . . . Colonel John Mulholland, . . .** Hagenbeck.
2. **Under his command . . . only forty-nine days.** *The Mission,* by Dana Priest, published by W.W. Norton and Company, Inc., p.143 . . . **Special Forces' finest hour.** Special Forces are not the same as special operations forces, a term which includes not only Special Forces (often called—but never by themselves—"Green Berets") but also special operations aviation units, Rangers, Navy SEALs (the acronym stands for Sea, Air, and Land), Air Force special operators and other commando organizations.
3. **. . . Task Force K-Bar.** A K-Bar is a knife particularly popular with sailors.
4. **According to Lieutenant Colonel Mark . . . eight weeks."** Rosengard.
5. **The TF Dagger leaders . . . in the north."** Rosengard.

Chapter 4

1. **In late November . . . Tora Bora.** Edwards.
2. **There were strong . . . also there . . .** Task Force Dagger source.
3. **$5 million reward.** On December 13, 2001, the State Department raised this reward, in place since October 1998, to $25 million. The announcement had been in the works for several weeks and had nothing to do with Tora Bora, according to Andy Laine, a spokesman for the State Department's Diplomatic Security Service.
4. **Dagger's success . . . to the Pushtun heartland.** Task Force Dagger source.
5. **From the very start . . . Afghanistan.** Edwards.
6. **This approach . . . Rumsfeld.** A Pentagon official who participated in video-teleconferences on this issue.
7. **"The message . . . our psyche."** Edwards.
8. **"We don't want . . . field-grade officers in Afghanistan.** Bello. I heard this line repeated numerous times during conversations with U.S. officers in Afghanistan. The Bush Administration version of the same notion was presented by Deputy Defense Secretary Paul Wolfowitz in testimony to the Senate Foreign Relations Committee

on June 26, 2002. The transcript can be found at: http://www.defenselink.mil/speeches/2002/s20020626-depsecdef2.html.

9. **120,000 troops . . . in the 1980s.** *Stumbling Bear—Soviet Military Performance in Afghanistan*, by Scott R. McMichael (London: Brassey, 1991).
10. **Inside the Pentagon . . . for their service.** White; Keane. The secretary of the Army is the top official in the Army. A civilian political appointee, the secretary's primary job is to make sure the administration's policies are implemented by the service. His boss is the secretary of defense. The chief of staff is the Army's most senior officer, whose job, in concert with the secretary, is to plot the strategic direction of the Army in areas like doctrine, modernization, and personnel policies, and to advise the president as one of the Joint Chiefs of Staff. The vice chief of staff is the chief's second-in-command, and runs the Army on a day-by-day basis.
11. **But when Shinseki . . . White said.** White.
12. **It didn't help . . . the Army leadership.** "A Different War—Is the Army Becoming Irrelevant?" by Peter J. Boyer, *The New Yorker*, July 1, 2002; "Pentagon Faces Transformation," by Tom Bowman, *The Baltimore Sun*, March 13, 2001, p. 1A; "Wolfowitz: More Resources, Better Management Keys to Defense Transformation," by Hunter Keeter, *Defense Daily*, August 9, 2001; "The 'Revolution in Military Affairs' has an Enemy: Politics," by Michael Catanzaro, *The American Enterprise*, October 1, 2001.
13. **The Pentagon's—and, by . . . work on the ground.** Edwards; senior officer involved in planning in the Pentagon; *10th Mountain Division (Light Infantry)—Operation Enduring Freedom, Afghanistan*, Joint Center for Lessons Learned Final Report, 6 June 2003, Colonel George Bilafer, team chief, p. 8; numerous other U.S. military sources.
14. **Thus the attack . . . tried to escape.** Rosengard; Task Force 11 source.
15. **It seems incredible . . . flee outta there."** Edwards.
16. **A few days . . . bin Laden himself.** U.S. special operations source.
17. **But even then . . . Franks]."** Edwards.
18. **American surveillance . . . over the border.** Bishop; Edwards.
19. **At least two . . . effort foundered.** Bishop.
20. **The Pakistanis intercepted . . . bin Laden was at Tora Bora.** "U.S. Concludes Bin Laden Escaped at Tora Bora Fight," by Barton Gellman and Thomas E. Ricks, *The Washington Post*, April 17, 2002, p. A1.
21. **Deputy Defense Secretary . . . allowing them to flee.** Wolfowitz's June 26, 2002, testimony to Senate Foreign Relations Committee, op.cit.
22. **But among . . . conventional forces.** Edwards; Task Force Dagger source; another U.S. special operations source; Gellman and Ricks, *The Washington Post*, op. cit.; a senior officer involved in Pentagon planning said bin Laden "probably escaped" from Tora Bora.
23. **Rosengard was more . . . all people in Afghanistan."** Rosengard.
24. **But to planners . . . do the mission," Edwards said.** Edwards.

Chapter 5

1. **In the cold, muddy . . . on the plate."** Fletcher; Rosengard; other Task Force Dagger sources.

2. **The disappointing performance . . . a new approach.** Task Force Dagger officer . . . **accepted bribes . . . safe passage.** Wolfowitz's June 26, 2002, testimony to Senate Foreign Relations Committee, op.cit. "Bribery is an Olympic sport throughout Afghanistan," commented a Dagger officer.
3. **By mid-December . . . Campbell, Kentucky:** Fletcher; another Dagger source.
4. ***The Bear*** **. . . best against them.** *The Bear Went Over the Mountain—Soviet Combat Tactics in Afghanistan,* by Lester W. Grau (London: Frank Cass, 1998); *Afghan Guerrilla Warfare—In the Words of the Mujahideen Fighters,* by Ali Ahmad Jalali and Lester W. Grau (St. Paul, Minn.: MBI Publishing Company, 2001) (originally published as *The Other Side of the Mountain* by the U.S. Marine Corps Combat Development Command); Fletcher; other special operations sources.
5. **While most . . . brilliant," Rosengard said.** Rosengard; other special operations sources . . . **working as an information operations specialist . . .** Some Army officers are trained in two fields: their primary branch (infantry, armor, aviation, etc.) and their functional area (operational support, information operations, institutional support). In Sweeney's case, his branch was Special Forces, but in his LIWA job he was working in his functional area.

Chapter 6

This chapter is based entirely on interviews with special operations sources familiar with events in Gardez.

1. **Texas 14 . . . ODA 594.** Each A-team in Afghanistan had two names. One was its three-digit team number, which tells someone familiar with the numbering system a lot about the team. The first digit refers to the team's parent group, the second digit to the team's company and battalion—there are three battalions in a group, and three companies in a battalion; for the purposes of the team numbering system, A Company, 1st Battalion, is 1, A Company, 2nd Battalion is 4, and so on—and the third digit to the team's number within that company. Thus ODA 594 was the fourth team in C Company, 3rd Battalion, 5th Special Forces Group. The other name given to the team was its call sign or code name. This only lasted as long as the mission. In Afghanistan, many of the teams were given the prefix "Tiger." But when the eleventh team went in, Dagger decided to change the prefix to "Texas," to avoid anyone confusing a team called "Tiger 11" with "Tiger 1" in a broken radio transmission.
2. **"He was not interested . . . of moxy."** Rosengard.
3. **The town into . . . in the 1990s.** Larry Goodson, a professor at the Army War College and one of the United States' foremost experts on the Afghanistan; McHale.
4. **Like many . . . was combat.** Sources familiar with operations in the Gardez safe house. The description of the safe house is informed by photographs I have seen of it.

Chapter 7

1. **The bulky . . . moonlit landscape.** Source is someone present in Bagram the night that Blaber arrived.
2. **The first American troops . . . October 21.** "Special Forces OD Alpha-555," by Lance M. Bacon, *Soldier of Fortune,* September 2003.

3. **Bullets had pockmarked . . . beside the runway.** My personal observations, February through April, 2002.
4. **In fact, many . . . dangerous enemies.** Task Force 11, JSOC, and other special operations sources; *Pitfalls of Technology: A Case Study of the Battle on Takur Ghar Mountain, Afghanistan,* by Colonel Andrew N. Milani. An experienced special operations aviation officer, Milani conducted Joint Special Operations Command's investigation into the Takur Ghar episode, which occurred March 4 during Anaconda. His extensive report is classified. However, while attending the Army War College, in Carlisle, Pennsylvania, in the 2002–2003 academic year, Milani drew heavily on his report to write his strategy research project (essentially a short thesis that all AWC students must write). He kept this paper unclassified by giving pseudonyms to the various Task Force 11 components. He referred to Task Force Blue, for instance, as Task Force SEAL, and AFO as Task Force RECCE. He also referred to Task Force 11 members only by their positions, ranks, and initials. During my research, I cross-referenced the Milani paper with interviews with CJTF Mountain staff and members of the special operations community.
5. **Established . . . a few dozen . . .** *Delta Force,* by Colonel Charlie A. Beckwith (ret.) and Donald Knox (New York: Avon Books, 2000).
6. **. . . almost 1,000 . . . for the CIA.** Special operations sources.
7. **The first Delta squadron . . . Task Force Blue.** Special operations sources; *Pitfalls of Technology.*
8. **Formed in 1980 . . . from the ground up.** *Brave Men, Dark Waters—The Untold Story of the Navy SEALs,* by Orr Kelly (New York: Pocket Books, 1993) pp. 208–236; retired Army special operator.
9. **It took a few years . . . Delta's.** Retired Army special operator.
10. **Some of the bitterness . . . coming apart."** Navy officer who has worked extensively with both Army and Navy special operations forces.
11. **Joint Special Operations Command . . . outright animosity.** Retired JSOC staff officer.
12. **Many strong . . . each organization.** Special operations sources.
13. **Nevertheless, JSOC . . . Army special ops source.** Special operations sources.
14. **But Dailey . . . for success.** Senior Army officer.
15. **Dailey applied . . . Gregory Trebon.** TF Sword source; other sources in the special operations community.
16. **Curiously . . . Air Force or joint staffs.** Trebon's Air Force résumé; sources in the special operations community. **. . . over 7,000 flight hours in fifty-five different military and civilian air frames.** Asked how Tebon amassed flight hours in so many different aircraft, Major Cynthia Teramae, the spokeswoman for his next command, Special Operations Command—Pacific, said, "It is common for a pilot who commands many different units to conduct familiarization flights in the different types of aircraft assigned to each unit in which he commands."
17. **His specialty . . . Dailey's boss.** Retired officer who served on the JSOC staff in the 1990s; a TF Sword officer; other special operations sources; senior Army officer.

18. **A barrel-chested man . . . warn visitors about.** I have shaken hands with Gary Harrell on numerous occasions, and on at least one was warned by one of his staff officers beforehand to beware the general's grip. Mark Bowden made the same point in *Killing Pablo* (New York: Penguin Books, 2002, p. 149).
19. **He had spent all . . . between 1998 and 2000.** Harrell's Army résumé.
20. **Harrell was no stranger . . . Aidid in Somalia.** *Killing Pablo,* ps. 149, 150, 152, 153; *Black Hawk Down,* by Mark Bowden (Boston: Atlantic Monthly Press, 1999) passim.
21. **Despite his . . . "door-kickers" in Afghanistan** . . . Edwards.
22. **Since July 2000 . . . "fusion cell."** Harrell.
23. **. . . that would take . . . back to Franks.** Edwards.
24. **The CENTCOM commander . . . could match.** Gray; Harrell; other CJTF Mountain, special operations, and intelligence sources; Edwards; I walked past the detention facility several times a day during my stint at Bagram.
25. **Nested inside Bowie . . . enemy territory.** Special operations sources. *Pitfalls of Technology.*
26. **AFO was not . . . familiar with AFO.** Special operations sources.
27. **Although AFO was small . . . in the 1990s.** A source who served on the JSOC staff in the 1990s; other sources in the special operations community.
28. **Prior to taking . . . Bagram with TF Bowie.** Special operations sources.
29. **In briefings . . . positively shone.** CJTF Mountain sources; special operations sources; my own observations watching Dagger, Bowie, and TF 11 personnel in briefings at Bagram in the days leading up to Anaconda.
30. **But beneath . . . deploying into Afghanistan.** JSOC officer; other sources in the special operations community; Edwards; retired officer who served on JSOC staff in the 1990s; senior Army officer.
31. **Edwards, the deputy . . . operational control."** Edwards.
32. **Some in TF 11 . . . Afghanistan experience."** Special operations sources. **. . . rising to command B Squadron.** Because of the Rangers' status as the Army's most elite airborne infantry, officers command Ranger battalions only after successfully commanding another infantry battalion. Thomas was the first to follow a Delta squadron command with a Ranger battalion command. For Thomas, the opportunity to command and mold young infantrymen proved irresistible.
33. **TF Red had been . . . a waste."** Special operations sources.
34. **This was the situation . . . Another former Ranger,** Special operations sources; CJTF Mountain sources; Special operations time line—this ninety-nine-page document, a detailed account of many special operations activities related to Operation Anaconda compiled by some of the participants, was mailed anonymously to me. Henceforth it will be referred to as "special ops time line."
35. **Jimmy was in . . . movie-star good looks.** I met Jimmy very briefly in Bagram before Anaconda.
36. **A 10th Mountain . . . *Serpico*.** CJTF Mountain staff officer.
37. **Indeed in some . . . Jimmy that guy.** Special operations sources; CJTF Mountain sources.

Chapter 8

1. **For a week . . . point in the war.** Source familiar with the meetings in the Ariana; special ops time line.
2. **Since mid-December . . . that region.** Edwards; Rich's biographical background is from *Ghost Wars,* by Steve Coll (New York: The Penguin Press, 2004).
3. **Now, a month . . . highest priority.** Special ops time line.
4. **"In no conversation . . . really did."** Edwards.
5. **After receiving . . . assembling in Gardez.** Thomas; Southworth.

Chapter 9

1. **By January 20 . . . U.S. allies.** Task Force Dagger source.
2. **By now . . . in the works.** Fletcher; another Task Force Dagger source.
3. **After studying . . . wants to do."** Rosengard.
4. **Despite the evidence . . . all these Afghans."** Rosengard; Fletcher.
5. **The second reason . . . understood it.** Rosengard.

Chapter 10

1. **At his Kuwait . . . varied wildly.** Mikolashek; Edwards.
2. **For a long time . . . around the valley.** Source in the special operations community.
3. **To Mikolashek . . . enemy in the Shahikot.** Mikolashek, Task Force Dagger sources; another source in the special operations community.
4. **Based on intelligence . . . (IMU).** Mikolashek.
5. **The IMU fighters . . . run with it.** Mikolashek. **". . . the main effort . . ."** Army doctrine defines "main effort" as "the activity, unit, or area that commanders determine constitutes the most important task at that time. Commanders weight the main effort with resources and priorities and shift it as circumstances and intent demand." (Army Field Manual 3-0, *Operations*).
6. **. . . by early February . . . about that time."** Mikolashek.
7. **However, CENTCOM . . . blocking positions."** Mikolashek; Edwards; Task Force Dagger source. Mikolashek's comments, echoed by several other knowledgeable sources, throw a harsh light on the following statement by Wolfowitz to the Senate Foreign Relations Committee on June 26, 2002: "So when in Anaconda we relied more heavily on American and coalition forces, it wasn't because we had, quote, 'learned a lesson,' but because we had more capability available."
8. **If the CIA . . . yet again.** Mikolashek.
9. **CENTCOM finally . . . Edwards said.** Edwards; Nocks.

Chapter 11

1. **It was a cold . . . dream posting.** Wiercinski; my personal observations from Kandahar.
2. **The Army had . . . twenty-five infantry brigades,** Monica Manganaro, media relations officer, U.S. Army Infantry Center, Fort Benning, Georgia. In addition to the twenty-five infantry brigades, the active Army also has twenty infantry "training" brigades, which are not combat formations.

3. **The 101st Airborne . . . the world's militaries.** The official 101st Airborne Division (Air Assault) Web site: www.campbell.army.mil/dhistory.htm.
4. **Such was the case . . . falling umbrella."** The official Web site of the 3rd Brigade, particularly the history pages at www.campbell.army.mil/3bde/3rdbde_history.htm and www.campbell.army.mil/3bde/187th_history.htm.
5. **The legacy of valor . . . was unrelenting.** Wiercinski.
6. **In early November . . . ranges at Jacobabad.** Sarat; Wiercinski.
7. **As the Rakkasans . . . operations," Mikolashek said.** Mikolashek; Edwards.
8. **. . . Forces Command . . .** Forces Command is in charge of all the Army's conventional war fighting units in the continental United States.
9. **In the 101st, these slices . . . military intelligence elements.** Cody.
10. **With all its components . . . 5,000 soldiers . . .** Wiercinski.
11. **But Franks didn't want . . . I can't get there."** Cody; Edwards; Keane; Mikolashek; Wiercinski; Burns.
12. **CFLCC and CENTCOM . . . missing artillery.** Mikolashek.
13. **. . . Mikolashek was telling . . . "full-spectrum operations,"** Wiercinski.
14. **When TF Rakkasan deployed . . . Al Qaida prisoners.** Cody; Marye; Wiercinski.
15. **The force package allotted . . . nowhere with Rumsfeld.** Cody; Edwards; Mikolashek; White; Wiercinski; senior officer involved in Pentagon planning; another Pentagon official.
16. **The chartered flights . . . the Sinai.** I was on this flight.
17. **Situated several . . . bargained for.** Larsen; Wiercinski; my personal observations from the six weeks I spent with the Rakkasans in Kandahar in January and February of 2002.
18. **As the Rakkasans adjusted . . . *to go to work.*** Cody; Edwards; Marye; Wiercinski; a general officer familiar with Franks's relations with the senior Army leadership.

Chapter 12

1. **The addition . . . handle on its own.** Mikolashek; special operations sources.
2. **He had already . . . spell Bagram."** Hagenbeck; Mikolashek; Edwards; Wiercinski; Larsen; Gray.
3. **Jim Larsen, in Bagram . . . disappeared inside.** Larsen; Fletcher.
4. **The Rakkasan officer . . . conducting in Uzbekistan.** Larsen; Gray.
5. **Larsen and LaCamera . . . and it showed.** Larsen; Nocks; my own observations driving from Bagram to Kabul and back. **The next morning.** The date of the meeting at the Kabul safe house is the subject of some confusion. Some documents state that it happened on February 8, others that it occurred February 9. The memories of the attendees' are similarly nonconclusive. Weighing the evidence, it seems more likely to me that it occurred February 8.
6. **The Toyotas pulled up . . . get ourselves into."** Larsen; Nocks; Harrell; Bishop; Haas; other sources familiar with the meeting in the Kabul safe house and with the safe house's design; special ops time line. . . . **Glenn . . . Mark . . .** In cases in which I have been unable to determine last names, or in which it is clear that the individ-

uals involved may be operating undercover at the time of this book's publication, I have only used first names, sometimes with last initials.

Chapter 13

1. **In the late . . . the puddle.)** Larsen; Wiercinski; Rosengard; another attendee at the meeting.
2. **Listening to Rosengard . . . trust and support.** Wiercinski; Larsen; another attendee at the meeting.
3. **The Rakkasan officers . . . battalion to Afghanistan."** Larsen.
4. **Wiercinski, Gibler, and Yates . . . of the infantry force.** Wiercinski; Larsen.
5. **Meanwhile, Bishop . . . *Anaconda*.** Larsen; Nocks; Bishop.

Chapter 14

Except where noted below, this chapter is based entirely on interviews with U.S. personnel familiar with events in Gardez during the prelude to Operation Anaconda.

1. **Only when the CIA . . . only as "Spider."** Special ops time line.
2. **"They went with . . . paramilitary guys."** Haas.

Chapter 15

1. **Blaber's decision . . . lay beyond it.** Special ops time line; sources in the Gardez safe house; other TF Dagger source.
2. **For signals intelligence . . . ambushes now.** "SIGINT Marines Help Fight War on Terrorism in Afghanistan," *Intelligence Community Newsletter*, Headquarters, U.S. Marine Corps Intelligence Department, February 2003; TF 11 source; Briley; another source in the CJTF Mountain TOC in Bagram; special ops time line; Gardez safe house sources; another TF Dagger source; Blaber briefing—this refers to a set of briefing slides I obtained that were used by Blaber to brief the story of Anaconda to many different audiences in Pentagon and around the U.S. military; I also spoke to several people who had attended one or more of these briefings for elaboration on the points made in the slides.
3. **Around this time . . . himself was in the Shahikot.** Special ops source; source in the Gardez safe house; "Ali Mohamed: The Defendant Who Did Not Go to Trial," by Judy Aita, U.S. Department of State International Information Programs, May 16, 2003, accessed on the Internet at http://usinfo.state.gov/regional/af/security/a1051502.htm; "The Infiltrator: Ali Mohamed Served in the U.S. Army—and bin Laden's Circle," by Peter Waldman, *The Wall Street Journal*, November 26, 2001.
4. **Another document . . . report stated.** I obtained a copy of this debrief.
5. **During this period . . . those missions.** Special ops time line; Blaber briefing; sources in the Gardez safe house.
6. **But when he . . . AFO's approach.** Special ops time line; a source familiar with the VTC.
7. **In fairness . . . element in Gardez.** TF 11 source in Masirah; special ops time line; source in the Gardez safe house; senior Army officer.
8. **As it was . . . went native.** TF 11 source.

9. **But to Chris . . . to us," Haas said.** Haas.
10. **Part of the reason . . . American in Gardez.** Special ops time line; Gardez safe house source; Blaber briefing.

Chapter 16

1. **The dark . . . to war again.** Hagenbeck; Edwards; Gray; Wille; Mikolashek. Details on MC-130 Combat Talon landings at Bagram were provided by Major Perry Panos, a Combat Talon pilot with the 919th Special Operations Wing who made over ten landings at the air base.
2. **The 10th Mountain Division had . . . (Light Infantry).** *The Army of Excellence—the Development of the 1980s Army,* by John L. Romjue, published by Office of the Command Historian, U.S. Army Training and Doctrine Command, pp. 15–16. The 10th Mountain Division Web site, http://www.drum.army.mil/history/divisionhistory.htm.
3. **In November 2001 . . . headquarters at K2.** Gray. **. . . a more intact division like the 101st . . .** The 101st's 2nd Brigade returned from a six-month deployment to Kosovo in November.
4. **When Mikolashek . . . division headquarters,** Edwards; Mikolashek.
5. **. . . but when . . . for operations.** Burns. That Cody commanded Delta's aviation squadron is from his official Army résumé.
6. **The generals and colonels . . . limited war with Iraq.** Mikolashek; another senior officer familiar with the plan.
7. **The response . . . Paul Wolfowitz.** Woodward, pp. 49, 60–61.
8. **But in October . . . or Saudi Arabia.** Mikolashek; another senior officer familiar with the plan.
9. **Burns was unaware . . . to train," Burns said.** Burns; Edwards; a senior special operations officer.
10. **Shortly . . . war was over."** Burns.
11. **As they would . . . auspicious start.** Gray; Bello, in a briefing he and Ziemba delivered at the Senior Fire Support Conference at Fort Sill, Oklahoma, October 3, 2002. I attended the briefing, hereafter referred to as "Bello at Sill," or "Ziemba at Sill."
12. **. . . "the culminating point" . . .** Lockwood.
13. **The draft plan . . . counterparts' requests.** Wille.
14. **. . . D-Day . . .** Although the general public tends to associate the phrase *D-Day* with the Allied invasion of Normandy on June 6, 1944, *D-Day* is actually the term used in every U.S. military plan for the day on which an operation is to commence. The *D* stands for *day*. Similarly, the hour at which an operation kicks off is known as "H-Hour."
15. **Nor did it help . . . in country.** Gray.
16. **. . . about eight modular olive drab tents . . .** Gray.
17. **The TOC soon . . . adventure."** Bello at Sill.
18. **The Mountain staff . . . "ad-hocracy."** Bello at Sill.
19. **"There were a lot . . . he added.** Lockwood.
20. **The common . . . two communities.** Gray; my personal observations at Bagram.
21. **Despite . . . previous jobs.** Bello; Hagenbeck, Wille.
22. **The most obvious . . . knew he did."** Wiercinski.

23. **But it was the Ranger . . . leader that he was."** Larsen; Wiercinski; Wille; Rosengard; Blaber; Grippe.
24. **Then Hagenbeck . . . doing," Wille said.** Gray; Hagenbeck; Wille.
25. **To reduce . . . from Hagenbeck's headquarters.** Gray.
26. **But there was only . . . pheasants."** Sources in the Mountain TOC; TF 11 officer in Masirah.
27. **(Despite the . . . in the Shahikot,** Bello; Briley; Wille; TF 11 source.
28. **. . . the very presence . . . cadre of guards.** Bello.
29. **This added . . . Harrell said.)** Lockwood; Harrell; numerous conversations I had with officers in the run-up to Anaconda.
30. **Blaber installed . . . raising his voice.** Sources in the Mountain TOC; TF 11 officer in Masirah.
31. **The first Mountain . . . occurred February 17.** Wille; Nocks; Hagenbeck; Gray.
32. **Hagenbeck was briefed . . . aside for Anaconda.** Bishop; Gray; Larsen; Nocks; Rosengard.
33. **(Mikolashek, however . . . forces,'" he said.)** Mikolashek.
34. **Finally, the leaders . . . (CJTF) Mountain.** Rosengard; Hagenbeck; Gray.

Chapter 17

1. **Pete Blaber had . . . otherwise have taken.** Special operations sources. **. . . handpicked these men . . .** The core of an AFO force was usually drawn from Delta's operational support troop, a unit trained to infiltrate cities under cover (sometimes using female operators posing as girlfriends or wives of male operators, because couples attract less suspicion than single males or groups of men), but the AFO commander also had the option of drawing personnel from Delta's three reconnaissance and surveillance troops.
2. **Blaber envisioned . . . between them.** Task Force 11 source.
3. **Juliet was the larger . . . peer, anywhere."** Task Force 11 sources; special ops time line. **. . . nickname "Speedy."** A Delta operator's nickname functions as an internal call sign. **. . . "SF baby," . . .** This was the name given to soldiers who joined Special Forces straight out of high school, instead of from another part of the Army. The Army ended the program, but revived it soon after Anaconda because of the high demand for Special Forces troops.
4. **Juliet had the northern . . . mountain streams.** Special ops time line; *The Bear Went Over the Mountain; Afghan Guerrilla Warfare*, p. 171.
5. **Twenty-five years . . . entire operation.)** Special ops time line; special operations source.
6. **The first phase . . . Task Force Orange.** Special ops time line; other special ops sources; http://www.specwarnet.com/americas/isa.htm.
7. **Once again . . . operations in the Shahikot.** Special ops time line; other special ops sources. The description of the Sate Kandow is from *Afghan Guerrilla Warfare*, p. 167.
8. **On February 20 . . . upon the Shahikot.** Special ops time line; other special ops sources. **. . . headlights off using night-vision goggles . . .** AFO's pickup trucks had infrared headlights that could be seen using the night-vision goggles, but the

operators rarely turned them on because they would have been visible to an enemy equipped with similar night-vision equipment.

9. **The Shahikot's terrain . . . and the finger.** Ziemba at Sill.
10. **From the Whale . . . the bag."** TF Dagger source.
11. **Juliet spotted . . . gathering in the Shahikot.** Special ops time line; other special ops sources; Thomas.
12. **This support . . . resources."** Rosengard.
13. **In a briefing . . . lifesaver.** Blaber.
14. **As night fell . . . time to start planning.** Special ops time line; other special ops sources.

Chapter 18

1. **What this plan . . . *Lincoln*.** CJTF Mountain slide briefing.
2. **The plan envisaged . . . operation,'" Wille said.** Gray; Wille; Bishop.
3. **Central to the plan . . . contingent at Gardez.** Briley; special ops source.
4. **Locals usually . . . operation, however.)** Briley; Wille; Ziemba at Sill.
5. **As to the . . . experience.)** Briley; Ziemba at Sill.
6. **The planners . . . might use.** Hagenbeck.
7. **Their biggest . . . later were low.** Ziemba at Sill; special ops source; rock drills I attended in the final days before Anaconda.
8. **Of greater threat . . . Hagenbeck acknowledged.** Hagenbeck.
9. **The Rakkasans and Zia's . . . air defense threats.** Ziemba at Sill; rock drills I attended; Rosengard.
10. **Worries over . . . fierce resistance."** Hagenbeck.
11. **(Rosengard . . . RPGs.** Rosengard.
12. **Ziemba's prediction . . . Ziemba said.** Ziemba at Sill.
13. **Like other . . . doubt the intel."** Hagenbeck.
14. **To help with . . . snatch him.)** TF 11 sources; Wille.
15. **Undeterred . . . "Goody."** Blaber; special ops time line.
16. **No sooner . . . into the Upper Shahikot.** Rosengard; Wille; Haas; other special ops source.
17. **From the moment . . . them," Wille said.** Rosengard; Wille; Larsen; Wiercinski.
18. **But, the Rakkasans . . . Wiercinski and Larsen.** Larsen; Wiercinski; Hagenbeck; Wille.
19. **Wiercinski also . . . to escape?"** Wiercinski; Larsen; Wille; Rosengard; Mountain staff officer; my observations of meetings and rehearsals I attended.
20. **Matters came . . . fuming mad."** Mountain staff officer; Antenori; two other SF soldiers reported hearing Mulholland make similar comments at other times.
21. **It appeared . . . Antenori said.** Special ops sources. . . . **Delta staff officer . . .** Many Delta staff officers are on short tours from elsewhere in the special ops community. These officers serve only at the headquarters and do not go through Delta's operator training course required for service in the assault or reconnaissance and surveillance troops.
22. **(Not all . . . could get.")** Bentley; Lundy.
23. **With Wiercinski . . . Lower Shahikot.)** Hagenbeck; another source in the Mountain TOC.

24. **That the Mountain . . . back door."** Mountain officer; Wiercinski; Rosengard; other special ops source.
25. **While the Dagger . . . into the Fishhook.** Wiercinski; Bello; Hagenbeck; Bentley.
26. **This plan reflected . . . be there."** Bentley; Bello; Wille; Rosengard.
27. **The inclusion . . . meetings, he said.** Gray; Wille; a source on the Mountain staff.
28. **The Mountain commander . . . good enough?"** Hagenbeck; Gray; Wille.

Chapter 19

1. **Amidst all . . . supporting artillery.** Dr. Richard Stewart, U.S. Army Center of Military History. The arguments made by senior officers in the Pacific to support their decision not to deploy artillery to Papua foreshadowed those made during the war in Afghanistan. "The artillery in this theater flies," one senior general told a subordinate in the Pacific, according to the official Army history of the campaign, *Victory in Papua,* by Samuel Milner, p. 135.
2. **The Mountain and Rakkasan . . . assets that we had."** Wille; Bello; Hagenbeck; Bentley; two senior Army officers.
3. **Bringing air power . . . Air Force channels.** Bello.
4. **However, there . . . of the war.** Gray; Bello; Bochain; Wille.
5. **But this wasn't . . . operation," he said.** Bochain.
6. **In the absence . . . air support."** Donnelly; Gray.
7. **But to Mountain . . . the debate.** Donnelly; Bochain; sources in the Mountain TOC.
8. **But even . . . or imagery.** Bentley.
9. **But it was . . . haystack."** Bello; Ziemba at Sill.
10. **When the war . . . missions in Anaconda.** Air Force pilot who flew missions over Afghanistan.
11. **But Louis . . . gave me."** Bochain.
12. **The Air Force's . . . Air Force officer said.** Air Force pilot who flew missions over Afghanistan; Mikolashek.
13. **That Anaconda . . . Over."** Air Force officer; a senior Army officer said that while Renuart may not have been "asleep at the wheel," he was "overloaded and didn't use his staff well."
14. **Word of . . . component.** Corley; Stutzriem.
15. **Donnelly acknowledged . . . operation," Donnelly said.** Donnelly.
16. **Hagenbeck, Mikolashek . . . a deal."** Wille.

Chapter 20

1. **There were reports . . . Tohir Yuldeshev.** Mikolashek; Briley.
2. **A skilled . . . hideouts of eastern Afghanistan.** *Jihad—The Rise of Militant Islam in Central Asia,* by Ahmed Rashid (New York: Penguin, 2003); interview with Ahmed Rashid on National Public Radio's *All Things Considered,* March 25, 2002, accessed at: http://gencturkler2.8m.com/MISC/ahmedrashid.html.
3. **By late . . . in that way."** Mikolashek; Bello; Briley; TF 11 officer. More evidence that Yuldeshev was in the valley came after the operation. U.S. forces found "battlefield litter" indicating that he had been there and some of the few Al Qaida

prisoners taken also indicated that Yuldeshev had been present. "We had pretty solid information that he was there," the TF 11 officer said.

Chapter 21

1. **Obsessing over . . . back to the Shahikot.** My personal experience. The military gave journalists ridiculously contradictory advice to "pack for a high-altitude, cold-weather mission, and pack light."
2. **U.S. forces . . . forces, Ziemba said.** Ziemba at Sill; Rosengard.
3. **The Rakkasan company-grade . . . returning to Bagram.** My observations.

Chapter 22

1. **Every few . . . latest discoveries.** Source present when Blaber and Spider arrived at the Mountain TOC.
2. **By now . . . with Dailey.** Special ops time line; special ops sources; Hagenbeck; Edwards.
3. **But in Dailey's . . . commitment," he said.** Senior Army officer.
4. **However, the perception . . . control setup.** Special ops sources; sources on the Mountain staff.
5. **By late February . . . different organizations.** CJTF Mountain slide briefing; special ops time line; McHale; Blaber; Haas.
6. **It was now . . . destiny."** Special ops sources in Gardez; special ops time line.
7. **The two A-teams . . . into the battle."** McHale; Haas; Thomas; Antenori. . . . **"jinga" . . .** The trucks are also known as "jingle" trucks, on account of the decorative chains that rattle off their sides as they move.
8. **But if the SF officers . . . coffins.** Special ops source.

Chapter 23

1. **There was an eerie . . . plan anyway.)** My personal observations—I attended all the briefings and rehearsals mentioned; Rosengard; Wille; Gray. **. . . confirmation brief . . .** According to Army doctrine, a confirmation brief is where the subordinate commanders repeat back to their commander their understanding of his intent for the missions he has assigned them. In this case, the confirmation brief became something of a back brief, in which the battalion commanders went into more detail than is normal for a confirmation brief.
2. **As for engaging . . . infantry-on-infantry fight."** My personal observations.
3. **Once the crowd . . . about," Rosengard said.** McHale; Rosengard; another Dagger source.
4. **But the result . . . idea," McHale said.** McHale; Thomas; Rosengard; Haas.
5. **Between all . . . Bagram and Tampa.** Bilafer, p. 8; Gray; Edwards.
6. **Some officers . . . important."** Wiercinski.
7. **But others . . . [with fewer]?"** Mountain staff officer; *Operation Anaconda—Lessons for Joint Operations*, by Richard L. Kugler, Michael Baranick, and Hans Binnendijk, National Defense University, p. 20.
8. **Edwards, the CFLCC . . . number."** Edwards.

9. **But many . . . issues with it.** Gray. Moseley, traveling, was called by his nighttime CAOC director Brigadier John Corley shortly after Corley was briefed on Anaconda February 23. Moseley received his first formal briefing on Anaconda February 25, five days after the CAOC was informed of the operation (source: "Operation Anaconda: Command and Confusion in Joint Warfare," by Major Mark Davis, June 2004. Davis, a Special Forces officer, wrote this thesis paper while at the School of Advanced Airpower Studies at Maxwell Air Force Base, Alabama. It is a superb effort to "peel back the onion" to get to the heart of the close air support issues during Anaconda.)
10. **The first misunderstanding . . . attack Serkhankhel.** My personal observations; Hagenbeck.
11. **That was not . . . support," Haas said.** McHale; Haas; another TF Dagger soldier; other sources in the special ops community.
12. **But the officers . . . that," he said.** Bentley; Bello; Wille; Rosengard; Haas.
13. **The final . . . operations" purposes** McHale; Bentley; Army Field Manual 100–106, *Information Operations.*
14. **While scores . . . presence in Gardez.** Special ops time line; another special ops source.
15. **None of this . . . but ignored.** Hagenbeck; Wille; Gray; Haupt; Briley; Harrell.

Chapter 24

1. **On the morning . . . before D-Day.** Wiercinski; Gray; Larsen.
2. **Of all . . . were pros."** Wille; Burke; other TF Mountain officers.
3. **The Australian SAS . . . transportation," Bishop said.** Bishop; other special ops sources.
4. **At the Gardez . . . course of the operation.** Special ops time line; other special ops sources.

Chapter 25

1. **On the morning . . . 36 hours away.** Special ops time line; Blaber; other special ops sources. **. . . MBITR . . .** The acronym stands for Multiband Inter/Intra Team Radio.
2. **By the evening . . . up the tab."** My personal observations.

Chapter 26

1. **Shortly after . . . horrifying life.** Special ops time line; other special ops sources; Blaber; photographs taken from an AFO PowerPoint briefing.
2. **"The success . . . heart of Operation Anaconda.** Blaber; my personal observations; Bello.
3. **The SEAL snipers . . . mountain perch.** Special ops time line; other special ops sources; photographs taken from an AFO PowerPoint briefing. **. . . Adidas sneakers . . .** An investigation based on a sales sticker found on one of the shoes revealed them to have been purchased at The Underground mall in Atlanta, Georgia.
4. **The AFO reports . . . to adjust.** Special ops time line; Rosengard; other special ops source; source in the Mountain headquarters; Wiercinski; Larsen; Hagenbeck.

5. **The reports from the AFO . . . around the civilians.** Special ops time line; other special ops sources; my observations of Rakkasan briefings.
6. **Why not?...in the Shahikot.** Special operations sources.
7. **One officer . . . about it.'"** Special operations source; a source in the Mountain TOC.
8. **At 12:30 . . . present itself?** My personal observations; Quinlan. **. . . entire 1,700-soldier task force . . .** This includes headquarters and support troops, as well as the 1,411 who went into the Shahikot.
9. **Late that . . . all concerned.** Mikolashek; another CFLCC officer.
10. **As the infantry . . . was gone.** Nielsen.

REACTION TO CONTACT

Chapter 1

1. **On the road . . . they said.** McHale; Southworth; Thomas; Haas; other special ops sources.
2. **Finally . . . showtime.** Special ops time line.
3. **The Americans . . . platoon leader."** McHale; special ops time line; source in the special operations community.
4. **Behind them . . . of it," McHale said.** McHale.
5. **Joining Harriman's . . . back to Gardez.** Special ops time line.
6. **Next in . . . engineer squad.** McHale.
7. **There was also . . . south of the Shahikot.** Thomas.
8. **Bringing up the rear . . . at the Fishhook.** Special ops time line.
9. **There were also . . . breakdowns.** McHale.
10. **As they drove . . . into the valley.** McHale.
11. **The Zermat Road . . . local hospital.** McHale; other sources in the special ops community; *Weapon of Choice—ARSOF in Afghanistan,* by Charles H. Briscoe, Richard L. Kiper, James A. Schroder, and Kalev I. Sepp, published 2004 by the Combat Studies Institute Press, Fort Leavenworth, Kansas, p. 285. This book, written under the guidance of Briscoe, U.S. Army Special Operations Command's historian, is a quasi-official history of Army special operations forces in Afghanistan. It avoids all but the vaguest mentions of classified special ops units, and repeatedly uses pseudonyms in place of soldiers' real names.
12. **No sooner . . . to the U.S. troops.** McHale; special ops time line; other sources in the special ops community.
13. **The two A-team leaders . . . "racing time."** McHale; other sources in the special operations community.
14. **Nevertheless . . . 2.55 a.m.** Special ops time line.

Chapter 2

1. **Shortly after . . . overhead.** Special ops time line; other special ops sources.
2. **Once they . . . bloodstream.** Special ops time line; CENTCOM investigation report; special ops sources.
3. **For the SEALs . . . yet again.** Special ops time line; special ops sources.

4. **The SEALs . . . mountainside.** Turner; other special ops sources; report.
5. **The sound . . . peaks."** Special ops time line and other special operations sources.

Chapter 3

Herman; Ryan; Hardy; Chenault; Hurley; Hamilon; Pebsworth; Pierce; author's general knowledge.

Chapter 4

1. **A quietly religious . . . relented.** Bishop.
2. **Now the short . . . problems.** Report; special ops time line.
3. **Both . . . purposes.)** Report; *Pitfalls of Technology.*
4. **Grim . . . instantly.** Report; Turner.
5. **Mako 31 . . . before sunrise.** Report; Turner; http://www.specialoperations.com/Memorial/spirit.html.
6. **The crew . . . evening.)** Report; Turner.
7. **Investigators . . . left.** Report; Turner; Thomas.
8. **McArthur . . . target.** Report.
9. **The Grim 31 . . . Shahikot.** Turner; report.
10. **It took . . . vehicles.** Report; Thomas.
11. **Harriman's . . . hip.** Report.
12. **Inside . . . another round.** Turner; report.
13. **Again . . . mortar fire.** Report.
14. **"I'm taking . . . radio,** Fletcher.
15. **a transmission . . . Grim 31.** report; Turner.
16. **Then . . . bone.** Special ops time line.
17. **The truck . . . over.** Report.
18. **As soon . . . fire.** Report.
19. **"Chief . . . radio.** Haas.
20. **Their colleagues . . . over the radio.** Report.
21. **At first . . . north.** Report.
22. **Meanwhile . . . radio.** Special ops time line.
23. **The Grim . . . sign.** Special ops time line; report; Turner.
24. **A few . . . situation.** Report.
25. **Back . . . life.** Special ops time line; report.
26. **About . . . auspiciously.** Report; McHale.

Chapter 5

1. **Despite . . . recalled.** McHale; Haas.
2. **The original . . . Whale.** McHale; Southworth.
3. **It was about . . . start.** McHale; Haas.
4. **The Americans . . . deepened.** McHale; Haas; Southworth.
5. **Zia Lodin . . . planes?"** Source in the special operations community; *Weapon of Choice,* p. 286.

6. **The events . . . valley.** *Operation Anaconda: Command and Confusion in Joint Warfare;* Murray; Blaber; Coe; Donnelly.
7. **With Task Force . . . unrealistic.** Hagenbeck.
8. **We can . . . progress.** Bentley.
9. **Colonel . . . Bello said.** Bentley; Bello.
10. **When . . . radio.** Report.
11. **The helicopters . . . flew on.** Apache pilots.
12. **In fact . . . call.** Marye.
13. **The smoke . . . again.** Anderson; Fichter.
14. **The medevac . . . incident.** Apache pilots.
15. **One . . . loose.** Chenault.
16. **By . . . 372.** report.
17. **Once . . . Bagram.** Report; special ops time line.
18. **After . . . wounded.** Report.
19. **John . . . body.** report; special ops time line; McHale.
20. **Onboard . . . difference.** Anderson; Fichter; Morgan; Boehm; Moore.
21. **McHale's . . . problem.** McHale; Southworth.
22. **Hearing . . . dust.** Apache pilots.
23. **That . . . of it.** McHale.

Chapter 6

1. **Sergeant . . . doorway.** Mendenhall; Harry; Chapman; Nielsen; Baltazar.
2. **But . . . shorn.** Nielsen; Chapman; Tucker; Harry; Baltazar; Koch; Wiercinski.
3. **Outside . . . Apache.** Baltazar; Koch.
4. **As Apache . . . Mr. Hardy."** Hardy; Hurley; Pebsworth; Chenault; Hamilton; Ryan et al.
5. **As sounds . . . *positions*.** Preysler; Nielsen.
6. **The southernmost . . . of the LZ.** Luman; Helberg.
7. **About . . . elsewhere.** Crombie.

Chapter 7

1. **The scene . . . fight."** Grippe.
2. **One of . . . that."** Ropel.
3. **Scrunched . . . remained.** Perez.
4. **Frank . . . *into*.** Grippe.
5. **What . . . subordinates.** Kraft.
6. **Seated . . . targets.** LaCamera.

Chapter 8

1. **Chalks . . . moved out.** Higley; Kraft.
2. **As . . . spots.** Grippe.
3. **Higley and . . . Contact, he said.** Kraft; reference: FM 7-8, *Infantry Rifle Platoon and Squad.*
4. **Kraft . . . zone.** Kraft.

5. **Once in . . . back.** Kraft; Hall.
6. **He called . . . fire.** Kraft.
7. **O'Keefe's . . . guns.** Ropel.
8. **Task Force . . . needed.** Kraft.
9. **The man . . . little about.** Peterson.
10. **Peterson . . . place.** McGovern; Higley; Peterson.
11. **Kraft . . . over."** Kraft.
12. **With . . . Halfpipe.** Kraft; Peterson; Ashline; LaCamera.
13. **Peterson's . . . whatsoever.** Peterson; Ashline.

Chapter 9

1. **As the Al . . . attention.** Murray; Savusa; Marye; Overbaugh; special ops time line; Wiercinski.
2. **With the . . . valley.** Ryan.

Chapter 10

1. **After . . . Halfpipe.** Ropel; Peterson.
2. **Ropel . . . element.** Ropel.
3. **Helberg's . . . Diane.** Helberg.
4. **Luman's . . . position.** Luman; Schmitz; Nielsen.
5. **Luman . . . making it.** Schmitz; Luman.
6. **Luman . . . 240.** Schmitz; Luman.
7. **It was . . . ammunition.** Luman; Schmitz.
8. **For . . . crack."** Luman; Schmitz.
9. **By 10:30 . . . *tomorrow*.** Baltazar; Nielsen; Preysler.
10. **LaCamera . . . Army."** Kraft; Peterson.
11. **When . . . happen."** Kraft.
12. **Kraft . . . safety.** Higley; Kraft; Grippe; Peterson.
13. **Grippe . . . whatsoever."** Grippe; LaCamera; Hagenbeck; Kraft.
14. **Among . . . decade.** Perez; Kraft.
15. **Perez . . . *there?*** Perez.
16. **The Army's . . . day."** Grippe; Perez.
17. **"He . . . Perez."** Kraft.
18. **Up and down . . . of there."** Grippe; Kraft.
19. **But as . . . fight."** Peterson; another 1-87 infantry mortarman; Perez.
20. **The plan . . . fixed."** Grippe; LaCamera.

Chapter 11

1. **The FARP . . . Hurley said."** Pebsworth; Hardy; Bardwell; Hurley; Wiercinski.
2. **A couple . . . saviors.** Achey.
3. **The pilots . . . lot worse."** Ryan.
4. **Roger . . . position.** Specialist Jason Gonzalez; Alcaraz; Peterson; Crombie.
5. **When . . . tally.** Alcaraz; Crombie.

6. **Lying . . . upbeat.** Special ops time line; other special ops sources; *Pitfalls of Technology.*
7. **When . . . telephone.** Bello.
8. **Already . . . afternoon," Hagenbeck said.** Hagenbeck; my personal experience waiting with the second lift.
9. **But as . . . night.** Hagenbeck; other sources in the Mountain TOC.
10. **By early . . . thought.** Nielsen; Helberg; Baltazar; Crombie; Luman.
11. **But then . . . done.** Special ops time line; Hagenbeck; another Bagram source.
12. **Jimmy . . . dark.** Hagenbeck.
13. **To Hagenbeck . . . initially.** Source in the Mountain TOC.

Chapter 12

1. **As . . . rucksacks.** Ropel.
2. **As the . . . forget.** Kraft.
3. **Bullets . . . slope.** Ashline; Peterson.
4. **Others . . . fell.)** Healy; Grippe.
5. **In the . . . ankles.** Perez.
6. **Unlike . . . Bagram.** Kraft; Peterson.
7. **Lying . . . wondered.** Kraft.
8. **Where the . . . ignored.** "Afghanistan—Fire Support for Operation Anaconda, by Robert H. McElroy, *Field Artillery,* September-October 2002; COMACC Sight Picture—Joint Air-Ground Operations (a December 2002 press release from Air Combat Command); "Left In Dark for Most Anaconda Planning, Air Force Opens New Probe," by Elaine Grossman, *Inside The Pentagon,* October 3, 2002.
9. **Lost in . . . targets."** LaCamera; Achey.
10. **By seizing . . . combat.** Achey.
11. **However . . . unanswered.** Thomas; McHale; Haas; Kraft; special ops time line.
12. **The problems . . . Iraq.** Davis, p.88.

Chapter 13

1. **Back . . . hill."** McHale.
2. **"Fires priority . . . after the battle.** Bentley.
3. **By the time . . . minutes.** McHale; Haas; Southworth.
4. **The overall . . . MRE.** McHale.
5. **While the SF . . . Carwazi.** McHale; Southworth.
6. **McHale and . . . truck.** McHale; another TF Hammer source.
7. **The two . . . support.** McHale.
8. **Haas . . . cover.** Haas.
9. **Task Force . . . bomb."** McHale; Haas.
10. **Other . . . Whale.** Southworth.
11. **Soon . . . minutes.** McHale.
12. **In the . . . pass.** McHale; Haas.
13. **It was there . . . Haas said.** Haas; McHale; another TF Hammer source.

14. **Then RPGs . . . convoy.** McHale; Haas; special ops time line.
15. **The Special . . . his men.** Haas. **"Kojast planes?!?"** Kojast is a Dari, not Pushto, word, and Zia was a Pushtun. However, like many Pushtuns, he spoke some Dari, and knew that while Haas spoke no Pushto, he did speak a little Dari also. Therefore, after venting in Pushto, Zia switched to Dari in order to make himself understood.
16. **The SF officers . . . support McHale said.** McHale.
17. **For . . . be."** McHale; Haas.
18. **Haas eventually . . . them down.** Haas; McHale; Rosengard; *Weapon of Choice*, p. 286; special ops time line.
19. **Hammer's . . . Zia.** Bentley.
20. **"The bottom . . . day."** Rosengard.

Chapter 14

1. **Night . . . ass."** Kraft; Ropel.
2. **Then, during . . . in the Halfpipe.** Kraft; Ropel; Healy; Peterson; Beers; Brault.
3. **Knowing they . . . binos."** Kraft; LaCamera.
4. **Word came . . . another day.** Healy; Ropel; Kraft.
5. **What LaCamera's . . . blessed."** LaCamera; Kraft; Peterson.
6. **The night . . . bitches."** Murray; Savusa; Wiercinski; special ops source.
7. **When . . . light.** Nielsen; Koch.
8. **Helberg's . . . watch.** Helberg; Luman.
9. **After . . . protectively.** Crombie.
10. **While . . . failure.** special ops time line; other special ops sources.

Chapter 15

1. **At midnight . . . to love.** Butler; my personal experience.
2. **In the middle . . . up and moving.** Baltazar.
3. **Butler's . . . in their chests.** My personal experiences. Hagenbeck.
4. **By 8 a.m . . . .returned fire.** Butler; Baltazar.
5. **Roger Crombie . . . to their north.** Crombie.
6. **Baltazar had just . . . over their heads.** Butler; my personal observations.
7. **To Baltazar . . . couple of wadis.** Baltazar.
8. **As the incoming . . . added dryly.** Butler; Ouditt; Blossom; my personal observations.
9. **Watching . . . to the wadi.** Musella; Celano.
10. **There, Kevin Butler . . . pal replied.** Butler; my personal observations.
11. **Baltazar's 3rd . . . heavy fire.** Baltazar; Luman; Schmitz.
12. **As his men . . . recover the rucksacks.** Crombie.
13. **Baltazar's 2nd . . . creek bed.** Baltazar.
14. **Hagenbeck had intended . . . to show up.** 1-187 Infantry After Action Review; special ops time line.
15. **March 3 began . . . than in Gardez.** Special ops time line; other special ops sources.

TAKUR GHAR

Chapter 1

1. **As dawn . . . was an order.** Special ops time line; other special ops sources; senior Army officer.

Chapter 2

1. **While the SEALs . . . to the valley.** Special ops time line.
2. **That plan . . . back in, tonight."** McHale; another ODA 372 source; Thomas; Haas; special ops time line.
3. **With Trebon and . . . about four hours.** Special ops time line; other special ops sources; *Pitfalls of Technology*, pp. 7–8.
4. **Glenn P. gave . . . any different.** Special ops time line; Al.
5. **In and of itself . . . to the airstrip.** *Pitfalls of Technology*, pp. 13–14; a JSOC officer; another special ops source.
6. **In Bagram, Hagenbeck . . . winter bite.** Hagenbeck; another source in the Mountain TOC; a special ops source; special ops time line.

Chapter 3

1. **The two Chinooks . . . fighting for."** Al; *Pitfalls of Technology;* special ops time line; sources in the special ops community, *Weapon of Choice*, pp. 296–297. **. . . pilot-in-command . . .** There were two pilots on a 160th Chinook. The more experienced of the two was referred to as the pilot-in-command; the less experienced pilot was referred to simply as the pilot. In the civilian world the less experienced pilot would be referred to as the *copilot* and I have used that word here, with the understanding that in strict Army terms, the word copilot has a different meaning. If more than one helicopter is flying a mission, an air mission commander flies in one of the helicopters to provide command supervision and ensure all pilots-in-command are following the plan.
2. **Of course . . . version of events.** *Pitfalls of Technology*, pp. 7, 14, 36; special ops time line; special ops sources.
3. **(However . . . minimal.)** *Pitfalls of Technology*, p. 10.
4. **But the realization . . . any combat operation.** Wille; Bello; two other sources in the Mountain TOC; special ops time line; special ops sources.
5. **At 2:20 a.m . . . landed there.** *Pitfalls of Technology*, pp. 8, 10, 11; Haas; *Weapon of Choice*, p. 297. **. . . apparently consisted of eight personnel . . .** The number of personnel in Mako 30 has been shrouded in mystery, due to the reluctance of the Pentagon to acknowledge the existence of Gray Fox, and hence, the presence of a TF Orange man on the initial infil on Razor 03. I concluded there were eight team members on the aircraft by working backward from the number of five SEALs and one combat controller (Chapman) Milani says went back to the mountain to look for Roberts after dropping off the aircrew plus Thor at Gardez.
6. **At 2:38 a.m . . . left of the Chinook.** Al; *Pitfalls of Technology*, p. 11; Milani report (the chronology of the Takur Ghar battle put together by the official U.S. Special Operations Command investigator of the event, Colonel Andrew Milani, and released to

me in redacted form under the Freedom of Information Act) pp. 10–11; special ops time line; a source in the special ops community; "Bravery and Breakdowns in a Ridgetop Battle," by Bradley Graham, *The Washington Post*, May 24, 2002.

Chapter 4

1. **In Bagram . . . couldn't miss.** Hagenbeck; another source in the Mountain TOC.
2. **The RPG slammed . . . cabin window.** Al; *Pitfalls of Technology*, pp. 11–12; Milani report, pp. 10–11; special ops time line; *Weapon of Choice*, p. 298; "Bravery and Breakdowns in a Ridgetop Battle," by Bradley Graham, *The Washington Post*, May 24, 2002.
3. **Al's copilot . . . from Takur Ghar.** Al; *Pitfalls of Technology*, pp. 11–12; Milani report, pp. 12–13; special ops time line; *Weapon of Choice*, pp. 298–299.
4. **The landing . . . went to work.** *Pitfalls of Technology*, p. 16; Milani report, pp. 13–15; a source in the special ops community.
5. **About 50 miles . . . he was alive."** Turner. **. . . Grim 32 . . .** An AC-130 crew's call sign changed from night to night. The numbers reflect which aircraft took off first from K2 (Grim call signs) or Masirah (Nail call signs).
6. **Thinking the Chinook . . . friendly forces.** *Pitfalls of Technology*, p. 17; Milani report, pp. 13–14.
7. **At this time . . . and Mako 30.** Turner.
8. **Once Slab understood . . . on the radio.)** Milani report, p. 15; sources in the special ops community.
9. **Slab called . . . *mountain*, he thought.** Blaber.
10. **As they soared . . . forever.** Turner.

Chapter 5

1. **Battlefield friction . . . *top of the mountain*.** *Pitfalls of Technology*, p. 17.
2. **Other than Slab's . . . aviators and SEALs.** *Pitfalls of Technology*, p. 19; Blaber; other special ops sources; Preysler.
3. **Blaber and Slab . . . was inbound.** *Pitfalls of Technology*, pp. 19–20; Blaber.
4. **Colonel Joe Smith . . . events on the battlefield.** Hagenbeck; Donnelly; another source in the Mountain TOC.
5. **Suddenly another . . . guy on the ground.** Special ops sources; sources in the Mountain TOC; *Pitfalls of Technology*, pp. 19–20; special ops time line.
6. **Perhaps acknowledging . . . transport aircraft.** Special ops sources; a senior Army officer.
7. **It took Razor 04 . . . saving Neil Roberts.** Al; special ops time line; sources in the special ops community; *Weapon of Choice*, p. 300; "Bravery and Breakdowns in a Ridgetop Battle," by Bradley Graham, *The Washington Post*, May 24, 2002.
8. **Razor 04 flew . . . last to Takur Ghar.** Special ops time line; a source in the special ops community; *Weapon of Choice*, p. 301.
9. **It took Grim 32 . . . was not so.)** Turner; other special ops sources.
10. **When Razor 04 . . . neared the peak.** Sources in the special ops community; *Weapon of Choice*, pp. 301–302.

Chapter 6

1. **Roberts hit the snow . . . Roberts was dead.** *Pitfalls of Technology,* pp. 16–18, 26–28; Donnelly; Milani report, p. 18; two sources in the special operations community. In the wake of the battle, rumors circulated that Roberts had been tortured and mutilated in hideous ways. These rumors were not true. Roberts also sustained a neck wound at some stage during his ordeal, but it was the head wound that was almost certainly fatal.
2. **Razor 04 was . . . 4:55 a.m.** Milani report, p. 22; *Pitfalls of Technology,* p. 21; Turner; *Weapon of Choice,* p. 302.
3. **Before the helicopter's . . . nearby knoll.** *Weapon of Choice,* p. 302; Milani report, p. 22; "Bravery and Breakdowns in a Ridgetop Battle," by Bradley Graham, *The Washington Post,* May 24, 2002.
4. **The whirling of . . . nonflyable.** *Weapon of Choice,* p. 302; special ops time line.
5. **As the helicopter . . . in the bunker.** Milani report, pp. 22–23; *Pitfalls of Technology,* pp. 21, 29; *Weapon of Choice,* p. 302; Turner.
6. **To Grim 32 . . . about it," Turner said.** Turner.
7. **Another SEAL climbed . . . quick reaction force.** Milani report, pp. 22–24; *Pitfalls of Technology,* pp. 21–22; Turner; Self; *Weapon of Choice,* p. 302.

Chapter 7

1. **At 3:45 a.m . . . .Captain Nathan Self.** *Pitfalls of Technology.*
2. **Born and raised . . . and their weaknesses.** Self.
3. **By the time Trebon . . . all the details straight.** Self; Canon; Don. **. . . tacsat . . .** Tactical satellite radio.
4. **Meanwhile, in Bagram . . . of misunderstanding."** *Pitfalls of Technology,* p. 22.
5. **As Razor 01 bucked . . . about the AC-130.** Self.

Chapter 8

1. **On the side of . . . monitoring the call.** Turner.
2. **Radio and phone . . . with Mulholland.** Special ops time line; sources in the special ops community; Donnelly.
3. **The folks most worried . . . might run into.** Turner.
4. **Yet again . . . out of the sky."** Special ops sources.
5. **At 6:07 a.m. Razors 01 and 02 . . . assaulted at 6:07 a.m.** *Pitfalls of Technology,* pp. 25–29.
6. **Slab said that . . . continue the fight.** *Pitfalls of Technology,* p. 29; Self.
7. **Nate Self, who . . . could have made.** Self.
8. **Chapman sustained . . . in that situation.** *Pitfalls of Technology,* p. 29; a source familiar with Chapman's wounds; a special operations source.
9. **Milani said . . . broke contact," he said.** *Pitfalls of Technology,* p. 29.
10. **If the man . . . over the mountaintop.** Self.

Chapters 9 through 12

All the material in these chapters came from the following sources: Self; Canon; Cory; Don; Greg; other sources in the special ops community; *Pitfalls of Technology*; Milani report; *Weapon of Choice*, pp. 304–319; Hagenbeck.

WINDING DOWN

1. **On March 3 . . . no casualties.** 1-187 After Action Review.
2. **The change in . . . attack helicopters.)** My personal observations in the Shahikot and at Bagram.
3. **The demonstrated value . . . down," he recalled.** Peterson; Ashline.
4. **After the Takur . . . be pulled out.** Special ops time line; other special ops sources.
5. **Juliet Team left . . . leave the Shahikot.** Special ops time line; other special ops sources; my personal observations (I flew out of the Shahikot on the same helicopter as Juliet Team).
6. **There remained . . . and waited."** Larsen.
7. **Encouraged by . . . finest," Rosengard said.** Rosengard; Haas; other special ops sources.
8. **Afghan forces finally . . . something to see."** Haas.
9. **Unfortunately . . . executive officer, said.** Larsen.
10. **Meanwhile, Blaber . . . enemy corpses.** Blaber.
11. **Blaber and his men . . . But where?** Blaber; special ops time line.
12. **Many never . . . body parts.** My conversations with U.S. generals, and personal observations. I walked on patrol down Ginger Pass with 4-31 Infantry on March 18.
13. **A better estimate . . . as died there.** Special ops sources.
14. **On March 13 . . . hosts poorly.** Special ops time line; Blaber; other special ops sources.
15. **The only enemy . . . security forces.** Mikolashek; Hagenbeck; "Al Qaida's Uzbek Bodyguards," by Owais Tohid, *The Christian Science Monitor*, September 28, 2004; Blaber; special ops time line; other special ops sources.
16. **No intelligence . . . in 2004.** Special ops time line; other special ops sources.
17. **But for AFO . . . found succor.** Special ops source.

INTERVIEWEES

The following individuals were interviewed on-the-record during the research for this book:

HEADQUARTERS, DEPARTMENT OF THE ARMY

Army Secretary Tom White
General John Keane

U.S. ARMY FORCES COMMAND

General John Hendrix
Major General Julian Burns

COALITION FORCES LAND COMPONENT COMMAND

Lieutenant General Paul Mikolashek
Major General Warren Edwards
Colonel Michael Longoria
Lieutenant Colonel Craig Bishop
Lieutenant Colonel Andy Nocks
Major Ignacio Perez

COALITION FORCES AIR COMPONENT COMMAND

Brigadier General John Corley
Colonel Larry Stutzriem

101ST AIRBORNE DIVISION (AIR ASSAULT)

Major General Richard Cody

TASK FORCE MOUNTAIN

Major General Franklin "Buster" Hagenbeck
Brigadier General Gary Harrell
Colonel Becky Halstead
Lieutenant Colonel Chris Bentley
Lieutenant Colonel Jasey Briley

Lieutenant Colonel Pete Dagnes
Lieutenant Colonel David Gray
Lieutenant Colonel Mike Lundy
Lieutenant Colonel Ronald Smith
Lieutenant Colonel Kat Stone
Major Lou Bello
Major Ed Burke
Major Pete Donnelly
Major Bryan Hilferty
Major Jonathan Lockwood
Major Paul Wille
Chief Warrant Officer 2 Thomas Baxter

TASK FORCE RAKKASAN

Colonel Frank Wiercinski
Lieutenant Colonel Jim Larsen
Major Michael Gibler
Major Sherrie Bosley
Major Dennis Yates
Captain Eric Haupt
Captain Paul Murray
Command Sergeant Major Iuniasolua Savusa

2-187 Infantry (Headquarters)

Lieutenant Colonel Charles "Chip" Preysler
Chaplain (Captain) Mike Shellman
1st Lieutenant Glen Helberg
1st Lieutenant Matty Lowen
1st Lieutenant Justin Overbaugh
Command Sergeant Major Mark Nielsen
Staff Sergeant Marc Richard
Sergeant Jim Jorgensen

A/2-187

Captain Kevin Butler
1st Sergeant Jonathan Blossom
Sergeant Corey Daniel
Corporal Jared Cave
Corporal Jason Fisher
Specialist Justin Celano
Specialist Jeremy Gaul
Specialist Justin Musella
Specialist Tim Ouditt
Private First Class Joseph Borgia

Private First Class Daniel Cunningham
Private First Class Steven Moisan
Private 2 Robert Garcia

C/2-187

Captain Frank Baltazar
Sergeant First Class Anthony Koch
Sergeant First Class Kelly Jack Luman
Staff Sergeant Chris Harry
Sergeant David Dedo
Sergeant Scotty Mendenhall
Sergeant Henry Schmitz
Sergeant John Tucker
Specialist Dan Chapman
Specialist Matthew Edwards
Private First Class Joseph Gallagher
Private First Class Pablo Quirindongo
Private First Class Jason Wilson
Private 2 Jason Bird

1-187 Infantry

Lieutenant Colonel Ron Corkran
Major Paul Sarat
Captain Robert Kuth
Sergeant First Class Chuck Nye

1-87 Infantry (Headquarters)

Lieutenant Colonel Paul LaCamera
Major Jay Hall
Captain Adam McLaughlin
Command Sergeant Major Frank Grippe
Sergeant First Class Robert Healy
Sergeant First Class Michael Peterson
Sergeant Jorge Alcaraz
Sergeant Ryan Brown
Sergeant Raul Lopez
Specialist Jason Gonzalez
Specialist James Patterson
Private First Class Jason Ashline

A/1-87

Captain Roger Crombie
1st Lieutenant Anthony Passero
Private Eric Estrada

C/1-87

Captain Nelson Kraft
Staff Sergeant Robert Brault
Staff Sergeant Randel Perez
Staff Sergeant Andrzej Ropel
Sergeant Jerry Higley
Specialist Thomas Beers
Specialist Eddie (Antonio) Rivera
Senior Airman Stephen Achey
Private First Class Kyle McGovern

C/4-31 Infantry

Captain Glenn Kozelka
1st Lieutenant Benjamin Croom
Staff Sergeant Steven Johnson
Sergeant Corey Reed
Sergeant Michael Angelo Rodriguez
Sergeant Ioasa Tavae
Specialist Jarrod Taylor
Private 2 Max Coryell

TF TALON

7-101 Aviation

Lieutenant Colonel Jim Marye
Captain Eric Moore
1st Lieutenant Justin Aaronson
1st Lieutenant Nicholas Meister
Chief Warrant Officer 3 Loyd "Blayne" Anderson
Chief Warrant Officer 3 Brett Blair
Chief Warrant Officer 2 Jeffrey Fichter
Staff Sergeant Denny Daughtry
Staff Sergeant Charles Kidd
Staff Sergeant Mark Stanley
Sergeant Todd Boehm
Sergeant Carl Moore
Sergeant Eddie Wahl
Specialist Jess Morgan
Private First Class Bo Blankenship

3-101 Aviation

Captain Joey Herman
Captain Bill Ryan
Chief Warrant Officer 4 Jim Hardy
Chief Warrant Officer 3 Rich Chenault

Chief Warrant Officer 3 Keith Hurley
Chief Warrant Officer 2 John Hamilton
Chief Warrant Officer 2 Stanley Pebsworth
Chief Warrant Officer 2 Emanuel Pierre
Staff Sergeant Chad Bardwell

B/159 Aviation

Chief Warrant Officer 3 Scott Beslin
Chief Warrant Officer 2 Kyle Evarts
Chief Warrant Officer 2 Ken Gunter
Chief Warrant Officer 2 John Quinlan
Staff Sergeant Torino DeGuzman
Staff Sergeant Timothy Johnson
Sergeant Michael Cillo
Sergeant Christopher Tichenor

2ND BRIGADE, 10TH MOUNTAIN DIVISION

Colonel Kevin Wilkerson

4-31 Infantry

Lieutenant Colonel Steve Townsend
Captain Christopher Johnson
Captain Joseph "Sepp" Scanlin
1st Lieutenant Andrew Exum
Command Sergeant Major Daniel Wood
Sergeant First Class Matthew MacClellan
Sergeant First Class Ray Montoya
Specialist Carl McCauley
Private First Class Joshua Mackay
Private 2 Albert Buentello
Private 2 David Gahris
Private 2 David Vasquez

TASK FORCE 11

Advance Force Operations

Lieutenant Colonel Pete Blaber

Task Force Brown

Chief Warrant Officer 5 Don _____
Chief Warrant Officer 4 Al ____
Chief Warrant Officer 3 Greg _____
Sergeant First Class Cory ____

Task Force Red
Captain Nathan Self
Staff Sergeant Arin Canon

TASK FORCE DAGGER
Lieutenant Colonel Louis Bochain
Lieutenant Colonel Chris Haas
Lieutenant Colonel Mark Rosengard
Major D. J. Turner
Captain Tim Fletcher
Captain Matthew McHale
Captain Glenn Thomas
Sergeant First Class John Southworth

TASK FORCE K-BAR
Sergeant First Class Frank Antenori

TASK FORCE 64
Technical Sergeant Jim Hotaling

274TH Forward Surgical Team (Airborne)
Doctor (Lieutenant Colonel) George Peoples
Doctor (Major) Bob Craig
Doctor (Major) Brian Burlingame
Doctor (Major) Tad Gerlinger
Captain Herman Allison
Captain Paula Lastoria
Captain Paul Maholtz
Sergeant Joe Civitello
Sergeant Marty Contreras
Sergeant Jamison Gaddy

15TH Reconnaissance Detachment
Major Matt Weingast

U.S. ARMY CENTER OF MILITARY HISTORY
Dr. Richard Stewart

U.S. ARMY CRIMINAL INVESTIGATION COMMAND
Chief Warrant Officer 2 Danny Thomas

13TH Marine Expeditionary Unit Cobras
Lieutenant Colonel Gregg Sturdevant
Major Shane Stover
Captain Chad Comunale
Captain Chris Roe

919TH SPECIAL OPERATIONS WING

Major Perry Panos

OTHERS

Jon Anderson
Major Richard Coe
Ahmed Rashid

BIBLIOGRAPHY

BOOKS

Afghan Guerrilla Warfare—In the Words of the Mujahideen Fighters, by Ali Ahmad Jalali and Lester W. Grau, published 2001 by MBI Publishing Company (originally published as *The Other Side of the Mountain* by the U.S. Marine Corps Combat Development Command).

Afghanistan's Endless War, by Larry Goodson, published 2001 by the University of Washington Press.

The Bear Went Over the Mountain—Soviet Combat Tactics in Afghanistan, by Lester W. Grau, published 1998 by Frank Cass.

Black Hawk Down, by Mark Bowden, published 1999 by Atlantic Monthly Press.

Brave Men, Dark Waters—The Untold Story of the Navy SEALs, by Orr Kelly, published 1993 by Pocket Books.

Delta Force, by Colonel Charlie A. Beckwith (Ret.) and Donald Knox, published 2000 by Avon Books (originally published in 1983).

Ghost Wars, by Steve Coll, published 2004 by The Penguin Press.

Inside Delta Force, by Eric L. Haney, published 2003 by Dell (first published in hardcover in 2002 by Delacorte Press).

Jihad—The Rise of Militant Islam in Central Asia, by Ahmed Rashid, published in 2003 by Penguin (first published in the United States in 2002 by Yale University Press).

Killing Pablo, by Mark Bowden, published 2002 by Penguin Books.

The Mission, by Dana Priest, published 2003 by W.W. Norton and Company, Inc.

Stumbling Bear—Soviet Military Performance in Afghanistan, by Scott R. McMichael, published 1991 by Brassey's.

Taliban, by Ahmed Rashid, published 2001 by Yale University Press.

Weapons and Tactics of the Soviet Army, by David C. Isby, published 1988 by Jane's Publishing Company Limited.

NEWSPAPERS AND PERIODICAL ARTICLES

"The 'Revolution in Military Affairs' has an Enemy: Politics," by Michael Catanzaro, published October 1, 2001, in *The American Enterprise.*

"The War's Bloodiest Battle," by Sean D. Naylor, published 18 March, 2002, in *Army Times.*

"Intel Take From Enemy at Shah-e-Kot Great, MIs say," by Sean D. Naylor, published 25 March, 2002, in *Army Times.*

"In Shah-e-Kot, Apaches Save the Day—And Their Reputation," by Sean D. Naylor, published 25 March, 2002, in *Army Times.*

"Anaconda Winds Down," by Sean D. Naylor, published 25 March, 2002, in *Army Times.*

"Deadly Find," by Sean D. Naylor, published 1 April, 2002, in *Army Times.*

"In Search of Casualties," by Sean D. Naylor, published 15 April, 2002, in *Army Times.*

"What We Learned from Anaconda," by Sean D. Naylor, published 29 July, 2002, in *Army Times.*

"Pentagon Faces Transformation," by Tom Bowman, published March 13, 2001, in *The Baltimore Sun.*

"Al Qaida's Uzbek Bodyguards," by Owais Tohid, published September 28, 2004, in *The Christian Science Monitor.*

"Wolfowitz: More Resources, Better Management Keys to Defense Transformation," by Hunter Keeter, published August 9, 2001, in *Defense Daily.*

"Left In Dark For Most Anaconda Planning, Air Force Opens New Probe," by Elaine Grossman, published October 3, 2002, in *Inside The Pentagon.*

"Losing the Peace?" by Michael Massing, published May 13, 2002, in *The Nation.*

"A Different War—Is the Army Becoming Irrelevant?" by Peter J. Boyer, published July 1, 2002, in *The New Yorker.*

"Special Forces OD Alpha-555," by Lance M. Bacon, published September 2003 in *Soldier of Fortune.*

"The Infiltrator: Ali Mohamed Served in the U.S. Army—and Bin Laden's Circle," by Peter Waldman, published November 26, 2001, in *The Wall Street Journal.*

"Bravery and Breakdowns in a Ridgetop Battle," by Bradley Graham, published May 24, 2002, in *The Washington Post.*

"A Wintry Ordeal at 10,000 Feet," by Bradley Graham, published May 25, 2002, in *The Washington Post.*

"U.S. Concludes Bin Laden Escaped at Tora Bora Fight," by Barton Gellman and Thomas E. Ricks, published April 17, 2002 in *The Washington Post.*

OFFICIAL U.S. GOVERNMENT PUBLICATIONS AND DOCUMENTS

Afghanistan and the Future of Warfare: Implications for Army and Defense Policy, by Stephen Biddle, published November 2002 by the Strategic Studies Institute, U.S. Army War College, Carlisle Barracks, Pennsylvania.

"Ali Mohamed: The Defendant Who Did Not Go to Trial," by Judy Aita, published May 16, 2003, by U.S. Department of State International Information Programs; accessed on the Internet at http://usinfo.state.gov/regional/af/security/a1051502.htm.

The Army of Excellence—the Development of the 1980s Army, by John L. Romjue, published 1993 by Office of the Command Historian, U.S. Army Training and Doctrine Command.

"Afghanistan—Fire Support for Operation Anaconda," by Robert H. McElroy, published September-October 2002 in *Field Artillery.*

COMACC Sight Picture—Joint Air-Ground Operations (a December 2002 press release from the U.S. Air Force's Air Combat Command).

Emerging Lessons, Insights and Observations—Operation Enduring Freedom, published 2002 by the Center for Army Lessons Learned, Fort Leavenworth, Kansas.

"Enduring Freedom: An Air Force Combat Controller's Experience," briefing by Technical Sergeant James Hotaling, September 2002. Text accessed at http://www.afa.org/media/scripts/afsoc.pdf.

"Lessons Learned From A Light Infantry Company During Operation Anaconda," by Captain Nelson G. Kraft, published Summer 2002 in *Infantry,* the official magazine of the U.S. Army Infantry Center and School, Fort Benning, Georgia.

Infantry Rifle Platoon and Squad—Army Field Manual 7-8, published by the U.S. Army.

Information Operations—Army Field Manual 100-6, published by the U.S. Army.

"Investigation Report for Suspected Friendly Fire Incident Involving AC-130 Spectre Gunship and U.S./Afghan Forces Near Gardez, On or About 02 March 02." The Central Command investigation; redacted version released November 2002 and obtained via the Freedom of Information Act.

JSOTF-N Command Briefing, a PowerPoint slide briefing produced by Task Force Dagger.

"SIGINT Marines Help Fight War on Terrorism in Afghanistan," *Intelligence Community Newsletter,* published February 2003 by Headquarters, U.S. Marine Corps Intelligence Department.

"Texas14 Monogram of Activities in Support of Operation Enduring Freedom (12 October 2001–26 March 2002)," an unpublished paper by Captain Glenn Thomas.

"10th Mountain Division Observations—Operation Enduring Freedom."

"The Milani Report," by Colonel Andrew N. Milani, the official U.S. Special Operations Command chronology of the Takur Ghar battle, released to me in heavily redacted form.

"Operation Anaconda," briefing by Lieutenant Colonel Pete Blaber, given to many different military audiences.

"Operation Anaconda" CJTF Mountain Command Briefing.

"Operation Anaconda—CJTF Mountain C2 Plans," a briefing by Major Francesca Ziemba.

Operation Anaconda: Command and Confusion in Joint Warfare, an unpublished paper by Major Mark Davis, June 2004.

Operation Anaconda—Lessons for Joint Operations, by Richard L. Kugler, Michael Baranick and Hans Binnendijk, published September 2003 by National Defense University, Washington, D.C.

Operations—Army Field Manual 3-0, published by the U.S. Army.

Pitfalls of Technology: A Case Study of the Battle on Takur Ghar Mountain, Afghanistan, an unpublished paper by Colonel Andrew N. Milani.

"Special Operations Forces in Operation Anaconda, 1-14 March 2002," a briefing by Dr. Richard Stewart, U.S. Army Center of Military History.

"TF 1-187 IN AAR: Operation Anaconda," unpublished "Memorandum for the Commander" dated March 21, 2002.

10th Mountain Division (Light Infantry)—Operation Enduring Freedom, Afghanistan, Joint

Center for Lessons Learned Final Report, published June 6, 2003, by Joint Forces Command.
*Victory in Papua,*by Samuel Milner, published 1957 by the Office of the Chief of Military History, Department of the [U.S.] Army
Weapon of Choice—ARSOF in Afghanistan, by Charles H. Briscoe, Richard L. Kiper, James A. Schroder, and Kalev I. Sepp, published 2004 by the Combat Studies Institute Press, Fort Leavenworth, Kansas.

INDEX

Abbott, Thomas, 233, 236, 240, 253, 254
Achey, Stephen, 271
Advance Force Operations. *See* AFO
Afghan Military Forces. *See* AMF
Afghanistan. *See also* Operation Anaconda; Al Qaida; Shahikot; Takur Ghar
  Bagram in, 4, 33–39, 44, 49, 56, 59–62, 64, 66, 67, 69, 74, 80, 82–83, 87–95, 99, 113, 117–20, 126, 131, 133–35, 137
  Chechens in, 42, 118, 157, 191, 318, 376
  Gardez in, 10, 24–28, 27–28, 39–45, 40, 41, 42–43, 47, 48, 60, 64, 65, 67, 70–74, 70–75, 76–78, 77–78, 80–82, 81, 82, 93, 95, 96, 98–102, 99, 100–107, 105, 106, 109, 111–17, 112–13, 117, 125, 138–44, 142, 145, 150–51, 154–57, 156, 159–60, 162–68, 165, 167, 170–71, 174, 177, 179, 184–85, 187, 203–4, 204, 208, 262, 264, 274, 279–81, 280, 286–89, 297, 299–305, 300, 302, 304, 306, 307–11, 317–19, 321, 323, 325, 330–33, 340, 352, 360, 368, 371–73, 376
  Kabul in, 8–12, 9, 14, 16–17, 26, 28, 39, 40, 46, 63, 64, 66, 67, 69, 73, 78, 91, 92, 112, 115, 117, 134, 154, 155, 213, 277, 304, 377
  Khowst in, 39, 40, 48, 58, 60, 65, 77, 78, 98, 99, 101, 104, 123, 149, 177, 329
  Rasul in, 71, 101, 112, 113, 185, 187
  Serkhankhel in, 44, 46, 119, 122, 124, 125, 127, 137, 146, 149, 154, 159, 164, 169, 176–77, 179, 192, 199, 211, 226, 235, 243, 249, 262, 272, 371–72
  Tora Bora in, 10, 12, 17–21, 22–24, 45–46, 48, 65, 119, 155
AFO (Advance Force Operations), xvi, 34, 39–41, 60, 64, 65, 68, 70, 73–76, 78, 80, 81, 87, 92, 93, 96–117, 122, 124–27, 137, 141–44, 151, 159–60, 167–68, 171, 173–80, 182, 184–85, 191, 197, 203–5, 208, 212, 214, 217, 235, 260–61, 263–66, 271, 275, 280, 286–89, 297, 300–303, 305–7, 309–17, 319, 322–23, 334, 352, 371–72, 374, 376–77
Air base, in Bagram, 4, 56, 82–83
Al Y., 105, 112, 160, 185, 214–15, 299, 308–09, 311–15
Alcaraz, Jorge, 260
Allen, Brian, 205
AMF (Afghan Military Forces), xvi, 45, 47, 48, 113, 140, 164–65, 185, 204, 206, 209, 211–12, 214–15, 273, 277–78, 281
  awards for, 304–5
Anderson, Loyd Blayne, 210–14, 226
Anderson, Marc, 341–43
Andy, 166, 189, 190, 244
Antenori, Frank, 126
Apaches, 210–11. *See also* Helicopters, in Operation Anaconda
ARCENT (Army Component of Central Command), 12
Ariana Hotel, 8–9, 11, 29, 39, 40, 60, 64
Army Component of Central Command. See ARCENT
Ashline, Jason, 241, 269
Australians, 26–60, 58, 87, 89, 118, 140–54, 158–59, 185, 377

Bagram
  air base in, 4, 56, 82–83
  as military headquarters, 33–39, 44, 49, 59–62, 64, 66, 67, 69, 74, 80, 87–95, 99, 113, 117
  Operation Anaconda relating to, 117–20, 126, 131, 133–35, 137
Ballard Sean, 205, 209, 211–12

Baltazar, Frank, 6, 217–18, 226, 251, 284, 290–92, 294, 296–97
Bardwell, Chad, 256–59
The Bear Went Over the Mountain (Grau), 24
Beaudry, Earl, Jr., 294, 296–97
Bello, Lou, 88, 128, 131, 134, 136, 155, 174, 209, 264
Bennett, Sam, 257–58
Bentley, Chris, 83, 93, 126, 128, 131, 134–35, 153, 155–56, 209, 272, 273, 281
bin Laden, Osama, 10, 17–21, 37, 40, 46, 76–77, 103, 142, 169, 172, 272
Bishop, Craig, 63, 67, 69, 70, 159, 198
Blaber, Pete
  in Operation Anaconda, xiii, 10, 28, 34, 38–40, 60, 64–68, 73, 75–76, 78–81, 90, 92–93, 121–22, 127, 137, 141–44, 160, 166–67, 169–70, 173–77, 180, 191, 203–4, 208, 262–64, 266, 285–88, 371–77
  in reconnaissance mission, 95, 96, 98–99, 101, 104, 109, 112–17
  Takur Ghar relating to, 302–3, 305–7, 309–11, 317–19, 321–22, 332, 334–36, 338
Blair, Brett, 3, 4, 5, 6, 7
Blocking Positions, 41, 48, 62, 93, 119, 122, 125, 140, 147, 152, 172, 193, 209, 210, 217, 228, 251–52, 264–66, 267, 283, 304
  Amy, 289–90, 297
  Betty, 266
  Cindy, 369
  Diane, 226, 251, 369
  Ginger, 234, 236
  Heather, 234, 236, 238
Bob H., 97, 101–02, 109, 115, 117, 165, 285
Bochain, Louis, 133–34, 136
Brault, Robert, 282–83
Brian, 346, 348, 354–56, 359
Briley, Jasey, 75, 118, 153, 157
Brossoie, James, 296
Brown, Gabe, 332, 347, 351–52, 356–57, 361, 363
Browning, Charles "Todd," 200
Burke Ed, 158
Burns, Julian, 85, 86
Bush, George W., 18, 85, 172
Busko, Rick, 172, 228
Butler, Kevin
  in Operation Anaconda, 288–95, 297
  at Takur Ghar, 305, 315, 320–21, 367, 369–70
Byrne, Thomas "Doc," 252, 253

Calland, Albert, 15
Canon, Arin, 329–30, 332–33, 341, 352–61, 363
CAOC (Combined Air Operations Center), xvii, 137, 152–53, 208, 317
Carr, Bob, 193, 194, 196, 218, 256, 258
Carwazi, 207, 212, 214, 273–76, 303
Casenhiser, Caleb, 197, 202–03, 205, 209, 211–13, 304
Celano, Justin, 293
CENTCOM (U.S. Central Command), xi, xii, xvi, 12–14, 18–21, 33, 36, 37, 48, 52–57, 59, 60, 68, 81, 85, 86, 88, 91, 92, 94, 95, 102, 120, 123, 131, 133, 135, 136, 152–53, 182, 271, 319, 369
Central Intelligence Agency. *See* CIA
CFACC (Coalition Forces Air Component Command), xvi, 134–36, 271
CFLCC (Coalition Forces Land Component Command), xvi, 12, 14, 18, 20, 21, 36, 40, 46, 48, 52, 55, 59, 61, 63, 64, 67, 83–87, 94, 120, 129, 131, 134, 136, 142, 152–53, 159, 182, 198
  Edwards in, xiii, 18, 20, 21, 36–37, 40, 48, 54, 56, 58, 59, 86, 142, 153
  Mikolashek in, xiv, 12–15, 18, 20, 34, 45–48, 52–55, 58–59, 61–62, 69, 82–86, 94–95, 118, 130–31, 134, 136–37, 152–53, 159, 182, 198, 271, 272
Chapman, Dan, 6
Chapman, John
  death of, 325–28, 339–40, 358, 360, 367
  in Operation Anaconda, xiii, 311, 316
Chechens, 42, 118, 157, 191, 318, 376
Chenault, Rich, 192, 194, 209, 211, 216, 220–22, 246–47, 258–59
Chuck, 333, 340, 342–43, 345, 348, 351, 354–55, 362
CIA (Central Intelligence Agency)
  Operation Anaconda and, 6, 9–11, 14, 16, 17, 19, 23, 25–28, 30, 33, 38–41, 43, 48, 60, 64, 65, 67, 70, 72–76, 78, 80, 87, 91, 94, 145, 150, 156, 157, 184, 267, 287, 2 98–99
  reconnaissance mission and, 95, 98, 99, 101, 108, 112, 115
  "Spider" in, xv, 73, 75, 78, 80, 101, 122, 127, 141, 143, 156, 276–77, 302, 304, 317, 372, 373
  Takur Ghar and, 303, 311, 376
Cifers, Mike, 6, 7
CJTF (Coalition and Joint Task Force) Mountain. *See* Task Force Mountain
Clark, Perry, 23, 61–63, 65
Clark, Wesley, 196

Coalition Forces Air Component Command. *See* CFACC
Coalition Forces Land Component Command. *See* CFLCC
Cody, Richard, 52–54, 58, 84, 129, 292
Combined Air Operations Center. *See* CAOC
Commons, Matt, 343, 346
Contant, Stu, 192, 194, 220–24
Corkran Ron, 66, 128, 147, 174, 242–43, 284, 290, 297, 369
Corley, John, 137
Crombie, Roger, 228, 234, 259–60, 266, 290–91, 295–96
Crose, Brad, 343, 346
Cunningham, Jason, 343–45, 349, 354, 355, 362–67

Dailey, Dell, xiii, 31, 32, 33, 35–37, 80, 81, 95, 141–43, 301, 365
Daniel, Cory, 341, 344–45, 348–49, 354–55, 362–65, 368
Dave, 341, 344, 348, 349, 355, 361
Dave H., 97, 160, 162, 168, 262
Deane, John, 275, 277
Deaths
  of Chapman, J., 325–28, 339–40, 358, 360, 367
  of Harriman, 209–14, 275–77, 304, 316
  of Roberts, 321–24
Dedo, David, 172, 217
Delta Force. *See also* India team; Juliet team
  Blaber in, xiii, 10, 28, 34, 38–40, 60, 64–68, 73, 75–76, 78–81, 90, 92–93, 95, 96, 98–99, 101, 104, 109, 112–17, 121–22, 127, 137, 141–44, 160, 166–67, 169–70, 173–77, 180, 191, 203–4, 208, 262–64, 266, 285–88, 302–3, 305–7, 309–11, 317–19, 321–22, 332, 334–36, 338, 371–77
  "Major Jimmy" in, xiv, 39, 90, 93, 99, 127, 141, 150, 175, 178–79, 182–83, 260, 262, 265–66, 307, 310–13, 316–22
  in Operation Anaconda, 10, 15, 19, 28, 30–36, 38, 39, 73, 76, 79, 84, 87, 90, 122, 126, 141–43, 158–60, 162, 165–66, 183, 244, 260
  reconnaissance mission and, 95, 97, 98, 102, 104–5, 109, 112, 117
  "Speedy" in, xv, 97–98, 101, 109, 111, 113–17, 144, 165–68, 171, 176, 260–63, 285, 288, 297–98, 376
  Takur Ghar and, 301–3, 312, 317, 323, 371, 377
DePouli, Ray, 34, 330, 342, 345–47, 351, 353, 355–56, 358–63
DevGru, 31
Don, 332–34, 340, 343, 347–49, 351–52, 354–55, 362, 364, 367
Donnelly, Pete, 134–35, 137, 153, 195
Dupuy, Trevor, 66

Edwards, Matthew, 2
Edwards, Warren, xiii, 18, 20, 21, 36–37, 40, 48, 54, 56, 58, 59, 86, 142, 153
Egerer, Fred, 74–75, 171
Ewadzkhal Valley, 98, 101, 103, 104, 108

Fichter, Jeff, 210–13, 226
Finch, Thomas, 239, 268
Fletcher, Tim, 22, 23, 281
"Force cap," 53, 56
Franks, Tommy
  as CENTCOM commander, xiii
  Operation Anaconda and, 12, 18, 19, 33, 34, 36, 46, 48, 53–60, 82, 86, 91, 94, 95, 118, 131, 134, 136, 137, 150, 152–53, 182, 266, 365
  Tora Bora and, 20, 21
Freedom of Information Act, xi

Gardez, 10, 24–28, 39–45, 47, 48, 60, 64, 65, 67, 70–75, 77–78, 80–82, 93
  Operation Anaconda relating to, 125, 138–44, 150–51, 154–57, 159, 162–68, 170–71, 177, 179, 184–85, 187, 203–4, 208, 262, 264, 274, 279–81, 286–89, 297, 299–305, 307–11, 317–19, 321, 323, 325, 330–33, 340, 352, 360, 368, 371–73, 376
  reconnaissance mission relating to, 95, 98, 99, 100–107, 111–17
  safe house in, 39, 41, 42, 70–74, 76–78, 81, 82, 96, 98–102, 105, 106, 109, 112–13, 117, 142, 145, 156, 159–60, 165, 167, 174, 184, 204, 280, 300, 302, 304, 306
  Task Force Dagger in, 27–28, 39, 40, 42–43
Gibler, Michael, 66, 67, 69, 242, 243, 284
Gilliam, David, 346–47, 349, 356, 362
Glenn P., 65, 75, 96, 99, 117, 203–04, 208, 262, 302, 305–06, 310, 312
Golden, Maurice, 276
Goody (Mike), 122, 160, 166, 171, 173–76, 189, 190, 198, 243, 244, 306
Grau, Lester, 24, 25, 76
Gray, David, 83, 93–95, 129, 130, 149, 153, 157

Gray Fox
in Operation Anaconda, 126, 143, 160, 165, 169, 171, 177, 185, 262, 297, 300, 311–15, 321
in reconnaissance mission, 102, 104, 106, 109–12, 117
Greg, 333, 340–45, 349, 354–55, 362, 368
Grim 31, 190, 198–206, 208, 272
Grim 32, 316–18, 320–24, 326–27, 335–38, 360
Grim 33, 317, 320, 321
Grippe, Frank, xiii, 69, 90, 95, 228, 234, 236, 238, 253–56, 283, 336
Grooms, Christopher, 215
Gurgel, Jonathan, 213
Guthrie, Bill, 215–16

Haas, Chris, xiii, 40, 60, 65, 67–68, 73, 81, 88, 115, 142–45, 151, 154–56, 185, 187, 200, 203–4, 206–8, 212, 273–78, 280, 302, 304, 317, 372–74
Hagenbeck, Franklin "Buster," xiii, 11–14, 60–61, 75, 82–83, 84, 86–90, 91–95, 118, 120–21, 123, 126–33, 136–37, 139, 141–42, 145–46, 149–50, 153, 157–58, 170, 172, 175–76, 178–79, 182, 208–9, 253, 256, 259, 264–67, 270–71, 290, 297, 304–5, 307, 312, 319, 365
Haidar, Gul, 372–74
Halfpipe, battle of, 237–38, 240–41, 246, 248–49, 251–56, 259–60, 266–71, 281–83, 289, 307, 370
Hall, Brandon, 242
Hall, Jay, 234
Hamilton, John, 193, 213, 222, 256
Hans, 104, 105, 109–11, 113, 117, 160, 165, 185, 197, 204, 299, 311
Hardy, Jim, xiii, 192–93, 196, 211, 218, 222–26, 256–58, 260
Harrell, Gary, xiv, 33, 34, 36–37, 64, 66, 74, 91, 93, 94, 130, 142, 149, 156, 170, 264, 266, 312, 319, 335
Harriman, Stanley
death of, 209–14, 275–77, 304, 316
in Operation Anaconda, 184–85, 187, 197–98, 200–206
Harry, Chris, 2, 217–18, 292
Harward, Robert, 15, 47, 94, 129, 360
Haupt, Eric, 149, 157, 179
Hazrat, Ali, 19, 20, 24
Helberg, Glen, 226, 228, 249, 285, 290–91, 296
Helicopters, in Operation Anaconda, 312–18, 319–25, 328–35, 341–49, 351, 353–55, 360–61, 363–69. *See also* Apaches
Henderson, Steven, 249
Hendrix, John, 86
Henrey, Mark, 260
Herman, Joe, 192, 246–47
Higley, Jerry, 236, 239–40
Hodges, John, 173
Holland, Charlie, xi, 33
Hoskheyar, 71, 72, 96, 145, 185, 187, 273, 281
Huber, Reginald, 228, 296
Huff, Randy, 257
HUMINT (human intelligence), xvii, 74, 102, 108, 135
Hurley, Keith, 192, 194, 196, 209, 216, 218, 220–25, 258, 259
Hussein, Saddam, 3, 85
HVTs (high-value targets), 29, 37, 39, 44, 65, 81, 92, 120, 138
Hyder, Vic, xiv, 300–302, 305–7, 309–11, 321, 352–53, 358–59, 366, 371

IMU (Islamic Movement of Uzbekistan), xvii, 46, 47, 65, 138, 139
India team
in Operation Anaconda, 97–98, 101, 104, 107–9, 122, 142–44, 159, 160, 164–69, 171, 174, 176–78, 185, 189, 261–63, 285–87, 297–99, 302, 311, 371, 376
in reconnaissance mission, 96–99, 101–2, 104–5, 107–9, 113–17
Intelligence, 41–48, 59–95, 77–82, 83, 92–93, 95. See also HUMINT; SIGINT
IPB (intelligence Preparation of the Battlefield), 8, 73
Isaac H., 112, 160, 185, 205, 212
Islamic Movement of Uzbekistan. *See* IMU
ISR (intelligence surveillance, reconnaissance), xvii, 101, 104

Jason, 102–04, 106, 112, 160, 162, 169, 177, 262
Jay, 102, 104, 112, 159, 160, 162
JDAM (Joint Direct Attack Munition), 132
John, 9, 10, 40
John B., 105, 112, 117, 160, 164, 165, 185, 204, 205, 212, 299, 311
Joint Special Operations Command. *See* JSOC
Jones, Mike, 91, 304, 312, 319, 266130
JSOC (Joint Special Operations Command), xi, xvii, 31–36, 80, 81, 92, 141, 143, 286, 301, 320, 365
Juliet team
in Operation Anaconda, 122, 142–43, 159–65, 168–71, 176–77, 185, 199, 205,

208, 262–63, 286–87, 298–99, 302, 305–6, 318, 328, 352, 366, 371–72, 376
in reconnaissance mission, 97–107, 109, 112, 117
Takur Ghar relating to, 302, 305–6, 318, 328, 352, 366

Kabul, 8–12, 14, 16–17, 26, 40, 46, 66, 67, 73, 78, 91, 92, 112, 115, 117, 134, 154, 155, 213, 277, 304, 377
safe house in, 9, 28, 39, 63, 64, 69
Kalashnikov, xvii, 9, 168, 189, 219, 222, 242, 246, 254
Kandahar, 12, 14, 17, 23, 26, 38, 47, 49, 55–59, 64, 66, 69, 112, 121, 131, 139, 145–46, 257, 329, 338, 360–61, 377
Karzai, Hamid, 16, 17
Keane, Jack, 18, 53–54, 59
Kearney, Frank, 80
Kernan, Joseph, xiv, 33, 80, 121–22, 286–87, 300–301, 305, 309, 365
Khowst, 39, 40, 48, 60, 65, 77, 78, 98, 99, 101, 123, 149, 177
safe house in, 58, 104, 123, 329
Kilburn, Jody, 193, 247
Kisner, Frank, 43, 335, 336
Koch, Anthony, 3, 6, 218
Kraft, Nelson, 234, 236, 237, 238, 240, 255–56, 269, 282–84, 297
Kris K., 69–71, 97, 159, 160, 162–65, 168, 177, 262

LaCamera, Paul, xiv, 62–63, 67–69, 89, 90, 91, 93, 146, 148, 167, 180, 228, 234–36, 238–40, 243, 246, 248–49, 251–53, 255–56, 264–67, 269, 271, 282–84, 289
LaFrenz, Matt, 329, 363–67
Larsen, Jim, xiv, 58, 61–69, 90, 94, 95, 122–23, 125–26, 178, 244, 372, 374
Lee, William C., 50–51, 66
Leister, Barry, 67
Lockwood, Jonathan, 89
Lodin, Zia, xiv, 26–28, 40–42, 45, 47–48, 59–60, 65, 67, 70–74, 93, 95, 112, 118–20, 122, 124–25, 127–28, 135, 139–40, 143–46, 148, 150, 154–56, 160, 184–87, 192, 197–98, 204, 207–9, 211, 212, 264–65, 273, 275–78, 280–81, 302–3, 317, 372–75
Longoria, Mike, 134, 137
Lopez, Raul, 239, 269
Luman, Kelly Jack, 226, 228, 250–51, 285, 290, 294–95, 297

"Major Jimmy"
in Operation Anaconda, xiv, 39, 90, 93, 99, 127, 141, 150, 175, 178–79, 182–83, 260, 262, 265–66
Takur Ghar relating to, 307, 310–13, 316–22
Mako 21, 300, 305, 308, 310, 311, 318, 371, 372
Mako 22, 297, 298, 305, 372
Mako 30, 300, 303, 305–12, 316–19, 321, 322, 324–26, 328, 335–39, 345, 347, 353, 358, 360, 365–68
Mako 31, 122, 142–43, 147, 160, 164–77, 185–89, 199, 200, 241–44, 263, 284–87, 297, 299, 311
Marcinko, Richard, 31
Mark O., 64
Maroyka, Brad, 234, 236, 238–40, 253
Marriott, Gabriel, 193, 196
Marye, Jim, 123, 174, 224, 241–42
Masirah, 32, 34, 35, 37, 80, 81, 170, 175–76, 261, 286, 302, 310, 318, 320–28, 333–38, 364–66
Massoud, Ahmad Shah, 8, 15, 40, 138, 374
McArthur, William "Buddy," 200–201, 205
McGovern, Kyle, 239–40, 253
McGraw, Brian, 237
McHale, Matthew, 70–71, 78, 118, 144–45, 150–52, 162, 184–85, 187–88, 198, 206–7, 214–16, 272–79, 304
McNeill, Dan, 86
Mendenhall, Scotty, 7, 217
Merkloff, Jim, 63
Miceli, Anthony, 345, 347, 351, 356–58
Mikolashek, Paul, xiv, 12–15, 18, 20, 34, 45–48, 52–55, 58–59, 61–62, 69, 82–86, 94–95, 118, 130–31, 134, 136–37, 152–53, 159, 182, 198, 271, 272
Milani, Andrew, 310, 339, 340
Military headquarters, in Bagram, 33–39, 44, 49, 59–62, 64, 66, 67, 69, 74, 80, 87–95, 99, 113, 117
Miller, Keary, 331, 348–49, 363–64, 367
Mingus, Jim, 329–32
Mohammed, Ali Abdelsoud, 76–77
Moore, Carl, 1, 2, 4, 5, 6
Moseley, T. Michael "Buzz," 136, 137, 152, 154, 271, 272
Mujahideen, 8, 9, 13, 17, 25, 29, 73, 76, 77, 78, 98, 120, 138, 157, 275, 278, 376
Mulholland, John, xiv, 14, 15, 22, 24, 27, 42, 43, 45, 47–48, 59–61, 67, 68, 93–94, 122, 124–28, 130, 146, 154, 159, 209, 264, 274, 280, 304, 335–36
Murray, Bill, 301

Murray, Paul "Dino," 174, 242–45, 284, 301
Musella, Justin, 293

Nail 21, 308, 316
Nail 22, 308, 310–12, 316
Naler, Chris, 322, 337, 338
National Security Agency. *See* NSA
Navarro, Eric, 211
Nelson, 105, 112, 165, 185, 197
Nielsen, Mark, xiv, 3, 4, 7, 90, 172, 183, 226, 251–52, 266, 285
Nocks, Andy, 63, 67, 69, 70, 137, 204, 211
Northern Alliance, 8–11, 14–17, 19, 23–24, 29, 47, 135, 138, 372, 373
NSA (National Security Agency), xviii, 74, 75, 171

Objective Remington, 5, 118, 124, 125, 251
Observation posts, 160–67, 167–79, 302–3
Ogilvie, John, 237
O'Keefe, Aaron, 238, 248, 252, 268
Omar, Mullah Mohammed, 16, 37, 142
Operation Anaconda, xi. *See also* Blocking Positions; Shahikot; Takur Ghar; specific Task Force entries
- Apaches used in, 191– 197, 210–11, 216, 218–26, 246, 248, 256, 257, 268, 298, 360, 365, 369
- Australians involved with, 26–60, 58, 87, 89, 118, 140–54, 158–59, 185, 377
- Bagram relating to, 117–20, 126, 131, 133–35, 137
- Blaber in, xiii, 10, 28, 34, 38–40, 60, 64–68, 73, 75–76, 78–81, 90, 92–93, 121–22, 127, 137, 141–44, 160, 166–67, 169–70, 173–77, 180, 191, 203–4, 208, 262–64, 266, 285–88, 371–77
- Butler in, 288–95, 297
- Chapman, J. in, xiii, 40, 258, 311, 316, 325–28, 339, 360, 367
- CIA relating to, 6, 9–11, 14, 16, 17, 19, 23, 25–28, 30, 33, 38–41, 43, 48, 60, 64, 65, 67, 70, 72–76, 78, 80, 87, 91, 94, 145, 150, 156, 157, 184, 267, 287, 298–99
- Delta Force in, 10, 15, 19, 28, 30–36, 38, 39, 73, 76, 79, 84, 87, 90, 122, 126, 141–43, 158–60, 162, 165–66, 183, 244, 260
- Franks and, xiii, 12, 18, 19, 33, 34, 36, 46, 48, 53–60, 82, 86, 91, 94, 95, 118, 131, 134, 136, 137, 150, 152–53, 182, 266, 365
- Gardez relating to, 125, 138–44, 150–51, 154–57, 159, 162–68, 170–71, 177, 179, 184–85, 187, 203–4, 208, 262, 264, 274, 279–81, 286–89, 297, 299–305, 307–11, 317–19, 321, 323, 325, 330–33, 340, 352, 360, 368, 371–73, 376
- Gray Fox in, 126, 143, 160, 165, 169, 171, 177, 185, 262, 297, 300, 311–15, 321
- Haas in, xiii, 40, 60, 65, 67–68, 73, 81, 88, 115, 142–45, 151, 154–56, 185, 187, 200, 203–4, 206–8, 212, 273–78, 280, 302, 304, 317, 372–74
- Hagenbeck in, xiii, 11–14, 60–61, 75, 82–83, 84, 86–90, 91–95, 118, 120–21, 123, 126–33, 136–37, 139, 141–42, 145–46, 149–50, 153, 157–58, 170, 172, 175–76, 178–79, 182, 208–9, 253, 256, 259, 264–67, 270–71, 290, 297, 304–5, 307, 312, 319, 365
- Halfpipe battle in, 237–38, 240–41, 246, 248–49, 251–56, 259–60, 266–71, 281–83, 289, 307, 370
- Harrell in, xiv, 33, 34, 36–37, 64, 66, 74, 91, 93, 94, 130, 142, 149, 156, 170, 264, 266, 312, 319, 335
- Harriman in, 184–85, 187, 197–98, 200–206, 209–14, 275–77, 304, 316
- helicopters used in, 312–18, 319–25, 328–35, 341–49, 351, 353–55, 360–61, 363–69
- India team in, 97–98, 101, 104, 107–9, 113–17, 122, 142–44, 159, 160, 164–69, 171, 174, 176–78, 185, 189, 261–63, 285–87, 297–99, 302, 311, 371, 376
- issues relating to, 122–30, 154–58
- Juliet team in, 122, 142–43, 159–65, 168–71, 176–77, 185, 199, 205, 208, 262–63, 286–87, 298–99, 302, 305–6, 318, 328, 352, 366, 371–72, 376
- LaCamera in, xiv, 62–63, 67–69, 89, 90, 91, 93, 146, 148, 167, 180, 228, 234–36, 238–40, 243, 246, 248–49, 251–53, 255–56, 264–67, 269, 271, 282–84, 289
- Lodin in, xiv, 26–28, 40–42, 45, 47–48, 59–60, 65, 67, 70–74, 93, 95, 112, 118–20, 122, 124–25, 127–28, 135, 139–40, 143–46, 148, 150, 154–56, 160, 184–87, 192, 197–98, 204, 207–9, 211, 212, 264–65, 273, 275–78, 280–81, 302–3, 317, 372–75
- "Major Jimmy" in, xiv, 39, 90, 93, 99, 127, 141, 150, 175, 178–79, 182–83, 260, 262, 265–66
- McHale in, 70–71, 78, 118, 144–45, 150–52, 162, 184–85, 187–88, 198, 206–7, 214–16, 272–79, 304

Mikolashek in, xiv, 12–15, 18, 20, 34, 45–48, 52–55, 58–59, 61–62, 69, 82–86, 94–95, 118, 130–31, 134, 136–37, 152–53, 159, 182, 198, 271, 272
Mulholland in, xiv, 14, 15, 22, 24, 27, 42, 43, 45, 47–48, 59–61, 67, 68, 93–94, 122, 124–28, 130, 146, 154, 159, 209, 264, 274, 280, 304, 335–36
observation posts in, 160–67, 167–79, 302–3
planning sessions for, 65–74, 117–37, 145–56, 179–82
preparations for, 26–60, 138–54, 159–60
Preysler in, xiv, 3, 90, 127, 171–72, 178–48, 217, 226, 243, 246, 250–52, 262, 265, 269, 284–85, 290–91, 295, 297, 369, 371
Al Qaida relating to, 4, 8, 10, 11 8–122, 12–14, 16–21, 23–26, 28, 29, 34, 39–40, 42–43, 45–48, 55, 61, 64–65, 67, 69, 72–77, 80, 81, 85, 86, 135, 137, 139, 140, 145–49, 153, 155–57, 162, 164, 167, 174, 177, 188–91, 195, 214, 216–17, 219–20, 223, 225, 238–42, 244, 246–48, 251, 259–60, 262–63, 267–69, 271, 274, 282–83, 285, 289, 290, 292–94, 296–98, 369–70, 375–77
Rangers in, xi, 2–3, 32, 33, 36, 37, 38, 63–64, 67, 69, 90, 91, 114, 121, 148, 182, 234
reconnaissance mission relating to, 96–117
Roberts in, 312–18, 321–24, 327, 332, 338–39, 347, 358, 360, 367
Rosengard in, xv, 15, 19–23, 25, 27, 43–45, 61, 67–68, 70, 90, 93–95, 113, 119, 121–28, 140, 147, 150–52, 155, 209, 264, 280–81, 289, 372–73
SEALs in, xviii, 15, 30, 32, 37, 38, 41, 58, 87, 88, 118, 121, 122, 143, 160, 165, 166, 173, 175, 185, 189–91, 198, 200, 243–44, 247, 253, 284, 286–87, 297, 371, 372
SF in, xix, 4, 9–11, 14–15, 19, 22–25, 36, 45, 47–48, 58, 60, 62, 64–65, 70, 72, 73, 76, 87, 95, 102, 118, 126, 128, 142–46, 150, 151, 154–56, 184, 185, 187, 188, 202, 204, 206, 213, 214, 278, 279, 281, 287
Takur Ghar and, 303–5
"Speedy" in, xv, 144, 165–68, 171, 176, 260–63, 285, 288, 297–98, 376
"Spider" in, xv, 73, 75, 78, 80, 101, 122, 127, 141, 143, 156, 276–77, 372, 373
Taliban relating to, 8–12, 14, 16, 17, 19–20, 23–24, 26, 29, 34, 40, 43, 46–47, 55, 64–65, 69, 76, 80
Wiercinski in, 49–59, 62, 66–69, 89–91, 94, 119, 122–28, 130, 132, 145–48, 150, 152, 156, 157, 158, 172, 174, 178–81, 191, 193–94, 218, 235, 241–45, 251–53, 259, 265–67, 287, 289–90, 369
Operation Enduring Freedom, 69
Operation Payback, 304
The Other Side of the Mountain (Grau), 24, 25
Overbaugh, Justin, 243

Pacha Khan, 71, 157
in reconnaissance mission, 99, 101, 103
Pakistan, 2, 8, 10, 12, 16, 17, 20–21, 23, 24, 27, 44, 46, 48, 52, 65, 70, 77, 81–82, 85, 117
Paktia, 10, 23–27, 43, 47, 48, 65, 77–78, 98
Pazder, Randy, 359, 363
Pebsworth, Stanley, 192–93, 218–19, 222–23, 225, 226, 256
Pecawul Ghar, 98, 108, 111–15
Pentagon, 8, 12, 18, 19, 30, 49, 50, 52, 53, 56, 57, 81, 85, 102, 120, 131, 136, 196–97, 232, 319, 377
Perez, Randel, xiv, 231–34, 253–55
Peterson, Michael, 239–41, 248, 252, 255, 260, 270, 283–84, 370–71
Pierre, Emanuel "Manny," 193, 194
Preysler, Charles "Chip"
in Operation Anaconda, xiv, 3, 90, 127, 171–72, 178–48, 217, 226, 243, 246, 250–52, 262, 265, 269, 284–85, 290–91, 295, 297, 369, 371
Takur Ghar relating to, 318, 321
Prickett, Shawn, 93
Pushtun tribesmen, 1, 14, 16, 17, 19–21, 26, 28, 45, 47, 48, 71, 106, 138

Al Qaida
Operation Anaconda relating to, 4, 8, 10, 11 8–122, 12–14, 16–21, 23–26, 28, 29, 34, 39–40, 42–43, 45–48, 55, 61, 64–65, 67, 69, 72–77, 80, 81, 85, 86, 135, 137, 139, 140, 145–49, 153, 155–57, 162, 164, 167, 174, 177, 188–91, 195, 214, 216–17, 219–20, 223, 225, 238–42, 244, 246–48, 251, 259–60, 262–63, 267–69, 271, 274, 282–83, 285, 289, 290, 292–94, 296–98, 369–70, 375–77
reconnaissance mission relating to, 96–117
Takur Ghar relating to, 302, 307, 313–14, 320, 324, 327, 329, 333, 338–41, 351, 354, 356, 361, 363

Quinlan, John, 179

Rakkasans. *See* Task Force Rakkasan
Rangers
in Operation Anaconda, xi, 2–3, 32, 33, 36, 37, 38, 63–64, 67, 69, 90, 91, 114, 121, 148, 182, 234
Self in, xv, 328–35, 339–42, 345–47, 349, 351–67
Takur Ghar relating to, 301, 324, 328, 330–32, 338, 341–48, 351, 353, 354, 357–58, 360–67
Rasul, 71, 101, 112, 113, 185, 187
Razor 01, 332–34, 336–40, 345–47, 353–54, 360, 365
Razor 02, 332–34, 336–38, 340–41, 352, 353, 360, 367
Razor 03, 307–13, 317–18, 320, 324, 328–29, 331, 333–34, 342
Razor 04, 307–8, 311, 317, 319–25, 328–29, 331, 334
Reconnaissance mission, in Shahikot. *See also* Operation Anaconda; Shahikot
AFO working with, 96–117
Blaber involved with, 95, 96, 98–99, 101, 104, 109, 112–17
CIA involved with, 95, 98, 99, 101, 108, 112, 115
Delta working with, 95, 97, 98, 102, 104–05, 109, 112, 117
Gardez relating to, 95, 98, 99, 100–107, 111–17
Gray Fox in, 102, 104, 106, 109–12, 117
India team in, 96–99, 101–02, 104–05, 107–9, 113–17
Juliet team in, 97–107, 109, 112, 117
Pacha Khan working with, 99, 101, 103
Al Qaida relating to, 96–117
SF working with, 95, 102
"Speedy" involved with, 97–98, 101, 109, 111, 113–17
Taliban relating to, 99, 103, 108
weather during, 105, 108–9, 114–16
Renuart, Gene, 136–37, 182
Rich, 40, 65, 67, 68, 73, 78, 94, 115, 304
Roberts, Neil
death of, 321–24
helicopter fall of, 312–18
at Takur Ghar, 327, 332, 338–39, 347, 358, 360, 367
Ropel, Andrzej, xv, 229–31, 238, 248, 249, 252, 255, 267–68, 282
Rosengard, Mark, xv, 15, 19–23, 25, 27, 43–45, 61, 67–68, 70, 90, 93–95, 113, 119, 121–28, 140, 147, 150–52, 155, 209, 264, 280–81, 289, 372–73
Rumsfeld, Donald, 18, 19, 55–59, 85, 131
Ryan, Bill, 192–95, 197, 226, 246–48, 247, 258–59

Sabus, Greg, 276
Safe house
in Gardez, 39, 41, 42, 70–74, 76–78, 81, 82, 96, 98–102, 105, 106, 109, 112–13, 117, 142, 145, 156, 159–60, 165, 167, 174, 184, 204, 280, 300, 302, 304, 306
in Kabul, 9, 28, 39, 63, 64, 69
in Khowst, 58, 104, 123, 329
Sakisit, Bill, 236
Sate Kandow pass, 98, 99, 101–3, 105, 112
Savusa, Iuniasolua, 50, 174, 180, 241–42, 244–45, 284
Schmitz, Henry, 250, 251, 294–95
Schwartz, Mark, 185, 200, 201, 204–5, 211–12, 276–77, 280
"Screaming Eagles," 2, 50, 52
SEALs
Hyder in, xiv, 300–302, 305–7, 309–11, 321, 352–53, 358–59, 366, 371
Kernan in, xiv, 33, 80, 121–22, 286–87, 300–301, 305, 309, 365
in Operation Anaconda, xviii, 15, 30, 32, 37, 38, 41, 58, 87, 88, 118, 121, 122, 143, 160, 165, 166, 173, 175, 185, 189–91, 198, 200, 243–44, 247, 253, 284, 286–87, 297, 371, 372
Roberts in, 312–18, 321–24, 327, 332, 338–39, 347, 358, 360, 367
"Slab" in, xv, 303–19, 321–22, 324–28, 335–39
in Takur Ghar, 300–303, 305–7, 309–14, 316–18, 320, 321, 323–27, 332–37, 339, 340, 358–60, 366–68
Self, Nathan, xv, 328–35, 339–42, 345–47, 349, 351–67
Serkhankhel, 44, 46, 119, 122, 124, 125, 127, 137, 146, 149, 154, 159, 164, 169, 176–77, 179, 192, 199, 211, 226, 235, 243, 249, 262, 272, 371–72
SF (Special Forces)
Haas in, xiii, 40, 60, 65, 67–68, 73, 81, 88, 115, 142–45, 151, 154–56, 185, 187, 200, 203–4, 206–8, 212, 273–78, 280, 302, 304, 317, 372–74
in Operation Anaconda, xix, 4, 9–11, 14–15, 19, 22–25, 36, 45, 47–48, 58, 60, 62, 64–65, 70, 72, 73, 76, 87, 95, 102, 118, 126, 128,

142–46, 150, 151, 154–56, 184, 185, 187, 188, 202, 204, 206, 213, 214, 278, 279, 281, 287
Takur Ghar and, 303–5
Shahikot, 7, 11, 13, 14, 21, 24–25, 40–48. *See also* Operation Anaconda
attack on, 184–299
Carwazi near, 207, 212, 214, 273–76, 303
Ewadzkhal Valley near, 98, 101, 103, 104, 108
Franks and, 46, 48, 53–60, 82, 86, 95
intelligence about, 41–48, 59–95, 77–82, 83, 92–93, 95
Masirah near, 32, 34, 35, 37, 80, 81, 170, 175–76, 261, 286, 302, 310, 318, 320–28, 333–38, 364–66
operation in, 60–61, 63, 65–70, 72–75
Pecawul Ghar in, 114, 115
reconnaissance mission in, 95–117
Sate Kandow pass near, 98, 99, 101–3, 105, 112
Takur Ghar in, 44
Task Force Dagger in, 117, 122–30, 133–34, 136, 139, 142, 144, 146, 150, 154, 155, 178, 180, 199, 201–04, 209, 230, 250, 267, 280–81, 372–73
Task Force Rakkasan relating to, 62, 64, 118–28, 130–32, 135–59, 171–74, 178–81, 185, 188, 192, 194, 205, 208–09, 270–74, 281, 284–85, 287, 289, 292, 297–98, 306, 321, 360, 369–74, 377
Tergul Ghar in, 44
terrain around, 43–44, 75–76, 100–101, 106, 109–14
Upper/Lower Shahikot Valleys in, 43–44
Yuldeshev in, 138–39
Zawar Ghar near, 104, 108, 109
Zermat in, 98, 99, 101, 105, 106, 113, 117
Shawn, 341–42, 349, 361
Shinseki, Eric "Ric," 18, 19
Short, Kevin W. "Speedy"
in Operation Anaconda, xv, 144, 165–68, 171, 176, 260–63, 285, 288, 297–98, 376
in reconnaissance mission, xv, 97–98, 101, 109, 111, 113–17
SIGINT (signals intelligence), xix, 74, 75, 102, 104, 105, 108, 135, 139
"Slab," xv, 303–19, 321–22, 324–28, 335–39
Smith, Joe, 94, 179, 266, 319
Southworth, John, 216
"Speedy." *See* Short, Kevin W. "Speedy"
"Spider"
in Operation Anaconda, xv, 73, 75, 78, 80, 101, 122, 127, 141, 143, 156, 276–77, 372, 373
Takur Ghar relating to, 302, 304, 317
Stebner, Eric, 358–59, 361, 363
Stratman, Hank, 54
Svitak, Phil, 341, 344, 345
Sweeney, Brian, 25, 42, 65, 67, 78, 116

Takur Ghar, xi, 44, 170, 228, 234–35, 237, 260, 290
Blaber relating to, 302–3, 305–7, 309–11, 317–19, 321–22, 332, 334–36, 338
Butler at, 305, 315, 320–21, 367, 369–70
CIA relating to, 303, 311, 376
Delta Force relating to, 301–3, 312, 317, 323, 371, 377
helicopter down at, 319
Juliet team relating to, 302, 305–6, 318, 328, 352, 366
"Major Jimmy" relating to, 307, 310–13, 316–22
in Operation Anaconda, 309, 316, 320
Preysler relating to, 318, 321
Al Qaida relating to, 302, 307, 313–14, 320, 324, 327, 329, 333, 338–41, 351, 354, 356, 361, 363
Rangers relating to, 301, 324, 328, 330–32, 338, 341–48, 351, 353, 354, 357–58, 360–67
Roberts at, 327, 332, 338–39, 347, 358, 360, 367
SEALs in, 300–303, 305–7, 309–14, 316–18, 320, 321, 323–27, 332–37, 339, 340, 358–60, 366–68
SF and, 303–5
in Shahikot, 44
"Spider" relating to, 302, 304, 317
Task Force 11 at, 300–307, 310, 318–24, 326, 332, 334, 336, 337–38, 342, 352, 360–61, 364–66, 365
Task Force Blue at, 300–312, 318–22, 328, 331–33, 359–60, 364, 366
Task Force Brown at, 307–08, 312, 328, 330, 333, 360
Task Force Dagger at, 302–04, 336
Task Force Hammer at, 302–4, 311
Task Force K-Bar at, 303, 360–61
Task Force Mountain at, 307, 310, 318, 319, 321, 340
Task Force Rakkasan at, 306, 321, 360
Whale near, 44, 74, 106–7, 119–20, 127–28, 151, 154–55, 160, 164, 166–71, 177–78,

Takur Ghar, (*cont.*)
185, 187–88, 197–201, 205–8, 214–23, 225, 246, 260, 267, 272–76, 279, 281, 284, 289–91, 293, 298, 299, 302–3, 306, 371, 373, 374
Taliban
Operation Anaconda relating to, 8–12, 14, 16, 17, 19–20, 23–24, 26, 29, 34, 40, 43, 46–47, 55, 64–65, 69, 76, 80
reconnaissance mission relating to, 99, 103, 108
Task Force 11, 91, 160, 170, 176, 217, 261, 286, 375, 380–81, 392
planning of, 64, 118, 121
preparation of, 29, 32–37, 138, 141–43, 149
at Takur Ghar, 300–307, 310, 318–24, 326, 332, 334, 336, 337–38, 342, 352, 360–61, 364–66, 365
Trebon in, xv, 32, 33, 35–37, 80, 81, 94
Task Force Blue, 80, 92, 121, 286–88, 297, 372
preparation of, 30–33, 37–38
at Takur Ghar, 300–312, 318–22, 328, 331–33, 359–60, 364, 366
Task Force Bowie, 157
Harrell in, xiv, 33, 34, 36–37, 64, 66, 74, 91, 93, 94, 130, 142, 149, 156, 170, 264, 266, 312, 319, 335
planning of, 61, 63, 64, 66, 69
preparation of, 29, 34, 35, 37
Task Force Brown, 372
at Takur Ghar, 307–08, 312, 328, 330, 333, 360
Task Force Dagger, 15, 16, 23, 75, 78, 81, 82, 87, 88, 94
in Gardez, 27–28, 39, 40, 42–43
Mulholland in, xiv, 14, 15, 22, 24, 27, 42, 43, 45, 47–48, 59–61, 67, 68, 93–94, 122, 124–28, 130, 146, 154, 159, 209, 264, 274, 280, 304, 335–36
planning of, 59–67, 70–73
preparation of, 24–29, 39–40, 42–43, 45, 47–49, 54
in reconnaissance mission, 95, 96, 98, 101, 106, 112
Rosengard in, xv, 15, 19–23, 25, 27, 43–45, 61, 67–68, 70, 90, 93–95, 113, 119, 121–28, 140, 147, 150–52, 155, 209, 264, 280–81, 289, 372–73
in Shahikot, 117, 122–30, 133–34, 136, 139, 142, 144, 146, 150, 154, 155, 178, 180, 185, 199, 201–4, 209, 230, 250, 267, 280–81, 372–73
at Takur Ghar, 302–04, 336
in Tora Bora, 19–21
Task Force Hammer, 93, 159–60, 166, 168, 184–91, 206–16, 226, 235, 243, 264–65, 270–81, 289, 372
friendly fire attack on, 197–206
McHale in, 70–71, 78, 118, 144–45, 150–52, 162, 184–85, 187–88, 198, 206–7, 214–16, 272–79, 304
planning of, 118, 128, 146, 147, 150, 151, 154–56
preparation of, 139, 142, 144
at Takur Ghar, 302–4, 311
Task Force K-Bar, 15, 158–59
planning of, 64, 67, 70, 118, 126, 129, 130
preparation of, 29, 47, 58
at Takur Ghar, 303, 360–61
Task Force Mountain, 11–14, 18, 39, 48, 60–62, 82–84, 86–93, 95, 113, 118–31, 133–35, 141–42, 144–47, 149, 150, 152–54, 156, 158, 162, 171, 174, 176, 178, 180–82, 193, 209–10, 228, 234, 238–40, 260–61, 264–66, 272–73, 273, 279–81, 289, 295, 307, 310, 318, 319, 321, 340, 373
Bentley in, 83, 93, 126, 128, 131, 134–35, 153, 155–56, 209, 272, 273, 281
preparation of, 39, 48, 60, 133–35, 141–42, 144–47, 149, 150, 152–54
at Takur Ghar, 307, 310, 318, 319, 321, 340
Wille in, xv, 11, 13, 14, 25, 83, 93–95, 118, 122–24, 128–31, 137, 150, 155, 157–58
Ziemba in, 11, 13, 25, 83, 93, 118–21, 139–40
Task Force Rakkasan, xviii, 48, 50–59, 61–65, 62, 64, 66–70, 86–90, 93, 235–45, 247–50, 255, 256, 261–72
Larsen in, xiv, 58, 61–69, 90, 94, 95, 122–23, 125–26, 178, 244, 372, 374
planning of, 61–65, 62, 64, 66–70
preparation of, 48, 50–59
Ropel in, xv, 229–31, 238, 248, 249, 252, 255, 267–68, 282
Shahikot relating to, 62, 64, 118–28, 130–32, 135, 139–59, 171–74, 178–81, 185, 188, 192, 194, 205, 208–9, 270–74, 281, 284–85, 287, 289, 292, 297–98, 306, 321, 360, 369–74, 377
at Takur Ghar, 306, 321, 360
Wiercinski in, 49–59, 62, 66–69, 89–91, 94, 119, 122–28, 130, 132, 145–48, 150, 152, 156, 157, 158, 172, 174, 178–81, 191,

193–94, 218, 235, 241–45, 251–53, 259, 265–67, 287, 289–90, 369
Task Force Sword, 28–30, 32
Tergul Ghar, 44, 201
Terrain, around Shahikot, 43–44, 75–76, 100–101, 106, 109–14
Texas 14, xix, 25–28, 40–41, 47, 65, 70–71, 78, 112, 115, 151, 184–87, 200, 201, 205–7, 215–16, 273, 276
  Thomas in, xv, 26–27, 41–42, 47, 65, 74, 112, 115, 118, 150, 151, 156, 184–85, 198–201, 206, 274
Thomas, Glenn, xv, 26–27, 41–42, 47, 65, 74, 112, 115, 118, 150, 151, 156, 184–85, 198–201, 206, 274
Thomas, Tony, 38, 121, 287, 329
Thompson, James "Fred," 217
Thor, 185, 197, 204, 300, 311, 321
Tink, Rowan, 158
Tora Bora, 10, 12, 17–21, 22–24, 45–46, 48, 65, 119, 155
Totten-Lancaster, Aaron, 342, 345, 346, 351
Trebon, Gregory, xv, 32, 33, 35–37, 80, 81, 94
Turner, D.J., 202, 316, 322, 324, 326, 335, 336–38

Understanding Defeat (Dupuy), 66
Upper/Lower Shahikot Valleys, 43–44
U.S. Central Command. *See* CENTCOM
U.S. Special Operations Command, xi, xii

Van Antwerp, James, 206, 277
Vance, Kevin, 330–32, 342, 346, 351–52, 355, 357, 359, 361, 363–65
Vela, Omar, 359, 363

Wadsworth, Larry, 197, 202–04, 209, 211, 304
Wahl, Eddie, 2, 4, 5, 6
Wald, Chuck, 136
Walker, Joshua, 342, 345–46, 351, 355, 359, 363
Warfare, unconventional, 14–18, 21, 23, 24, 46, 47, 54, 55, 72
Weather, during reconnaissance mission, 105, 108–9, 114–16
Whale, 44, 74, 106–7, 119–20, 127–28, 151, 154–55, 160, 164, 166–71, 177–78, 185, 187–88, 197–201, 205–8, 214–23, 225, 246, 260, 267, 272–76, 279, 281, 284, 289–91, 293, 298, 299, 302–3, 306, 371, 373, 374
White, Tom, 18, 56–57
Wiercinski, Frank, 49–59, 62, 66–69, 89–91, 94, 119, 122–28, 130, 132, 145–48, 150, 152, 156, 157, 158, 172, 174, 178–81, 191, 193–94, 218, 235, 241–45, 251–53, 259, 265–67, 287, 289–90, 369
Wille, Paul, xv, 11, 13, 14, 25, 83, 93–95, 118, 122–24, 128–31, 137, 150, 155, 157–58
Wilmoth, Harper, 358–60, 363
Wilson, Jason, 2, 3
Winters, Ed, 65, 66, 81
Wolfowitz, Paul, 21, 85
World Trade Center, 8, 49, 57, 181, 230

Yates, Dennis, 66, 67, 69, 148, 153
Yuldeshev, Tohir, 138–39, 175, 376

Zachran, Pacha Khan. *See* Pacha Khan
al-Zawahiri, Ayman, 37, 76, 142, 377
Zawar Ghar, 101, 104, 108, 109
Zermat, 40–42, 44, 74, 77, 80, 81, 98, 99, 101, 105, 106, 112, 113, 116, 117, 118, 128, 145, 184, 185, 187, 189, 278–80, 311, 317
Zia. *See* Lodin, Zia
Ziemba, Francesca, 11, 13, 25, 83, 93, 118–21, 139–40